T0284856

The Wild East

NEW PERSPECTIVES ON THE HISTORY OF THE SOUTH

UNIVERSITY PRESS OF FLORIDA

Florida A&M University, Tallahassee

Florida Atlantic University, Boca Raton

Florida Gulf Coast University, Ft. Myers

Florida International University, Miami

Florida State University, Tallahassee

New College of Florida, Sarasota

University of Central Florida, Orlando

University of Florida, Gainesville

University of North Florida, Jacksonville

University of South Florida, Tampa

University of West Florida, Pensacola

MARGARET LYNN BROWN

The WILD

UNIVERSITY PRESS OF FLORIDA
Gainesville Tallahassee Tampa Boca Raton
Pensacola Orlando Miami Jacksonville Ft. Myers Sarasota

EAST

A Biography of the Great Smoky Mountains

Revised Edition

Cover: top, webcam photograph from the Great Smoky Mountains National Park website; *bottom*, photograph by George Masa, "Looking down Noland Creek Valley from Andrews Bald," circa 1920s.

Copyright 2000 by Margaret Lynn Brown
Revised edition 2024 Margaret Lynn Brown
All rights reserved
Published in the United States of America

29 28 27 26 25 24   6 5 4 3 2 1

LIBRARY OF CONGRESS CATALOGING-IN-PUBLICATION DATA
Brown, Margaret Lynn.
The wild east: a biography of the Great Smoky Mountains / Margaret Lynn Brown.
p. cm.—(New perspectives on the history of the South)
Includes bibliographical references (p.) and index.
ISBN 978-0-8130-1750-1 (cloth)
ISBN 978-0-8130-2093-8 (pbk.)
ISBN 978-0-8130-8086-4 (pbk.)
1. Great Smoky Mountains National Park (N.C. and Tenn.)—History. 2. Great Smoky Mountains National Park (N.C. and Tenn.)—Environmental conditions.
3. Human ecology—Great Smoky Mountains National Park (N.C. and Tenn.)
I. Title. II. Series.
f443.g7 w55 2000
976.8'89—dc21 99-089346

The University Press of Florida is the scholarly publishing agency for the State University System of Florida, comprising Florida A&M University, Florida Atlantic University, Florida Gulf Coast University, Florida International University, Florida State University, New College of Florida, University of Central Florida, University of Florida, University of North Florida, University of South Florida, and University of West Florida.

University Press of Florida
2046 NE Waldo Road
Suite 2100
Gainesville, FL 32609
http://upress.ufl.edu

For Charlie and Frank

We followed him down through the friendly
woods and none of us said anything until we
were almost at the clearing. He stopped, blocking
our way, and said, "They got some mountains
in California. You ought to see them sometime.
But it's not the same." He marched on a few yards
before halting again to declare, "Some way or
other, it just ain't the same."

FROM "THE POSSE," BY FRED CHAPPELL,
IN *You Are One of Us Forever*

Contents

Preface to the 2024 Edition

LIKE A CHILD LEAVING HOME, a book has a life in the world that the author cannot imagine. Many people have been inspired by the stories of land and people in the Great Smoky Mountains told in *The Wild East*. The "postcards home" I have received for two decades have come from family members searching for relatives, scientists studying mushrooms, and forestry students who value human connections to the environment. Author Ron Rash rendered an unforgettable portrait of the lumbermen who cut the big trees in his novel *Serena* (Harper Collins, 2008).

I hope you will be inspired, too.

Since I combed archives in five states to birth *The Wild East*, more sources have appeared. The Wilderness Society has reissued the journal of Harvey Broome, founder of the Wilderness Society, *Out under the Sky of the Great Smokies* (2001). In his descriptions of hikes from 1941 to 1966, Broome recounts adventures intriguing to both the avid hiker and the novice such as climbing through six inches of snow on April 5 to ascend Charlie's Bunion. A recent reprint of note is Paul Fink's *Mountain Days: A Journal of Camping Experiences in the Mountains of Tennessee and North Carolina, 1914–1938* (2019), with a foreword by Ken Wise, director of the Great Smoky Mountain Regional Project. With his clear-eyed, journalistic voice, Fink's 1974 manuscript *Backpacking Was the Only Way* influenced me in writing *The Wild East*.

In his 2003 documentary *The Mystery of George Masa*, filmmaker Paul Bonesteel was the first to point out the importance of photographer George Masa in the movement to create a national park. Born in Osaka, Japan, Masa came to Asheville, North Carolina, in 1915. Friend and hiking companion of the famous outdoorsman Horace Kephart, Masa took many of the beautiful nature photographs that became part of promotional brochures for the park. Ken Burns also told Masa's story in his 2009 PBS *National Parks* series. The poet and scholar Brent Martin followed the elusive trail left by Masa's photographs in *George Masa's Wild Vision* (2022), creating a portrait of North Carolina, a century ago and now. And as this new edition of *The Wild East* goes to press, Janet McCue and Paul Bonesteel have cowritten the biography *George Masa, a Life Reimagined* (2024).

The Burns PBS *National Parks* series also celebrated the colorful Horace Kephart as a major figure of the park movement. A thoughtful and nuanced biography of Kephart by George Ellison and Janet McCue, *Back of Beyond: A Horace Kephart Biography* (2019) depicts the St. Louis librarian as a man who followed his heart, leaving behind success and duty but retaining ties to both. He wrote to others who might be restored by the wildness he cherished. George Frizzell and Mae Miller Claxton edited a collection of Kephart's lesser-known essays and letters, *Horace Kephart: Writings* (2020).

Although the Cherokee have long been part of the Smokies story, recent scholars have expanded our knowledge of African Americans in the region. In 2018 the park initiated an African American History Collection. An examination of census records showed that each of the counties surrounding the Smokies were home to as many as 80 enslaved persons in 1860 as well as a few free families. Anthropologist Antoine Fletcher is filling in the gaps in the archival record with oral history interviews, locating African Americans who worked for Suncrest Logging Company, TVA, and Job Corps. In a new community study, *Oconaluftee: Shared Valley of the Smokies* (2022), author Beth Giddens weaves together both slaveholding Cherokees and enslaved people during the nineteenth century, rendering a view of this Appalachian farming community as a much more diverse place.

Another side of the families removed to create the park can be seen in an artful description of cemetery practices in *Decoration Day in the Mountains: Traditions of Cemetery Decoration in the Southern Appalachians* (2010) by Alan Jabbour and Karen Singer. The authors use oral interviews to explain how the children and grandchildren of former residents tend cemeteries and add flowers, then sing, eat, and tell stories to keep loving memories of the past alive. In addition, scholars brought together by Aaron Purcell for *Lost in Transition: Removing, Resettling, and Renewing Appalachia* (2021) show how Appalachian farmers who lost their land in the Smokies as well as in Mammoth Cave and Shenandoah National Parks remember lost communities and participate in the stewardship of park lands.

During all of this new scholarship, the Smokies transformed my life, too. I married my husband, Charlie, in a candlelight service under old-growth hemlocks near Cosby Campground. My son, Frank, grew up visiting elks in Cataloochee, paddling Fontana Lake with a Tremont camp, and celebrating birthdays in Smokemont campground. In every season, I hike a trail with my friend Kris, but we most often reflect on our lives near the roaring waters of Big Creek. In my new home south of the park, I became a gardener devoted to native plants that I first met on these adventures.

As you read this biography of the Great Smoky Mountains, I invite you to reflect on the tremendous changes the mountains have endured in a hundred years. Because we humans rarely live this long, studying a place for this length of time allows us to consider the impacts our own lives have on the land. W. M. Ritter barely visited the Smokies but built a logging empire that devastated the landscape in a season. George Masa and Jim Thompson took photographs of the mountains for a decade that helped park promoters achieve their dream. Boyd Evison lived and worked in the Smokies for only three years but managed to chart a course for scientific and environmental stewardship. Thanks to the career of park air-quality specialist Jim Renfro, all of us living in the Southeast and the Midwest can breathe easier.

One reason I chose to publish a new edition with a chapter 11 is that in the twenty-first century the Great Smoky Mountains have become a critical regional center for nature education and outdoor learning as well as scientific research. The All Taxa Biodiversity Inventory attracts scholars from all over the world to "Discover Life in America." The research done in the Great Smoky Mountains protects the lives of valuable species; the Smokies are a home for bears and other wildlife that still needs our advocacy. An important part of this advocacy has become Park Partners, cooperating associations that have helped the Great Smoky Mountains National Park continue to meet its mandate for historic preservation and resource protection as well as education. At the same time, a 2016 fire offers a cautionary tale about why our national parks remain global treasures that must be preserved for future generations.

Special thanks to Dan Richter of Duke University and his graduate students for encouraging me to update *The Wild East* in this new edition. Their questions helped guide what should be included. I am also grateful to Ann Linnea and Kris Johnson for believing in my writing. A toast to the Bread and Roses Writing Group, who gave the new epilogue its first edit: Laurel Anderson, Hilary Clark, Julie Daniel, Anita Leverich, Lisa Harris, and Molly Murfee. And special thanks to Michael A'Day, archivist for the park, and Frances Figart, creatives services director for Smokies Life, for their help in locating sources. Thanks to Michele Fiyak-Burkley and Larry Leshan at the University Press of Florida. And the patience of my editor, Sian M. Hunter, deserves special recognition.

Acknowledgements

"THERE'S NO SUCH WORD AS 'CAN'T,'" Miss Mary Brandt, my third-grade teacher, told our class, an attentive group of blonde Minnesotans. Although perhaps limited as philosophy, her words filled me with that wonderful power of the possible. Until that moment, what I couldn't do—see well, run fast, or talk in public—seemed like rapidly closing doors in my future. Kick those doors in, Mary Brandt seemed to suggest, or at least knock real hard.

Not all teachers hand you a short phrase full of ammunition; some show you the power in another way of doing things. The school librarian, Vy Thompson, suggested that since I had already read so many stories, I ought to try the books that no one checked out. My high school English teacher, Karla Sellers, amazed us with tales of living as a soldier on a kibbutz in Israel. And my journalism advisor, Rosalie Seltz, went over the basic rules of grammar so many times that writing a sentence fragment required concentration.

All of us learn from our families, of course, but it's rarely what the teacher intends. My father, a civil engineer, taught me the difference between cement and concrete. This fact came in handy when studying Hoover and Fontana Dams, but I recall most clearly Dad's annual argument with Grandma about whether Franklin Roosevelt was a good president: No one ever won. I am also grateful that my oldest sister, Ann Linnea, sincerely believed a bookworm wanted to climb sheer rock faces; canoe against the wind in the rain; or go winter camping in below-zero temperatures. She hoped I would enjoy the challenge; instead, I discovered the strength in facing fears. And my mother, who wishes I did not live so far away, now denies she ever said, "I just want you to be happy."

Still, it is hard to forget those people who tell you exactly what you need to hear during that long struggle toward adulthood. As one of 55,000 students at the University of Minnesota, I cherished Dr. Richard Horberg, who argued with me every day over Kurt Vonnegut or Bernard Malamud, yet ended up telling me I wrote with "sophistication." As an associate in the Knight Fellowship for Professional Journalists at Stanford University, I learned from Richard Gillam that history is not so much an analysis of former presidents as an argument we engage in to understand our past. When I graduated from the University of Kentucky, I got the encouragement I needed to finish this book from my advisor, Ron Eller, who set me loose on the world with this: "Write *your* book, not the book that any professional historians want you to write. This is the freedom of having the Ph.D. you worked so hard to get."

Not all teachers, however, come from institutions of higher learning or even from that learning institution called the family. I became a journalist and then an oral historian because I believe in the alchemy that happens when one person tells a story to another. Former employees Susan Bratton and Boyd Evison led me to documents that I otherwise would have passed by or not found at all, and I am indebted to all those who generously shared their stories with me. No scholar works in a vacuum, and this book builds on the pathbreaking work of others. Appalachian scholars, especially David Whisnant, Durwood Dunn, and Ron Lewis, not only contributed the insights cited in the book, but forced me to confront my own prejudices. Ethnohistorians, including Sarah Hill, Charles Joyner, William McKee Evans, Lewis Latham, and Richard White, made it possible for me to tell this story in multiple voices. At a meeting of the American Society for Environmental History, White told me not to simplify my story to fit a theory, and for this I will always be grateful. The diverse group of scholars and National Park Service employees who belong to the George Wright Society, particularly Richard Sellars, helped me understand the unwieldy government agency. And of course this is a work of environmental history, so I must credit pioneering works by William Cronon, Timothy Silver, Alfred Crosby, Arthur McEvoy, Donald Worster, Mart Stewart, and Carolyn Merchant. Over the past ten years, while working on this project, I also have been a student of women writers, many of whom faced far more daunting tasks than I did. Virginia Woolf, who struggled with childhood abuse, episodic depression, and an all-male publishing world, still had the courage to insist, for all of us, on a "room of one's own." I needed to read Zora Neale Hurston, Leslie Marmon Silko, Isabel Allende, Mary Oliver, and E. Annie Proulx to trust the uniqueness of a woman's voice, and consequently, my own.

In truth, the most powerful teacher we have is within, that simple desire to know and to appreciate that which is not us. Now-retired park archivist Kathleen Manscill recognized this in me and brought forward boxes of information in which to dig. I will never forget that wonderful afternoon that she took me into the collection room to view a stuffed passenger pigeon, iridescent in the eerie preservation light—a moment that made the past and the purpose of my research come alive. Park librarian and hiking companion Annette Hartigan got me out on the trails looking at wildflowers and trying to apply what I read. Kris Johnson led me toward encounters with the wild that became an inherent part of the work, including a six-pronged buck, a champion hemlock, and a rather irritated mountain rattler. Her tireless encouragement pushed this book forward in fallow periods.

In the process of completing *The Wild East*, I discovered that you can even learn from people you never met, like former employees Mary Ruth Chiles and John O. Morrell, who happened to save invaluable documents, against all ordinary procedure. Of course, I have many people to thank for their help with details. I am grateful to Wayne Moore at the Tennessee State Archives; Cheryl Oakes at the Forest History Society; George Frizzell at Western Carolina University; and Mike McCabe and his staff at the Brevard College Library for their thoughtful suggestions. Thanks to Sally Polhemus at the McClung Collection, Arlene Royer at East Point, Steve Massengill at the North Carolina State Archives, and Will Fontanez at the University of Tennessee. For financial aid in completing my Ph.D., I thank the University of Kentucky and my grandmother, Margaret Ann Brown, an educated woman who never completed high school. Many organizations made the travel to archives possible: the North Caroliniana Society at the University of North Carolina-Chapel Hill, the Franklin and Eleanor Roosevelt Institute, the Archives of Appalachia at East Tennessee State University, Brevard College, the University of Kentucky, the Great Smoky Mountains Natural History Association, the Forest History Society, and the University Press of Florida. Without the computer experts at Brevard College, particularly Paul Parker, the manuscript might still be trapped on an unusable hard drive. The support of Susan Bruno during the final writing process also deserves special recognition, as does Amanda Littauer for last-minute research.

Many readers have contributed their time to making this a better piece of writing. I thank Astrid Brown, Frank Brown, Ann Linnea, Dan Pittillo, Betsy Burrows, Mark Burrows, Preston Woodruff, Herb Reid, Ron Eller, Theda Perdue, Eric Christianson, David Hamilton, Kathi Kern, Richard Gift, Jennifer Frick, Dave Wetmore, Paul Elwood, and Sarah Hill for reading various drafts. I am indebted to Kris Johnson, Scott Perry, and Kitty Manscill for reading the entire manuscript under deadline. A special thanks to Pat Arnow for highlighting eminent domain in *Southern Exposure*. A toast to my supervisor, Helen Gift, for her patience and encouragement. And I am grateful to John David Smith for rediscovering me, to Meredith Morris-Babb for believing in this project enough to bless it with an advance, and to Gillian Hillis for her careful editing.

Throughout my life, I have been lucky to encounter amazing people as teachers. I thank Eric Black for introducing me to southern culture and a Welsh terrier named Kishke; Ted Olson for encouraging me to drive south; and Don Davis for giving me firsthand experience with mountain agriculture. I learned more from Nyoka Hawkins about gender analysis, and more from Craig Friend about frontier history, than I ever gleaned from scholarly tomes. As an assistant professor of history at Brevard College, I am lucky to work every day with a dedicated faculty, including a scholar in the history of science, Scott Sheffield; a southern historian, Tim Long; and a gifted poet and wordsmith, Ken Chamlee. I thank my students, particularly those in environmental history classes, for alternately confounding and enlightening me. Finally, I honor members of my merry tribe, who daily help me realize the joy of learning, however painful it sometimes can be: Claire Lewis, Anne Welsbacher, Kris Johnson, Tony Thompson, Kathleen Fluhart, Edie Quinn, Angela Faye Martin, Naomi Tutu, Betsy Burrows, Paul Elwood, September Fisher, Jon Gudmundson, Maureen Killila, Charlie Parsons, Natasha, and Rocky.

If a world-famous astrologer had told me, twenty years ago, that I would one day move to the southern mountains, study the history of the people, research the environment, encounter bears, boars, snakes, rangers, hunters, and scientists, and then write a book and teach about it, I would have laughed. A journalist, raised in the West and Midwest, I could not have seen how my talents applied. If she had further told me that my unique perspective would become an asset to these endeavors, I would have scoffed. But perhaps Mary Brandt's simple declaration ("there's no such word as 'can't'") would have suspended crippling disbelief. For this reason, the book is dedicated to all the teachers (mentioned and unmentioned) who believed in my abilities before I did. It's proof, in a way, that you can encourage the shy one to be a little bit bold.

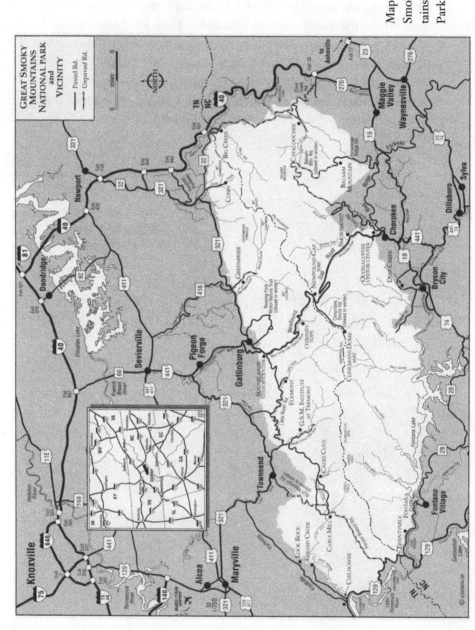

Map of Great Smoky Mountains National Park and vicinity.

Mountains of Story

*Born under another sky, placed in the middle of
an always moving scene, himself driven by the
irresistible torrent which draws all about him, the
American has no time to tie himself to anything,
he grows accustomed only to change, and ends up
regarding it as the natural state of man.*

ALEXIS DE TOCQUEVILLE, *Democracy in America*

Although his words ring true for us at the turn of the
twenty-first century, the French traveler Alexis de Tocqueville described an America he witnessed in 1836. I first read
Democracy in America more than 150 years later, while on
a journey of my own to the Great Smoky Mountains of
North Carolina and Tennessee. I remember how astounded
I was that someone who lived so long ago could describe my
own world so well.

Like the persistent migrants in de Tocqueville's chronicle,
my maternal grandparents left Sweden for the lumber
camps of Washington and the golden promise of California. My father's people emigrated to North Carolina during
the early nineteenth century but left in the next generation
for Tennessee, then Missouri and Oklahoma. My great-
grandfather ran a general store in Colorado; his son roamed
the Rockies as a liquor inspector. Even my own parents,
born in Denver, traveled to Minnesota for my childhood;
my earliest memories include tracing the Nebraska landscape in the dusty back window of our station wagon.
Change surely seemed like the natural business of humans

to me, and I never knew which place to name when people asked me about home.

I wasn't, in fact, looking for home on that dazzling May day in 1987, when I crammed a mound of luggage into a rusted Dodge Colt and drove south from Minneapolis. At that moment, the South brought to mind only images of civil rights workers facing off against Klan members. Even at age twenty-eight, I regarded the cities east of the Mississippi as one big encroaching megalopolis. The road trip held all kinds of surprises, though: on the bluffs of Iowa, I saw the magnificent Effigy Mounds; in Missouri I watched the Mississippi of my childhood stretch out as wide as any lake; and on the road to Chattanooga rolled miles of green hillsides speckled with purple princess trees.

Not long after I crossed the North Carolina state line, I had an experience I will never forget. Without warning, I felt my entire being drawn forward in anticipation. My little dog stood up on the seat and looked out the window. All at once out of the mist rolled blue-and-green mountains, layered like the limbs of enormous women lying together in a steam bath, or perhaps crumpled carpeting full of sleeping children. The closer I got, the more entranced I became. Unlike the stern and craggy faces of the more familiar Rockies, these gentle giants brimmed with every shape and shade of green vegetation, the lushness punctuated with tiny flowers called bluets.

The following day, I hiked the Polls Gap Trail into Cataloochee Valley in Great Smoky Mountains National Park. Tropical-looking rhododendron sheltered roaring whitewater streams. A canopy of giant hemlock and tuliptrees towered above. Reaching open land, I saw the soft rolling ridges, thrown into relief by that inscrutable mist, the source of the name Smoky Mountains.

The Smokies, as they are affectionately nicknamed, are a distinct family of mountains in the Southern Appalachians. Extending into both North Carolina and Tennessee, they include some of the highest mountains (Clingmans Dome, 6,642 feet) and most dramatic scenery in either state. Since the 1930s, the 540,000 acres they cover have been cared for by the National Park Service. The agency's largest unit in the eastern United States, Great Smoky Mountains National Park is a treasure of biodiversity. These magnificent forests include fifteen of the nation's largest specimens on the National Register of Big Trees and some 1,600 species of vascular plants. Scientists have identified 30 species of salamanders; 675 butterflies and moths; and a single tree, the northern red oak, has 468 insects and 54 spider species associated with it.[1]

In the western United States, fellow hikers tell you about the miles they've covered and the elevation gained. On top of Mount Sopris in Colorado, for example, a stranger told me that my harrowing descent couldn't compare with that experienced at Capitol Peak. So the people I met in Cataloochee Valley surprised me very much. One urged me not to miss a yellow trillium. Another described a former homesite. A fisherman claimed he knew every ripple of the creek, because he was "practically born in it." On that particular May day, it rained without warning, as if someone had taken a bucket and poured it over our heads. Without rain gear I was drenched, my camera ruined, and the trail became an obstacle course of gooey mud and water. As darkness gathered, I was a candidate for hypothermia, but I sang like an idiot, entranced by the endless variety of green.

This lushness can in part be explained by the prodigious rainfall and drenching mists in the Smokies; the peaks receive annually some 80 inches of rain, and even the valleys, 50. Tremendous biodiversity also can be linked to ancient geologic forces. The Smokies escaped the continental glaciers of the Ice Age, which in part explains their height. For thousands of years, then, the ground on the highest peaks remained frozen year-round: tundra grew on the permafrost and mammoths and mastodons walked the valleys. As the earth warmed, deluges eroded the hillsides, and the alpine plants and animals gave way to a spruce-fir forest that remained for the next 10,000 years. About 2 percent of the Smokies—the 13,000 acres on the tops of the highest peaks—are covered with this spruce-fir forest, making it the southernmost example in the United States. Only at high altitudes can certain lichens, mosses, wildflowers, and warblers that tolerate cooler temperatures live; hence, the spruce-fir forest is often described as an "island of the North inside the South." For the same reason, the northern hardwoods—maple, birch, and beech—start at 4,300 feet and intermingle with the spruce-fir.

A cove hardwood forest comprises most of the park. This uniquely southern forest includes 130 deciduous trees, but especially yellow-poplar, American basswood, white ash, and Carolina silverbell. Found in moist areas reaching up to 4,500 feet, the cove hardwood forest associates with a distinctive understory of dogwood, spicebush, witch hazel, clethra, and sweet shrub, and a lush and diverse herbaceous layer. The more acidic sites between 1,000 and 5,500 feet sport stands of eastern hemlock with some white pine and a typical understory of rhododendron and dog-hobble. Lower and middle elevations include stands of mixed pine-hard-wood and mixed oaks. Steep rocky south-facing slopes support Virginia pine-pitch pine conifers, mountain laurel, and huckleberry. Each com-munity—in fact, some scientists count sixty-seven of them—nurtures a specific understory as well as wildlife and insects that favor those plants. Each community also follows spring and summer rhythms. During the short period in the spring when the leaves have not yet sprouted, the extra sunlight reaching the ground enables many wildflowers, such as trillium, to flourish; in the shady days of summer, ferns dominate the forest floor.[2] The combined presence of the northern and southern forest communi-ties gives this section of the Blue Ridge a biodiversity unparalleled in North America.

During that first summer, I waited tables at Granny's Restaurant in Cherokee, North Carolina. A white family managed operations, al-though a Cherokee woman owned it and many Cherokees worked in the kitchen. Our customers included an interesting mix of tourists, Chero-kees, and local whites. My friends in the restaurant teased me about being a Yankee, but they also filled my life with stories about the place where they lived. My favorite customer, who ordered pie and coffee no matter the time of day, told me he once saw footprints of the Little People, magi-cal folks of Cherokee legends, on the banks of Soco Creek. On my days off I hiked with another new friend, a park ranger, who introduced me to the colorful names of southern mountain plants, animals, and places—doghobble, "preacher birds," and Little Greenbrier. When I shared these discoveries in the restaurant, one of my coworkers joked, "I know what you are—you're one of those flower children." "A late bloomer, at least," I shrugged.

To supplement my salary I wrote articles for the *Waynesville Mountain-eer* and the *Christian Science Monitor.* In addition to bear experts and hunt-ers, elderly people and Cherokees, I interviewed Gay Webb, a hardware store owner in Cocke County, Tennessee. Although he called himself an environmentalist, he didn't resemble activists I had previously encountered. The Webb family had lived in the mountains for generations; in fact, a mountain and a creek in the park bear their name. Webb talked with a comforting drawl and teased every customer who came into the store that day. Champion's paper mill filled the adjacent Pigeon River with a smelly industrial effluent, he told me, and he wanted to see the water run clear before he died.

Although I had lived in the region only a few months, I recognized something new and valuable in the store owner and my Cherokee friends. I have since spent years in libraries and archives trying to understand what was, in fact, part of that first impression. The people of the Smokies touched me because they daily manifested something I myself do not yet have: a sense of place. Their personal stories were woven together with a larger narrative we call history, and this history bound them with a particular place on earth.

And so why would a late-twentieth-century pilgrim, caught in de Toqueville's "irresistible torrent," wish to write a book about mountains where her ancestors never lived? I am in search of a memory that my people cannot give me, and I am dissatisfied by much of what I read about the Smokies. Searching the bookstores in Gatlinburg, Tennessee, I found shelves of Civil War memoirs, audiotapes of dulcimer music, and folksy accounts of quaint people who played the banjo and ate corn bread. None of this approached the complexity of a Cherokee waitress who worshiped in the Mormon church; a mountain store owner who marched in protests; a fisherman who claimed to be born in a national park; or a government employee proud of her Tennessee roots. None of this explained the stone fences and cemeteries, old homesites and jonquils on the trails.

Adjacent aisles bulged with books and videos about the Smokies, filled with glossy images of waterfalls, black bears, and Mount LeConte. They seemed to suggest that the park had no history—as if miraculously, in a region well populated and cultivated, this wilderness was preserved. The only history I came across was *Birth of a National Park*, an account of the park's founding. Author Carlos Campbell, a member of the Great Smoky Mountains Conservation Association, which led the campaign to bring a national park to the South, celebrated park champions, such as David

Chapman, "dynamic leader of the movement," and Mrs. Willis P. Davis, "Mother of the Park." In the Haywood County library I found *Strangers in High Places*, an account of the many visitors to the Smokies, from William Bartram to the park founders to the exotic wild boars. An activist in the 1966 campaign to gain wilderness designation for the Smokies, author Michael Frome benefited from firsthand meetings with environmentalists Harvey Broome, Ernie Dickerman, and ranger John Morrell. Neither Frome nor Campbell, however, wrote much about the people who were not strangers to the land, the mountain people and Cherokees who called the region home. Both books perpetuated the notion that valiant preservationists somehow protected this rare example of a Wild East.[3]

In 1900, when this book begins, the Great Smoky Mountains were no longer a wilderness. Wolves, mountain lions, and white-tailed deer, which once roamed these valleys, had become a rare sight. Even the giant clouds of passenger pigeons that once filled the sky, and for which the Pigeon and Little Pigeon Rivers were named, faced extinction. An agricultural people, the Cherokees, had farmed the valleys for several centuries. European farmers began settling the area by 1820. In no sense could the Great Smoky Mountains be called a "frontier" in the beginning of the twentieth century; it was part of a diverse pastoral landscape, the rural Appalachian South.

Four centuries earlier, Cherokees lived in parts of what today we call Tennessee, North Carolina, South Carolina, and Georgia, but they called a place in the Smokies *Kitu'wha*, meaning "mother town." They farmed the valley lands, burned the woods for pest control and game management, and hunted in the forests above. During the sixteenth century, Spanish conquerors Hernando de Soto, Juan Pardo, and Tristan de Luna invaded the region. Though they did not reach the Smokies, their trade goods, plants, and diseases did. Old World crops, such as peaches, watermelons, pears, and cowpeas, came with the Spanish, as did cattle-raising practices. Increasingly committed to European trade, Cherokees began hunting more intensively, which led to the disappearance of bison and elk. As they expanded animal husbandry, they cleared more fields. Trade also brought exotic species, such as Spanish bayonet, which encroached on disturbed woodlands.[4] By the eighteenth century, English colonials entered the fur trade with the Cherokees, which further reduced the white-tailed deer and beaver populations.[5]

The Cherokees, like most North American tribes, owned their land collectively. During the American Revolution, they sided with the British, and then faced retribution from American troops. The soldiers burned their houses, destroyed their crops, and massacred families. "We proceeded by Colonel Grant's orders, to burn the Indian cabins," wrote Lieutenant Francis Marion. "Some of the men seemed to enjoy this cruel work, laughing heartily at the flames, but to me it appeared a shocking sight. But when we came, according to orders, to cut down the fields of corn, I could scarcely refrain from tears."[6] Some of these soldiers were rewarded with 100- to 2,000-acre land grants—in many cases the same land they saw on their campaigns.

One of the largest land grants in the region—including most of the Haywood County portion of the Smokies—was given to Revolutionary War hero Robert Love, who represented Buncombe County in the North Carolina Senate at the time. Another influential citizen, William Cathcart, received 33,280-acre grants from the North Carolina assembly in 1796. In the Tennessee Smokies, a single speculator, Drury Armstrong, obtained 50,000 acres in the Little River section by registering the land "in the names of members of his family and others" and transferring the titles to himself. Armstrong, Cathcart, and Love heirs amassed large fortunes by selling the land or renting it to settlers. Some of the earliest farmers in the Smokies, including John and Lucretia Oliver in Cades Cove, William and Jane Huskey Ogle in Tennessee, and Samuel Cable on Hazel Creek, squatted on land not yet ceded in treaties. They then sought preemptive rights, since their early arrival guaranteed them mill sites, forge sites, the most fertile land in the valley, and hence productive farms.

Americans elected Andrew Jackson in 1828 on a platform advocating the removal of Native Americans to the West. Whites wanted to open more land in the Southeast for white settlement, and Jackson made an exception for the Cherokees, even though the Cherokee Nation had adopted a U.S.-inspired constitution, the sovereignty of which was recognized by the United States Supreme Court. Jackson also chose to ignore his own close relationship with the Cherokees and their help to him in the Muskogee, or Redstick Creek Wars. He "forgot" their assistance in negotiating with the Seminoles. Congress passed the Indian Removal Act of 1830, forcing the Cherokees along the Trail of Tears to Indian Territory.[7]

Contemporary visitors to the region will wonder, then, why so many Cherokees remain in the area immediately adjacent to the Great Smoky Mountains. In the early nineteenth century, a small settlement of more traditional Native Americans living on the Oconaluftee River separated from the Nation and declared themselves citizens of North Carolina. Under the leadership of Chief Drowning Bear, his white adopted son, William Holland Thomas, made repeated trips to Washington, D.C., to exclude the Oconaluftee Cherokees from Indian removal. It helped that Thomas's people lived on rocky, mountainous lands. Through Thomas's maneuvering and aided by the fact that they did not live near gold mines or cotton plantations, the Oconaluftee Cherokees avoided removal.[8] The Cherokees who remained in the Smokies became the Eastern Band, but they faced years of political battles in order to remain. The Cherokee Land Act of 1850 formally opened up much of the remaining land in the Smokies, and speculators bought tracts of 5,000 to 10,000 acres and in some cases more. Not until after the Civil War (in which most Cherokees fought on the Confederate side) did North Carolina allow them to seek justice in state courts, and not until 1924 could they vote. Repeated efforts to remove the Eastern Band made the Cherokees wary of their white neighbors.[9]

For the rest of the nineteenth century, both whites and Cherokees shaped the Smokies as they farmed the lower elevations. With a land grant from the state of North Carolina, German immigrants John Jacob and Sarah Mingus moved into the valley above the Cherokees and began to work the fertile bottomland of Raven Fork. With English or Scots-Irish ancestry, most early white farmers relocated from farms in Burke, Surry, Lincoln, or Wilkes Counties, North Carolina; a few others arrived from South Carolina, Virginia, Georgia, or other parts of Tennessee.[10] Like other nineteenth-century Americans, they perceived the wilderness as threatening: the forest loomed as a dark place filled with panthers and wolves. State governments attempted to eradicate the predators. In Tennessee, hunters received $6 for each wolf pelt ("over four months old") and $1 for each red fox pelt. A "wild cat" hide could be "received by the tax collector in payment of the poll tax" for one year. By the 1870s, bounty hunters so greatly reduced the number of predators that the price of the bounties fell: wolves brought $2, wildcats $1, and foxes, 50 cents. Bounties disappeared by 1900, but the price on the head of a wolf persisted until 1917.[11]

The absence of predators and the expansion of cleared fields led to an increase in squirrels, crows, possums, raccoons, and even pigeons. In frontier Tennessee, squirrels became such a nuisance that farmers pressured the general assembly to take action; they passed a law requiring each adult male pay a "tax" in squirrel or crow scalps.[12] Indeed, the popularity of fried squirrel stew in mountain subsistence diets may have resulted from this simple necessity—nobody ate squirrel in Europe. A native of Cataloochee Valley in North Carolina, Jonathan Woody, said his grandfather rode his horse to the state capital in Raleigh to pressure the governor to pass bounties on these troublesome animals.[13] Early residents of Pigeon Forge and the surrounding mountains shot passenger pigeons for sport and also to keep them from eating their crops. Lucretia and John Oliver, early residents of Cades Cove, built dikes to divert water from wetlands. These improvements along with cattle and hog raising diminished the native canebrakes, which the Cherokees used for everything from blowguns to baskets.[14]

After the Civil War, both Cherokees and mountain whites faced a new influx of settlers. Sons, now grown, returned from the war looking for their own land. Former soldiers settled their families in the smaller valleys or rented speculation lands. In 1887, the United States Congress passed the Dawes Act, requiring the division of Indian lands into individual allotments rather than communal holdings. Whites claiming Cherokee ancestry flooded the land of the Eastern Band, called the Qualla Boundary, in hopes of gaining an "allotment." At the end of the nineteenth century, both white and Cherokee communities faced constant incursions from small investors as well as the get-rich-quick schemes of local residents who wanted to develop the timber or mining resources of the region for a burgeoning Industrial Revolution. For only a brief time remoteness kept them at bay.

Despite poor roads and few rail lines, no one could claim in 1900 that the Smoky Mountains were "pristine." But the American that de Tocqueville described, who "grows accustomed only to change," still wanted to believe that somehow something stayed wild. The first national parks— Yellowstone, Yosemite, Sequoia—once belonged to native peoples, yet this was neatly forgotten. The western parks did not brim with networks of farms or abut industrial cities. Only a certain audacity, then, could locate a national park where nature had been plowed, logged, and conquered. If a Wild West, why not a Wild East? The history of the Great Smoky Mountains is not the simple story of preserving a wilderness, but rather the complex narrative of restoring—and even creating—one.

Forest Economies

At first the earth was flat and very soft and wet. The animals were anxious to get down, and sent out the Buzzard and told him to go and make ready for them. This was the Great Buzzard, the father of all the Buzzards we see now. He flew all over the earth, low down near the ground, and it was still soft. When he reached the Cherokee country, he was very tired, and his wings began to flap and strike the ground, and wherever they struck the earth there was a valley, and where they turned up again there was a mountain. When the animals above saw this, they were afraid that the whole world would be mountains, so they called him back, but the Cherokee country remains full of mountains to this day.

FROM "HOW THE WORLD WAS MADE," A CHEROKEE
MYTH COLLECTED BY ANTHROPOLOGIST JAMES
MOONEY IN THE 1890S

Ye make springs gush forth in the valleys
they flow between the hills,
giving drink to every wild animal;
wild asses quench their thirst.
By streams the birds of air have their habitation;
they sing among the branches.
From your lofty abode you water the mountains;
the earth is satisfied with the fruit of your work.

PSALM 104:10–13

SEPARATED BY GREAT forested ridges—and vastly different historical and spiritual traditions—white and Cherokee farmers created a patchwork of homes, fields, and woodlands in the valleys of the Smoky Mountains in 1900. They also coexisted with a remarkably diverse environment and a mammoth old-growth forest. In every watershed below 3,400 feet, the land evoked a pastoral scene: framed or log homes surrounded by swept yards; bounded by kitchen gardens, stone fences, grazing cattle, and cornfields; connected by spiderwebs of dirt roads. "Back then it was cleared fields and when children would lie for a talk you could hear them for miles," described Lucinda Ogle, born and raised in the Junglebrook area. "Same way with church bells. They would vibrate from mountain to mountain." Almost 7,000 people called this Smoky Mountains landscape home in 1900 (see table 1).[1]

Visitors to the Smokies, however, always commented on the forest above and its extraordinary chestnut trees, sculpting the hillsides with their giant canopies, reaching 80 to 100 feet and comprising in places 75 percent of the forest. When they burst into cascading white blooms each spring, people said it looked like snow had fallen on the mountains. Combined with white oak, scarlet oak, northern red oak, chestnut oak, black oak, and hickory, this primeval oak-chestnut forest shadowed mountain laurel and a lush herbaceous layer of ferns and wildflowers. Forest communities from the tops of the ridges to the bottoms, including spruce-fir, northern hardwoods, cove hardwood, hemlock, and mixed pine, all fit the description of an old-growth forest, which implies a 150-year minimum age standard. A botanist who visited the Smokies in the late nineteenth century reported a greater number of indigenous trees than could be observed between Turkey and England, through Europe, or from the Atlantic Coast to the Rocky Mountain Plateau.[2] And so although residents populated the valleys, they're called *mountain people* for the forested ridges that indeed brought much character to their lives. Economists have labeled them marginal to the world economy, but their knowledge of and folklore about the land still captures contemporary imaginations, still baffles and intrigues modern scholars and scientists.[3]

As farmers, they shared the concerns of other rural Americans in 1900: they worried about children who went off to work in a mill or factory, low prices, bad weather, and the evils of an increasingly urban nation. They were not isolated; many read a newspaper and made regular trips to the

Table 1. Great Smoky Mountains Communities in 1900

Community	County	Population
Big Cove (Cherokee)	Swain	381
Oconaluftee	Swain	275
Noland Creek, Deep Creek, Medlin,		
Hazel Creek, Forney Creek*	Swain	1,350
Cataloochee	Haywood	764
Greenbrier, Mill Creek, Roaring Fork,		
Sugarlands, Baskins Creek, Junglebrook*	Sevier	1,716
Cades Cove	Blount	709
Catons Grove, Cosby Creek	Cocke	
Webb Creek, Gilliland Town		1,800
	Total	6,995

Source: 1900 Federal Population Census.

*The Census District does not delineate the population in these individual communities, so numbers involve some estimation, based on family names and genealogical sources.

county seat. "The folks on Deep Creek, they mostly worried about what was going on in Deep Creek," said Winfred Cagle, who grew up in this North Carolina valley. "They didn't care too much what was going on in Alarka or down in Georgia or Mexico or all them places. They let them folks live and be happy and we did the same thing." To a person from New York, or even Raleigh, though, the Smokies in 1900 surely seemed remote. Railways barely reached adjacent communities, so a traveler could expect hours on a wagon after the railway ride. In rainy weather, even the main county roads were transformed into a sea of mud. Cherokee did not get its first paved road until 1927.[4]

Cherokee and white farmers shared this outlying landscape, but history kept them divided. The ancestors of white farmers participated in the forced removal of the Cherokee Nation to Oklahoma along the Trail of Tears in 1838. During the Civil War, the Thomas Legion of Cherokees served in the Confederate army, whereas many mountain whites remained loyal republicans. At the turn of the century, Cherokees faced continual pressure from the government to send their children to boarding schools, which sought to eradicate all native cultural traditions. They also battled for the right to hold their lands communally, as federal policy pushed for allotment or parceling the land out to each individual. Whereas two-thirds of white farmers owned their land and one-third rented from somebody who did, Cherokees held their lands in common, with individuals paying county taxes for the land they farmed. Such differences should not be downplayed.[5]

An ethnographer who lived with the Eastern Band in the late nineteenth century, James Mooney, often commented that Cherokee traditions were dying. But the resiliency of practices relating to land use remained remarkable, particularly in Big Cove, the traditionalist community in the heart of the Smokies. Only 48 percent of the residents of Big Cove could speak English well enough to carry on "ordinary conversation." A Cherokee Indian Agency (CIA) superintendent lamented in 1906 that the Cherokees "still cling to many of their superstitions, conjuring for the cure of the sick and to bring them good luck."[6] Subsistence practices probably kept many Big Cove residents connected to their traditions, as they still planted their cornfields with the help of *gadugi*, or traditional work groups. Simply traversing the landscape, in fact, could remind Cherokees of the ancient myths, as many used specific locations as their settings. In the "Origin of Disease and Medicine," for instance, the bears met on Clingman's Dome, or *Kuwa'hi*, to discuss the problem of mankind hunting them. In other stories, the Great Rabbit, chief of all the rabbits, held council on Gregory Bald. The Nunnehi, a race of spirit people known to bring back lost children and hunters, lived in a ridge above the Oconaluftee River. Cherokee cosmology divided the universe into This World, the Upper World, and the Under World. Supernatural beings, like the Monster Turtle and Uktena, visited This World through pools and rapids of the Oconaluftee or Tuckaseegee River. The prominence of the land in their lives—its role in subsistence as well as sacred landmarks—may explain why only 28 percent of Big Cove adults belonged to a Baptist or Methodist church.[7]

White mountain people did not have a mythology set in the Smokies, but they did locate their central metaphors and points of reference in the wooded ridges. They distinguished between every feature of mountain topography—bald, butt, bottoms, cove, gap, hollow, knob, sink, swag, and top—and gave each such feature a name: Silers Bald, Round Bottom, Charlies Bunion, Laurel Top. They peppered their conversation with metaphors from the environment. A person could be "as mean as a black snake" or "as ugly as a fence daubed in tadpoles." A child should return home "as straight as a martin to his gourd." To "groundhog it" meant to live in poor circumstances, and "waiting for the bees to swarm" was a euphemism for pregnancy. Even their humor rose from the mountains. Mountain people have to "tie growing pumpkins to stakes so they don't endanger those passing below," claimed one pundit, and "many a mountain family gets its firewood by throwing it down the chimney."[8]

Geography figured into the faith of mountain whites, too, as most belonged to independent Baptist churches, governed by members who chose a minister who had a "calling" rather than divinity school credentials. Primitive Baptists separated from the Freewill and missionary movements in 1832 to continue full immersion for baptism, church on weekends only, and no missionary work or Bible societies. Each member became "saved" as an adult, when he or she could choose to be baptized and join the church. Like the Cherokee purification rituals, this coming-of-age ceremony took place in the creek that was also the lifeblood of the members' farms. White preachers reminded members that they could have only what nature might grant them; human beings must conform to the pattern nature set. "In the mountain view of things," writes Catherine Albanese, "there is some space for free will, but overwhelmingly God controlled the basic lot of people. . . . Thus prayer for mountain people was not a plea for earthly benefits. Rather it was an attempt to move into a condition which a person was thought to yield freely to God." Despite the Calvinist nature of preaching, which reminded members of their sinfulness, primitive Baptists, like the Cherokees, saw nature as a sanctuary where spiritual power could be found. Between the harsh blows of climate and the endurance required to survive on limited means, mountain Baptists looked for moments of grace.[9]

In a way foreign to a modern reader, Cherokees and white mountain residents did not separate themselves from community and place. However mediated through different cultural traditions, for both groups knowledge of and love for the land came from *use*, indeed the need to use it to survive. Unlike contemporary notions of nature appreciation, which suggest "leave only footprints and take only photographs," Cherokees and white mountain people relied on what they could harvest again and again from their gardens, the meadow, and the forest. Each elevation of the Smokies from balds and ridges to forests and bottomlands had special meaning to them, a meaning related to what the land provided. "The land was grandpa's life and wealth," writes Nora De Armond, from Cocke County, Tennessee. "He had great courage in his own ideas, a chance to carve out life of his choosing."[10]

Ridge Tops and Balds

The highest elevations of the Smokies remained the most wild in 1900. Neither whites nor Cherokees harvested wood in the alpine spruce-fir forest, where the "he-balsam" (red spruce) and "she-balsam" (Fraser fir) dominated the canopy, and "pot scrapings" (lichens) hugged the rocks and tree trunks. Only trappers, hunters, and fishermen climbed regularly to these cool, misty regions. The lucrative days of fur trapping had long passed at the turn of the century, or as Greenbrier native Clon Ownby put it, a few people ran traps "after coon and possum hunting quit for cold weather." Lona Parton Tyson remembered that her father trapped muskrat in the winter near Greenbrier Pinnacle, but J. Roy Whaley said, "There wasn't a lot of fur there in the mountains." Centuries of trapping had all but eliminated otter, mink, and wolves, and tanneries had switched to cattle and hogs for their source of leather.[11] Still, Whaley noted that "two or three good possum hides" would buy a pair of shoes at the store.[12]

Not everyone trapped, and only occasionally did anyone climb this high to fish. Most mountain people supplemented the family diet with "speckled trout" (native brook trout) caught closer to home. Carrying a sack of cornmeal, bacon, and blankets, young men and women walked upstream to fish and camp overnight. A mountaineer cut a sourwood sapling, stripped the leaves, tied a string and a straightened safety pin to the end. For bait: red worms, spring lizards, minnows, hornets, bread crumbs. Cherokees found this hook-and-line method useful, but some added the old formulas. "Take fish hawk whiskers and wrap them around the hook," said Awani'ski. "It has drawing power. You let the fish play on the line a while before you pull him up and he'll attract others."[13] Cherokees also still built fish traps, into which unsuspecting trout swam but could not leave, but both Tennessee and North Carolina outlawed the ancient practice of poisoning the water with pounded walnut bark or buckeye to catch fish. One white man living on Forney Creek reported his full-time occupation as "fishing," but he may have been making a joke at the census-taker's expense. In fact, many mountain people expressed concern about overfishing by outside sportsmen. In 1885, Cataloochee farmer Will Palmer helped get a law passed in North Carolina making it illegal for anyone to offer trout for sale or to fish in Cataloochee Creek or any of its tributaries without permission from the residents. Not long afterward two Cataloochee boys, Glenn Palmer and Bob Ewart, told their families they would be searching for lost cattle on Beech Ridge when they "stole out" fishing on Lost Bottom Creek. They caught ninety-seven speckled trout, fried and ate all but two. Glenn Palmer always told people this was the meanest thing he had ever done, but the worst he suffered from his father—Will Palmer—was a stern lecture.[14]

Although their fathers and grandfathers seriously diminished large mammal populations, mountain people expressed concern about over-hunting by sportsmen. One outsider hired a mountain man just to collect bear hides, raising the ire of some of the neighbors. "While . . . most of the big game has been killed, there are still a few black bear left in the more remote and inaccessible mountains, in pursuit of which much sport can be had," wrote one local historian during the period.[15] In 1896 Tenn-esseeans made it illegal to hunt any animal for profit in Sevier, Blount, or Cocke County. Laws reflected the shortage of deer as early as 1871, when North Carolina forbid anyone in Haywood or Jackson County "to hunt with gun nor chase with dogs any deer."[16] "We could kill a deer any time we took a notion to," Newton Ownby recalled of the Little River area in the 1880s. "Our smokehouse was full all the time." Most mountaineers, however, regularly hunted smaller animals—rabbit, coon, possum, squir-rel, and turkey—found closer to home. "If you did any hunting much it was usually squirrel hunting," said Robert Woody. "It really was just not so much for the sport but to have some squirrels to eat." While men dominated hunting, women such as Eunice Smelcer also brought home fresh meat: "I liked to squirrel hunt. I killed six in one day. I have good luck any time. I take my kids with me and I have as much fun as they do." On the other hand, Herman Matthews said his father didn't hunt at all. "[Our] family didn't eat much wild meat," he said. "My dad didn't allow us to bother the wildlife. . . . He said that if it wasn't preserved it'd be de-stroyed and the coming generations wouldn't see the wildlife. He didn't hunt, and he didn't allow us to. He didn't want people to hunt on his place, but they did anyway, but he didn't like it."

Cherokee formulas for hunting required the hunter to fast, to travel without eating or drinking, then to conduct ceremonies and recite prayers at his campsite that night. Then the next morning, he could hunt. While it's difficult to say how many Cherokees continued the old practices, Elsie Martin remembered as a child that "when hunting or fishing men don't eat a meal. It was the practice that you don't eat before going hunting or fishing." Cherokees may have been less likely to hunt for sport, as even in the early part of the century a few mountain men did. Eugene Lowe described as a young boy fox hunting with his grandfather: "Way most people fox hunt is to go on a ridge and build a fire and listen to the dogs run. . . . You don't catch one of them. Foxes can outrun them dogs."[17]

Mountain people hunted bear most often to protect stock. Bounties on predators, including panthers, wolves, and foxes, disappeared by 1900, because these animals no longer existed in numbers great enough to threaten cattle or sheep. A sheep missing from the balds or hog meat stolen from a smokehouse are, in fact, the two most common openings to bear hunt stories. Hattie Caldwell Davis recalled one bear Cataloochee farmers nicknamed Honest John, because "he only killed one [cow] and ate what he wanted, then carried the rest of it off and put it behind a log for his next meal."[18] In hunting tales, the cattle owner contacted the best-known hunter in the valley, who disappeared into the woods with a pack of dogs. Bill Walker, for whom Walker Valley is named, cornered a bear in a cave, then proceeded into the blackness with his gun ("Old Death") cocked. He fired when he felt "warm moisture on his face" and he didn't miss. Turkey George Palmer of Cataloochee, a legendary bear hunter, claimed he killed so many bears that he feared revenge: he ordered a steel casket for his funeral, so bears wouldn't dig up his bones. Men told these stories to entertain rather than record history, but they make clear that residents considered bear hunts something out of the ordinary and bear hunters, legendary characters. Most farmers did not have time to hunt bears. "Back them days you didn't see 'em, rare for a bear to get in close," said Seymour Calhoun. "When we lived in here [Cades Cove], we had to go halfway up Smoky Mountain to find a bear," agreed Maynard Ledbetter. "Bears were scarce," said P. Audley Whaley, who grew up in Cataloochee. "Cattle owners hunt down and kill a bear." Bear hunt stories indicate that the chase involved long waits and intelligent bears, which disappeared into "slicks" (rhododendron thickets) or led pursuers through dog-hobble, named for its desired effect on hounds. Because of the wily nature of bears, some cattle owners used a deadfall trap made of logs, which fell when the animal went for the bait.[19]

Bears and their pursuers probably carved the earliest network of trails that became the basis for the famous Appalachian balds. Ancestors of the Cherokees burned small areas to observe game and enemies, and old myths typically mention balds as specific locations, such as Lizard Place and Rabbit Place. For instance, the story of U'la'gu, a yellow jacket as large as a house that snatched up children and wild game, took place above the Nantahala River. Hunters followed the monster to its cave and built fires around the hole. U'la'gu died in flames, but thousands of smaller yellow jackets escaped all over the world. Later versions of the same myth linked this incident to the creation of the balds: "the Great Spirit declared that all high mountains would be devoid of trees so the Cherokees could always see their enemies." As one scholar has guessed, this later version was probably altered to explain phenomena that grew to prominence just before the storyteller's lifetime.[20]

By the middle of the nineteenth century, both Cherokees and whites herded cattle and sheep to the balds each spring. The annual presence of animals created a disturbance, which spread non-native plants, such as English plantain, dandelion, and white clover, across the balds. On the rim of the open land, the forest sprouted orange flame azalea, which made the view from the balds spectacular, especially in May. "You could see . . . a long ways," said Maynard Ledbetter, making use of a dramatic pause to emphasize his words. "[There were] oak trees and chestnuts here and there, but the cattle kept the brush down." Annually taking domesticated animals to a wild place, mountain people learned a great deal about the ecology of the mountains, as all the balds are above 4,900 feet. When lamb's tongue appeared on the balds "as thick as a meadow" in the spring, Cades Cove farmers knew to herd cattle to Spence Field. On the way up Bote Mountain (from Cades Cove) or Shanty Branch (from Cataloochee) some people put wire muzzles on their cattle to keep them from eating rhododendron. Paul Woody remembered the cattle enjoying early-season ramps, the wild leeks of the Smokies. "Cow's milk from a cow fed on wild plants had a peculiar taste," said Herb Clabo, "but we got used to it." If they took cattle to the balds too early, however, the overheated animals might get caught in a snowstorm and the chill could kill them. Bone Valley Creek in North Carolina received its name for cattle that died in this manner in the spring of 1902. In general, though, mountain people believed that cooler air and fewer insects kept the animals healthier. Milk sickness, a fatal disease to cattle and people who drank the cattle's milk, seemed less frequent when animals spent the summer on the mountain tops. White snakeroot, which caused the ailment, is in fact a low-elevation plant.[21]

Absentee landowners held the high country above Cataloochee, so community members treated it as something of a commons. Large landowners in Cades Cove leased Russell Field and Spence Field to other farmers. Above Big Cove, Cherokees grazed communally held lands or sought rent from white people who wanted to pasture their animals. Of the three communities, the Cherokees showed the most concern for the impact of animals on the semi-alpine environment. In one rental agreement, they allowed cattle or horses "but no hogs or sheep," as the latter trimmed grass to a nub. Farmers from Haywood County ranged their cattle on Cherokee lands for $10 per year in 1902, and sometimes pastured upwards of 800 cattle. "Some parties are ranging without attention to the terms, others are paying for a few head and pasturing many more," complained a government agent, who threatened a civil suit on behalf of the Cherokees.[22]

All three communities shared herding responsibilities. Cherokee and Cades Cove farmers pooled their resources to hire a herder. Bessie Jumper, a Cherokee woman, told a story of an old woman charged with finding cattle when she ran into the Little People, who told her exactly where the missing animals were. She wasn't supposed to mention their help, however, and when she related the story she didn't live long. Above Cataloochee, farmers simply left cattle without a herder. "[My father] had a little feist that always used to take his cattle up the mountains," recalled Paul Woody. The dog walked behind his father, and when one of the cows stepped off the trail, "he'd nibble at the heels. That feist learned to lay down flat so the cattle couldn't kick him." Farmers returned once a week to "salt" the animals, or leave the necessary mineral in a log. "When you salted your cattle, you salted everybody's cattle," remembered Raymond Caldwell. In addition to providing a needed nutrient, the salt kept the cattle from wandering too far from the mountaintop. According to

Woody, a trip to "salt the cattle" turned into a kind of holiday; men would hunt and fish along the way and camp for as long as a week. "And it seemed like when he got home [my father] wasn't behind, nothing was pushing," Woody said. "I just can't account for it. We're all pushing, you know [today] for time, but that was a relaxing day of life." At the end of the summer, herders gathered the animals into a "gant lot," and farmers came and picked up their livestock.[23]

The Great Trees

The richly diverse oak-chestnut and cove hardwood forests, which spread across the ridges below the balds and the spruce-fir zone, grew resplendent chestnut and yellow poplar trees in enormous sizes. "In this region nearly all trees attain their fullest development," said Horace Kephart, who hiked the Smokies between 1904 and 1913. "In cool rich coves, chestnut trees grow 6 to 9 feet across the stump; and tulip poplars up to 10 or 11 feet, their straight trunks towering like gigantic columns, with scarcely a noticeable taper, 70 or 80 feet to the nearest limb." By 1900, a few lumber companies had extracted valuable trees, such as walnut and cherry, for the burgeoning Piedmont furniture trade. Because of transportation problems, though, even the famous forester Gifford Pinchot wrote, "commercially these forests are at present unimportant."[24]

To the communities surrounding the Smokies, however, the forests—especially those of chestnut trees—were very important. The American chestnut covered a full 31 percent, or 159,165 acres, of the Smokies and grew to mammoth sizes. A fallen chestnut above Cosby on Indian Camp Creek, for example, measured 9 feet, 8 inches in diameter 6 feet above the ground. "The hollow portion is so large that [an adult] could stand up in it," described a naturalist. "This hollow runs more than 50 feet up the trunk and at its narrowest point is not less than 3 feet. This must be the tree of which I heard. A man lost some stock during a snowstorm and later found them safe inside a hollow chestnut tree." Enormous trees produced epic quantities of chestnuts. "This is an unbelievable thing: how many chestnuts there were," said Paul Woody. Alie Newman Maples agreed: "As a little girl, me and my brother Ray would take a sack or a pail and go out to the woods. Strong winds blew in the night, and we would pick up gallons of chestnuts under each tree. So delicious and sweet." Families baked chestnuts in the fireplace; Delce Mae Carver Bryant remembered sackfuls hanging on nails outside the door, ready to be baked. Johnny Manning, who grew up in Greenbrier, remembered as a child trading his pocketfuls of chestnuts for school tablets and pencils. John McCaulley, who grew up in Cades Cove, recalled seeing 100 bushels of chestnuts piled near the herder's cabin at Rich Gap and four men packing them off to sell. His own family gathered seven bushels, and with the help of mules, carried them to Knoxville, where they received $4 per bushel.[25]

In turn, the animals that residents most often mentioned as game—squirrels, wild turkey, deer, and bear—depended on this annual mast production. The large oak and chestnut trees above the Smokies settlements provided excellent gray and red squirrel habitat. Woodlots and fencerows offered a home for fox squirrels. Walter Cole recalled that "bears got fat on chestnuts, coons got fat on chestnuts, and the woods was filled with wild turkey, coon; most all game ate chestnut and got fat." A former Cades Cove resident, Maynard Ledbetter, boasted that "back when there were chestnuts, bear got so fat they couldn't run fast; now the poor bear run like a fox."[26]

To a great extent, mountain subsistence depended on the chestnut tree. Builders found chestnut wood to be remarkably insect-proof and rot-resistant, so chestnut logs made the best fence rails and posts as well as caskets. "It was soft wood and worked good: you could split it," said Seymour Calhoun. And chestnut trees grew so large that in one documented cabin a single tree contributed all the logs for the main structure. "But my father built our cabin of oak," said Calhoun, "because that's what he had to cut down to build it." Martha Wachacha, born in Cherokee in 1910, said her father also preferred oak for log cabins. "He didn't use poplar; it would decay soon," she said.[27]

The huge annual mast production made woodland grazing possible, and seasonally, mountain people let their hogs run loose in the woods. "We used the woods as pasture," explained Herb Clabo. Because farmers kept 60 percent of their land in woods and unknown speculators owned the ridges, woodland pasture was everywhere. "There were about a hundred pigs when I first moved here," said Maggie Wachacha. In Big Cove, the average farm ran just two hogs, but seven households owned ten or more. "Now you don't see any pigs. Pigs and hogs were so fat. There were plenty of chestnuts back then. That's what they lived on," Wachacha said.

To keep the hogs from wandering too far away and to facilitate catching them in November, farmers put out a ration of corn at regular intervals. Wachacha's father would blow a horn whenever he did this, which trained the hogs to come down for a meal. "Pigs would come and form a row there were so many of them," she said. Mark Hannah, who grew up in Cataloochee, said that his family used dogs to round up the hogs. "Sometimes, after they were fat on mast, they went wild," he said, "and we had to catch them with a dog. This was fun, but dangerous!" Feral hogs became legendary characters, such as the Brushy Mountain Sow, Old Chiltose, and "the old-bellied sow on Little Fork Ridge."[28]

Woodland pasture shows up in fence laws, which required ground under cultivation to be surrounded by a fence 5 feet high. "In place of fencing the cattle," explained Pink Sutton, "they fenced the garden up. Cattle out." The law even specified acceptable fence materials, and only "notoriously mischievous stock" that were "known to be in the habit of throwing down and jumping fences" had to be contained. Anyone caught trying to "kill, maim, or injure" livestock "lawfully running at large" was guilty of a misdemeanor, and in Haywood County, a felony. In the nineteenth century, this practice tied mountain farmers to lowland economies, as hogs, cattle, and even turkeys were rounded up and driven hundreds of miles to market. In the 1880s, John E. Roland remembered drovers gathering cattle, hogs, and even turkeys in big lots in Bryson City to herd to Richmond, Virginia. As railroads entered the region, they challenged fence laws and broke drovers' markets. Common law made railroads responsible for animals killed by trains, but fencing a right-of-way was prohibitively expensive. Beginning in the 1880s, railroads began pushing through stock laws, which required farmers to control their animals. A North Carolina judge ruled that if a county tried to pass a "no stock law" bill, the entire county would have to be enclosed at county expense. Tennessee finally linked stock laws to population to force counties to comply; John Davis, a Tennessee farmer, actually moved to the sparsely populated Smokies to escape stock laws.[29]

To run hogs in the woods required managing the woods with fire. Prehistoric Native Americans burned to clear undergrowth and promote hunting grounds, the Cherokees continued this practice, and by 1900 it was commonly done by both white and Native American farmers. Burning kept down the undergrowth and controlled rats, ticks, chiggers, and snakes. "Before the logging companies came in, before the timber was cut, you could start a fire and it just burnt the leaves around the trees," said Seymour Calhoun. Low-grade fires also promoted the growth of large oak trees, as their thick bark protected them from fire damage, and they sprout prolifically where other species fail. Because oak acorns germinate rapidly and root quickly, the trees adapt easily to the dry conditions following a fire. Table mountain pine, found most often on steep south-facing slopes, actually requires fire in order to germinate. For this reason, the species probably became much more common during this historic period. Although burning sometimes scorched the bottoms of tree trunks, it converted leaf mulch to necessary minerals, which "greened up" the new growth, and the lack of woody underbrush gave the woods an open appearance. "You could just ride on through [on a horse]," Calhoun said.[30] Just as farmers needed the oak-chestnut forest, the oak-chestnut forest profited from the farmers.

Since farmers heated their homes with fireplaces or woodstoves, they also cut firewood from the deep woods. The Cherokees in Big Cove estimated that they cut between five and fifteen cords of firewood per household each year. At a rate of ten cords per year per household, Smoky Mountains residents consumed as much as 13,510 cords per year. Not all of this meant cutting down green trees, however, as waste wood in construction, dead snags, blowdowns, and trees cleared for gardens made the easiest firewood.[31]

Even before major lumber companies entered the region, small portable mills gave residents access to construction goods. In Cherokee, residents added glass windows to their log cabins after the portable mills arrived. Several portable mill owners visited Cades Cove in 1904, for example, and contracted to supply the lumber for framed houses. Because of the great number of trees larger than 20 inches in diameter, portable mills were not as practical for extraction as they were in other parts of the Southern Appalachians. Mom-and-pop operations, however, could turn a profit. Jarvis Connor's father bought 300 acres for $1,000 by setting up a small sawmill and cutting the best timber on it. No one marveled at his success more than the man who put up the money: "I thought for sure I'd get that Connor farm as soon as I loaned that $1,000," he reportedly said.[32]

The counties surrounding the Smokies supported about 100 small sawmills in 1884, but less than 1 percent of the residents were employed by sawmills in 1900. In the last decade of the nineteenth century, several large lumber companies entered the mountains looking for valuable species, particularly walnut and cherry. The Glasgow-based Scottish Carolina Timber and Land Company, for example, constructed a mill on the Pigeon River and purchased stumpage from area farmers. Clon Ownby remembered his father describing a company that cut only very tall trees for gunwales on barges. "The logs were so long they couldn't take them around the curves," he said, so they maneuvered the tall trunks on separate wagons. Such labor-intensive logging did not prove profitable; the Scottish Carolina company lost a million dollars before it folded. Land records show that several landowners conveyed "certain timber" on their wooded lands to small lumber companies.[33] Small logging operations did leave their mark on the Smoky Mountains where loggers rolled or "ball-hooted" lumber down cleared lanes into streams or built splash dams. The J. L. English Lumber Company, owned by a prominent Knoxville judge, built a series of splash dams along the Little River watershed in the 1890s. The brief use of splash dams in the Smokies did cause some suffering to both land and people. Splash dams restrained small streams until a holding pool formed; when the water was released through the gate, it carried the logs downhill toward the main river or another dam. The pressure of heavy logs and turbulent water made a "veritable arroyo of torn shores and skimmed stones out of the mountain streams." This was the case on Hazel Creek, where "the logs went rolling and tumbling and the water roaring." According to Granville Calhoun, "you could hear it for a mile. It was like a great storm, the logs bumping one another and hitting the logs." The eruption killed so many trout that Hazel Creek residents walked along the creek banks and picked up bucketfuls.[34]

As the railroads edged closer to the Smokies, mountain men made extra money by cutting crossties out of locust trees and selling them by the wagonload. "We would cut the right-sized board with a broadaxe; they sold for about 60 cents apiece," explained Winfred Cagle. "You could make about two or three in a day, then it took a day to take 'em [to the company]." Along the railroad lines, entrepreneurs built tanneries in Sylva, Hazelwood, Asheville, Brevard, and Andrews, North Carolina; and in Knoxville, McCookville, and Walland, Tennessee. Tanneries required the acidic bark of hemlock and chestnut oak trees to tan and loosen the hair from the hides. Between 1902 and 1931, Shlosser Leather Company in Walland processed 300 to 400 hides per day using acid wood.[35] One man in Swain County described his full-time occupation as "tanbark peeler," but most families thought of it as seasonal, supplemental work like making crossties. Aaron and Nancy Moore, residents of Little Greenbrier, paid off the balance of what they owed John Stinnet for their land by hauling tanbark. The Cherokees regularly sold tanbark in Andrews, North Carolina, but many disputes arose over whose bark it was to sell and where and when it could be collected. Whites sometimes collected tanbark on Indian land. "It is true there are many trespasses on these lands and the lands are being continually depreciated in value on account of these trespasses," wrote a Bureau of Indian Affairs (BIA) agent. "Nor do the Indians receive anything for the use of these outside lands. In many cases, when the matter is traced out, it is found that some of the Indians [whose land it was not to sell] have sold the timber or bark and pocketed the cash for [their] own use."[36] In one case, the superintendent recommended selling a parcel of land because so "much timber, tanbark, and chestnuts have already been removed by trespassers." Other whites wanted to contract with the Cherokees to cut timber, but this immediately caused problems. Legally, no sales could be made without the approval of the U.S. Department of Interior, which administered the BIA. The Cherokees, naturally, believed their land was theirs to contract. In 1904, the Eastern Band allowed Charles Fuller to cut timber on Indian land without U.S. Department of Interior approval, and the government agent threatened to sue in court. Over the next decade, BIA agents spent much of their time threatening white trespassers and preventing illegal cutting of timber by Cherokees and "white Indians." The tribal council approved several such contracts and looked the other way when certain Cherokees allowed cutting on tribal lands.[37]

Despite the conflict over and use of the great trees, which foreshadowed the century ahead, in 1900 the understory still sustained many plants that both the Cherokees and white mountain people found essential to daily life. One of the first signs of spring in the Smoky Mountains was the edible greens that appeared in the woods. "Ma filled her apron with poke stalks growing everywhere," remembered Dorie Cope.

"Nature's garden was ready long before our garden produced anything edible. The fresh greens were a delicious, welcome change from our winter fare of dried or canned vegetables." An important early spring food, pokeweed (*Phytolacca americana*, sometimes called "poke sallet") provided greens more than a month before a garden would sprout. Mountain people also enjoyed branch cresses, crow's feet, and dock. Both whites and Cherokees favored European imports, including beets, chard, watercress, and garden cress. Cherokees did, however, reject two other exotic greens that whites enjoyed—dandelion and chicory. Both groups boiled greens with several drainings and then fried them; however, Cherokee women did not believe in nibbling tidbits of greens as they were being harvested, as they saw their white neighbors do. Both Cherokee and white farmers also collected ramps in early April or May in dark, moist areas above 3,000 feet. Some folks believed that raw ramps and sassafras tea worked on the system like a spring tonic.[38]

Before a canopy of leaves darkened the forest floor, wildflowers bloomed in profusion. Cherokees and white mountain people found many of these plants useful as well. Juanita Ownby's family dug bloodroot to dye Easter eggs red. Mayapple, though bitter by itself, and passion flower fruit added flavor to special drinks. Mountain women made a ginger-like candy by boiling the root of little brown jug and then dipping it in a heavy syrup. "Ginger root" flavored breads and desserts, and a tea made from the same plant reportedly cured menstrual cramps. Before store-bought cloth became commonplace, women dyed wool with walnut root; indigo to create blue, and maple bark for purple dye.[39]

Most people who grew up in the mountains can remember their grandmothers giving them spicewood or sassafras tea, but they don't often remember why. Martha Crisp, who lived on Mingus Branch, used ground ivy (*Glechoma hederacea*) for kidney and bladder troubles, and black snakeroot and boneset tea for pneumonia. As P. Audley Whaley said, "mother was the doctor," at the turn of the century, and mother often got her remedies from the woods. Patent medicines arrived with small valley stores and peddlers, and many people mention mustard poultices and castor oil, but they still found available herbs a major source of medicine. Dora Proffit Williams, who grew up in Greenbrier, documented eighty native plants that her mother regularly used. "I can remember people bringing their little babies to mother for her to doctor them," writes Williams. "Mother could [also] make a salve out of a weed she called 'sheep sorrell.' It would cure up most any kind of sore. Many people in the community who had sores that would not heal would come to mother for a treatment of her salve." Winfred Cagle quipped, "I believe [my mother] could've cured leprosy if there'd been any around, with the salves and medicines she would make." Where did white mountain women learn their remedies? Though evidence is meager, it seems likely that Cherokee women shared some of their secrets or white women observed what worked for their Native American neighbors. Government agents, who frowned on traditional practices, complained that Cherokee women were always out gathering leaves and roots. In 1898, a Cherokee midwife delivered Dorie Cope's older brother, and according to her family "the Indians were fine herb doctors and kind, sympathetic midwives." Cherokees had a centuries-old tradition of using some 500 medicinal plants; one did not have to be a conjuror or shaman to treat colds and menstrual problems, or to devise formulas for hunting, fishing, or love problems. Similarities between their system and white women's use of medicinal plants support the idea that this was their ultimate source.[40]

Mountain people made money from herbaceous plants as well. For several hundred years, the most profitable herb collected each fall in the Smoky Mountains was ginseng. Cherokee shamans addressed ginseng as a sentient being, *Yunwi Usdi'* (Little Man), but tribal members also collected the intricate roots for sale at the local stores, destined for markets in China. "There used to be a good bit scope of 'sang on the mountain," said Turkey George Palmer. "I could fill a tow sack in half a day and sell it for 15 cents a pound green or 25, dry." Anthropologists recorded a ceremonial Cherokee method of hunting ginseng, which included "passing by" the first three plants and "paying" the spirit for the fourth plant with a small bead. But white mountaineers also replanted their favorite patches and cultivated ginseng, which takes seven years to harvest. "I raised sang, too . . . had a patch of it measuring 6 by 18 feet," Palmer said. He relied on making $50–$60 a season selling wild and cultivated ginseng every fall in the Caton's Grove store in Cocke County, Tennessee. Because prices rose substantially during the second decade of the twentieth century, mountain residents later had trouble with competitors stealing their patches and failing to replant. Storeowners complained about sellers who brought them the wrong roots or sold cultivated ones masquerading as the more valuable wild ginseng. Gudger Palmer remembered his mother being fooled by a Big Cove resident, who sold her what turned out to be withered poke roots as the sacred root.[41]

A small market also existed for holly and galax. "Mr. Carl Baum, the florist in Knoxville, would have us children and Dad gather things for his florist business. They would pay us 25 cents a tow sack full for galax leaves or ground pine," writes Lucinda Ogle. "I think they used them in wreaths. We also gathered rosin to sell . . . This was used in medicine." All six children in Ogle's family hunted galax in the fall, when they didn't have to worry about running into poisonous snakes. Delce Carver Bryant, who spent her childhood above Cosby, remembered her mother helping out with the bills by collecting mountain holly.[42]

The edge of the woods, like the disturbed areas around the balds, grew up in blackberries and huckleberries, which both Cherokees and whites gathered for their own use. "The food supply is materially and pleasantly varied by the abundant and choice product of wild berries, strawberries, raspberries, blackberries, whorttleberries and the service, all in their season," described the superintendent of Cherokee schools. Old fields proved a fine environment for strawberries especially. Pearl Caldwell, also of Cataloochee, said that she usually harvested a 10-quart bucketful of strawberries and made jam and wine. She also made wine out of wild grapes and rhubarb. "They was raspberries and strawberries and June apples and all sorts of fruit, and it was more like living in the Garden of Eden than anything else I can think of," concluded Charlie Palmer of Cataloochee.

In addition to offering this bounty, the old-growth forest provided much of the character to daily life. Enormous stands of great trees, after all, made life in the Smokies different from life in other rural areas in the South. Eighty-four percent (eighty-two species) of the known Neotropical migratory birds nest in an old-growth oak-chestnut forest. It is not much of a stretch, then, to suggest that this enormous stand would have supported prodigious numbers of warblers, vireos, scarlet tanagers, and wood thrushes.[43] These, in turn, became a source of folklore: for example, the red-eyed vireo, which called repetitively in the middle of the afternoon, was known as the "preacher bird." Since owls find greater nesting habitat in old-growth forests, their numbers would have been greater than the present. And the horned owl *(tskĭlĭ')*, the barred owl *(u'guku')*, and the screech owl *(wa'huhu')* all played starring roles in Cherokee tales.

Both groups favored stories set in the woods above their homes. Traditional Cherokees, for instance, referred to *tskili* and *u'guku'* as witches, and to all night-singing birds, including the mysterious whip-poor-will, or *wagulĭ'*, and Chuck-will's-widow as evil omens or ghosts. Scary stories, called "haint tales" by mountain residents, typically opened with a description of the forest at night and the call of the whip-poor-will. Both species of nightjars, or nocturnal, ground-nesting species, prefer the open woodlands that the Cherokee and white farmers created.[44]

Open Valleys

Below the great trees, the open valleys in each watershed of the Smokies supported the daily rhythm of small neighborly farming communities and a varied ecosystem of meadow and woodlot. On the flattest, most fertile land in the richest coves, a few farmers, such as Will Messer in Cataloochee and John Oliver in Cades Cove, created large, profitable farms of more than 400 acres. Farmers of this class rebuilt frame houses at the turn of the century on the land where their ancestors lived in log cabins. They sold corn, apples, and sometimes tobacco to local markets. The farther up the watershed, the smaller the farm and the less likely that the resident owned his property. In Big Cove, Cherokee households cultivated an average of just 10.5 acres per household in the summer of 1900.[45]

Mountain residents, whatever the size of their land, located their homes near a creek or spring. They needed accessible drinking water, and in Cherokee they also made use of plants grown near the springs. Mandy Walkingstick said that her family protected golden club near the springs, because crushed roots from the plant made an effective poultice for sore muscles.[46] Whites and Cherokees diverted water through a tiny building called a spring house, which kept fresh perishable foods, particularly milk. In the early twentieth century, the typical mountain farm included not just a home, spring house, and barn, but a yard scattered with small outbuildings: a smokehouse, corn crib, chicken house, woodshed, outdoor toilets, washhouse, and sometimes a grist mill. The buildings that showed the most creative architectural design and adaptation to the Smokies environment, though, were the cantilever barns. These multipurpose buildings, first invented by an innovative Sevier County farmer, supported a second floor that overhung the first. In the damp mountain environment, farmers could store fodder and corn above the ground, keeping it free of insects and molds. Animals rested in pens below, and a wagon rig could be kept dry under the large overhangs.[47]

Around the house and outbuildings, farm women kept a yard of firmly packed dirt, which children swept every day; when weeds were eliminated, the ticks and chiggers also disappeared. "Daddy sent us out to get sackfuls of pennyroyal and we'd throw that around the floors and in the dogs beds, and it would keep fleas away," remembered Lucinda Ogle. "Nightshade and pans of buttermilk would catch the flies." Women kept straight-backed chairs, looms, and spinning wheels on the porch, but except in the coldest winter weather, they worked and socialized in the yards. To brighten outdoor living, they planted flowers in front of the house, especially daffodils, gladiolus, tiger lilies, daylilies, and periwinkle. Gourd vines or English ivy trailed over a paling fence or trellis, and flowers framed the yard. A few plants, such as yucca and multiflora rose, probably proliferated simply because of all the disturbance to the land. The three most common yard trees families planted in Cades Cove included eastern red cedar, black walnut, and apples. Cedars, especially, made a good roosting place for chickens and guineas, and walnuts made a brown dye, a delicious treat, and drew squirrels to the yard for easy hunting from the porch. Older Cherokees believed that the birds that often hung around homeplaces carried messages. The chickadee, called *tsikilili'*, was a truth teller that would warn you of trouble ahead or predict that a friend long absent would soon return. On the other hand, the tufted titmouse, or *utsu'gi*, brought false messages.[48]

Around the yard, farmers pieced their land into woodland, pasture, and fields. They practiced a cycle of land rotation in which land was cleared, then planted in row crops until soil fertility dropped, when it became pasture. Without mowing or heavy use, the forest quickly invaded with saplings, and in five years the field could be covered in black locusts. When the soil regained its fertility, a later generation might clear the same field by girdling trees and burning the undergrowth. "Deadenings," as farmers called these fields of scarred trees, were used as evidence of poor farming methods by extension agents, but leaving the tree roots helped prevent erosion and burning restored nutrients to the soil by releasing minerals in the form of fertilizing ash. In Cades Cove, at least one farmer built earthen dikes to reclaim wetlands for pasture.[49] "They made a new ground, cleared off a field, and just planted it there," described Emmaline Driver, a native of Cherokee. "The ground was rich. . . . They had all kinds of beans and they didn't have no bugs or anything like we do today." In some communities, breaking "new ground" became a neighborhood activity. "They called it workings," said Cauley Trantham. "They'd get ten or fifteen men and they'd get together and clear it out. They had axes and they'd chop it out by hand and then dig out the roots and stumps with a mattock where they were able." It took four things to "make it" in those days: "a turning plow, a mattock, a hoe, and muscle power." On some of the largest farms, tenant farmers and sharecroppers were hired to do the back-breaking work of clearing land. Less prosperous renters, such as Lona Parton Tyson's family, cleared land for large property owners and then moved on. "Most of the time we would stay . . . a year, long enough to grow a crop of corn and potatoes and a garden," recalled Lona Parton Tyson. "[Then] we would be moving to another old house with the same old job of cleaning the house and loading our furniture, such as it was."[50]

Extension agents and foresters blamed mountain people for ruining soil fertility, but those who remained on one piece of land for two or three generations acquired knowledge of how to improve nitrogen content. In addition to burning and the slower process of land rotation, mountain people reclaimed some land with compost and animal manure; many people mention using lime for acid soil and planting cover crops to return nitrogen to the soil. "Most of the time they sowed grass and clover," said George Beck, describing farmers in Oconaluftee Valley. "My daddy sowed a lot of clover." On Noland Creek, Eugen Lowe's father spread wheat bran on the ground to help fertilize the soil. The superintendent of the federally run Cherokee Indian School ordered one ton of "Land Plaster" and "Superphosphate" each year; whereas he had to order many exotic seeds from Virginia, the fertilizer was available in nearby Waynesville. After 1914, state agricultural agents encouraged the use of red clover as a cover crop and nitrogen fixer, but at least one noted that farmers in Sevier County already grew cowpeas in corn at the last cultivation, which were "picked by hand for seed" and "logged down" to replenish the soil.[51] And mountain farmers did *not* plow downhill, as their humorous tales sometimes suggested or proponents of scientific agriculture later claimed that they did. They preferred non-draft horses for plowing, because they were lighter, could maneuver in steep terrain, and didn't cause as much erosion. Horses pushed single-, double-, or bull-tongue plows "*around* the hill" (my emphasis), and in steep places they used a hoe to break a small section of land. The farmer shouldered rocks to the side of the field, and children often had the tedious task of stacking them to make a stone fence around the field. Although the mountain people did not use mortar for rock walls, they so carefully sized and placed the stones that many of them remained standing for more than a century.[52]

Both Cherokee and white mountain farmers relied on corn. Big Cove farmers produced 19 bushels of corn for each bushel of wheat. BIA officials frequently complained about the way that attendance dropped during planting and harvest times, when parents needed children at home to help. One bemoaned the impossibility of interesting Cherokees in "raising something besides corn and beans." Throughout western North Carolina and eastern Tennessee, at least three times as many acres were planted in corn as in the next ranking crop, wheat. Corn delivered more yield per acre, required a minimum of equipment, would grow among "rocks, stumps, and deadened trees on the hillsides," and could be left standing before harvest for weeks, even in the ever-present rainy weather. Surplus corn could be sold as stock feed or used in making whiskey.[53]

Nonetheless it was a challenge to cultivate plants in such a wooded environment. The closer the woodlands, the more critters that viewed corn as a delicacy: crows, coons, opossums, turkeys, squirrels, and groundhogs, as well as domestic chickens, cows, hogs, and mules. Coal tar–covered seed would keep chickens out of freshly planted corn, because they "didn't recognize it." Some people soaked their corn in whiskey for the same reason. Jim Shelton said that to keep crows out of the garden, "run a horsehair through a grain of corn and tie it," which would choke the bird. While fences kept large domestic animals out of the corn, mountain women and children complained about the constant task of chasing crows and the neighbor's chickens out of the corn. Both Cherokees and white mountain people hung rows of large gourds to attract purple martins, swallow-like birds that nest in colonies and eat thousands of insects. Because these birds are fiercely territorial, a martin colony could keep away pesky corn-eating birds, with the added advantage of minimizing insect pests. The other drudgery women and children complained about most was hoeing the weeds. It seemed that "by the time you got through with it, it was time to do it again," according to Mrs. Cauley Trentham. Because they used no agricultural chemicals, if it rained a little bit (and it rained a lot) the weeds got "knee high in there." Large landowners could afford to hire teams of men, women, and children to hoe corn; paid by the day, they worked from dawn to dusk. In Cherokee, Bessie Jumper remembered being hired to hoe corn for 50 cents a day, though "sometimes [we] got chickens for hoeing corn."[54]

Every person as well as every domesticated animal relied on corn. Robert Woody described eating cornmeal mush ("boiling water and cornmeal") for breakfast, cornbread with a big noon meal, and cornbread and milk for supper. Farm animals, especially horses, ate the dried stalks and leaves of the plants (called "fodder"). Families that could not afford ducks or geese used corn shucks to stuff mattresses. While many mountain people made whiskey out of their corn surplus, most refused to drink alcohol for religious reasons. "In all of our ramblings in the mountains I never did see a moonshine still," said Velma Ownby Lamons, "but I know there were people in Greenbrier who made whiskey. This does not say that these men were, by nature, criminally inclined. Many of them were God-fearing men, trying to make a living by earning a little extra cash for a large family." The federal government placed a tax on whiskey and required distillers to obtain licenses; such fees would render small-time operators insolvent, so periodically "revenuers"—federal tax collectors—raided mountain stills. Lucy Black Ownby claimed that some women even made moonshine: "People had to feed their families and clothe them." Paul Woody, on the other hand, recalled that his father's copper still bothered his mother so much that she tricked her son into telling her where it was located. "She cut that still down," Woody remembered. "Daddy never did make it any more." Because stills required such a great amount of hardwood to keep the fire hot, they had to be moved frequently and probably caused a greater impact on the woods during Pro-

hibition, when cases of moonshine were sold in Knoxville and other surrounding communities.

In Big Cove and Snowbird, Cherokees organized a *gadugi*, a group of
community members who worked together to plant everyone's corn and
worked members' fields during illness or death. People preferred to wait
until the strawberries came out, to keep the birds off the young seeds.
Gadugi members were bound by what anthropologists call a "harmony
ethic," which was to treat each other with nonaggressiveness and non-
competitiveness, "particularly if the goal was individual success." In 1910,
Cherokees still celebrated the green corn ceremony during late September in honor of the fall harvest. White mountain farmers lacked a religious festival such as the green corn ceremony, but they did look forward
to corn-shucking parties every fall. Every Saturday during September in
Cataloochee, neighbors would go from one farm to another shucking
each family's corn. Women made large dinners with chicken and dump-
lings, someone brought a fiddle, and children played in the piles of
shucks. Communities held contests to see who could shuck the most, and
"if you shucked one with some red greens [sprouted grain] in it," a young
man could kiss his girlfriend. Many other subsistence practices, for example, building barns and killing hogs, required this kind of neighborhood cooperation and so involved an all-day festival, much like the corn-
shucking.[55]

To grind corn into meal, Cherokees and whites on the North Carolina
side of the Smokies used pounding mills, very simple watermills that operated mortars and pestles. Some Cherokee women continued to use the
hand tools of their ancestors, but a pounding mill could be left to do the
work all afternoon. In four or five hours with no supervision, 2 gallons of
corn would be meal. Farmers built 111 tub mills, which operated on
small, high-velocity streams, throughout the Smokies. Mingus Creek
and Cades Cove offered larger custom mills, which included a dam, race,
flume, and vertical shaft. Because the Smoky Mountains mills operated at
a community level—"you're so and so's son, you need fine meal"—they
never became large commercial operations.[56]

To store grain for milling, every farmer built a corn crib high above the
perpetually wet ground. Some families tolerated a black snake under the
corn crib to keep mice away from this stash. Others preferred dogs or

cats: "You couldn't live without a dog," said Calhoun. "If you didn't have a dog around the place you had possums." Dogs also helped keep marauding animals away from chickens and ducks. Most mountain women kept a flock of chickens for eggs; every Big Cove household included a small flock, though twenty-five farmers had forty or more. Like most rural women at the turn of the century, mountain women kept a mixture of breeds, such as Plymouth Rocks, Rhode Island Reds, Buff Orphingtons, and Domineckers, but they regularly lost chickens to weasels, hawks, opossums, skunks, and snakes. Jim Shelton told a story about his mother-in-law, who was awakened in the night by a squalling hen. Grabbing a lantern, she went out to investigate, but at first all she could see was the thrashing bird. Picking it up, she saw a weasel that had the hen around the throat, and before she could move, it grabbed her. She had to choke the weasel to death to loosen its grip from her.[57]

Whereas men, women, and children worked together to care for corn patches, women took primary responsibility for vegetable or "kitchen" gardens. Women selected vegetables that could be preserved all winter: pumpkins and field peas could be dried; beans, strung into "leather britches;" beans or cucumbers, pickled in large crocks; cabbage became sauerkraut; beets, sweet potatoes, and Irish potatoes stored in a "tater hole." Callie Wachacha, of Cherokee, said that her mother even dried greens, such as poke salad. "She would just spread them on a sheet," recalled Wachacha. "When they dried we put them in paper bags. We put them away by hanging them here and there." Until canning jars became commonplace, women dried apples—along with huckleberries, blackberries, gooseberries, raspberries, and strawberries—in the sun. Lucinda Ogle's grandmother spread the fruit on a "whopper rock," a boulder with a flat top about 12 by 20 feet the family termed "Granny's drying rock." Some valuable herbs, in fact, were not just collected in the mountains but cultivated on mountain farms. Ella Jackson, born in Cherokee in 1904, grew lady's slippers in her yard. "Aunt Sarah was the one who told me about lady's slippers," she said. "I was going to the hospital for heart problems." Jackson planted six roots from the mountains in her herb garden. She said that she had to get dirt with the roots when she dug them out because "dirt here is different from mountain dirt." Her comment can be substantiated with biology, because these orchids live only in a symbiotic relationship with a fungus, and to be transplanted they require the original soil. To cure heart problems, Jackson said, "boil the root and drink the tea."[58]

Some Smokies residents believed that kitchen gardens grew healthier if planted during the phases of the moon and the signs of the zodiac. Whereas some of these "rules" came down from oral tradition—"plant all root crops in the dark of the moon and those that bear above ground in the light of the moon" or "plant beans on Good Friday"—others probably originated from the *Farmer's Almanac*, a popular publication that traded on these ideas.[59] Whatever method they used, women raised prolific gardens in mediocre soil, and filled their cellars with earthenware crocks and later blue canning jars with zinc lids and rubber washers. They carefully collected and saved seeds each season; most had preferred varieties that could be shared and propagated. Lucy Black Ownby, who grew up on Cosby Creek, believed that rich gardens and the lack of artificial preservatives kept people healthier. "You didn't have a bunch of junk to eat," she said. "You ate beans and cornbread and vegetables." Paul Woody also believed that because they didn't use chemical sprays on vegetables, there were fewer pests. "We wasn't bothered with bugs back then. The bugs didn't come in 'til later on. When they did come in we had to go out there and catch 'em and put 'em in a jar. Then they kept, of course, getting worse and worse." The lack of pests also made orchards easier to care for. "At the time there was not anything to destroy the trees, and they didn't have to be sprayed," recalled Evolena Ownby about Greenbrier. "Sometimes the cold [however] killed the fruit in early spring. Almost every farm had an apple tree and sometimes grapevines, peach, walnut, and butternut trees. "What you used more than anything back then was old winterjohns," said Wesley Reagen, who grew up near Roaring Fork. "They're a fall apple . . . and real sour." Winterjohns, which many former mountain residents remember, could be stored until March without rotting. Sour-juicy apples made excellent apple cider if combined in a 1:4 ratio with sweet apples. If families had a second tree, they preferred a sweeter apple that could be eaten, out of the hand, right away. According to a Cherokee Indian agent, a pomologist could not even recognize all the varieties of apples grown in the area. After peeling and slicing two dishpans of apples into a huge barrel, a farm woman would lay a pan of sulphur on top of the apples and light it, quickly covering the barrel with a clean cloth. The sulfur smoke "bleached" the apples white, and they were considered a special treat all winter for desserts, such as stack cakes and fried pies. Cooked apple butter and pressed apple cider helped mountain women make use of every apple on the trees.[60]

Many people listed sugar or molasses as one of the few necessities they purchased at a store, although others emphasized the importance of raising "syrup cane." "Everybody made a good cane patch," said Seymour Calhoun. "They put up enough syrup to do 'em from one year to the next." The lengthy week-long process required boiling cane, pressing out the sap, and boiling down the syrup; no wonder this practice was abandoned early when cash became more readily available. Both Cherokee and white farmers retained honeybees or a favorite bee tree, however, because of the popularity of sourwood honey, often found in chestnut and poplar trees. One Cosby Creek resident, Will Webb, worked full-time as beekeeper or apiarist in 1900, trading with his community for the other goods he needed. Although North Carolina state foresters promoted commercial development of sugar maple-tapping, the practice never caught on in the Smokies. Individuals did make maple syrup for themselves, and Clon Ownby remembered his grandfather designing a complicated system of homemade poplar troughs on the hillside to help collect syrup in a vat.[61]

The other important task in food preservation was smoking meat. Usually neighbors worked in teams to process each other's hogs. After the first heavy frost in November, they penned up several free-ranging hogs in preparation for the kill. The messy work could only be done in the sanitary conditions of cold weather. A hole was dug for a barrel, which made the top of it at ground level. The barrel was filled with water, kept warm by red-hot flint rocks. One man knocked the hog in the head with a hammer, then helped another dip the animal in the hot water until the hair fell off. Another cut up backbones and ribs with a knife and handsaw, while still another salted down the hams and hung thin strips in the smokehouse. A trench in the middle of the floor contained a fire, which the men smoldered with oak, hickory, or other green, wet wood to create fire that would smoke for days without flaring up. During the week, women collected the lard in barrels and used this and entrails to make lye soap.

Children who grew up watching these endless seasons of work remember best a great deal of time outdoors and most of it unsupervised. "We children in the Sugarlands . . . had so much fun outdoors," Alie Newman Maples remembered. "We would play up and down the rivers jumping from rock to rock and our feet would get so tough we could crack chestnut burrs with our heels." When Alice Moore Posey recalled similar times on Hazel Creek, she got so choked up that she couldn't speak. Arlie Trentham remembered "riding the pine trees" on James Bohannon's land: "We'd get up in the top of 'em and ride from top of one to the top of another. "That is, until Mr. Bohannon cussed us out," he added. It is significant how confident children felt alone in the woods. Former residents remember crossing the mountains by themselves at nine years of age, from Cherokee to Snowbird or from Curry He Mountain in Tennessee to Hazel Creek, North Carolina.[62] Such descriptions reflect, in part, nostalgia toward youth, but perhaps childhood seemed more idyllic because it was so precious; records show that death in childhood was commonplace. Between April 1881 and February 1882, 28 percent of all recorded deaths in Sevier County were of children under one year of age; 56 percent were of those under twenty-one. Pneumonia, cholera, and diphtheria epidemics often took children's lives. At the same time, parents who allowed their children to freely explore the natural world, its risks and dangers, no doubt influenced who they became as adults. Lona Parton Tyson recalled as a child seeing snow blow in through the cracks in the chinking of her log cabin. "It kept us healthy and ready to get out and make snowmen and skate on the creek when it was frozen over with ice," she reported. Whether or not this produced some kind of heartiness, it certainly created people sensitive to and conscious of the changes in the weather and the passing of the seasons. They grew closer to the land and more dependent on each other, but life without central heating or electricity required endless hard work. Charlie Palmer described Cataloochee as the "Garden of Eden," but Gladys Trentham Russell remembered more clearly the daily toil: "We were able to live because we worked—and we worked hard."[63]

Neighborhood Economies and a Sense of Place

In recent years, much has been written and debated about mountain people's involvement in the market economy. No one would seriously argue anymore that they were "self-sufficient" or outside the rapidly incorporating world system; ginseng, galax, crossties, tanbark, hogs, and especially the nascent timber industry pulled them into it. Nor does anything about their choices suggest that they shunned capitalism or the American dream of owning their own land. Class and race surely divided people in the mountains as it did everywhere else in the American South. Economist Paul Salstrom has argued that Appalachia's rural population faced a "subsistence crisis" in the late nineteenth century because of population increase, subdivision, and soil depletion. This crisis, then, pushed them into the lumber trade, which began exploiting the forests of the Southern Appalachians after the Civil War.

In 1900, however, population pressure did not present a crisis for landowners in the Smoky Mountains. Tenants living on more marginal agricultural land, such as Dorie Cope's family, felt pushed toward mill towns and lumber camps. But mountain people living on finer bottomlands such as Cataloochee and Cades Cove had no incentive to work for the lumber companies until land ownership patterns shifted or their environment was dramatically altered. And emphasizing national economic trends tends to diminish the importance of kinship relations, community values, and neighborliness in shaping small-scale economies—"informal economies," in Salstrom's words—and, in turn, the significance a sense of place played in their lives. "Everybody was everybody's neighbor," explained Winfred Cagle. "Everybody loved everybody." Specifically, he explained:

> In the fall of the year, say, if one neighbor didn't have any hogs to kill for the smokehouse, well, if a neighbor had one extra, they'd swap it with them. Now they wouldn't give it to 'em! . . . a bundle of firewood for a 50-pound hog. They wouldn't just give it to you, that was bad luck.

Swapping firewood for a 50-pound hog may not be an even trade economically, but it allowed the poorer neighbor to survive with his pride intact. Maybe everybody didn't love everybody in some Christian utopian sense, but on Deep Creek folks understood that the health of everyone in the community affected them all. Besides, in a community of several hundred people, it's not hard to learn who is trustworthy and who is not—in mountain terms, whose "word" you could count on. This had implications for credit as well as community. Paul Woody described how a man or woman's "word" figured into borrowing money:

If a man come to borrow money from you that had a twofold meaning. In the first place, I thought of you as a friend or else I wouldn't of went to your house. And in the second place, it give you a chance to prove that you was my family . . . your word or my word or anybody else's word was just like [a signed agreement] and you could depend on it.

If community and the common good had such concrete meaning for mountain people, did this extend to special care for the environment? After all, if they truly knew this kind of interconnectedness with human beings, did it extend to nature? "We talk about environmentalists today, but I was *raised* an environmentalist," said Henry Posey. "I was raised if you skid logs on a stream, you covered the banks with limbs to keep the water clean. You take care of game. I was told how many squirrels I could get. If I got any more, I'd have a hide on my back." The oft-quoted mountain expression, "raise what you eat and eat what you raise" is looked upon as a statement of self-sufficiency, but it is also an acknowledgment that one cannot be improvident and survive. "You didn't waste nothing," said Cagle. His family didn't generate garbage because they didn't buy packaged food and used table scraps to feed the chickens and hogs. "People back then learned themselves right off the bat not to be wasteful," he commented."[64]

Both Cherokee and white farmers in 1900 manifested a powerful sense of place in the Smoky Mountains, one that made them loathe to leave. "Perhaps this rural heaven did not offer the ideal life, but it seemed good to those who lived it and they wished for little else," wrote southern historian Robert Woody.[65] Without romanticizing what indeed was a very difficult life, it is accurate to say that this sense of place resulted from great ecological knowledge borne of use and spiritual traditions that encouraged them to imbue that use with meaning. They cleared land, ran hogs, and planted gardens, and this lifestyle depended on the thickly forested ridges above them. They harvested wild plants and cut trees from the woods, but they did not *extract* them; they tried their best to be satisfied with "the fruit of God's work." Their relatively small population and organic woodland agriculture supported significant "agrodiversity:" biologically diverse ecosystems, including mature old-growth forest communities, open grazing land, managed woodland, and cultivated fields.[66]

At the same time, although individuals like Henry Posey show concern and knowledge of environmental consequences, such as overhunting and overfishing by outsiders, they don't in oral histories use the word "wilderness," meaning untouched land. There is no evidence that they collectively developed anything like a "land ethic" that would cause them to question new technology or industrial development. Survival depended on use, and while Christian belief supported the idea of stewardship and endurance in the face of suffering, nothing in their beliefs suggested that intensive use might cause more suffering. The American dream for each family to support itself on its own farm still held the horizon. Cherokee tradition, on the other hand, called for "strong talk" or public debate about environmental consequences such as the overuse of fire, because of the effect of these consequences on everyone in the tribe. However, only the Big Cove and Snowbird communities remained traditional in 1900. "Strong talk" in the Eastern Band during this century would include the voices of government agents who wanted to eradicate tradition and "progressives" who pushed the tribe to become Christian and develop economically. Cherokees surely tried to limit commercial use of the balds and forests, and no one in Big Cove seemed inclined toward large commercial farm production. Communal landholding still shaped the Eastern Band, still differentiated them from their white neighbors. No one thought about wilderness protection, or reserving large tracts of lands free of producing commodities. In a world where use remained moderate and population low, the forested ridges above them looked endless.[67]

1.1. Sheep grazing on a high-elevation grassy bald in the Great Smoky Mountains, about 1910. Although travel writers still refer to the origins of the grassy balds as a "mystery," they were largely created by animal grazing. Courtesy of Great Smoky Mountains National Park.

1.2. Farmers on their way to the balds; photo taken at Indian Gap, 1911. Mary Lindsay Collection. Courtesy of Great Smoky Mountains National Park.

1.3. Cherokee boys hauling chestnut wood for fuel for their school, Cherokee, North Carolina, 1900. Courtesy of the North Carolina Division of Archives and History.

1.4. Before logging companies moved into the region, farmers carved a patchwork of field and pasture in the lower elevations, with an old-growth forest above. Little Greenbrier, Tennessee, probably 1910. Dame Olive Campbell Collection. Courtesy of University of North Carolina, Chapel Hill.

1.5. Although often depicted as hillbillies, mountain folk appear as ordinary rural Americans in their own photographs. George H. Caldwell Family, Cataloochee, North Carolina, 1902. Courtesy of Great Smoky Mountains National Park.

1.6. Young farmer hauling store-bought items on a homemade sled, Little Greenbrier, Tennessee, about 1910. Dame Olive Campbell Collection. Courtesy of University of North Carolina, Chapel Hill.

1.7. Mountain residents supplemented the family diet with brook trout. Little River, about 1910. Dame Olive Campbell Collection. Courtesy of University of North Carolina, Chapel Hill.

1.8. The Walker sisters and Jim Shelton of Little Greenbrier, Tennessee, in front of a hollow chestnut tree. Photo by Jim Shelton. Courtesy of Great Smoky Mountains National Park.

A Lumberman's Dream

*The present age is called a commercial one, a
going, driving age. There was no past age in
which there was so much and so strenuous
industrial, commercial, or mental activity as
this, or if so history gives no account of it.*

STANLEY HORN, *Southern Lumberman*, 1907

UNBEKNOWNST TO THE Cherokee and white farmers
in the Smokies, two visitors who arrived at the turn of
the century heralded permanent transformations for
the mountains and the people who lived there. Representing the new U.S.D.A. Forest Service (USFS),
Horace B. Ayres and William W. Ashe surveyed the
Southern Appalachians in 1901 in search of undeveloped timberlands.[1] They reported to Gifford Pinchot, the Progressive forester who predicted that all
the timber in the United States would be gone in
twenty years if lumbermen did not heed his call for
scientific management. The first step of management,
Pinchot believed, was this kind of survey of resources.

Ashe later became an enthusiastic naturalist; he
discovered more than 100 new species and documented many others, now rare or extirpated. On this
trip, though, the two men did not mention the tremendous biodiversity, the number and variety of
plants and animals, they found in the region. They
barely noted the human residents, except to miscalcu-
late the population and to chide them for damaging
timber by burning the woods. In Cataloochee, for example, they reported that only about 30 families lived

"scattered through the mountains," when, in fact, 764 people (136 households) resided in the valley lands around Cataloochee Creek, Little Cataloochee Creek, and its tributaries. The foresters turned their eyes to the vast ridges above and calculated their value in board feet: Cataloochee Valley had only "slight" agricultural value, they claimed, while the surrounding mountainsides would yield an astounding 161,280 board feet per acre, 80 percent of which would be chestnut and oak (6,000 to 12,000 board feet was considered typical).[2] In each watershed, Ayres and Ashe emphasized the low land prices (see table 2). "The best farm in the valley can be bought for $5 per acre," they wrote of Cades Cove. "Fifty cents an acre is considered a good price for mountain land." They did not see the Smoky Mountains as a woodland pasture or a rich complex of old-growth forest communities but as a natural resource ready for efficient extraction—then followed by scientific management for future harvest, of course.

The nation's press immediately picked up on Ayres and Ashe's report. Magazine and newspaper articles, quoting the two foresters, talked about the need for scientific management of the remaining forests. Their study helped enact the Weeks Law of 1911, through which Congress granted $2 million per year for five years to create a forest reserve in the East by purchasing "forested, cut-over, or de-nuded lands within the watersheds of navigable streams." To gain the support of the timber industry, the Weeks Law included only already cutover lands, but foresters themselves also did not support the idea of wilderness protection. Federal forester William Hall actually wrote about the "great menace" of forest fires found in virgin forests and the increased timber production guaranteed under "the care of man."[3] In truth, by calculating the tremendous timber possibilities available at bargain-basement prices, Ayres and Ashe probably helped promote the Smokies' rapid industrial development.

In any case, shortly after the team finished its report, eight large corporations seized upon the financial opportunity. "The Smokies were a lumberman's dream," described Thomas Edward Maxey, an engineer for Montvale Lumber Company. "They were a wilderness of virgin timber, the finest stands of hardwood in the country." By 1911 Montvale had finished a band sawmill in Fontana, at the mouth of Eagle Creek. The Whiting Lumber Company began construction on a double band saw, a planing mill, and dry kilns in Judson, with plans to employ 400 men. On

Table 2. Timberlands in the Smokies, 1901

District	Land Prices (per acre)	Expected Yield (board feet)	Chief Trees
NORTH CAROLINA			
Alum Cave	$10	57,778	chestnut, oaks
Big Creek	$2–$5	74,240	hemlock, poplar
Cataloochee	$2	161,280	chestnut, hemlock
Deep Creek	$2–$10	3,000	hardwoods, hemlock
Eagle Creek	$2.50	4,000	oak, chestnut
Forney Creek	$2–$5	4,000	oak, chestnut
Greenbrier	$2–$10	138,240	chestnut, mixed
Hazel Creek	$.50–$2	3,000	oak, chestnut, hickory
Noland Creek	$2–$5	3,000	oak, chestnut
Oconaluftee	$1–$5	1,700–3,000	oak, chestnut
Twentymile	$2.50	2,000	oak, chestnut
TENNESSEE			
Abrams Creek	$.50	90,662	pine, oak, hemlock
Cades Cove	$.50	96,960	chestnut, oak, pine
East Fork of Little River	$2–$5	29,747	oak, maple, linn
Jakes Creek	$2–$5	17,715	chestnut, oaks
Laurel Creek	$1	18,624	oak, maple, hemlock
Little River Middle, West Prong of Little River	$1–$5 $5	105,366 117,056	chestnut, hemlock oak, maple, hemlock

Source: *The Southern Appalachian Forests*, Ayres and Ashe, 1905.
Timber is measured in board feet. One board foot is a piece of timber 1 foot long, 1 foot wide, and 1 inch thick. The working unit is 1,000 board feet or M bd. Ft.

Hazel Creek, W. M. Ritter employed 250 men, who lived in the company town of Proctor and turned out 100,000 board feet per day. The Norwood Lumber Company sent 400 men into the woods on Forney Creek to cut trees and build 10 miles of railway. Mason Lumber Company used three portable and band sawmills to ship several hundred cords of acid wood each month to the new Champion Fibre Company in Canton, North Carolina. And in Tennessee, W. B. Townsend moved his operations farther into the east fork of the Little River, where company engineers developed new steam-powered skidders to reach the highest slopes.[4]

Consolidation and combination in the lumber industry along with new technology made this rapid industrial development of a remote location possible. Companies originating in the Northeast forced out small operators through trusts and pricing advantages, then sent timber buyers south. (For a summary of corporate loggers in the Smokies, see table 3.)[5] William Whitmer, for example, entered his family's Pennsylvania lumber business, then became president of William Whitmer & Sons when his father died in 1896. Two years later, with the help of an insurance trust, he combined operations with Parsons Pulp & Paper Company. His various operations employed upwards of 1,000 people and annually produced about 100 million board feet of hardwood lumber. He was attracted to the area by John C. Arbogast, a West Virginia speculator, who bought 33,000 acres of prime timberland from the Eastern Band of Cherokees for $245,000 in 1906, supposedly to build a railroad. Three years later, Arbogast sold the same acreage to Whitmer for $630,000. Government agents said that this sale "disposed of all the good timber land owned by these Indians." Whitmer got additional bargains from landowners in the Oconaluftee Valley, whom he bought out to build Ravensford, a mill town that housed 100 employees.[6]

Timber giants such as Whitmer raised the capital necessary to invest in railroads, the key to extracting timber profitably. In 1907, W. M. Ritter extended the Smoky Mountain Railway past Fontana to Kitchinsville, near the mouth of Twentymile Creek. Two standard Shay engines ran between his new mill town, called Proctor, and the Southern Railway line at Andrews, North Carolina. Ritter, born on a Lycoming County, Pennsylvania, farm in 1864, grew up admiring a "proud and aristocratic" lumberman, who later hired him. With $1,700 in capital, he started his own sawmill in Mercer County, West Virginia, in 1890, and within a decade operated eighteen circular mills. In the Hazel Creek Valley, his buyers purchased most of the forest "on the stump," or timber rights only, from speculators, who retained title.[7] At the turn of the century, the W. M. Ritter Company ran four divisions, representing West Virginia, Virginia, Kentucky, and North Carolina.

Wilson B. Townsend, another Pennsylvania lumberman, became interested in the Little River area after the Schlosser Leather Company

Table 3. Lumber Companies Operating in the Great Smoky Mountains, 1928

	Technology	Species Taken
NORTH CAROLINA		
Big Creek		
Suncrest	band sawmill,	ash, basswood, beech,
150,000 board feet	planing mill,	birch, buckeye, cherry,
per day	edger, trimmer,	chestnut, cucumber,
	electric light	black gum, hemlock,
	plant	hickory, locust, maple,
		oak, poplar, spruce,
		walnut
Fontana Area		
Kitchen Lumber Co.	band sawmill,	ash, basswood, beech,
100,000 board feet	edger, trimmer	birch, buckeye, cherry,
per day		chestnut, black gum,
		hemlock, hickory,
		maple, oak, pine,
		poplar
Montvale	band sawmill	ash, basswood, beech,
Baltimore, Md.		birch, buckeye, cherry,
50,000 board feet		chestnut, cucumber,
per day		black and sweet gum,
		hemlock, hickory, holly,
		locust, maple, oak, pine,
		poplar, sassafras,
		sycamore, walnut
Forney Creek		
Norwood	band sawmill,	ash, basswood, beech,
50,000 board feet	edger, trimmer,	birch,
per day	dry kiln,	buckeye, cherry,
	electric light	chestnut,
	plant	hemlock, maple, oak,
		poplar, spruce
Proctor Area		
W. M. Ritter	band sawmill,	ash, basswood, beech,
Columbus, Ohio	planing mill,	birch, buckeye,
100,000 board feet	edgers, trimmers,	butternut, chestnut,
per day	dry kiln,	black gum, hemlock,
	electric light	hickory, locust, maple,
	plant	oak, poplar, walnut

continued.

Table 3 — continued

	Technology	Species Taken
Ravensford		
Whitmer-Parsons	double band saw,	ash, basswood, birch,
Pulp & Lumber	resaw, edgers,	buckeye, butternut,
Philadelphia, Pa.	trimmers	cherry, chestnut,
		hemlock, maple,
		oak, poplar, spruce
Smokemont		
Champion	band sawmill,	ash, basswood, beech,
Cincinnati, Ohio	edger, trimmer	birch, buckeye, butternut,
35,000 board feet		cherry, chestnut,
per day		cucumber, black gum,
		hemlock, hickory,
		maple, oak, poplar,
		spruce
TENNESSEE		
Townsend		
Little River	two band sawmills,	ash, basswood, birch,
	planing mill,	buckeye, cherry,
	edger, trimmer,	chestnut, hemlock,
	dry kiln,	maple, poplar, oak,
	electric light	spruce
	plant, ice plant	

Source: Southern Lumberman's Directory of American Sawmills and Planing Mills (1928).

financed a railroad into nearby Walland. Townsend already controlled major logging operations in Pennsylvania and coal, clay tile, and railroad holdings in eastern Kentucky when he moved into Tuckaleechee Cove in 1901. He built a railroad, mill, and company town, which residents named Townsend in his honor. Like Ritter, he could afford the latest technology and so switched his operations from circular saws to band saws, which allowed cutting very thick logs with less waste. Townsend invested in steam-powered skidders, which could profitably transport oak and chestnut trees as small as 10 inches in diameter as far as 5,000 feet.[8]

Although Townsend purchased much of his land from speculators, he also bought tracts from mountain people. A mountain man, William M.

Walker, at one time claimed as many as 5,000 acres in Walker Valley, though he never held clear title to that much land. A cattleman and occasional bear trapper, Walker also kept bees and made oak buckets and barrels, earning a good enough living to send several daughters to Maryville College. A stroke disabled him in 1918, and according to the family story this is what forced him to sell his land to Wilson B. Townsend. Townsend visited Walker at his cabin not long after he became infirm and persuaded the mountain man to sign away 96 acres, "more or less," for $1,500 cash and a promise not to cut the great trees on Thunderhead Prong. The old man sold his land for a song, one family member lamented, and the lumber company "sang it." Walker died one year later. Townsend kept the promise until his own death in 1936, after which the Little River Lumber Company took all the trees on Thunderhead Prong. Dollie Burchfield Nelson described a land agent working for the Morton Butler lands, much of which Townsend later purchased. The agent tricked her illiterate father out of his land by befriending him and then asking him to "witness" a document supposedly to an adjoining piece of land. Eager to help a friend, the unsuspecting farmer actually signed away title to his own land.[9]

Cheap land, technological improvements, and railroad investment also moved the Champion Fibre Company into the Smokies. Organized in 1893 by a Cincinnati, Ohio, businessman, Peter Thomson, Champion Coated Paper Company appointed law school graduate Reuben Robertson, Thomson's son-in-law, head of its new plant in Canton, North Carolina, in 1905. Robertson purchased the Tennessee and North Carolina Railroad and began building the new plant, which used chestnut wood to make white paper pulp. It shortly became the largest such operation in the world, and, according to Robertson, accomplished in 1908 what the rest of the industry would not achieve until the 1930s. Champion contracted a lot of its timber from extraction companies, such as W. T. Mason. Mason purchased stumpage rights on an old land-grant tract purchased by the Eastern Band of Cherokees. The tribal council sold the timber off 30,000 acres for $15,000—a breathtaking 50 cents per acre—in 1893, before the commercial possibilities and extraction methods skyrocketed. The contract gave the company *fifteen years* to complete the job, and the company waited until it was profitable to do so. After the contract expired, the tribe had to threaten a lawsuit to get Mason off the site. The company extracted between 3 and 4 million board feet.[10]

When Champion officials finally started buying land for their own operations in the Smokies, they had to hire a lawyer to untangle the claims of speculators and landowning farmers. Original state land grants in the Smokies frequently overlapped, because the early federal government, the state of North Carolina, and, after the War of 1812, the state of Tennessee sometimes gave away the same tract. Nineteenth-century land speculators, such as Robert Love, then parceled out small farms, sometimes serving as their own bankers to early settlers. Nobody in the nineteenth century could make money off the steep woodland, so title problems were sorted out informally or went uncontested. A land speculator, George W. Pack, visited Big Creek and upper Cataloochee in 1887 to consider the Love lands for speculation. Although he could get the land for a mere $1 per acre, he considered the title problems so hopeless that he walked away from the deal. Title problems eventually made the region a "great field for lawyers."[11] To clear titles, lumber companies and speculators typically gained "possession" by hiring someone to live in a cabin on the land and attain legal occupancy. Lumber agents made regular visits to the cabins and filed reports to their home offices about the progress of the "claims." The elaborate process to gain clear title could be well worth an investor's time, as speculation would be almost as profitable as logging. The 16,983 acres purchased by the Norwood Lumber Company in 1910 changed hands at least four times among different Swain County investment groups, each of which made profits on the arrangement.

Effluents from the Champion plant rendered the Pigeon River as dark as tea, but a by-product of the operation, tannic acid, offered additional opportunities for profit. "At that time our plant was the largest one anywhere in operation using chestnut," Robertson said. "We supplied the bulk of the British requirements. British Tanners, Ltd., was an aggregation of twenty of the big tanners, and we supplied all their needs. It was our most profitable operation."[12]

In words that spoke for all the corporate loggers, Robertson said, "We came to the Great Smoky Mountains for two reasons. The first was spruce and the second was the enormous stand of chestnut." On further consideration, Robertson might have added a third: a non-union workforce of stable, low-wage laborers. In 1912, the average wage per hour in Washington state for lumber workers was 22 cents per hour, compared with 12 cents per hour in North Carolina. The average number of working hours per week in the Pacific Northwest hovered between 59 and 60, whereas lumbermen in North Carolina could expect to work 62.7 hours each week. In the West and Northwest, lumber workers increased their wages and improved their hours with the help of the International Workingman's Association, the Knights of Labor, and several well-publicized strikes. Southern lumbermen kept unions out by hiring entire families to work in well-controlled camps, exploiting racial differences, and, in the case of Champion, offering considerable pay incentives to people not previously tied to wage labor. *Southern Lumberman*, the trade association newspaper, labeled labor organizers "agitators," "bomb-throwers," or "reds." "The appearance of a branch of [the Brotherhood of Timber Workers]," according to the industry publication, "will be the instant signal for the shutting down of that plant."[13]

And market pressures eventually increased the attractiveness of the Smokies. During the 1890s, timber barons cut over more accessible forests, and continued orders for timber forced them into more and more remote areas. "When Europe burst into the horror of warfare in 1913," demands on the forest mounted," wrote a government forester, "and postwar reconstruction saw no letup. So the large sawmills . . . marched across the face of the remaining Appalachian wilderness." To meet this world demand for hardwood timber, logging giants in the Smokies extracted the great forest on 200 miles of freshly built logging railroad during what became the peak extraction period for the industry. If big profits weren't enough to encourage the timbermen, North Carolina and Tennessee officials also welcomed development. City boosters in growing urban areas, such as Knoxville, Tennessee, fought to improve railroad connections to their cities and to attract New South business to the region. County elites linked economic development with railroads, whether or not the money truly benefited the majority of the residents. A Knoxville businessman, William J. Oliver, obtained a loan to build a railroad by pledging stocks and bonds, including $150,000 squeezed from Sevier County Court. To help the company, the state supreme court validated a dubious bond election in the county. Throughout the construction, delays for nonpayment plagued the line; instead of making Oliver or Sevier County a great fortune, the line was sold for payment of debts in 1921.[14]

In some instances, legal problems actually spared the Smoky Mountains environmental destruction. Shortly after the Civil War, a Dillsboro man prospecting for mica on Hazel Creek discovered a rich vein of copper. Much to his disappointment, the land already belonged to Bryson City Sheriff Everette. Everette sold the land to W. S. Adams, a New York mineral developer, who built a small mining village on Sugar Fork and hired a crew of local men. To make the site profitable, he planned to transport a copper smelter to the site—a move that would have rendered much of the Hazel Creek watershed a lifeless desert. However, another post-Civil War land speculator from New Orleans laid claim to the same land. As Adams sunk his shafts, George Westfeldt sued to halt operations. Westfeldt won the first suit, but a new trial was granted, and the case remained tied up in courts for twenty-six years. By the time it was settled, in favor of Adams, both men were dead.[15]

Although historians have depicted them as examples of the worst kind of robber baron, at least two of the timber giants in the Smokies, Robertson and Townsend, gave considerable lip service to scientific forestry and government forestry reserves. Robertson early on hired industrial foresters and decried the waste of other lumber companies. As president of the Hardwood Manufacturers' Association, Townsend described the "noble work" of the USFS in acquiring lands for the national forests. "If it were possible for an individual or a corporation to be exempt from taxation and interest charges on investments, they could well afford to buy these lands," Townsend wrote, with a belief in the ability of the forest to regenerate itself over thirty to fifty years. "The purchase of this land in the Southern Appalachians is a magnificent business proposition for the government," he said. Townsend clearly planned to sell his own cutover lands in the Smokies to the USFS, as he allowed a government forester to set up the first crude fire tower on his land near Townsend and invited government attorneys to delve into his land titles.[16]

For their part, professional foresters felt optimistic about the future of the forests under the care of these large corporate loggers. They believed that economies of scale would provide more incentives for efficient, scientific management and the purchase of large tracts by the government.[17] *Southern Lumberman* crusaded for the national forest and against the waste represented by poor forestry practices and the tax burden of cutover lands. "The fact that timber has been cheap and abundant has made us careless of its productions and reckless of its use," one writer asserted. Regular features by foresters (including Ashe) as well as profiles of progressive loggers who advocated scientific management (Townsend) filled the pages of the publication.[18]

Southern Lumberman regularly chided its readers for wasteful practices, advocated the use of sound, scientific forestry techniques, yet at the same time compared the lumbermen's rapid extraction of the forests with "the astounding works of the mythical gods, heros, and demons." "The present age is called a commercial one, a going, driving age," wrote Stanley Horn, editor of *Southern Lumberman*, and his words surely rang true in the woods of the Smoky Mountains during the 1910s and 1920s. "There was no past age in which there was so much and so strenuous industrial, commercial, or mental activity as this, or if so history gives no account of it," said Horn.[19] Whether they were gods or demons, captains of industry or timber barons, after they left the Smoky Mountains, the old-growth forest and the communities below it would not be the same.

The Mountains Looked "Skinned"

The lumbermen built railways into each watershed, with spur lines into the finest groves of trees. Where the land rose too abruptly for the railroad, men built tramlines for winch-powered cars called "Sary Parkers," affectionately named for a particularly strong woman.[20] In the gorge at the mouth of Meigs Creek, the Little River Lumber Company built a swinging bridge of cables and logs held together by crossties and rails. A Sary Parker moved up the suspension with the help of a Shay engine (called a "sidewinder") and a heavy cable secured to a giant stump. Timber crews remember jumping into the river when the heavy load quivered precariously; miraculously, no one was killed this way. On Hazel Creek, W. M. Ritter also built a logging chute, or a giant trough of hewed timbers, which carried logs out of the woods. "They'd put maybe fifty or seventy-five or more logs in that slide, the largest logs in the rear, [attached to] a j-grab and a good pair of horses," explained Dillard Wood, who, at age thirteen, got a job greasing the chute with black oil. "Sometimes a log would run off and leave the horses," he remembered.[21]

The giant trees fell with 6- and 8-foot, two-man crosscut saws (called "misery whips"); "grandaddy" trees took a special 11-footer. Raymer Brackin remembered his crew cutting one giant poplar thicker than the saw was long: they had to remove the handle from one end and let a single man saw it. In the steepest areas, even large lumber companies used horses or oxen to drag logs to the railroad. In large basins, though, the extractors preferred steam-powered skidders. Men hooked the sawed logs with chains called "chokers," which could be attached to a cable. Some of the trees were so large that it took two 8-foot chokers to surround them.[22]

Skidders, each a system of cables run by a steam-powered vertical boiler, pulled the logs down the hill. The Clyde overhead skidder, used on Lynn Camp Prong, for one, not only took down the cut trees but also devastated every smaller tree in its path. "It just destroyed everything," said Seymour Calhoun, describing a skidder used by Ritter. "They destroyed more timber than they got out with 'em because it just knocked the trees down and bushes and everything and just leave the destruction of it." Raymer Brackin agreed: "You hardly ever left a tree of any size standing and all the little ones was torn down." Photographs taken of the Smokies region confirm that most of the corporate loggers engaged in clear-cutting rather than "high-grading," which implies taking just the largest, most attractive trees. Jennie Bradshaw Abbott, whose father worked for the Little River Lumber Company, said the landscape looked "skinned." Cable lines from the skidders so deeply eroded the hillsides that their herringbone marks remain visible today. In the ridge tops above Cataloochee, the Suncrest Lumber Company used a Lidgerwood type overhead skidder, which could carry logs for a mile. Here the tracks ran parallel to the crest of the mountains and the machine pulled the logs up the slope by a line anchored to a lower ridge, often more than a mile away. For this reason, spruce and fir dangled 400 feet above the ground and caused less damage to the valley floor. Although both types of skidder differed in how much erosion they caused, both resulted in unnecessary dead trees. "When you start uprooting trees . . . 15, 18 inches [in diameter] you're gonna take everything. It just tears the whole works up," said

Curt McCarter, who remembered Little River Lumber Company Operations.[23] The sight of a completely cutover valley was not easily forgotten. Backpacking from Mount Collins in 1919, Paul Fink encountered Suncrest logging operations on Balsam Mountain:

> A great shock it was to us to travel for days through a magnificent, truly virgin forest . . . and then step suddenly into the utter devastation the spruce logger leaves behind him. In the years just gone the whole basin of Big Creek, draining the eastern ends of the Smokies and the Balsams, had been cut over. Everything of any size had been taken, for the paper mills can handle anything above sapling size. Then, as usual, fire had gotten out into the slash and completed the devastation, burning everything, even the organic matter in the forest floor, leaving the bare soil to erode and wash away under the heavy rainfall.[24]

Fires routinely followed large timber operations; a spark from a skidder boiler or the metal wheels on rails easily lit fields strewn with slash. According to Louis McCarter, who worked for the Shea Brothers on Laurel Creek, an ember from the hooded stack of a train would touch dead limbs like a spark igniting gunpowder. "It was like building a bonfire and just piling wood on it," Seymour Calhoun commented on the frequent fires around Ritter's operations. John Parton, who worked twenty-five years for Little River Lumber Company, said that part of the job was fighting fires "every once in a while" and virtually every fall.[25] In the 1920s and 1930s, the Smokies experienced the most dramatic forest fires in its history. Albert Siler remembered a fire around Suncrest operations that men escaped although it burned up four or five teams of horses. A single fire in 1924 burned from Yellow Creek and Sinking Creek to the top of Mount Guyot, destroying green trees and ground cover as well as the leftover timber. Shea Brothers finally had to remove all the dead timber around the railroad right-of-way. "They tried to keep [fire] out," said Louis McCarter, an employee. "But it'd get away sometimes in spite of them." Fire did not limit itself to railways or lumber camps, either. Horace Trentham remembered a Jakes Creek fire that almost reached a friend's homeplace. The man carried all of his possessions onto several big rocks on the creek. According to Trentham, the fire destroyed all his possessions but left the man's home intact. Lucy Black Ownby, who grew up near Cosby, recalled a fire that swept from one ridge to another during the 1930s. "It was so smoky you could barely breathe," she said. Her family wet down quilts and threw water on their board roof to keep it from burning. A logger who worked in Black Camp Gap told about a farmer who was fishing with his son when fire broke out. The two waded to the middle of the creek and remained completely submerged except for handkerchiefs over their faces. Between the frightening scene and the frigid creek, the boy wanted to bolt, so his father practically held him underwater.[26]

Neither before nor since has the Smokies suffered such tremendous fires, because of its spectacular annual rainfall. Only the huge quantity of slash and spark-generating railroad and skidder equipment can explain this rash of fires. Whereas intentional fires set by nineteenth-century farmers to control undergrowth remained small and of low intensity, timber fires following logging operations burned hot and fast. In 1925, a fire on upper Oconaluftee Creek burned for days from North Carolina over to Tennessee, igniting green trees over a wide area. At the same time, logging operations could render the farmers' practice of burning woods more dangerous. A forest fire survey done by the North Carolina state forester found that brush-burning and moonshine operations caused almost as many fires between 1918 and 1920 as lumber companies and railroads, yet few of these fires would have occurred without the available slash and dead trees. Without noting logging history, foresters blamed farmers for the destruction. They aimed new laws, such as North Carolina's Forest Fire Law of 1915, squarely at local "carelessness" rather than at lack of prevention by lumber operations. Tennessee too set fines for anyone who "willfully or accidentally" set fire to adjoining woodland or cut or destroyed timber on state land. Foresters did convince Townsend, at least, to appoint wardens and to build lookout towers to control the spread of fire.[27]

Predictably, floods followed the fires. "Timber removal followed by fires in the debris resulted in excessive high and low stream flow," wrote a forestry student, observing timber operations in western North Carolina. Because trees use a tremendous amount of moisture, without them the heavy annual rainfall simply washed humus and topsoil into the creeks. A 1917 fire, caused by a skidder at the cutting line, almost destroyed Dorie Cope's home. The next day, dirt and debris slid into the river, transforming it into a muddy, sluggish mess. Smothered by the ashes and mud, trout washed belly-up onto the shore. The 1925 Oconaluftee fire left a barren area, over which torrential rains removed the topsoil.[28]

The combination of corporate logging, fires, and sometimes grazing or cultivation proved deadly for the flora and fauna of the Great Smoky Mountains. If a fire reaches such high temperatures, it destroys the humus or "duff" in the upper layers of the soil. Hot fire, combined with skidder erosion, changed the character of the affected spruce-fir forest. The land grew back with either northern hardwoods or fir, but essentially it lost the red spruce component. One former clear-cut site, Upper Forney Creek, for example, today supports small fire cherry and yellow birch trees, but few Fraser fir and no red spruce. Many rare flowers and plants, such as Rugels ragwort (*Rugelia nudiculis*), which prefer the acidic soil of this northern-like clime, still do not grow on Upper Forney Creek.[29]

Likewise, plants and wildlife favoring deciduous communities diminished with logging. In every mountainside cut, herbaceous plants, wildflowers, and ferns died. Some plants, such as the lady's slipper, can't tolerate the increased sunlight; others become crowded out by the blackberries and fire cherries that quickly move into the opening. In turn, the animals that relied on mast also disappeared. After so many years of hunting, the white-tailed deer could not survive the onslaught of logging too. The loss of white-tailed deer was so complete by 1927 that the North Carolina legislature announced a complete ban on deer hunting for five years. Deer, like turkeys, squirrels, and woodland mice, relied on the beechnuts, chestnuts, acorns, and other mast provided by the trees that the lumbermen cut. During the 1910s and 1920s, North Carolina and Tennessee established state game and wildlife commissions, as the devastation generated by logging made the need apparent. In 1913 Tennessee and North Carolina both ordered closed seasons on fur-bearing animals. All animals, birds, and fish became property under the protection of the states. As with fire, the new state agencies aimed wildlife laws at controlling further hunting and trapping by individuals rather than at recovering habitat or challenging the practices of lumbermen.[30] A disturbance of this magnitude would have had long-term effects on Neotropical migrants, commonly called songbirds. About ninety-eight songbird species, including warblers and vireos, migrate every year from the tropics to the Southern Appalachians to nest. Baby songbirds suffer nearly 100 percent mortality from predators if their parents try to nest in places, like the woods near clear-cut sites, with a high proportion of "edge." Although a few species, such as the indigo bunting, seem to thrive in the second-growth forests that follow clear-cutting, most declined significantly. Not surprisingly, the first laws protecting songbirds follow the path of timbering in North Carolina and Tennessee, when a drop in their numbers became noticeable.[31]

To understand how loss of habitat affects an individual species, scientists in recent years have studied the impact of clear-cutting on salamander species. Because their skin must be kept cool and moist to facilitate gas exchange, salamanders cannot withstand the loss of shade, reduction of leaf litter, increase in surface temperature, and reduction of soil moisture that accompany clear-cutting—let alone fires and floods. Studies show that salamanders take thirty to sixty years to return after mature hardwood forests are clear-cut.[32] The inevitable sedimentation and deterioration of streams where timber cutters take trees all the way up to the banks of streams also contribute to loss of this species. In Southern Appalachian sites, biologists concluded that clear-cutting destroyed more than 75 percent of the salamander population in an area.[33] Although salamanders may sound like one small and unglamorous species, their importance to mountain ecosystems is only now being realized. Major insectivores, salamanders consume ten times the amount of insects that birds do for their biomass. A major loss in salamanders like this may explain why people in the logging camps complained so much about gnats and other flying pests.

Even nonscientific observers recall tremendous changes in the wildlife. Earl Franklin, who worked for the Little River Lumber Company, observed the impact on owls, which require large trees for nesting. "'Fore we cut that timber in there them old big-horned owls, you couldn't sleep a night for them [calling]. They's everywhere. Just as quick as the timber's cut them owls left," he said, "And they're just now beginning to come back there. . . . And they've been gone ever since back in the early 1930s." When people complained of the loss of birds, *Southern Lumberman* offered nonsensical editorials that disassociated extinction from logging. The editor claimed birds and animals went extinct because of "their community breeding places" and "their habit of foraging for food in flocks."

One *Southern Lumberman* article even stated that the world was better off without these birds, because they frequently roosted "in such numbers as to break the largest limbs off giant oaks."[34]

Increased siltation in the streams coupled with the water warmed by increased sunlight despoiled trout populations and other species, such as otters, that relied on trout. Early twentieth-century naturalists and later scientists did not find otters in the Smokies, despite the suitability of the environment. Sportsmen deplored this loss and lobbied for stream improvement. Tennessee established a fish hatchery in Elkmont in 1917, funded by fishermen's fees, and called for a closed season on both native brook and rainbow trout. Walter Cole, who grew up in the Upper Sugarland Valley, recalled only brook trout during his childhood, before non-native rainbow trout—called "California fish" by local people—came to Elkmont. "They brought 'em up on the train," he said. "And we hauled them over with a team of mules and a wagon and put them in the [Little] Pigeon [River]. Later we had plenty of rainbow."[35]

Some mountain men also took matters into their own hands. Two years later, North Carolina opened a fish hatchery in Erwin, Tennessee, and Granville Calhoun ordered 5,000 rainbows, which came on the train to Bushnell. "I took some old wooden barrels, not having any experience at the time about how to care for fish," he recalled. "I lost most of the fish before I could get home. Got home with about 300 alive." Calhoun poured them into Sugar Fork Prong of Hazel Creek and waited. "They looked like they were dead," he said, "but I saw life in some of them." According to Calhoun, he got his neighbors to agree not to fish below Hazel Creek Falls for three years, and his children fed the fish with bread crumbs. At the end of three years, the entire community came out for a trout-fishing day. Calhoun's wife caught eighteen that morning, and his son caught one 16 inches long.[36] The government, sportsmen, and small farmers paid for and took the responsibility for losses due to habitat destruction by corporate loggers.

Whether or not clear-cutting caused permanent damage to the mountains is a subject of considerable debate. Until recently, biologists and plant ecologists accepted the notion that even the more complicated ecosystem represented by a cove hardwood forest would eventually grow back in "succession" to reach, once again, the "climax forest." After an area was cut over, small bushes and brambles invaded the area. Small trees, called stump sprouts, rose from the cutover trees. "The next thing, these blackberry briars come up, and then generally followed that was the wild cherry," observed a mountain resident. "We called them friendly briars,'" said Raymer Brackin. "They didn't have no stickers on them hardly." Small trees slowly invaded the bushes. Backpacker D. R. Beeson described the spruce-fir forest, several years after it had been cut over. "The mountain is so densely wooded here, covered with small balsams about 4 feet apart, that you can't see out over the surrounding region except in a very unsatisfactory way," he wrote in his journal.[37] Different animals thrived in each succeeding habitat. "Where you log out an area, or burn an area, they may not been a darned groundhog," Earl Franklin described. "The next year after you cut the timber, every rock, every big stump, and everything's got a groundhog under it." Finally, after several generations of smaller hardwoods, a climax of giant hardwoods or spruce and fir could again be established.

Succession certainly did occur, but ecologists do not know how long it will take to create an old-growth forest, and they no longer feel certain that these forests will recapture the diversity they supported before corporate logging. The beech groves or beech gaps that once prospered on Newfound Gap, for example, never returned. On places such as the Middle Prong of the Little River, where logging with a steam-powered skidder took place fifty years ago, forests did not return to the same number of trees recorded on mill tallies.[38] Depending on the extent of fire, steepness of the land, degree of mechanization used, and whether the land was cultivated or grazed after cutting, the soil could not necessarily support a forest of giant trees. Scientists who compared uncut with clear-cut sites in the Smokies almost nine decades after deforestation found that only half the species diversity and one-third of the canopy returned. "Neither community characteristic showed any trend toward recovery with age," the ecologists concluded; "if anything, both richness and cover appear to be decreasing." Ramsey Cascade, Upper Porters Creek, and Porters Flat, which were never reached by corporate loggers, remain qualitatively and quantitatively different from similar sites above Elkmont. Some aquatic species also have not returned to previous diversity in logged watersheds. Scientists suggest a number of reasons for this, but the long-term effects of this dramatic turn-of-the-century disturbance should not be underestimated.[39]

The Smokies had entered the Industrial Age. In just twenty years, lumbermen clear-cut 60 percent—300,000 acres—of the Smoky Mountains; they removed an estimated 2 billion board feet of lumber.[40] They uprooted the farmers living in Oconaluftee, Deep Creek, and Walker Valley, and created communities, including Ravensford, Proctor, Judson, and Townsend. They erected a network of temporary lumber camps, which appeared and then disappeared when extraction was complete. They accomplished these tremendous changes while amassing large fortunes for themselves. By 1917, W. M. Ritter had been named the "father of southern hardwoods" and at his death in 1952 he was worth in excess of $3.7 million. In addition to accumulating tremendous profits, they received accolades for their contributions to society. After World War I, W. M. Ritter was selected as one of six "big business men" who formed an advisory organization for the development of post-war relations between government and industry. In 1926, President Herbert Hoover appointed Reuben Robertson chairman of the National Committee on Wood Utilization in the U.S. Department of Commerce.[41]

Ritter credited his meteoric rise to following "Christian principles," including honesty, hard work, and long-range planning. "The more perfect the service one renders," he explained, "the greater and more certain will be the reward flowing back to him."[42] He encouraged Christianity among his employees, particularly the compunction to work hard, by hiring preachers to serve in the lumber camps. Like most lumbermen, William Whitmer declared himself a Republican, but "declined political preferment and contented himself with the conscientious execution of his various commercial duties." *American Lumberman* described Whitmer as a "thorough optimist," because in the words of the writer, "the true optimism . . . is that which accomplishes."[43]

Southern historian Robert Woody, who spent his summers in Little Cataloochee between 1910 and 1928, said that "in all that period of time you saw very little change" beyond the mowing machine that replaced hand-held scythes for cutting hay. Each improvement in farm technology arrived slowly, after much sweat and savings. Despite the general perception that life didn't change much between 1910 and 1928, records show that life, indeed, was in the midst of economic and environmental transformation. Even in Cataloochee, where landowners refused to sell their own woodlands to the lumber companies, agriculture changed in response to their presence. Large and mid-size farmers prospered, as lumber companies brought new markets for apples, corn, pork, and beef. Barbed wire appeared on even the smallest farms, as no one could resist the profits to be had selling beef to the lumber companies. Between 1890 and 1925, the number of farms in all the Smoky Mountains counties steadily increased. The population of Cataloochee alone grew from 764 people in 1900 to 1,251 in 1910.[44]

After 1910, some Cataloochee and Cosby farmers substantially improved their incomes by providing apples to the large lumber camps in Oconaluftee Valley and Big Creek, and eventually to regional markets, such as Knoxville, as well. Will Messer became the wealthiest man in Cataloochee this way; his neighbors told him that he ought to "cross his honeybees with lightning bugs so they could work day and night." Messer built an apple house that would hold 2,500 or more bushels of apples. The sawdust from commercial logging operations provided apple growers with cheap insulation for storing their crops. The disadvantage of poor roads, in this case, was outweighed by cooler high-altitude temperatures: apples could be stored and hauled to market one wagonload at a time as needed. Bill Proffit, from the Mountain Rest community of Cocke County, moved to the area in 1900 for a logging operation and stayed to raise an orchard. His granddaughter, Delce Carver Bryant, remembered her father taking his apples to sell in Knoxville. A clever pomologist, he grafted as many as five varieties onto a single tree. "We didn't even have an apple [variety] that went all the way to the top of the tree," she recalled.[45] In 1925, a commercial operation, Cherokee Orchard, joined the apple production in the Smoky Mountains. A middle Tennessee man, W. O. Whittle, purchased the 1,000-plus-acres operation from several small farms. In addition to 6,500 apple trees, Whittle started a nursery that included more than 100 native plant varieties, propagated from stock taken from the surrounding mountains. Even small operators benefited in the short term from logging operations. Because of the logging economy, one Cherokee agent requested permission to buy corn, oats, and hay outside the Qualla Boundary. "I am told that the lumber companies operating near here are paying higher prices than we are offering," he explained, "and consequently the supply of these articles is almost exhausted in this locality." Greater access to goods and cash meant that more consumer goods, and hence more packaging and garbage, entered the mountains with the lumber camps. The first truck appeared in Swain County in 1916, and by 1926 there were eighty-two.[46]

Both Cataloochee and Cades Cove farmers sold cattle to the lumber companies, but they faced increasing competition from lowland farmers who wanted to do the same thing. Between 1900 and 1930, the number of cattle produced in Haywood County doubled, and the farmers of Cataloochee increased the sizes of the balds. After Suncrest Lumber Company cleared the spruce-fir forest on Mount Sterling, they allowed farmers to graze this land as well.[47] Grazing after logging, however, had much more serious and long-term effects on the land than grazing alone. The combined effect would deplete the soil and make it slow for trees to grow again on "the balds."

And so, what mountain people and Cherokees felt about the devastation of their environment was complicated by their economic role in it. The lumber companies provided wages or "public work," and this in some cases purchased loyalty. A scholar who spent much of the 1920s in Bryson City, wrote, "The true mountaineer has no respect for a tree, feeling merely that the timber is there to be exploited and he is glad for the lumber operations that afford employment." Whether or not the scholar referred to the mountain men who held land for generations is difficult to judge. The lumber companies also attracted young men from urban industrial centers, such as Knoxville, who preferred outdoor work to the textile mills. Of nineteen men who served as engineers, surveyors, and site managers for Suncrest operations in the Smokies, not a single one grew up in the mountains.[48]

And the employment afforded by lumbering was neither secure nor well compensated. Although lumbermen worked under safer conditions than railroad men or miners, the rate of fatal accidents was 1.5 per thousand workers in 1913, compared with a rate of 0.25 in other manufacturing industries. The lumber industry in Great Britain, Norway, Germany, and Austria all claimed better safety records, and neither North Carolina nor Tennessee required compensation to injured workers. Even living in a lumber camp could be dangerous, as the base camps, called "string towns," consisted of railroad cars set off the track by a giant crane, for which a family paid $3 a month. Horace Trentham remembered a log loader accidentally turned out a load on top of a shanty car. "Tore that house all to pieces," he described. Just minutes before, he saw a woman inside the car; for a minute, he felt certain the load had killed her. Then she emerged from the bushes in which she had jumped, in the split second as the logs began to roll. "Boy she's lucky," he commented.[49]

Many of the companies did not pay workers in cash; rather they offered "scrip," which could only be used in the company-owned store. "The most of the people that worked for the [lumber companies] hardly ever drawed any money," said Audley Whaley. "They took it all up in groceries and overalls." Employees who lived in company towns such as Judson, Proctor, Ravensford, and Townsend also received wages in scrip. The design, economy, and subsequent odor of the town was dictated by the mill, and the company even paid for local law enforcement and approved local "elected" officials. At the end of a hiking trip to Mount LeConte in 1921, Paul Fink stayed at the company hotel owned by Little River in Townsend. As he and his friends relaxed in their room, a town marshal suddenly walked in, without knocking. "He questioned us closely as to who we were, whence we came, our business in the town, and the like," wrote Fink. "Then it developed that word had come to him some rum-runners were expected in town that night. So when he heard that three hard-looking characters, with bulging packs had arrived on the evening train, we were suspected." Fink's companions convinced the company man of their real purpose, but they left with a good idea of how social control in W. B. Townsend's community worked.[50]

Many who chose this life had no other options. Sam Whaley, who grew up in Greenbrier, was one of the youngest sons of ten children. After his father died, his mother, brother, and younger sisters had all they could manage just running the farm. "My twin brother would stay at the house and help tend the corn, and I'd go and work to get enough money to buy our books and shoes," he said. Still a teenager, Whaley joined the men crossing the mountains to a lumber camp in Oconaluftee Valley. "There wasn't as many ways of getting money in those days as there are now," he said. "We didn't have no welfare then." Johnny Manning also underlined the economic necessity of wage labor: "That's the only jobs we had," he said.[51]

Many Cherokees went to work in the logging camps because the economic devastation that accompanied timber operations made it more difficult to continue subsistence farming. Government agents recommended hiring a "forest guard" not just to protect timber from trespassing but to end grazing in the woodlands. One agent even wrote Gifford Pinchot, suggesting that the U.S. Forest Service take over administrative care of Cherokee timberlands. Maggie Wachacha, born in Cherokee in 1892, cooked for Cherokee men in a logging camp near Andrews. In addition to three meals a day, she washed their laundry—all for $1.50 a day. "As of today I wouldn't do that," she commented. "It's hard work. I wouldn't wash a pair of socks now for a dollar and fifty cents." Government agents further used the poor timber deals and timber destruction to justify allotment, the dividing up of communally held land into individual property rights. Although they did not succeed, every Cherokee Indian Agency (CIA) annual report recommended this, and agents made repeated appeals to the council.[52]

Some mountain men viewed lumber work as temporary, like their own seasonal tree-cutting, a means to an end. Carl Woody, for example, labored as a tenant farmer in Cataloochee until volunteering to fight for his country during World War I. When he returned, Woody thought of only one thing: buying a small farm in the valley he called home. Because a lumber operation in nearby Oconaluftee Valley offered good wages, Woody situated his new wife with her family and "commuted" to the lumber camp. The purchase price seemed too high to Woody, but he "wanted a home so bad" that he put down his entire $700 savings. He moved his family onto the new farm, then returned to Oconaluftee for four months to earn the remaining $200. "You just don't know how good I felt," he later told his son, "when I was sitting on my *own* porch."[53]

Some long-time residents of the mountains, however, chose not to work for lumber operations. As a young man, Mark Hannah left Cataloochee to seek his fortune in a lumber camp. "Roughest place I've ever seen. Overhead skidder pulling logs dropping them down. Big bunch of rough men," he described. "That just wasn't my type a business." Hannah went home to the farm.[54] In most cases in the Smokies, corporate loggers bought the land they clear-cut. Mark Hannah said that people in Cataloochee weren't happy about the loss of the forest, the woodland pasture, ginseng, and chestnut crop, but "they couldn't do anything about it—all they could do is go to work for [the lumber companies]. It wasn't their land." Another scholar who traveled in and wrote about the region echoed Hannah's remarks. "Indians and white mountaineers alike have an affectionate regard for their forests I have not found in the North," wrote Henry Canby, "They regard with a certain melancholy the invasion of the lumbermen, who since my first visit . . . have hacked their way to the top of the Balsams, and peeled off great areas of spruce." Although some received short-term economic benefits, others, Canby argued, "deplore the slaughter of the forests." A herder he met in his travels said: "It seems as if they just naturally tear up everything. Soon there'll be no more big woods."[55]

A point often missed by those who sentimentalize trains and crosscut saws is that the lumber companies always intended to leave. Turn-of-the-century lumbermen had no long-term plans for the communities that they built. As much as residents of Proctor, Ravensford, Judson, and Townsend created a sense of community among themselves or loved the mountains, they were at the mercy of the market. Those who wanted to stay after the lumber companies finally pulled out would sometimes purchase small areas of cutover land and try to resume farming. "All these people they tried to grow some food up there," remembered Arnold Thompson, a logger. "And people you know they had to get wood, too. They'd clean up [the slash] on these old hilltops you know for the wood."[56] Because this soil was so much poorer and the steep land so easily eroded, grazing and cultivation accelerated flooding and made it more difficult for the land to recover.[57] In the following years, foresters and government agricultural agents decried "mountain farming" by pointing to these desperate people, who moved into cutover areas to survive.

As historian Ronald L. Lewis argues, the loss of the bountiful old-growth forest eliminated the means for traditional subsistence life. Although wage employment and consumer goods surely pulled mountain people away from subsistence, the loss of the forest made it impossible to return. Daughters forgot which herbs their mothers hunted in the woods, due, in part, to the fact that the woods weren't there any more. Sons did not carry on the tradition of bear hunting, because the mountains supported fewer bears. Environmental catastrophe, from this perspective, also brought death to communities, as deforestation, a decrease in farm size, and an end to woodland pasture accompanied the loss of the forest. "Railroad and timber development did not stimulate the growth of a vibrant agricultural sector," Lewis writes, "but rather, forced farmers to either abandon the countryside for a new life in the industrial towns or face a life of rural marginality at the periphery of the American, and now global, economy."[58]

The increasingly global economy in which lumbermen lived gave them little knowledge of or appreciation for a sense of place. With the exception of Townsend, who built a residence in his mill town, the Smokies represented little more to them than a location on a map. This tremendous distance allowed them to convert forests into the abstraction "natural resources," which could be "extracted" for maximum profit. People become "labor" rather than individuals or even members of a community. Once a forest or a village loses its complexity—the "preacher birds," potscrapings, lady's slippers, possums, and dogwoods cease to exist—all becomes a mere object for the actions of the capitalist. Domination of humans and nature go hand in hand, as many writers have pointed out; intrinsic values, such as wildness, claim no currency.

Theoretically, Townsend and Robertson at least represented a new generation of lumbermen more concerned with scientific forestry. The impact of their ideals cannot be seen in the Smoky Mountains. "There is great waste in the manufacture of timber from the forest to the consumer," noted J. S. Holmes, and in the Smokies he would find many examples. On steep and uneven ground, lumbermen lost much timber in cutting, because trees broke or split when falling and were left to rot. In Champion's "state-of-the art" spruce operations, Holmes recorded that trees not harvested were "so broken and crushed" that they would not regenerate.[59] Townsend considered himself a leader in "scientific" methods, but the devastation would be as complete on the Little River as on any watershed in the Smokies. Robertson did show considerable long-term commitment to the distant mill town of Canton, North Carolina, but Townsend intended to sell his denuded mountain lands to the U.S.D.A. Forest Service.

Neither lumbermen nor government foresters knew or cared about the central role the forest played in semi-subsistence mountain farming. "Agriculture," wrote Holmes, "which in most parts of the State stands first among the important industries, takes third place in the mountains, and, if only those farm products which bring a cash return are counted, is unimportant."[60] Just fourteen years before, his colleague Gifford Pinchot declared the mountains "commercially unimportant" for lumbering. Foresters tried to prevent waste, fires, and floods, but their conservation still arose from concern for the timber market. A fundamental shift occurred when Ayres and Ashe entered the mountains in 1901: once within the range of marketable vision, the great forests of the Smoky Mountains were reduced to quantities of board feet.

2.1. Corporate loggers built railroads into every watershed of the Smokies; lumbermen then clear-cut the mountainsides and left the land to erode. Courtesy of Great Smoky Mountains National Park.

Above: 2.2. Mill and millpond of W. M. Ritter operation in Hazel Creek, Swain County, North Carolina. North Carolina Collection. Courtesy of University of North Carolina, Chapel Hill.

Left: 2.3. W. M. Ritter, one of the lumbermen who made a fortune on the old-growth trees in the Great Smoky Mountains, owned operations in five states. Austin Brooks Collection, Ramsey Library. Courtesy of University of North Carolina, Asheville.

2.4. Crestmont Lumber Company mill and town site on Big Creek, North Carolina. Courtesy of Great Smoky Mountains National Park.

2.5. Bill Walker, who owned the old-growth forest on Thunderhead Prong, persuaded lumberman W. B. Townsend to spare the largest trees. After Townsend died, the Little River Lumber Company broke the promise. Dame Olive Campbell Collection. Courtesy of University of North Carolina, Chapel Hill.

2.6. Laying track up the Little River Gorge, Tennessee, 1906. Courtesy of Great Smoky Mountains National Park.

2.7. Little River Lumber Company log loader hoisted a mammoth tree. Dame Olive Campbell Collection. Courtesy of University of North Carolina, Chapel Hill.

Scenery in the Eminent Domain

The world's oldest mountains ... have been waiting for thousands of years for the multitudes that will inevitably make their way to gaze upon the wonder of Nature.

BROCHURE PROMOTING A NATIONAL PARK IN THE GREAT SMOKY MOUNTAINS, 1928

LUMBERMEN WERE NOT the only ones to discover the Smoky Mountains at the turn of the century. Even as speculators moved in to purchase the exquisite stands of old-growth forest, the first tourists appreciated the woods for different reasons. "Beyond Townsend we entered a wooded gorge and were snaked up the stream. The wheels screamed on the curves," Knoxville attorney Harvey Broome described his first trip on the logging railroad into Elkmont. "Such thrills! We looked down on raw boulders in water, foaming and clear. The cars crossed the stream on a bridge and everybody moved as one to the windows on the opposite side to continue a love affair with the river." Hikers like Broome looked on scenery as more than a natural resource; they cherished the mountains as a spiritual retreat, a place to encounter the "love of the beautiful."[1] As the United States moved from a rural to an urban nation—from a pastoral landscape to a collection of industrial, multicultural cities—many citizens longed for a haven, a simpler time they imagined out of America's past.

In his memoirs, Harvey Broome later rejected the notion that he was a big-city dweller who, seeing the "shambles of the natural world" in urban areas, "sought to protect and restore it elsewhere." Born in Knoxville, the young lawyer quickly developed a passion for the Smokies. He later would serve as president of the Smoky Mountains Hiking Club (SMHC), director of the Great Smoky Mountains Conservation Association, and one of the founders of the Wilderness Society. Broome said he experienced an intrinsic beauty, "intensely desirable" in the Smokies. Others, however, such as writer Horace Kephart, embraced the connection between urbanization and escape: "The East is a land of swarming industrial centers," he wrote. "The millions of people hived in cities have learned that it is a matter of self-preservation for them to have wing room, every now and then, in the open air. They must have vacations out-of-doors."[2]

Whether it was a need for recreation or spiritual retreat, the Smoky Mountains began to inspire literary works, long pilgrimages, and great loyalty on the part of those who traveled to see them. "I was born in the Rocky mountains and reared to contemplate the glorious colors of scenery," wrote a Princeton professor. "After [a lifetime of travel] I looked from the summit of Mount LeConte. It was wholly unique; in its blending of color, its multiplicity of outline, enveloped in that fairy, ghostlike veil and haze, there is nothing else on the face of the earth like it." It was, in the words of Kephart, "an Eden still unpeopled and unspoiled." "We have never seen a section of the country where the vegetation is so varied or abundant," claimed one magazine writer, "or where the land is so richly threaded with mountain streams."[3] Such rhapsodies inspired tourists, and in tourism others saw financial opportunity. If the Smokies were as unique as the writers claimed, then money could be made selling lodging, tours, and eventually gas and automobiles to those who came to visit. When enterprising men sold the economic benefits of tourism to their congressmen, a national park was born.

Early Visionaries and Health Enthusiasts

"It is not far from the truth to say that the Southern Appalachians were rediscovered at the end of the 19th century," wrote one forester. Surprisingly, he was talking about enthusiastic tourists and writers, rather than lumbermen. Among the primary considerations of these urbanites, from

Maine to Georgia, was access to railroads and healthful mineral springs. According to travel guides published at the time, mineral springs relieved people with chronic conditions, such as dyspepsia, hysteria, rheumatism, tuberculosis, gout, liver complaints, and other "cutaneous affections." Just outside the Smoky Mountains, a Mississippi planter built an enormous three-story, seven-gabled hotel and cottages to accommodate 300–400 guests at Montvale Springs, Tennessee. Sterling Lanier, grandfather of poet Sidney Lanier, owned and operated the "Saratoga of the South" for wealthy visitors until the hotel burned in 1896. Nathan McCoy, a Civil War veteran from Illinois, in 1886 opened the Allegheny Springs Hotel in Blount County, featuring velvet-upholstered furniture, brocade drapes, crystal chandeliers, marble-topped dressers, and hot and cold water on every floor. A more modest hotel, called Mt. Nebo, offered twenty-two rooms for guests between 1877 to 1937 and advertised "strong chalybeate water" as well as hot and cold baths. In Sevier County, a lawyer, James R. Penland, established the Dupont Springs Hotel. "The names of almost every prominent man and woman from cities throughout the South could be found on the [hotel's register] between March and October," according to a former guest.[4]

More adventurous and sporting travelers ventured farther from the railroad lines. Mountain men sometimes hired themselves out as guides to sportsmen's expeditions and their families boarded guests. At the foot of Shields Mountain, the Reverend James Seaton opened his farm home as a boarding house for visitors in 1884. He also sold land to individuals, who built one-season cottages on a flat-topped ridge above the house—it became known locally as "Seaton's Summer City." Water from the mineral springs ran through a gun barrel into a stone basin, then through a wooden trough with a hinged lid that served as the family's refrigerator for milk and butter. Around the spring, Seaton constructed a platform with benches for guests to gather—but no bathing was allowed.[5]

A famous early traveler to the Smokies, Mary Noilles Murfree, stayed in an informal arrangement with a family in Cades Cove. Murfree, who published under the name Charles Egbert Craddock, wandered the mountains on horseback in search of tales and scenery. She wrote popular romances that used the Smokies as an exotic, virtually foreign setting. Almost every chapter of *In the Tennessee Mountains* and *The Prophet of the Great Smokies* opens with a poetic description of mountains and trees, and her characters typically became so inspired by a beautiful sunset that they found their true loves—or had a change of heart. "The woods . . . were all aglow with color, and sparkling with the tremulous drops that shimmered in the sun," she wrote. "Above all rose the great 'bald' still splendidly illumined with the red glamour of sunset and holding its uncovered head so loftily against the sky that it might seem it had bared its brow before the majesty of heaven." There are few specific species in her descriptions, beyond "a wilderness of pine." Still, future visitors looked for the spectacular places she described, and they no doubt wondered about the "uncouth creatures" Murfree wrote of who lived there. Mountain residents, according to Murfree, were "roughly clad" and disinclined toward work, because here on the frontier "humanity is an alien thing."[6]

An early magnet for the readers of Mary Noilles Murfree became Asheville, North Carolina. Florida developers wooed upper-class people from the Northeast by promoting the mountain air and water for health and recreation. Tuberculosis sufferers, called "lungers" by local people, filled the huge hotels built in Asheville during the 1880s and 1890s. They were joined by urbanites wanting to escape hectic city life and sportsmen looking for wild places to hunt and fish.[7] Some, such as Chase Ambler, decided to stay and start small businesses in the prospering community devoted to good health. An Ohio physician, Ambler spent his weekends hunting and fishing in rural Buncombe County and soon became appalled at the floods, fires, and wildlife devastation—not to mention the associated health problems—he witnessed around logging operations. In 1899, Ambler and other concerned citizens formed the Appalachian National Park Association to do something about it. At their first meeting, Ambler declared, "[It] would be reckless stupidity, negligence of the grossest kind, if a portion of this grand and picturesque place be not preserved in its natural condition for the enjoyment of the people." The *Asheville Citizen* joined his cause by displaying a front-page cartoon, graphically depicting the mountains stripped of trees and vegetation.[8]

In its first petition before Congress, the Appalachian National Park Association declared the urgency of its idea. The cause gained support from residents, visitors, schools, and newspapers; it was backed by North Carolina Senators Jeter C. Pritchard and Marion Butler. Lumber companies, land speculators, and foresters quickly stepped in, though. George Smathers, a prominent lawyer for railroad and timber companies, joined the association and his influence may have been one reason that the first convention promoted "a Southern National Park and Forest Reserve," indicating the area should not be exempt from future timber harvest. Use of the latter term pleased Gifford Pinchot, chief forester of the United States, who wrote, "If I can be of use, I hope you will let me know." In 1900, Pritchard petitioned Congress, extolling the rare natural beauty, the superb forest, and the excellent climate of the Smoky Mountains, but suggested that the "park" should act primarily as a forest reserve and a location for a school of forestry. Forester W. W. Ashe and state geologist Holmes, both powerful forces in the state, wanted to protect the economic potential of timber in the western counties. As they completed their surveys of the mountains that summer, they tried to slow down Ambler's publicity campaign. Smathers and another man, dispatched to convince the North Carolina legislature to support a resolution, mysteriously lost it in the shuffle.[9] And so, early outcries for a national park to "preserve" the Smoky Mountains were overridden by foresters and lumbermen who wanted to "conserve" trees for future cutting.

Four years later, in 1904, the most famous early tourist of all arrived in the Smoky Mountains—Horace Kephart. A librarian from St. Louis, Missouri, who lost his job due to drinking and periodically roaming in the woods, Kephart wanted to recover his senses in the wilderness and forge a literary career. Placing his finger on the "emptiest spot" of a map of the eastern United States, Kephart left his wife and children and set off for adventure in the mountains of North Carolina. He arranged to stay in a cabin on Hazel Creek near the abandoned Everett copper mine but arrived in such poor condition that he had to be nursed back to health by Granville Calhoun, a well-known mountain man. As soon as Kephart recovered, he began camping, hunting, and fishing in the woods, and from these adventures published articles in *Sports Afield*, *Field and Stream*, *Forest and Stream*, *Outing* magazine and others. Nothing of his puny condition or alcohol problem appears in the robust, even swaggering articles. Eventually, he produced two popular books, *Camping and Woodcraft* (an outdoors manual) and *Our Southern Highlanders* (about the mountain people).[10]

The Great Smoky Mountains in Kephart's work contained few logging operations and a scant number of farmers. Although he compared them with the Rockies, Kephart's Smokies held a magic all their own. They were, in summer, "warm, soft, dreamy, caressing, habitable" he wrote, but at the same time "inexpressibly lonesome, isolated, and mysterious." Kephart's notebooks do include entries about wildlife and vegetation as well as Cherokee and white subsistence practices, but his published work emphasizes bear hunts, raids on moonshine stills, feuds, and murder mysteries. Kephart and presumably his readers admired a frontier-like ability to conquer nature, to survive in a place without "civilization." Rather than reading an accurate description of diverse white and Cherokee farming communities, they wanted to hear about gun-toting mountain men.[11]

Other travel writers equated themselves with eighteenth-century explorers. Although thousands of people lived in the Smoky Mountains and logging operations riddled the area in the 1920s, historian Paul Fink maintained that "only a limited number of hardy spirits had climbed the high peaks and penetrated the deep valleys, and many were the spots that human eyes had never looked upon." To the "explorers," permanent mountain residents were objects of the scenery. The Smokies, one writer asserted, were "peopled by a race of gallant mountaineers who live in a world of three hundred years ago." Another writer described them as "interesting *chiefly* because they preserve traits and manners that have been transmitted unchanged from ancient times [emphasis added]." A "fiery and vindictive race," Horace Kephart wrote, in words that concocted lasting stereotypes, "fell into feuding and warring among themselves because state and federal law could not reach them." Even a thoughtful observer like Harvey Broome saw the mountaineers as more rarefied than himself. "We were met by grizzled mountaineers, whose clothes carried the odor of sweat and of earth," he remembered. "The scent was not unpleasant but I was aware of it whenever I came near them."[12]

As these literary careers bloomed, middle- and upper-class citizens of Knoxville, Tennessee, began to suffer the same problems that had troubled eastern cities since the early nineteenth century. During the 1910s and 1920s, citizens in the growing mill town began to see pollution, ghettos, and race riots, and they looked to the mountains in their own backyard for sanctuary and escape. The hotels in this second wave of tourism also capitalized on mineral springs, but they more often emphasized fishing, scenery, and firsthand experience with mountain culture. Owners called the Line Springs hotel in Wear Valley "one of the best watering places in the world," and Henderson Springs Hotel published a handbill detailing the mineral content of its water. The latter also offered banjo music and tall tales of mountain feuding after supper each evening.[13]

Industrialists saw tourism as a way to maximize profits from facilities. The Schlosser Leather Company, located in Walland, built an eleven-room boarding house for employees in 1906 but later began to advertise for other guests. Promotional materials recommended the fine food, fishing, electric lights, hot and cold water, and a mineral spring. Guests from Knoxville or Maryville could reach the Chilhowee Inn from the Knoxville and Augusta and the Little River Railroads. At the same time, W. B. Townsend advertised his employee boarding house for traveling salesmen, teachers, and those interested in "excellent fishing." He charged his employees with keeping the roadway neat, not allowing slash piles along the excursion route "so as not to mar the scenery."[14] Farmer John Oliver built a log lodge in Cades Cove with eight bedrooms, a kitchen, and a dining room. Oliver's advertisement stressed "good clean moral people; drunks and immoral people strictly prohibited." During the 1920s tourists from every state in the Union and a few parts of Europe visited this family operation. Willie and Hattie Myers ran Ekaneetlee Lodge, near what is today Parson Branch Road in Cades Cove. Both Eleanor Roosevelt and John D. Rockefeller later stayed in the "immaculate home" of the Myers, who served air-cured ham, beans, biscuits, mountain honey, coconut cream pie, and coffee.[15] At Ogle's general store in Gatlinburg, Justice of the Peace Ephraim Ogle supplemented his income by marrying couples who traveled to the area for their honeymoons; usually a store customer was pulled in to witness the event. Also in Gatlinburg, Andrew Huff opened the two-story, six-bedroom Mountain View Hotel in 1918. Visitors took the train to Sevierville and met Andy and his horse and buggy. They rode into Gatlinburg on a narrow, rough dirt road. One visitor recalled that when the wagon got stuck, Huff simply got out, applied his strong shoulders to the rear axles, and lifted the wheels out of the rut. Huff's son, Jack Huff, developed a lodge and small cabins on the top of Mount LeConte (6,593 feet) in 1925. The strenuous 16-mile hike from Gatlinburg was not for the faint of heart, but the views from Mount LeConte soon became popular.[16]

Apparently, 1920s tourists sought a somewhat rustic experience: indeed, sleeping on "beds of balsam" seemed part of the wilderness experience for the "jolly vagabonds." "A great many . . . so-called hotels are merely semi-public," wrote one visitor, "that is, the family of the host sits at the same table." One such homey place was Hotel LeConte, located in Greenbrier. J. W. Whaley, a local resident, built a two-story, tin-roofed, frame building situated on two prongs of the river with a large swimming hole in front. "The ceaseless, restless, hollow roar of this stream made a welcome music for our outdoor-living souls," wrote Harvey Broome, one of the first guests. "Its clientele came from all over the country; local patrons were practically nil," remembered another visitor, yet it was only "advertised by word of mouth." In 1925, Ray and Oscar Bohannon and their brother-in-law, I. Lillard Maples, built a three-story hotel at the top of the Sugarland Valley overlooking the Chimneys and Sugarland Mountain. Porches on the upper floors extended the full width of the aged-gray building; slight gaps separated the floor boards. "If you wanted to know what they were having for breakfast," recalled a guest, "you just looked through the cracks in the floor, and you could tell that they were having bacon and eggs or corn."[17]

Although the Cherokees did not build hotels, they too began to profit from the tourists that ventured into the mountains. The annual Cherokee Fair, established in 1914, attracted visitors to view stickball tournaments, home demonstration projects, and agricultural products, and to purchase food and crafts. BIA agents saw the fair as an economic opportunity for the Cherokees, although they worried that it would cause them to "regress" into primitive activities.[18] Despite this discouragement, young Cherokees such as Rebecca Youngbird taught themselves to make pottery in the tradition of their ancestors and then sold their wares to the new tourists. "I priced them at what I thought somebody would pay me," Youngbird said. By 1926, tourism made basket-weaving and other crafts an important part of the economy in Cherokee.[19]

Most tourists viewed the Cherokees and whites with a charitable if somewhat paternalistic attitude. Alie Newman Maples remembered a tourist giving her and her playmates a sack of toys out of the window of the car. "I guess they thought those little mountain children will appreciate them," she said. "[They probably] saw a lot of pictures of dirty tacky kids and felt so sorry for them. But they didn't know what a good time we children had up there in the mountains." Mountain people, for their part, sometimes enjoyed "putting one over" on the tourists. One mountain man told a Johnson City resident, D. R. Beeson, about a "joint snake." If you beat the snake with a club, he told Beeson, it breaks apart as if brittle. "The most curious thing about the snake is that if you go away and leave it, it will get together and grow back into a snake again," Beeson wrote in his diary. "I'm not stretching this story a bit."[20]

Despite enterprising mountain men and railroads, tourists in the 1920s already had discovered the joys of traveling by automobile. Paul Adams, a naturalist who spent several years camping on Mount Leconte, said that in 1923 "it was not an uncommon occurrence to see car tracks in the [Indian] gap." By taking a network of logging trails, a Model T could spiral up the North Carolina side of the mountains. Small hotels, such as Henderson Springs, advertised "driving" along with fishing and croquet as recreation. The balds became a popular destination for adventurous automobile drivers, and road traffic no doubt helped maintain these roads. Within a few years, Andy Huff had expanded his hotel and replaced the buggy with Henry Ford's miracle of middle-class transportation. In the Sugarlands, Sam Newman opened the Sky-u-ka Hotel and installed the first gasoline pump in 1927. The small store next to the pump still, however, took chickens and eggs in trade for lard, salt, coffee, condensed milk, and canned vegetables.[21]

Although the environmental impact of 1920s tourism did not compare with that of lumber operations, outsiders did introduce new plant and animal species that began to dominate parts of the forest. In 1920, about 100 European wild boars escaped from a 500-acre tourist hunting preserve near Hooper Bald, just outside the Smokies. Although the same species as the domestic hog, the wild boar had bristly, long fur, a wedge-shaped head, and longer legs. The boars competed with bear and deer for mast in the fall, then thrived upon snails, larvae, salamanders, or the eggs of turkey and grouse. As the boar population increased, it eventually threatened the delicate bulbs and roots of wildflowers.[22] Another introduced species, the rainbow trout, came with the fishermen who demanded stream improvement after logging operations. Rainbow fingerlings adapted readily to the new environment, and they soon dominated creeks where they were introduced. Between logging operations and rainbow introductions, native brook trout retreated to the headwaters of streams. A third introduced species, the Japanese honeysuckle (*Lonicera japonica*), arrived with the tourists—probably planted as an ornamental by the hotels, from which birds carried away the seeds. First introduced into the United States in 1864 from Asia, it escaped from gardens and quickly spread along roadways and fencerows. Although it was called a "pernicious and dangerous weed" by some, Cherokee women found honeysuckle useful for making light baskets, impractical for heavy service, which they sold to tourists.[23]

Over the next two decades, tourists from Tennessee to Ohio purchased cutover land above an old lumber camp, Elkmont. Calling themselves the Appalachian Club, the up-and-comers built summer homes on the land. "Whole families went to the mountains for the entire summer, taking with them trunks of clothes and canned goods," wrote one historian. "Fathers of families took the [timber company's] train to Elkmont for the weekend, bringing with them fresh vegetables and replacements for staple foods." In 1920 a second group, calling themselves the Wonderland Club, purchased a nearby hotel and constructed summer homes as well. Apparently such rivalry developed between the Appalachian Club and Wonderland Club members that they refused to acknowledge each other on the train. Local people referred to the whole Elkmont area as "Club Town."[24] Two Club Town rivals—David C. Chapman, president of a Knoxville drug company, and James B. Wright, an attorney—soon stood at the center of a controversy about whether the region should become a national park.

Tourists for a National Park

As tourism perked along in the Smoky Mountains, Congress established the National Park Service (NPS) under the U.S. Department of Interior. Unlike the national forests, which the government managed for future harvest, the NPS preserved forests for tourism, health, heritage, and recreation. By the 1920s, national park enthusiasts in the western states had learned that a strong economic rationale in the form of tourism development could be used to gain much wider support for national parks. The first director of the NPS, Stephen Mather, sold the idea of economic development through tourism to major philanthropists.[25] In the summer of 1923, a prominent Knoxville couple, Anne and Willis P. Davis, visited Yellowstone National Park and noted the booming small businesses around the park.[26] They returned full of enthusiasm for getting a national park in Tennessee, and quickly won the support of friends and colleagues. Members of the local auto clubs, merchants aware of the tourism possibilities, members of the chamber of commerce, and real estate companies created the Smoky Mountains Conservation Association and hired a New York publicity firm to promote the national park and solicit donations. It may have been the publicity firm that pushed the word "Great" in front of "Smoky Mountains," but not long afterward the organization and its documents adopted the label GSMCA—and changed the name forever. Newspaper articles listing the benefits of tourism to other states appeared in city newspapers. David C. Chapman, elected president of the GSMCA, quickly proved his ability to maintain the support of local media. A tireless civic promoter, Chapman also served as director of the chamber of commerce and the East Tennessee Automobile Club; the Knoxville papers portrayed him as a valiant hero, fighting for a noble national park.[27]

As soon as they contacted the U.S. Department of Interior, Chapman and his Knoxville boosters discovered that thirty other cities were trying to do the same thing. Secretary of the Interior Hubert Work appointed the Southern Appalachian National Park Commission to investigate the sites and select one. The inspection tour did not actually include the Smokies, but when investigators arrived in Asheville, Chapman and several others appeared with an album of scenic photographs. Chapman himself had not visited any part of the Smoky Mountains except the Little River area, but his hyperbole was hard to resist. Several delegates agreed to tour Mount LeConte, and as a result of either the hike or the hyperbole ended up recommending a national park in the Great Smokies—that was, as soon as Shenandoah National Park could be established.[28] Rather than elation, the boosters felt dismayed to be "second" to Shenandoah, but the announcement brought Asheville into the park movement. (Before this, Asheville wanted the Linville Gorge-Grandfather Mountain area to be the first national park in the East.) By 1925 both cities campaigned vigorously for a national park in the Smokies, and they gained the unqualified support of newspapers in both towns. "Asheville has come out flat-footed for the Park and one of the most ardent boosters is Mrs. Vanderbilt,"

Horace Kephart told Chapman. "Our hardest job was to convince our own folks in and around Bryson City that the Park would be worthwhile. They could not see what the coming of hundreds of tourists daily through the park in Swain County would mean for Bryson City."[29]

Indeed, regional fund-raising lagged throughout the campaign, because local economies remained tied to logging and farming. "Not only is there no real benefit, but on the contrary there is serious injury done by an imaginary and exaggerated hope of taking money from wealthy tourists," wrote a citizen in *Montgomery's Vindicator*. The writer mentioned the reduction in taxable property and the increased taxes on remaining properties. Other county governments touted the good roads that would result and the vibrant tourism economy that could replace departing lumber operations. "Three years ago the people of Graham County were elated over the fact that a large lumber operation was soon to start in that county," an editorial writer mentioned. "Today these people realize the problems they will face when the company moves out, but they have no choice in the matter."[30] People still working for lumber companies felt threatened by the national park movement. Another Appalachian Club member, James B. Wright, regularly represented at least two lumber companies and became the unofficial spokesmen for their views on the national park. Before the Davises visited Yellowstone, the Knoxville lawyer had worked for several years to bring a national forest to the Smokies, enticing a small USFS office to the Little River area. USFS employees worked on several roads and trails within the proposed purchase area, examining titles to purchase the land after cutting. By 1925, they concluded that overlapping claims would cause too many problems for the federal government.

The reluctance of the USFS may have been one reason that Tennessee Governor Austin Peay convinced W. B. Townsend to grant the state an option on 76,000 acres of his land for a state or national park. A Democrat, Peay established the first state forestry department and made state forests and wildlife protection one of his priorities as governor. Peay promoted state parks, because they "produce revenue, stimulate travel to and through a state, and in other ways react to the benefit of the entire community." Townsend, for his part, always intended to sell the land to the government, but he did not plan to give up logging: he reserved the right to remove the timber from Middle Prong, Cars Creek, West Prong, East

Prong, Laurel Creek, Cupshaw, Briar Branch, Eldorado, Pigeon River, and Cades Cove "within a reasonable period" [fifteen years]. Joe Barnes, a lumberman for Little River, recalled the day the deal was consummated. His supervisor told the men, "Boys, we sold it," and added: "Log her." Barnes and his crew started cutting, "and when we got done," he described, "that poor little ridge there wasn't a toothpick left on it."[31]

When the U.S. Department of Interior showed support for a national park in the Great Smokies, opposition from the remaining lumber companies solidified. Reuben Robertson, president of Champion, took out a full-page advertisement in the *Knoxville News-Sentinel* and *Knoxville Journal*. "We recognized that it was a desirable thing from the standpoint of the community and of the states," Robertson later recalled. "But we had a duty to our stockholders to protect their investment." At a meeting of the Western Carolina Lumber and Timber Association, members concluded that they did not oppose government purchase of lands, but they preferred a national forest. "In a National Park, no timber may ever be sold for any purpose whatever, and no minerals or water power may be developed," they moaned. "Much less talk about the need for national parks in the Appalachians would be heard if the distinctions between the Park and the Forest were thoroughly understood," wrote Verne Rhoades, forest supervisor for the nearby Pisgah National Forest.[32] Wright testified against the national park movement and tried to make the distinction between a national park and a national forest clear by publishing his testimony. "Just why the people of Tennessee have been called upon to issue $1.5 million in bonds to purchase property which the Federal Forestry Department has for years wanted to buy, I never could understand," he said.[33]

But Chapman and fellow Knoxville promoters realized that a national park brought publicity that a national forest did not. Preservationists, such as Harvey Broome and Paul Fink, knew that few areas in the eastern United States remained untouched by logging operations. Both groups gained approval in the press, where distinctions between what was logged or not logged, between a national forest or a national park were quickly lost. Early on, park promoters persuaded newspapermen that the Smokies were as beautiful as any natural monument in the West. "I have tramped the Catskills, the White Mountains, the Green Mountains, the Berkshires, and the amazing Rockies," wrote one journalist, "but nowhere have I beheld anything so lovely and at the same time so majestic as the incomparable Great Smokies." One writer told of the "exceedingly steep mountain slopes, the deep v-shaped valleys, and the zig-zag alignment of these valleys," as if he were describing the Swiss Alps. Later, the promoters described the tremendous boon a national park would bring to the states' economies. One newspaper claimed that "50,000 tourists a day" would visit Knoxville, "the Great Smoky Mountains city." An increased demand for everything from apples to automobiles, they argued, would result from the proposed national park.[34]

Park promoters also induced scientists to join the crusade by emphasizing that the mountains would become a museum of zoology, forestry, and botany. "We want a place where the wildlife of our mountains will be preserved and made accessible for study," wrote Jesse M. Shaver, a biologist at George Peabody College. "When you look with prophetic vision into the future, you can see one of two things," asserted G. R. Mayfield, a scholar at Vanderbilt University, "the Great Smokies saved for this generation and all generations, or the Great Smokies barren and denuded." Chapman and his associates put their own twist on the reports of scientists. The Smokies, they claimed, would be "an inviolable sanctuary for all decently behaved wild animals; objectional ones [will be] exterminated by Park officials duly charged with the task." While the scientists estimated that more than 50 percent of the proposed park was already cut over, the boosters described "primeval scenery" with "3,000-year-old trees."[35] Like the local color writers before them, park promoters made white and Cherokee mountain residents into part of the frontier attractions. "They are fascinating people these mountaineers," wrote one journalist. "[T]hey are descended from pre-revolutionary backwoodsmen and still live in the eighteenth century." In the *New York Times*, another writer claimed that he saw "at the very top of LeConte . . . a boy living alone in a cabin made of slabs." The boy cherished a single volume, namely, Thoreau's *Walden*. Mountain residents, in these accounts, lived in log cabins without windows, reared families of fifteen children, and had "practically no contact with the outside world." One reporter invited by the park commission stated that "the [Cherokee] inhabitants of the area will greatly add to the picturesque nature of the park, though the school children and younger inhabitants may be transferred to a western reservation." On the radio, a prominent Greenville citizen said he visited

Cherokee, where he saw an Indian, obviously lost, and inquired whether he could help. The Cherokee reportedly said, "Indian not lost. Wigwam lost." After telling this joke, he commented that Cherokee would be one of the attractions of the park. Whether conscious or not, these stereotypes raised one of the most important issues of the movement for a national park. What would happen to the people who lived there and farmed the land? Unlike western parks, carved out of public lands or reservations, the Smokies had to be etched from the holdings of eighteen unwilling timber and mining companies and the homesteads of more than 1,100 small landowners. Yet the use of the state's power of eminent domain for a national park was unprecedented in American history.[36]

Scenery in the Eminent Domain

Eminent domain, the power of the government to take private land for a perceived public good, originated in English common law. The Fifth Amendment of the U.S. Constitution states, "nor shall private property be taken for public use, without just compensation." Clearly, the Founding Fathers saw roads as a compelling "public use," but since then the phrase has been the subject of much debate. When foresters first proposed the Weeks Act, for example, which allowed for the purchase of lands for a "forest reserve" with the power of condemnation, the House Judiciary Committee defeated the measure as unconstitutional. "We are unable to find, and our attention has not been called to any grant of power to the federal government which includes even indirectly these purposes," wrote the chair of the committee. To sidestep the constitutional issue, forest reserve proponents put the emphasis on "protecting stream flow" by purchasing lands "within the watersheds of navigable streams." Because so much trade took place on the river systems, this public use, they argued, came under the authority of the federal government to regulate commerce. Mather also did not believe that parks could be created with the taking power of the government; the land east of the Mississippi River, he thought, would have to be donated. Assistant NPS Director Arno Cammerer, on the other hand, suggested that individual states might gain taking power and then, in turn, donate the land to the federal government.[37]

Attorney James B. Wright raised the issue of forcing people off their land and informed the mountain people that their farms could be taken, whether they wanted to sell or not. The Knoxville newspapers ridiculed Wright, naming him the "foe of the park." When signs reading, "We Don't Want Our Homes Condemned" appeared in the Smokies, the newspapers blamed Wright for putting mountain people up to it. Although Wright probably did use concern for local people to aid timber company interests, he was not incorrect about the potential use of eminent domain. Early in the promotion, Governor Peay, a Wonderland Club member, traveled to the mountains to reassure farmers that their land would not be grabbed by the state. As Peay made his promises, however, Cammerer drew the first "taking line" on a map: he included 704,000 acres in western North Carolina and eastern Tennessee and well over 15,000 people and their homes.[38]

The promotional map published by the GSMCA, in contrast, showed Cades Cove, Gatlinburg, Pigeon Forge, Townsend, Walland, Millers Cove, Elkmont, Wear Valley, Pittman Center, Proctor, Bushnell, and Judson judiciously left out. Chapman repeatedly told the media that people would not be forced out of their homes. "We want the park. We must have the park," stated a newspaperman in the *Knoxville Free Press*. "But we will not be party to visiting upon the people in the park area such a cold-blooded fate as that planned to deprive them of the only home they know." Park promoters finessed the issue at the national level as well. "We are assured that when the park is finally established the native mountaineer farmers as well as the Cherokee will remain unmolested," reported the *New York Times*. "Like the mountaineers, our Indians will retain possession of their abodes within the park," said one publicity brochure, "and—perhaps—enjoy their new dignity, if such it is, of being objects of interest to millions of tourists."[39]

Wright, joined by several large landowners, the Appalachian Club, local judges, and the state representative from Sevier County, R. S. Seaton, objected to the "Cammerer line" and the power of eminent domain that the state now sought. A Knoxville labor publication came out in support of the park but opposed takings because it would "put a hardship upon innocent people, yes even upon unsuspecting people." The editor also reprinted Peay's 1925 and 1926 promises that the mountain people's homes "would be held sacred." The major newspapers in the city, however, accused Seaton of "wrecking the greatest asset ever offered Sevier County."[40] A local judge who supported Seaton received threatening telegrams. Several landowners who spoke out against losing their land were treated with contempt by reporters.

With the help of James B. Wright, the "park foes" struck a deal with state politicians. Large orchard and nursery owners around Gatlinburg and Wear Valley as well as the major hotels were left out of the "taking line." The power of eminent domain could not be used on "improved property" unless the secretary of the Interior notified the park commission that the land was essential, and "all reasonable efforts to purchase the land" had to be exhausted. With these changes, Seaton declared himself "staunchly for the bill." Chapman, for his part, continued proclaiming long after the bill passed in both North Carolina and Tennessee that the power of eminent domain would never be used.[41]

By 1927, park promoters had raised about $1 million in private donations and $2 million each in appropriations from North Carolina and Tennessee. According to their calculations of land prices, this left them with less than half of what they needed. Land-buying halted, and those who had already sold to the states had to wait for payment. Meanwhile, at the national level, the new NPS director, Horace Albright, began to woo John D. Rockefeller Jr., son of the Standard Oil magnate. Unlike his father, John D. Rockefeller Jr. rejected the idea that wealth was to be used only for personal gain. As a schoolboy, he absorbed the early American literature of James Fenimore Cooper and Henry David Thoreau, and during the grimy years of industrialization he grew to believe that all Americans needed time outdoors. According to Albright, "It could be summed up in a word: fitness. His philosophy was somewhat like that of the Chinese with their balanced yin-yang or again with the Navaho belief of harmony or walking in beauty. Humans need [he believed] a quiet, peaceful atmosphere. A communion with nature." Eventually, Rockefeller would make critical contributions to Acadia National Park as well as Shenandoah, Mesa Verde, the Grand Canyon, Yellowstone, the Grand Tetons, Yosemite, the Virgin Islands, Redwoods, and Colonial Williamsburg.[42]

Persuaded by promoters who claimed that 60 acres of primeval forest per day fell under timber axes, Rockefeller granted $5 million to the

Great Smoky Mountains, as "a living memorial" to his mother, Laura Spelman Rockefeller. This generous donation made the Great Smokies a reality two years before Shenandoah became a national park.[43] Soon after the donation, however, Rockefeller grew concerned about reports of continued timber harvest in new park lands and demanded that such cutting be stopped at once. Cammerer forwarded this urgent message to the park commission, with the request that "every standing tree be saved, and that the continuance of lumbering operations now is incompatible with the plans of the two states." With this pressure, the park commission filed suit against Little River Lumber Company to try to force them to stop. But Townsend had been guaranteed the right to cut trees in his contract, and by the time the case appeared in chancery court, the giant trees on Thunderhead Prong were already gone.[44]

A friend of the timber companies, Wright did not give up even after the Rockefeller contribution. He continued to needle the park promoters, and he even convinced the state legislature to investigate the buying procedures of the Tennessee Park Commission. Whereas the North Carolina Park Commission was staffed with a congressman, a USFS representative, and public officials from other parts of the state to ensure impartiality, Tennessee appointed Chapman and other local individuals—including owners of a real estate firm that stood to profit from sales—to its commission. Wright challenged Chapman's power, the "propaganda" in the newspapers, and the method of buying land in the valleys first and the "primitive uplift" second. He published a memorial to Bruce Keener Sr., a "friend and neighbor" at Elkmont, whose dying wish was to keep his mountain home.[45] At one point the investigators interviewed Cammerer, who explained why Cades Cove, Cherokee Orchard, and Elkmont were "absolutely necessary" for the park: "You can't put tourists on mountain tops. You must give them conveniences." He dismissed talk about a "condemnation threat" against the mountain people: "Why call it a threat? It's a power we already have." Privately, he told Rockefeller that "if there was any attempt made to eliminate Cades Cove from the park it would not be acceptable to the Secretary of the Interior and the park would fail." The investigating committee remained unimpressed by Wright and those who testified and released a statement praising Chapman, who privately told people he was perturbed to have suffered this inconvenience. The newspapers echoed his disgust. Knoxville residents attended a "mass meeting" denouncing the "sob stuff" Wright offered. One citizen attacked Wright for protecting the "sentimental mountaineer," who, in his eyes, was "grasping at golden opportunities to enlarge his pocketbook with gains from vast golf courses, snobbish hotels, and hot dog stands."[46]

The Rockefeller gift did blunt resistance from lumbermen, though, who turned their attention to getting as much money as they could from the states for their land holdings. Champion officials, for example, claimed that because the land would be removed from logging before all of the virgin timber could be cut, the company should receive as much as $7 million for the land. Park officials instead offered $1 million. To resolve the dispute, Tennessee park officials decided to file a condemnation suit. An extensive, seventeen-day hearing took place in the circuit court in Sevierville, with witnesses from both sides. The jury of view awarded Champion $2.6 million for the Tennessee side alone. "And I think some of them wet their pants over it!" Robertson recalled. Chapman refused to pay more than $1.5 million for the entire tract, and Robertson and Chapman nearly came to blows over the matter. With NPS officials acting as arbitrators, the lumber company agreed to take $3 million dollars for all of the land. According to a forester for the company, Champion needed the cash to purchase new machinery and did not want the negative public relations associated with killing the park. Champion lawyers, charged with clearing title to the land, reported that more than 300 adverse claims had to be compromised to clear the Champion boundary.[47]

Emboldened by the Rockefeller money and support in the courts, the Tennessee Park Commission filed its first major condemnation suit in July 1929. The year before, when park land buyers offered Cades Cove landowner John Oliver $20 per acre, he asserted that "real estate here sells for $40–$50 per acre." Oliver clearly did not want to leave his home or community. The prominent Cades Cove resident appealed to the buyer's conscience, reminding him of his duty to act "perfectly square with people who have been dispossessed of their homes in order that city people might have a playground." Oliver was well known to Knoxville residents, many of whom had stayed at his lodge, so the condemnation of his land brought the mountain people their first positive attention from the newspapers. "While this territory is miles from any railroad connections and is beyond the reach of telephone and telegraph, many of the farmers residing within the coves are progressive," reported the *Knoxville Journal*, "in many instances the farms being equipped with power tractors, lime pulverizers, and other modern machinery."[48] Oliver challenged the state's right to exercise the power of eminent domain on behalf of the federal government. Although the Blount County Circuit Court agreed with Oliver, the Tennessee Supreme Court saw no reason that the power of eminent domain "be exclusively the necessity of the particular sovereignty seeking to condemn." This case and a similar one filed by Mack Hannah in North Carolina greatly discouraged others from defending their farms. Still, as many as sixty-five tracts had to be condemned in North Carolina alone, most of them owned by small farmers. Many others were discouraged by the immense power of the federal government to defeat men such as Oliver and Hannah: in the words of Zenith Whaley, a resident of Greenbrier, "With the big dog gone, they knew they couldn't handle the bear."[49]

"At that time people didn't know anything about parks," Winfred Cagle remembered. "They thought it was awful, to just drive people out of their homes like they drove the Indians out at one time. People didn't understand about preserving a forest. . . . They thought they were just being drove out." According to Alie Newman Maples, many of the younger people wanted to sell, but older, more established farmers did not. "Like anyone who has a home where they're happy, you hate to give it up and sell it." Moreover, the year 1929 was not a good one to convert land to cash, and some farmers, including Zenith Whaley's father, lost their money in bank failures.[50]

All in all, it took more than twelve years to buy the 1,132 small farms and 18 large tracts in the Great Smoky Mountains, and the two state commissions accomplished this with decidedly different styles.[51] The North Carolina Park Commission paid a standard $6–$12 per acre for woodland, $20–$30 per acre for cleared, flat farmland; making separate valuations for houses, barns, and orchards. They also kept careful records of appraisals and payments, which indicate they paid approximately 1.6 times the conventional tax valuation for the property.[52] The Tennessee Park Commission, by comparison, did not keep diligent records and employed more "tactics" in acquiring land. As one agent noted, "the average price of $16 per acre can be shaded if the negotiations [are] drawn out and condemnation proceedings employed." Like other state agencies, the Tennessee Park Commission understood that condemnation power was most important as leverage. "To take over some of the property proves that you can," said Chapman to a buyer.[53] The North Carolina Park Commission did have fewer small farms to buy (263 compared with 879), and the Tennessee Park Commission often suffered from Chapman's heavy-handed methods. After 1931, when the federal government began management of the area, the NPS also encouraged the Tennessee Park Commission to buy "unsightly" homes that might become "hot dog stands" at the entrance of the national park.[54]

The "Cammerer line" originally included a major portion of Big Cove and Cherokee lands. "The map plainly shows that the boundary between the park and the reservation is very poor from the administrative standpoint," said the first superintendent. The Cherokees agreed to sell a 75-acre tract on Lambert Branch in 1929 for $903, a price comparable to those paid white farmers. When the park commission first proposed a swap of Big Cove with other lands, the BIA agent viewed it as another way to modernize traditional Cherokees and get them out of a remote section "to points nearer the school and hospital." The tribal council was indignant, however, and viewed these negotiations as another eviction. Instead, the NPS actually sold the Cherokees a small tract known as the Boundary Tree. And so, at least this time, white people would be removed and the Cherokees would be allowed to stay.[55]

An estimated 5,665 people left their homes for the creation of Great Smoky Mountains National Park. Of these, 385 were tenant farmers who received nothing from either commission; neither the state nor the federal government aided them in relocation.[56] All schools and churches were removed, but cemeteries became the permanent responsibility of the U.S. Department of Interior. Congress established circumstances under which the secretary of the Interior could lease land for up to two years, and land buyers reassured people that they could probably stay until all the land was turned over to the federal government. A few took lease arrangements as part consideration for the price, but this proved disastrous as they then found it difficult to find comparable land for the cash in hand. To help relieve the situation for older mountain residents, Congress in 1932 passed a bill granting certain individuals leases for the rest of their lives. The lifetime leases certainly helped many older people who did not want to leave their homes, but they soon discovered it was a mixed blessing.[57] Under the jurisdiction of the federal government, lessees could no longer cut firewood, dig herbs, hunt, or clear fields on what had been their land. And, of course, their friends and the pattern of community life vanished.

Lifetime leases also prevented further resistance from the seventy-two summer-home owners in Elkmont. Residents of the Appalachian Club and Wonderland Club cottages used the legislation to negotiate half of the appraised purchase price plus a lifetime lease for their summer homes. Although legislators intended to soften the blow of removal, the lease arrangement allowed summer residents to transfer title to their children, which ensured a long-term summer cottage community in the park. To Chapman's credit, his influence in Elkmont prevented Appalachian Club members from erecting small hotels or larger residences on their lands, which would have greatly inflated prices. But Chapman himself obtained such a lease. When controversy arose about this privilege, he transferred title to a relative stationed in Panama. And he also used the lease situation to benefit elites with other inholdings. A wealthy industrialist named Louis Voorheis looked all over North Carolina for the perfect summer home, then discovered it as a 102-acre orchard on Twin Creeks, outside Gatlinburg. He hired Clifford Oakley, a local man, to manage the estate and a German furniture maker to design the house, gardens, and a pond. In the pond Oakley described, there was "a dolphin with water coming out of his mouth placed out in the middle with rocks and all. He had ducks, but it was hard to keep the foxes from catching them." Voorheis negotiated a lifetime lease on his property, where he entertained superintendents and park officials until his death in 1952.[58]

A Blight on the Mountains

As park advocates and lumbermen, state commissions and mountain people fought over land tenure, signs of an environmental catastrophe began to appear in the mountains. As early as 1925, a fungus later named *Cryphonectria parasitica* arrived, dooming the remaining stand of American chestnut in the Smokies and permanently altering the character of the forest. A pathologist working for the federal government in 1929 found that 99 percent of the chestnut trees in the Smokies were infected, but that less than 50 percent were actually dead. Individual dead trees began to appear as land surveyors, appraisers, and land buyers entered the coves.[59]

The chestnut blight came to the United States at the turn of the century on infected nursery stock. A forester at the New York Zoological Park first noticed in 1904 an immense number of dead and dying chestnut trees on the land he supervised. It took five years for the first bulletin to appear on the exotic disease, new to science. Scientists figured out that microscopic spores formed in cavities on the bark of trees infected with the blight. In summer, these "cankers" exuded sticky masses like toothpaste from a tube. After the spores germinated, the fungus sent fine threads, called hyphae, into the inner bark, killing each cell it invaded. A year after the bulletin came out, *Southern Lumberman* first made reference to a "mysterious blight" in Pennsylvania and New York and a "new fungus" that was the topic of a forestry meeting. "Large timbered sections of [Pennsylvania] are already and in an alarming manner affected by the disease," the report said. By 1912 all the chestnut trees in New York City were dead and the chestnut blight had reached ten states. Although many of them thought it futile, frantic scientists in Pennsylvania launched a vigorous control program, which included burning dead trees, monitoring the advance of the disease, and spraying the cankers with a "Bordeaux mixture." This effort, a scientist later commented, was a little like using toy swords to battle an enemy equipped with atomic bombs. At the time, pathologists publicly proclaimed that control of the chestnut blight would "sooner or later become a real accomplishment." With faith in science and the zealous reports of control efforts, *Southern Lumberman* recounted that a "check" on the blight had been found by the Pennsylvania Chestnut Blight Commission.[60]

Nevertheless, the relentless disease spread south at an astounding rate of some 50 miles per year. "That's light speed for a disease organism," said Steve Oak, a plant pathologist. "It's more or less overnight."[61] Perhaps aided by other introductions, the blight first entered North Carolina near Stokes and Surry Counties about 1913, then spread west. North Carolina lumbermen used the coming destruction as a last-ditch effort to defeat the proposed national park: "Certainly nothing could be more unsightly than the gaunt and naked trunks of these dead trees, standing like skeletons in every vista to which the eye turns," they wrote, pointing out that within a national park "no machinery is provided to cut or dispose of these dead trees." The lumbermen's concern masked their true motives, as they knew that a chestnut tree was worth money, dead or alive. The blight could not be stopped, but foresters determined quite early that the timber left standing for one year after death was "nearly as good as green timber." Because the wood retained its sap for so long, they could manufacture lumber from dead standing chestnut for "at least four years after the death of the tree and ten or more years in some areas." Once they discovered the blight, Little River and Champion stepped up production to get all the trees before they rotted. Reuben Robertson claimed that Champion cut chestnut trees for twenty years after the blight arrived. Eventually, "the pulp yield decreased," he said, and "then synthetic tannin materials came in and the price dropped." Champion sponsored a few experiments with blight-resistant Chinese chestnut trees, but this soon became unnecessary. "[Only] if we could restore that original balance by which the extracted material paid for the wood, chestnut would be desirable," he added. With both the blight and the park inevitable, Champion cut trees at record rates.[62]

In the late 1920s, the forest still showed few signs of the impending disaster, because the blight did not kill a tree instantly. After the orange, yellow, or reddish brown masses appeared on the bark, some leaves withered and died. Next, a few small limbs waned, followed by the death of larger and larger branches. It took as long as ten years for a mighty tree to finally perish.[63] For mountain people, the national park controversy probably at first turned their attention away from the dying forest. When the trees finally died, the cumulative changes—logging, a national park removal, the blight—all ran together in people's consciousness.

"The worst thing that ever happened in this country was when the chestnut trees died," said Walter Cole. "Turkeys disappeared, and the squirrels were not one tenth as many as there were before." Deer, bear, squirrels, turkeys, and other birds that escaped to unlogged, old-growth areas of the Smokies now suffered another loss of habitat. Several species of moths that relied on chestnut trees became extinct. Those species already suffering from loss of habitat due to lumber operations—the wild turkey, goshawk, Cooper's hawk, cougar, bobcat, and white-tailed deer—did not recover because the blight continued the destruction. Unlike other nut-bearing trees, chestnuts bore "fruit" annually and at far greater yields than the oaks and hickories that replaced them. Wildlife that depended on the chestnut would never achieve their previous populations.[64]

As the Great Depression descended on the region, the chestnut trees and the people who relied on them left the Smoky Mountains together. Families loaded wagons and trucks with their belongings, and the skeletons of old trees stood in silent grief for a world transformed. For more than 100 years, Smoky Mountain people had built homes, cleared the land, raised cattle, hogs, and sheep, harvested apples and corn, and gathered plants in the woods. "The hard work had really been done," said Gudger Palmer. "Then the government came along and said 'we're taking over.'" "When families moved out, their hearts were broken," Paul Woody remembered. "There was such brotherly love [in Cataloochee], you just can't walk away from that very easily." "Most of them left crying," agreed Roy Whaley.[65] Although newspaper articles and even scholarly studies claimed that the mountain people happily left the Smokies for better agricultural lands, this was not the reality for most.[66] Small farmers went to work in the new ALCOA aluminum plant, migrated to the textile mills, or, if they were lucky, became a part of the new tourism economy. And the loss of agricultural lands in the region around the Smokies caused a permanent change in the landscape.

The preservationists and park boosters had won a great victory. Against powerful opposition, the largest national park in the East would be protected from further logging. Because of their hard work and enthusiasm, the Great Smoky Mountains would get a chance to recover from intensive logging and become an invaluable preserve of old-growth forest and a sanctuary of biodiversity in a rapidly developing region. Without a doubt, this is one of the grandest natural and historical treasures in the United States. But admiration of the breadth and long-term value of this tremendous achievement should not obliterate the cost incurred to make it happen. To be sure, a handful of former mountain residents would profit enormously from the new national park—as the *Knoxville News-Sentinel* predicted, they wanted to "enlarge [their] pocketbooks." Many would say that the world of wage labor, washing machines, and canned goods represented an improvement, but most agree that something, as well, was lost.

The citizens of Tennessee and North Carolina who helped create the park quickly wrote their names across the landscape. The U.S. Geological Survey required that all duplication in local names be eliminated—

there were ten small streams named Big Branch, for example, in local usage—but neither local whites nor Cherokees served on the nomenclature committees. The committees did add a number of Cherokee names to the landscape, but they also memorialized the "founding generation," so that Greenbrier Knob became Mount Davis, Little Bald became Mount Squires, White Rock became Mount Cammerer, and Old Smoky, Mount Chapman. In the scenic vistas they chose to celebrate—individual peaks and waterfalls—they copied a wilderness aesthetic found in the western national parks they emulated. In the small farmers they removed, they projected the attitudes and lifestyles of nineteenth-century frontier America.[67]

As for the dozens of tenant families and those who could not afford to move, they remained in the Smokies. Some farmed their own land, now tenants of the North Carolina or Tennessee Park Commission and soon-to-be lessees of the NPS. A few moved to vacant farms, better situated in the valleys. Because of the economic hard times, some turned increasingly to bootlegging to make ends meet. A few destitute people actually moved into the vacated park just to avoid being homeless. "Most of the landowners are moving out leaving less responsible and in many cases lawless people," David Chapman wrote in an urgent telegram to NPS Director Horace Albright. "We are dealing with people who have occupied 3,000 separate pieces of land and in this twilight zone that now exists it is imperative that general policies be more clearly outlined."[68] Although the park would not become an official unit of the NPS until 1934, Chapman pleaded with the agency for help in policing the land. Immense problems partly created by Chapman himself landed in the lap of the man the agency sent in response—the first park superintendent, J. Ross Eakin.

3.1. Turn-of-the-century tourists did not necessarily dress for strenuous activity. Guests at Melrose Springs Hotel, Blount County, 1886. Courtesy of the University of Tennessee library.

3.2. Local-color writer Horace Kephart, with a timber rattler he killed. Courtesy of Hunter Library, Western Carolina University.

3.3. The Granville Calhoun family, who lived on Hazel Creek, looked after Horace Kephart when he arrived in the valley in poor health. Courtesy of Hunter Library, Western Carolina University.

3.4. Not exactly low-impact camping. Tourists in the 1920s created a major high-elevation disturbance. Photo by Jim Thompson. McClung Historical Collection, Knoxville, Tennessee.

3.5. Little River Railroad train delivered tourists to Wonderland Park, July 1914. Photo by Jim Thompson. McClung Historical Collection, Knoxville, Tennessee.

3.6. Members of the Appalachian Club dined in finery at Elkmont, probably 1917. Photo by Jim Thompson. McClung Historical Collection, Knoxville, Tennessee.

3.7. An Appalachian Club swimming hole on the Little River, 1914. Photo by Jim Thompson. McClung Historical Collection, Knoxville, Tennessee.

3.8. Hikers made the grassy balds a popular destination. Gregory Bald, with Cades Cove and Rich Mountain in the background, 1934. Photo by Carlos Campbell. Courtesy of Great Smoky Mountains National Park.

3.9. David Chapman (right foreground) led a group of early park promoters to the summit of the peak named for him. (Left to right) Harvey Broome, Mrs. Charles Myers, Miss Mildred Query, and James Thompson. Photo by Jim Thompson. McClung Historical Collection, Knoxville, Tennessee.

3.10. Jim Thompson, whose photographs sold the Smokies to the Southern Appalachian National Park Commission, favored images reminiscent of the West, such as this one of the Chimneys. Photo by Jim Thompson. McClung Historical Collection, Knoxville, Tennessee.

3.11. Large chestnut tree before the blight. Photo taken by Laura Thornborough, a popular writer who promoted the park, 1926. Courtesy of Great Smoky Mountains National Park.

Landscaping a Park
out of the Wilderness

*The CCC was one of the best things any government
ever did, but they overdid it in the Smokies. They
built endless numbers of fire roads up every big
hollow, and too damn many automobile camps, and
[800] miles of trails.*

ERNIE DICKERMAN, ENVIRONMENTAL ACTIVIST

IT'S EASY TO SEE that J. Ross Eakin, the first superintendent of Great Smoky Mountains National Park,
faced a difficult task in January 1931. The Great Depression had tightened its grip on the region, and
long lines of people looking for jobs greeted him at
the entrance of his new Gatlinburg office. An engineer by training and a detail man by temperament,
this West Virginian worked at both Glacier and
Grand Canyon National Parks before he took charge
of the Smokies. According to one contemporary, the
first superintendent "didn't have much to say, but
what he said he meant." That first week as he looked
over the applications, Eakin realized that the park
founders had promised almost everyone a job in the
new national park. "I have been astonished at the
number of very high class men available [for construction work]. We are overwhelmed by applications," he said. He commanded funds to hire just four
people. "The fact that we have announced no applications will be received, makes no difference. They
go home and write a letter making application."[1] To

make matters worse, he did not technically have jurisdiction over the land. He knew that it would be physically impossible with such a small staff to protect so much acreage from hunting, trapping, and plant-gathering, "especially when it is considered that there is a dense population around the park and many people residing in the park." If he also realized that he would be reversing centuries of land-use practices and halting activities that people considered part of their cultural heritage, he might have been discouraged.[2]

Despite these obstacles, Eakin saw that the new park attracted visitors. In the darkest days of the nation's economy, area hotels and cabins turned away people most nights. An outpouring of publicity proclaimed the "beautiful scenery and floral variety" of the Smokies. One magazine called it the "World's Greatest Flower Garden." The new park even appeared as the backdrop in advertisements for the flashy Lincoln-Zephyr automobile.[3] But how long would tourists continue to come, when the park still lacked improved roads and campgrounds? And what if the scenery failed to measure up to expectations? Those who ventured from Mount LeConte would soon discover that the land was far from being a primeval wilderness. Joe Frank Manley, one of Eakin's early employees, toured the Smokies in June 1933. Manley's first impressions included neither beautiful scenery nor floral variety. He called it "the most fragmented ecosystem" he had ever seen. "The chestnuts were dead. The people were farming the land," he described, "the loggers were still in there—they were still logging Middle Prong of the Little River. It made you wonder just what it was that drove the founders to create a national park out of *such a mess as this*."[4]

A Home for Bears

Into this hodgepodge landscape, Eakin brought NPS rules for protection. The new director of the NPS, Horace Albright, called national parks "the most complete and magnificent laboratories imaginable" and invited scientists to explore and research them as "field schools." Albright realized that ranger protection and restocking did not solve all the problems created by human history or tourism, and that the government needed scientific help to figure out what to do. And yet wildlife management and ecology remained relatively unknown fields; in fact, official policy allowed the extermination of wolves and coyotes (not considered good for tourists) until 1931. Neither men like Eakin, though, nor scientists invited into the Smokies during the 1930s had any idea just how complex and contradictory the goals of protection and tourism could be.[5]

And so for the first time in history, the U.S. government banned hunting on (then) 300,000 acres in the Southern Appalachians. Although a complete cessation of hunting would prove impossible for decades, the rules had immediate effects. Less than two years after hunting was halted, the eastern cottontail population, for one, exploded. "These animals infest farm land, old fields, and thickets, and the forest is not their natural habitat," remarked a researcher from the Chicago Academy of Science. Because natural predators, such as foxes and wildcats, preferred dense thickets, he reasoned, "control measures" would have to be undertaken to suppress the rabbits until the area became reforested. Nature, nonetheless, asserted her own control measures. Rangers complained of incessant numbers of dogs and house cats entering the park. Unfamiliar with the no-hunting rules, domesticated animals knew a field day when they saw it. Later that year, the Chicago mammalogist noted his own mistake, as the red fox population increased enough to take care of the rabbits. He added, however, that the red foxes might soon "need control." By the middle of the decade, bobcat sign picked up as well. Loss of habitat from logging and the chestnut blight rendered white-tailed deer so rare that any sighting got mentioned in the monthly *Superintendent's Report*, but they recovered at an extraordinary rate, too. "Apparently my estimate of there being only three deer in the park area was wrong," Eakin wrote. "One man whom I consider reliable informed me that he had seen one herd of seven deer." Deer, like turkeys, rabbits, and skunks, can prosper in the early succession forest and so quickly increased. With no concept of ecological ebb and flow, however, or the cyclical nature of animal populations, the superintendent used the scientists' comments to recommend importing deer from Shenandoah National Park and Pisgah National Forest and the trapping of foxes, cats, and skunks.[6]

Farmers surrounding the park also reacted to the increased wildlife, particularly bears. Not long after Eakin arrived, Fonz Cable killed a large bear near Ekaneetlee Gap (not at that point acquired by the park) that reputedly attacked cattle weighing 800 pounds. Because former mountain residents still grazed sheep and hogs under lease arrangements on

Spence Field and Gregory Bald, they worried about young animals being lost to bears. The ubiquitous blackberry, a succession species, proved a spectacular environment for recovering black bear populations. "Before the park came, we never saw bears," said Lucy Black Ownby, who lived near Cosby. Bears truly seemed to prosper, especially in the highlands. Black bears became "bold enough to tolerate man's presence and accept food," the park naturalist reported. "The situation, however, is by no means alarming—in fact it is encouraging to see the come-back of this fine fur-bearer." Bears regularly sharpened their claws on new park signs. "Is it possible that the bears are attracted by oil used in the paint, or are they simply opposed to signs in a national park?" Eakin joked. By the late 1930s, bears became frequent visitors to Cosby. Delce Mae Carver Bryant, whose widowed mother leased an orchard in the area, recalled the bears as one reason her family finally decided to move in 1941. "The woods kept closing in on us," she explained, "and the bears at that time, well, there were a lot of bears. They begun to come in and carry off the cattle, getting in our smokehouse, getting our meat." In one month, bears killed a 90-pound pig belonging to W. M. Baxter and a young bull belonging to Lem Ownby on Jakes Creek. In the orchard leased to Jane Denny at Elkmont, several cherry trees were destroyed by bruins, which would sharpen their claws on the young trees, girdling them. Responding to these and other complaints, NPS workers constructed a three-rail boundary line fence, which stretched across open country to prevent grazing stock from damaging the woods and to help reduce the number of losses to bears on the balds. "What they done is put up a fence," reported one character in a Fred Chappell short story, "but the Park Service won't put you up no barbwire fence because it ain't what they call rustic-like, they don't want no tourist looking at a barbwire fence. . . . And it wasn't two days later . . . there was a bear setting in a tree [having climbed the fence] looking down like he owned that tree and the U.S. Park Service too."[7]

Just as bears followed blackberry bushes, poachers seemed to follow bears. "It just came natural to some people to poach," Lucy Ownby said, referring to the hard economic times. "They figured the land belonged to them as much as anybody else." "We were mostly game wardens at that time," agreed early park ranger and local resident P. Audley Whaley. "[P]eople were used to doing as they pleased in the park—they hunted and fished whenever they got ready and so we had to stop that . . . and that's quite a chore." In general, Whaley did not feel that his friends and neighbors resented him; "they didn't seem to hold too much of a grudge against me," he said. "They'd say, 'well, you're just doing your job. You caught me.'" In the 1930s, local judges remained sympathetic to the poachers. A case against a leaseholder caught bear-trapping was dismissed on the grounds that the governor of the state of Tennessee had not been notified that the park would assume police powers. But this did not discourage rangers from prosecuting bear poachers and confiscating traps. In one busy month, rangers confiscated twenty-five steel traps, one box trap, and three "deadfalls," the latter primarily used for bears. "The poaching season got into full swing," the superintendent wrote, wryly, "necessitating diligence on the part of the ranger force to suppress the increased poaching on park lands brought about by an increase in fur prices." Trappers traveling through the woods left very little sign, and they hid the traps more carefully. Yet rangers regularly caught and prosecuted people for illegal trapping in the park.[8]

Despite official NPS policy to avoid introducing non-native species, the park imported rainbow trout fingerlings throughout the 1930s.[9] Rangers and members of the Izaak Walton League "planted" millions of rainbow trout, grown in federal hatcheries, into the streams of the Smokies. The Izaak Walton League also maintained hatching ponds for rainbow at Forney Creek, Elkmont, and Deep Creek. This cornucopia proved too much for the many animals that feed on trout. Rangers noted that "the kingfisher was the greatest enemy: 27 kingfishers were killed during the period that the fish were in the [Deep Creek] ponds." Other animals doomed by preying on fish ponds included water snakes. In one month, rangers killed thirty water snakes near the Forney Creek pond; an "autopsy" of one revealed fifty trout fry inside. "An intensive campaign must be waged against water snakes if good fishing is to be provided," said Eakin. And so, creating good fishing for tourists took precedence over protecting these predators too. The superintendent purchased three .410-gauge pistol-grip shotguns and one .32-caliber rifle for the sole purpose of killing reptiles. Snakes in general just did not seem to meet rangers' criteria for good park animals, as killing them became a common practice even great distances from the rearing ponds. On a visit from Washington D.C., Arno Cammerer, with the help of Eakin, killed one large rattlesnake, and the rattle traveled home with Cammerer and his wife as a souvenir. In June 1934, rangers exterminated 226 snakes in Tennessee alone, 11 of them timber rattlesnakes. That summer rangers encountered two mature rattlesnakes, fifteen young ones, two mature copperheads, and ten young ones under a large rock and promptly destroyed them all. Not until 1939 did the NPS formally adopt a policy that stated that "no native predator shall be destroyed," after which it officially halted all extermination campaigns against individual species. No one can say how long the informal practice of dispatching snakes continued.[10]

To help watersheds devastated by logging operations, new NPS rules also ordered streams "open" or "closed" to fishing. A 1933 press release announced limits of twenty fish per person per day; a 6-inch minimum for brook trout and for rainbow, 7 inches. According to regulations, all fishermen must carry a license. Fish populations steadily increased in park waters. Improved fishing received considerable notice in local newspapers and new travel guides. "Men who have fished in the park for years state that fishing is much better than ever before," rangers reported, and two-thirds of the 500 fishermen who came opening day 1936 caught their (by then) limit of ten.[11] In those early years, Smoky Mountain streams still contained rock and small-mouth bass, which found homes in the small mill ponds and other dams built by mountain residents.[12] Fishing rules, like a lot of the new regulations, fell hardest on local people, who fished as a way to feed their families. The park limited bait to artificial lures, which mountain people rarely used. Not surprisingly, the majority of fines imposed on fishermen hit local people. In 1934, two local men took a little whiskey and a fishing seine to a favorite spot and got arrested for possession of both as well as "camping without a permit."[13]

Except for the special agreement with the Little River Lumber Company, NPS rules forbade cutting wood for home use. "We had to buy coal [to heat our house], because we couldn't get enough firewood," remembered Raymond Caldwell, whose father leased land in Cataloochee.[14] The new edicts made digging up plants and other herbs illegal as well. Three men living on Mingus Creek were indicted for cutting down a bee tree for honey, but the judge released them, as title to their land had not yet passed to the state. A Cherokee woman—referred to as a "squaw" by the ranger—was caught removing four small boxwoods from park land and "made to plant them back." But tourists also removed plants—in this case, for their own yards or nurseries. It became such a problem that the *Knoxville News-Sentinel* agreed to publish license plate numbers of those caught carrying wildflowers, dogwood, or red buds out of the park to deter them further. "Decent people in this country are determined to break up this practice," Eakin stated.[15]

The new NPS authority also governed the lives of park tenants, the former landowners. Three deputy sheriffs and the assistant chief ranger searched one man's home in Little Greenbrier for stolen goods; finding none, they turned their attention to seven green possum hides and one groundhog hide drying on frames. The man claimed that he caught the animals outside the area, but he was "warned not to keep hides in his home so long as he lived inside the park."[16] A leaseholder on Twentymile Creek, functioning as an unpaid deputy park warden, tried to arrest a man for fishing violations. The violator struck the deputy with a blackjack and ran, whereupon the deputy drew a gun and brought the fugitive down with a bullet through the shoulder. "We are hopeful that he will come clear [of charges for assault]," Eakin said of his deputy," as he is an excellent game warden." In another incident, a Smokemont man hired to help fight fires "discovered" 6 1/2 gallons of liquor in the home of another leaseholding couple in 1934, and they were charged with possession of liquor for sale. Because the park also held the lease on their Bradley Fork home, the unfortunate pair was "notified to vacate the premises."[17]

In addition to legal leaseholders, a growing number of "squatters" lived in the park. When the states purchased the land from farmers, they made no provision for tenants, who in some cases had no place to go. Because of the dire economic times, others simply moved into the empty cabins and began taking advantage of the empty lands. Whatever the circumstances, Eakin worried a great deal about the squatters. Two men recently released from the state penitentiary (where they were serving time for liquor manufacturing), he reported, eluded park rangers who tried to catch them at a still. In fact, Eakin arrested dozens of "squatters" in Cosby, for everything from public drunkenness and carrying a concealed weapon to stealing government saws and axes. "So far as [legitimate] residents of the Cosby Creek section of the park are concerned," Eakin wrote after taking these measures, "conditions are vastly improved. These arrests will have a good effect in that it will restrain the disorderly element, all of whom live outside the park, from making the park a hangout." But the new park rangers also tried to get rid of anyone who fit the description of a vagrant, regardless of whether the person had committed a crime. Officials warned "an undesirable outfit" living on Big Creek that "anyone . . . on park property that couldn't show some visible occupation would stand a poor show with park authorities." And a divorced woman and her daughter living on Forney Creek—known for "loose morals," according to the superintendent—were told that if they did not leave, they would be evicted. "Without exception the better class of local people approve this action," he commented.[18]

To discourage landless people, the superintendent posted notices that non-leaseholders must leave, and in a few months thirty-eight families departed. He also ordered the razing or destruction of empty homes, a practice that roused "considerable ire" among the legal leaseholders, forced to watch their communities go up in flames. In one month of 1931, for example, records show that the park sold twenty-one houses in North Carolina for $152 and gave away twenty-seven others for "removal and cleanup." In Tennessee, the park sold ten empty buildings, and rangers torched thirty-nine others. In desperate economic straits, one man, Pharis Trentham, tried to return to land he claimed through his grandfather. He started clearing a site and told officials he was building a cabin when they arrested him. A federal commissioner informed Trentham that he had no vestige of title in the land.[19] In these hard times, many people did not have the cash to buy another farm or even to migrate someplace else. "You see a lot of people moved from the land they sold us to better located property, thinking that this would be all right," a land buyer complained to Chapman, who passed the problem on to Eakin. "Some of their houses have been either sold or burned. They are asking me to help them to get to stay." Chapman almost apologized for handing him this problem. "It seemed inhuman to run them away" as economic conditions worsened, he explained. "We were waiting for a better day and of course things are now vastly worse."[20]

The economic picture did not improve for more than a decade, and problems with people living inside the new park continued. "This matter of leasing has given me more concern than any other feature," Eakin said. "The difficulty of permitting so many destitute people in the park is that the longer they remain the more destitute they become and drastic action must some time be taken to clear up the park."[21] Shortly after the NPS gained full jurisdiction over the land in 1934, the new director, Cammerer, announced that the federal government would no longer accept any park lands from the states until all inhabitants had left the area. The edict was more easily rendered than enforced, however. Tourists, it turned out, liked the colorful rural people, and their enthusiasm soon made the former landowners one of the new park's chief "attractions."[22] Travel guides mentioned how to find a real mountain person to visit, and travel writers described them as fascinating examples of living history. The *Tulsa World* called the Smokies "one of the last strongholds of individualism"; *National Geographic* claimed that the mountaineers were "until recently isolated from the machine age"; and the *Winston-Salem Sentinel* recommended viewing the "primitive ways" visible in the park by visiting the Cherokees or white farmers. The *State Magazine* described an elderly lady who lived "where white men had never set foot," existing on "quail and deer and possums." At least one writer to the *Asheville Citizen-Times* pointed out the absurd exaggerations some of these stories contained: "We mountain whites in Western North Carolina long ago became accustomed to have our visitors from above the Mason and Dixon line sojourn in our midst for a few weeks and then go back to their northern homes and write all sorts of preposterous stuff about us and our ways," he wrote, but [the *State Magazine* article] "is as preposterous as anything I have ever read."[23]

Although the Great Depression caused preservation problems, ironically, it also saved the Great Smoky Mountains. For one thing, it slowed the pace of those who wanted the park to become a full-blown tourist attraction. The esteemed founder David Chapman, for example, wanted landing fields for small planes in Cosby, Greenbrier, and Cades Cove. He advocated flooding a portion of Cades Cove to create a lake for fisherman. Even Albright told the *Knoxville News-Sentinel* that he had nothing against the idea of a golf course in the park. "It so happens that there are at present no golf courses in the national parks," he said, "but that is no reason why this park should not set a precedent."[24] Lack of funding, mercifully, defeated these grand schemes. The two states that purchased the park, in fact, wanted to make every remote area accessible by automobile. In 1931 the North Carolina State Highway Commission with federal Bureau of Public Roads funds began work on a new road from

Smokemont to Newfound Gap. The park superintendent objected to the tremendous cuts and fills required for the road, and he tried to get Tennessee to slow down approach highways until interior roads could be at least "oiled" to eliminate "dust nuisance."[25] The North Carolina highway commissioner complained about the "needless roadside damage" done by Tennessee and pledged to protect the roadsides in North Carolina. This proved to be more a case of state rivalry than concern for the scenery, though, as Eakin complained that the North Carolina department was neither "landscape conscious" nor "interested in acquiring this virtue." The first tourist passed over Newfound Gap in April 1932, and the highway department moved on to approach roads 112, 10, and 107. Both states pushed for a skyline highway, similar to the one in Shenandoah. Senator Kenneth McKellar (Democrat-Tennessee) pushed so hard for this that Albright, who opposed the plan, worried that he would lose his job when Franklin D. Roosevelt was elected. The ridgetop drive failed, however, because of the expense involved; at the time, the two states did not have funds to finish buying land for the park, let alone enough to build precarious roads at the highest elevations.[26]

Within a year, the Great Depression also would bring Eakin a park development team that surpassed anyone's wildest dreams, sponsored by Franklin Roosevelt's New Deal. Elected with an extraordinary mandate, Roosevelt swept into office with optimism, a belief in government-led economic recovery, and a commitment to conservation. "Anyone who has read the history of our country knows how in our rush to acquire land and subdue the forests many of our natural resources were destroyed for all time," Roosevelt wrote. The new Democratic president believed "America [was] ashamed of the heedless exploitation of natural resources in the past," and asserted that "from now on conservation and wise use shall inform every act and policy of the government." In the Smokies, Eakin soon found himself at the helm of Roosevelt's Civilian Conservation Corps (CCC), the Public Works Administration (PWA), the Works Progress Administration (WPA) and an astonishing team of NPS landscape architects. Since he had always voted Republican, you have to wonder how he felt.[27]

The Tree Army

Emergency conservation work was not, technically, Roosevelt's idea. The much-maligned Herbert Hoover in fact pumped money into construction work with the same intentions as his successor. Some of this money made it to North Carolina and Tennessee, channeled through state directors into Great Smoky Mountains National Park. With these modest relief funds, Eakin built a network of short "fire trails," and he improved some trails blazed earlier by the forest service. Hiring local people under the state director of emergency relief proved difficult, however, because the officer "certified" recommendations according to political reward; county registrars also siphoned money out of the labor funds for their own use.[28] Eakin's notes show that he made moving fire equipment over the trails his chief concern, and trail crews hired under emergency relief funds were laid off in November until spring. Nevertheless, during these transitional months park engineers built the first scenic public trail, the mile-high horseback trail from Newfound Gap to Mount Kephart. Under the supervision of NPS landscape architect Sheridan West, construction began in September 1932, cost about $500 a mile, and set the standards for the rest of the trails in the Smokies. Workers used only hand tools, relying on picks and shovels. With a maximum grade of 15 percent and a minimum width of 4 feet, one journalist commented that "it looks more like a narrow gauge [rail] road." No boulders, tree stumps, or other obstacles defaced the trail. According to NPS standards, workers wove unsightly sticks, rocks, and earth carefully into the landscape. They even replaced the moss on stumps, logs, rocks, and boulders to "heal the wounds" of new construction. "We called it mossing the stump," recalled Bob Brown, a federal worker.[29]

Finishing such projects proved difficult, however, as funding disappeared and manpower with it. But the new national park would not remain understaffed or underfunded for long. Instituted during the first hundred days of Roosevelt's administration, the CCC, or Tree Army as it was called, employed single men between the ages of eighteen and twenty-five for six months of conservation work. His goal was to put 250,000 youths to work in the outdoors by July 1, 1933. A lifelong advocate of conservation, FDR believed that the CCC would "conserve and develop natural resources and at the same time give unemployed young men practical training." The enrollees' mission, in the words of the president, was to engage in "clean life and hard work" and emerge "rugged and ready for entrance into the ranks of industry."[30] They received $30 a month, $22 of which was sent home to their families. Jointly administered by the U.S. Department of Labor and the U.S. Army, the young men hired by the "three C's" were trained and housed in camps run by army captains. By 1942, when World War II forced the cancellation of this highly successful program, two and one-half million young men had served in it.

Within two months of the legislation, the CCC began building a camp on Laurel Creek; by July, nine camps dotted the Smokies, and within a year, seventeen camps, employing a total of 4,350 "physically fit" young men, filled the mountains. The Great Smoky Mountains National Park soon had more CCC camps than any other two national parks combined.[31] Although CCC administration required local "quotas," the majority of men came from other parts of Tennessee and North Carolina, anyway. Two exceptions Eakin enumerated were the camps transferred from Idaho and a contingent of "New York boys." The superintendent seemed to feel that local young men worked harder than the "New York boys;" in fact, he claimed that local men added to one camp improved the "New York boys" by 200 percent. More than 500 Cherokees applied for 100 positions offered by the CCC under Indian Emergency Conservation Work funds, but most of their work went toward erosion control and construction projects on Qualla Boundary lands.[32]

This sudden great boon in able-bodied young men created a few managerial headaches. Early on, Eakin grew concerned about the "astonishing number" of men kept in camp constructing mess halls, barracks, and officers' quarters. Of 186 young men at Camp No. 2, he lamented, "an average of 84 per day or 45 percent were kept in camp by the Camp Commander." Eventually, he got at least one camp commander dismissed for this practice. In spite of all this construction, though, the CCC cleared little additional land for the camps; most camps stood on former fields or lumber camp sites.[33] By 1942, Eakin probably wished that the youths spent more time in camp, as with their increasing confidence in the woods and enthusiasm for the Smokies came an assortment of mischievous behaviors. Over the decade, CCC boys were caught fishing and hunting illegally, drinking moonshine liquor, driving government vehicles without permission, and generally having the time of their lives.[34]

As the CCC men began to fill the trails and roadways of the Smokies, the NPS sent Eakin the park's first naturalist, Arthur Stupka. "I don't need a naturalist," Eakin complained, "because I don't want any more visitors [until construction was finished]." And so Eakin told Stupka to get acquainted with the park: "This is your baby," he said. Stupka spent four years hiking, building a natural history collection, and making connections with scientists before he offered a single public hike or evening program. With a master's degree in zoology from Ohio State, Stupka worked as a seasonal in Acadia National Park before arriving in the Smokies. "I was lucky to be first on the scene," Stupka reflected later. "I was my own boss." With twenty-two CCC camps of young men whirling around him, Arthur Stupka set out to understand this biological treasure he had inherited.[35]

Two other New Deal programs sent conservation workers into the Smokies: the PWA and the WPA. Both programs attempted to revive local economies by giving unemployed men construction work. Secretary of the Interior Harold Ickes administrated these funds, and he allocated some $40 million for NPS projects, including road and trail construction, campground development, museum construction, and restoration activities. An additional $24 million came into the NPS through the Works Progress Administration (later changed to Work Projects Administration). The WPA sponsored the Federal Writers' Projects, whose authors gave the Great Smoky Mountains generous coverage as an important new tourist attraction. The WPA also sponsored work camps, which were involved in road and trail construction and other projects. Because Roosevelt also expanded NPS jurisdiction over all historic sites, battlefields, monuments, and other parks previously administered by other departments, the agency suddenly had 161 sites to manage rather than 63. Few parks benefited in as many ways as the Great Smoky Mountains from all these new programs; in turn, few bear quite the same stamp of 1930s design and philosophy.[36]

Wildlife responded immediately to the presence of all these well-fed conservation workers: adept panhandlers appeared at every camp. Several camps reported ravens, apparently attracted by "an easily gotten meal to be gleaned from the remains of lunches of CCC boys." Cosby Creek (Camp NP-6) adopted a wild turkey. Wesley Ogle, a park warden who grew up in the area, may have come across the same turkey, which not only showed no fear but took a piece of bread from his hand. "After 25 years of roaming the Smoky Mountains," Ogle said, "I would say that this was the most amazing event I have ever witnessed." One CCC camp had a "bear exhibition" each night at the garbage dump, and cooks demanded bearproof storage facilities for food.[37]

Eakin first directed his new troops toward the dead and dying chestnut tree snags that dotted the landscape. During his second winter, mountain windstorms blew down more timber than any old-timer could remember. "Well it was disfigurement. The mountains looked awful," recalled Frank Jackson, one of the first CCC enrollees. In addition to the eyesore, Eakin worried about the potential fire hazard from acres of dead, drying wood. Jackson remembered being assigned to "fire hazard duty" for days, and his crew alone cut enough chestnut timber to build two CCC camps. The CCC used the dead trees for fuel in the barracks and donated much of the rest to area residents, which, Eakin claimed, "contributed materially to the relief of local people." The men laid other chestnut logs flat on the ground, parallel to the contours of the mountains, then they cut off the limbs and scattered them to retain a neat appearance, reduce fire hazard, and promote decomposition. Although not part of their strategy, this practice contributed to the building up of a strong humus layer, as rotting trees serve as "nurse logs" for many plants. Over the first two years of the CCC, as much as one-third to two-thirds of crew time was spent on this kind of cleanup.[38] Trained in the arid West, Eakin probably worried more about fire hazard than he needed to in the profoundly wet climate of the Smokies. However, when combined with a drought year, the dead timber and slash left by the chestnut blight, road-building, and lumber operations *could* be a fire hazard. In 1936, twenty separate fires crept onto park lands, and with the help of high winds burned 929 acres. That same year the CCC spent 19,442 man-hours putting out blazes on park and exterior lands. Careless campers started a few fires; a CCC crew, which left burning brush unattended, provoked a second; and another ignited from the Little River Lumber Company's train. The majority of fires in the 1930s, however, were labeled "incendiary"—a result of arson.[39]

During their first months in the new park, rangers preached the gospel of fire prevention to residents of the park, who were required as a condition of their leases to help fight fires, even after the CCC boys arrived. A year later Eakin angrily declared that "10 out of 12 fires are of incendiary origin" and he blamed specifically a former Deep Creek family "antagonistic to the park." "A court might question bloodhound work as evidence," he remarked, but "such action would have a beneficial moral effect." The truant fires started in many corners of the Smokies: anger over the park's removal of residents and management policies often sent the forest into flames. Other fires were probably accidentally caused by local residents burning brush on their own land.[40] By 1936 the situation had not improved and the superintendent began turning over investigations to the NPS's Division of Investigation. On the one hand, the superintendent praised the fire-fighting efforts of local people. On the other hand, when incendiary fires began to decline in 1938, Eakin commented that this represented only a local "firebug's holiday."[41]

Bootleggers, who had discovered some new business among young CCC enrollees, used fire as a way to avoid detection. To be sure, sometimes the fire at an unsupervised moonshine still accidentally caught the neighboring woods on fire, but the operators also understood that fire-fighting rangers had no time for liquor control. Poachers soon figured out how the principle worked, too. In one case, a fire actually got away from federal tax unit officials burning a still in Cosby. Seizing moonshine stills preoccupied rangers throughout the 1930s. In one month of 1935, for example, they captured stills in Greenbrier, on Dudley Creek, and on Cosby Creek. All the operators got away. P. Audley Whaley, a local man who became a park ranger in 1938, said he usually just left a note on stills he discovered, asking that the operation be moved. This way Whaley avoided retribution, and the stills always disappeared. Paul Adams, an avid hiker, said he often ran across stills. Under these circumstances, he recommended, "the most appropriate and safest thing to do is to poke a few pieces of firewood under the pot."[42]

The young men in the CCC regularly attended fire school in their camps, eventually building lookouts or fire towers on Cove Mountain, White Rock, Greenbrier Pinnacle, Mount Sterling, Rich Mountain, Blanket Mountain, Straight Fork, Shuckstack, and Spruce Mountain. Set on prominent points, lookouts appeared like cabins with a lot of windows and balconies or little cabins on eight-story steel stilts. Trenches lined with copper wire around the buildings provided lightning protection. Cherokee CCC enrollees built such a tower on Barnett Knob, which the new park agreed to man. In addition to constructing the towers, CCC and other public workers strung telephone lines from the towers to CCC base camps and the Gatlinburg office. Because of the rolling landscape, steamy climate, and heavy vegetation, the Smokies were not as well suited to fire towers as many places in the West. During a 1939 drought, small fires often broke out, but the hazy smoke pattern made it impossible to see anything from a tower.[43]

Once CCC men "cleaned up" the chestnut trees and finished the fire towers, Eakin relaxed somewhat. "Undoubtedly," he remarked, "the . . . CCC camps stationed in this park have helped develop this park at a more rapid rate than any other park ever built by the federal government." In a little more than two years, by his estimation, the park had advanced at least ten. But the most permanent contribution of the conservation workers was yet to come. On the heels of this CCC "army," a veritable legion of landscape architects arrived. Three assistant landscape architects, three junior landscape architects, eleven landscape technicians, and three planting foremen descended on the Smokies. The NPS engineers planned trail shelters, campgrounds, amphitheaters, comfort stations, observation towers, and picnic areas, and, when Ickes approved the permanent facilities in 1938, construction accelerated to include visitor centers and a park headquarters. By 1942, this group rebuilt and landscaped Newfound Gap Road, the Clingmans Dome Road, the Newfound Gap Overlook and Rockefeller Memorial, Sugarlands Headquarters, the Oconaluftee Ranger Station, the Mount Cammerer Fire Lookout, 700 miles of trails, nine shelters on the Appalachian Trail (AT), and the Little River/Laurel Creek Road.[44]

Like virtually every landscape architect in the 1930s, the men who redesigned Great Smoky Mountains National Park were influenced by Frederick Law Olmsted Sr., who designed Central Park in New York City. Olmsted borrowed the English gardening tradition of the nineteenth century, which sought to create informal pastoral landscapes rather than impose a geometric design on the land. During the 1920s, the Landscape Division at the NPS developed design standards that similarly tried to harmonize the landscape with the automobile—guardrails, bridge abutments, culverts, and comfort stations that looked "natural" in a meadow. "Whether the plan be for a group of buildings, a front yard, a camp site, a collection of fireplaces or any other group of objects," stated U.S. Department of Interior guidelines, "we cannot place the developments helter-skelter. There is always a serious danger of going wrong at this point, particularly since many persons have the notion that such helter-skelter is more natural than to place objects in an orderly system." The Bureau of Public Roads provided technical engineering skills, and the NPS landscape architects tried to create scenic views, follow natural contours, minimize cuts and fills, avoid steep grades, and restore the land to a natural appearance using native plants.[45]

To meet NPS standards of "visual harmonization," they established at Ravensford a large nursery for collecting, sizing, and propagating pine, spruce, and locust trees, as well as rhododendron. CCC workers rescued plants along road and trail construction for the landscape architects' nursery. Occasionally the architects also sent them to the balds to collect seeds, because the NPS strictly enforced planting of only native species; the architects failed to realize, however, that exotic grasses also grew on the balds.[46] In just two months of 1937, for instance, the Ravensford operation donated 40,000 seedlings to the Cherokee CCC camps, planted 35,000 in Cataloochee, worked 30,000 into erosion control on Tennessee roads, and gave 100,000 to the new Blue Ridge Parkway. Sometimes the conservation workers created something a little less naturalistic than the landscape architects imagined, and heavy-handed formality quickly aroused criticism from visitors, who complained to park authorities. After the completion of the Newfound Gap parking area, for example, CCC workers returned to the area with extra plantings to mitigate the "bareness and formality" of the landscape. After this reconstructive work, the site was declared "less objectionable" by the superintendent.[47]

The bulk of public conservation work during the late 1930s, however, went toward roads, trails, picnic areas, campgrounds, and park administration buildings. Almost every mile of the 700 miles of trails as well as the motorways and park headquarters was constructed or at least improved by CCC, WPA, or PWA funds. Some trails, such as the stretch of the Appalachian Trail from Mount Guyot, cost $1,000 for just 650 feet of trail. The workers blasted through solid rock in this "Saw Tooth Country," and then built up a permanent bed and retaining walls for the trail.[48] "The hardest one was the Trillium Gap Trail," reminisced Amos Reagen,

Table 4. Trees and Shrubs Planted along a State Highway between December 1, 1933, and April 15, 1934, by One CCC Camp

	Planted	Thrived	Died
Dog-hobble	2,565	2,515	52
Mountain laurel	934	912	22
Rosebay	1,422	1,401	21
Hemlock	159	128	30
Black birch	854	840	14
Silver birch	910	900	10
Sugar maple	151	145	5
Red maple	1,156	1,126	30
Striped maple	84	82	2
Dogwood	1,278	1,158	120
American hornbeam	94	65	29
Witch hazel	86	80	6
Silver bell	59	57	2
White ash	41	39	2
Staghorn sumac	43	40	3
Sourwood	583	568	15
Serviceberry	11	6	1
Buckeye	7	6	1
Tulip tree	29	24	5
Sassafras	4	3	1
Black locust	5	4	1
Spicebush	3	4	1
Sourgum	5	4	1

Source: J. Ross Eakin, *Report on Emergency Conservation Work, April 1 to June 30, 1934,* CCC Records, GSMNP Archives.

a local man who went to work with the CCC. "Ropes, scaffolds, switch hammers," he listed the necessary implements as proof of the difficulty. Enrollees frequently had to make long hikes to the work site each day, build elaborate bridges out of chestnut logs, and construct stone retaining walls in precarious locations. "Hard place to work high up on the mountain," said Reagen, who supervised a large crew, "cold weather, lots of rain up there. Boys they want to come in during the weekend, two or three of them got sick every week. Hard job moving these CCC boys."[49]

The rapidly constructed network of trails spiraled toward the most popular monument-like locations, such as the summit of Mount Le-

Conte. With so many workers, NPS officials barely had time to inspect the progress. Prodigious CCC photographers did, however, dutifully record examples of unnecessary grading and blasting. "Too wide!" an NPS official wrote on a photograph of the newly completed Brushy Mountain Trail. "Might as well be called The Broadway of America!"[50] The other major work done by the CCC involved building motorways out of old logging railroads. They removed ties, scrap metal, rocks, and slides; installed culverts; dug drainage ditches; and then smoothed the surface. Some sections were strengthened with shale or crushed rock. The trees cut during construction ended up as telephone poles or lookout towers or bridge reinforcement. Above each bridge the men "cleaned up" disorderly logs and drift, to protect the new bridges from washouts, and of course they "mossed the stumps."[51] CCC enrollees also followed behind the last logging operations on Middle Prong and Tremont, conducting erosion control. "As soon as the skidder is moved away from the site," Eakin reported, "the crews move in and do whatever work is possible to prevent erosion and decrease the fire hazard." A crew followed behind the truck-hauling operation, as well, to keep the trucks from damaging roadside trees and to clear debris along the road. Throughout the park, the crews built dams, seeded grasses, planted small locusts, sloped and mulched banks, installed culverts, and built drainage ditches to prevent continued loss of topsoil. They even guyed young trees at Forney Ridge with wires to protect them from high winds.[52] Road and trail construction proved dangerous work for these young men. A rockslide buried three public workers at a quarry on the Newfound Gap construction project; only one survived. A dynamite blast killed the water boy on another road project. One young enrollee from Powell, Tennessee, apparently died of heart failure or shock after he cut himself on the leg with an axe. Although a tourniquet stopped the bleeding, when the army doctor began dressing the wound, the sight of his battered leg proved too much for the boy. The most horrifying accident happened when a bus transporting men to Smokemont ignited as the fuel was being dispensed. Since the gas tank was under the right front seat, flames cut off their avenue of escape. "All more or less roasted alive," the superintendent wrote, although the men kicked out the windows and only two finally died. Young men joyriding for the first time on mountain roads often collided with the steadily developing stream of visitors, and the mountains saw increased traffic accidents almost every year.[53]

To achieve NPS standards of "cultural harmonization," the CCC established a rock quarry and hired stone masons. All structures had to be handcrafted from local, rough-hewn materials with lines reminiscent of, if overscaled from, pioneer or "primitive" construction techniques of the region.[54] In the park headquarters plans, the designers used rugged stone blocks and heavy squared porch timbers to suggest early-nineteenth-century eastern Tennessee stone houses; they graded the lawn in front of the building to create the illusion that it sat on a slight rise. The Oconaluftee Ranger Station also had a full-façade front porch with six chestnut posts and stone chimneys on each end to give it a "rustic" character like a mountain cabin. Even the eight comfort stations designed by the landscape architects and built by the CCC used large slabs of locally quarried stone and wooden roof shingles. The comfort station at Newfound Gap included privacy walls extending from the building at both ends in the same fine stonework. By using larger stones at the bottom and battering the walls for a rugged look, designers created the illusion that the comfort station grew naturally out of the mountain. As a concession to the prevailing culture, the comfort station also included separate facilities for African-American tourists.[55]

"Cultural harmonization" also meant preserving buildings that portrayed a frontier or pioneer history. Landscape architects supervised the removal and reconstruction of old log homes in several locations, to create pioneer history exhibits. Before the park, no two homes in the mountains looked alike, as a visitor could see log cabins, boxed houses, and all manner of frame construction. To expedite the removal of squatters, Eakin destroyed 100 buildings in May 1931 alone.[56] Now the architects wanted a few pioneer structures to remain: by removing more modern framed buildings, barbed-wire fences, and unsightly boxed buildings, they reasoned, the park could add "human interest" to scenic beauty. The park sold the remaining contemporary box and frame buildings (except for a few in Cataloochee) at public auction, such as the old Richwood School on Abrams Creek, for which the park received $5. CCC workers removed and reassembled other structures, such as in the Oconaluftee Pioneer Village, which contained an interesting assortment of "typical" buildings supposedly to represent a mountain farm. CCC enrollees reconstructed Mingus Mill in 1936 and the Cable Mill in 1937, both of which had fallen into disuse. Around the mill they demolished any modern-looking homes and replaced them with more primitive alternatives. Around the remodeled homes, they cut barbed wire and reconstructed old rail fences. These actions created the appearance that places like Cades Cove had not changed in 100 years and that mountain people remained hearty pioneers until the park arrived.[57]

To further promote the cultural history of the new park, North Carolina and Tennessee organized committees to collect artifacts from the "settlers" so recently removed. The park appointed H.C. Wilburn, an engineer with the CCC, and the park wildlife biologist, Willis King, to assist ranger Charles Grossman in creating a development plan for the historical resources of the park. An NPS museum curator, sent down to the Smokies for a month, also helped author the plan, which called for preserving artifacts, interpreting them, and creating displays of mountain culture in the vacated homes and farms. The expert suggested leaving the empty cabins to "serve as shelters for hikers," and to show "the complete isolation" and "very limited quarters" of the mountain people to curious tourists. Wilburn also wanted to collect appropriate stories about the mountain people for interpretation "before they moved from the area." Despite a tendency to stereotype the mountain people, Wilburn in particular collected more than 1,300 valuable historic tools, utensils, guns, and other items, which the superintendent barely acknowledged.[58]

The park historians argued, however, about whether mountain culture was something that could or should be preserved. One thought that "certain aspects of material culture can be perpetuated," but another worried that "many undesirable characteristics of the mountaineers' culture" should not be preserved. Still another wondered whether the NPS could expect some mountain people to be content with "crude, rigorous surroundings following the hard way of producing their handcrafts solely for the intangible reward of being a scientific guinea pig, particularly when their neighbors can have cars, radios, and new dresses." Eakin did not want to enter this fray. Only reluctantly and after repeated complaints by Wilburn did he send CCC boys to clear young trees and saplings from the abandoned farms, so they would not return to forestland. The superintendent termed this "meadowland maintenance." Eakin was not interested in preserving the history of the mountain people. He viewed the lessees and the empty cabins as management problems. Wilburn grew quite angry when CCC enrollees ground up an old stone fence on Palmer Creek for road gravel, but he got no response from the superintendent. The museum advocate also tried to convince the superintendent to let more lessees remain, occupying preserved buildings and farming the land, to "make the exhibits live."[59] Museum plans, drawn by a curator for the NPS, arrived in November 1935: one, located in Smokemont, would relate archeology and culture. The other, near Gatlinburg, would emphasize natural history. Wilburn even obtained newspaper coverage for his museum ideas, but in the end the new park emphasized roads, trails, and campgrounds—not history. "Violence is being done and there might result damaging public criticism," he wrote the NPS, but here, too, he got little response. Although the NPS had already begun to emphasize historic battlefields and presidents' homes in other places, the agency could not yet envision that the lives of ordinary people also can be history. The museum sketched on the first Master Plan was never constructed.

Despite the tremendous amount of development work accomplished by the CCC, the original park boosters, amazingly, were still not satisfied. The Knoxville promoters who made the national park a reality wanted even more roads and amenities in and around their Smokies. As the CCC constructed campgrounds and picnic areas with intricate, durable stonework, David Chapman tried to convince another New Deal agency, the Tennessee Valley Authority (TVA), to dam Abrams Creek and create a lake for fishing and boating in Cades Cove. Preservationists throughout the country became outraged when they heard about the plan and accused the NPS of letting state politicians arbitrate "a road here, an artificial pond there, each with some special reason." Harvey Broome, founder of the Wilderness Society, organized a letter-writing campaign against the proposed 60-foot dam and summoned experts to prove that "the area had never been occupied by water." In the face of scientific proof and the national pressure, Cammerer stated he would "refuse this appeal to state politics."[60] There would be no new lake in Cades Cove.

Senator McKellar's influence as the acting chairman of the Senate Appropriations Committee proved critical, however, in getting the funds necessary to complete land purchases for the park. In 1933, Roosevelt announced that the government would appropriate $1.5 million to finish land purchases for Great Smoky Mountains National Park. When Tennessee had difficulty finishing the job even with these additional funds, McKellar got an amendment to an appropriation bill for a western park to the tune of $743,265 in 1937. The New Deal also supported park development by featuring the Smokies in the Federal Writers' Project tourist guides. In *North Carolina: The WPA Guide to the Old North State*, writers promoted the Smokies as the "wildest highlands in eastern America."[61] The flamboyant Senator McKellar was still not satisfied, however, and in 1939 he dramatically announced an investigation of the first park superintendent. He objected to the fact that Eakin was not a resident of the state, and he disagreed with the way the park, and particularly Eakin, misallocated CCC funds. McKellar wanted to bring more political favors to his constituents and may have been trying to secure a greater price for two tracts of land that remained to be purchased for the park. The primary sponsor of legislation authorizing parks in the Southern Appalachians, he wanted his home state of Tennessee to be a big beneficiary of tourism dollars. The U.S. Department of Interior and a U.S. Senate investigating committee cleared Eakin of any wrong-doing, and Senator McKellar backed off from charges that a "Republican" and a "West Virginian" damaged Tennessee's development plans.[62] The NPS called Eakin to Washington, D.C., however, and soon thereafter he was involved in a serious car accident. In 1944 he suffered a stroke and remained in a coma a year before he died.

Mountains Take Back the Land

As the NPS struggled over proper development, the mountains slowly began to take back the abandoned farmland, the clear-cut slopes, and the bare spots created by dead chestnut trees. Early seral stages of succession, as ecologists call them, bring pioneer species that can tolerate the sun. In the spruce-fir zone, sedges and grasses moved into the newly timbered areas. Blackberry, fire cherry, and yellow birch soon covered the muddy and eroded slopes, interrupted here and there by young spruce.[63] In some places, the adjacent canopy trees, such as red oak, chestnut oak, and hemlock, slowly grew larger to fill in the opening again. Catbirds and chipping sparrows, which flourish in these kinds of clearings, began to increase.[64] Where a large number of chestnut trees died or suffered a clear-cut, a different kind of succession occurred, starting with saplings of sweet birch, black locust, and sassafras. Ferns spread across upturned tree roots. In an Appalachian oak-hickory forest, the early species are tulip poplar, black locust, shortleaf pine, hemlock, black cherry, and white and Virginia pine. Several birds that adapted well to this early succession forest were the bobwhite, grouse, and ruby-throated hummingbird. According to naturalist Paul Adams, who hiked the Smokies especially during the 1920s and 1930s, ruby-throated hummingbirds became more common because of the habitat changes. Adams speculated that "flowering shrubs and flowers, some introduced by horses and hay, have further altered the landscape, and on the whole, made it more favorable for ruby-throats."[65] Over the next decade, red maples replaced early succession species, especially in the middle elevations of the Smokies. In the humid and verdant valleys, new species grew even faster. In the first two years, little blue stem grass, wild strawberries, and fleabane daisies entered farmers' unattended fields. Greenbrier (*Smilax*) and sumac also began to appear, followed by shortleaf pine, Virginia pine, and sassafras. After just ten years, abandoned fields were covered with successful stands of young pines, and the yards of homeplaces were scattered with small trees sticking up in unusual places. Even after rangers destroyed almost all of the homes or exiting farmers dismantled them, visitors could tell where they once stood, because of the thousands of peach, pear, plum, and apple trees planted by mountain people. Each spring when the trees flowered, the former communities would appear, ghostly white to a knowledgeable observer, through the green forest.[66]

With the increase in pine stands at lower elevations came the destructive southern pine beetle. A native pest, the southern pine beetle tends to be cyclic, and depending on weather, affects primarily Virginia pines, pitch pines, and table mountain pines every five to seven years. Whereas surveys done in the early 1930s showed no sign of the beetle, by 1938 "numerous individual pines in widely separated areas" of Cades Cove and Mount Harrison showed infestations. By the end of the decade, the NPS began eradicating trees infested with the southern pine beetle. Workers also faced white pine blister rust, an exotic species, which uses gooseberry as an alternate host. Because blister rust attacks only white pines, which are rare above 3,500 feet, the outbreak was unusual. Park technicians yanked 15,438 gooseberry bushes infected with blister rust on 66 acres of

Cataloochee. In fact, the CCC "invited in" the blister rust, by planting white pine in this high-elevation valley.[67]

Slow reforestation helped some wildlife, such as the red squirrels. On one day in December, the park naturalist counted twenty-five red squirrels ("boomers") on the 5 miles between Grassy Patch and Mount LeConte. The deer population picked up more slowly, although one ranger cited a large herd of twenty- five deer on Tobes Creek.[68] Although it is not logical that raccoon populations would have increased with reforestation, park records show a large number of poachers in search of them. P. Audley Whaley remembered catching a coon hunter who said: "Mr. Whaley, I've always lived up here. . . . I've hunted and fished it, and I'm gonna do it as long as I live." The next time Whaley caught him, the mountain man inquired what would become of the confiscated raccoon carcass. "Give it to some old person," Whaley snapped, as he wrote up the incident. The next morning, the coon hunter showed up at Whaley's home with his father. "My daddy's the oldest person in these parts," he said, expecting Whaley to return the coon.[69]

As shade improved on the streams of the Smokies, colder water temperatures made trout introduction more successful. The CCC constructed more permanent, scientifically designed rearing pools at the Chimneys for Tennessee and on Kephart Prong for North Carolina. The park continued to obtain tens of thousands of fish from federal hatcheries, and they "planted" 300,000 to 400,000 mostly rainbow trout in Smoky Mountain streams each year. CCC boys carried 6-inch rainbows to the streams in milk canisters, and the exotic species soon reproduced in the waters of the park. Since brook trout, which stay along quieter banks, and rainbow trout, which can swim into turbulent falls, can occupy the same pools, wildlife technicians assumed that the two would not interfere with each other.[70]

An assortment of odd problems haunted the new fish-rearing pools. One morning fish at the new Chimneys location began to die at an alarming rate. An estimated 45,000 trout died in a matter of hours. The park superintendent suspected that a "local man charged with illegal fishing" had poisoned the water, though he had no evidence of this. The water was tested, and no reason for the incident could be ascertained. Just three years later, several such incidents in a row occurred at the Kephart Prong location. Rangers tested for clogged drains or faulty pipes, and still tens of thousands of trout died. They lowered the water temperature by providing additional shade, but any trout replanted in the rearing ponds died in a matter of hours. Only decades later did scientists establish what had happened in these repeated trout maladies. Apparently, the heavy blasting work disturbed Anakeesta rock formations, composed of pyritic and carbonaceous slate and phyllite. When exposed to air and water, Anakeesta forms a toxic combination of ferrous sulfate, sulfuric acid, and metals. This drastically lowers the pH of the water draining from the site, killing macroinvertebrates, salamander larvae, and fish. Because brook trout are even more sensitive than rainbow trout to changes in pH, they suffered greater losses both in the streams and in rearing pools. And streams contaminated with Anakeesta take a long time to recover: twenty years after a construction contaminated the water of Beech Flats Creek, researchers still found lowered numbers of stream-breeding salamanders in the area.[71]

The early rangers also conducted one reintroduction experiment, returning a species absent but formerly present in the bioregion. In 1934, they liberated two golden eagles in Tennessee, but one of the two had grown too accustomed to captivity. "When not hungry, it soars around like any other eagle, but when hungry it lights and takes meat from a ranger's hand," Stupka reported. "The ranger says apparently it has quit hunting for its food and has gone to panhandling for a living." A month later the "tame" eagle was shot in the wing by a lessee. It recovered, but the mountain man "was immediately notified to vacate the premises and move out of the park." Two years later, the Tennessee Board of Game and Fish sent three additional golden eagles. One was shot by a farmer in Highland, Virginia, and another eagle, which arrived in fragile condition, died. When yet another eagle arrived half-dead from the same agency, Eakin wrote them "not to ship the poor birds any more."[72]

The park also got one unusual request for exotic relocation from the president himself. An amateur naturalist, Roosevelt collected birds on his family farm in Hyde Park during his youth. All his life he loved to travel, and one of his favorite locations was where the giant sequoia and redwood trees grew in Northern California. Roosevelt wanted to see if redwoods would grow in the Smokies. "Unfortunately, there does not appear to be any area in the East where these unusual and interesting trees will do well," responded Secretary of the Interior Harold Ickes gently. Since the soil and climatic conditions in Cherokee are similar to those in the Smokies, Ickes got the BIA to try the experiment to avoid planting of nonindigenous species in a national park. "My dear Mr. President," Ickes addressed FDR. "The giant sequoia, like the redwood, does not seem to thrive in areas where the summer precipitation and humidity are high."[73]

Between 1931 and 1940, four federal agencies and two state governments literally developed a park in the Great Smoky Mountains. With generous budgets and prodigious numbers of workers, they built amenities for tourists and carved as much as 800 miles of trails and four major road systems within the park boundaries. They accomplished all this using minimal heavy equipment and exhibiting sensitivity to native species, scenic beauty, and harmony with the landscape. Using skilled craftsmen, they built structures that lasted and embodied a significant period of conservation history. Because they constructed so many beautiful buildings in such a short period, the park is blessed with continuity of design that transcends budget shortfalls and quirky NPS directors' tastes. They were, however, creating a scene, a rustic image, a vision of what America should be. To accomplish this, they revised and adulterated history in a way that suited their own interests and tourists' aesthetics. The Smokies no longer existed as a *place* of intimate knowledge and memory: in fact, only Stupka seemed to know very much about the new ecology being created within the boundaries. The park had become a modern if absentee "paradise for the hiker, horseback rider, and angler," managed for their enjoyment by the government.[74] In addition, because government funds kept flowing, they kept on building. "The CCC was one of the best things any government ever did, but they overdid it in the Smokies," commented environmentalist Ernie Dickerman. "They built endless numbers of fire roads up every big hollow, and too damn many automobile camps, and [800] miles of trails."[75]

Almost as quickly as the NPS constructed this park, people arrived to use it. The first statistic monitored by the new park was the number of visitors. In the single month of June 1934, in the middle of the Great Depression, 40,769 people from forty states and one foreign country visited the new park. In the same month six years later, 128,533 people visited the Smokies, and almost half of them were from states other than Tennessee and North Carolina. On a single day in 1937, 3,738 vehicles including 20 busloads of Tennessee Home Demonstration Club members wound up and down the new Smoky Mountain roads. Motorcycles were so common that at the end of a frigid December 1940 rangers recorded the first month that none had visited the new park. After just six official years of park operation, citizens of Blount, Sevier, and Cocke Counties met to discuss the "bottleneck" of traffic that occurred in busy summer months between Pigeon Forge and Gatlinburg.[76]

As each of the campgrounds was completed, tourists appeared to fill it. Early on, the superintendent noted that despite the lack of sanitary conveniences, primitive campgrounds overflowed with visitors. One month in 1935, Eakin was forced to allow temporary campgrounds at Smokemont, Deep Creek, below Elkmont, and in Cades Cove. "The situation is rapidly getting out of control," he protested. CCC boys barely evacuated two camps in Cosby, when tourists converted them into public campgrounds. In the middle of dire economic times, the park superintendent had to put a one-day-only restriction on camping in the national park to control visitation. He also had to initiate regulations preventing people from sight-seeing in large, 1 1/2-ton trucks. Loaded with fifteen to twenty-five persons standing up in the bed, the trucks descending mountain roads gave park rangers a turn, although no one actually got hurt this way.[77]

With these throngs of people came the first records of wildlife destroyed by cars and accidents involving animals.[78] As early as 1942, the Smoky Mountains Hiking Club (SMHC) complained about litter. "The minds of many of us are turned to religious thoughts when we enter the glorious mountains," remarked one writer. "How incongruous, how futile, how shocking to this frame of mind to come face to face with broken bottles, tin cans, gum and candy wrappers, old newspapers and lunch bags in the midst of nature's wonderments." Although the crowds "appreciated" the mountain people, they also pushed many to finally leave the area.[79] Younger people moved away, so most of the people living in the park after 1940 were elderly. "But they were left up there alone," Lucinda Ogle remembered, "they couldn't be happy back in there all by themselves." When Tom Campbell died in his cabin above Gatlinburg, a group of CCC enrollees carried his body down the mountain. The Walker sisters, five women who decided to remain in Little Greenbrier, sometimes saw more than 300 visitors a day. "August visitors found the sisters in the field topping corn, weaving their homespun garments and poke bonnets," a newspaper reporter chirped. "But they are not to be disturbed. They are one of the park's greatest assets now."[80] The Walker sisters themselves soon felt otherwise. They eventually asked the park service to remove the sign directing traffic to their door.

One of the last major projects completed by CCC boys was the official dedication wall and plaque for the new park. For almost a year, the now-expert stonemasons worked on the permanent memorial, which stood on the state line at Newfound Gap, half in North Carolina and half in Tennessee. "For the enjoyment of the people," the bronze plaque said, reminding visitors that money for Great Smoky Mountains National Park came from the people of the two states and the federal government as well as the generosity of John D. Rockefeller Jr. In a radio address on the eve of the dedication, Director Arno Cammerer extolled the park, "the most centrally situated wilderness area in the United States." He praised the wildflowers and the virgin forest. "Until very recent years all this region was a land of unexplored mystery," he said. "Even the Indians left untrodden hundreds of thousands of acres of inaccessible lands. . . . To walk today through the dim, shadowy depths of these primeval forests is in many places altogether impossible." Thus the myth continued that the Smokies remained an untouched wilderness—in Cammerer's view, the pioneering NPS had carved a park out of the wilderness.[81]

On September 2, 1940, President Franklin D. Roosevelt came to deliver a dedication speech at the new monument. That morning, the 12 miles from the park headquarters to Newfound Gap were policed by the president's tree army—CCC enrollees stood 1,000 feet apart all the way up the mountain. Thousands of people crowded into Newfound Gap to see the motorcade and hear the message broadcast by radio over a nationwide hookup. Secretary of the Interior Harold Ickes presided. Behind the president sat Eakin, and not far behind him McKellar, the senator who wanted to fire the superintendent for not developing the park enough. Beneath the plaque sat David Chapman and the governors from both states.[82] First the governor of North Carolina, Clyde Hoey, spoke. He described the great variety of flora and fauna in the Smokies and told the assembled group that this new park represented a chance for all citizens to dedicate themselves to "the high purposes of our republic as we battle for the preservation of our heritage of liberty and freedom." The governor of Tennessee, Prentice Cooper, then called the park "a strategic factor in national defense, a natural barrier to an enemy, a natural protection to the inland country." Everyone, it seemed, thought more about the impending conflict with Germany than any miracle of landscape architecture, ecological recovery, or preservation. Finally, Franklin D. Roosevelt, whose programs constructed the park, moved to the microphone. Oddly enough, he didn't mention his CCC boys at all. He spoke briefly about trees, then cut to a shrinking earth, "so diminished by the airplane and the radio that Europe is closer to America today than was one side of these mountains to the other side when the pioneers toiled through the primeval forest." His talk concerned mostly the coming war, new army bases, and conscription of manpower. When he mentioned defending a way of life that allowed men "to hold up their heads and admit no master but God," the crowd cheered. "I hope that roads and paths and trails will still be built in the cause of liberty and recreation," he said, ominously, "and not confined to the ulterior purpose of a war machine controlled by an individual or an oligarchy."[83] The Great Smoky Mountains stood dedicated to the free people of America, and young men were now trained for the real business of war.

4.1. Superintendent Eakin (front row, center) and his rangers. Courtesy of Great Smoky Mountains National Park.

4.2. Site of the Trillium Gap Trail to Mount LeConte *before* CCC construction. Courtesy of Great Smoky Mountains National Park.

4.3. Trillium Gap Trail to Mount LeConte *after* CCC construction. Courtesy of Great Smoky Mountains National Park.

4.4. CCC worker drying and cleaning native seeds, collected on the balds, 1935. Photo by P. M. Wentworth. Courtesy of Great Smoky Mountains National Park.

4.5. CCC enrollees mowed Cades Cove to prevent woody succession, 1939. Photo by Willis King Courtesy of Great Smoky Mountains National Park.

A Lake in the National Defense

We are building this dam
To make the power
To roll the aluminum
To build the bombers
To beat the bastards

TVA MOTIVATIONAL POSTER

WORLD WAR II gave the federal government imperative to create a lake next to the Great Smoky Mountains. Just as the Great Depression gave President
Roosevelt a mandate to develop conservation resources such as the CCC, World War II gave another New Deal agency, TVA, the public support
necessary to build what would be the highest dam
east of the Mississippi. For twenty years, the Aluminum Company of America (ALCOA) considered
building a large hydroelectric dam on the Little Tennessee River to supply its power needs. In fact,
ALCOA purchased some 15,000 acres of land toward this goal, but war gave TVA the money for the
job. Waving the flag of national defense, TVA purchased an additional 55,000 acres, relocated 1,311
families, and inundated 11,800 acres of private land
to create Fontana Dam on the slopes of the Great
Smoky Mountains.

However, TVA officals did discuss the recreation
possibilities of a lake in the Blue Ridge before the
war. At a National Conference on State Parks during

the 1930s, TVA employee C. M. Terry extolled the "rich natural heritage of rugged mountains and peaceful valleys," the "wave after wave of rolling hills topped by crests of flowering shrubs," and the mild climate. "Yet there is one feature lacking," he said, "to round out the recreation potentialities of the region: lakes." In the eight reservoirs created by TVA to date, Terry stated that 5,000 pleasure crafts with a combined value of $1 million were cruising the lakes.[1]

And TVA certainly had economic development as its ultimate goal, even with Fontana. When he took office, President Roosevelt labeled the South the nation's number one economic problem; in the first hundred days of the New Deal, TVA received a virtual mandate from Congress to improve navigation and flood control along the Tennessee River and to promote "the economic and social well-being" of the people living in the greater watershed. By the end of the decade, the *Asheville Citizen-Times* reported that Swain County, on the North Carolina side of the Smokies, was the state's "no. 1 economic problem." All but 406 of the 2,300 families in the county were on relief rolls. "Sticking a salted thumb into an open wound," reported the newspaper, "the state of North Carolina acquired and deeded to the federal government 57 percent of the county's total area as a part of the Great Smoky Mountains National Park, thus exempting it from taxation."[2] From TVA's perspective, such statistics made the Fontana area the poorest of the poor.

TVA legislation emphasized the need for flood control, but nobody mentioned the fact that flooding resulted, in large part, from intensive logging; in fact, TVA advisors tended to downplay any connection at all. Although the U.S. Army Corps of Engineers suggested that the goals of navigation and flood control could be accomplished by lower dams, which inundated fewer acres of valuable bottomland, TVA continued to promote high dams—primarily used for the production of electricity—as its total "system of reservoirs."[3] One of three TVA chairmen, Arthur E. Morgan, strongly disapproved of the U.S. Army Corps of Engineers and envisioned an agency that could keep above local politics and contribute materially to the lives of people who lived in the valley. At Norris, Tennessee, where TVA built its first dam in 1936, Morgan, former president of Antioch College, and his staff planned a model village of low-cost, "modern, efficient" homes for displaced farmers. TVA staffers prepared voluminous statistics about the 3,000 rural families displaced by the dam and the "suburb in the wilderness" Morgan wanted to build.[4]

But Morgan's approach angered some elites in the region. David Chapman, the early promoter of Great Smoky Mountains National Park and a Knoxville civic booster, became irritated with TVA planners when they would not hire land buyers and surveyors whom he recommended from the Great Smoky Mountains project and failed to support his idea for a dam in Cades Cove. An influential citizen, he was not used to being ignored. "If they want somebody to help with improving the economic social conditions of the Tennessee Valley, they will have to get somebody who knows the people who is one of them," he wrote, in what appears to be a rough draft of an unsent letter. "Yankees . . . and town fellows will rub [local people] the wrong way—can't do it," he scribbled. "It will have to be done by somebody who can talk our language and understands us." Chapman, of course, had done his share of rubbing local people the wrong way, but he clearly resented the fact that TVA would not take his advice.[5]

From the other side of the spectrum, another TVA chairman, David Lilienthal, found Morgan's approach too human-centered. An attorney who served on the Wisconsin Public Utilities Commission, Lilenthal agreed that TVA should be above local politics, but he disapproved of Morgan's social planning. The production schedule for Norris Dam slowed because of social research and haggling over land prices, and Morgan could get sidetracked on unworkable ideas, such as establishing a special currency in TVA towns and recombining Tennessee counties. By the time TVA completed Norris, Lilienthal and Morgan bumped heads over who would actually control the agency. Each began positioning himself in the president's favor. About this time, Morgan was negotiating with ALCOA for the Fontana project, but he worried about the private company obtaining a monopoly on the "vast electric power potential of the upland area." To power its aluminum plant in nearby Alcoa, Tennessee, the company built Cheoah Dam in 1919, Calderwood in 1930, and Santeetlah in 1928. ALCOA wanted to retain control of the Little Tennessee Valley, not share it with a government agency. The company grew very hostile toward Morgan, and at one point even planted a spy in the chairman's office. Meanwhile, Lilienthal worked against the project, because, according to Morgan, he had "an intimate relationship with ALCOA" and wanted to protect the company's interests. "This was by far the most important single project on which I came into conflict with the other members of the board," the chairman later wrote. Unbeknownst to Morgan, Lilienthal slowly discredited Morgan with Roosevelt and used his influence to cancel the Fontana project altogether in 1936.[6]

After Morgan protested the cancellation of Fontana, he was charged with insubordination. But Lilienthal had already maneuvered himself into position with the president, and he used congressional investigations of TVA as an opportunity to further damage Morgan's reputation. To his "horror," Lilienthal testified, Morgan's proposed agreement with ALCOA included "the proposition that the aluminum company should receive a share of the benefits."[7] Roosevelt urged Morgan to resign, which he did. Abandoning Morgan's idealistic notions of social planning, Lilienthal courted southern businessmen by speaking frequently on a topic he called the "Restoration of Economic Equality Among the Regions of the U.S." He traveled to nearby Waynesville, where he talked to business, civic, and farm leaders about improving conditions in the South. He argued that the region was plagued by inadequate industrial research, discriminating freight rates, and a tendency to be a producer rather than a processor of natural resources. All these problems, of course, could be solved by TVA and the industries it would attract to the Southeast with cheap electric power.[8]

Fontana, in fact, fit perfectly with these goals, but ALCOA remained hostile toward TVA and actually tried to negotiate funding for the construction through Roosevelt's Reconstruction Finance Corporation. The advent of World War II, then, proved particularly useful to Lilienthal. As the Axis powers signed a military pact and war broke out in Europe, demand for war materials in the United States increased. Senator Harry S. Truman, chairman of the Senate Committee on War Production, declared, "I want aluminum. I don't care whether it comes form ALCOA, the Reynolds Metal Company, or Al Capone!" If ALCOA refused to negotiate with TVA, the company looked like a fat-cat monopoly standing in the way of the war effort. ALCOA needed Fontana Dam, so Lilienthal reopened negotiations with a lot more power in his corner. By this time, ALCOA worried less about losing control and more about getting government assistance for this massive project. In return for donating the

15,000 acres ALCOA had already purchased and allowing TVA to maintain the new dam, ALCOA would receive all the electric power it needed. TVA agreed to purchase the remaining 53,292 acres for the dam and to foot the bill for the $70 million structure.

When newspapers in Swain and Jackson Counties got wind of the potential dam construction jobs, they came out in full support of it. "Most of the vicinity has been logged, anyway," reported the *Bryson City Times*. "With the park on one side and the huge lake on the other, this should be the camping recreation center of western North Carolina." The newspaper eagerly reported when TVA engineers arrived in town, although "whether they were here to do preliminary surveying and investigating is not known." The *Jackson County Journal* emphasized "power to turn the wheels of national defense plants" as well as the "lack of electric power which blocks the establishment of big industry in the county." Neither newspaper mentioned the potential effects on the Little Tennessee River, nor did they comment on the impact on communities, some of which appeared in other regular newspaper features. On Hazel Creek stood the former lumber town of Proctor, and, following the Southern Railway down the Little Tennessee, a traveler would come to Bushnell. At the confluence of the Nantahala and the Little Tennessee, the scenic farms of Judson and Almond stretched along gentle hillsides with the mountains towering in the background. Across the line into Graham County were Japan (pronounced "JAY-pan"), Stecoah, Brock, and Tuskeegee.[9]

With community support and the national defense argument, TVA and ALCOA signed an agreement in August 1941, a document that differed little in content from the one Morgan negotiated five years previously. Nevertheless, federal officials called the agreement "a milestone in relations between government and business." As soon as the agreement was signed, Lilienthal sent confidential reports to the major newspaper editors of the region. "To overcome the critical shortage of power for national defense," he stated, TVA needed to provide an additional capacity of 400,000 kilowatts, which included the Fontana project. "This project involves a *minimum of interference* with the critical needs of other vital defense activities," underlined the report. In a press release accompanying the report, editors were authorized to announce on January 1, 1942, the agency's "major contributions to defense." During the next year, Lilienthal pressed the business community for support, emphasizing the success of previous projects and warning against criticism. He also pledged business leaders to prevent the agency from being the "victim of local politics," as "your eternal vigilance," he said, "is the price of low cost energy."[10]

Local business leaders in Swain and Jackson Counties seemed to take his advice. Within a month Bryson City held a meeting to help with housing and road construction to the dam. The chamber of commerce started a Build Fontana Dam Club, the membership fees of which went toward promotion. "Every citizen in Swain County interested in the development of this project should become a member of this club," urged the editors of the *Bryson City Times*. "By doing so you will be rendering yourself and your county a great service." As construction began in 1942, every movement in personnel, the arrival of survey and clearance crews, as well as the efforts toward land acquisition received glowing reports by the paper. Reporters noted the "large check" paid for the Almond school property, the minuteman flag given to TVA employees for the purchase of war bonds, and the progress of poured concrete.[11]

Despite the other reasons TVA and ALCOA wanted to build the dam—industrial development and tourism—TVA made ample use of the "demands of national defense" throughout the project.[12] Whether it involved justifying construction costs or keeping employees to a grueling schedule, Lilienthal would trot out the national security argument, how Fontana was "essential to defense power needs." The new federal agency issued edicts to employees and press releases to newspapers that made supporting the dam sound like an essential part of American patriotism. "OF COURSE YOU WANT AMERICA TO WIN THE WAR, EVERY GOOD AMERICAN DOES," TVA project manager F.C. Schlemmer said [capitalization in original document]. "In order to win the war our armed forces need plenty of guns, planes, tanks, ammunition, and supplies. It takes power to manufactor [sic] these things. THAT IS WHY FONTANA DAM IS BEING BUILT—TO PRODUCE THIS POWER."[13]

Building Boulder in the East

Commenced less than a month after Pearl Harbor, Fontana Dam was scheduled for completion in just twenty-one months, a record time frame for such a large hydroelectric dam, public or private. Within a year, the agency hired 6,337 workers, which gave the site a population greater than the sum of every man, woman, and child in Graham County. Unemployed white and Cherokee men from all over western North Carolina, Tennessee, and northern Georgia flocked to the jobs at rates ranging from 50 cents to $1.25 per hour. TVA policy also attracted 697 African-American workers, whose presence caused a riot by whites the night they arrived. Although some left as a result of the violence, most stayed in the segregated quarters the government built for them. Project managers needed every able-bodied man they could get. With a seven-day, twenty-four-hour work week, turnover remained high throughout construction; the project averaged 389 "exits" each month. Workers who wanted to see their families or rest had to quit for a time and hope to be rehired. Systemwide TVA managers struggled to maintain this production schedule: in one year, 1942, the agency was constructing thirteen dams. "We were doing planning on all those dams at one time. That really was a madhouse at that time because we just had to make progress on all of them," recalled Don Mattern, a senior civil engineer. TVA literature made high productivity sound as important to the war effort as troop movements, and slacking off, as one historian put it, "was tantamount to treason." Driving workers this hard resulted in high accident rates; Fontana workers suffered 472 accidents and 14 fatalities during construction.[14]

Because of the large number of workers, the first project on TVA's Fontana agenda had to be construction of an actual town. Within sight of the dam, the agency built Fontana Village, named for a lumber camp and mining town that would soon be underwater. As excavation began for the dam, TVA cleared a level spot along the river to erect the village. TVA's built environment included two tent camps of 76 and 125 four-men tents, a trailer camp with 127 units, eleven men's dormitories, two women's dormitories, 25 permanent houses, 155 temporary houses, 100 "demountable houses," medical facilities, dining halls, two schools, and a sewage treatment plant. Unlike the ideal communities Morgan earlier envisioned, Fontana Village looked temporary, even though it contained modern conveniences, such as electricity and telephone service. In addition to the segregated tent camp and dormitory for African Americans, the village included separate dining rooms and recreation facilities.[15]

Before TVA finished Fontana Village, people poured into the region to obtain the defense-related jobs offered at the site. When the new employees could not find housing in the village, they rented almost any empty building available. On Hazel Creek alone, "transients," as their employer called them, rented thirty-five trailers, thirty-five shacks, and five tents on Nantahala Power Company land. In Bushnell, they occupied a deserted gas station and an unused warehouse. Almost immediately, TVA's Population Readjustment Division began to receive complaints from the North Carolina state health officer about the lack of sanitary facilities and the "grave danger of epidemics" posed by the makeshift settlements. In response, the agency sponsored a Shack Development Control Program to funnel the "transients" into the village and to prevent families from settling "permanently" in the shacks. Within a few months, the shack controllers aided by the state health department served notice on the shack residents to vacate the premises. About 167 of the 256 shacks surveyed "did not meet sanitary requirements."[16]

TVA's ambitious construction activities soon brought the agency into conflict with the adjacent national park. A month after the project started, TVA surveyed the area, including park lands, for potential quarry sites. To improve roads at the dam site, the agency wanted to unearth about 25,000 cubic yards of rock, and officials proposed using a 150- by 600-foot stone outcropping on Great Smoky Mountains National Park lands near Twentymile Creek. Reluctantly, the park agreed to sacrifice the rock. The TVA also negotiated a 110-foot-wide, 6-mile-long right-of-way across the national park for a telephone line to the dam site and transmission lines to the aluminum company. Although he considered the construction of such a corridor "entirely foreign to park policies," Eakin acquiesced to the demands of national defense and accepted this easement.[17]

Fontana required not only a tight time schedule, but also a bold engineering feat. Situated in a narrow, steep-walled gorge rare in the Tennessee Valley, the Fontana site is probably one of the only places in the entire Tennessee Valley watershed where this huge 480-foot dam could have been built. To construct a dam this tall and narrow, TVA borrowed knowledge gained from engineering achievements at Boulder (later Hoover) Dam on the Colorado River. Engineers directed workers to drill two 37-foot tunnels, which diverted water during construction and served as spillways when the dam was completed. They also adopted the Boulder method of quick-cooling concrete in 50- and 100-foot sections.[18] For the 2.6 million cubic yards of concrete needed for this structure, TVA used dynamite at a quarry site 5,000 feet downstream, where workers crushed 15,000 tons of rock daily. TVA planners estimated that the total excavation for the dam, spillways, and "improved" river channel required 1.5 million cubic yards of rock and dirt, most of which they blasted and jack-hammered from the gorge. "The whole job at Fontana is like a vast digestive system whose task it is to get the food—concrete—into the muscles of the dam," said TVA foreman Charley Cathey, interviewed on the site by a newspaper reporter. On the same "inaccessible wilderness" where Cathey once cut timber for W. M. Ritter, he now helped supervise construction of the mammoth dam.[19]

To prevent the dam, once built, from becoming clogged with vast amounts of rock, trees, housing materials, and debris, workers cleared the acreage behind the structure. In 1942, TVA contracted with a lumber company for the removal of 2.9 million board feet of hardwood and pine lumber from 5,125 acres, only some of which they used in Fontana construction. Using two portable sawmills, the contractor extracted an additional 1,275 cords of pulpwood. Workers trimmed any trees growing above the draw-down altitude so that their tops would not protrude above the water; some species, particularly sweet gum, can continue to grow for years partially submerged. Photographs of the cleared hillsides show that not so much as a sapling remained.[20] Then the clearance crews even burned the piles of slash left by timber operations. In 1942, a fire broke out from slash-burning operations and blackened 150 feet of land for about a mile and a quarter inside the nearby national park boundary. NPS officials charged TVA with carelessness and inadequate employee training in fire prevention. "I assure you that the Great Smoky Mountains National Park is very dear to the hearts of all of us, and to permit it to be ravaged by fire would be little short of sacrilege," stated the TVA division superintendent, trying to smooth over relations with the park superintendent. The following year, however, Eakin again complained about the "menace to the park" from clearance operations because enormous piles of dry timber bordered the railway running to the copper mine. He worried about the temptation to "firebugs," who might use incendiary fires as a way to channel angry feelings toward the park. TVA's division superintendent stated that he shared Eakin's concern about "firebugs" and recommended controlled burning, particularly in the Eagle Creek district, where he said TVA had encountered incidents involving vandalism.[21]

Disgruntled employees committed at least one act of arson; they were caught when the FBI was called in to investigate "disruption of power to defense plants." Other acts of arson and vandalism resulted from TVA's land-buying activities, however, which angered many people and proceeded simultaneously with the construction of the dam. Based on calculations, dam builders predicted that Fontana would back up water for 30 miles along the river and cover more than 10,600 acres of land. Water would inundate the villages of Fontana, Bushnell, Japan, Stecoah, Judson, and Almond, or, in the words of TVA's documents, the communities would "lose their identities." As construction workers began pouring concrete, the fate of the farms above the high-water mark in Proctor and Hazel remained undecided. The road to these farms would be covered with water, so if they were allowed to remain, North Carolina Highway 288 would have to be rerouted around the edge of Fontana Lake. Eventually, TVA officials contacted the park to discuss the situation. Should they "take" the Proctor communities or rebuild the road? Superintendent Eakin gave the officials a measured response. On the one hand, the park would "gladly administer" and protect the additional land. Controversy and a shortage of funds during land acquisition caused the Great Smoky Mountains National Park to be smaller than originally planned. From the beginning, Eakin considered Eagle Creek and Hazel Creek management problems, because bear hunters entered the Smokies from this side and a number of incendiary fires crept into the park from these two watersheds. David Lilienthal visited the superintendent, reminding him of TVA's mission to participate in reforestation and erosion control.[22]

On the other hand, park officials worried that the lake would be polluted and an eyesore, because an effluent from a paper mill in Sylva flowed down the Tuckasegee River into the Little Tennessee. "Polluted waters are bad enough," commented Eakin, "but to add to this unsightly condition, provision is being made for a pull-down of 185 feet in the level of the reservoir in the development of power." Because of the periodic draw-down of water required by hydroelectric dams and the steep banks surrounding the sides, Fontana would be less than scenic and not really accessible, Eakin argued. To improve the possibilities, the park service proposed that TVA dam some "arms" of the reservoir so that a system of clear water lakes would surround Great Smoky Mountains National Park.[23] By emphasizing the high cost of "auxiliary" dams and the shortage of adequate shoreline on the proposed sites, TVA convinced park leaders that extra dams were not needed. After all, the officials reasoned, the "pollution phase" would probably not be that serious, and an educated public would understand that periodic draw-downs benefited flood control elsewhere. By this time, though, Eakin resolved that Fontana was a reality and that the overpurchase plan would benefit the park. He began calling the extension "logical," even though he knew that many residents living in this section would be hostile to the idea. And, Eakin reasoned, a new road might be a scenic route "very helpful to the park by relieving congestion." Privately, Eakin worried that if the NPS didn't agree to take the lands, TVA might take them, anyway, and give them to the NFS, which Eakin believed would be "embarrassing" for the park. Although in previous projects TVA planners replaced inundated roads, with wartime financial pressures they argued it was "futile to restore the road at so great a cost for so sparse a population."[24]

Swain County political leaders, however, vigorously objected to the additional loss of taxable property. Already irritated that an entrance to the park at Deep Creek had been scrapped, they wanted a piece of the economic development going on in Cherokee and Gatlinburg. And so TVA outlined plans for a scenic parkway around the edge of the lake, which could be built after the war. To satisfy Swain County, the park agreed to include the construction of a road between Bryson City and Deals Gap in its next Master Plan. As soon as the War Production Department freed up funds for road-building, the park would construct a scenic road to make cemeteries and homeplaces accessible to the former residents and to allow the county further benefits from tourism. NPS officials allowed that the land would be a "desirable addition to the park" and might be required, anyway, for a proposed "parkway around the park." On July 30, 1943, the U.S. Department of Interior (under which operates the NPS), TVA, the state of North Carolina, and Swain County joined in a Quadripartite Agreement, which stated that TVA would purchase the extra 44,400 acres and transfer the land to the NPS. The U.S. Department of Interior agreed to construct a dustless surface road no less than 20 feet in width "as soon as funds are made available for that purpose by Congress after the cessation of hostilities."[25] The 1943 Agreement, as it is usually called, seemed to satisfy Swain County, as local politicians believed that the increased revenue in tourism would make up for the loss of tax revenue. A similar situation arose in Graham County, as a small community of about thirteen homes called Cable Cove would be without road access after inundation. Isolating Cable Cove, in turn, would cut off Poison Cove, a 450-acre community accessible by dirt road farther up the mountain. Rather than rebuild this road, TVA also decided to invoke its heavy purchase policy. At no time did the county government or local newspapers show concern for any of these displaced farmers or relocated communities.[26]

While government agencies bartered the fate of those above the high-water mark, TVA continued to purchase the other communities above the dam. Since the earliest planning stages of the project, TVA had done social research on the Fontana area. TVA documents labeled Graham and Swain Counties "submarginal," because land sold for less than $22.50 per acre in these "southern rural slums." Whereas "slum dwellers of the city at least have access to up-to-date and efficient municipal services in education, public health, and recreation," a report stated, rural slums lack such services "since poverty is such that the public revenues barely support the minimum functions of government." Urban planners saw "grave social and spiritual deficiencies" among people living in the mountains, where "social and cultural life is at a low ebb." Because TVA officials believed that these mountain people lived without meaningful social institutions, they emphasized family case work—"divide and conquer," if you will—in getting them to leave.[27]

New Powers of Eminent Domain

Although TVA documents emphasized the "submarginal" nature of these communities, the agency's own facts and figures describe lively and productive communities. Not unlike Cataloochee or Cades Cove, Judson and Almond, North Carolina, supported 143 families in 1940. About 33 percent of the Judson residents had lived in the community all their lives, and 70 percent had fewer than three children. All but four heads of household in the community could read and write; ten had attended college, and six of these held bachelor of science degrees. Five families in these two communities already had electric lights run on small water-powered generators, including Calhoun Welch, whose ingenious waterwheel ran lights and a small circular saw in his woodshop. Eight small grocery or general merchandise stores served Almond and Judson and the surrounding area, and three Baptist churches as well as the Almond elementary and high school were at the center of community life. Here TVA caseworkers couldn't fail to note the "fertile bottom land" that would be inundated when the two communities disappeared underwater. "The extremely rugged nature of the adjacent lands makes it impossible for farm families to re-establish themselves on the steep, unproductive land above the reservoir margin," a caseworker admitted.[28]

When copper mines on Hazel Creek and Eagle Creek still sent the valuable mineral over the mountain to Copperhill, Tennessee, for processing, the spur line run by the Southern Railway prospered, and along with it Bushnell, North Carolina. A caseworker from TVA described the residents of Judson, Almond, and Bushnell as "pioneers living for many years practically isolated from the rest of the world," but photographs show them in typical 1940s dress, living in neat, white-framed farmhouses. On Gunnar Branch, George Gunnar set up a small homemade shower system, and on Goldmine Branch, Chas Cole designed a gravity-run water system for his family. The two-room, cinder-block Bushnell School, built in 1917, had indoor plumbing and served grades 1–7 until TVA closed its doors in 1943. The area around Bushnell included the Forney Creek Baptist Church and the Chambers Creek Baptist Church, where families regularly held revivals in addition to twice-weekly services. Area churches also sponsored young people's get-togethers and an annual old-time singing convention. County agents established home demonstration clubs for women at Roxy McClure's home, agricultural meetings for men, and 4-H clubs for children in the area. The nearest doctor lived in Bryson City, but "Tiny" Kirkland, an experienced midwife, served all three communities.[29]

Founded by Montvale Lumber Company in 1902, Fontana embodied the temporary boom years at the turn of the century. A logging camp that all but vanished when Montvale sold out to Great Smoky Mountains National Park, Fontana was described as "transient" by caseworkers. Still, a school, community recreation center, hotel, church, and store remained. Communities on the edge of the Smokies—Hazel Creek and

Proctor, and, over the mountain in Graham County, Stecoah, Brock, Tuskeegee, and Japan—also had seen more prosperous days during the timber/mining/tannery boom. About thirty families living on Panther Creek (served by the Japan post office), for example, lost their land for Fontana Dam. Somewhat poorer than people in neighboring communities, only two of the thirty residents lived in painted houses, and none had running water or electricity. Fewer children reportedly went to school, but most families regularly attended the Panther Creek Baptist Church. Because of their less-fortunate circumstances, TVA caseworkers recorded more negative descriptions of Japan. "Chickens roost in the shade trees," "pigs run loose around the house," and "flies breed unmolested around the house," one TVA official complained. "All of these unsanitary practices point to the reluctance of the mountaineer to make modern improvements and develop a cooperative community spirit."[30]

Residents in these small places would have been baffled by such derogatory descriptions, as TVA did not record a community without a church. "Lacking cooperative community spirit" seemed to mean disagreeing with TVA policy. Although the smaller communities indeed suffered greater poverty than did Judson, Almond, and Bushnell, those who remained on the land were adept at making do on semi-subsistence farming and occasional cash work. Although small, these communities had well-developed systems of spiritual and social support. As Hazel Creek resident Alice Moore Posey recalled:

> It was in the depression days, but those that had property could get out wood, cut cross-ties, and acid wood to buy their flour and the things they had to have. They had cows, chickens, and gardens. They made a good living. There wasn't much money to be had, but people didn't starve. You know, in these larger cities, there was lots of people on starvation. They couldn't get the food. We were poor back then, but we did have food on the table.[31]

TVA targeted Bushnell, Judson, and Almond first, because soon after the gates of the dam closed, all three would be underwater. To achieve these removals, TVA exercised extraordinary powers of eminent domain. Because of the high valuations a few individuals received when the states purchased land for Great Smoky Mountains National Park, TVA founders sought greater land acquisition powers.[32] Whereas the U.S.

Department of Justice historically handled condemnation proceedings for other federal agencies, Section 25 of the 1933 TVA Act permitted the agency to conduct its own land condemnation. By statute, TVA could decide which lands were needed, employ its own appraisers, and make a nonnegotiable offer to landowners. If an owner refused to accept this one-time offer, his property was condemned and a "declaration of taking" was issued, allowing the Authority to take immediate possession. Despite the fact that all challenges to eminent domain in the United States went before a jury, TVA received the power to forego jury trials as a means of determining fair compensation. By TVA's own calculations, this aggressive approach to land-buying saved the agency 60 percent off fair market value for property.[33]

With so much power in the buyer's hands, farmers had little choice but to accept the sale price. In the words of Eugene Lowe: "You didn't have to sign anything, the judge done it for you." Added to these facts was the pressure of dam construction already going on downstream. No longer just a proposal, every day the dam became a more concrete reality. A homeowner reluctant to deal with TVA negotiators might watch his next-door neighbor's land cleared and home burned. To further complicate matters, many residents living on smaller farms—or their sons or daughters or nieces or nephews—found employment with TVA. "The three-year period from 1941 to 1944 was a bitter-sweet time for the residents of Hazel Creek and the surrounding areas," wrote Duane Oliver, whose family lived on Hazel Creek. Everyone who wanted a job had one, for the first time since Ritter and Whiting Lumber companies left in 1928. "The bitter part came," Oliver said, "when everyone realized that they would have to sell their land and move, for when the lake was filled they would have no road to the outside world."[34]

From their vantage point as the principal employers in the valley, TVA officials instructed land buyers to pressure employees who lived above the reservoir to move. "From the beginning an effort is made to eliminate unemployment," a TVA relocation expert mentioned, emphasizing the importance of employment connections to speedy, cooperative removal. State and county governments actually provided TVA with lists of families receiving public welfare and those delinquent on taxes. The agency also put pressure on the WPA to get its clients living upstream to relocate as well. "The idea that every person must be satisfied is a fallacy which results in disaster," remarked a TVA official speaking on public relations as related to property management. "We are a public organization in a democracy wherein the rule is by the majority. Obviously, programs designed for the good of the majority will affect adversely individuals or minorities."[35]

By the end of 1943, TVA employed as many as 89 of the 771 people living in Judson and Almond, which greatly complicated local feelings about removal. Abraham Cole Hyatt, for example, saw his seventeen-year-old son join TVA clearance crews. Hyatt and his family had "every comfort of a city dweller" in their "beautiful seven-room home," considered "above average" for Bushnell by TVA caseworkers. A farmer most of his life, Hyatt eventually took a job as one of four caretakers for Philip Rust, a wealthy businessman from New Jersey who owned a 3,000-acre hunting and fishing reserve. In return for watching over the lands, Hyatt received free lodging and the right to farm on Rust's land. Hyatt also improved his standing by renting his own land, farther up the valley. W. W. Jenkins, Hyatt's tenant, worked twenty-five years for the W. T. Mason Lumber Company and like Hyatt was "dead set" against removal. Because of the men's longtime residence in the valley, TVA officials worried that they might exert a "great influence on other families."[36]

Formal TVA policy used at other locations allowed occupants to stay on their land as long as possible to harvest crops, and if dam construction destroyed a fall harvest, the agency would pay for the loss. Because of the imminent closing of the dam's gate, however, Fontana removal operated on an accelerated schedule. "As tracts are purchased the families are visited at once and urged to start looking for relocations," a TVA official instructed his staff. As soon as a family had a definite relocation, TVA workers discussed plans for final removal work, such as selling buildings, moving whole houses, burning fields, and removing fences.[37]

Because of the inflammatory language of official reports, it's not difficult to imagine unpleasant encounters between TVA caseworkers and local people. Andy Chicklelee, a Cherokee man, lived in western North Carolina all his life and worked nineteen years for Southern Railway as a member of the section crew. He cooperated with TVA caseworkers, stating he only wanted to remain close enough to Southern Railway to keep his job. Chicklelee sold a 40-acre tract of land he owned outside of Japan to TVA for $849, and the Cooperative Extension Service found him another farm, but because he had to wait so long for payment he temporarily rented a home in Almond with his daughter's family. The money finally came through for Chicklelee in 1945. His son-in-law, however, continued to bicker with the Cherokee Council, and at one point locked the doors and refused to turn over possession of the property. "By some means," the record mysteriously stated, "Mr. Walker's house and household goods caught fire and burned down."[38]

When the 1943 Agreement was finally reached, the November 7 inundation date was only a few months away. And so TVA quickly moved to finish land acquisition in Proctor and the farms scattered along Eagle Creek, Hazel Creek, Forney Creek, and Noland Creek. Superintendent Eakin lobbied to retain some of the homes for use as fire warden housing and ranger stations. The park also expressed interest in the hydroelectric plant and small water systems owned by residents for the same reason. Because Superintendent Eakin actually asked rangers to investigate their soon-to-be-acquired facilities before they were even vacated, these informal "surveys" caused some consternation among the residents.[39]

Approximately 10 percent of Proctor would be flooded, but the majority of the 163 residents watched their homes and above-water lands become part of the national park. TVA caseworkers portrayed Proctor as "a unique picture of community decadence and disorganization" and depicted the "natives" as "residue of the more prosperous periods of lumbering and mining." The lumber boom period, according to the TVA reports, meant that "schools have made remarkable progress" and "feuds have practically disappeared." Some of these comments even made their way into local newspapers, which supported removal after the 1943 Agreement. "Some of those who lived deep in the mountains have never been far from home," reported the *Sylva Herald and Ruralite*. "For instance, there is an old woman who lives back in the Proctor area, two miles up in the cove, where it is impossible to take a car. She's rather feeble. . . . [Her son] said his mother had not been to Proctor in 40 years and had never been to Bryson City, 25 miles away. She had never been in an automobile."[40]

Of course, Proctor residents didn't consider this woman typical, and they would have bristled if they saw themselves in reports where they were labeled "residue" or "decadent." There is no historical record of feuds ever existing in the area. About thirty Proctor men worked for the

Fontana Copper Mine, and another group ran a small sawmill in town. A few found work with the railroads; others farmed or worked for TVA. Most importantly, Henry Posey emphasized, "People cared for one another, people loved one another, people was neighbors." Posey's father owned 365 acres, and less than 3 acres of it would be flooded, so his father offered to give TVA the land if only the family could postpone their departure. More than the land, Posey recalled, his father wanted to stay in the community. "They run us out," he commented, "but they ain't never got my heart out of there."[41]

For most of his sixty-three years, Arnold Bradshaw lived in the Epp Springs area above Proctor. During the lumber company years, Bradshaw ran a store on Noland Creek, but since 1933 he mostly farmed and occasionally harvested timber from his property. He and his wife and three daughters lived in a small four-room house where he farmed four small tracts and rented another to a tenant. Bradshaw clearly did not want to leave, and he circulated a petition in Bryson City protesting the removal. His actions seemed to contradict the words of the TVA official assigned to Proctor, who described literacy in the area as "only the ability to sign relief receipts." Faced with the resistance of Bradshaw and others, the TVA caseworker noted contemptuously: "Even in a guarded dependency they may be better off on the little pieces of land so many of them love so much." Reports showed further hints of the resistance TVA encountered around Proctor. "Because of the definite lack of fraternal and social organizations" and the "clannish attitude of the natives," an official document stated, "we were necessarily forced to de-emphasize group action."[42]

At least one resident of the area asked TVA whether he could obtain a lifetime lease on the property, as many elderly residents dispossessed by the national park had done during the 1930s. Whether or not the NPS was influenced by the anger on Hazel Creek or past problems with life-leasers in the rest of the park cannot be determined by the public record. In any case, the acting director of NPS told TVA officials that granting lifetime leases on the soon-to-be park lands would be "repugnant to the purposes and intent" of the transfer agreement. Still, TVA did grant several temporary leases, and "for public relations purposes" the national park continued to honor them after the lands shifted to their control.[43]

As families left and removed their homes, communities were reduced to "unsightly heaps of unwanted lumber and buildings," and then burned by TVA clearance crews. "I recall standing on the graveyard hill in Possum Hollow and watching the Franklin store and warehouse being put to the torch by TVA," wrote Oliver. "We children found this exciting, not realizing that a town and a way of life was dying." Oliver's family actually salvaged enough fine lumber from the vacant houses in the area to build their new home in Hazelwood, North Carolina.[44]

Despite the overwhelming power of TVA, Arnold Bradshaw decided to challenge the legality of the 1943 Agreement between TVA and Great Smoky Mountains National Park. Bradshaw, Hyatt, and Rust joined S. Columbus Welch, John Burns, and Fred Lollis in a lawsuit against the Tennessee Valley Authority. The six men charged that the Authority had no power to condemn their lands, because their property would not be inundated. The land was being taken, not for defense purposes or dam construction, but to benefit another federal agency, the NPS. Represented by an Asheville law firm, they accused TVA of exceeding its power in the agreement with the national park. Four months after the gates of the dam were closed—water was literally beginning to lap at Highway 288—the U.S. district court agreed with them. Shortly thereafter, the Fourth Circuit Court of Appeals upheld the lower court's decision against TVA.[45]

While TVA appealed the decision, the status of the North Shore lands remained in doubt. The six litigants waited on their land, but the two federal agencies bickered over who should take care of the North Shore until the case was decided. TVA granted the NPS "permission" to occupy homes on certain tracts for the use of fireguards, but which agency would take over law enforcement presented a problem. At the same time, TVA negotiated with representatives of Swain and Graham Counties as to what would become of land on the south shore of the lake. TVA proposed transferring this to the USFS, but county representatives favored a state or county park or even selling the land back to private individuals. Although the chairman of the Swain County Planning Board and officials of Graham County exerted all the influence they could to have the property returned to them, private memos within TVA show that federal officials considered this a "very shaky deal" by "weak local agencies." The State Planning Board even urged TVA to allow the counties the chance to develop the south shore as a recreational facility. Despite this interest by the county, the 5,027 acres south of Fontana Reservoir became part of the Nantahala National Forest in 1947.[46]

As the first power unit of Fontana Dam went on line, TVA's appeal for the North Shore lands reached the U.S. Supreme Court. The opinion, not rendered until March 25, 1946, by Justice Hugo Black, reversed the lower court's decision and reaffirmed TVA's position. Black, a southern conservative, noted that all other landowners in the area sold voluntarily, and that the area became "practically isolated" after the highway was submerged. In broad strokes upholding TVA's prerogative, Black quoted the original provisions of the acts creating TVA, which he said "show a clear congressional purpose to grant the Authority *all the power needed* to acquire lands by purchase or condemnation which it deems necessary for carrying out the Act's purpose [emphasis added]."[47]

Those families that continued living on Hazel Creek, including Gamey Burns and his wife, lingered until the Supreme Court's decision before finally moving from the property. By 1947, they moved to Lands Creek, about 5 miles from Bryson City. Bradshaw moved to a farm in Cherokee County between Andrews and Murphy. Some families migrated to textile mills in Gastonia, North Carolina, and Kingston and Decatur, Georgia. Increase in property values and the influx of war-industries workers made it difficult to relocate farmers. "Only a few acres of accessible land would cost about the same as many acres of inaccessible mountain land," a TVA official admitted. Because TVA, the NPS, and the USFS also took so much land in Swain County out of private ownership, reports noted that Fontana residents "have spread over a wider area than the families of any other reservoir." "One older lady had never been off of Hazel Creek in her life, and within a month [of leaving] she died, and within another month her husband died," said Alice Moore Posey, who grew up "in" Hazel Creek as she likes to say, and had five of her six children there. Her own mother, afraid of boats, never returned. "We can't help but feel hurt over the way they did us," she concluded. Henry and Alice Posey, who moved to Macon County, waited so long to leave that they were not able to return across Highway 288 for their last load of belongings. "TVA, you know what that stands for, don't you? Tennessee Valley AUTHORITIES, that's what took our land away from us," said

Henry Posey. "War was going on, people was tore all to pieces. If there hadn't been a war going on, there would've been a war up there!"[48]

TVA finally spent just $43.82 on each of the 1,311 families removed to create Fontana Reservoir. Most of this money went toward referrals, either to the Agricultural Extension Service or the Farm Security Administration. Planners predicted that the reservoir would affect 2,043 graves in sixteen cemeteries, and caseworkers consulted with families about which graves should be moved where. If the cemetery would not be underwater, families generally did not want their ancestors dug up and reinterred. By the end of the project, TVA relocated 1,047 graves. The NPS then agreed to maintain the cemeteries on the North Shore lands and to provide transportation, by boat, to former residents who wanted to visit family graves.[49]

Underwater Farms

By the time the water lapped across Highway 288, both World War II and the battle for Hazel Creek had almost ended. "On February 1, 1945, the period of critical war power demand ended with the addition of the Fontana project," TVA records state, "followed by a leveling off of power requirements." As soon as the water reached 1,500 feet, what had been the Little Tennessee River looked very much like a lake. As the waters began to top the hills above Judson, all unexcavated archeological sites in what had been Cherokee homelands were lost. The pioneer history of the valley, and that which can be studied through archeological digs, were destroyed.[50] The inundation of land wiped out the terrestrial population—an estimated 1,500 organisms in each square meter of land. Dead and decaying plant food caused a temporary boost to certain fish populations, which immediately skyrocketed. "The number of bass taken from Fontana [in 1946] was amazing," wrote one fisherman after that first season. "In the spring and early summer of its second year, it was not uncommon to see the majority of fishermen unhitching strings loaded with fat bass." The "superabundance" of fish did not last, however, as the productivity of the reservoir eventually stabilized.[51]

At the same time that the reservoir quickly supported certain game fishes, other freshwater species disappeared altogether. Whereas the river supported seventy to ninety species of native fishes, only fifteen or twenty adapted to the reservoir. Whereas the river maintained more than 100 species of aquatic insects, only about one-fifth could live in the reservoir. As the gravel beds at the bottom of the Little Tennessee filled with sediment, freshwater mussels lost their habitat and an unknown number may have even become extinct.[52] Many nongame fishes, including mirror shiners and blueside darters, and perhaps even snail darters that once lived in the lower valleys of Hazel Creek, Eagle Creek, Twentymile Creek, and Noland Creek, vanished. These bottom-dwelling fish require large fast-moving rivers; without silt-free nesting sites and the aquatic insects that favor this habitat, they cannot survive. "They can't eat and they can't reproduce," explained David Etnier, a prominent ichthyologist, "and it doesn't get much worse than that." Eventually, they were eliminated from the Little Tennessee watershed altogether by TVA's dams. Like the darters, the Smoky madtom, yellowfin madtom, and spotfin chub also became threatened or endangered in North Carolina or Tennessee.[53] In fact, writes Etnier, "The fishes that depended on the river in its natural state will never be completely known. Fourteen native fish species are known to be extirpated from the river and some species that were never known to science may no longer be with us."[54]

The newly impounded waters also diminished migrating fish species. Scientists in the early 1940s noted that paddlefish and lake sturgeon once lived in the Little Tennessee River, but after the construction of Fontana Dam they disappeared from the area. Sometimes called "spoonbill catfish," paddlefish do survive in impoundment waters more frequently than lake sturgeons, but juvenile paddlefish get crushed against the screens that cover the intake valves when the power plant goes on line. Lake sturgeon no longer exist in Tennessee; paddlefish are "of special concern." All the TVA dams put together made them much rarer species in the Southeast. Another freshwater species, the American eel, actually traveled from the Little Tennessee to the deep Atlantic near Bermuda to spawn before TVA disrupted the fish's route.[55]

Fontana and the other TVA dams also may have even altered the patterns of migrating waterfowl. Before construction of the TVA dams, Canada geese and black ducks flew east of the Tennessee Valley on their way south, and pintails and mallards followed the Mississippi Valley. "None of these long, narrow bodies of water has attracted any appreciable number of shore or waterbirds," park naturalist Arthur Stupka wrote in the years after the area was flooded, "due, in part, to their newness, their fluctuating water levels, and other reasons." After several decades, however, all four species used the man-made lakes as a stopping-off point, and many stayed through the winter season.[56]

"Reservoirs are biologically very, very strange habitats," described Etnier, "There's nothing adapted to them, because they're not lakes and they're not rivers."[57] Despite the loss of biodiversity and the profound ecological changes that accompany the flooding of the land, artificial lakes such as Fontana sometimes achieve a kind of ecological stability. Largemouth bass stocked in combination with bluegill, sunfish, and catfish can stabilize their populations in a reservoir like a miniature food chain. Very large, cold-water storage impoundments such as Fontana, however, do not support the same number or combinations of fish. Drawdowns, the erratic releases of water needed to produce hydroelectric power, keep the temperature of the lake unstable, which inhibits some fish. During the fall and winter months, the water surface of Fontana drops 130 feet, leaving an unsightly steep and barren shoreline. During the spawning season, changing water levels can kill large numbers of bass.[58]

The state of North Carolina began stocking Fontana Lake in 1945, even before the water reached its high-water mark. During the 1950s and 1960s, the state department of fisheries stocked largemouth bass, smallmouth bass, crappie, bluegill, and a large number of walleye in the lake. Because of TVA's clearance operations and the draw-down, it was more difficult to stabilize erosion in the lake, and because of the deep water it was difficult to build the brush shelters and shallow water most bass prefer. Finally, during the 1970s and 1980s the North Carolina Wildlife Resources Commission introduced a northern lake species called white bass, which has stabilized in Fontana along with small and largemouth bass, crappies, walleye, and a small number of muskellunge.[59]

Essentially, no aquatic plants can live in Fontana except for unicellular algae, which fluctuates and, in turn, affects both the fish populations and the available oxygen in the lake. Until the paper mill located in Sylva, North Carolina, shut down in 1975, TVA hydrologists found that Fontana occasionally suffered from oxygen concentrations lower than 1 milligram/liter (5 milligrams/liter is considered healthy). Fisheries technicians estimated that at least 5 percent of the total reservoir capacity did not have enough oxygen to support fish. Environmental systems engineers later found that Fontana Lake contained large quantities of heavy metals; surveys found manganese, copper, and zinc all in concentrations similar to those in areas receiving industrial pollution. Although the heavy metals may have resulted in part from the old paper mill and mining activities, scientists believe that Anakeesta formations in the mountains contributed to this pollution. As the metals continue to accumulate, they may in the future cause a hazard to fish and the people who eat them. For fifty years now, the natural runoff from the creeks of the Great Smoky Mountains has built up sediment in Fontana Lake. Free-flowing rivers carried a great deal of suspended sediment, and the still water of the reservoir allowed this to accumulate. The lake will gradually become shallower and warmer, and with this eutrophication, or aging, it will fill up with plants, eventually containing too much nitrogen and phosphorus to support fish. Accumulated PCBs, once used as fire retardants in electrical transformers, may cause further problems as the lake ages. The reservoir already has a high mercury level. Although Fontana remains among the least eutrophic of TVA's reservoirs, the agency still must find ways to control the process, or one day the lake will disappear altogether. In the future, policymakers face expensive decisions about dredging, aeration, or chemical control of sedimentation.[60]

But did Fontana, the wilderness lake, ever bring prosperity to Swain County? In 1946, TVA leased Fontana Village to a private company for the development of a recreation center and boating facilities. Slowly the lake gained a loyal following of vacationers, and local people who once fished with cane poles took to boats and lures. By 1950, though, the village was filled to only two-thirds of its capacity. The economic boom from lake traffic that Swain and Graham Counties hoped for never arrived. As for the scenic North Shore road promised in the 1943 Agreement, it was never built. A 1948 document finalized the transfer of lands, and over the next twenty years, the park constructed a 1-mile spur, then two sections 2.5 miles long, a 2.1-mile extension, and then a tunnel, which alone cost $2.2 million. By this time, though, environmental groups started to object to excessive road-building in the park, and budget cuts kept the road's progress down to these fits and starts.

From the historical record, it is clear that a particular bureaucracy, TVA, dealt with individuals in a capricious manner. At the same time, county elites did not object to this—indeed, they supported the removals. If NC 288 had been constructed, no newspaper or local politician would have grieved the loss of Judson, Almond, Bushnell, Proctor, or Hazel Creek. Economic advancement of the richest members of the county would not compensate those who suffered from removal. Even an agency with conservation as one of its goals—as TVA clearly had at one time— did not value long-term environmental impact over its expeditious short-term goals. The "wilderness lake" that covers one side of the Smokies has nothing to do with wilderness. And so this story should serve as a caution-ary tale for government planners: even with laudatory goals such as de-feating Hitler or improving the living conditions of a region, too much power in the hands of a few often results in arrogant disregard. Progres-sive reformers such as the employees of TVA glorified efficiency over the worthwhile, if messier and more complex goals of social justice and de-mocracy. "The idea that every person must be satisfied is a fallacy which results in disaster," as the TVA official so frankly put it. "Obviously, pro-grams designed for the good of the majority will affect adversely individu-als or minorities." Yet this supercilious attitude and the actions arrogated by it came with a cost—events of the 1940s would haunt Great Smoky Mountains National Park in ways that nobody could have predicted.

5.1. Judson, North Carolina, 1943, now under the waters of Fontana Dam. Photo by Arnold J. Hyde. TVA Records, East Point Record Center for the National Archives.

5.2. John Montieth family and home on Forney Creek, 1943. The family was removed for the creation of Fontana Dam. Photo by F. L. Derthick. TVA Records, East Point Record Center for the National Archives.

5.3. Almond School, 1943, now under the waters of Fontana Dam. Photo by Z. B. Byrd. TVA Records, East Point Record Center for the National Archives.

5.4. Phillip Rust home. Rust, who used this summer home for hunting, led the lawsuit against TVA's "heavy purchase" policy, 1943. Photo by F. L. Derthick. TVA Records, East Point Record Center for the National Archives.

5.5. Construction of Fontana Dam, 1943. Photo by C. L. Blee. TVA Records, National Archives.

5.6. Fontana spillway, looking south, 1944. Photo by J. E. Fair. TVA Records, East Point Record Center for the National Archives.

5.7. Remains of the Hazel Creek copper mine, 1944. Photo by Portland P. Fox. TVA Records, East Point Record Center for the National Archives.

Drive-in Wilderness

*Here you can have your cake and eat
it too. You can have both automobile
roads and wilderness trails*

1950S TRAVEL WRITER

WILDERNESS SOCIETY co-founder Harvey Broome
hiked the Smokies in 1950 with a great deal of pride.
In just two decades, tremendous recovery had occurred in the forests that Broome helped preserve as
a national park. In his notebooks, he described walking through the ubiquitous young poplars, sweet
gums, maples, and other saplings of a second-growth
forest. "The old pattern of field and forest was being
erased," he wrote. "It was almost all forest—young
forest set in old, except for the ordered rows of the
fruit trees in [old orchards]. So rapid is the growth
in the well-watered and well-sunned Smokies, the
young forest is no longer too evident." Although a
few former residents remained in the park as leasees,
the forest had quickly moved in to create a tangle out
of old pastoral landscapes. Birds that preferred a second-growth forest, such as chickadees, titmice, and
oven birds, prospered. Small mammals often found
in old fields, such as rabbits and groundhogs, became
regular parts of the monthly *Superintendent's Report*.[1]

For most 1950s tourists, especially those whizzing
through the green mountains in their automobiles,
the Smokies looked like a forest, and therefore a "wil-

derness." Most thought that when the *North Carolina Guide* called it "the best surviving remnant of the forest that once extended from the Atlantic to the prairies of the middle west" the authors referred to the entire park. As the *Christian Science Monitor* put it: "[a traveler] can be swallowed in a wilderness as primitive as it was in the day of Columbus." A few hiked to the old growth that existed in more remote locations, but most wanted scenic vistas they could quickly relish. Because of the early emphasis on road-building by the two states and the role of automobile tourism in area development, landscape architects designed overlooks around almost every curve where motorists could pull off and get a photograph. "Everything that is possible for nature to do for roads, she has done," gushed one enthusiastic writer, crediting a mythical female with what, in truth, the CCC had accomplished. "Lined with countless varieties of trees, shrubs, and flowers, [the roads] lead along beautiful streams with lovely waterfalls, through cool shadowed gorges, virgin forests, and fertile valleys."[2] From the overlooks, a standard set of vistas began filling photo albums: Above the gateway city of Gatlinburg, Tennessee, stood Mount LeConte, one of the few distinct peaks in a landscape that otherwise looked like a sea of ridges. In Cherokee, North Carolina, parents recorded their children with Indian "chiefs." On the western end of the park, tourists circled the Cades Cove loop road, where open land met a backdrop of mountains. As one journalist put it, the Smokies helped "Americans satisfy their growing desire for the out-of-doors." Another claimed: "Here you can have your cake and eat it too. You can have both automobile roads and wilderness trails." Or, as *National Geographic* declared, this was "drive-in nature," because only 6 percent of the visitors actually took to the trails on foot.[3]

In the decade of "Gunsmoke" and Korea, McCarthy and *The Man in the Gray Flannel Suit*, Great Smoky Mountains National Park succeeded beyond its founders' wildest dreams. Across America after the war, GIs came home, got married, started a baby boom, bought cars, and took to the road to see national parks on their vacations. Between 1941 and 1952, visitation in the Smokies nearly doubled; in 1954, the park drew 2.4 million tourists. As the founders predicted, proximity to major metropolitan areas soon made the Smokies the Yellowstone of the East. Families who got out of their cars, not surprisingly, wanted to pursue activities like those found in western parks. "Mountain climbing, horseback riding, walking, motoring, swimming, boating and fishing will ever be the favorite sports" in national parks, an early NPS memorandum stated. "All sports within the safeguards thrown around the national parks by law, should be heartily endorsed and aided wherever possible."[4]

Despite this enthusiasm, the war years brought a serious decrease in funding and man-hours to the NPS, with the loss of the CCC and the drop in the federal work week (forty-eight to forty-four and finally down to forty hours). The Fontana controversy also weakened political support for funding. Smokies Superintendent Edward Hummel believed that "conditions were desperate." At the same time that the park enjoyed the success its founders desired, the rangers couldn't serve the burgeoning numbers of tourists. "These people want to spend less money for sleeping and eating accommodations. They want to camp in the park. This means we need to increase our camping facilities," Hummel declared. "We're having a hard time keeping the facilities in line with the demand." With similar situations in the other national parks, NPS Director Conrad Wirth sought a special meeting with President Eisenhower to gain more support. After showing a film of the overcrowded facilities nationwide, he said, "What we have just seen is a plant operating at 200 percent capacity. How long would a business concern continue to operate its plant at a 100 percent overload? If it is to stay in business, it must plan and develop for the demand ahead." Eisenhower pledged funds for Mission 66, a ten-year construction program aimed at improving facilities in the national parks by the agency's fiftieth anniversary in 1966 (or "everything fixed by '66," as rangers put it). In the Smokies, Superintendent Hummel claimed that this "conservation program," as he called it, would produce the Foothills Parkway, paralleling the northern side of the park; two new visitor centers, improvements on Newfound Gap Road, a tower on Clingmans Dome, expansion of Smokemont campground, housing for employees, four new campgrounds, the Roaring Fork-Cherokee Orchard road near Gatlinburg, and utility facilities. The NPS deemed that land should be "preserved for all time unimpaired to be made available for the enjoyment of the people," said Hummel. He paused, catching the apparent contradiction: "[reconciling] the two things [has] been one of our major headaches ever since."[5]

At a Knoxville Rotary meeting, the superintendent went on to point out another reason that the Smokies, in particular, should be the special recipient of Mission 66 funds. The Smokies had more need for employees, according to Hummel, because of its continual problems with local residents. Visitors who came hundreds of miles in their automobiles sometimes picked flowers illegally, Hummel stated, but primarily local fishermen broke the rules by going over their limits or fishing in forbidden streams. Most of the vandals who carved their initials on the trees, cut trees for firewood, and wrote their names on Appalachian Trail (AT) shelters were "locals," he claimed. Most of the car wrecks, he scolded, were caused by "motorists who know how to drive in the mountains." He did not mention, however, that park problems with area residents resulted from the park's history and attitudes like his. To lighten the mood, Hummel concluded that wildlife could be as much of a problem to enforcement as the nearby mountain people. "And that includes the bears," he said. "They often break the signs."[6]

Despite these special problems, Hummel seemed confident that a projected 4 million visitors by 1966 would guarantee the park an unending stream of federal money. He quoted a travel study by the North Carolina and Tennessee State Highway departments that reported 94 percent of all park visitors came through Smokemont campground and Gatlinburg, Tennessee. "The prospect of additional traffic volume poured onto the already over-laden road system within the park would be discouraging if it were not that proposed construction will open new areas," researchers agreed. Visitors spent $4.5 million in the area in 1955, $1.6 million in North Carolina and $2.9 million in Tennessee. A closer look at the funding, however, revealed that Gatlinburg alone brought in $2.4 million, making it the premier gateway city. How visitors viewed the Smokies would be shaped a great deal by what they saw on their way into this northern entrance. And those who came in through Smokemont primarily spent money in Cherokee, the Qualla Boundary of the Eastern Band, where tourists could have a unique cultural encounter before facing the "wilderness" in their Fords and Chevrolets. Overwhelmingly, these travelers on their way to discover America came for (in this order) the scenery, wildlife, climate, and "nature study." They believed that the area did not have enough restaurants, lodges, or other tourist accommodations, but they did not go away disappointed. In the words of a popular guide to the area: "Here one may temporarily forget the woes of a war-torn world, or think things through, get a better perspective, a truer sense of values, gain inner peace and fortitude, and meet tomorrow's problems and the tasks ahead."[7]

A well-informed naturalist and gifted writer such as Harvey Broome knew that the Smokies could not be called a forest as primeval as the one that greeted Hernando de Soto. He might agree that a hike brought "inner peace and fortitude," but he understood the Smokies as a forest in recovery. He was *not* a motorist-tourist; rather, he got out of his car to investigate firsthand everything from the "inhumanly beautiful wizardry of winter" to the azaleas on Gregory Bald in June, those "ranks of spiked, claret buds." Even Harvey Broome, though, could not help drawing comparisons to the West. He found the "sawtooth zone of evergreens" in the spruce-fir zone reminiscent of the High Sierras of California. Like those who promoted wilderness in the western states, he saw a restored Smokies as part of a lost Eden, so that an encounter with wild turkeys became "a thrilling glimpse of a prodigal past." To describe his experiences in the Smokies, he quoted photographer Ansel Adams, a lifelong advocate for the national parks: "The earth promises to be more than a battlefield or a hunting-ground; we dream of the time when it shall house one great family of cooperative beings." Above Cades Cove, Broome marveled at "massive hay fields . . . so far-reaching they reminded us of western meadows." As he gazed across the mowed valley, Broome continued his reverie: "Here on a Sabbath, with the noisy tractors tucked away in the barns, the Cove was the embodiment of peace and harmony between man and nature."[8]

The coalition of preservationists, such as Broome, and promoters of tourism, such as the auto clubs, that created Great Smoky Mountains National Park still agreed on a few things in the postwar years. They agreed that Cades Cove, with its pioneer ranch-like appearance, depicted an ideal in American heritage. They agreed that the vistas from open balds, such as Spence Field and Gregory Bald, provided scenic views that cleansed the spirit. They wanted to listen to Gatlinburg resident Wiley Oakley, the "Will Rogers of the Smokies," tell stories of a simpler lifestyle. They wanted the unique cultural experience provided by an Indian reservation. In short, this unlikely consensus, developers and preservationists, for a few decades still agreed on what a national park should look like: as Smokies Superintendent Hummel put it, "the idea of a national park originated in . . . Yellowstone."

Horsy Concessions

In the West, where cattle ranching forged settlement, horseback riding became a historical tradition. For this reason, it was promoted as a national park activity, and, in turn, Smokies entertainment. Although some tourists in the early part of the century rode horses, mountain people did not trail ride for recreation. Most families could afford only to feed one horse—the plow horse—and reserved riding for special occasions, such as courting a wife. Park founders brought the idea of trail riding to Mount LeConte in August 1924. A commission appointed by the secretary of the Interior visited the area to determine whether the Smokies could be considered scenic enough to become a national park. The party rode on horseback from Gatlinburg up LeConte Creek Valley to about 1 1/2 miles above Cherokee Orchard, where the existing trail became impassable for horses. On foot they proceeded up the Rainbow Falls trail, newly cut by mountain guide Wiley Oakley, down to Alum Cave and then to Grassy Patch, where the wrangler met them with horses for the ride back to Gatlinburg. David Chapman, leader of the Tennessee promoters, gave the wrangler poor instructions, though, so the group spent a sleepless and supperless night on the mountain huddled around a campfire, until a logger rescued them. Of course, the commission enthusiastically recommended what surely must have seemed like a primitive wilderness for national park designation.[9]

Soon after the NPS took over the land, officials opened the door for horseback riding concessionaires, private companies to lease land for running this western recreational activity. The same year that Eakin arrived to manage the Smokies, an early travel writer reported that "horseback riding is one of the pleasantest diversions offered to visitors in Gatlinburg." In Cataloochee, an Atlanta man and his wife, Tom and Judy Alexander, leased the Preacher Hall place at the lower end of the valley for trail rides in 1932. "For me, the craving of the mountains is an incurable disease," wrote Tom Alexander, "comparable to the craving for whiskey by an alcoholic." As they built their concession, Alexander and his wife well remembered the Cataloochee removal: "It was heart-rending to see these excellent families, some crying, with their household goods piled in wagons, leaving their beautiful valley."[10] Nevertheless, Alexander funded development of his ranch by working for the CCC, and the assistant chief ranger accompanied the first Cataloochee Trail Riders trip in 1935, providing both natural history information and instructions on how to pack horses for a mountain excursion. The NPS even loaned Alexander several saddles, and, in fact, continued to do so for the rest of the decade.[11]

Although Superintendent Hummel stated that most park management problems came from local people, he had reason to know better. One of the most persistent problems for Hummel, and his predecessor, John Preston, were the concessionaires. Alexander, and the first superintendent, Eakin, early on became irritated with each other. Both men told different stories, but the minor nature of the insults would seem to indicate a personality conflict. In 1937, for example, Eakin criticized Alexander for breaking park rules by walking his fox terrier, unleashed, to Mount Leconte. Alexander resented the reprimand and wrote an angry letter to the superintendent. He received another reproach from the superintendent for plowing a field without auhorization. The same year, Eakin complained that Alexander did not submit concession reports, even after repeated reminders. Because the Atlanta man bitterly griped about the park to his customers, Eakin eventually feared that he was "poisoning the minds of visitors against the National Park Service." This proved too much for Tom Alexander. He moved out of the park and established Cataloochee Ranch adjacent to the park, though he continued to borrow pack saddles. "After five generally happy years at Cataloochee," he recalled, "we too grew increasingly hampered by Park Service restrictions and the year-by-year lease arrangement that discouraged us from improving and enlarging Cataloochee Ranch."[12]

After several years in Florida, Alexander returned to buy a new ranch adjacent to the national park. In 1938, 1942, and 1944 he requested that all the trails in the vicinity of his ranch be improved. They were. In 1940 he requested that truck trails be improved to permit him to bring his supply trucks over Cabin Flats, Walnut Bottoms, Cataloochee, and Round Bottom Roads. They were. The following year, he broke the lock on the Mount Sterling fire tower cistern to supply his horses with water.

An involved correspondence followed, wherein Alexander claimed he needed water, and the park developed an alternative source for him. For their part, rangers grew dissatisfied with Alexander and his demands. They claimed that he took too many horses on one trip, cut trees for tent poles, mocked the park service while rangers talked to his guests for free, served bear steak suppers to his guests within the park, and sprayed DDT on yellow jacket nests in the paths of horses. Superintendents Eakin, Blair Ross, and John Preston all complained to the park service about the demands Alexander made on the park maintenance staff. They also noted that the ubiquitous trail riders made muddy ruts in the centers of the trails; to avoid the ruts, riders went around, widening the trails.[13]

Surrounding Tom Alexander's Cataloochee Ranch on lands also adjoining the park, some twenty-one property owners raised cattle and sheep. They frequently complained about bears stealing their animals. During the 1940s, sixteen of the twenty-one owners estimated they lost 59 cattle and 159 sheep to bears. Fewer than half of the owners said that the situation grew "worse each year"; the others found that by moving their stock to lower pastures, stalling them at night, using vigilant herders, or erecting electric fences the problem could be eliminated. All of the Cataloochee farmers told ranger Mark Hannah, who had grown up in Cataloochee himself, that they would cooperate with the park service to control killer bears by live-trapping and relocation. One man, an employee of Alexander's, stated that all bears should be outlawed. When asked if it would help to have a twelve-month bear hunting season on the mile-wide strip adjoining the park, all the landowners objected because "dogs would kill more stock than bears."[14]

On May 24, 1952, a group of Cataloochee Ranch trail riders noticed the carcass of a red-and-white heifer near Purchase Knob. The heifer, owned by farmer Dick Moody, appeared to have been killed by a bear, because bruins will typically hide a carcass for a return visit. Something or someone killed the heifer, dragged it into the park, and covered it with leaves. Without contacting park officials, Alexander ordered his employees to place steel traps around the carcass on park property. The next morning the carcass and traps lay untouched, but a 500-pound steer lay dead about 300 yards from the park boundary. "I decided to take some dogs and hunters and to pursue and kill the bear," Alexander said, knowing that hunting was forbidden in the park. When a ranger later asked why he didn't call Superintendent Preston or rangers stationed in Cata-loochee, he said, "I didn't have time and it wouldn't have done any good to call you . . . I took the law into my own hands."

Thirteen men, including Alexander, followed the bear's tracks with dogs along Snaggy Ridge and downhill toward Caldwell Fork. When the hunters finally confronted the bear, every member of the party shot it. "The bear was shot 18 or 20 times before it was killed," Alexander said. "All the shooting was done under my instructions." When they returned to Cataloochee Ranch, the owner cut up the bear and divided it into eigh-teen portions. To the amazement of the assistant chief ranger, who visited the ranch the next morning, Alexander assumed full responsibility for the action taken by the hunters and his employees.[15]

Superintendent Preston filed charges against the owner of Cataloochee Ranch.[16] Because of his straightforward defiance of the federal govern-ment, Alexander became a hero to some. When publicity on the event reached a national audience, people from as far away as New Jersey wrote Superintendent Preston on behalf of Alexander. "We like Tom Alexander and have known him for years," Preston responded to one letter writer. "We do not seek to persecute him nor any person, but have simply charged him with a violation of the law." At a meeting Preston called to help area farmers, the North Carolina Department of Conservation agreed to hire a man to patrol the southeastern boundary of the park to prevent bears from stalking stock. If he discovered an attack or its imme-diate aftermath he would "summarily kill the bear." If the bear retreated into the park, federal employees and state game wardens would pursue it. Despite these efforts, the case further crept into the national conscious-ness through an article in the *Saturday Evening Post*, "Bears Are No Good," depicting noble farmers defending life and limb from rapidly multiplying bears, which attacked property at will. Director of the NPS Arthur Demaray wrote a disapproving letter to the editor of the *Saturday Evening Post*, calling the article "a vicious attack on American wildlife and the principles of the national park program." In the midst of the furor, however, Demaray moved Preston to Yosemite and brought in Edward Hummel, superintendent of Colonial National Historical Park in York-town, Virginia, where he was popular with the local residents.[17]

When the trial finally took place in November 1952, the *defense* curi-ously refused to seat any jury member from Haywood County. "[Alexander's] refusal to take the stand and his actions in the past month would indicate that the great crusade he started on was not the vehicle he thought it would be," said the chief ranger. The men who went on the hunt testified that they had no knowledge of who killed the bear—they all shot into the bear at once. No one denied Alexander's participation. Alexander's attorney closed with the biblical story of David the shepherd protecting his sheep. "If a man can protect property from a thief why cannot a man protect property from a wild animal," reasoned the defense. The prosecution pointed out that Alexander was "an old friend" but that nevertheless he "was as guilty as he could be." The judge carefully instructed the jury—ten white men, one African-American man, and one woman, all "well-to-do folk" from the Asheville area—to remember that however one's sympathies lay, the case hinged on whether a man had taken the law into his own hands. The jury hung twice, after heated arguments that echoed loudly down the hallway. Finally, the jury acquitted Alexander. The North Carolina State News Bureau reported that "newspaper readers and radio listeners from coast to coast agreed that acquittal of Tom Alexander on the charge of killing a Great Smoky bear made a happy ending to a celebrated case."[18]

The next week, Alexander visited the NPS regional director in Richmond, Virginia. "You fellows sort of tried to put the bee on me, didn't you?" he taunted the director. "There had been an open and flagrant violation of the regulation and we had no course than to take the action which we did," replied the official, stiffly. Alexander advanced two proposals: first, regulations should be revised to permit the killing of bears to protect livestock; second, Alexander should be appointed deputy warden to patrol the boundary for killer bears. When the official pointed out the new policy for protecting wildlife, Alexander wrote state Senator Willis Smith, asking him to intervene and pressure the park to meet these demands. "We ask for the simple right to immediately pursue the killer bear ourselves and destroy him, in the park if necessary," Alexander said, and he got support from a state senator. "The National Park is a wildlife sanctuary by law and by public desire, and hunting of any species or individual animals will nullify this status," the director countered. "We feel that any move to abrogate this sanctuary status would be highly undesirable and that it would be violently opposed by many persons."[19]

Relations with Cataloochee Ranch under subsequent superintendents remained difficult. Alexander had pulled several trump cards, and it had cost John Preston his position. In 1961, Alexander reported that a bear killed some of his cattle. When rangers investigated, they found three dead cattle, two killed by "black leg" and the third gnawed by a bear. A veterinarian informed the rangers that the cause of the death of the third cow could not be determined. Bears finished off what remained of the cattle, as no one buried them, and rangers refused to hunt down the bear. Both parties remained dissatisfied with the situation.[20]

Surely the 1950s public loved national parks, but pleasing that public proved no small task. Folks wanted horseback riding and trails, and concessions to serve those activities, but the protection of bears fell second to this. As much as the public longed for a wilderness experience, they did not, to give another example, want to see poisonous snakes. Throughout the first three decades of the park's history, rangers and maintenance men continued the extermination of poisonous snakes—in the Smokies, timber rattlesnakes and copperheads—initiated in the CCC years. Predatory mammals theoretically achieved protection in the national parks in 1931, but this did not help the vipers.[21] As Preston and future superintendents discovered, tourists proved fickle taskmasters.

Who Killed the Brookies?

Another western experience tourists came to expect in the Smokies was trout-fishing. In a region known for slow-moving rivers and catfish, visitors could see cold rushing streams like a creek in Wyoming. Praising the rainbow trout, local tourism bureaus attracted anglers, and the park service accommodated them. Because of heavy turn-of-the-century logging, however, this did not prove an easy task: the streams required stocking in order for the trout population to recover.

Superintendent Eakin consulted scientists during the 1930s for help with the trout problem. Because water snakes mined the trout-rearing ponds, he and many fishermen felt convinced that they must hurt fishing in the park. Eakin, along with wildlife technician Willis King, instructed rangers in the dispatching of all water snakes. Fishermen strongly approved of this policy, in fact, even put pressure on the NPS to continue. "This past year more than 200,000 small trout were planted and we hope this year to plant at least an equal number," said M. G. Thomas, president of the Tennessee Federation of Sportsmen, "but I say very frankly to you unless the snakes are held in complete subjection, it will do no good whatsoever for us to continue to spend our money, the state's money, and the government's money for this purpose." The Knoxville chapter of the Izaak Walton League expressed similar concerns about wasting its money to feed water snakes. The NPS sent Dr. Harold Bryant from the Washington Wildlife Division to investigate the situation. Bryant could understand controlling snakes in the vicinity of trout-rearing ponds, but he reminded everyone that "water snakes are a natural element of the fauna" and that the fundamental purpose of the NPS was that of "protecting all native forms of wildlife." Skeptical that trout represented even a small portion of the snakes' diets, he left the door open for predator control. Based on his report, Demaray ordered the destruction of 500 water snakes in order to examine their stomachs. As rangers set about killing snakes, they probably looked the other way when fishermen took matters into their own hands.[22] Did water snakes really have anything to do with the trout mystery? With brown, tan, gray, or red bands along its body, the northern water snake, the most common species in the Smokies, appeared menacing enough. *Neorodia sipedon* presents no hazard to human beings, yet members of this species strike and bite (without venom) if cornered or seized. They feed largely on salamanders and fish, but young water snakes also provide food for larger fish. Today, scientists think they especially improve the health of trout populations by feeding on diseased or stunted fish.[23]

Despite water snake control efforts and stocking, trout streams in the Smokies did not quickly recover under protection as expected. Particularly disturbing became the brook trout, whose range didn't improve at all. Before corporate logging devastated the streams, brook trout thrived in nearly every stream above 2,000 feet in elevation. Robert Burrows, a biologist who surveyed Great Smoky Mountains watersheds in 1935, concluded that "there is some doubt regarding the amount of natural reproduction in these streams." At best, he estimated that the brook trout retreated to streams above 3,000 feet, which translated into a total loss of more than 160 miles of range in thirty years. "It will probably be necessary to stock quite heavily," he said, and recommended brook trout for small headwater streams and rainbows for nearly all of the other streams. The following summer 50,143 brook and rainbow trout were "planted" in park streams.[24]

In his reports, wildlife technician Willis King did not blame the water snakes. Increasingly, though, he worried about "fishing" as a possible cause of the poor brook trout's demise. This could be disastrous, as fishing promoted the sacred cow, visitation. King recommend a step-up in the annual stocking program to help the trout: approximately 400,000 4- to 6-inch trout per year; rainbows below 3,000 feet, and brook trout above.[25] His plan seemed to work, as opening day in 1941 brought record crowds from all over the country. The superintendent even agreed to a temporary campground in Elkmont to accommodate the hordes. At the close of the season, rangers planted an additional 208,960 fish in the park stream—but only 95,115 brook trout.

The most heavily stocked fish in the park, rainbow trout, or "California fish" as some of the locals called them, had become a popular game fish from coast to coast. Unlike the native brookies, rainbows hailed from the western states. Under supervision of the wildlife technician, CCC enrollees first took rainbow fingerlings in 10-gallon milk cans and 55-gallon drums from Kephart Prong, Cades Cove, and Chimneys rearing pools to the streams. Rainbows multiplied in the protected streams; anglers followed the fish. In July 1942, a leaseholder caught a 21-inch rain-bow weighing 3 3/4 pounds in Abrams Creek. Every year, the number of anglers grew. On opening day in 1953, park rangers spent the entire day directing traffic. "I've never seen anything like it," said park ranger Ralph Shaver, mopping his brow. "Planted fish were much in evidence," the *Knoxville Journal* reported. "Results of the heavy stocking of park rangers showed up everywhere."[26]

While sportfishing improved with the rainbows, the brookies still did not fare so well. After more than three decades of stocking and reforestation, the brook trout range actually *declined* another 15 percent. Scientists were baffled: protection supposedly improved conditions for both wildlife and tourists. They began to fear that fishermen indeed created the real problem. Trying to put a positive light on what they thought might be an overfishing problem, park officials lowered creel limits and planned a catch-and-release program. They designated certain streams for sportfishing only; tourists could bring the brook trout out of the water, but they were obligated to set them back in the water. "Fishing for Fun," as the NPS dubbed the program, began in 1954 in the West Prong of the Little Pigeon River in Tennessee and Bradley Fork in North Carolina. The literature for this project, part of a national program to relieve overfishing in the national parks, emphasized that "a trout is too highly prized to be caught only once." After the first experiment, rangers pronounced the program a "big success" and extended it to two additional streams in 1958. However, the thrill seemed to pass quickly, particularly for tourists. Superintendent Fred Overly estimated that 95 percent of the participants by the 1960s were locals, and that didn't help the trout situation enough. He told the Region One director of the NPS that his rangers were "trying to make it work" but perhaps "more regulations would be necessary." [27]

To further improve fishing opportunities, park managers decided to "restore" two streams crowded with "rough" fish. Since ALCOA completed the Chilhowee Dam, carp and other fish undesirable for tourism had migrated into the lower sections of Abrams Creek and Indian Creek, tributaries of the 1,690-acre lake. The Tennessee Game and Fish Commission and the U.S. Fish and Wildlife Service (USFWS) met with NPS managers to discuss improving game fish opportunities in Cades Cove, along the 14.6-mile section above Chilhowee Lake. Using a method previously experimented with in lakes and ponds, state biologists wanted to poison the "rough" fish from the creek and introduce rainbow trout. As official documents put it, "reclamation with rotenone is feasible and practical." Preliminary tests showed that just about everything but goldfish could be killed in a five-hour exposure of 4 parts per million (ppm) of PRO-NOXFISH, the poison's brand name.

And so, in April 1957 biologists released canisters of rotenone in 5 ppm on a 7.5-mile stretch of Indian Creek for an hour, then decreased the dosage to 1 ppm for five hours. In June the scientists used PRO-NOXFISH to poison a 14.6-mile stretch of Abrams Creek. Official documents stated that the poison left "no survivors." The USFWS took measures to keep black bear from feasting on the dead poisoned fish, but forty-seven known fish species died in the experiment, including the spotfin chub and the smoky mountain madtom. The latter may have become an endangered species because of this project. In July, the park planted 1,000 legal-sized rainbow trout and 12,000 fingerling brookies into Indian Creek, now "cleaned" of other fish species.[28] Soon thereafter, 2,400 adult rainbows were released into Abrams Creek, followed by an additional 30,800 fingerlings. One year later the park service declared reclamation a big success. Rainbow, in particular, had achieved such a strong position that the superintendent canceled restocking that next fall. "The results obtained in the reclamation of Indian Creek and Abrams Creek demonstrate conclusively that populations of preferred game fish can be restored or established quickly and practically in streams by eliminating rough and competitive species," claimed the chief of Appalachian Sport Fishery Investigations with the USFWS.[29]

Despite these pronouncements, the brook trout continued to lose ground. Several veteran fishermen suspected that the park's own policies hurt the native brook trout. Although research had yet to prove it, rainbow trout compete with the native brook trout for stream habitat. Rainbow and brookies can live in the same pool, but brookies tend to stay along the sides, facing downstream; rainbows swim in the turbulent water near the heads of pools. Brook trout spawn in the fall and hatch in February or March. Rainbows, in contrast, spawn and hatch in the spring, but by the fall they catch up to the brookies in size. In one year, rainbows reach adulthood, 2 to 3 inches longer and 1.8 times heavier than the average adult brook trout. With a higher reproductive rate and larger size, rainbows gain an advantage in competition for mayflies, stone flies, and caddis flies. As the park stocked rainbows, the bigger fish gradually crowded out the brookies, forcing them above natural barriers or headwaters.

The first researcher to suspect the rainbows was Robert Lennon of the USFWS. To verify his hunch, Lennon proposed removing all the rainbow from Ramsey Prong and Indian Creek and stocking them with brook trout, but records do not show whether this experiment was carried out.[30] Meanwhile, trout-fishing continued to be one of the park's big attractions; creel census work showed a catch rate per hour of 2.7 fish, with brook trout being a little easier to catch than rainbows. Hazel Creek, which flowed into Fontana Lake, became famous for rainbow trout. Although a dozen streams in the park had comparable fishing, anglers who took boats across Fontana Lake to gain access to the remote area associated this trek with better fishing.[31]

Despite stocking, and even "reclamation" efforts on Abrams Creek and Indian Creek, brook trout kept vanishing. The accelerated road-building completed under Superintendent George Fry may have released the acidic Anakeesta formation into park watersheds, worsening the situation. Robert Lennon surveyed the brook trout situation again in 1967. "Brook trout are scarce," he concluded, "found only in remote, headwater streams." Official NPS fish policy in 1936 stated: "In waters where the introduction of exotic species threatens extinction of native species in an entire national park or monument area, such plantings should be discontinued and every effort made to restore the native species to its normal status."[32] As late as 1971, the park still planted 20,700 rainbow trout in twenty-seven streams. "Any increase in exploitation of the brook trout in the Park or damaging alterations of the habitat might have serious consequences for the remnant populations," Lennon warned. Because of the popularity of fishing, especially in Abrams Creek and on the Little River, stocking continued on these streams until 1975. Until a superintendent challenged the primacy of tourism, the park muddled forward, stocking rainbows and making the problem worse.[33]

How far would the park go to please the public? In 1957, the owner of a Knoxville soft drink company and his son-in-law tried to build a $1 million chairlift from Cherokee Orchard to Mount LeConte. Although skiing, too, hailed from the West, Charles M. Brown said he wanted to shoulder the entire expense of chairlift construction just so "more people could see Mt. LeConte." The park rejected Brown's humanitarian offer, as did the Great Smoky Mountains Conservation Association. "Much damage has already been done to the flora on the summit of Mt. Leconte by the hikers and backpackers who go to that great vantage point," a GSMCA official said. Then he suggested, "If a chair lift is needed, why not build one to the top of the ridge just across the river from upper Gatlinburg? This is outside the park and no permission of the Park Service would be needed." And so in 1958, Gatlinburg got its first ski lift, and soon thereafter, its own ski resort. Following another trend in western tourism, ski clubs sponsored Austrian instructors to help Atlanta and Chattanooga residents learn how to tackle this new recreational activity. Never mind that snow rarely stayed more than a week in the South: "in the meantime, the operators have turned on the snowmaking machines," according to the *Chattanooga Times*. Self-proclaimed gateway to Great Smoky Mountains National Park, Gatlinburg (or the "Cinderella City," as one historian dubbed it) cashed in on 1950s notions of mountain wilderness. The park followed this lead.[34]

Gateway America

Recreating the East in the image of the West did not originate solely with the NPS. Gateway developers in Gatlinburg and Cherokee pushed the image they thought America would buy. An estimated 40 percent of the 3.2 million visitors to Great Smoky Mountains National Park in 1959 passed through Gatlinburg, Tennessee, which developers designed to look like an Aspen-style Swiss village. More than one-third came through Cherokee, on the North Carolina side of the park. Here, they could see plastic Plains Indian crafts made in Japan, a white version of Cherokee history, or a small building with genuine exhibits. Travel writers, visiting both cities, called the Native Americans and the native white mountaineers "living memorials to the past."[35]

Appropriately, the village of Gatlinburg got its name from an enterprising nineteenth-century storeowner, Radford Gatlin, who offered to house the post office if residents changed the name of the town from White Oak Flats. Although it remained a farming community until the national park came along, at the turn of the century the village attracted northern philanthropists, who wanted to teach mountain children to read and write and to improve family health care practices. The ambitious founders of the Pi Beta Phi School eventually hoped to teach mountain women how to regain skills, such as spinning and weaving, employed by their grandmothers.[36] When the national park became a reality and tourism a viable economy, local women actually became interested in their roots, and they crowded into classes where they could learn to weave coverlets and make baskets to sell. Their husbands and fathers learned to carve and whittle for tourists, who wanted quaint regional goods. Although Sevier County residents continued farming until the 1960s, craftwork became a popular way to earn extra money. During the 1930s and 1940s county extension programs pushed craft instruction as well, funded by a federal program intended to make mountain people more "independent." Ironically, one federal agency, the NPS, believed that mountain people would be better off leaving their farms; another federal agency, the U.S. Department of Agriculture (USDA), encouraged them to "Live at Home." Such contradictory images of Appalachia permeated U.S. government policy.[37]

In the early years of the park, a few local people found new work serving as guides for tourists. Four men who had grown up in the area—Will Ramsey, Wiley Oakley, Arthur Ogle, and Blake Carver—were "much in demand" as they would provide a homey commentary on the woods along with a hike or trail ride. Wiley Oakley became the unofficial "town character" of Gatlinburg, because of his honesty and colorful descriptions. As his daughter, Lucinda Ogle, recalled, "He was the type that would fascinate you with everything, like one time we was up on Clingmans Dome with a group and they said, 'Wiley, what's beyond them mountains.' He said, 'I don't know. Them mountains just keep on keeping on.' He was descriptive. If he didn't know the name of something, he'd give it a name." Oakley reputedly coined the name hearts-a-bustin' for a shrub with a bright red, heart-shaped flower. His humor and colorful speech made him such a popular guide that women's groups from Knoxville would call to make appointments ("Mama'd send me along to keep his reputation," Ogle said.). His autobiography, called *Roamin' and Restin'*, provides memorable descriptions of life in Gatlinburg before tourism: "I like to hear the water trinkling down the mountain all night long so I can sleep well and in the morning hear the chickens crowing for day light to come and then I know there is another new day in the early break of light." It also shows that Oakley understood tourism was rapidly changing the character of the farming community: "now bringing you up to the minute Gatlinburg is gitting to be a buisy place and two many people thrashing the streets all the time." Wiley Oakley did not stay a poor man, however poor his spelling habits—as his son Harvey said, "We owned half them mountains up in there. He divided it all up among the kids."[38]

Other local entrepreneurs expanded on the pioneer color and native craft theme. E. L. Reagan, a longtime resident of the area, opened his own fine furniture shop, specializing in cherry, walnut, and maple creations. In 1941 Alan Stalcup, a North Carolina man, moved to the area and opened Stalcup Industries, which employed women and girls weaving purses and other basketry for his three shops. A former Oak Ridge scientist, Douglas Ferguson, opened Pigeon Forge Pottery, and soon the area developed a national reputation for crafts and pioneer culture. During the 1950s, many tourists came to the mountains to glimpse what they viewed as American frontier heritage, and some believed that that heritage was white. "Gatlinburg is unique due to the fact that it is almost a 100 percent American community," wrote one chronicler of this native handcrafts boom in 1960. "Here exists the purest strain of Anglo-Saxon stock to be found anywhere in America. There are no negro families; only a few residents of foreign birth."[39]

Until the 1980s, land in Gatlinburg stayed in relatively few hands. Most of it, in fact, can be traced to Andrew Huff, Stephen Whaley, and Charles Ogle Sr. Andy Huff established the first hotel, the Mountain View, in 1916, later enlarged by his son, Jack. Stephen Whaley ran the commercial apple orchard, Cherokee Orchard; after he sold it to the park, he opened a successful boarding house in town. He and his oldest son, Dick Whaley, built the Riverside and Greystone Hotels; when the town incorporated in 1945, Dick Whaley served as the first mayor. Whaley, in particular, felt strongly about retaining as much Gatlinburg land as possible in local hands and merely leasing to outsiders. "How can anybody determine what this land is worth when it isn't for sale at any price?" Whaley explained, although the lease arrangements also made him wealthy and kept the family in control. All three men traded on Gatlinburg's frontier image. "Anyone meeting Huff in the lobby of his Mountain View hotel today," wrote a reporter in 1953, "would hardly think of him as having played a major role in developing the multi-million dollar tourist business which sweeps in a mighty flood over the once-sleepy little town of Gatlinburg." By all accounts, these families had a great deal to say about the direction tourism took in the community and even the superintendents the park hired.[40]

After park visitation for a single year—1950—topped 2 million, Gatlinburg elites became more intent on attracting tourist dollars. They hired a professional manager for the chamber of commerce and sponsored billboards as far away as Rockefeller Center calling Gatlinburg "Gateway to the Smokies." Although the themes of "mountain hospitality" and "cool mountain air" dominated brochures and the city still sponsored events that included women dressed in homespun and men in plaid shirts, the members of the new City Advertising Department had bigger plans. They had already captured the craft theme from nearby Townsend and Cosby; they had already topped Cherokee as the premier gateway. They wanted to bring bigger money to Gatlinburg: conventions. With this in mind, the more rustic boarding houses of the 1920s and 1930s in Gatlinburg gave way to a Swiss-village image. Another import from the western states, faux Bavarian architecture and ski chalets—even the name, with "burg" at the end—fit 1950s ideals of what a visit to a mountain wilderness should include.

Journalists quickly caught on. Gatlinburg in the 1950s was "a clean, new city that looks as if it has just been built and is waiting to be dedicated," declared the travel editor for the *Orlando Sentinel*.[41] Another writer hailed "the new Gatlinburg, conscious that it has a precious inheritance to share with touring Americans, has modernized its facilities for feeding and housing guests." This writer even seemed to understand the importance of playing down the rustic aspect of the frontier image. "The so-oft presented picture of these people as fiddlin' and feudin' hillbillies is correct only to a fractional degree," she wrote. "In reality, they are a people with a certain aristocratic bearing, with an ancient and honorable background, and a philosophy that places a high premium upon simplicity and serenity." A *Philadelphia Inquirer* reporter seemed a little more cynical about this hillbilly/frontier image. "And how are these mountaineers doing?" he asked. "Well, a lot of them are vacationing now down in Miami and the rest of them are polishing up fleets of Cadillacs and adding new wings to their luxury hotels in preparation for next summer's business. If these are hill people—and they sure enough are—they've outslickered the slickers from the flat lands in one of the most bodacious places in the country."[42]

The winding road from Sevierville into Gatlinburg followed the Little Pigeon River and crossed one-lane bridges, but it soon became plastered with busy signs, advertising everything from paint to snuff. "Gatlinburg has lost its native charm by cheap commercial development, no zoning, and no roadside planning," said a city planner from Virginia, prophetically. Within a week, however, Carlos Campbell, one of the park founders, wrote a letter to the *Knoxville Journal* defending the city: "NPS officials have said repeatedly that so long as adequate accommodations are provided outside the park, no commercial development will occur in the park." In other words, keep building so the park won't have to become tacky. After the profusion of signs, a 1950s visitor came around the corner to see new, taller hotels—the Gatlinburg Inn, the French Village, the Mountain View, the Greystone, and the New Riverside—suddenly appear. "There are 1400 people in this place . . . and they've built themselves an $11 million town, corralled most of the people who stream into the Smokies at the rate of two million a year and set up just about everything a body could want," said Oliver Crawford, the *Philadelphia Inquirer* reporter. Crawford did not exaggerate the dollars coming into Gatlinburg, but the number of local residents able to afford Miami vacations would have been small. Less than half of all women in the area and less than two-thirds of the men found employment year-round, and seasonal unemployment could zoom to 14 percent. For those who did not own hotels, higher-paying jobs could still be found in agriculture.[43]

Elite landowners in the middle of the valley sat on a gold mine. The number of buildings in Gatlinburg jumped from 641 in 1942 to 1,114 in 1956; the number of businesses doubled. In 1956, Gatlinburg got its first convention center, and the following year, a country club. When Bruce Whaley remodeled the Riverside in 1953, he called it "southern mansion style" with tall porch columns; in truth, it was a combination of stone, stucco, glass, and heavy timber that Americans associated with informal but expensive ski chalets. "The death knell of quaintness," historian Ed Trout quipped, "was probably best manifest by the new ordinance prohibiting 'the keeping of chickens or other domestic fowl within 300 feet of any public eating place.'"

Not to be outdone by the local developers, the park used Mission 66 funds to create a drive-in wilderness just outside the city. In 1963, construction began on a connecting spur between Cherokee Orchard and Roaring Fork Roads to form a loop motorway. The 5.3-mile spur was 10 feet wide with no shoulders, so that it would accommodate only slow, one-way traffic. Construction crews were instructed to avoid straightening the twists and turns so that the motor road would follow the natural terrain as much as possible. "We look at it as an automobile nature trail," said Superintendent Fred Overly. "On this new road we are making an effort to keep the natural wilderness as much as possible." Of course, Overly noted, it would also help the economy of Gatlinburg.[44]

By 1963 the Smokies drew 5.2 million visitors, and the Gatlinburg city limits expanded to incorporate 2,000 acres including 47 restaurants, 73 swimming pools, 153 motels, and 13,000 beds. Loyal tourists from previous decades, who wanted to listen to Wiley Oakley's stories or meet real mountain people, were turned off by the new Gatlinburg—their complaints were lost, however, in the din of cash registers. In fact, researcher Jerome Dobson posited that early Gatlinburg growth (1930–1967) closely followed park visitation—hence the frontier and chalet themes were at least related to the mountains—whereas later growth had more to do with Gatlinburg itself as a place to go. In 1967, a *Chicago Tribune* travel writer still called Gatlinburg "one of the relatively few places in the United States where you can be downtown and in the wilderness at the same time." The following year, however, a space needle thrust upward in the middle of town (a replica of the one built for Seattle's world fair) and in 1973, an aerial gondola made its way from downtown up the mountain. By the 1970s, those who wanted serenity and communion with nature or a shower after several days of camping stayed someplace else.[45]

Across the mountains, the gateway at the southern entrance to the Smokies developed in Cherokee, the Qualla Boundary of the Eastern Band. As in Gatlinburg, 1950s tourists wanted to see something of a frontier American past, and the Cherokees soon served this market. As this passage from the 1951 *North Carolina Guide* shows, tourists wanted contact with a unique culture, but they wanted to be reassured about the true Americanism of native people:

> This is the largest organized Indian reservation east of Wisconsin. It is estimated that 15 percent of the 3,700 residents are full-blooded Cherokee; 31 percent are ¾ or more full-blooded. The lands are held in common for the tribe under the supervision of the Office of Indian Affairs. Domestic matters are administered by a chief, assistant chief, and a tribal council of 12, all of whom are elected. . . . Most of the Cherokee are members of the Baptist or Methodist churches. Nevertheless, traces of their pagan past are evidenced by the 15 or more practicing medicine men and the survival of conjuring societies. . . . In and about the reservation the swarthy, impassive, solemn-visaged Indians go about their everyday pursuits. They have for the most part adopted modern attire, though the tribal dress is used on festive occasions.[46]

The writer of this state-sponsored publication impressed on readers the Cherokees' racial purity. They were safely supervised by the federal government in this account, and domestic matters sound American—at least "elected." Most twentieth-century Cherokees practiced Christianity, but the writer made them pagan enough to be a curiosity. They looked like anybody on the street or in the grocery store, but with three-quarters full blood and "swarthy, impassive" looks, one could experience a safe "otherness." This tremendous ambivalence—wanting otherness, however reassuringly familiar and American—very much characterized the 1950s tourist in Cherokee, North Carolina. Serving this market, Cherokee entrepreneurs began serving up a strange mix of Sitting Bull, Tsali, and Tonto. As with Gatlinburg, tourism brought a renaissance in authentic Cherokee traditions, such as basketmaking and pottery, but it also brought a ready market for brightly colored feather headdresses, plastic tomahawks, and reproduction Navaho blankets mass-produced in Asia.

Until the 1930s, federal Indian agents promoted agriculture and worried that the return to native arts and crafts would cause Native Americans to "regress." The official policy of the United States attempted to eradicate native culture by sending young people to boarding schools and encouraging allotment, or the breakup of communally held lands into individual tracts. John Collier, commissioner of the Bureau of Indian Affairs under the New Deal, reversed this policy. Collier believed that native handicrafts could provide economic uplift while preserving the "distinctive contribution" Native Americans made to American society; he believed that communal ownership of land promoted a community-mindedness that should be retained. Collier proved something of a visionary for Cherokee, with its proximity to the new national park and ready tourist markets. However, his follower's cheery and poetic descriptions of communal life brought charges of communism from more conservative factions of the Eastern Band.[47] Meanwhile, native arts boomed, as every tourist wanted to bring home a souvenir of Cherokee history and culture. In 1937 a home economics teacher in Cherokee and the boarding school principal convinced Cherokee weaver Lottie Queen Stamper to teach basketweaving in the school. By 1938 craft classes received so many Christmas requests that the school brought in other adults from the community to meet the demand, and two generations of basketweavers ultimately learned the craft, popular with tourists, from Stamper. The annual Cherokee Fair, started in 1913, became a popular tourist attraction, where basketweavers could sell their wares, and many motorists from

Charlotte and Atlanta and Florida planned vacations to see the fall colors in the mountains and to watch the Cherokee ball game, an original dance, or the "cash award to the prettiest full blood Indian baby." The state department of tourism annually promoted the fair, and it became a routine newspaper feature all over North Carolina. "The revival of tribal dances gives the visitors an insight into the original Cherokees in their native environment," as one reporter put it. Seeing an opportunity to make money, the tribe voted to include a carnival company at the annual event, with rides, hot dog stands, and cotton candy. Tourists had no trouble with this strangely postmodern combination of cultures. Everyone seemed to agree that economic uplift brought by tourism was a good thing for the Eastern Band, a necessary thing, even. But as soon as the tribe made money, it faced charges of crass commercialism. "[The carnival company] gives an air of modernity which is entirely out of keeping with what should be the dominant note," Superintendent Eakin complained, indicating he didn't approve of too much modernity.[48] Nevertheless, after the completion of U.S. Highway 441 across Newfound Gap, the Blue Ridge Parkway, and Highway 19, life in Cherokee became slowly more and more oriented toward the tourist's dollar. Entrepreneurs sought flashier Plains Native American traditions. During the 1930s at the Cherokee Fair, the Cholocco Dramatic Club created a dramatic pageant, "The Spirit of the Great Smokies," which told the history of the Cherokees from their first meeting with whites. At one point, 500 tribal members took part in the show. In the summer of 1937, however, the white superintendent of Indian schools wrote to the *Asheville Citizen-Times* that the now-biennial Cherokee pageant would be much improved. "We are doing our best to get away from the rather drab outfits our Indians have used in the past," he said. "We have sent to Pawnee Bill's in Pawnee, Oklahoma, for elaborate outfits." If the new look lacked authenticity, it produced the desired effect.[49]

The war understandably brought about a drop in tourism. Many Cherokees found work on Fontana Dam; more than 250 men and women enlisted. The price of timber soared, so the council voted to cut more than 2 million board feet from the tribal forests. Cherokees who still depended on the forest for subsistence practices found themselves further driven toward cash work. In her important study of Cherokee basketweavers, Sarah Hill discovered that craftswomen could no longer find white oaks they needed to make splints for their useful and sturdy baskets. Betty Lossiah, whom Hill interviewed, recalled sitting down in the woods, discouraged that she could not find any white oak. There she noticed the early successional species, maple. She cut the slender maple saplings, and took them home. "I make the basket up and everybody learn," she said. "Reshaping customs to create and sustain different markets, basketweavers turned to . . . red maple, developing another tradition of basketry," wrote Hill.[50] Even prolific basketmakers still relied on other means of support. During the 1940s, 553 out of 593 families in Cherokee still raised gardens extensive enough to have income from them; about two-fifths planted winter gardens. The federal government continued to put money into community improvement clubs, which emphasized soil conservation, profitable livestock practices, home preservation, and scientific crop cultivation. In 1948 milk cows, chickens, and apple orchards were still common in Cherokee; even guidebooks noted that typical Cherokees lived "on small farms and in ordinary rural communities." As another reporter, sent to find "the true picture of the red man," behind the "fake glamour and paint," said: "Some of the old nature worship crops out in the Cherokee Christian practice at times, but all in all the Cherokees are decidedly spiritually and religiously inclined."

At the end of the war, the federal government sent an Indian agent who saw the tribe's future in tourism. Joe Jennings, a University of Tennessee graduate with a Ph.D. from Peabody College, served as a regional promoter of roads and tourism development. Predecessors warned him that when the 300 Cherokees who served in the armed forces returned, "you'll be sitting on a volcano," because western North Carolina offered only poverty and discrimination, and the Cherokees now exercised their long-denied right to vote. Jennings, however, proceeded to worry that tourists might not find enough accommodations on the boundary. "We drove over the mountains from Knoxville [on July 4]," he told an officer in the Department of Indian Affairs, "and nearly every 'turn out' in the highway was occupied by one to three cars with sleeping tourists in them."[51] He wanted the tribe to attract tourists of a higher class than those who frequented the novelty shops, and he deplored "chiefing." Enterprising Cherokee men discovered that they could earn a reasonable income in the summer by standing on the highway dressed in Plains Indians war bonnets, rented from a Baltimore costume shop, accompanied by a snake or stuffed bear. Unlike Jennings, the tourists didn't seem to notice the faux culture, and paid handsomely to stand next to a "chief" for a photograph.

A reformer in the tradition of Collier, Jennings expressed concern that none of the five new tourist courts was owned by Cherokees; instead, the council leased land to whites. Presently, he helped Chief Jarrett Blythe borrow $150,000 from a revolving fund of the Indian Service to build a tribal motor court, called the Boundary Tree. The tribal council appointed a business committee to be in charge of building and running the court. According to a report written in 1954, the enterprise cleared $13,500, beyond the payment on the debt. By that year, Cherokees also owned and operated twenty-three motor courts, thirty-three shops selling handicrafts and souvenirs, ten service stations, eight grocery stores, and five restaurants. With help from Jennings, about sixty Cherokee craftworkers established the Qualla Arts and Crafts Cooperative in 1946 to promote high-quality work and to serve as a buying cooperative. Through the Southern Highlands Handicraft Guild, the co-op placed some crafts in shops off the reservation. White buyers, including a prominent teacher at the school, supervised the basketweavers during the 1950s, dictating low prices but demanding the use of natural dyes.[52]

Although Jennings helped create lasting institutions, which provided year-round, rather than seasonal income, he could not change the Hollywood-inspired tastes of tourists. Nostalgia for a Wild West still pervaded travel accounts about the community. "Gone are the happy days of fruitful hunting and fishing," lamented one Cherokee "expert." "The Cherokees today are lovers of natural beauty. They like to climb the mountains over the old trails made famous by their warring ancestors. While their entire manner of life has changed to the modern, Indian traits and instincts remain intact in the fullbloods of the reservation." Another travel writer waxed poetical about the return to nature a tourist could experience among the Cherokees, when she described the ball games at the annual Cherokee fair: "The players wear only athletic trunks. As their naked bronze bodies twist and turn, the muscles rippling and swelling, it reminds us of ancient masterpieces of art sprung into life and action." "The Indians have set up archery ranges and not only entertain the visitors with their skill but give lessons in the sport," said one reporter, "and they stand ready to sell bows, quivers and arrows." He added that "racial imperturbability" quickly gives way to "affability," when the Cherokee storeowners "see the visitor bearing wampum."[53]

Did Jennings help the Cherokees, or simply provide aid to tourists? In his spare time he offered assistance to the Asheville Rotary Club, AAA of New York, Louisville Auto Club, Carolina Motor Club, and Parkersburg (West Virginia) Automobile Club in planning trips to the area. As president of the Western North Carolina Associated Communities (WNCAC), he promoted regional development.[54] To make the pageant into a more permanent outdoor drama, WNCAC incorporated the Cherokee Historical Association (CHA). Although he had strong support from Chief Blythe, Jennings and all of the other administrators of the CHA, except the secretary, were white.[55] A full two years before builders completed the outdoor amphitheater, newspapers proclaimed *Unto These Hills*, a historical drama offered nightly in the summer time: "It will attract many of the visitors to the Great Smoky Mountains National Park who otherwise may not come into North Carolina and it will induce them to stay longer."[56] Produced by the CHA, the drama received funds from eleven individuals who contributed $20 million, the tribal council, the Indian Service, and the state of North Carolina. Fabulously successful for the rest of the century, *Unto These Hills* reflects the contradictions of the 1950s in an amalgamation of history, fiction, and patriotism. The story blames corrupt Washington politicians and turncoat Andy Jackson rather than frontier pressure and greedy Georgians for Cherokee removal. It emphasizes a small gold rush in Dahlonega, Georgia, rather than a major land grab as the cause of the tragedy. Innocent victims but true Americans, the Cherokees dress like western frontiersmen and square dance in the middle of the pageant. No Cherokee participates in tribal betrayal; they were duped. Although tribal members make cameo appearances, white college students wearing dark makeup comprise most of the actors.

The CHA also employed University of Tennessee, North Carolina, and Georgia anthropologists and historians to design a museum and the Oconaluftee Indian Village. Constructed to resemble a Cherokee village in 1750, the village employed tribal members to demonstrate crafts and provide the history of subsistence practices. The third CHA project, a museum, collected artifacts held privately by wealthy whites in Knoxville and Asheville. By returning pieces of heritage to the tribe, the museum granted Cherokee young people the chance to retain contact with the past. Private funds, state grants, and federal assistance made this possible, because of tourism. Ironically, this same force—tourism—everywhere distorted history. One professor of education who wrote about Cherokee history for a tourist pamphlet said that "the Cherokees are sure now of a home in the mountains of North Carolina," explaining that this is "due in large part to the fact that [they] are a great tourist attraction."[57] Wearing identical calico costumes, Cherokees in the "living history" museum demonstrate crafts, positioned in "work stations" rather than clans or family groups.

As with Gatlinburg, Cherokee money remained in a few hands. While the federal government technically held the reservation in trust, individual Eastern Band members purchased or traded their land with other members. Highly acculturated Cherokees bettered themselves by getting well-located property, and a "strong feeling of ownership" developed toward their share of property. "The divergence between tribal haves and have-nots was becoming increasingly apparent," historian John Finger wrote regarding the 1950s, "adding another element to factionalism and mounting tensions." The majority of Cherokee residents, especially conservatives or traditional tribal members, lived in poverty. Full-time jobs in the tourist industry paid no more than a dollar an hour and laid off workers at the end of the season. The most well-paid conservative Cherokee in Big Cove made $3 per hour running a bulldozer for the NPS. A 1955 survey found that 90 percent of the 600 homes in Cherokee did not meet healthful standards for water, sewage, and garbage facilities. The CHA employed 220 Cherokees and spent much of its surplus on community improvements, but income disparities remained sharp.[58]

The push for tourism dollars also created conflicts between the culture portrayed and the exploitation of nature. On the one hand, guidebooks during the 1950s described the close relationship with nature that the Cherokees enjoyed. "Industrial society makes the same demands everywhere," one writer sadly noted. "Even the remnant of a simple life in the forest has nearly vanished. The advance of civilization restricts and binds. Every one, white man and red man, has to buckle down to a job." However, the same writer claimed, in Big Cove far back in the reservation, it was possible to view "a few Cherokees who still live close to nature," in an "outpost of the past."[59] At the same time, though, the tourists who wanted to see snakes and bears, live and stuffed, created a market for poachers. As

John Collier explained to the secretary of the Interior: "Reaching Chero-kee, visitors observe and frequently join in the misery of the caged and trained bears which are trader bait. To obtain these bears . . . scoundrels enter the national park, murder the parent bears, and drag the youngsters down to their purgatory." The *Chattanooga Times* carried an article about bears housed in small, hot cages for the gawking tourist in Cherokee. Jennings also received angry letters from visitors, who worried about one bear housed in a souvenir shop where tourists could "watch Sam drink" and pay to feed him soft drinks. "I spoke with the Indian who manages the bear," wrote the concerned man. "I wanted him to know I had only the highest thoughts of the Cherokee Reservation . . . but the Indian told me off." Jennings replied that "the treatment of caged animals on the reser-vation has been a matter of great concern to me" and that he would take this up with WNCAC. Jennings tried to draft a regulation to forbid li-censed traders to keep wild animals as tourist attractions. "The consider-ation is not only humanitarian," Collier noted. "A bad impression is made by the Indians and Indian Services, contrasting badly with that made by the national park."[60]

Between Cherokee, North Carolina, and Gatlinburg, Tennessee, American tourists in the 1950s purchased the image of the frontier they expected. While Cherokee became a Plains Indian outpost and Gat-linburg perfected the art of looking like Vail, Colorado, the NPS catered to automobile tourists most effectively in Cades Cove. In spite of overall disregard for preserving the agricultural history of the park, the NPS quickly followed the lead of tourists, who wanted the open landscape of the former farming community retained. Even though park officials clearly viewed the park's mission in terms of natural history, tourists in search of a mythical "pioneer history" pushed the agency toward unusual management practices for a wilderness refuge.

Drive-in Wilderness

After the creation of the park, the first superintendent, Eakin, enforced NPS policy, ordering the cessation of all subsistence practices, including firewood-cutting and grazing. Eakin understood that a pristine wilder-ness couldn't be touched. His move made life difficult for leasees remain-ing in the park, who wanted to continue traditional practices. By 1936, so many people had moved from the area that his order was enforceable. The former agricultural lands began to grow up in large shrubs and saplings. Tourists complained about the loss of the view, so the superintendent sent in CCC workers to mow the fields. In 1937, heavy rainfall on top of the years of grazing caused erosion problems in the streams, so the CCC sloped and mulched the streambanks to keep the water clear. Historian Hiram Wilburn, hired by the park to collect artifacts, promoted a decidedly different view of wilderness. Wilburn wanted to turn Cades Cove into an outdoor museum of mountain life, "after the Norwegian and Swedish manner," and the NPS took this "under study." While a somewhat skeptical Eakin continued to follow a policy of "meadow maintenance" or "open meadow" in Cades Cove, the NPS considered a more direct application of Wilburn's idea.[61]

The park, in cooperation with the U.S. Soil Conservation Service (SCS), in 1946 initiated a "historical" program to "perpetuate the scene of Cades Cove area as it was when the park was established." Soil conservationists estimated that the open land in 1935 stretched approximately 2 by 5 miles: to achieve a near approximation, they recommended managing it as "one big farm." In the central and western portion of the cove, they suggested planting a grass-legume combination, which included exotic species, not native to the area, rotated with clover, soybeans, and alfalfa (other exotics). For this project, the park straightened stream channels and cleared trees and shrubs from the banks to provide quick drains and to prevent "unnecessary flooding." In the eastern portion of the cove, which had rockier and less fertile soil, the agriculturists recommended a "permanent pasture" by cutting down trees and planting Sericea lespedeza, another exotic species. "Difference in soil classes alone would impose a Herculean task of developing uniformity of vegetation," the scientists reported. "Nature is unable to do so." The report also approved maintaining the old orchards, because "if deer ever become established in the cove it may result from their fondness for apples."[62]

Rangers and soil conservationists interviewed the nine Cades Cove community members still leasing land in the cove to determine "their qualifications, interests, and respective abilities" to render assistance in maintaining the open character of the land. John Birchfield, one of the farmers, kept several historical buildings for the park but could not clear land and mow fields, because of his age. "He is respected and would not willingly leave the cove," a ranger noted. Because of Birchfield, the park preserved one large "virgin meadow," with wild native grasses, forbs, mosses, and other plants that did not subsequently become plowed, seeded, limed, or fertilized. Kermit Caughron negotiated with the park to greatly expand the area under pasture and to grant himself and the other lessees ten-year contracts. He also tried to get the park to provide lime to improve soil acidity. Another resident, Labe Myers, did not consider himself a farmer and preferred to work for the park. His son, recently released from a German prison camp, took charge of several fields for small grain, hay, and pasture. All the residents favored a conversion from crop farming to livestock production, because the prevalence of coons, crows, groundhogs, and squirrels made it impossible to grow the most popular mountain grain, corn. "Let no one suppose all permittees are stupid," warned O. B. Taylor, one of the soil conservationists. "I might have believed that from a casual tour of the loop road. To meet them and talk about land uses is convincing they have a very good working knowledge of their profession."[63]

At the end of the first season of Cades Cove cattle ranching, rangers inspected the results. Former residents paid a small cash rent and paid for fertilizer and lime, which ran as high as $15 to $20 per acre. Visiting rangers were concerned that lessees did not seem "cognizant of the need for maintaining buildings and lands in a manner creditable to the Service." Some lessees further had to clear land, which had already begun to grow up in trees before they could introduce an estimated 800 to 1,000 Aberdeen Angus and whiteface Herefords. Inspecting rangers cautioned officials about retaining good relations with cove farmers, because "people living in isolated regions tend to develop rather unusual concepts of public relations."[64]

The local newspaper approved of the new open land policy, but reporters knew that the scene concocted by the park service bore little resemblance to the original. "While in its well populated days the cove included diversified farming," the *Daily (Maryville) Times* noted, "practically all of the land now is used for grazing beef cattle."[65] Whereas once farmers managed small farms in a patchwork of woods, crops, and meadow (separated by fences), the cove became one large ranch of grazing cattle. The park ranger manual from the 1950s gave seasonal employees tips on interpreting this new policy. Why was the park service, dedicated to preserving the wild deer and turkey or helping a visitor find a campground, engaged now in "clearing fields, cattle grazing, and plowing fields?" The manual provided rangers with an answer to this potentially thorny question:

> In going back to the beginning and before the park was established, Man had become a part of Cades Cove. He loved the land, the hills, and the cove. To him it was God's good world. It has been felt by the National Park Service that here in the Great Smoky Mountains National Park a part of the world should be conserved as man had made it.[66]

The manual went on to explain that the "slow, easy, one-way road is symbolic of the way of life of those who lived in the Cove." In fact, the official explanation continued, seven "special use permits" were granted to maintain 2,500 open acres of tillable land. "Those people who live in the Cove are in some instances descendants of the original settlers, but they are not part of the exhibit," tourists were warned. "They are there to aid all of us in doing a job—to enable the National Park Service to more fully accomplish its objectives."[67] Local newspapers generally praised the restoration of Cades Cove and the plans to build Laurel Creek Road into the area. Before this construction, the main approach was a winding gravel road over Rich Mountain and a narrow, graveled loop road circled through the cove from a parking lot. Soon visitors could enjoy a paved trip all the way from the Sugarlands Visitor Center. When the "one big farm" project to maintain open land neared completion, park officials erected a sign at the cove entrance:

> This was an American frontier. To this valley in the early 19th century came the pioneer settlers. Isolated from an outside world, they became self sufficient. Sturdy log structures, their timbers hewed with a skill now lost, remain as memorials to a way of life. The fine frame buildings show self-taught advance in construction methods. Elsewhere the frontier passed on yielding to change and innovation, but here a pioneer culture has persisted. Offering to future generations 'A sense of the land from which their forefathers hewed their homes,' Cades Cove with its visible record of man's struggle with the wilderness is a valuable heritage of the American people.[68]

From the opening day of the park, tourists went to Cades Cove to see the former residents, now lessees, of the national park, representing this "valuable heritage." The *Knoxville Journal* depicted a "mountain-locked" Cades Cove with a photograph of an elderly couple. "In a backwoods cabin in Cades Cove," the article stated, "this barefoot couple continues to live. Asked how old he was, Aaron Crawford replied, 'I don't know; I can't read or write.'"[69] The new land management policy encouraged the cove to become an "animated museum," as one magazine put it, where tourists could see "actual descendants of original pioneer families who lived in that happy valley for generations." *Friends* magazine encouraged readers to meet the grandchildren of white settlers in the scenic valley, "which remains almost unchanged from the way it looked in the 19th century." The NPS preserved this valley as a record, the writer said, "of man's struggle with the mountain wilderness." The *Ford Times* encouraged customers to enjoy "a drive-in look, not only at farms, mills, and churches of a century ago, but *at the people themselves* [emphasis in original] tilling the soil, grinding meal, carrying on the ways of their pioneer ancestors." On the route, the author noted, "you cross original fords"— Tater Branch, Whistling Branch, Olive Branch—in your car.[70] Charlie Myers told an *Atlanta Journal and Constitution* reporter that he liked tourists; in fact, in June 1961 he got 26,791 of them to sign his guest book. "The U.S. Government has put the wilderness back, to preserve the area and show this and future generations how this continent used to look," the reporter wrote. That same year Supreme Court Justice William Douglas traveled to Cades Cove and interviewed individuals who had grown up in the cove, including Kermit Caughron, John Oliver, Randolph Shields, Charlie Myers, and Mrs. John Coada, for a special *National Geographic* feature. He marveled at the "verve and flare of Elizabethan England" found in their speech and described many of the subsistence practices used at the turn of the century in the cove. "Deep in the Great Smoky Mountains, a rustic valley cups a remnant of pioneer America," the magazine advertised. "Here Justice Douglas reports on a way of life that has almost vanished."[71]

No doubt reminded of the Ponderosa or the Big Valley in television shows about lands farther west, tourists strongly approved of the "one big farm" policy. However, the land responded less favorably. Whereas small farmers traditionally owned 10–20 cows, one leasee eventually ran a large

herd of 800 cattle on 800 acres. The cattle overgrazed the fields and damaged streambanks, causing a serious loss of water quality. In 1964 members of the SCS grew concerned enough about turgid water in Cades
Cove to direct the park in further "channel improvement" on Abrams
Creek. They supervised the removal of all trees, shrubs, brush, stumps,
logs, and other woody growth from the stream. To decrease flooding and
the tendency of nature to re-create wetlands, they eliminated all the
plants, logs, limbs, and stumps that kept erosion in check. They ignored
the cattle, the primary cause of poor water quality. A 1980 study of Cades
Cove found that effluent from agricultural practices could be detected on
Abrams Creek 15 kilometers away from the site; fecal coliform levels frequently exceeded state of Tennessee standards. Visitors regularly swam,
waded, and fished in Abrams Creek, but because of the unhistorical cattle
ranching, nutrient levels and bacterial loads were undesirably high.[72]

Because of the planting program, tall fescue soon dominated the open
land in the cove, crowding out native grasses and wildflowers. Fescue may
have caused sickness in wildlife because it served as a host to the toxic
fungi ergomine and ergovaline. Whereas native grasses grow as tall as 8
feet and provide travel lanes, forage space, and nesting cover, fescue for
hay was mowed twice a year. Because fescue was mowed during June and
August, it destroyed the homes of ground-nesting birds, such as killdeer,
bobwhite, and eastern meadowlark. The most profitable way to raise hay
also proved destructive to newborn animals, like fawns, which are often
concealed in tall grasses. Only John Birchfield's untended meadow preserved orchids, grasses, rushes, ferns, a sunflower, and a buttercup species
not found in the mowed fields. According to an NPS document from
1997, more than 35 percent of the species in the abandoned field are
considered rare in the rest of the park.[73]

Deer multiplied, attracted by the wide fescue meadows, and became
popular with tourists. By 1960, a maintenance foreman working in Cades
Cove counted a herd of fifty-six deer in the cove, a record number seen in
one place in the park. By 1977, scientists counted 2,172 deer in the cove
and recommended removing some to prevent overpopulation. Soon
thereafter, they recorded an outbreak of disease from the overcrowding.
Because deer liked to browse on the leaves, buds, and succulent twigs of
deciduous trees, the area they favored became dominated by pines; red-
bud, oaks, and dogwoods became uncommon in the woods around the

cove fields. Deer also destroyed rare plants, including the wahoo, or burningbush, American columbo, and Virginia chain fern. With an absence of major predators, deer populations can easily outstrip a forest's ability to support them; still, a 1981 study showed that cattle had a much greater impact on the cove than deer. Nevertheless, tourists loved the deer, which fit nicely into the nostalgic scene. When the last lessee finally left the cove, visitors focused their cameras on deer and cattle.[74]

"Cades Cove achieves such reality that visitors never stop to think of it as a synthetic creation designed to force back the wilderness for a show of history and folk culture," wrote conservationist Michael Frome, seemingly unaware that the "synthetic creation" derived from the minds of 1950s America and represented neither history nor folk culture.[75] Without a doubt, Cades Cove lent a little glamour to the lives of 1950s superintendents, as they entertained the stars Ingrid Bergman and Anthony Quinn, who worked on *A Walk in the Spring Rain* in Cades Cove. In its own way, the scenic frontier created on the loop road complemented western trail riding in Cataloochee, the ski resort in Gatlinburg, and the Wild West show in Cherokee.

At the end of the 1950s the NPS used Mission 66 funds to improve roads and campgrounds to Cades Cove, and to construct the Foothills Parkway, intended to take the traffic burden off U.S. Highway 441. Between 1955 and 1965, the monthly *Superintendent's Report* read like the annals of a construction company. Considerable pride glowed from reports about the number of completed miles and quantity of installed guard rails. In one month of 1965, for example, the report announced that the Foothills Parkway was "progressing nicely," despite five slides successively wiping out the work in one small area.[76] The success of the cove, however, prompted the park to complete the Pioneer Exhibit at the Oconaluftee Visitor Center near Smokemont. In July 1955, 84,571 tourists poured into the exhibit; on a single Sunday on the July 4 weekend, 5,079 visitors were counted. Just as they loved Gatlinburg and Cherokee, tourists clearly enjoyed the forays into history created by the NPS, but the park soon closed the Pioneer Exhibit because it created traffic problems.

Harvey Broome called the mowed fields of Cades Cove, surrounded by dramatic mountains and balds, "the embodiment of peace and harmony between man and nature." Even Harvey Broome could not escape the lure of a manufactured scene that reflected a romantic American landscape ideal. One thought brought a shadow to the conservationist's face, however, when plans for Laurel Creek Road and the new 2,000-person Cades Cove campground still existed only on the drawing boards. As early as 1950 he wrote:

> The serene peace which has been the hallmark of the Cove for a century will yield to the frenetic restlessness of the machine age. The black, slow-moving bodies of the beef cattle, which harmonize with the Cove's single spirit, will be overshadowed by the racing of mechanical monsters.[77]

The North Carolina Department of Conservation and Development called the ubiquitous signage on gateway highways a "hideous blot upon the gorgeous scenery."[78] Although traffic, litter, and signage may seem incongruous with uninhabited wilderness, the rapidly increasing tourism in the park was not shocking at all. Without the "mechanical monsters"—or the forces behind automobile tourism—no park would exist. A powerful coalition of preservationists such as Broome, and regional promoters, had created the Smokies in the image of Yellowstone. Can the "wilderness" be experienced from the window of an automobile? Do tourists preserve the environment while gassing their vehicles? Could they, as 1950s travel writers claimed, "have their cake and eat it too?" Harvey Broome would be among the first to doubt it.

6.1. An activity common in western parks, horseback riding arrived with a national park in the Smokies. Tom Alexander's trail riders, 1940s. Cataloochee Ranch Collection, North Carolina Division of Archives and History, Raleigh, North Carolina.

6.2. Photo taken for a 1959 park exhibit promoting rainbow trout fishing; rainbow trout were an import from the West. Courtesy of Great Smoky Mountains National Park.

6.3. Managing Cades Cove like "one big farm" made it look like the Ponderosa. Charlie Myers's Herefords, 1952. Courtesy of Great Smoky Mountains National Park.

6.4. The loop road in Cades Cove, ever popular with tourists, became the ultimate "drive-in wilderness." Courtesy of Great Smoky Mountains National Park.

6.5. Here the Tennessee Department of Conservation created the impression through promotional photos that the Cherokees wore headdresses common among the Plains Indians. Tennessee Department of Conservation. Courtesy of Tennessee State Archives, Nashville, Tennessee.

Left: 6.6. "College girls" wearing shuck hats, belts, and bags, typical of "mountain crafts," according to the Tennessee Department of Conservation. Courtesy of Tennessee State Archives, Nashville, Tennessee.

Below: 6.7. The Annual Wildflower Pilgrimage, which began in 1950, originally promoted caravans of cars through the Smokies to look at wildflowers. Courtesy of Great Smoky Mountains National Park.

Bearly Managing Tourons

Where do you keep the bears?

TOURIST IN SUGARLANDS VISITOR CENTER

NOTHING WILL TEST your patience quite like a job working with the public. As anyone who has worked in retail or information services knows, people can ask idiotic questions even after you've given them a good explanation and decent directions. On any given day behind the counter in the Sugarlands Visitor Center, park rangers still hear tourists ask where Sugarcreek is. With a map containing the correct names laid in front of them, tourists wonder aloud about "Kingman's Doom" (Clingmans Dome) or "Codes Cave" (Cades Cove). Although proper park etiquette in the 1950s and 1960s required rangers to call every traveler a "visitor," privately they joked about individual "tourons" (a combination of tourist and moron).[1] One common situation in which park employees found themselves with tourons can be described as damned-if-you-do-or-don't. John Morrell, one of the park's early rangers, loved to tell about finding a family alongside U.S. Highway 441, their picnic lunch spread out near the overlook. In the middle of the tablecloth sat a bear, "making fast work with their fried chicken and a frosted cake." The frantic woman begged Morrell to do something to drive the bear away. Her husband, on the other hand, busily recorded the entire epi-sode on a movie camera. "Leave the bear alone," he said. "We can get more food in Gatlinburg, but this film will be the highlight of our whole trip."[2]

The more Great Smoky Mountains National Park succeeded in visita-tion, the more difficult ranger Morrell's balancing act became. Whereas official Mission 66 plans projected 4 million visitors by 1966, the park actually topped 5.2 million in 1962. While keeping concession owners such as Tom Alexander in line, rangers had to break up "bear jams" (traffic jams caused by people stopping to see a roadside bear), catch moon-shiners, crack down on poachers, stop posey-pickers, put out fires, write traffic tickets, nab people breaking fishing regulations, and prevent the burgeoning numbers from otherwise destroying the park. As early as 1944 NPS Director Newton B. Drury understood that improved trans-portation to the national parks would bring hordes that could "destroy the very things we are charged with preserving."[3] Even agency-sponsored reports showed the contradiction between attracting large numbers of tourists and taking care of the land.[4] But park managers still celebrated numbers as a sign of success: in the world of government funding, visita-tion proved public satisfaction. "Growing as a ministry of tourism," wrote critic Alston Chase in *Playing God in Yellowstone*, "the Park Service became a bureaucracy less capable of satisfying its mandate for preservation."[5]

Unprepared to acknowledge this contradiction, the NPS nationally just kept expanding the system during the 1960s. By its completion, Conrad Wirth's Mission 66 construction program seemed out of touch with a new national consciousness about taking care of the environment. But Wirth's successor, George Hartzog Jr., took advantage of President Lyndon Johnson's Great Society money to add eighty-seven new units into the NPS system. His agenda, "Parkscape U.S.A.," led to an increased concern about law enforcement, as many of these new units came from urban areas, such as Golden Gate Park in San Francisco. By the time Hartzog stepped down in 1969, he had established a law enforcement office and greatly stepped up law-enforcement training of seasonal and entry-level rangers. As Chase described the 1960s, "Rangers became a force of policemen rather than wildlife scientists or historians, and most wildlife-management policies came to be designed, not to preserve parks as pristine, but to attract visitors."[6]

To compound the problem, most superintendents felt their first loyalty was to Wirth, Hartzog, and therefore tourism, rather than to advancing notions of environmental protection. To rise to the position of superintendent, employees had to demonstrate not knowledge of the bioregion, not innovation in protecting wildlife, not wisdom in balancing preservation with tourism, but loyalty to the National Park Service. Each advance in rank involved a move, often across the nation, to another park or historic site. George Fry, who became superintendent in 1963, worked as a park ranger at Crater Lake, an assistant chief ranger at Rocky Mountain, a chief ranger at Mammoth Cave and the Everglades, and a superintendent at Isle Royale before he came to the Smokies. The short-term superintendency arose to prevent park leadership from bedding with local developers; in the case of Fry, it made him more loyal to director Hartzog than to any single policy or park. In his published journal, Fry recounted that when he took over at the Smokies, Hartzog handed him a list of goals to accomplish. He was to remove the slides from the Gatlinburg spur, finish acquiring the right-of-way for the Foothills Parkway from Interstate 40 to Walland, acquire the right-of-way and construct the Gatinburg bypass, remove commercial buses and trucks from park roads, complete a new Master Plan for the park, finish the Bryson City-Fontana road, reorganize park operations under an improved management plan, and initiate new bear management. When he began work on the Gatlinburg bypass, he wrote in his diary, "one of the director's objectives was finally getting underway." Fry could become the superintendent of Sequoia National Park, an example of what he considered an advancement, if he successfully completed all the goals. With dismay he noted the staff he had inherited, because they paid too much attention to the backcountry. "They were not doing law enforcement and public relations work I would have preferred," he complained. According to ranger Morrell, Fry liked meetings: rangers could predict the length of the meeting by the size of the cigar Fry brought with him. When he first came to the park, the superintendent met with members of business groups, environmental organizations, conservation clubs, and civic assemblies. A former Eagle Scout, Fry also spent time with various troops. In fact, his journal reads like a steady date book of appointments. He may have listened intently to each of his constituencies, but in truth he came to the park to do what Hartzog told him to do.[7]

Charged with finishing roads, Fry made it his first priority. Over the previous decades, Swain County officials put pressure on the park to complete the North Shore Road around Fontana Lake promised in the 1943 Agreement with TVA. County officers showed patience when the war tied up construction money. In 1947 the park completed 1 mile of the road, but soon the funding crisis directed money toward campgrounds and other overcrowded facilities. During the 1950s, Bryson City residents watched as Cherokee and Gatlinburg flourished. Between Great Smoky Mountains National Park, the USFS, TVA, and the Cherokee lands, only 25 percent of Swain County remained open for taxable development. Robbinsville, in Graham County, fared even worse. The richer the Tennesseeans got, the more these North Carolina communities nursed a grudge against the park and pinned their hopes on the long-promised North Shore Road.[8]

While Great Smoky Mountains National Park proceeded with Mission 66 and responded to Swain County demands, however, the nation rapidly hurtled in a different direction. As the park recommenced work on the eastern portion of the North Shore Road from the park boundary to Canebrake Branch, Rachel Carson published *Silent Spring*. As road contractors battled incessant slides, Americans listened to new studies showing how polluted and overdeveloped their country had become. When 2.5 miles of the North Shore Road finally saw pavement in August 1963, a liberal consensus in Congress passed landmark environmental legislation, including the Clean Air Act and the Clean Water Act. Under George Fry's direction another 2.5 miles of the road, including a tunnel, reached past Noland Creek; meanwhile, membership swelled in the Sierra Club, the Wilderness Society, and Friends of the Earth. In short, as the North Shore Road proceeded in fits and starts, the nation's view of roads and development drastically changed.[9] Fry met regularly with local officials about the road, reporting his progress to Hartzog; in 1965, his salary rose to $17,645.[10]

As Fry finished Mission 66 construction, he unintentionally created a formidable adversary named Ernie Dickerman. A Chicago native, Dickerman graduated from Oberlin College and went to work for TVA in Knoxville, traveling around rural areas and telling people how great electricity would be for them. In 1936, while working for a plastics company, Dickerman joined the Smoky Mountains Hiking Club (SMHC); on his first hike in the Smokies, he found "what I was looking for on this planet."[11] Soon famous for leading hikes off the beaten paths, Dickerman described a trip up Dunn Creek: "There is no artificial path for most of the distance here, folks. You just clamber up a beautiful creek bed of moss-covered rocks, overflowed by a swift, gleaming mountain stream." Once he led a hiking expedition up the steep north side of Mount LeConte, bushwhacking from one rhododendron bush to another, and the group didn't arrive at the top until nearly dusk. And so Dickerman persuaded them to spend a chilly night on the mountain, rather than risk the descent in the dark. Like a lot of urbanites who felt disgusted by the impact of humans on the environment, Dickerman found hope and a feeling of freedom in the woods, what contemporaries began calling "a wilderness experience." On his frequent trips out West, Dickerman described his adventures in letters to his friends, Harvey and Anne Broome. "Such tremendous richness one feels as he looks about himself in East Tennessee!" he exclaimed once, on returning. When he was forty-five years old, his aging father wrote Anne Broome, asking if she knew where he was. "I assume he is travelling in his station wagon automobile," his worried father inquired. "Ernest can be rather bumptious and self assertive at times."[12]

Until the 1950s Dickerman didn't direct his "bumptious" nature against the park service. He did become president of the SMHC in 1950, and he created a Parks Committee (later renamed the Conservation Committee), through which he wrote Park Superintendent Hummel about extra preservation for the Greenbrier area. At first he only complained about the park's constant road-building: "This nibbling process, Ed," he addressed Superintendent Hummel, "as represented by the proposed enlarging of the upper section of the Pinnacle fire road, is the sort of practice which in the course of time can destroy an appreciable portion of the park's wilderness area."[13] Because of his long-term friendship with the Broomes, Dickerman joined the national movement for the Wilderness Act of 1964, which would give more permanent protection to designated areas.[14] "Perhaps the continued destruction of our remaining wilderness is a symptom of society's basic incompatibility with earth's environment," wrote conservationist Michael Frome, an author and activist who supported the Wilderness Act. Under the act, recommended areas with "outstanding opportunities for a primitive and unconfined type of recreation" could be declared closed to motorized traffic and equipment, after a lengthy government process including local hearings, review, and a separate act of Congress. Wilderness designation permitted hunting, fishing, and camping, but except in emergencies no motorized equipment or vehicles. Before the Wilderness Act, the NPS remained virtually the only federal property devoted to preservation; environmentalists such as Frome, Dickerman, and the Broomes saw a chance for new enclaves of wild places and greater protection for existing ones.[15]

The excitement generated by Harvey and Anne Broome and Ernie Dickerman proved contagious. Because of the Broomes' charisma, two engineers, Leroy Fox and Ray Payne, became involved in the Conservation Committee. Born in Pennsylvania, Fox moved to Knoxville during World War II to work for Rohm & Haas, a plastics company, as a chemical engineer. An amateur photographer, Fox began exploring the Smokies to find wildflowers, and he joined the SMHC in 1963, where he met Harvey Broome.[16] "He got interested in me before I got interested in him," said Fox, who compared Broome with a mountain preacher. "His love for wilderness and the outdoors caught me at a time when I was weak I guess!" Because Fox had participated in several local clean air activities, Dickerman drafted him for the Conservation Committee. Payne, a native of West Virginia, moved to Tennessee in 1957 to work for the Oak Ridge National Laboratory as a mechanical engineer. Another avid hiker, Payne joined the SMHC in 1964, about the time Harvey Broome and Ernie Dickerman began considering the Smokies for a potential wilderness area.[17]

Not long after the Wilderness Act passed, Superintendent Fry met with some of these new "purists in the conservation field" as he called them. The superintendent clearly did not trust these "environmentalists" [quotation marks Fry's].[18] At the time, Fry was proceeding with another one of Hartzog's goals, the Master Plan. Hartzog handpicked five administrators from across the country, who visited the park in 1964 and toured the Gatlinburg ski lodge, all the campgrounds in the park, paved and unpaved roads. They did one exit interview with staff members. On their second visit, the director's Master Plan Study Team stayed overnight on Mount LeConte and Hazel Creek; then they met with local politicians and representatives of the tourism industry.[19] Not realizing what a pow-der keg this issue would become, Fry also invited Dickerman to meet with the Master Plan Study Team.

That summer the NPS also announced that the Smokies would be the first park to go through the public hearing process for possible wilderness designation. Because of the push by local politicians and tourism interests for continued development, Hartzog figured the agency would encounter little interest in wilderness designation in the Smokies. Dickerman and other members of the SMHC, in the meantime, came up with a proposal for two large wilderness areas, covering most of the land above the 2,400-foot contour line and excluding the Newfound Gap Road (U.S. Highway 441) and the Clingmans Dome Road corridors. "The mountain wilder-ness of the Great Smokies Park constitutes the prime feature of the park," the environmentalists asserted. "Automobiles today constitute the most serious threat to wilderness."[20] Dickerman managed to get an issue of *Living Wilderness*, the Wilderness Society's quarterly magazine, devoted to the Smokies, urging the park service "to exhibit a kind of leadership in which it has frequently excelled." A great "abundance and variety" of rec-reational opportunities already existed in the park, and therefore more did not need to be developed. "The basic issue is what kind of a park we want the Smokies to be," Dickerman challenged. "Do we want it to be the kind of wild park that it is today or do we want it to become an automobile pleasuring ground?" Throughout the fall, representatives of the environ-mental groups continued to speak out against a park service proposal, which excluded a large corridor from Monteith Branch, North Carolina, to Townsend, Tennessee, a site for a second transmountain road (the first being U.S. 441). "We feel that the basic values of a park as small as this one will be impaired if it is fragmented by a road," commented Harvey Broome.[21] "Each time we build a road . . . we drive out the animal wildlife we are trying to preserve," wrote Paul Adams, who, like Broome, partici-pated in the founding of the park.[22] Columnist Carson Brewer noted that Smokies visitation had doubled three times in thirty years, and some people suggested it might double in another ten years. "Since we're talk-ing of the need for two transmountain roads for six million, won't it be necessary to have four roads for 12 million?" he wrote. "And then eight roads in another 10 years to handle 24 million?"[23]

Although environmentalists knew that the area where the second transmountain road was proposed had been heavily logged by W. M. Ritter during the 1920s, they considered it part of the wilderness they wanted to preserve. Soon Knoxville newspapers reported on "opposition" to park development. "Don't say we are the opposition," Dickerman retorted. "We're positive. We want the Smoky Park wilderness areas left as they are. It's the National Park Service itself that would whittle the size of the wilderness. NPS is the opposition."[24] To dampen the Dickerman argument, the park service proposed to create six small wilderness areas: Abrams Falls, Blockhouse Mountain, Meigs Mountain, Clingmans Dome, Mount Guyot, and Cataloochee Divide. This would comprise about half the acreage in the park and still leave massive corridors open for park development, including the second transmountain road. "You can't just order a visitor to get out of his car," Hartzog criticized the environmentalists. "You have to entice him out of his car. We may be able to show, through motor-nature trails, short nature walks, lookouts, outdoor exhibits, or other methods of interpretation the meaning of wilderness and what it can offer."[25] Fry echoed this rationalization. "I'm a wilderness enthusiast and always have been," he said. "The Park Service's guiding principle is to make national parks available to the public and at the same time preserve their natural state," he noted, unaware of gainsaying. He reminded everyone of the incremental road construction intended to satisfy the 1943 Agreement, which had already been abandoned several times because of constant landslides on the terrain. With this alternative, he said, there would be "no longer any need" for the remaining North Shore Road.[26]

Director Hartzog and Superintendent Fry seriously underestimated Ernie Dickerman's power of persuasion and how much American attitudes had shifted in favor of preservation. Imagining himself in a position of power, Fry unveiled the Master Plan written by Hartzog's team The Master Plan included a marine area, campground and picnic area, livery stable, store, and amphitheater on Fontana Lake; a LeConte-style lodge in Spence Field; a ski run using the abandoned section of U.S. Highway 441 down the eastern slope from Newfound Gap; sixteen new picnic areas; vista clearings; new campgrounds at Big Creek, Townsend, Tremont, Mount LeConte, Montieth, Proctor, Lost Cove, and Round Bottom; the expansion of Abrams Creek, Cades Cove, Elkmont, Greenbrier, Cosby, and Cataloochee campgrounds; and the much-disputed second transmountain road from Montieth Branch to Townsend. In December, Fry sat down with the Swain County officials and negotiated the Montieth Branch-Townsend transmountain road as an alternative to completion of the North Shore Road. Fry also recommended finishing the Foothills Parkway, which would run along the northern boundary but outside the park from the western end eastward to Interstate 40. Despite his promotion of this extensive development, Superintendent Fry believed that the primeval areas of the park would remain "unspoiled" and that the Master Plan simply "opened up" more of the park to 6 million annual visitors. The park service, he believed, should concern itself with the entire public, not simply a "minority group who wants to escape from civilization."[27]

The *Chicago Tribune*, not exactly a minority group, blasted the plan because it "illustrates how conservation values can be and are betrayed in the house of presumed friends." The editor further argued, "What the army engineers have done to the Everglades and want to do to the Grand Canyon are sad instances of sabotage by government of public lands presumably guaranteed for conservation by the government. But for the park service itself to assist rather than resist destructive designs on one of its own major holdings is even more shocking." Dickerman called it a "street plan" for the park; he quit his job to become a full-time organizer for the Wilderness Society. "If that is the plan to be followed by the Park Service, what is going to happen to our park?" he asked.[28]

Amazingly, Fry and Hartzog thought the public hearings about wilderness designation would be simple. "Little did we realize," Fry reflected later, "that our proposed transmountain road was a 'no no' with the purists, the so-called wilderness people." Meanwhile, the Wilderness Society sent out an SOS, for "Save Our Smokies," to the nation. Organizers did not oppose access for the "lame, halt, sedentary, aged and weak." Rather, they believed that the halt, lame, and aged "did not want to be run through a bumper-to-bumper parking lot." In a special memorandum from the executive director, the Wilderness Society asked that the 35,000 members either attend the public meetings or send a letter to Fry. "The wilderness areas proposed by the Park Service appear to have been gerrymandered to avoid sites which had been chosen for intensive development," the conservation group declared. Author Wilma Dykeman noted the expansion of the Foothills Parkway and the construction of nearby Interstate 40 "thrusting through the mountains." "What I am saying is that nothing comes without a price, not even 20th century speed and travel," she told her weekly Newport, Tennessee, readers, "and there are times when we need to sit down and consider the price we pay for what is sometimes mislabeled as progress."[29]

The public hearings brimmed with passion. More than 150 people attended the meeting on June 13, 1966, in Gatlinburg. The mayor of Townsend, John Wilson, came with forty residents to speak on behalf of Fry's Master Plan, as did Donald McSween, a Newport native on the Tennessee Conservation Commission. With an estimated 10 million visitors by the 1970s, McSween said, "steps must be taken at once to provide for such an influx." Fry and an Eagle Scout, both in uniforms, lined up to testify. Carlos Campbell, one of the park founders representing the old coalition of conservationists and developers, supported the park service and reminded the audience of the 1943 Agreement with Swain County. "Any person who asks that neither road be built clearly indicates, it seems to me, that such person is either grossly ignorant of the historic background of the controversy or he is asking the Park Service to violate a valid contract, thus asking it to take a position of sheer dishonesty!" Representatives from the Wilderness Society, Trout Unlimited, Smoky Mountains Hiking Club, Boy Scouts, Isaak Walton League, National Parks Association, Wildlife Federation, Appalachian Trail Club, and Sierra Club all spoke against the road and in favor of more wilderness. One Illinois man said he drove 500 miles to speak on behalf of the wilderness areas. Ed Clebsch, assistant professor in the University of Tennessee botany department, termed the proposed plan of a second transmountain road "an inadequate wilderness" because development in the remaining sectors could destroy the park's ecology. He was cheered for forty-five seconds. The issue sparked dozens of letters to the Knoxville papers as well, including many that chided the editors for supporting the park over the wilderness advocates.[30]

More than 115 people testified on June 15 in Bryson City. In North Carolina, where Fry commanded more support, the superintendent lobbied key players in the community to speak on behalf of the NPS position. Robert Leatherwood, chair of the Swain County Board of Commissioners, supported the second transmountain road as a fair compromise to the 1943 Agreement. North Carolina Congressman Roy Taylor as well as representatives of the state's park committee, the Swain County Planning Board, the superintendent of North Carolina state parks, the *Atlanta Journal*, chambers of commerce, the Rotary Club, the Lion's Club, the Bryson City Women's Club, and the Carolina Motor Club all spoke in favor of the park's Master Plan. Despite such illustrious support, Dickerman had done his homework. The pro-transmountain road forces had fancier credentials and more political power, but the environmentalists had "more troops," Fox recalled. He, Dickerman, and Payne sent letters and made phone calls to every environmental, recreational, and scientific group they could marshal.

On the pro-road advocates' home turf, they attracted the Carolina Mountain Club, Carolina Bird Club, Georgia Appalachian Trail Club, and Defenders of Wildlife as well as a variety of well-spoken college professors. "No road on earth is important enough to destroy the last large wilderness area in the United States," said C. H. Wharton, a vertebrate ecologist at Georgia State College. "There is no commitment to any local group . . . which can override the fact that the Great Smoky Mountains is the proud possession of all Americans from coast to coast."[31]

While conservationists and developers waited for the results of the hearing, George Fry announced the opening of four new gravel roads for automobiles: the Heintooga picnic area, Parsons Branch Road, the East Prong of the Little River above Elkmont, and the Ramsey Prong Road from Big Greenbrier to its end at Eagle Forks Prong.[32] In August he flew to Washington to meet with the director about the wilderness hearings.

That fall, Dickerman kept the issue before the public by organizing a "Save Our Smokies" hike. "Ernie called me one night and said where can we hike in the vicinity of the proposed transmountain road," recalled Fox, "and I suggested coming from Clingmans Dome to Buckeye Gap on the Appalachian Trail, then down the Miry Ridge to Elkmont." Fearing a riot, the park service sent rangers to patrol the area. After an inspiring speech by Broome and Dickerman, an estimated 600 orderly people walked part of the seventeen-mile route. Stationed at Buckeye Gap, Fox counted 234 hikers. George Fry reported skeptically that whereas 475 started the hike and 100 made it to the lunch break on Silers Bald, only 25 or 30 completed the hike.[33]

After the strong environmental showing at the public hearing and an avalanche of mail, Secretary of the Interior Stewart Udall rejected the second transmountain highway on December 9, 1967. Legend has it among environmentalists that he actually signed his first name to the agreement, thought better of it, then didn't sign his last name.[34] Environmental groups were elated by the cancellation of the road, and in this victory Ernie Dickerman forged a lifelong career in activism; he left for the Washington office of the Wilderness Society and would one day be known as the "granddad of the Eastern wilderness." The following March, Harvey Broome died suddenly. The two engineers, Ray Payne and Leroy Fox, came out of the memorial service together and stood there under the foggy streetlight. "Well, it looks like it's up to us to carry this on," Fox said. Payne nodded.

With the help of Dickerman, now in Washington, and Bill and Liane Russell, founders of the Tennessee Citizens for Wilderness Planning, the engineers cinched an audience with President Nixon's secretary of the Interior, Walter Hickel, in 1969. Two busloads of ninety-one hikers, from Knoxville, Asheville, Oak Ridge, and Kingsport, descended on Hickel's office in support of wilderness designation.[35] "The Great Smoky Mountains National Park represents a land area of extraordinary quality, of special and superlative characteristics," Fox said in his presentation. "The science of ecology has been forced into the position of accepting the fact that most of man's problems today are ecological in nature," added biologist Ed Clebsch. "That science desperately needs undisturbed and recovering areas of landscape and seascape for performing baseline studies related to man's influence on earth." Frank Singer of the Carolina Mountain Club addressed the road issue directly: "It is important and just that Swain County be given a greater role in the overall regional planning in the future. Many thousands of interested persons . . . have endorsed alternatives to the transmountain road which would better fit in the present and future philosophy and practice of park management."[36]

After listening to all the prepared statements, Hickel said he would come to a decision at 3 p.m. At the appointed hour, Hickel stood on a table in the conference room, so that wilderness advocates and members of the press could see him, and announced an eighteen-month study, which supposedly would settle the matter. The advocates traveled home, cautiously optimistic. When the U.S. Department of Interior finally released the results in an attractive publication, called *Transportation Concepts*, they were stunned. The 1971 report, with an introduction by George Hartzog, offered several options for more or less wilderness designation, but the "recommended option" closed Newfound Gap Road (U.S. Highway 441), the main artery through the park. "It was shocking when we first heard about it, and to this day it reverberates in Cherokee," said Fox. "We didn't agree with it, and we never asked for this."[37] Fox and Payne got their first hard lesson in politics. Hickel and Hartzog knew that closing the main road through the park would cause such an uproar with Gatlinburg and Cherokee developers that the public would soon associate wilderness with this extreme position. With the publication of this booklet, the old coalition of developers and preservationists effectively vanished for the rest of the century.

Trouble brewed in Bryson City, anyway, as local residents fumed about losing the second transmountain road. "We've been treated worse than the Cherokee Indians were in Andrew Jackson's day," said a Bryson City druggist, Kelly Bennett. "The Indians were chased off their land, finally given some trinkets for it. We gave our land for a promise—a promise that hasn't been kept for 25 years." Since 1969, an 8.1-mile section of highway in Great Smoky Mountains National Park has ended abruptly just beyond the back of a dark tunnel. Nearby, local residents hung a sign that read, "Welcome to a Road to Nowhere . . . Broken promise 1943." Although North Carolina State Highway 28 connected Bryson City with Tennessee outside the park, the charge remained. The "Road to Nowhere" has become the highway's nickname and a kind of alternative tourist attraction.[38]

By this time Fry was under attack for closing U.S. Highway 441 to commercial traffic, another one of Hartzog's goals. With the completion of Interstate 40 between Knoxville, Tennessee, and Asheville, North Carolina, and the Gatlinburg bypass, NPS policy required that no buses or trucks be allowed through the park. Many truckers tried to run the closure, so rangers kept busy chasing them down and taking them to court. This second round of public criticism gave Fry a bitter tone in his diary. "So now, after five years of managing the park and meeting the goals of the director, there was still a lot of controversy, not of my making, but in the direction the director had steered us," his pen steamed. He blamed his failure to get "our transmountain road" on Ernie Dickerman, environmental groups, and the *Knoxville News-Sentinel*, which kept "criticism of the park action in the public eye." At least Fry still felt he understood what the Smokies needed, even if "purists" like Dickerman wanted to ruin it and ungrateful "wheelers and dealers in Gatlinburg" criticized him. Before moving on further goals, Fry took a few days off to take the Ordeal for the Vigil Honor, a meditation retreat in the woods at Camp Pellississippi. In a ceremony initiating him into a new level above an Eagle Scout, he was named *TSJWAYI*, meaning "Great White Heron."[39]

Yogi and the Picnic Baskets

The last Hartzog goal Fry tackled, improving bear management, proved what a thorny task preserving the wilds and pleasing the public at the same time could be. In his reminiscences, ranger John O. Morrell devoted an entire chapter to bear stories. At the height of his career, Morrell spent a lot of time protecting visitors from bears, and vice versa, because during the 1950s and 1960s they had become the park's chief attraction. Although the view from Mount Le Conte was splendid, the trip through Cades Cove breathtaking, and the annual wildflower pilgrimage exceedingly popular, what really got people out of Gatlinburg and Cherokee was: bears. Unfortunately, though, for Morrell, Fry, and the park service, what tourists wanted—bears—was not necessarily good for bears, or tourists either, for that matter.

As the first major sanctuary for *Ursus americanus* in the East, the Great Smoky Mountains soon protected some 400 black bears. About 6 feet when standing, a female black bear weighs 120–130 pounds; a male, about 200–240 pounds. Normally tolerant and not ferocious toward human beings, male black bears become hazardous to one another each June, when they compete for the most attractive female bears. After mating, a female ovulates, but the fertilized egg does not implant in her uterus until she finds her den, usually a cavity high in a mature tree. Males generally pick a den nearby but on the ground. By January or February the female gives birth to one to four cubs, which leave the den with her in March. Over the winter, bears lose one-third or more of their body weight, and so they emerge each spring ready to eat—for a mother bear, the situation is even more critical, as she must support her cubs too. In the wild, a black bear dines on berries, mast, ants, beetles, yellow jackets, and small mammals. In the 1940s in the Great Smoky Mountains, though, bears began to prefer picnics, or whatever food they could panhandle from tourists.[40]

In the early years of the park, scientists still knew very little about the life cycle of a wild black bear, let alone the habits of a panhandling bruin. Certainly no one imagined how quickly bears, once protected, could adapt themselves to human beings. In 1938 bears already tied up traffic on Newfound Gap Road. Lured onto the road with food by a motorist in search of a photograph, a bear could soon stop an entire line of cars. "Largely because they are unacquainted with our policy which makes bear-feeding a violation of the rules, some tourists toss food to the bruins," Superintendent Eakin complained, "and the animals, now, apparently associate human beings with a potential and choice food supply." Eakin issued a press release for local newspapers, pointing out the reasons for the policy. The day after the press release, a bear bit a man who got too close with his camera.[41]

Just three years later, roadside bears became a major attraction in the park, and along with popularity came increasing bear "incidents" like the one in 1938. One bear, which made his debut on May 5, 1940, became such an adept panhandler so fast that the park decided to move him on May 29 to a more remote section of the park. Although Roscoe, as the rangers dubbed him, traveled ten miles in the back of a park vehicle, he returned to the same section of highway by May 31. This time rangers marked him with white paint and gave him another ride in the back of a pickup, and he returned by June 6. Three days later the repeat offender was picked up, taken eighteen miles "by air line" and again released. You guessed it, by June 13 he arrived at his old haunts. Although the record does not say what became of Roscoe, in August a visitor suffered the worst incident yet. A woman from Savannah, Georgia, followed by a small, yapping dog, stopped to watch a mother bear and her cubs. The bear went for the dog, as did the woman. Although the tourist rescued her dog, the bear's revenge required nine stitches, three drains, a tetanus shot, and painkillers. In his report, the superintendent said she "escaped destruction of considerable muscle tissue only because she was very fat."[42] The next summer, bears chewed up three saddles belonging to a horseback party at Little Indian Gap shelter cabin. A bear got into a spring house in Elkmont and drank 4 gallons of milk, then got his head stuck in the pail and couldn't get loose, "in which unfortunate condition he was found, and it was another case of a ranger to the rescue—of the bear." A few days later, a bear destroyed a tent and camping equipment in Cosby campground, and another established himself in Chimneys campground, "hav-

ing found living accommodations much to his liking there." The following day, he was taken to Deals Gap, at the extreme western end of the
park, marked with paint, and released.[43]

By the end of the 1940s, visitors reported seeing as many as eighteen
different bears in a single trip from Gatlinburg to Smokemont. All the
early guidebooks mention the bears. "The dangerous thing about the
bears," one reporter noted, "is that visitors regard them as harmless pets,
habituated to humans."[44] While official policies forbade the creation of
tame bears, superintendents understood their popularity. Every spring
the park put up signs reading, "Do Not Feed the Bears" and sent press
releases on the topic to local newspapers, which dutifully printed them,
unedited. Every summer, people came to feed the bears and rangers
looked the other way, busy directing traffic. Superintendents Eakin and
Russ reported even serious encounters with a good deal of mirth:

> On June 25, Dr. Burlin of Bryson City and party were camped at the
> Bryson Place on Deep Creek and experienced an unusual incident
> with a bear. They had gone up the creek a short distance from their
> camp, leaving their personal possessions in the tent. Upon their
> return they found that a bear had visited the tent taking Dr. Thomp-
> son's pants, all the bread, meat, butter, frying pan, and all the Camel
> cigarettes, leaving the Lucky Strike cigarettes. Dr. Thompson for-
> tunately had a second pair of pants which relieved his embarrass-
> ment. The only item retrieved was the frying pan, which was found
> approximately half a mile from their camp. The bear to date has not
> shown up on the highway wearing Dr. Thompson's pants.

While the bears did seasonally disappear for wild foods and hiberna-
tion, just before they left they would "enjoy a bountiful Thanksgiving
repast at the hands of visitors, who fed them anything from chocolate
candy to fruit cakes."[45]

According to Morrell, rangers named all the roadside bears and knew
their habits well. One bear with a brown face, nicknamed Sadie, became
aggressive only if someone tried to take her photograph. Morrell recalled
one afternoon on the Clingmans Dome Road, when a tourist with a camera tried to get a close-up of Sadie. The tourist's wife cautioned him, but
he persisted. "Who's afraid of a tame bear?" he said. He got within ten
feet of Sadie, squatted, then Sadie charged the photographer, and in so

doing bent a sapling so that it struck the tourist in the head. He tried to run, but landed in the middle of the road with his pants torn. "To my surprise," Morrell said, "the man's wife was delighted, laughing and taunting him with: 'Now who's *not* afraid of a bear?'" Another bear, nicknamed Old Tom, weighed 450 pounds and developed a scenic and tasty range near Mount LeConte. Trapped on August 11 and taken to Cosby (thirty-six miles by road and fifteen miles as a crow might do it), he returned to his favorite spot by late afternoon the next day. Despite regular transportation, Old Tom grew old as a successful panhandler. Near the end of his life, he was nearly deaf, and he "walked down the center-line of the highway, completely disregarding traffic." Not surprisingly, bear jams became a regular part of a Smokies vacation, and not until October, when acorns were plentiful, did the panhandlers wander back into the woods. "Only one bear, Diana the Dimwit, remains along the highway to snarl up Sunday traffic," the superintendent reported in the late fall. According to Morrell, Diana the Dimwit got her name because she didn't seem to have sense enough to go into the woods even in bad weather. "As gentle as a dog," she was often the first bear visitors saw in the Smokies. Morrell requested permission to move her off the road. "Why do you want to move her?" the chief ranger asked. "She has never even offered to hurt anyone." "That's why I want to move her," Morrell answered. "She is the first bear the visitors encounter, and they think that ALL park bears are tame." His request was denied—bears like Diana were too valuable as tourist magnets. Evidently, bears, tourists, rangers, and their supervisors had all become habituated to the situation.[46]

During the 1950s panhandling bears graduated to major property damage. Lessees had long complained of bears stripping corn and apple trees or stealing pigs and calves. Soon some wealthy Knoxville residents, who had maneuvered privileges to maintain summer homes for themselves in Elkmont, complained about bears repeatedly breaking into their cottages for food. Rangers spent hours trapping and removing bears from the area, as well as from Cades Cove and Smokemont, where "certain bears appeared to be destructive and vicious." Rangers noticed that mother bears taught their cubs how to panhandle, and soon there was more than one generation of bears adept at breaking into picnic baskets, even cars. In 1957 rangers trapped a number of bears "suspected of unprovoked attacks on sleeping campers at Elkmont," shot them, and turned their carcasses over to an orphanage. Reports about these incidents no longer showed much mirth, but park officials clearly had managed themselves into a dilemma.[47]

A new official NPS policy stated that "fed bears become bums, and dangerous," but no one in the Smokies seemed to mind their mooching.[48] Did roadside bears become dangerous? Although there exists no confirmed case of a human killed by a black bear in Great Smoky Mountains National Park, tourists reported seventy-one personal injuries between 1960 and 1966, the first period for which such statistics were recorded. The vast majority of these incidents occurred on roadsides, where bears associated humans with lunch. Visitors reported the nabbing of 182 picnic baskets over this same period, which doesn't sound too serious until you note an additional ninety-six incidents where bears broke into automobiles and house trailers to get to food. Two Georgia residents reported that bears ripped open the top of their new 1967 Ford Mustang, broke the side mirror, dented a fender, and flattened a tire. Because of traffic pileups and aggressive behavior toward humans or cars, 229 bears were relocated and 54 bears destroyed between 1960 and 1966.[49] Bears proved themselves hazardous to Ford Mustangs, but would they attack people? Researchers Janet Tate Eagar and Mike Pelton, a University of Tennessee graduate student and her professor, showed that panhandlers learned to charge humans, because startled tourists repeatedly dropped the box of crackers or cookies and ran, leaving the bear with a reward. Unless visitors repeatedly harassed a bear, or a person came between a bear and its escape route or a mother and her cubs, nothing serious happened. In the 392 panhandling sessions Eagar observed, she recorded no serious injuries, even though she witnessed 624 aggressive behaviors, such as charging. In one example, three young boys pursued Phoenix, a female roadside bear. First she seemed to warn the boys by twirling around rapidly and making noises in her jaw. When one of the boys tantalized her by holding food out of her reach, she grabbed the cookie in her mouth, actually pushing him away with her front paws. When the boys persisted, she knocked one of them to the ground and bit him on the neck. "This was not so gruesome as it sounds," wrote the researchers. "She did not even puncture the skin, and there were no superficial wounds visible immediately thereafter."[50]

Bears did cause traffic problems, however, and this became a growing concern with increased visitation in the 1960s. In July 1963, the chief ranger reported 493 bear jams on the Tennessee side of U.S. Highway 441 alone. On one day in July 1965 Superintendent George Fry counted twenty-two bears and five traffic jams between Cherokee and park headquarters. "Somebody feeds the bears against regulations," Fry told a reporter, but of course this was nothing new. Ignored regulations in regard to panhandlers had been the unofficial policy for almost three decades. "And that just teases them. No more food and the bear is maddened, slapping at anyone within range," he explained. Under Fry, rangers such as Morrell were supposed to get the bears off the road as soon as possible. "My boss told me to get the bears back in the bush so the traffic would clear," he told a reporter.[51] As soon as the traffic (and especially the ranger) cleared, he might have added, the bear would return.

Then in the summer of 1967 bears brought the NPS its worst nightmare. A horrific incident in Glacier National Park that summer threatened the image of the national parks as a safe place to encounter nature. Though the tragedy involved grizzly bears, which typically weigh five times as much as the average male black bear, in the media blitz that followed such distinctions disappeared. On August 13 two grizzlies each attacked a campsite in Glacier National Park, killing and mutilating two nineteen-year-old girls. Eerie coincidences made it an especially good news story. One victim, Michele Koons, worked in the park gift shop, and she had asked her parents' permission before joining her four friends on an overnight camping trip to Trout Lake. A grizzly raided their camp early in the evening, so the young adults built a fire and huddled in their sleeping bags all night. Just before dawn, the grizzly attacked again, and as everyone tried to run to a tree, Koons screamed that her zipper was stuck, as the bear started tearing her arm. "Oh my God I'm dead," her friends remembered her last words, as the grizzly dragged her into the woods. Ten miles northeast of this site camped Roy Ducat and Julie Helgeson, a sophomore at the University of Minnesota. Helgeson also worked for a park concession, and she too was dragged into the woods in the early morning hours. Ducat ran to a nearby chalet to get help, but his companion died of puncture wounds in her throat and lungs shortly after rescuers arrived.[52]

No major network, newspaper, news magazine, or outdoors publication missed this story. Photographs of the two attractive girls and descriptions of their outstanding academic records appeared juxtaposed with menacing stock photos, illustrations, and footage of mammoth grizzlies, snarling and looming. The press demanded an explanation. These were the first deaths from grizzlies in Glacier's history (only three bear deaths had occurred in the entire history of the NPS), and no one seemed to have a clue why it happened. Renowned naturalists Frank and John Craighead, who had studied grizzlies since 1959, said that even these large bears generally retreat from humans unless injured, sick, or cornered. "This whole thing, the coincidence of two attacks at almost the same time, leaves us at a loss," said Glacier's chief ranger. The superintendent proposed the ludicrous notion that a lightning storm had excited the bears to violence. Since this was the late 1960s, some suggested that hippies gave the bears bait laced with LSD. Never an official story, ranger lore insisted that both girls were having their menstrual periods at the time of attack. The park service buried the incident in a mountain of reports, official autopsies, and FBI special-agent investigations. Even at the time, however, officials knew that a garbage-dependent bear had killed Julie Helgeson. The park actually fed bears at the dumps so tourists could get a closer look at them.[53] As many as 75 percent of Glacier's grizzlies relied on the dump feedings. As the number of visitors to Glacier and indeed all the national parks increased, and bears lost their fear of humans through park and tourist feeding, the potential for such disasters increased. Something clearly had to be done. In April 1968 the NPS held a closed meeting of research scientists and management biologists at the Horace M. Albright Training Center in the Grand Canyon. Starker Leopold, chief scientist of the park service, called for a return to wild bears not dependent on garbage. Within weeks of the park service meeting, Glacier, Yellowstone, and the Great Smokies all moved on new bear-management plans.[54]

In the Smokies, however, the 1968 bear-management plan still reflected all the conflicts between resource management and tourism. With a stated objective to "maintain bear populations in their natural environments," the report demanded that rangers "provide conditions for visitors to observe [them] in safety." Apparently, no one saw the potential contradiction. The program ordered the immediate removal of all bears seen in campgrounds and along U.S. Highway 441. If a tagged and released bear returned to the park, rangers would "determine the disposition of the animal." When a bear became "belligerent, hostile, or overly aggressive," it would be removed. At the same time, as soon as the first bear appeared on the roadway, rangers were to "start instilling fear in the animals." Visitor education, bearproof garbage cans, and assistance to researchers completed the management plan on paper. An article in the *Knoxville News-Sentinel* detailing these initiatives illustrated them with a cartoon of a bear in a jail car driven by "the park bear patrol." Park ranger Marion W. Myers stated that harmless television bears, such as Yogi, Gentle Ben, and Smokey, compounded the problem. "Their cute antics stick with the public," Myers said, but in the previous year tourists suffered sixty-five bear incidents, with injuries resulting to twelve persons. Although none was serious, Myers said, forebodingly, that "scalps have been laid open." Rangers needed to reawaken bears' "normal inherent fear of humans" by hitting them with clubs.[55]

Whether it was the comic illustration of the "bear patrol" or ranger Myers using Yogi's name in the same paragraph as a club, public outrage over the article and the new policy rapidly reached fever pitch. Tourists wrote Superintendent Fry. They wrote Secretary of the Interior Stewart Udall, the Tennessee Department of Conservation, the North Carolina Department of Conservation and Development, their senators, their governors, President Nixon, and even former First Lady, Lady Bird Johnson. The majority of writers called the new policy a "grave mistake," because "each year as we visit the Smoky Mountains we enjoyed the bear jams." Another writer protested "the removal of black bears" from the park (this had not been proposed), as they were "the chief attraction for tourists and natives." "One of the reasons we like to visit the park is to see the bears," said another woman. "It is very thrilling to get to see a mother bear with her young cub and to see the mother protect her cub just as our mothers protect us." One man stated parents took their children to the park primarily to see bears: therefore, "evacuation of the bears" would result in the loss of "hundreds of thousands in revenue." One woman addressed the superintendent as "Dear Sir (loosely speaking): I am surprised someone such as you who would resort to such cruelty toward animals could keep your job very long." Postcards tended to be more cryptic: "Dear Jackass Fry" and "Go away, leave, resign, anything just so you go, go go . . . we much prefer the bear, they are not half as dangerous."

Many of these letters attacked irresponsible tourists for ruining every-one's fun. "Anyone with an ounce of common sense knows that a bear is one of God's wild creatures and you do not attempt to pet one as you would a cat or dog. Superintendent Fry's argument that the bears may molest visitors is his idea. In 95 percent of the cases I would say the visitors are molesting the bears." As another woman put it: "May we respectfully suggest that you remove the offensive tourists instead?"[56]

Fry's defensive responses to all these letters contained numerous underlined words. "Your vociferous letter," most of his responses began, "leads to the conclusions that you have no experience in handling people with bears around and that you are unacquainted with Federal Tort Claims Act (60 Stat. 843; 28 U.S.C. 1964 ed Sec. 2371, et seq., as amended)." His condescending tone caused bear lovers to share the responses with a Knoxville Journal columnist, who furthered this public relations fiasco. The columnist referred to the relocation rules as "George Fry's black bear extermination policy" and stated that it was "common knowledge around Gatlinburg that every bear sighted by park officials is a bad bear." "That is," he explained, "an attempt is made to trap and ship away every bear. There are few bears left and perhaps will be none by the end of the summer."[57] The entire psychology department at the University of Tennessee wrote Superintendent Fry on the subject of hitting bears with clubs to train them to be afraid: "all of us, on the basis of professional knowledge, question the effectiveness of such a method. In fact, it may more probably result in greater aggressiveness toward humans by the bears." Fry wrote back, lecturing them about his twenty years of experience with animals, and reassuring them that the "club" was merely a "stick" used to tap them on the nose. "This does not result in aggressiveness toward humans, but instills in them a respect for humans, keeps them at a distance, yet permits visitors to see free, roaming bears."[58]

Fry did receive some supportive mail. A biology professor wrote, suggesting that the park build a fence between visitors and bears. "What surprises me, indeed I find it appalling is that the commonest argument is nothing should be done because after all many fewer people are injured or killed each year than by cars," the professor commented, "as though you were to argue that because fewer people are killed by leukemia every year than by cars nothing should be done about such diseases!"[59] One woman defended the park service, saying, "If the government would get rid of the bears, then people could enjoy the park. After all, who is the park for, and whose taxes are paying for it?" Another man wrote asking whether under the new circumstances the park might give up bear cubs for adoption. "If so please give me full details on how to get one." A Texas high school student wrote, requesting one of the discarded bears for a school mascot.[60]

The majority of tourists and newspapers that needed tourism dollars condemned the policy. The *Waynesville Mountaineer* reminded the superintendent that the bears represented a major attraction to the 5 to 6 million visitors per year. Statements about injuries and maulings tend to "frighten people unnecessarily," an editorial commented, because if people "obey the regulations and use common sense the chances of getting even near a bear are remote, unless by choice." Although the editorial writer praised the park service's policy of trapping pest bears and relocating them, he concluded that "the idea of separating people and bears defeats the basis on which national parks were developed."[61] The North Carolina director of travel and promotion, however, put the issue more directly:

> We hear continuing rumors that the National Park Service hopes to gradually eliminate all bears from the Great Smokies. Naturally, we hope this is not true. I realize that the bears must cause your rangers a few headaches now and then, but I believe the problems they cause are more than offset by the great attraction which they provide our travelers. The entire travel industry in North Carolina will be vitally concerned with this . . . and to do a story for the *Travel Bulletin*, I would appreciate your views.[62]

Don't tamper with tourism, the subtext read, a theme echoed by a *Knoxville Journal* story. The lead referred to George Fry's "Get-Rid-of-the-Bears" campaign. The reporter interviewed two vacationing newlyweds from Valdosta, Georgia. "We've been roaming through the Smokies for almost four days and have yet to see the first bear," complained Mrs. Stansell in the story, which included a photo of the couple with a stuffed bear. "I've been to the park twice previously and always saw a bear," Stansell continued, "but this is my husband's first trip and he is anxious to get a glimpse of one. It looks like he won't however, because we have to leave tomorrow."[63]

Despite his prolific correspondence with bear lovers and bear haters, Fry didn't mention this trouble in his daily log. To his credit, the number of bear incidents declined that year. Establishing dominance with a club seemed to work so well that eventually, Morrell recalled, all a ranger had to do was swing the club in the air—sometimes, he was convinced, the bears responded to his uniform—and the animals fled into the woods. They became afraid of rangers, and they disappeared when they saw them. The majority of tourists, though, did not want bears to run away. They wanted to feed bears. One hiker described a Sunday in June 1968, when she emerged from a backpacking trip on the AT at Newfound Gap. Because of the publicity furor over bears, a ranger at the overlook valiantly tried to field questions about bears. "All the way down the mountain road on the way to the airport," she said, "I saw no other ranger and no warning signs but I did see all too many bear jams with up-ended bears in garbage cans surrounded by gawking tourists." The policy also had little effect on the backcountry, where bears proved an especially big problem on the Appalachian Trail. Another hiker from Indiana saw sixteen black bears on his hike through the park on the AT. "Fifteen of those bears reacted normally and moved away with a shout or a well-aimed stone," he wrote. "However, we spent 45 minutes shaking in a tree because of the 16th bear. Shouts and stones only made her advance faster swatting at trees as she came." Although the hiker bore the bear no ill will, he asked the superintendent if he could carry a gun loaded with blanks or tear gas next time. (Fry said no.) A responsible UNC-Greensboro student wrote about spending the night with her friends in an AT shelter. They carefully hung their food in a tree, yet in the middle of the night a bear lifted a pack of empty cans off the top bunk next to one of the sleeping campers. When the group made loud noises to frighten her, she charged at them. No one was hurt, but the young woman wrote that if her charges ever became "real attacks, there could be problems." That fall, the chief ranger recommended that the park service cover the front of each AT shelter with cyclone fencing to protect sleeping campers. Panhandlers that could not survive without human food probably wandered out of the park to get it, where they were easily killed by poachers or hunters.

Whether the new management plan created happy tourists or unhappy bears, in 1969 Fry had completed most of Hartzog's goals. He failed to complete the Master Plan and the Fontana Road, but the director wanted him to move to Olympic National Park. In fact, developers in Gatlinburg put pressure on Hartzog to remove Fry. Five Gatlinburg businessmen filed suit against Fry for closing U.S. Highway 441 to commercial traffic. (The judge threw the case out of court, as soon as Fry recited the legislative mandate.) "[This] was his program I was carrying out," Fry wrote, "but Hartzog did not have the guts to tell them it was his doing. It was easier to put the blame on me." Fry wanted to stay in the Smokies, and he felt bitter toward Hartzog: "Why should he care about my feelings, when he was the king on the throne?" At age fifty-eight, after thirty-six years in the NPS, Fry could have retired but at Hartzog's insistence he decided to go to the regional office in Atlanta instead.[64]

No one who made a serious inquiry into the bear situation in the Smokies could deny the conflict between managing for tourists and the environment at the same time. "The history of resource management in the National Park Service has often been one of trial and error where success was due more to individual personalities than sound guidelines and good information," wrote one NPS official. In short, he said, the focus on promoting tourism pushed the park toward "crisis management" when it came to the land, because nothing would be done about problems, such as the panhandling bears, until a crisis proved that no other options existed.[65] By 1969, even the NPS could see the inherent contradiction between tourism and preservation. In fact, a whole host of unattended resource-management problems, such as the vanishing brook trout, lurked beneath the surface. After the intensive promotion of the road-building program of the 1960s, Tennessee developers still remained unsatisfied, while in North Carolina, Swain County residents grieved the loss of their North Shore Road. These same roads created a new generation of environmental activists, suspicious of the park's commitment to preservation. In the next decade, they would be joined by young scientists within the agency, who became increasingly vocal about those problems. Back at Sugarlands Visitor Center, the most common daily question rangers faced was: "Where are the bears?" followed closely by "What did you do with them?"[66]

On Friday, June 13, 1969, the Clyde Martin family of Knoxville arrived for their annual hike to Spence Field. The two youngest members of the clan, Doug, age nine, and Dennis, age six, chased each other through the woods, appearing and disappearing from their parents' view. The trip was uneventful except for the appearance of a scruffy bear, which snorted several times at the group. The family spent the night on Russell Field, then proceeded on to Spence Field. The next afternoon, as adults looked on, the children played on a grassy knoll near the AT. Although he was out of sight only a very short time, Dennis suddenly did not come when called. A frantic father and grandfather searched the trailside. They found no sign of him. They returned to the ranger station, and over the next sixteen days, hundreds of volunteers, including a detachment of Green Berets, combed the mountains in a grid pattern. They found no sign of the boy. The family believed their son was kidnapped, a story confirmed by psychics called in to investigate the case. Ranger Dwight McCarter, who participated in the search, suspected that a bear may have carried the boy's body away. No one ever solved the mystery, but in 1985 a ginseng collector discovered the bones of what might have been a little boy.[67]

7.1. "Bear jams," or traffic jams caused by panhandling bears, became a daily occurrence in the Smokies during the 1940s. Courtesy of Great Smoky Mountains National Park.

Above: 7.2. Against NPS policies, panhandler bears became the most popular attraction in the park, 1957. Courtesy of Great Smoky Mountains National Park.

Left: 7.3. Superintendent George Fry, whose shift in bear policy angered many tourists, posed in front of the park headquarters. Courtesy of Great Smoky Mountains National Park.

Left: 7.4. Ranger John Morrell, who loved to tell bear stories, depicted here in the 1940s. Courtesy of Great Smoky Mountains National Park.

Below: 7.5. Before bearproof garbage cans. Courtesy of Great Smoky Mountains National Park.

7.6. Fry wanted his rangers to do more "public relations" work, exemplified by ranger Saul Schiffman talking to tourists in Elkmont campground. Photo by Jack Boucher. Courtesy of Great Smoky Mountains National Park.

7.7. Rapid road-building for NPS's Mission 66 program led to extensive rock slides, such as this one on the Little River Road. Courtesy of Great Smoky Mountains National Park.

7.8. Activist Ernie Dickerman (with microphone) spoke at a "Save Our Smokies" rally, 1966. Dickerman became Fry's nemesis as the leader of the movement to gain wilderness designation for park land. Wilderness Society cofounder Harvey Broome is second from upper right. Courtesy of Leroy Fox.

Still Not a Wilderness

*I have always felt that if you do the right thing for
the right reasons and you avoid being arrogant about
it, people will eventually see what you're doing. When
you can show clearly that it's for the common good,
eventually you will win. People will stand by you.*

BOYD EVISON, PARK SUPERINTENDENT, 1975–77

WHEN HE RETIRED from Great Smoky Mountains
National Park in 1964, park biologist Arthur Stupka
had a clear notion of what science in a national park
meant. Few if any scientists worked for the NPS
when he started in 1935, and he received nearly free
rein to carve out the occupation as he saw fit. Since his
teenage years in Ohio, Stupka had kept a nature journal, in which he recorded everything from spring's
first arrival of birds and wildflowers to little-known
species of moths and salamanders. And so wherever
Stupka hiked in the Smokies, he carried the journal,
binoculars, an altimeter, and a cyanide jar, and the
resulting twenty-eight years of records provided a
wealth of biological information about the park, unparalleled in its depth and accuracy. "I liked the area.
It was more interesting than Ohio," the park naturalist shrugged, a man of considered words. His taxonomic skill with trees, wildflowers, and insects became legendary among the academic scientists who
visited the national park, who became his closest associates. He authored or coauthored five books about
natural history—"you could hardly call them books,"
he said, with characteristic modesty—and apprecia-

tive scientists named eight species for him. After exhaustive study and collection, Stupka saw his most important role as an interpreter, leading public hikes and giving public talks to share his knowledge of the environment with visitors.

Consequently, Stupka understood science as a pursuit above politics. "I don't fool with them," he exempted himself. He did not share contemporary notions of wilderness; if he saw a poisonous snake where a visitor might step on it, he killed it. He did not see the need to incorporate cultural history and natural history; to him, the mountain people were until recently "primitive" and not a source of information about the natural world. When Superintendent Hummel told him in 1960 that the newly formed Great Smoky Mountains Natural History Association must sell books and postcards to help fund the park, he told Hummel he no longer wanted to be the naturalist. The new edict from on high forced interpreters to minimize lengthy educational programs, to breezily "entertain" visitors: as one biologist put it, the new ethos "put natural history on the back burner, if not the waste bin." For the last four years of his career he became the park biologist to avoid becoming involved with public relations and money. "I retired because I didn't want to have anything to do with financial things," he said. For the next three decades, Stupka divided his time between a home in Florida and the Hemlock Inn in Bryson City, where he continued to give daytime hikes and evening talks into his nineties.[1]

While Stupka's position sounds uncomplicated and straightforward, it prevented him from challenging park policy. Promoting tourism at the expense of the environment proved costly for bears, brook trout, and Cades Cove ecology, but even someone as well respected as Arthur Stupka could not do anything about it. As he retreated to work on his collections, however, change brewed at the national level. When rangers in Yellowstone got caught in the public limelight shooting herds of elk to control overpopulation, the park service asked for an outside study of its wildlife policy, to be led by biologists and ecologists. The committee, which included University of Tennessee Professor Stanley Cain, produced a widely quoted document called the *Leopold Report*. The author of the study, Starker Leopold, exhorted the NPS "to recognize the enormous complexity of ecological communities" and recommended that scientific research "form the basis of all management programs."[2] The year after the *Leopold Report* came out, Arthur Stupka retired at age fifty-eight. Younger men—and women—would have to change the role of science in Great Smoky Mountains National Park.

Reinforcing the *Leopold Report*, another study by the National Academy of Scientists (NAS) similarly sought the elevation of scientists in the agency. Although university scholars had long done research in the parks, resource management often operated without knowledge of their work. Research scientists, for their part, showed little interest in management problems. The chair of the NAS committee, biologist William J. Robbins, called scientific research in the parks "piecemeal," "fragmented," and "anemic." Solid science required knowledge of local ecosystems and in-park scientists who understood from fieldwork how research was being conducted. He recommended that the park service change its organizational structure, personnel, and budget to give scientific research "line responsibility." Director Wirth and his successor Hartzog chose to ignore these reports, which in truth challenged the direction the two men had taken the park service.[3] Likewise, Smokies Superintendents George Fry and his successor, Vincent Ellis, paid it little mind. It would take more than some paperwork in Washington, D.C., to get Great Smoky Mountains National Park oriented toward scientific research and preservation. It would take a bold new superintendent, a graduate student from Cornell University, and a new research unit called the Uplands Field Research Laboratory.

The Uplands Invasion

The first Ph.D. in the park came in through the back door. A native of Maryland, Susan Power Bratton graduated from Barnard College, Columbia University, and collected several research appointments before entering the Ph.D. program at Cornell University, under Robert Whittaker, the eminent ecologist. Whittaker, who did seminal research on the Smokies during the 1950s, encouraged Bratton to do her research in the park. In the summer of 1972, Bratton stayed in park housing, hiked the trails, and became increasingly disturbed by the rooting and digging of the exotic Russian wild boar in the park. Her dissertation, which began as a study of herb niches at high elevations, ended up incorporating the hog disturbance. "During this stay," Bratton recalled, "I also did some volunteer trail work for the rangers, since the AT was a madhouse and there was almost no patrol. Even after the permit system was established, the shelters were often flooded with people who were off-schedule or simply did not bother to get a permit."[4]

Concerned about impacts on the fauna, Bratton sent her review of hog literature to the park, free of charge, and included a letter, expressing concern about the lack of research on management issues. Rather than dismissing her as an idealistic graduate student, regional chief scientist Jim Larson wrote back, saying he shared her concerns. His successor, Ray Hermann, actually recruited Bratton to become the park biologist, even though Superintendent Ellis did not think the Smokies needed one. Hermann charged her with creating the Uplands Field Research Laboratory, which would oversee research for parks in the southern mountains environment. "Looking at it in retrospect," Bratton commented, "I believe that my sudden rise from volunteer grad student to GS-11 was difficult for the all-male Ranger Division to deal with." Parks such as the Smokies still did not employ many researchers except by outside contract, and the only female employees were secretaries. In the 1970s area newspapers reported on three new "girl rangers" and identified Bratton as the "pretty" and "attractive blonde" in charge of scientific research. If a male researcher accompanied Bratton to a backwoods research site, rangers kidded him about being alone in the woods with a woman.[5] To change an institution with a lot of centralized authority into a model of responsiveness and affirmative action would not be easy.

A further complication was incorporating Bratton and her Uplands crew into NPS culture. Most employees in management worked their way up the ladder by conforming to policy and moving from one park to another. Even the chief ranger and superintendent wore uniforms. Bratton and the technicians she hired arrived about the same time backpacks, hiking boots, and facial hair for men took hold of the nation's youth, and 1970s aesthetics did not sit well with the Ranger Division. Local newspapers commented on Bratton's "faded denims and simple button-up flannel shirt." To save money on the nonexistent budget, Bratton recruited graduate and undergraduate students to do research and hired technicians when money became available. The Uplands crowd held barbecues and covered-dish suppers and were known to sing while camped out on the balds. "We were accused of recruiting tenors," she joked. They went mountain-style square dancing and contra dancing, and Bratton herself was a clogger. On the one hand, students often came into conflict with rangers; if the students parked their vehicles incorrectly at a trailhead, for example, the rangers would cite the vehicles and have them towed. "On the other hand, we had a fast and solid start using less funds than most park operations would for a single project," said Bratton, pointing out the work done on grassy balds, hogs, gap phase, and under-story structure. And no one could argue with their publications: in those early years, management reports and magazine articles as well as master's theses, dissertations, and scholarly articles flowed out of the new Uplands Field Research Laboratory.[6]

Superintendent Ellis located his new biologists in run-down trailers, leftovers from a Mississippi flood relief operation, at the site of the old Tremont lumber camp 14 miles from headquarters. Bratton was issued a beat-up pickup, which frequently broke down; she used her own car for fieldwork without reimbursement. If the graduate students she recruited couldn't get into seasonal housing, they slept on the floor in her house. "I [had] serious trouble getting cooperation and getting anything done," she recalled, as the facilities did not compare favorably with the state-of-the-art Cornell laboratories. "This was partially due to being a single scientist outside the main sphere of political engagement," said Bratton. "I also think the park administration was hoping that if science remained 'out there' somewhere, they would not be responsible to act relative to its findings." Working closely with Hermann, Bratton set research priori-ties: (1) scientific research should reflect park needs, not researcher inter-est; (2) it needed to be prioritized so the more important problems could be addressed first; and (3) project areas needed to be open to multiple research interests to maximize what the park would find out. During her first year, she began visiting universities and held a scholarly meeting for scientists doing research relevant to the park. Since Stupka's departure, research in the park had fallen off. "Getting more scientists into the park was an easy trend to initiate," said Bratton. "Making management more dependent on sound science was far more difficult."[7]

And Uplands research soon challenged that staple of park policy: at-tract more visitors. Between 1964 and 1975, the park saw a 63 percent increase in visitation, a 33 percent increase in hiking, and a 63 percent increase in horseback riding. But in just three years, 1972–1975, the trails saw a 53 percent increase in backcountry camping.[8] Shortly after her arrival, Bratton's researchers began documenting the tremendous effect that overuse had on the Smokies environment. The Uplands Field Research Laboratory quantified the erosion that horses caused on Cataloochee Divide, where the horses created a "muddy corduroy" out of the soft soil, which made for "very difficult walking."[9] They studied the total number of illegal campsites, which widened the disturbance in Big Creek, Forney Creek, Elkmont, and Heintooga campgrounds.[10] On the Appalachian Trail, through-hikers detoured around obstacles, trampling the undergrowth and creating a virtual roadway. As Bratton noticed her first summer, the permit system simply increased the number of illegal campsites. In a single twelve-bunk trail shelter in 1971, an estimated 132 backpackers spent the night. Bratton's observations, widely circulated through newspaper interviews, made her very unpopular with the park's Maintenance Division, in particular, because she noted the frequent use of motorized "management roads" for trail maintenance work. At the time, rangers actually policed the backcountry with motorbikes.[11]

Luckily for Bratton, her research dovetailed with articles in the national press, which argued that success was spoiling the national parks. When these articles mentioned the Smokies, they noted George Fry's limit of seven days on staying in campgrounds and new camping fees as an attempt to deal with traffic. The new director of the NPS, Gary Everhardt, understood that the promotional activities of Wirth and Hartzog put the park service in an terrible position. "We have reached the crisis point in some areas," he told a *U.S. News and World Report* reporter. "We will simply have to find more ways of controlling visits, or else the parks will no longer be worth visiting." Power had clearly shifted at the top of the agency when Hartzog resigned in 1972. However, because none of his successors in the 1970s stayed more than a couple of years, the park service did not incorporate structural or administrative changes that could support the scientists. For example, none of the seven divisions reporting directly to Everhardt represented resource management or research; both subjects still fell under Management and Operations with maintenance and law enforcement.[12] Likewise individual parks, including the Smokies, could be more or less supportive of resource management, depending on the predisposition of the superintendent. Susan Bratton and the other scientists who started dedicating themselves to research in the

Smokies found that protecting the park put them in an adversarial position with their supervisors. That first year Bratton told Arthur Stupka, the park's longtime naturalist, that she would "advertise some of the park's problems to the scientific community," and that she was concerned about the "lack of management" in the park.[13] Superintendent Ellis, probably aware of her hostility, kept her excluded from major meetings by the distance to the trailer. A change of heart with regard to science in general and Uplands in particular arrived in 1975, when Everhardt chose Boyd Evison to be the new superintendent. However, both Evison and Bratton underestimated how difficult changing policy could be in the strange political arena of eastern Tennessee and western North Carolina. Neither imagined the power of history to undermine the best intentions of scientists and superintendents.

Exotic European Boars and Native North Carolina Hunters

About twenty years before the Uplands Field Research Laboratory existed, ranger John Rogers saw the first sign of the European wild hog (*Sus scrofa*) in Great Smoky Mountains National Park. "This was a very large track," he recalled. "Later in the early fall [of 1951] some smaller tracks were seen, and I finally saw three shoats [young hogs] that year."[14] Since they first escaped from a private hunting reserve on Hooper Bald in 1912, the hogs made their way steadily toward the park boundary. With bristly fur, wedge-shaped heads, and long legs, the wild boars looked bigger and ran faster than domesticated pigs. Plowing up the ground like rototillers, they ate insects, salamanders, bird eggs, snails, and the roots of wildflowers. In the fall, they thrived on acorns and hickory nuts and competed with black bears for food. Since wild boars often root near streams and springs, they caused soil erosion and siltation. Worst of all, without a major predator their population grew annually at an astounding rate. Producing five piglets a litter sometimes twice per year, their yearly reproduction averaged 178 percent. The president of the Smoky Mountains Hiking Club first noticed boar activity on a hike to Blockhouse Mountain in 1958. He was amazed at the effect on vegetation. Two years before, Haw Gap had a beautiful meadow, but on this visit the "grubbing operation" left hardly a "patch of grass large enough to camp on."[15]

The park took action in 1959, when rangers trapped the first hog on Gregory Bald; the following year, rangers noted a trail the hogs rooted along Parsons Branch in the western end of the park. Although rooting and damage increased exponentially with the hog population, only sixty-one boars were trapped by 1962; all were released in nearby national forests, where they became popular game animals with regional hunters. Throughout western North Carolina and eastern Tennessee, hunters chased the European wild boar with specially trained dogs. Soon they labeled boar-hunting a "popular tradition." Eventually, the state wildlife commission captured hogs and even started a breeding program to aid hunters.[16]

Of course, the state didn't appreciate the fact that another government agency, the NPS, wanted to remove hogs. In January 1964, the North Carolina Wildlife Resources Commission questioned the park's authority to manage the exotic Russian wild boar through live-trapping and relocation as well as "direct reduction" (read: shooting them). Representing local hunting clubs and regional sportsmen, the commission believed that the park should serve as a reserve to produce hogs, much the way it did with bears. George Fry ordered all trapping and shooting to cease until a decision could be obtained from NPS lawyers. Because official park policy mandated that the park protect native species, such as the rare Jordan's salamander and the bulbs and roots of trilliums, from exotic ones, such as the marauding boar, the solicitor could find no legal basis for the hunters' objections.[17] The North Carolina Wildlife Resources Commission did not give up easily, though. While Fry ordered a $19,900 study in 1964 "to develop an effective wild hog elimination program" and a $39,500 study in 1969 "to develop a more practical and effective management program," the North Carolina Wildlife Resources Commission funded its own study.[18] In a joint effort with the Tennessee Game and Fish Commission, the North Carolina commission reported that live-trapped animals did not seem to have the "homing" instinct often reported in bears. Of the ninety-one wild boars transplanted from Great Smoky Mountains National Park, none returned to their original capture sites.[19] Whereas the state leaned toward live-trapping and releasing the hogs to benefit the hunters, at $207 per boar for trapping and relocation the park found it more cost effective to shoot them. For example, a 1972 study by

University of Tennessee Professor Mike Pelton and the Tennessee Division of Wildlife Management compared the effectiveness of various NPS control efforts. They concluded that trapping and "direct reduction" of hogs did not begin to keep the hog population in control; the NPS estimate of 500 animals living in the park was "likely very conservative."[20] The battle of studies echoed years of grudges between the park service and residents of Swain and Graham Counties in North Carolina.

In 1969 the park removed 155 hogs. According to the park ranger at Twentymile, this unusual success could be attributed to a poor mast crop, which made trap bait more enticing. By the fall, however, the population recovered. A ranger in the Little River district wrote that "the potential exists for explosive increase of the population" and he recommended more research into control efforts. By the time that the Uplands Field Research Laboratory opened, European wild boar had spread to Cades Cove, to park headquarters and Cherokee Orchard, and as far east as Oconaluftee and Cosby.[21]

Into this scientific and political fray walked Susan Bratton, who in 1974 produced her voluminous report on the scientific literature on the European wild boar. Because the hogs already had caused problems in other national parks and because scientists in Great Britain, Germany, and Poland had published a great deal about their biology, she found the impacts of wild boars on vegetation and their prolific reproduction well documented. "Even if the Park Service cannot possibly hope to exterminate the hogs, the population should be kept well below the carrying capacity . . . to alleviate the effects of competition and predation on other species," she wrote. European scientists also concluded that control of hogs *required* hunting, because live-trapping just did not keep the numbers down. According to farmers arrested for illegal hunting in the park, poaching probably worked better than anything else, as they took some 100–300 hogs per year. "The hunters know that the Park Service is trying to reduce the hog population and they are perfectly aware that the Park Service has failed in the attempt," she concluded. "As far as the hunters are concerned they are doing the Park a favor by shooting hogs, and they therefore can easily rationalize killing a deer or bear. The large hog population has also renewed interest by the hunters' lobby in creating a legal hunting season in the park. Their arguments are becoming difficult to ignore, as the hogs take over more and more of the Park." She recommended a regular census program the following year to get an accurate idea of population and control of the estimated 800 hogs.[22]

No one at first paid attention to Bratton's study, and most of the research would be replicated in the Smokies before it became part of policy. Her conclusions were left, in her own words, to "chance and personalities."[23] As chance would have it, Director Everhardt sent the Smokies a new personality in Superintendent Boyd Evison.[24] Son of an NPS employee, Evison grew up in Washington, D.C., traveling on family vacations to the Smokies, which he called "the greatest wilderness east of the Rockies." After graduating in forestry from Colorado State University, Evison worked in public relations for a few years, then became a park ranger and eventually director of the Horace Albright Training Center in Arizona. At age forty-one, he became the youngest man to serve as superintendent. Sitting on the porch of the superintendent's home in Twin Creeks above Gatlinburg, Evison could not help being impressed by the "lush abundant life, the sight, smell, and feel of it; the green canopy overhead," he recalled. "There probably were more green cells in sight than existed in Arizona (from whence I came)." Among his first impressions, he also could not forget the way the forest floor appeared "plowed, disked, and harrowed" by wild boars. Everhardt expected Evison to make changes; he also knew that the dynamic young superintendent would tell him things he didn't necessarily want to hear.[25]

Evison grew up believing in wild places; when he was a child, his father read aloud to him from Ernest Thompson Seton's *Two Little Savages* and Rudyard Kipling's *The Jungle Book*. As an adult, he was influenced by Aldo Leopold's *Sand County Almanac* and Joseph Sax's *Mountains without Handrails*. When visitors questioned him about the safety of undeveloped tracts of roadless land, he was not afraid to declare risk as part of the wilderness experience. An avid runner and hiker, Evison kept a backpack by his desk for quick escapes, and articles about him included the mileage in the backcountry he covered in what he described as the "finest wilderness area in the east." "Lean and quick-witted," as one article called him, Evison believed in the *Leopold Report's* new emphasis on ecosystem management. At the same time he noted, along with Everhardt, the danger of overuse. Rotting historical structures, rutted trails, and littered roadsides send a signal to the public, Evison told a reporter during his first week at the park, that "America doesn't care enough to husband its most distinctive natural and historical resources. Why then should people treat those resources with care? Neglect begets neglect."[26] His obvious pro-wilderness philosophy caused Gatlinburg developers to blanch when, shortly after his arrival, he posted contamination warning signs along the West Prong of the Little Pigeon River between Gatlinburg and Pigeon Forge to alert tourists that the city dumped raw sewage into the crystal-clear mountain stream below. "I'm sorry we had to do it, but we have an obligation to the public," he said about the signs. He repeatedly refused to sugarcoat his message for the sake of developers. In contrast to his predecessors, he said that high visitation was a *problem:* "We have to preserve the resources, or there will be nothing left to enjoy," he said. "It should still be possible 100 years from now for people to go out in the back country here and hike for a couple days without seeing anybody else. If it's going to be possible anywhere in the eastern United States, this will be where it is."[27] And he could be blunt about the abuses of tourism: "People should be aware that if they feed bears they are helping to sign their death warrants."[28]

Within the first week Evison observed that "Susan Bratton and her doughty band were exiled to a decrepit trailer at Tremont, and she had been essentially excluded from the park's management core." Almost immediately, he offered the scientists the superintendent's house, just outside of Gatlinburg, and he moved his wife and two daughters into what had been the district ranger's house. "Interestingly, local rumor was that we moved because my wife was upset by the snakes around the house," Evison remembered. "Not true. In fact, we had kept snakes as pets for years!" The Twin Creeks facility sat next to a creek in two channels and grew very moldy in the summertime. All the baseboards carried a greenish tinge, and it had a poor history as a residence. For Bratton, though, Twin Creeks represented a "breakthrough in terms of science legitimacy," and the group had a party to celebrate when they got stationery and a sign. Under Boyd Evison, Uplands got a brochure, explaining its function in research coordination, collecting baseline data, monitoring research, project research, and management application.[29] And the gestures turned out to be more than symbolic, as Evison also supported Bratton's work on trail erosion and stream siltation from overuse. Allowing Bratton into the circle of decision making, though, would bring him into conflict with the park's Maintenance Division.

At first Evison made simple administrative changes geared toward conservation. He started a paper-recycling program at the headquarters. In park restroom facilities he replaced paper towels with blow-dry equipment. He began replacing full-size cars with compacts and ordered that he and the assistant superintendent drive the smaller cars. He mandated a "rigorous" physical fitness program for park employees "so that they will be capable of handling such strenuous jobs as search and rescue." Although some employees surely grumbled, these changes reflected real national concerns about energy conservation and a growing awareness of recycling. No one would call them revolutionary.

In January the following year, however, he took a step toward protecting the trails, in support of Bratton's research. Three backcountry roads used by the Maintenance Division and "special park friends" would be closed to vehicles of all kinds. "Anything we can do to reduce stream siltation is important to water quality and fish habitat," the press release stated. "Conversion to trail status should reduce non-vegetated surface and the silted water run-off to adjacent streams." A few privileged employees used the roads to go fishing, and they didn't appreciate the loss. To make sure that the order was obeyed, large boulders—soon dubbed "Boyd's Boulders"—were placed at the entrances of three backcountry roads. One Gatlinburg resident wrote the *Knoxville News-Sentinel* to express his gratitude for the closings, calling it a "heartening sign that there is a sincere effort taking place to preserve the parks as real sanctuaries." Because the park service had previously paid so little attention to environmentalists, this move did seem revolutionary to them. The Maintenance Division did not hold his move in high esteem, however, as for workers the change meant hand tools and backpacking.[30]

To many, the road closings looked like little more than a symbolic gesture. "I never understood the local reaction," recalled Don Defoe, who worked as an interpretive ranger at the time. "After all, those roads were not open to the public, anyway." Defoe and his family lived in the park, but when he went to Gatlinburg to shop, everyone grumbled about the roads.[31] Some people simply resented the loss of "special privileges," such as the college professor who liked to use vehicles to take his students on field trips in the backcountry. But Evison had done more than move a few large rocks; he had announced a pro-wilderness policy; since George Fry's road-building days, any road, paved or unpaved, represented potential tourism development. Within a few months, John Anderson, an official of the East Tennessee Development District (ETDD), wrote to the NPS calling the road closures a "drastic action." Evison replied: "It hardly seems drastic to reduce by 7.1 miles a public road system totaling 234 miles." But Evison was not naïve: "That ETDD guy wanted the management roads opened up, permanently."[32]

Anderson charged that closing the primitive roads was "not consistent" with the park's commitment to reduce traffic on U.S. Highway 441. "If these roads are closed for one summer, it is most unlikely that they will be reopened for many years, if ever," he said. Evison countered that closing road sections in Elkmont, Tremont, and Greenbrier would make these areas more attractive to hikers. "There remains ample opportunities elsewhere in the region for dirt road driving in mountainous surroundings," he said. Anderson sent copies of his letter to the Cocke, Sevier, and Blount County Chambers of Commerce and the local newspapers. A group of Cosby residents started a petition drive protesting the road closings as an "invasion of people's rights" and sent the documents to Tennessee Senators Bill Brock and Howard Baker. Although the Walnut Bottoms Road in Big Creek had been officially closed to the public for decades, letter writers claimed that "people were still allowed to take two-wheel carts up there; the old people could ride in them and we could cart our trash out on them after we finished picnicking." Supported by local tourist-related businesses, the petitioners accused the park of taking "fixtures" (towel dispensers) out of the Cosby campground restrooms. Evison may have understood the sacred nature of road-building to area developers, but he did not count on their ability to marshal local people, who because of the park's history were willing to believe just about anything about the federal government, including a conspiracy to remove towel dispensers. Evison stuck to his plans: the boulders remained. "In its time, that practice [motor vehicle access to remote areas by special individuals] may have been okay," he said. "That time is past." He kept up an exhaustive speaking schedule at regional organizations; he believed that petty politics could be defeated by careful statements of clear purpose. And at first it seemed to work. "Some like what the new Park Superintendent is doing and some don't," wrote a *Sevier County Times* reporter, "but it is hard not to like the Superintendent himself, a young, clean-cut outdoorsman whose goal it is to see that more park rangers walk the back trails instead of riding in cars." He continued to have philosophical discussions with reporters, who wrote up his comments, probably knowing how they would be received by area development interests. The conflict between preservation and use presents "the ultimate dilemma," he told an *Asheville Citizen-Times* reporter. "Where do you draw the line of using and preserving? No matter where you draw it, people on either side are unhappy."[33]

Such earnestness reflected, in part, 1970s sensibilities, but Evison in retrospect said: "I have always felt that if you do the right thing for the right reasons and you avoid being arrogant about it, people will eventually see what you're doing. When you can show clearly that it's for the common good, eventually you will win. People will stand by you." As the director of the Horace Albright Training Center in the Grand Canyon, he frequently went hiking and camping where he could hear the full array of natural sounds, without the intrusion of human-generated noise. Early one morning, he stopped to hear "wrens singing, ravens gurgling while they danced above the rim, the zip of swifts." Suddenly, a group of Boy Scouts jogging in line appeared, shouting a relay of messages up and down the line like soldiers. His reverie destroyed, Evison felt that more people needed to be educated about peace and solitude. "Later, I told some employees I was talking to that if I broke a leg, I would crawl out on my hands and one knee before I'd call in a helicopter," he said. "I assumed they knew what I meant. Wrong! Later, someone told me that they heard I was afraid of helicopter travel!"[34]

About a year after the road closures, Evison took aim at Maintenance Division procedures again. To save $30,000 a year in fuel, he reduced mowing on park roadsides. "Having been used to seeing our roadsides mowed as if this were a city park instead of the East's greatest remaining wildland area, it no doubt seems to many that allowing the return of natural vegetation is evidence of a problem," he announced. "It isn't, though—and already visitors are seeing a greater abundance of wildflowers, increased lushness of vegetation, and a reduction in the helter-skelter pulloffs along the scenic park routes." For the park's Maintenance Division, however, mowing meant jobs and security. The director of maintenance told the General Accounting Office that it didn't save money to cut one bar's width once a year (to keep woody growth back), instead of all the rest multiple times. When asked how that could be, he referred to accounting procedures that based annual budgets on how much went unused at the end of the year. If the Maintenance Division mowed, "we don't have any money left over at the end of the year." For Evison, unmowed roadsides sent "a message to visitors that they are in a natural area, a place where nature—not man—determines what grows." When the maintenance men "forgot" and mowed, Evison recalled later, "I was too easy on [the maintenance chief]. I even found TRAILS with wide-mowed swaths along each side."[35]

If Evison made enemies, it didn't seem to affect his belief in what he was doing or his commitment to preservation: new ideas and press releases announcing them flowed out of his office. A test showed that consolidating litter collection not only eliminated the slow-moving garbage trucks along U.S. Highway 441 but resulted in less littering and fewer opportunities for bears. So, Evison removed most of the garbage bins at overlooks. Again, this move did not go over well with the Maintenance Division, concerned with retaining jobs. However consistent and appealing he sounded, Evison sometimes made enemies where he didn't need any more. In a press release, he urged that those using cemeteries in the park bring no plastic flowers or non-biodegradable containers, because "what is intended as a sign of respect so quickly becomes a sad and unsightly castoff." He asked that cemetery visitors assure the "historic integrity" of the cemeteries by not replacing gravestones "without first discussing it with park historians." To local people, already miffed at a park unresponsive to their needs, this official mandate probably appeared insensitive.[36]

With such wilderness values in mind, Evison reversed the ranger/maintenance employee practice of killing snakes. Rattlers, copperheads, and nonpoisonous snakes deserved as much protection as any other species, he reasoned, and his move drew praise from scientists and environmentalists. However, local people who took snake-killing and ranger protection from snakes for granted were not so pleased. He ordered that everyone leave the snakes alone unless they posed "an immediate threat" to someone; he added that the mere presence of a snake beside a trail is not an "immediate threat." Not long afterward, a Bryson City man was taken to court for killing a copperhead. Ronnie Dowthit said he was driving into Deep Creek campground, when he saw the snake "viciously striking at everything that came near it." He stopped his car to investigate and discovered that because it had been hit by an automobile it could not crawl off the road. "I stomped the snake's head and killed it," said Dowthit, who was wearing boots, "but about that time a park ranger walked up and said he would have to give me a ticket for killing wildlife in the park." The ranger would not listen to Dowthit's explanation, so outraged Bryson City residents requested that representative Roy Taylor investigate the matter. Although the park dropped all charges, the incident stuck in local people's minds as punitive park rangers harassing citizens about practices they themselves used to promote.[37]

Shortly after the snake announcement, Evison took a closer look at the park's strange brook trout history. Tom Harshbarger, a fishery biologist with the U.S. Forest Service Southeastern Experiment Station near Bent Creek, North Carolina, helped prove what Bob Lennon had long suspected: rainbow and brown trout crowded out the native brook trout. "And remember, we introduced these other species—the brookies were the only trout here," said Harshbarger. "It's just possible that this subspecies . . . can't maintain competitive standing." In response to this new information, Evison banned brook trout fishing for the 1976 season. Fishing for brown and rainbow continued, but the most sensitive brook trout streams in the park were closed to ALL fishing.[38] Old-timers had long expressed concern that the brookies—or speckled trout—were losing ground to the exotic rainbows. A USFWS study showed a 50 percent decline in the range of the native species over the past twenty years. "We are aware of the decreasing number of speckled trout and have noticed that their existing numbers have been forced steadily upstream," wrote one fisherman, who actually recommended increasing the scope of the ban. William Lollis, a dedicated fisherman who grew up in Deep Creek and moved to Candler, called the superintendent to tell him that he approved of the protection for brook trout. None of the articles about the ban pointed out, however, that the park itself had caused the brook trout to decline by stocking rainbows. And one columnist implicated "fishing pressure" as a cause of the rapid regression. Lollis, at least, was not fooled by this: he told the superintendent in no uncertain terms that rainbow caused the decline, and he recommended that the park build barriers or waterfalls to keep the rainbow downstream. He was thanked for his observations and told that "research" was looking into these questions. Despite this early support from fishermen, park officials still thought that fishing might be part of the problem; as one scientist put it, "fishing in a national park is a privilege and not the primary purpose." Other fishermen took this personally, as they felt that they could distinguish between a rainbow and a brookie and that killing a protected fish was poaching, not sportfishing. "Ironically, were a motorcycle rider caught biking on the famed Appalachian Trail in the Great Smoky Mountains National Park," said columnist Don Kirk, "the trail would not be closed. Finding litter around a table doesn't close the Chimneys Picnic ground."[39]

The first study completed after Evison closed the streams showed the situation to be even worse than expected. A June 1978 report revealed that brook trout occupied only 125 miles of streams, a decrease of 38 miles since 1950, all due to stocking. In contrast to the 50 percent loss reported earlier, scientists predicted a 70–75 percent loss of the brook trout from their original range. It also appeared that brook trout were becoming genetically fixed because of inbreeding within small isolated populations. Such inbreeding results in fewer alleles, or genetic variations, the scientists confirmed, which decreases the ability of the species to adapt to changing environmental conditions.[40] To further protect the Smokies brook trout, Evison applied for threatened status. In 1977 a research group at Cornell University reported that the native brook trout of the Smokies has blood serum and other protein differences that make it a subspecies of the New England brook trout commonly used in stocking. "Those local guys who fish for specs [a nickname for the speckled trout] have been saying they can always tell a Smokies fish from a stocked fish," said Evison. "Now the scientists agree with the fisherman." From a management perspective, the declaration by the Cornell scientists would seem to make special status for the brookies permanent. NPS policy since 1962 required stocking of native species, "where they have become eliminated or seriously depleted by natural or man-made causes;" Smokies brook trout had become a native species, distinct from the usual stocked fish. Armed with the new study, Evison tried to convince the NPS that special status would help the brook trout. "The fear of some who are involved in the research and restoration effort is that future administrations of the park . . . may not be as sympathetic with these programs as we are," Evison wrote the NPS regional director, "and that they may be pinched off unless threatened population status is established." Because a Tennessee Tech study conflicted with the Cornell study, however, the NPS did not support the plan.[41]

That same summer, enthusiastic young resource managers proposed delivering electric shocks to rainbow trout and moving them downstream. To study the rainbow-brook trout situation, resource managers and student volunteers experimented with this procedure in 1976 and 1977. When two electric wands with opposite charges were placed on the water, all life in the stream become temporarily stunned; biologists moved into the water, quickly sorting the fish and putting them into containers. Before the rainbows knew what hit them, they were transported below a physical barrier, such as a waterfall, that prevented them from moving upstream, leaving the brookies to multiply. The pilot project covered Road Prong and Taywa, Silers, Beetree, Sams, Starkey, and Desolation Creeks. Because of the success of this pilot, Evison supported the proposal to make electrofishing a regular part of management procedures. The National Environmental Policy Act (NEPA) required that no project proceed without an environmental assessment, which included a public comment period. Using one-tenth-mile sections above waterfalls or other barriers, rainbows would be removed from 100 miles of streams in an effort to expand the range of the brookies, and about 10 percent would be sacrificed for research. At the first public hearing in Maryville, Tennessee, only eleven people showed up, most of them representing the Sierra Club. They expressed concern about the effects of shocking on the fish and building any unnatural barriers, but overall they supported the plan. Alan Kelly, a USFWS biologist, spoke in favor of the restoration project. "Brook trout range has dwindled from 465 miles before the turn of the century to around 125 miles today," he said. "This is marginal habitat, at best. And with rainbows moving upstream at the rate of about half a mile, annually, there's the distinct chance that brook trout could be eliminated from the park if something isn't done."[42]

At the second public hearing, held in Sevierville, old grudges in Cosby over law enforcement and road-closings emerged. Wayne Williamson, a Cosby native who had fished in the Smokies for thirty years, argued that "the National Park Service is trying to put fishermen out of the park altogether. You're asking for local support and you won't get it." Bob Lee

Trentham, a Sevier County native, expressed skepticism that the reduction of rainbows could be carried out successfully. "Why not turn trout fishermen in those streams," said Williamson. "I'll guarantee you we could knock down those rainbows." Kelly said that the USFWS had tried to get the park service to raise creel limits and drop the size limit on rainbows with that very objective, but that it was nixed. Danny Maner, a Sevierville resident, argued that once the brook trout responded the park service wouldn't necessarily allow fishing again, and this seemed to be the greatest concern. Dr. John Jacobs, a Sevierville physician, stated that if you looked at the history of relationships between the park and local people these fears were justified. "How do we know that up in Washington, plans won't be changed and more and more water closed to fishing?"[43] The overwhelming public sentiment and fear caused the national office to balk. It decided to postpone the recovery program until the furor died down. Evison immediately appealed the decision, calling it a "mistake." In fact, he said, the park service could face greater flak if the brook trout disappeared. He said the agency should not be party to "letting our population of a distinctive native species slide without doing all we can to help it survive."[44] The music had stopped at the top of the agency, and William Whelan, who replaced Gary Everhardt as director, did not take the same strong stance for protection.

Boars Again

In one of his first interviews with the *Gatlinburg Press*, Evison mentioned the European wild boar, which rooted up the ground everywhere in the park. "I saw endless acres of forest that almost looked as if they'd been strip-mined," he commented. "We [were] working with a scant amount of people, but we hope[d] to come up with a miracle. The wild boar is unnatural to the Park and essentially destructive, incredibly so."[45]

At first Evison simply stepped up control efforts in the backcountry. During 1976, all boars taken in the park were killed and dissected for research at the Uplands Field Research Laboratory. Scientists analyzed stomach contents, for example, to prove food habits; they examined lower jaws, to age the animals. Every boar was measured for chest girth, neck, hind foot, and total length. Upland's first wildlife biologist, Francis J. Singer, kept voluminous information on the boars. Employees who

trapped and hunted kept detailed records of time spent in different activities (trap-building, repairing, moving, trapping, hunting) to determine
the most effective control method. The researchers learned that hogs
spent the summer in high elevations and the winter in low elevations.
They could be successfully trapped at the low elevations, but hunting
each summer in the high country remained the most effective way to
control their numbers.[46]

Based on this research, Evison decided to try hiring professional hunters. Two teams of men, each with a native mountaineer and a wildlife
biologist, would commence hunting the hogs. After contacting local
hunters who refused to participate, the park hired C. R. Todd of Jessup,
Georgia, to hunt with dogs. The purchase order gave Todd fourteen days
to capture 100 boars, but after four days of hunting he captured only
one hog and local hunters were incensed. Leonard Lloyd, a Robinsville,
North Carolina, lawyer, said he planned to lead a campaign to stop the
destruction of wild boar herds. "By anyone's common sense definition,
the wild boar has lost and long since given up his alleged exotic status,"
said Lloyd, pointing out the exotic brown and rainbow trout in park
streams. "Under park service regulations requiring destruction of all exotic species within the park, it would be necessary for park personnel to
remove all of the brown trout and rainbow trout." U.S.D.A. Forest Service officials weighed in that they didn't believe the boar caused any problems on lands they managed. "We want the herds remaining in the park
protected in such a manner as to assure the continued propagation of this
wonderful animal."[47]

Under pressure from North Carolina hunters, on September 1, 1977,
the U.S. Department of Interior ordered Evison to stop killing the hogs.
The ban angered Tennessee environmentalists, concerned with the destruction caused by an estimated 2,000-hog army devouring the wildflowers in the park. "The whole system—the Department of Interior, and
the director of the National Park Service—cannot act. They can only
react," charged Michael Frome. One of the park founders, Carlos Campbell, called it a "sell-out to hunters." On October 19, Evison reached an
agreement with the director of the North Carolina Wildlife Resources
Commission: near the USFS lands, hogs would be live-trapped and transferred; distant from these points, wild boars could be killed "for research
and other purposes."[48] At the same time, the NPS decided to study the

problem, and Director Whelan sent in an outside investigator to determine whether Evison or the park had done anything wrong. "While the
bureaucratic process grinds," noted columnist Carson Brewer, "the exotic wild hogs increase their population in the Great Smoky Mountains
National Park, wallow in the creeks, root up wildflower beds, and gobble
up native species of plants and animals."[49] Unfortunately, Evison had created another powerful enemy, the Swain County and Graham County
hunting community.

The evaluator from the U.S. Department of Interior interviewed everyone who opposed the NPS, including area hunters and the North
Carolina Wildlife Resources Commission, and wrote a confusing document summarizing their accusations. She concluded that because the
European wild boar cannot be totally eliminated from the park, it should
be removed from "fragile and sensitive areas, whereas in other areas of the
park where boars have become indigenous for 30 years, such efforts may
be futile or not necessary." Since the boars roam and reproduce quickly,
her recommendation made little sense. She also did not seem to understand how the NPS policies promoting preservation differed from USFS
policy for multiple use, such as hunting. The NPS "has not defined what
constitutes an exotic," she claimed, whereas "boars are considered game
residents of Tennessee and North Carolina."[50] Despite such inconsis-
tencies, her document does accurately reflect the concerns of Graham
County and Swain County hunters. "Local residents of North Carolina
and Tennessee are culturally attached to wild boars. For three generations, hunting has brought them pleasure," the evaluator reported.
"Hunting in this area has enhanced the economy of Swain and Graham
counties." Urging local environmentalists to remain quiet on the matter,
Evison released an Interim Wild Boar Management Program in March
that spelled out his agreements with the North Carolina Wildlife Resources Commission. When possible, the park would transfer animals to
the national forest; when this proved impractical, rangers could shoot the
hogs. According to park documents, researchers also investigated the use
of biological control, such as "baits containing sterilants" or "introducing
an infectious agent which is host specific," but because of the potential
threat to livestock outside the park, Evison rejected these ideas.[51]

No sooner had Evison put out this fire, when the North Shore Road issue reemerged. The Great Smoky Mountains still did not have a Master Plan or wilderness designation, and Evison was charged with sustaining the process to its completion. Because of the continual rockslides and poisoning by exposed Anakeesta rock formations along the North Shore, constructing the infamous road looked impossible. The U.S. Department of Interior rejected a second transmountain road. And so, environmentalists, local politicians, and park service officials tried to work out a compromise that would satisfy the disgruntled North Carolinians and prevent them from blocking wilderness designation—and the Master Plan.

Because of the 1966 uproar about how little the park supported wilderness, Evison's predecessor, Vince Ellis, supervised a wilderness study team that formally recommended 390,500 acres for wilderness designation, or 76 percent of the park. Congressman Roy Taylor made it clear he would not support any wilderness designation that included the North Shore land, so this the NPS judiciously excluded. Ellis expressed concern that wilderness management would add to maintenance costs, because legislation required less mechanization and more man-hours. He believed only virgin forest should be declared wilderness. At the same time, Swain County officials threatened to bring suit against the U.S. government, to force construction of the North Shore Road.[52] No such suit was ever filed.

Meanwhile, environmentalists developed a "Circle the Smokies" parkway to satisfy tourism interests yet prevent the construction of a second transmountian road. Ted Snyder, a Sierra Club leader, and Frank Ball, a Carolina Mountain Club member, advocated paying Swain County a cash settlement in reparation for the broken 1943 Agreement.[53] The various environmental groups joined forces in a coalition called the Great Smoky Mountains Wilderness Advocates, which favored the circumferential road system but did not offer a solution to the 1943 Agreement problem. The coalition did not want the 44,000 acres of the North Shore lands excluded, describing it as "prime wilderness."[54] The wilderness folk pointed out that the previously logged areas had shown "remarkable recovery" in forest regeneration. They recommended that 475,000 acres in the park be designated wilderness, compared wioth 395,000 acres in the NPS plan that President Ford forwarded to Congress in early 1975. Representative Roy Taylor (N.C.), who served as chair of the House subcommittee on parks and recreation, refused to approve any bill about wilderness designation until the road issue was settled.[55]

In the summer of 1975, North Carolina Governor James Holshouser attempted to work out a solution that would satisfy Swain County and Congressman Taylor. Representatives of both sides plus the NPS met at the governor's residence in Asheville. Secretary Joel E. Harrington of the N.C. Department of Natural and Economic Resources met with Swain County officials in an effort to come up with a compromise. Harrington's ten-point plan included an extension of the Blue Ridge Parkway, two other road projects, and a $15 million cash payment. "Everyone agreed that we would not nickel and dime Swain County over the amount, that clearly they deserved to be compensated," remembered Ted Snyder, who later became president of the Sierra Club. Swain County Commissioner Odell Grant appeared reluctant to settle, but the commission diligently revised and re-revised the ten-point plan.[56]

Dickerman, who by this time worked for the Wilderness Society in Washington, D.C., arranged a meeting with Nat Reed, the assistant secretary of the Interior, to draft a settlement. Snyder, Dickerman, representatives of Swain County, the NPS and others all met in an Interior Department conference room. Reed turned to the Bryson City attorney and asked what dollar amount the county needed to settle the case. Everyone held their breath. "$25 million," the attorney said. Reed had a pile of information on an open manila folder on the table in front of him, and at the outrageous request, he simply closed it. "'Thanks for coming to Washington,' he told us," Snyder recalled. Reed did not express willingness to go to bat for even a small sum, as the budget was so tight. Compromise and the possibility of resolution disintegrated.

When Congressman Roy Taylor retired in 1975, the Great Smoky Mountains Wilderness Advocates renewed its efforts for wilderness designation by lobbying Lamar Gudger, Taylor's successor.[57] Evison favored the environmentalists' wilderness plan, but he could not openly support it. Behind the scenes, he worked to get the long-debated and much-delayed Master Plan in harmony with wilderness designation; his draft indicated that the roads he had closed in wilderness management would stay closed. In February 1977 another round of public hearings invited public comments on this new version of the Master Plan. Just as the county attorney derailed discussions of a dollar settlement, Swain Countians turned out en masse to protest the superintendent's proposal. At the Sylva meeting, former clerk of Swain County Court at Bryson City Henry Truett announced four new priorities: (1) build the North Shore Road; (2) build the transmountain road; (3) return 44,000 acres within Great Smoky Mountains National Park to Swain County from whence it came; or (4) face legal action to force compliance. Odell Grant told Evison that if the road wasn't built the park would "burn." Several participants brought up the hog problem. One member recommended managed hunts. Another suggested wild hog meat obtained on the hunts could be given to food banks and shelters. "If a citizen can't hunt the boar," one said, "stop park rangers from doing it."[58]

Across the mountains in Tennessee, the Master Plan hearings could not have been more different. Ron McConathy, an Oak Ridge resident, advocated closing all roads to vehicles, with public transportation provided to trailheads. Fred Norris, a University of Tennessee botany professor, named the Smokies "a priceless heritage." He called for greater preservation through wilderness designation. John Duffy, a University of Tennessee student, said there were roads everywhere but true wilderness existed only in a few places. "If we are to have Wilderness Areas in the park, we should have as many as feasibly possible," wrote Paul Adams.[59] The vast majority of the 325 who attended the meeting in Knoxville favored greater wilderness designation and fewer roads.[60] In Sevierville, Clint Bach spoke out against the way Evison challenged traditional uses by closing the roads: "NPS is stepping on the public's foot, eliminating footlogs over the creeks, in effect closing such swimming holes as Brownlee, Abernathy and Sugarlands by banning vehicle parking. Let people use the park. They love it too."[61]

While NPS officials digested the comments, the Uplands Field Research Laboratory completed a study about extending the Blue Ridge Parkway, one of the proposals suggested in the ten-point plan compromise. Because of the grave possibility of Anakeesta poisoning, the park no longer supported this part of the compromise. The NPS environmental review left the ten-point plan in "shambles," as the local newspaper put it. Another round of meetings took place including the park, TVA, and state and local officials to try and create a new settlement.[62] "I'm about convinced now we won't get any roads through that park," said Grant. "After

34 years would you be optimistic?" asked one of his aides. However, they put off the lawsuit and attended more meetings.[63]

In 1978 Tennessee Senator Jim Sasser proposed a bill supporting wilderness designation of the 475,000 acres, excluding the North Shore lands, but North Carolina Congressman Gudger would not support the bill without settlement of the 1943 Agreement.[64] Meanwhile, Swain County residents whose ancestors rested in cemeteries across Fontana Lake organized the North Shore Cemetery Association and held the first Proctor Cemetery Decoration Day. More than 100 people were ferried across the lake to the Proctor area near the mouth of Hazel Creek, where they hiked to the graveyard. Those not physically able to make the journey were transported by a horse-drawn wagon paid for by the NPS. "We're strong enough to do something now," said Helen Vance, a 1943 graduate of Proctor High School, and organizer of the cemetery association, told the assembled group.[65] The cemetery association got the attention of Cecil Andrus, secretary of the Interior under Jimmy Carter. At a picnic at the Deep Creek campground, Andrus promised that he would resolve the famous North Shore Road controversy. He examined all of the proposals, including a new one to pave Galbreath Creek Road as a segment of the "Circle the Smokies" plan. Newspapers expressed relief that Andrus might find a solution, and environmentalists appeared optimistic.[66]

Emboldened by Andrus's apparent support, the Swain County Board of Commissioners publicly called for the removal of Boyd Evison. In a letter addressing Andrus, they declared that Evison gave "no consideration to the voice of the local population in management decisions regarding park operations" and had "virtually turned the North Carolina side of the park into wilderness without the consent of Congress." The writers claimed that restrictions on hiking trails "have reached the point of being ridiculous" and that trail crews (by using manual equipment, such as axes, rather than mechanized equipment) cost "taxpayers several times the amount the use of modern equipment for maintenance would cost." They even claimed that Evison's "antics" were "directly responsible" for four incendiary fires within the park in the spring of 1978, destroying 400 to 500 acres of plant life. "I don't believe any additional restrictions on public use of hiking trails have been imposed since I became superintendent," Evison responded. "No roads that were providing a regular public access by motor vehicle on the North Carolina side of the Park when I arrived have been closed nor are they in the process of being closed." (The three roads closed to maintenance were on the Tennessee side.) He calculated that reduced mowing and use of motorized equipment actually saved taxpayers money, and he wondered how he could be blamed for someone else's arson. "I'd be interested to know how you can say that my actions regarding boars were responsible for the four fires," he said, losing his measured tone. "If you can truthfully make such a statement, one must necessarily wonder if you might be able to furnish information that could lead to the arrest of felons. I hope you will consider your legal and moral obligations carefully."[67]

Like Eakin, Preston, and Fry, Evison was called to Washington, D.C. When he returned, he announced that he had accepted the post of assistant director of the NPS and would leave the following month.[68] In retrospect, he said he did not feel he should remain at the Smokies. "Several environmental groups offered to protest the removal," he said, "but I told them to pick their battles. I had lost my effectiveness." Because many of the management policies Evison started were retained—particularly the elevation of the Uplands Field Research Laboratory—he would feel proud of his short tenure in the Smokies.[69] His only real frustration, he claimed, was not finishing the draft of the Master Plan.[70]

Newspapers on the Tennessee side of the park gave Evison a royal send-off. "As much as anything, the boulders symbolize Boyd Evison's philosophy of park management," said columnist Carson Brewer, who praised his devotion to wilderness management. The headline in the *Maryville-Alcoa Times* declared that Evison's ingenuity had improved the park. "Many may not have agreed with some of the things which he has done in seeking to improve the park, but he has had the initiative and willingness to face some of the problems and attempt to find solutions," praised an editorial writer, who was especially impressed with the roadside trees cleared for scenic vistas. "Some of them, such as not mowing the roadsides and centralizing trash receptacles, have not only saved money for other needed items but have produced desirable side effects. There are now more wildflowers blooming along roadsides and less trash."[71]

As Evison left for his new job in Washington, D.C., the committee appointed to settle the North Shore Road issue continued to meet, hoping to come up with a cash settlement that would make everyone happy.[72] A new Swain County commissioner and a former NPS employee, William Rolen, wanted to help Andrus and North Carolina find a solution to the problem. "The 1943 Agreement . . . has turned out to be a bad bargain for Swain County," Leroy Fox wrote Rolen. "Even if the Northshore Road were to be built over many years it would do little material good for the County. To make the best of a bad bargain you feel that getting the most cash you can—and now—is the way to go." Fox made it clear that environmentalists would support Rolen in obtaining a cash settlement: "We agree with you, and we will help if there is a gimmick to get the support of national interests with which we have some influence."[73]

Initiated by Andrus, the committee was chaired by David Felmet of the North Carolina Parks, Parkway, and Forest Commission, and included some of the original task force participants as well as Helen Vance of the cemetery association, but no conservationists were invited. Swain County wanted an extension of the Blue Ridge Parkway, a visitor center at Deep Creek, and regular transportation to the cemeteries. Then they asked for a new industrial park near Bryson City, athletic facilities for the high school, and cancellation of an old FHA loan. As for the cash settlement, they agreed to accept the difference between the 1979 cost of construction of the North Shore Road and all their additional requests, or $14.7 million. "They were getting to the point where they thought that Uncle Sam had a big bag of money just for them," said Fox, who grew frustrated with the demands. "They were trying to get as much as they could for Swain County."[74] At one point, negotiations broke down, so the chair recommended that the county people hold a caucus; to everyone's surprise, they invited Ted Snyder, the Sierra Club representative, to attend the caucus. Despite their differences, the Swain County delegation trusted the lawyer and the environmentalist to get the new plan into acceptable shape. The committee did finally forge a document, containing a $9.5 million cash settlement, which it forwarded to Cecil Andrus. By the time this happened, however, it was too late. Jimmy Carter lost the election in the fall of 1979, and Andrus, in effect, became a lame-duck appointee. The Andrus Compromise bill passed the House but never cleared the Senate.

Although neither wilderness designation nor the 1943 Agreement were completely resolved, the legacy of Evison and Uplands Field Research Laboratory lives on in the 1982 General Management Plan. The plan established historic zones, developed zones (roads), and experimental research zones as well as the uses allowed in each one. The plan classified the bulk of the park as a "natural subzone," where both visitor uses and park management activities should be nonmotorized and noninvasive; for this reason, the Master Plan is often referred to as "de facto wilderness management," and it satisfied the environmentalists. But the mark of the Swain Countians also appears on this document. The plan required the park to provide access for those who wish to visit the North Shore cemeteries.[75]

With the help of Bratton and the other researchers at Uplands, Superintendent Boyd Evison made a fundamental shift in the management of the Smokies. Because of his leadership, for the first time in the history of the Smokies, resource managers from within the organization proposed policies. Rather than simply managing wildlife for popular appeal, the Uplands Field Research Laboratory under the direction of Bratton began doing historical research on the conditions of balds and former agricultural uses. Uplands recommended policy that protected native species from encroachments, such as the European wild boar and the rainbow trout. Bratton initiated a management report series to put research into print quickly and to make it more accessible to nonscientists.[76] Evison and Uplands Field Research Laboratory reversed a long history of management without science. At the same time, however, they could not erase fifty years of animosity between the park and area residents. Because people living in rural Swain and Graham Counties, and, to a certain extent, Haywood County, did not benefit economically from the park, they viewed any attempt at curbing development as insult added to previous injuries. A few towel dispensers and several miles of gravel road hardly seemed worth the trouble they caused; the trouble they caused, however, showed how the past shaped politics in the Smokies.

In 1983, Helen Vance, leader of the North Shore Cemetery Association, filed suit against the TVA and the NPS to force them to build the North Shore Road so that surviving relatives could visit the graves of loved ones. The group asked that if the court failed to order the new road built, TVA be ordered to lower the level of Fontana Lake to uncover old State Road 288. A federal judge dismissed the suit, pointing out that TVA had given relatives the option of having their loved ones reburied and that the park service accommodated the cemetery visitors. Vance appealed the decision, but the Court of Appeals affirmed the District Court. In 1985 Vance sought a Writ of Certiorari from the U.S. Supreme Court. She was denied.[77] Swain County now had no road, no cash settlement, and no legal standing. But that didn't mean that hard feelings disappeared.

8.1. Superintendent Boyd Evison was the youngest superintendent in park history and the most controversial, 1976. Courtesy of Great Smoky Mountains National Park.

8.2. To prevent "park friends" and maintenance workers from using motorized vehicles on wilderness trails, Evison placed large boulders at the trailheads. They are still called "Boyd's Boulders." Photo by author.

8.3. Ranger Ray Kimpel with a 75-pound European wild boar and an 18-pound shoat he shot on Parson's Branch, 1964, as part of the exotic control project. Courtesy of Great Smoky Mountains National Park.

8.4. Ranger-directed traffic at Sugarlands corner, 1975. Evison removed the traffic light in 1976, because it did not seem compatible with wilderness management; it also slowed traffic. Photo by Clair Burket. Courtesy of Great Smoky Mountains National Park.

8.5. Trail erosion caused by heavy use became one of Evison's concerns. Courtesy of Great Smoky Mountains National Park.

In Search of the Wild East

After removing our packs, setting up my camera and spotting scope, [my companion] made a statement that every naturalist east of the Rocky Mountains had been waiting to hear for many years: 'we have chicks in the nest.'"

DICK DICKINSON, WHO ACCOMPANIED DAVE
MORRIS, PARK WILDLIFE VOLUNTEER, AS HE
WITNESSED THE FIRST PEREGRINE FALCON
NEST IN THE SMOKIES IN FIFTY YEARS.

ON SUNDAY MORNING, December 7, 1975, William O. Harris, a retiree living in Sevierville, Tennesssee, noticed a movement in the woods near the Chimneys picnic area. He climbed down the bank near the parking area to get a view of the West Prong of the Little Pigeon River—and what turned out to be a panther with two kittens. After fifty-five years as an animal trainer for the Tampa, Florida, zoo, Harris knew his cats, and he would remember this encounter with the wild in great detail. He later told rangers about the spots on the kittens and the dark tip on the mother's tail. There could be no mistake, he told the ranger, he had seen a mountain lion.[1]

One of twenty-seven subspecies known, the eastern cougar (*Felis concolor*) once lived in North and South Carolina, Tennessee, and Kentucky. Because hunters eliminated the cougar so quickly through state bounty programs, biologists do not know the complete historical range of this secretive cat. Hunting as far as sixty miles to find small mammals and birds, mountain lions needed large undeveloped areas to survive. "No finer symbol of the eastern wilderness exists than this solitary lord of the mountains," wrote Susan Bratton, director of the Uplands Field Research Laboratory.[2]

Did mountain lions exist in the Smokies in 1975? Bratton wondered. The recently enacted Endangered Species Act obligated Great Smoky Mountains National Park to protect rare species and—if the big cats no longer existed—allowed for their reintroduction from outside the region. A reintroduction program, however, necessarily involved the Florida panther or the western cougar, a different subspecies. "I was not afraid to suggest reintroducing a big cat," Bratton later reflected, "but the trouble was it was not clear if the Appalachian subspecies was completely extinct. A reintroduction of lions from outside the region, if there were even twenty or thirty natives left, would be highly questionable."[3] Although as recently as 1967, George Fry told a visitor that "we can't support the claim that there are panthers still in the Smokies," rangers in the 1970s recorded a half dozen sightings by visitors *every year*.[4] Nicole Culbertson, a college student working for Uplands, studied the mystery by analyzing the forty-three recorded sightings of a panther in the park by visitors, rangers, and maintenance employees. Because twenty-eight of the forty-three clustered in the first half of the 1970s, Culbertson concluded that "three to six mountain lions" lived in the park in 1975. As further evidence of their existence, she co-related the sightings with "areas of high deer density."[5]

The mountain lion sightings, however, coincided with something besides deer density: visitors and scientists alike during the 1970s shared a desire to enhance or create new wilderness enclaves. Whether or not the big cats existed, visitors certainly hoped they did. Armed with new federal legislation and a commitment from the NPS to promote research, scientists in the Smokies at long last attempted to restore a wilderness that a mountain lion could call home. After more than a century of farming, logging, mining, road construction, and tourism development, the Smokies finally received a transfusion of the preservation ethic. "Americans have shown a great capacity for degrading and fragmenting native biotas," the *Leopold Report* chided, in words that traveled to the hearts of the Uplands crew. "So far we have not exercised much imagination or ingenuity in rebuilding damaged biotas. It will not be done by passive protection alone." To fully restore the wilderness, the report required historical research to identify which plants and animals once lived in the ecosystem, followed by ecological research to understand current plant-animal relationships. From this, managers came up with a "management hypothesis" to be tested by experimental introduction of native species or removal of exotics. Based on the results, the scientists could recommend resource-management policy. In addition to this recommended process, the *Leopold Report* gave scientists a mission: to create "an illusion of primitive America," maintaining landscapes "as nearly as possible in the condition that prevailed when first visited by the white man."[6]

Almost immediately, Bratton and the other members of the Uplands research team encountered difficulties with the *Leopold Report*. If the eastern cougar still existed, for example, reintroducing a western species spelled disaster for survival of the unique genetic strain. How do you prove something missing that keeps showing up? On top of this, the scientists soon realized that re-creating a pre-Columbian scene might not meet the approval of the visiting public. During a talk at Oak Ridge, an audience member slyly suggested that perhaps Bratton introduced the lions; after all, she seemed to arrive about the time the sightings began. ("I think my hours can be fully accounted for in the late 1970s," Bratton joked.) "Two paradoxes are apparent," wrote Peter S. White, another member of the early Uplands group, with Bratton in 1980. "Our goal is to preserve systems that must change and managing for preservation itself introduces human influence into natural systems even when its sole purpose is to correct or prevent human-related damage."[7] As White and Bratton warned, thorny questions faced scientists and resource managers charged with recreating history in a contemporary setting. As they and others sought to restore native ecosystems, such as brook trout habitat, and reintroduce species, including the red wolf, river otter, and peregrine falcon, hard lessons about the management and politics of wilderness awaited them. Still, rangers who entered resource-management training learned that while "re-creating 1492" might prove impossible, especially given the rapid development of the region, it remained a worthy goal.

In 1978 the USFWS began a concerted five-year effort with state and federal conservation agencies to locate positive identification of the cougar in the Southern Appalachians. A wildlife technician collected scat that Louisiana State University researchers identified as mountain lion scat, but the specimen deteriorated too much to be a reliable finding. Knoxville Zoo curators positively identified a baby panther killed by dogs, but they attributed the unfortunate animal's presence to exotic pet owners. By the end of the century, Mike Pelton, a University of Tennessee wildlife biologist, pointed out that he and trained graduate students never saw scats, footprints, or other cougar sign, even though they had hiked more than thirty years in the Smokies backcountry. All the sightings were short-lived, which seems to be further evidence that they are former pets released in the park. Bob Downing, author of the USFWS study, also registered skepticism but stopped short of declaring the elusive animal a complete ghost. "If we could ever declare the Eastern cougar extinct, that would open the door [for restocking]," he declared. "But I think there are always going to be those who are continuing to mistakenly report cougar sightings. It's going to take some guts to declare them extinct. It would be an unpopular decision."[8] And in the world of wilderness "management," public opinion played a major role.

When a Wilderness?

One of scientists' first lessons in public opinion and policy contradiction came while studying the famous grassy balds, the open meadows on the mountaintops. In Stupka's era, scientists who saw the park as a natural preserve considered the balds natural phenomena, somehow related to the high-country environment. Even the famous botanist, Richard Whittaker, assumed that the balds were related to alpine conditions or a retreat of the tree line during an ice age. Other scientists published theories about how the balds resulted from frost damage, windstorms, or even "gall wasps." Finally, in 1970 Philip Gersmehl, a geographer, produced convincing evidence that Native Americans burned and cleared the balds, and white settlers dramatically expanded them; in short, the grassy balds resulted from human contact. In fact, once the NPS took over the land and ceased grazing the balds, woody plants and shrubs began invading the open land, further evidence for the human-caused theory.[9] Managing for wilderness, then—minimizing human intervention—promised an end to the balds.

Whether or not caused by humans, hikers loved the balds. As early as 1963 members of the Great Smoky Mountains Conservation Association pressured the park service to beat back the wilderness on the balds. "The balds provide thrilling panoramic views that would be blotted out if the forests should be permitted to take over," they argued, emphasizing the balds' "great beauty and charm."[10] The balds became a management issue in the 1970s, when the park underwent public hearings for the new management plan. Even those who favored wilderness designation—which would make it difficult to burn and cut down trees—did not want the balds to grow over. And so Uplands Field Research Laboratory hired Mary Lindsay, a graduate student at Cornell University, to uncover the environmental history of these special habitats at high elevations by interviewing former herders, scouring archival sources and photographs, and measuring woody encroachment on the balds. When Lindsay spoke at the Knoxville Science Club, a descendant of Russell Gregory (from whom Gregory Bald received its name) attended. The researcher concluded that human beings created the balds, but "natural" or not, the public—as well as she herself—wanted to keep them.[11] "It was clear that all plant communities resembling a grassy bald in the Great Smoky Mountains National Park had a history of intensive human interference," Bratton concluded. "One of the most surprising results of the historic work was that burning was not a major factor in balds maintenance."[12]

During her second summer, Lindsay experimented with several methods of fighting back the wilderness. She and three other Cornell students, clad in blue jeans and hard hats, whacked and sprayed the briars, while sheep, cattle, and goats penned in 1-acre plots worked on the rest. Most of the hikers Lindsay met approved of the experiment, "although there are a few die-hard wilderness freaks who aren't sure if they want to have sheep up here," she admitted. "And a lot of hikers were worried about animals polluting the stream, but they won't be anywhere near the water." Some NPS employees pointed out the irony of restoring farm animals to a scene from which they were so recently extirpated; certainly no cattle appeared in the pre-Columbian Smokies.[13] In terms of the experiment, sheep proved the best browsers, but also the most susceptible to ambush by bears. As for maintenance, the scientists concluded:

> Wilderness values, such as lack of human interference, must be
> weighed against the uniqueness of the balds and their aesthetic
> appeal. Usually wilderness would have the greatest weight in terms
> of both uniqueness and aesthetic value. In this case, however, a plant

community that is of very limited distribution is being replaced by successional forest, and vistas are being obscured. The balds also provide habitat for some rare plants and the hybrid azaleas found only on Gregory Bald.[14]

As a compromise, Bratton recommended redesignating two of the balds as "historic." Evidence revealed Gregory Bald and Andrews Bald as the two oldest (recorded by white surveyors in the late eighteenth century), and excluding them from wilderness designation allowed technicians to chop down the briars and saplings to keep the meadows open. "If the balds were buildings," Bratton argued in a management report, "they would almost certainly be protected, just because of their age and their importance in local literature." NPS officials in Washington, D.C., rejected historic designation, because of the uncertain bald origins, but they agreed to classify them as "experimental research subzones," which allowed for their restoration. Eventually, Uplands recommended using power mowers and herbicides to keep the forest at bay and regular monitoring of the sites. Carlos Campbell, a park founder and author of *The Birth of a National Park*, considered this his last great victory. At the end of the century, the balds had not received historic designation, and travel writers still claimed their well-known origins a "mystery." Annually, the park vegetation management crew camped at the bald, felled trees, trimmed blueberries, sprayed herbicides, and planted native seeds on Gregory Bald and Andrews Bald.[15] While wilderness enthusiasts might long for a consistent "hands-off" policy, the real world of public opinion and resource management demanded compromise. Pre-Columbian history did not always satisfy modern aesthetics or preservation of rare plant communities.

The complexities of history and wilderness also became apparent to the Uplands researchers in the management of LeConte Lodge. Named for a Georgia naturalist who frequently visited the mountains during the nineteenth century, Mount LeConte first became the focus of public attention in 1924, when park founder David Chapman escorted the members of the Southern Appalachian National Park Commission on a trail ride to the top in order to convince them to choose the Smokies for a national park (see chapter 3). Paul Adams, who participated in the ride, later established a camp on Mount LeConte, accompanied by his German shepherd, Cumberland Jack. His journals, which contain records of birds and wildflowers observed on Mount LeConte, today reside in the Tennessee State Archives. One of the few distinctive peaks in the park, LeConte became a popular hiking destination and photo opportunity. Jack Huff, who founded the Mountain View Hotel in Gatlinburg, built the exceedingly popular LeConte Lodge with park blessings in 1936, shortly after marrying his wife at Myrtle Point, southeast of the site.[16]

No one considered the lodge a natural phenomenon, of course, and so wilderness supporters called its existence into question. During a joint meeting in January 1975, twenty-four environmental groups combined to form the Great Smoky Mountains Park Wilderness Advocates, demanding greater wilderness management of the park. They lobbied for the removal of the AT shelters, an end to mechanized equipment in trail maintenance, and the closing of LeConte Lodge. "Despite the nostalgia that many of us feel for LeConte Lodge," the group's spokesman declared, "we recognize that its continued existence creates problems which appear to be insurmountable." A failing wastewater system served 8,000 guests per year, and raw sewage polluted the fragile mountaintop environment. Requiring more than a cord of wood per day for heating and cooking, lodge managers sometimes cut green trees. "The Rainbow Falls trail already has been turned into a quagmire by the heavy horse traffic, making it unsuitable for foot traffic and requiring extensive maintenance and rebuilding," the wilderness advocates argued.[17]

Indeed, years of heavy use eroded the trails to Mount LeConte and degraded the woods around the lodge. A geographer recorded the frequent debris slides on the mountain, especially on the much-loved Alum Cave Trail. Exacerbated by sudden heavy rainfalls and the shaly Anakeesta formation of which Mount LeConte was a part, six major slides followed the trails.[18] At the same time, Uplands research showed that horse traffic, in particular, deeply eroded the trails. "Plain common sense, as well as the dilapidated condition of trails, such as Rainbow Falls, which are heavily used by horses, indicates that horse use contributes a disproportionate amount of damage to the park trail system," wrote Paul Whittaker, the Uplands researcher in charge of the project. Whittaker's study of a Cherokee Orchard hiking trail showed that 100 passes by a hiker had "little visible effect," whereas just 88 passes by a horse rendered parts of the trail "virtually impossible to negotiate."[19] Still another Uplands report revealed more than 50 acres of mountaintop land disturbed by green-tree cutting. Lodge owners admitted using trees blown down from storms, and even this, the report argued, prevented nutrients from returning to the soil and encouraged erosion. "Here we had official U.S. government park service reports saying that [the lodge] damaged the environment on top," recalled Leroy Fox, one of the wilderness supporters.[20] The lease on the lodge expired in 1977, and the owners felt ready to retire, as vandalism and ongoing maintenance proved expensive at the remote location. It appeared that wilderness advocates might succeed in removing the lodge.

The Smokies-traveling public, however, felt quite differently: they loved the lodge. Developers in Gatlinburg, not surprisingly, wanted it to stay. The historical nature of LeConte Lodge aroused a "torment of mixed emotions," as columnist Carson Brewer put it, even among those who advocated wilderness designation. "If the boobs in Atlanta and Washington close the lodge," one Gatlinburg resident said, more bluntly, "they will be doing the greatest misservice [sic] and unjust action to the future generations of Americans who will never know the pleasure of spending time in the peace and solitude of Mt. LeConte."[21]

Because of the strong show of public support, the environmentalists backed down. "We decided we would make a trade-off," explained Fox, "that we would oppose the removal of LeConte Lodge if [Gatlinburg developers] would not oppose further wilderness areas in the park." The superintendent at the time, Boyd Evison, also retreated from actually closing the lodge. He recommended strict use of a reservation system, reducing use of the trail by horses, limiting visitation by cutting back on parking space, and clamping down on illegal camping at the site.[22] At a Wilderness Management Symposium, Evison's successor, Dave Beal, tried to clarify the park's support for LeConte Lodge: "If a use is well established before efforts are undertaken to control it, much resistance will be encountered," he deciphered. "We are taking away rights or privileges previously enjoyed!" Although "we must guard against cheapening the concept of wilderness," he argued, reality must enter the picture:

The point is this: If wilderness is to be preserved there must be a constituency which supports the program. That constituency must be quite broad based and inevitably will contain disparate views that must be accommodated in our planning and management efforts. We cannot afford to be too pure or too permissive, but must always strive to be good stewards of the resources we are charged with preserving.[23]

And so LeConte Lodge slipped into the 1982 Management Plan, and the new owners used helicopters to transport major supplies to the site twice a year and llamas to carry weekly provisions. They agreed not to cut wood on the mountain. They pay three-quarters of 1 percent of their gross receipts to the federal treasury, so the park does not see any income from the concession.[24] And Beal's point made an impression on succeeding superintendents: wilderness management required the support of the public and, in this case, the public wanted to stay overnight on Mount LeConte. Why did superintendents during the 1980s and 1990s avoid limiting horse traffic on trails? For the same reason that Evison and Beal did not touch Mount LeConte: they needed constituencies to support the park, and horseback riders cared passionately about the Smokies. Although the 1982 Management Plan instituted what managers hence referred to as "de facto wilderness designation," or management not in conflict with future possible wilderness designation, in truth it maintained a compromise between management for tourism and wilderness. As the outcry for balds and LeConte Lodge indicated, the public hearing process taught park officials significant lessons about public relations. New policy needed scientific research *and* public support.

Uplands vs. Park Management

In addition to dealing with conflicts between wilderness and tourism, the Ph.D.s and graduate students who initiated the Uplands Field Research Laboratory during the 1970s and early 1980s proved themselves enormously productive: most published papers, articles, books, dissertations, master's theses, and management reports from their field research. In their late twenties and early thirties, largely without children, the Uplands staff had connections at major universities, did not mind working overtime, and cared passionately about preservation issues. "There was a lot of energy at Uplands, a lot of collegiality and a lot of dedication," remembered Chris Eagar, who joined the talented group in 1976 as a

University of Tennessee graduate student. He pointed out how many of the researchers went on to successful careers. "But we were a different breed than your typical park service employee."[25] With this no one disagreed. "Everyone was a field person to the core," said Susan Bratton, who left Uplands in 1980 to direct the NPS Cooperative Unit at the University of Georgia. She remembered one of the perennially rainy days when she picked up Mark Harmon, an expert in fire ecology, whom she met at a trail intersection to provide a ride back to the lab. He had cheerfully waited through at least one downpour. "I asked him why he was so willing to stay soaked and he just looked at the sky and said: 'I love it out here in the rhododendron. I don't want to go home!'"[26] However, the unconventional appearances and attitudes of the nature-loving scientists put them into conflict with park officials, who complained about everything from badly parked cars and illegal bunk beds to mice and dirty dishes in the lab. Science had taken the Smokies by storm, but management wished it looked neater and perhaps wore uniforms. Superintendents had enough trouble with wilderness advocates and preservationists *outside* the park.

After Boyd Evison left, scientists felt less supported by NPS officials. Uplands made them nervous, and Susan Bratton disquieted park service norms. "Susan is a very directed person; she was a good forceful person to start this program in the park," reflected Peter White, but "being a woman and a young person did not help when it came to dealing with park management."[27] White, who received his Ph.D. from Dartmouth College in 1976, met Bratton during his undergraduate studies at Columbia University, when she was a student at Barnard College. Bratton recruited White to become Uplands plant ecologist in 1978, about the time he finished postdoctoral research at the St. Louis Botanical Garden. With his taxonomic skills, White updated the park's checklist of plant species in the park and increased the records of known plants by 10 percent. He also started a list of rare plants, those designated or proposed by Endangered Species Act legislation or the states of North Carolina and Tennessee, which the park could monitor for the future effects of visitor use, road and trail construction, poaching, and acid rain or ozone damage. White and Bratton both felt strongly that the park needed vegetation mapping, or permanently designated plots in each ecosystem, so that disturbance history could be understood and threats, such as the exotic gypsy moth, monitored before they did too much damage. To overcome the vagaries of funding and the whims of superintendents, they tried to "group the plots around management questions," such as the effects of deer browsing in Cades Cove. They also found creative ways to pay for the labor, as in 1981 White hired Chris Eagar to lead a group of volunteers from Earthwatch, an environmental organization that plans working vacations for outdoor enthusiasts. Eagar led crews of six or seven dedicated and interested laypeople backpacking into the spruce-fir forest to set up vegetation plots; the park gained operating funds to run the project and free labor. "They brought a lot of energy and enthusiasm but not much technical skill, but it was easy to train them to use a compass," Eagar recalled. "And it was fun for me, because they wanted to learn as much as they could about the Smokies."[28] Through creative funding, over 300 permanent plots were completed in the western end of the park and in the spruce-fir zone, but money disappeared before the entire park could be plotted. Everyone missed Evison's advocacy. "I felt that park superintendents, not just in the Smokies but throughout the country, generally did not understand fully what it takes to do good science," White said. "It simply was not in their background or training to appreciate how to get that work done. With all the competing budget needs, this meant that they generally weren't supportive in terms of basic funding and infrastructure for in-house science labs." A good scientist, White believed, wants to collect data, use a computer to analyze that data, publish results in a peer-reviewed journal—"that's how you gain credibility as well as build your own career"—attend scientific meetings, and be integrated into the scientific community as a whole. Peer-reviewed scientific data also stand up in court cases when a legal issue comes up. "To me, I would say that the NPS managers were often satisfied with superficial science," commented White. "They just weren't trained to evaluate that science independently and rarely saw the need for such an assessment." White acknowledged that the Uplands group often appeared "skeptical of bureaucracy," but at the same time "we typically worked a twelve-hour day."

Beyond superintendents, science took a beating at the national level when Republican President Ronald Reagan hired James Watt as secretary of the Interior. Watt, a born-again Christian, opposed preservation and even tried to open up mining in the national parks. Watt abolished several agencies in the U.S. Department of Interior, and ordered that the NPS absorb employees from these other agencies. Inside Great Smoky Mountains National Park, Uplands disappeared under the auspices of the Science Division, which reported more directly to the superintendent, and White became the director of a new cooperative unit on the University of Tennessee campus. Across the nation, the NPS shifted field research to outside contracts by university-employed professors. Subsequent Secretary of the Interior Bruce Babbitt transferred some 1,950 scientists from in-house research stations and cooperative units of the U.S. Fish and Wildlife Service and the National Park Service into a new agency called the National Biological Service (NBS), charged with providing biological inventories, monitoring, research, development, and technical assistance throughout the country. Funding for the NBS increasingly came through private-public partnerships, such as a demonstration project initiated by Champion International Corporation. Further administrative musical chairs transformed the NBS into the Biological Resources Division under the U.S. Geological Survey. "I personally feel [that eliminating in-park research] was a great loss throughout the country," said White, who in 1986 became director of the North Carolina Botanical Garden at the University of North Carolina at Chapel Hill. As White lamented, field research in the parks by scientists who knew and loved individual ecosystems, like the Smokies, had been deemed impractical.[29]

Meanwhile, a new generation of resource managers, many of them trained by the Uplands scientists in the park, took over the job of restoration and wilderness management. Like White and Bratton, they negotiated the political ground of "de facto wilderness designation" and tourism. Because they had developed their careers within the NPS—typically, they wore uniforms and rose through the ranks of seasonal employment or law enforcement—they understood chains of command and looked like NPS rangers. Because most of them had grown up in the Southeast, they quickly adapted to local culture and established loyalty to the region. If they did not have doctoral degrees or time to engage directly in pure research, they believed in park management based on science and worked to enforce federal legislation with a creative blend of grants, appropriations, and public-private partnerships.

Not every wilderness restoration project became a political balancing act; increasingly in the last two decades of the twentieth century, resource managers learned to regard such projects as public relations opportunities. Their careers tied to the agency, the rising stars in Resource Management tried to restore wilderness without raising public ire. Steve Moore, a fisheries biologist in the division, began working with the Smokies during the 1976 controversy over using electrofishing to restore brook trout by removing rainbow trout. A graduate student from Tennessee Tech at the time, Moore made the brook trout restoration project his master's thesis and ended up with a career in the NPS. As a graduate student, he pushed for endangered/threatened status for brook trout as a way to get money to do research; he believed in a strong approach to protection. After twenty years of working in the system, however, he has become a part of NPS culture: he concluded that a "less confrontational" approach had value. Instead of pursuing further genetic studies to prove the brook trout's special status and engaging in political battles to get endangered species listing, Moore guided the Smokies toward working with anglers and developing alternative sources of funding. He still strove to improve brook trout habitat lost through rainbow stocking, but he did not see further regulation as the best route. "To be honest with you, given the constraints you end up with when you get a threatened or endangered listing, I'm not sure it's even a good idea. I don't think we want to lose the management options that we've got," he explicated. "It would tie our hands."[30]

Electrofishing rainbows and removing them downstream during the 1980s and 1990s, Moore and the fisheries technicians learned the challenges associated with restoration work. In some cases, they removed rainbows and replaced them below barriers, only to find that a tiny remnant population could still recover at the expense of the brookies. "We started out with a lot of ideals: we imagined, for instance, that we could go out with these magic tools and catch every fish in the creek," Moore recalled. "You might have all these fancy mathematical formulas that predict the population size for you, but it doesn't mean that they're right." Although electrofishing substantially reduced rainbow trout, it did not eradicate them, as the wily rainbows hid in rocky pockets of the stream, eluding fisheries technicians. "We found out through time that a lot of what happens is that the complex nature of the habitat allows fish to hide," said Moore. "We may only be getting 60 to 70 percent of the fish in the stream." Then the technicians discovered that the transplanted rainbows could be remarkably innovative at returning upstream, even if waterfalls stood in their way. Fish-management textbooks predicted that rainbows stopped short of a 5- to 8-foot barrier, for instance, depending on the nature of the waterfall or rock outcropping. "One of the things we have learned in a lot of this work, though, is that the fish haven't read the same book that the biologists did," Moore wisecracked. In several cases, Moore found rainbows that jumped 7-foot waterfalls. At one point, fisheries experts removed rainbows from Deep Creek, only to inadvertently invite upstream another exotic species, brown trout. With major barriers and repeated electrofishing, however, restoration work succeeded; five years after ceasing removals from Silers and Taywa Creeks, for example, no rainbow trout returned and brookies recovered habitat.[31]

While experimenting with improvements in the restoration program, Moore said that he was struck by the irony of removing fish with "fancy equipment," where anglers might want to fish. He also deplored the waste, as 2 to 3 percent of the rainbows didn't survive, despite best efforts to transport them quickly. Originally from Waynesville, North Carolina, Moore grew up fishing on the North Carolina side of the park, and so he hypothesized: Can anglers aid the process? Can they catch a significant number of rainbows to improve brook trout populations? In 1981, Moore invited local fishermen to catch and keep as many rainbows as they could harvest over nine weeks on Lynn Camp Prong. Eager anglers arrived to harvest some 5,655 rainbow trout.[32] "The thing that we found was that the fishermen crop off all the larger fish first, then most of the little guys are left," Moore said. "After four weeks of fishing, the effort drops off. The guys get tired of going and catching nothing but little fish, and they quit coming." Although his report called fishing a "cost effective alternative" to electrofishing, Moore said he worried about provoking animal rights advocates if the program continued. "I'm willing to take the risk to lose a few fish with my management action," he said, "to gain the long-term positive of reaching the goal to stabilize brook trout and prevent continued loss of range from rainbows."

Pragmatic and personable, Moore said he believed in research that answers specific management questions. "We're trying to get good research data, good management-oriented work that provides us with answers to questions that we can use to make intelligent recommendations to management," he said. "It's silly if you don't manage that way. I don't know how you manage without good science." He applauded the DNA research, for example, which classified the native Southern Appalachians brook trout as "genetically distinct" from hatchery brook trout, most of which originated in the Northeast.[33] However, he believed the appropriate venue for resource managers working in parks remained applied research. Admittedly, research can't always provide neat answers, but more than ten years of electrofishing experiments showed that removing rainbows twice in the same summer greatly increased the chances of ridding the fish from a stream. In just one summer, transplanting the rainbows twice accomplished in one year what previously the park accomplished in four or five.[34]

To increase support for brook trout restoration, Moore spent a considerable percentage of his time on both public education and fund-raising for species restoration. The "confrontational approach" of the 1970s, as he saw it, sometimes caused unnecessary animosity. At meetings with fishermen, he tried to make sure they understood that the park only closed streams on a short-term basis—with a goal of restoring brook-trout fishing: "I fish! If I'm the fisheries biologist, why would I do anything to mess up my own fishing?" Moore regarded restoration work as an "unfunded mandate"—an imperative under federal legislation that does not receive base funding from Congress. In 1988, he coordinated a fund-raising event to sell wildlife prints with the help of Trout Unlimited, the American Fisheries Society, Land Between the Lakes, and the Great Smoky Mountains Natural History Association. Ten years later, he raised $208,000 in grants for brook trout restoration through Trout Unlimited, Friends of the Smokies, the National Fish and Wildlife Foundation, Coors Pure Water 2000, Western Carolina University, the University of Tennessee, and Tennessee Tech University. "There's a growing awareness that parks are very special places," he said, "and people are willing to spend money and time to see that they stay that way."[35]

While the park devoted most of its fisheries attention to the popular brook trout and undoing the damage caused by rainbow stocking, scientists outside the agency drew attention to nongame fishes. The 1957 poisoning of Abrams Creek in Cades Cove by the USFWS eliminated the spotfin chub, yellowfin madtom, smoky madtom, and duskytail darter from the park. "It was the most catastrophic thing I know of that has happened in the park," Moore remarked. After the "reclamation," Abrams Creek contained only thirty-five of its original sixty-seven species. "It was pretty effective," David Etnier, a University of Tennessee professor, commented wryly. A native of Minnesota, Etnier first became interested in Tennessee through his graduate school textbooks, in which he noticed how many fish species were restricted to the headwaters of the Tennessee River drainage—the result of TVA dams. His research drew national attention during the 1970s, when he discovered the snail darter, a rare species that nearly stopped the Tellico Dam. Until the 1980s, Etnier believed that the infamous Abrams Creek experiment caused the extinction of the smoky madtom, a tiny member of the catfish family. In fact, the Abrams Creek poisoners put this unknown catfish in formaldehyde and sent it to the Smithsonian Institution, where a taxonomist later identified it as a new species. "It was identified after being driven to extinction," Etnier remarked.[36]

Much to Etnier's relief, a USFWS employee, Gerry Dinkins, in 1983 discovered a smoky madtom on nearby Citico Creek, which flows through the Cherokee National Forest. After Etnier provided a positive identification, he urged Dinkins to research the relatively unknown smoky madtom. An avid diver, Dinkins used a snorkel, fins, and flashlight to study the nocturnal smoky madtom and discovered its range to comprise 12 miles of lower Citico Creek.[37] He also discovered another rare madtom, the yellowfin madtom. His colleague in the graduate program, Peggy Shute, decided to do a similar underwater study of the yellowfin madtom, and in her research she discovered yet another rare species, the duskytail darter.[38] Etnier and his students raised the idea of helping these remnant species survive by reproducing them and restocking them in Abrams Creek. The Endangered Species Act urged federal land managers to restore native species "if a species is eradicated by man-caused activities."[39]

At the same time, because Citico Creek drained a watershed on USFS land, officials worried about becoming custodians of so many endangered species; they knew that a tiny fish with so much legislative power might stall management decisions that affected the creek. And so in 1982, the

USFWS, the USFS, and the NPS permitted Peggy Shute and her husband, Randy Shute, to collect 250–350 eggs (an estimated 5 percent of the egg production) from each species to rear them in a University of Tennessee aquarium, promising to release some of the fish back into Citico Creek and the rest, in the Smokies. The Shutes together with another graduate student, Pat Rakes, created a nonprofit organization, called Conservation Fisheries Incorporated (CFI), to fund the restoration project. It took three years to successfully reproduce the madtoms, and so in 1988 the Shutes released the first smoky madtoms and yellowfin madtoms in Abrams Creek.[40] After they began to find the madtoms reproducing in Abrams Creek, CFI produced the spotfin chub and the duskytail darter for potential restoration. "It's incredible, it opens so many doors," said Etnier, who with CFI searched for other relocation sites to get these fish off the endangered species list.

While nonprofit foundations and the USFWS initiated this restoration project, Great Smoky Mountains National Park enjoyed considerable good PR from their work. Not only do rare species enthusiasts such as David Etnier remind people of the enormous biological value of the park, but the public gains renewed appreciation for native ecosystems, beyond the high-profile mammals, such as bears. But it's hard to beat the publicity provided by a problem-free mammal that also happens to photograph well. No one denied that the greatest public relations bonanza for the park in the 1990s came from river otters, because they look, well, "cute." Resource Management Specialist Carroll Schell called river otter restoration a "no-brainer" for resource management, because technicians easily documented the otter's recent historical presence in the park and discovered few problems for its reintroduction, such as disease, competition, or habitat destruction.[41]

For all practical purposes, hunting, trapping, and habitat destruction extirpated the river otter from the Great Smoky Mountains, yet a few persisted into the twentieth century as if to prove their appropriate place in the ecosystem. During the 1930s, wildlife technician Willis King interviewed CCC worker Leander Parton, who remembered an otter trapped in 1921. King also located a Hartford resident, William Barnes, who shot an otter on Big Creek about the same time. In 1980, the Tennessee state geologist and a fish-and-tackle wholesaler claimed they saw an otter on

the Little River, just outside the park. With this and other evidence, resource managers declared a recent (historically speaking) niche in the
Smokies reserved for the furry mammals.[42]

Sponsored by TVA, the Tennessee Wildlife Resources Agency, the
Audubon Society, the Great Smoky Mountains Natural History Association, and the NPS, wildlife researchers in 1986 released eleven otters into
the park. A graduate student, Jane Griess, tracked eight of the otters for
eighteen months, until the transmitters implanted in the animals' bodies
died. By October, only six otters remained in the park, but they distrib-
uted themselves over the entire Abrams Creek watershed, enjoying a preferred diet of crayfish. One otter took up residence in Tellico Lake, and
another lost its life in a fish survey net in Chilhowee Lake.[43] Deeming the
experiment a success, the park released an additional twenty-six otters
into Abrams Creek, Little River, and Hazel Creek, with only occasional
complaints from local fishermen, who worried that "trout-eating otters"
would not only ruin their sport but further endanger the brook trout.
Griess's research showed that the otters preferred slow-moving fish, like
suckers and crayfish, and probably did not pose a threat to the trout.[44] In
fact, a Blount County commissioner, from west Millers Cove, accused
otters of raiding his catfish ponds. Wildlife specialists verified that otters
would have a tendency to look for other food sources each January, when
their preferred prey were limited.[45]

Nevertheless, in 1994 the park purchased an additional hundred animals from a Louisiana furrier at $400 each and released them on the Oco-
naluftee River, Big Creek, Cosby Creek, the Middle and West Prongs of
the Little Pigeon River, Cataloochee Creek, and Hazel Creek. "One otter
had never seen snow before," Schell recalled. "He sniffed it, rolled
around in it, then slid down the hill on it as if he'd been doing it all his
life." Over the entire program, the Smokies released 137 otters, and the
Great Smoky Mountains Natural History Association kept the otter in
the public mind with postcards, children's books, and even stuffed animals sold in the Visitor Center. In the world of restoration, where over-
coming public criticism can be a constant problem, it helps to have dark
eyes and an impish face.[46]

Whereas the otter took to the streams of the Smokies with very little
incident, the red wolf did not so easily blend into this Wild East. *Canis*

rufus once lived throughout the Southeast, but no concrete evidence located this species in the park. Hunting and indiscriminate killing eventually limited wolves to the Ozark-Ouichita Mountain region of Arkansas, southern Missouri, eastern Oklahoma, Louisiana, and Texas. Loss of habitat through logging and development further limited the red wolf to a few counties of Texas, and the animals began interbreeding with coyotes, which, because of their smaller size, can survive in more open landscapes. Finally, in 1980 the USFWS declared the species extinct in the wild and rounded up the remaining canines. Even before Congress passed the Endangered Species Act, wildlife biologists established the Red Wolf Recovery Project to start a breeding program, to educate the public about wolves, and to evaluate sites for possible reintroduction. Because of the interbreeding between wolves and coyotes, the program accepted only 43 of the 400 wild canines examined by wildlife technicians. Further morphological study left the program with just fourteen "good" red wolf "founders" to restore the population.[47]

Almost immediately, the Red Wolf Recovery Project faced two major challenges. First, red wolves bred in captivity often lost their fear of human beings. Second, anti-wolf propaganda, from Little Red Riding Hood to Disney's *Beauty and the Beast,* has created a lot of wolf-fearing human beings who don't want the canines in their backyards. Once the captive breeding program proved successful—thirty-seven zoos today claim red wolves—reintroduction programs tackled reintroduction problems. To acclimatize wolves, release experts discovered they had to leave them in pens on the site for at least six months. "We were flying by the seat of our pants" when the project began, confessed Gary Henry, red wolf coordinator for the Southeast Region of the USFWS. Despite many studies of the timber wolf, "we just didn't have biological information about the red wolf," said Henry. And no one in the world had successfully reintroduced a major predator. At one of the first reintroduction sites, the Land Between the Lakes in Kentucky, the USFWS discovered why. "Livestock owners thought the wolves would wipe out livestock. Deer hunters thought wolves would decimate deer populations," Henry remembered. "We even had opposition from humane society folks because coyotes had moved that far east, and we were going to have to do some coyote control to get the wolves started."[48] With so much opposition, the Red Wolf Recovery Project abandoned the site in 1984.

In the Smokies, public education came first. The USFWS chose the park because it represented the largest tract of contiguous federal land-holding in the Southeast, even though historically the red wolf probably did not live there. Henry met with various groups surrounding the park for almost a year before the first experiment to educate the public about red wolves. He published a newsletter for interested citizens and worked with the park public relations officials to gain publicity for the project. "For those people who visited the park during the project, and thousands of them saw wolves, because in Cades Cove it's pretty open country, it certainly demonstrated to them that wolves are not a threat to humans," observed Henry. Wolves proved an attractive draw for tourists, he added: "They came to see wolves and to hear wolves howl."

The biggest obstacle to red wolf success in the Smokies turned out to be something more basic than public acceptance—the habitat. Preliminary research showed that some coyotes existed in Cades Cove, but wild-life technicians hoped that they would retreat once wolves, the more dominant species, arrived. In January 1991, USFWS workers brought in the first two pair of red wolves, which stayed in pens until pups arrived. Then Henry and technicians fitted radio-transmitter collars onto the first pair plus their two seven-month-old female pups and released them on November 12. "At the end of that year it looked like it was feasible, they did okay," said Henry, "so we started a full-scale reintroduction in 1992." The second year, the USFWS put one family in the Cove and another in the higher-elevation forest, near Tremont. Almost immediately the wolves left the park and had to be recaptured. To encourage the canines to regard the Smokies as home, the following year USFWS technicians re-leased them with young pups. The wolves stayed, but the pups did not grow properly and the adult wolves suffered from malnutrition. In fact, over the seven years of the project, two-thirds of the adult wolves simply left the park in search of food, and twenty-nine of the thirty-three pups born did not survive. Hindsight made the reasons clear. "There's a very low prey base in the park," Henry explained; wolves prefer small mam-mals such as rabbits and raccoons. "The majority of the park is high-elevation forest; there isn't enough of the early-succession forest that supports rabbits, raccoons, and deer." Chris Lucash, another USFWS biologist, put it another way: "Unfortunately, there was only one Cades Cove in that park."[49] After seven years and $1.2 million in public funds, the wildlife experts declared the project a failure and rounded up the last wolves. Mysteriously, however, three of the large predators had removed their collars and disappeared.

Although the Smokies failed to support red wolves in the 1990s, it appeared from the recovery experiment that high-elevation forests never did. The program found more success in the Alligator River Reserve in eastern North Carolina, where habitat matched the wolves' historical range. A more successful and less costly reintroduction program to restore peregrine falcons began by accurately documenting the raptor's place in the forest. In the 1930s and 1940s, when Arthur Stupka still took nature hikes up the Alum Cave Trail, he kept one eye out for peregrine falcons, the small raptors known for their magnificent wind speeds and commonly referred to as "duck hawks." Stupka, an avid birder, recalled one such hike in 1942, when he and his lucky visitors saw a trio of young peregrines flapping their wings atop a ledge. Unbeknownst to the naturalist at the time, one of the last peregrine falcons in the eastern United States came from this nest. During the 1950s and 1960s, widespread use of DDT for mosquito control increasingly killed off the birds. The park did not use DDT, but the peregrines preyed on birds that encountered DDT outside protected lands. Unconfirmed sightings of peregrines took place in 1965, 1977, and 1983, but ornithologists agreed that the peregrines had disappeared from the East. In the Smokies, ravens slowly took over the Alum Cave Bluff.[50]

Outraged at the loss of the peregrine, scientists and falconry experts established the Peregrine Fund to research the bird, promote its recovery, and encourage public education about raptors. Cornell University researchers devoted a captive breeding program to peregrine recovery, and by 1975, the lab produced more than fifty birds a year. The researchers began working on a release method, called "hacking," which achieved a 74 percent success rate (four weeks after release). About this same time, the USFWS initiated an Eastern Peregrine Falcon Recovery team to evaluate sites for restoring the birds in the East. Because of the well-documented presence of peregrines and the Smokies' protected status, the coordinator rated it the best release site in Tennessee. A team released four young female falcons on Greenbrier Pinnacle in 1984 and kept a twenty-four-hour watch on them from a hidden screen until they disappeared.[51] By 1990, after thirteen birds were "hacked" in the park, a breeding pair finally chose Alum Cave Bluff, the place Arthur Stupka last saw the species. Probably because of the human disturbance or helicopter flightseeing, they did not successfully construct a nest, however.

When birders spotted another nesting pair in 1997, the park service closed the manway over Duckhawk Ridge and near the ledges. Volunteers protected the site, waited, and watched. On June 8, 1997, Dave Morris, park wildlife volunteer, climbed to the observation point below Peregrine Point to take his shift. "After removing our packs, setting up my camera and his spotting scope," recalled Dick Dickinson, who accompanied Morris to the site, "[Morris] made a statement that every naturalist east of the Rocky Mountains had been waiting to hear for many years: 'we have chicks in the nest.'" The three chicks, which Dickinson described as "fuzzy white tennis balls," didn't move for days. "Nothing I can write can describe the emotion level of witnessing an event that has not been seen in more than fifty years," Dickinson said. "Each time I tell the story, sit at the computer to enter this data, look at the pictures, or close my eyes to relive the event, cold chills run all over my body."[52]

Retraining Garbage Bears

While high-profile reintroductions grabbed the public's imagination, re-source managers also struggled to retrain bears to a wilderness without picnic basket repasts. Despite George Fry's best efforts, panhandling bears did not immediately unlearn their junk-food habits. The *Gatlinburg Press* still announced the first "panhandler bear of the season" in May 1975, and described a mother bear which, "we think, seems to actually send her cubs up a tree when she hears people approaching."[53] Under Boyd Evison, resource managers wrote a new bear-management plan that required bearproof garbage cans, public education, and more backcoun-try patrols and citations to ensure that visitors stored food properly and left campsites clean. "Actually, it's largely a people-management plan," described Evison. "And its central concern is with the need to keep the Smokies' bears wild and free—not dependent on garbage and junk foods. That dependence . . . has resulted in tragic injuries and frequently, is the direct cause of the bears' death." When visitors complained that they no longer got to see bears in the park, rangers pointed out that roadside bears are easy prey for "cub-nappers," those who steal bears for tourist attractions. Rangers have to shoot bears, they pointed out, if they become so accustomed to human beings that they destroy property or attack visitors.[54]

When the "people-management" bear program began, Kim Delozier worked as a hunter for the exotic wild-boar management program. He rose through the government ranks as a backcountry ranger, then spent time as a technician with the USFWS before landing a job in bear management. During the 1980s, he recalled constantly trapping and relocating panhandling bears. "If you had a problem bear, you caught him and moved him," Delozier remembered. "If he came back, like so many of them did, then you took him someplace outside the park." By the 1980s rangers no longer gave bears names, but even as numbers, bears became legendary. Bear 75, for example, developed an extraordinary attachment to Cades Cove. Captured eleven times, he traveled at least 1,500 air miles, including from a relocation to the George Washington National Forest near Harrisonburg, Virginia—400 miles from the cove! Delozier recalled transporting one family, a mother and two tiny cubs, from the Morton Overlook (on U.S. 441) to Cataloochee, and two years later both of the cubs had become regulars at the overlook again. "The species has a lot of behavioral plasticity," commented researcher Mike Pelton, "It can adjust and adapt just like that. And it's primarily focused on food!" As for the management policy during the 1970s and 1980s, Delozier said: "We moved a lot of bears in those years." However, bear incident statistics seemed at first to prove that the policy worked, as both personal injuries and property damage caused by bears declined between 1978 and 1980.[55]

Despite the bearproof garbage cans and visitor education, Delozier referred to the policy as still largely "reactive:" when rangers encountered a problem, they moved a bear. The year 1989 stayed in Delozier's mind, however, because property damage nearly tripled that year, and the number of injuries suddenly rose from three the previous year to seventeen. And one of the incidents proved quite serious. Phyllis Murphy, a Clinton County, Ohio, resident, stopped at the Chimneys for a picnic supper with her husband. After dining in the van, she walked by the creek, bent down to examine some rocks, and when she stood again she saw a bear. "I just hollered, 'Oh my God' and I turned," she recalled. "I was going to run, but my foot slipped and I went down between the rocks. Then it jumped on my back and broke my shoulder blade and grabbed me by the neck and just started swinging me. I thought I was dead." Other tourists threw rocks and eventually a large log at the bear, which ran off but then started eating out of the garbage again. Murphy had no food with her at the time of the attack; she was not even wearing perfume or deodorant. As an ambulance arrived, rangers evacuated the area, closed the picnic area, and tranquilized the bear.[56]

"We returned to spotlight the picnic area later that night and discovered twelve bears feeding on the garbage," Delozier recalled. "It was obviously out of control." Typically in a wild setting, scientists described bears as crepuscular, with late morning and early evening feeding patterns. "But if food [like picnics and garbage] is available during the middle of the day, bears can become diurnal," emphasized Pelton. "Or if they're harassed and hunted they will be strictly nocturnal." Although the Chimneys had bearproof garbage cans, maintenance crews typically worked from 7 A.M. to 3:30 P.M. Most picnic traffic happened after that time, so the bears, true to character, adapted. Some evenings people left tremendous mounds of garbage on top of the cans—in Delozier's words, "they looked like Christmas trees of garbage." Bears fed all night, then in the morning the maintenance crew cleared the area, so everything looked okay during the day. Meanwhile, Gatlinburg hotel owners told their guests to travel to the Chimneys if they wanted to see bears.[57]

As garbage bears slowly became habituated to human beings, they were less and less afraid, and constantly rewarded for fearless behavior by getting food. "Once they become highly habituated," Delozier explained, "there's almost nothing we can do—rubber bullets, sirens, rocks, pepper spray, almost nothing you can do has a behavior-changing effect on them," he said. While the aggressive bear that attacked Phyllis Murphy had to be destroyed, the other night active freeloaders at the Chimneys might be retrained to fear people. After using volunteers to help sanitize the picnic area at night, wildlife biologists experimented with a retraining method tried in Florida with black bears. Rather than simply moving the bears, they used traps to capture them, and then they gave the bears a complete medical workup, including weighing, measuring, tattooing, and pulling a tooth. Caught and released on the same spot, the bears relearned a healthy fear of humans.[58] Outwitting and retraining the bears

proved a constant job for resource managers, though, as in 1998–99 wildlife technicians installed special food storage cable systems at all backcountry campsites to keep food from bears.

Explaining to the public why they couldn't see bears all the time dominated Delozier's job, but he owned special skills for the public relations
task. "I'm a local," he said, from Seymour, Tennessee. "I went out to the
highway from my home and turned right to go to UT, then took a left and
went to work." He obviously enjoyed telling this story. An affable nature
and a regional accent helped Delozier defuse potential conflicts. At one
Rotary club meeting, a ranger explained the bear policy and why it's better for bears to be wild. Afterward, a motel owner confronted him, saying
that "For years, we sent people to the Chimneys to see bears. Now they
go home, never having seen a bear." The ranger explained that the bears
were still there, only now they no longer feed on garbage. "You are not
only hurting our business in Gatlinburg," the motel owner whined, "you
are negatively affecting the entire economy of Sevier County."

Dolly's Mountain Home

It's hard to imagine that Kim Delozier or even the entire bear population
of the Great Smokies in any way adversely affected the Sevier County,
Tennessee, economy. While scientists worked through restoration and
reintroduction projects to make the Smokies an increasingly wild place,
the gateway communities surrounding the park boomed. The great irony
of this Wild East during the 1980s was that a typical visitor got too busy
to see the park. Increasingly preoccupied with theme parks, bungee-
jumping equipment, music theaters, Elvis museums, outlet malls, motels,
restaurants, a gospel hall of fame, and even a casino, tourists only inciden-
tally drove through the Smokies, supposedly the inspiration for all the
development.

The long-touted economic bonanza that park founders envisioned
finally arrived, at least for Tennessee, during the 1980s. As park rangers,
now effectively the equivalent of traffic cops, raced to manage 10 million
tourists, Gatlinburg, Pigeon Forge (both in Sevier County, Tennessee),
and Cherokee (in North Carolina) competed to claim them as customers.
Whereas tourists spent $77 million in Gatlinburg during 1976, twenty
years later the town claimed $300 million in annual retail sales.[59] Begin-

ning in the early 1970s, Gatlinburg, Pigeon Forge, and Cherokee began to do business at a volume that attracted outside entrepreneurs. Before this, tight control by local developers, coupled with the "quiet village" image of Gatlinburg in particular, deterred outside investment. Beginning in 1973, chain motels and chain restaurants began to take off. "Gatlinburg is becoming a place for outsiders to do business with outsiders," concluded one researcher. "It has a destiny much more tied to the larger interurban economic system." And so, while the big money came into Sevier County, it increasingly poured into the pockets of corporations based someplace else.

While visitation figures continued to rise, tourists spent less and less time exploring the park. "For the vast majority," stated one report, "the park is largely a windshield and facility experience."[60] A typical visitor did not come from the area, spent most of his or her time in Gatlinburg, Cherokee, and Pigeon Forge, then drove up to Newfound Gap or Clingmans Dome in the national park to view the scenery. About half stopped at one of the pull-outs along the way to take a photograph, but they probably left their cars running. Almost 95 percent stopped only at man-made facilities. Hiking enthusiasts and local people used one of the fifteen finger entrances and continued to explore the backcountry, but the vast majority of visitors "saw" the Smokies in an afternoon, then returned to an entertainment center or shopping mall for the rest of their visits. Gross receipts increased each year in Gatlinburg and Pigeon Forge, even when the park experienced decreases in park visitation. By 1995, tourists cited "shopping" as the best reason to visit the area.[61]

The person most responsible for the boom at least sounded local. Born in Sevier County, country singer superstar Dolly Parton bought into a successful 400-acre theme park called Silver Dollar City, owned by Herschend Enterprises, in 1985. Prescient investors changed the name to Dollywood. "I can make money doing a lot of things," claimed Parton, who has residences in Nashville and Los Angeles, "but the whole dream was to do something to bring honor to my family as well as to my friends and relatives." The Pigeon Forge City Council apparently thought she was a good bet, because together with the state they put together $3 million for improvements in roads, sewer, and water facilities. The following year, their return looked obvious: sales tax earnings increased 100 percent. The theme park became the largest employer of the 600 tourism businesses in Pigeon Forge, with 1,300 employees. By 1990 a million and a half people visited Dollywood during its seven-month season.[62]

Just outside of Pigeon Forge, Parton built a replica of the shack in which she was born. (The family was so poor, she quipped, "the ants used to bring back food they'd taken from us because they felt sorry for us.")[63] Surrounded by a schoolhouse, church, and grist mill, the shack took on the romance of *Little House on the Prairie*. As tattoo parlors, T-shirt shops, personalized license plate stands, factory outlet malls, second-home developments, and other amenities carved up the rural landscape, inside Dollywood a fantasy of the past survived. On ten stages surrounding Dolly's "town," regional entertainers performed country, bluegrass, and gospel music, while in Craftsman's Valley, women in gingham dresses and men in overalls demonstrated and sold baskets, quilts, soap, and other homey paraphernalia. Beyond the music and crafts, Dollywood enticed visitors with a 1924 antique carousel, a whitewater ride, a trip on a runaway mine train, and Blazing Fury, "a fast-paced journey through a burning town," along with the usual bumper cars and the Tiltawhirl. "Through Dollywood, it's my hope that we can preserve the heritage and lifestyle of the Smokies that gave me my strength," Parton said, "and that we can create jobs and grow in this area, so we can all live better . . . I'm not just coming back to take; I'm coming back to give." Despite her optimistic view of preserving history, the appeal of Dollywood mostly relates to the star. In the Dolly Parton Museum, visitors watch a video of country music stars paying tribute to Parton. "I really have gone from rags to riches," a video Parton tells the audience. "I almost feel like Cinderella." Afterward, visitors can view more than 2,000 of her personal effects, including sequined gowns and gold records. Amazingly, Parton and Herschend Enterprises found that people will pay $20 per day to enjoy carnival rides, see a video of Parton, and gawk at her abandoned costumes.

According to an in-depth survey of Sevier County completed in 1989, "the principal benefits of the tourism boom in Sevier County appeared to have gone to a select group of businessmen." Although the county population surged since the 1970s, most of the financial benefits have gone to a managerial class that moved into the area. For those without extensive capital to invest, tourism offered minimum-wage jobs as food servers, hotel maids, and retail clerks. Because many businesses do not stay open all year, most employees are "part-time," which translates into few benefits and no job security. "Most tourism industry employees in Sevier County reported that they worked intensively, for long, arduous hours six months out of every year, then essentially waited for work for six months," said Michael Smith, author of the study. Smith found that whereas in 1970 Sevier County had an unemployment rate of 5.6 percent, by 1980 this more than doubled, reaching 11.6 percent. Moreover, the seasonal rate soared even higher: in 1986 the off-season average remained at 20.8 percent and the peak-season rate stayed at 8.8 percent. If a breadwinner with two dependents worked full-time at minimum wage in 1989, his or her annual salary fell $2,900 below the federal poverty line. Not surprisingly, over this same period more poor families in the county became dependent on public assistance. "Seasonal employment has helped in some sense but hurt in others," said Cheryl Seale, human resources administrator of the Douglas-Cherokee Economic Authority. "Effectively, all it does is knock them out of their Medicaid benefits."[64]

Ironically, Smith's report showed that in the county promoted as the home of "good, clean family fun," families suffered. One Gatlinburg woman interviewed for the report stayed home with her six children until her husband, a park janitor, died suddenly. For two years the family lived on social security benefits; then Marie Wheatley went to work for a hotel, cleaning rooms for $4.05 per hour. After working nine years at the same hotel, Wheatley injured her leg on the job; when she returned, her employer cut her hours and eventually fired her, warning other employers that she had "a bum leg." In 1988 she lived in the home purchased with her husband's life insurance money, along with two of her daughters, a son-in-law, and two grandsons. Because in a tourist economy housing costs stay inflated—as off-season cabins sit empty—Wheatley's daughter was skeptical about being able to live on her own. "You work all your life for something," she remarked, a woman in her early twenties, "and you never end up with anything." Like Wheatley and her daughter, a disproportionate number of the working poor in Sevier County were women.[65]

In Cherokee tourism lagged during the 1980s, prompting the tribe to spend $200,000 in advertising to promote the museum, the craft cooperative, and the outdoor drama *Unto These Hills*.[66] As with Sevier County, the money seemed to leave the area or concentrate in a few hands. Unemployment typically reached a staggering 40–50 percent in the winter months, and the average number of families operating below the poverty line ranged from 11 to 23 percent in Swain and Graham Counties.[67] "When I was a young man, the only wage work was off the reservation," said Ed Welch, a Birdtown resident. "When I wanted money I went to Tennessee and up to Asheville. I finished concrete on Henley Street Bridge and worked at Babcock Lumber Company in Louisville." As for tourism, Welch did not see this as an option. "Tourist trade? Now what kind of jobs are that? You can't feed the entire reservation for six months and expect it to go hungry for the other six because the white man won't come to look at him."[68]

In a move that sharply divided the tribe, the council voted in 1994 to sign a contract with Harrah's to bring gambling to Cherokee. Tribal leaders reached an agreement with the state of North Carolina to allow video gambling, as long as the games "require skill and dexterity" and "pay no more than a $25,000 jackpot." The agreement so angered tribal members, that they overthrew most of the council and the chief in the next election. The new chief, Joyce Dugan, could not renege on the casino contract, so she vowed to make sure that the money helped the entire Eastern Band. Even before the $82 million, 175,000-square-foot casino opened in 1997, each tribal member received payments from an interim casino. At the end of the first year of operation, per capita checks topped $2,200. According to Dugan, Harrah's brought 1,400 new jobs, entertainment, and a 36 percent increase in business on the reservation by the end of the century.[69]

Both Cherokee and Gatlinburg-Pigeon Forge failed during the last half of the twentieth century to attract more diversified industry that would have helped workers. In Cherokee, the federal government holds the land in trust, so businessmen do not own their land; many businesses, including Harrah's, considered this a major obstacle. In Tennessee, Sevier County benefited from sales tax revenues and inflated property values, so that county commissioners—often members of the tourism and real estate industries—did not encourage a diversified industrial base. County revenues, then, become swallowed up in the increased demand for water, roads, and utilities. A county that thrived on tourism looked the other way when developers put together shoddy second homes or built hotels in locations that violate good sense.[70]

Despite unsolved economic problems and traffic that slowed to a standstill for 20 miles between Sevierville and the park, development continued unabated in the 1990s. Each successive wave seemed to have less to do with the mountains, as Dollywood, Inc. proposed the idea of an entertainment park full of music theaters, which the promoters nicknamed Music Road. A small group of residents protested the development, but Pigeon Forge shelled out $8.8 million for the land, road construction, and utility installation. Council members gambled that revenues from Music Road would pay those expenses, as Dollywood began constructing its own Music Mansion theater.[71] In 1998 Dollywood announced plans for an $8 million roller coaster and a $3 million gospel music hall of fame. The assistant director of the Pigeon Forge Department of Tourism celebrated the "new categories of visitors" this would bring to the region, who she said might not otherwise consider Dollywood and Pigeon Forge for their vacation plans.[72]

By the end of the century, successive years of flat sales caused Gatlinburg, on the other hand, to question the carnival-like atmosphere of the town. The chamber of commerce along with businesses and community groups hired the Sonoran Institute of Tucson, Arizona, a consulting firm that specializes in gateway development, to come up with a new plan for the city. "The old formula for creating prosperity in Gatlinburg is not working," the report stated, "and has been stale for some time." The consultants surveyed visitors and found that "the current first impression made on visitors is that of a rundown, haphazard collection of buildings ranging from the good to the bad to the ugly." Although businessmen cringed at the word "tacky," the report pulled few punches: "Gatlinburg is widely viewed as one of the most unattractive and inappropriate gateways to a national park in the United States." The report recommended that the town tear down the space needle and ferris wheels and build something related to the mountains, such as botanical gardens, a natural history center, or an arts-and-crafts enclave. "We don't want to be noticed as T-shirt City, U.S.A.," commented Gatlinburg Mayor George Hawkins, but "evidently it's easier to make a dollar selling T-shirts than anything else." Meanwhile, Ripley's Believe It or Not Museum heralded plans to build a $42 million, 1.2-million-gallon aquarium, with sharks, sting rays, and other ocean-loving animals in it.[73]

And so as scientists in the Great Smoky Mountains infused the national park with a commitment to preservation and wilderness restoration, the gateway cities became riddled with development. As Alie Newman Maples, who grew up in the Sugarlands, put it: "I love our mountains, but it seems like we're building now so much and building up and hiding our beautiful mountains, which I really don't like at all." Lucinda Ogle, a native of Junglebrook, who saw her view of Mount LeConte destroyed by a high rise, said: "It disgusts me how they have to put high rises around."[74] Not all the gateway cities thrived on the wretched excess of Pigeon Forge. Nearby Townsend, Tennessee, advertised itself as the "peaceful side of the Smokies," and a healthy debate took place in the community as to how development should progress. City Councilwoman Sandy Headrick, owner of the Highland Manor Motel, believed that haphazard growth can threaten that peace. "This is a friendly, welcoming community," she said, "and we need to keep it that way."[75]

Despite the efforts of concerned citizens like Headrick, Great Smoky Mountains National Park increasingly appeared like a vast island of green in the middle of mindless sprawl. Setting aside, for a moment, the traffic, habitat fragmentation, and air pollution caused by development, what will happen to wilderness when at last no one gets out of the car? "To manage, to protect, to perpetuate living things in parks, they have to have value to humanity," Carroll Schell reminded us. "If they didn't, we wouldn't be here." Although wilderness advocates might take issue with Schell's pragmatic anthropocentrism, history supports his claim. Because the public wanted a wilderness, money became available to reintroduce river otters, red wolves, and peregrine falcons. Because people defined exceptions to wilderness management, LeConte Lodge stayed open and grassy balds got maintained. However idealistic and hard-working the scientists and resource managers employed by the NPS, it remained a federal agency, responsible to a public that doesn't always know what it wants. "It's easy for the U.S.D.A. Forest Service to calculate the wood products that come out of a forest stand," Schell said, hence justifying its existence. "But it's more difficult for us to calculate the value of a park experience, because it's so personal." And because it's so personal, land managers alternately educated people about nature and pulled together constituencies to support resource management. In the next century, the park's wilderness designation may be most in jeopardy from a public that, in the end, went shopping.

Because of the support for wilderness management by the park, Tennessee environmentalists in the 1980s decided to make another push for wilderness designation. "I had leverage at that time, because I was chair of the Tennessee Park Commission," said Leroy Fox. Because the park as well as the Wilderness Society celebrated its fiftieth anniversary in 1984, advocates focused their efforts on achieving congressional designation by that year. Senator Jim Sasser, a young progressive Democrat from Tennessee, offered to write the bill, and Senator Howard Baker, who had recently stepped down as Reagan's chief of staff, pledged to support it. The bill, introduced on October 7, 1983, included a provision to reimburse Swain County for the unbuilt Road to Nowhere. Leroy Fox invited George Fry, now retired, to join the delegation that lobbied the Tennessee governor, Lamar Alexander. "He was no longer working for George Hartzog," recalled Fox, "and we wanted to show there were no open sores in the park service." Fry heartily agreed. "To me, it was a personal triumph," Fox said. "It made me feel good that the controversy of 1966 was behind us. That there aren't any enemies in this story, only differences of opinions."[76] Superintendent John E. Cook fully supported the bills that would bring 467,00 acres of Great Smoky Mountains National Park into the wilderness system. "Some individuals have reservations about applying the wilderness designation to the 44,000 acres of former TVA administered lands," Cook told Fox. "We have no such reservations and strongly urge full 'instant wilderness' designation."[77]

Without alerting the congressional delegation from North Carolina, however, Jim Sasser took a bus tour to the Road to Nowhere. A group of Swain County residents, fearing Sasser's influence, met the bus and refused to let him disembark. Some perceived the trip as a violation of protocol: the Road to Nowhere runs through the district of North Carolina Senator Jesse Helms. Others felt the Swain Countians forced an unnecessary confrontation. "I still think we might have gotten the bill through, if it wasn't for Jim Sasser's ill-advised trip," said Leroy Fox. Up to that point, the only person uncommitted was Jesse Helms; in November, he came out with a bill of his own, which omitted certain lands from wilderness designation and provided funds to build the much-disputed North Shore Road. On March 6, 1984, a public hearing at the courthouse in Bryson City brought record crowds.[78] The North Shore Cemetery Association members attended, and local people filled the hallways. On March 27, environmentalists filled a Senate hearing room in Washington, D.C., in support of the Sasser-Baker Bill. Fox, who testified at the Washington meeting, recalled eating at a Chinese restaurant on Capitol Hill at the next table from the cemetery group. "We were friendly," he said, after so many years of meeting together, "despite the tension of the moment." At some point between the two meetings, Jesse Helms, who bore a grudge against Sasser, put pressure on Baker and Tennessee Governor Lamar Alexander, both of whom withdrew support. After testifying in favor of wilderness, Alexander reversed his testimony.[79] The bills died in the Senate.

Despite this failure, environmentalists tried again in 1987. The House wilderness bill claimed twenty-three sponsors and recommended that the 467,000 acres already managed as wilderness receive official designation, contingent on a $9.5 million settlement to Swain County. Senators Terry Sanford, Sasser, and Al Gore sponsored the companion bill in the Senate. Jesse Helms proposed his own bill, of course. He recommended that wilderness designation exclude the 44,000 acres transferred to the park service in the 1943 Agreement and made designation contingent on building the North Shore Road, appropriating $950,000 to pay for the road in addition to paying a $9.5 million settlement.[80] The Department of Interior did not state an official position, and therefore the park superintendent did not. The wilderness bill would not change visitor access, facilities, or activities in the park. Motorized equipment could still be used for search and rescue, and boaters could still enjoy Fontana Lake. No roads would be closed. As official publications put it, "The visitor experience will not change from the present." The bill made wilderness protection federal law, rather than an administrative decision.[81] Besides Helms's predictable opposition, the principal chief of the Cherokee, Jonathon L. Taylor, testified against wilderness at the public hearing, "We are opposed to any wilderness designation within the park," said Taylor. If wilderness designation had to be achieved, he preferred the Helms Bill, because it excluded lands immediately surrounding the reservation. "I want to ensure that tourism is not reduced to our reservation, that the roads are kept open, that the land directly adjacent to our reservation is not in wilderness status, and that restrictions are not placed on the types of activities our people, or those visiting our region may involve themselves with." He wanted language in the bill "guaranteeing that U.S. Highway 441 (the Newfound Gap Road) would never be closed. He also requested that Cherokees be allowed to collect native herbs in the park.[82]

The arguments in the 1987 Senate hearings rang familiar tones. "Along the north shore the forest now comes down to the lake waters, in an unbroken expanse of natural forest from the crest of the Smokies," testified Ted Snyder. "It would violate the integrity of a great tract of wilderness to have a road gouged out of it. Nothing destroys the sense of being at one with nature more than to come across an obtruding road." Leeunah Vance Woods, a member of the North Shore Cemetery Association, spoke against the Sanford-Sasser-Gore Bill. "I believe in conservation and preservation of the area," she said, "but I also believe in conservation and preservation of our heritage, and the two can be compatible. . . . If you don't have the leisure, the money, the physique or the commitment of a special lifestyle, then the wilderness recreation lobby doesn't want you to be allowed in anymore. If you can't afford to have your family learn backpacking, horseback riding, skiing, camping, or the mysteries of the white water canoeing, you are going to have less and less access to more and more public land."[83] Once again, through the influence of Jesse Helms, the wilderness bills died.

To the great frustration of both environmentalists and Swain County officials, the unbuilt North Shore Road had become a proverbial political football. One side or the other tried again in 1991 and 1995. As long as Jesse Helms remained in office, environmentalists saw little hope of gaining wilderness designation. As long as Swain County insisted on actual construction of the road rather than a cash settlement, there was little hope of compromise. By insisting on both preservation of the area and respect for human heritage, Woods unconsciously named the dilemma that has faced the National Park Service since the 1916 Organic Act. Somehow the park must conserve "natural and historic objects and the wildlife therein" while providing for unlimited enjoyment of the same. As White and Bratton described the paradox: "Our goal is to preserve systems that must change."

9.1. Peregrine falcons were restored to the Smokies in the 1990s, after a 50-year absence. Courtesy of Great Smoky Mountains National Park.

9.2. In the world of restoration, it helped to be as cute as these river otters: their reintroduction brought only positive PR. Courtesy of Great Smoky Mountains National Park.

9.3. The red wolf, shown here in a cage and wearing a transmitter collar, became a public relations success but a restoration failure during the 1990s. Courtesy of Great Smoky Mountains National Park.

Global Threats, Local Conspiracy Theories

This is one of the most polluted national parks in the country. It has the highest monitored deposition of nitrogen and sulfur pollution, which acidifies high elevation streams and forests and reduces visibility. It has the highest cumulative ozone exposures in the East. But the good news is there's something we can do about it.

JIM RENFRO, AIR RESOURCE SPECIALIST,
GREAT SMOKY MOUNTAINS NATIONAL PARK

ON A ROUTINE aerial survey of the park in 1963, rangers noticed a patch of dead trees near Mount Sterling. Pale snags thrown into relief against resplendent summer green turned out to be Fraser fir, the only native fir in the southeastern United States. Park officials called in an entomologist, who confirmed that an exotic insect had killed the trees. Like the American chestnut, the firs constituted a major component of the high elevation forest in the southern mountains; like the chestnut, the firs faced destruction by a species transported to the United States on unquarantined nursery stock. By October the chief ranger called the balsam woolly aphid (later renamed the balsam woolly adelgid) "our principal forest concern." Within a month, the park began cutting the infested trees to prevent the spread of the deadly insect.[1] The following year the Control Project cut down 4,827 Fraser fir of all sizes and ages. Workers sprayed the stumps with creosote and "the slash was well scattered and flattened" to maintain appearances. Without burning or in some way destroying the insects, however, the operations did not prevent the adelgids from spreading to the rest of the forest, which of course they did. In 1965 park workers cut down an additional 3,324 Fraser fir, but they no longer imagined they could keep acres of dead trees invisible.[2]

Whereas in the first half of the twentieth century changes in the Smokies environment came from localized development—timber operations and road-building—by the last decades before the millennium the mountains suffered impacts more global in origin. Following the expansion of world trade and aided by the lack of effective quarantine laws, exotic insects, diseases, and invasive plants from foreign lands increasingly became the greatest threat to biodiversity in the park. In addition to these biological invasions, the Smokies faced the brunt of air pollution and ozone damage produced by a rapidly industrializing South as well as the Ohio River valley. Although the growth of gateway cities made the Smokies increasingly look like a great refuge of green in an ocean of development, global threats reminded everyone that this was no island wilderness.

"We must make no mistake: We are seeing one of the great historical convulsions in the world's flora and fauna," forewarned British ecologist C. S. Elton about the increase of exotics in the United States.[3] As with the chestnut blight, exotic insects, diseases, plants, and animals transformed a disturbed area, like the heavily logged Smokies, very quickly. Called the "least reversible" of human impacts, exotic invasions loomed as the greatest threat to biological diversity in the late-twentieth-century landscape. Howard Stagner, chief of the NPS Natural History branch, first called attention to non-native species as early as 1962, but parks did not possess the funds to respond.[4] In 1979 the National Parks and Conservation Association, an advocacy group for the national parks, surveyed the conditions of national parks across the country. Listing the variety of "external threats" facing the park—exotic species, air and water pollution, clearcutting, and intensive development—the survey warned that superintendents managed their parks like "isolated islands."

The "External Threats to the Parks" survey prompted the NPS to submit its own *State of the Parks* report to Congress in 1980. The *State of the Parks* pulled no punches when it described the "significant and demonstrable damage" that continued "to degrade and destroy irreplaceable park resources." The report called 75 percent of these threats "inadequately documented" and warned about "endangered" air quality, "threatened" flora and fauna, and "significantly threatened" scenic resources. This report, and subsequent ones by the General Accounting Office (1987) and the National Parks and Conservation Association (1989), helped generate federal funding for protection and monitoring, but the threats seemed to multiply faster than the funding.[5]

Because of the work done at Uplands Field Research Laboratory, the NPS often cited the Smokies as a model of monitoring, a biological early warning system for exotics and air pollution. By the end of the century, however, the forest suffered from five major diseases along with a severe increase in air pollution, ozone, and acid rain—all of which threatened rare plants and altered the ecology of the Smokies. As tourists increasingly asked, "What happened to the trees?" scientists struggled to find out the mechanisms of tree death and its impact. As the highly visible Fraser fir vanished from the landscape, parallels to the chestnut blight stayed on everyone's minds. "Both [the chestnut blight and the Fraser fir] were high profile with the public and increased public awareness of exotic pests, if you want to look at the bright side," said Kristine Johnson, supervisory biologist in resource management. Johnson first became aware of the death of the fir as a graduate student at the University of Tennessee, where she wrote her master's thesis on the adelgid. "But both had an echoing effect on their ecosystem: many plants and animals were affected in ways we will never fully understand."[6]

A European native, the balsam woolly adelgid arrived in Maine about 1900, reached Shenandoah National Park in 1956, and attacked Mount Mitchell in 1957. The tiny insect—1/25th of an inch—sucked nutrients from living wood cells and injured them with a substance in its saliva. The substance caused abnormal cell division in the fir's cambium that resulted in hard, brittle wood, no longer capable of transporting nutrients to the limbs. The tiny adelgid spread with the wind and reproduced parthenogenetically, which is a fancy way of saying females required no male interaction; consequently, as many as three generations sometimes appeared in a single summer season. At first the fir's growth declined, then the foliage turned yellow, then brown. It took three to nine years to kill a Fraser fir, depending on the vigor of the tree.[7]

In 1961 the U.S. Forest Service Southeastern Experiment Station attempted to control the adelgid by releasing seven predatory beetle species from India and Pakistan. Unfortunately, however, the beetles did not survive a North Carolina mountain winter.[8] Only 65,600 acres of the unique spruce-fir forest still existed in the Southern Appalachians—74 percent of it in the Smokies—and by 1978 all of it showed signs of the adelgid.[9] The control method attempted in the Smokies at best only slowed the insect's rate of dispersal. Rangers found the adelgid above Cataloochee in 1964, on Mount Guyot in 1966, and on Luftee Knob and Spruce Mountain in 1968. Because of the firs' commercial value as a Christmas tree crop and international exports, private and public organizations cooperated: representatives of the USFS, the U.S. Fish and Wildlife Service, the North Carolina Christmas Tree Growers, the Mead Corporation, and various state agencies conferred on research.[10] In addition to the aerial surveys and clear-cutting, researchers trapped the insects and sprayed experimental pesticides. Everyone did cost analyses of these efforts, but no one found them effective. Finally, in 1975, Canadian researchers found that the fatty acids in a simple soap solution killed the insect by dissolving its outer shell. In order for the soap to work, however, the bark must be coated with a high-pressure hose; aerial spraying didn't work. The spray saved the Christmas trees, as the growers could protect rows of "crops."[11] But protecting a forest, remote from spray equipment, proved impractical.

And so a climb to Clingmans Dome, the highest point in the Smokies and a popular visitor destination, looked dismal by 1982. As naked firs ominously lined the favorite hiking trail, the public grew alarmed at the overall health of the forest. One concerned Franklin, Tennessee, woman wrote: "The Fraser firs are special friends of mine." She offered several suggestions, relevant to the California medfly. "I don't want to acquiesce to their death without at least one effort to help save them," she pleaded.[12] Although spraying the entire spruce-fir forest with high-pressure hoses could not be accomplished, the public did not want to see all of the Fraser fir die. And so the park began spraying the most visible and accessible Fraser fir trees, along the Clingmans Dome road and trail and Balsam

Mountain Road. Spraying a few trees along a roadway might be akin to fighting a forest fire with toy water pistols, but the public demanded that something happen. "We are not solving the overall problem," said Dean Berg, a resource management specialist, "but supporting the Clingmans Dome area, which is a prominent tourist attraction."[13]

By the time the park began spraying, tiny fir trees regenerated on the older sites, like Mount Sterling. As with the chestnut blight, a few young trees lived long enough to reproduce—about 10–20 years—before they succumbed to the infestation. Regeneration gave scientists hope that the beautiful fir would survive, and they continued monitoring research plots to measure success. Keith Langdon, another resource manager, comforted a worried public by explaining that the park could preserve a diverse gene pool. "By protecting firs in six far-flung locations, we hope to preserve a greater fraction of genetic matter," he told a reporter. "Firs growing at 4,000 feet may be slightly different from those in 6,600 feet. Saving some at both elevations will ensure that some of each will survive to reproduce."[14] In 1995 the park received a Christmas tree farm east of Cataloochee Divide as a bequest, and on this new site Langdon helped create a 600-tree plantation from Fraser fir seeds collected throughout the park to further protect genetic resources and to provide a place for scientific study.

When the nettlesome insect finally diminished the fir and hence declined itself, resource managers reduced the spraying program. Over the fourteen years of spraying, though, the program drew criticism from an environmentalist who disapproved of using untested sprays in a pristine area. "I'm not opposed to control of aphids in a national park," said Dr. Garrett Smathers, a former senior scientist with the NPS, "but I don't think it should be done unless they are sure it's safe. My questions are: has a definitive study been done on this, has it been done at this park, and do they have the data backing this up?" The park conducted no such environmental assessment, and no such studies yet existed. Resource managers confirmed that the soapy spray killed aphids, mites, and small insects without an exoskeleton and then broke down quickly before posing a hazard to watersheds.[15]

As the firs died, the environment at high elevations began to change as well. Since firs outnumbered spruce at the highest elevations, the higher the elevation, the more dead standing timber. Increased sunshine and forest floor temperature caused ferns and mosses to die back.[16] Blackberries, briars, and elders began to invade the drier, hotter forest in many places. Without shade and nesting places, wrens and warblers that favored these northern climes decreased as well. A bird census in 1986 showed 37 percent fewer birds (decreased population density) than at the same sites, studied in 1974. Birds that favored open fields, such as indigo buntings, began to make appearances in the spruce zone. Of the thirteen species of breeding birds recorded in Smokies spruce-fir forests in 1967, ten showed a decline in numbers: the Blackburnian warbler, American robin, black-throated green warbler, black-capped chickadee, veery, golden-crowned kinglet, black-throated blue warbler, solitary vireo, winter wren, and dark-eyed junco.[17] A lot of the long-term impacts remained unknown, however, according to Paris Lamdin, a University of Tennessee scientist, because of the complex ecology of the spruce-fir forest. "For example there are over 242 species of insects associated with the Fraser fir, 62 in the leaf litter alone," he said. Something surely happens to them when the host plant dies, but scientists have only begun to study the impact of such changes on forest ecosystems.[18]

As researchers struggled to understand the impact of a single exotic—the balsam wooly adelgid—a host of others invaded the Southern Appalachians. For trees not valued as timber species, the research—and hence the park's ability to piggyback onto it—has been slow and poorly funded. The butternut, never a major forest component in terms of frequency or wood product value, nearly disappeared as money for research failed to develop. Known for its straight trunk and broad, open crown, the butternut tree provided food for wildlife, and the brown husks yielded a yellow or orange dye. Closely related to the black walnut, the tree was valued by farmers for its nuts as well as for its timber, which made fine furniture. A mitosporic fungus specific to butternut arrived in the United States during the 1960s, but not until 1986 did anyone identify it in the southern mountains. In 1987, Keith Langdon, supervisor of monitoring and inventory, along with Bob Anderson of the USFS found seventy butternut trees to monitor for the disease; *all* of them already showed signs of the lens-shaped cankers, covering the trunk, limbs, twigs, and even the nuts. Because the fungus attacks the nuts, affected butternuts cannot reproduce. Some butternuts appear to keep growing and may fight the disease, but the USFWS nominated the tree for endangered species protection, and the USFS banned cutting of butternuts. Because so few remained, six federal agencies pledged to locate remaining trees, identify those with resistance, and preserve material for possible grafting or cloning.[19]

When a disease such as the dogwood anthracnose arrived and spread quickly, the park could do little to halt the rate of destruction. The delicate dogwood tree, which each spring sprinkled the forest understory with white flowers, faced demise in the 1990s from this fungus. In addition to their unique beauty, dogwoods supplied food for fifty-one species of migrating birds, which dined on the elliptical, shiny red berries. Containing a high level of calcium, dogwoods' decomposing leaves improved the soil. In winter, high-protein dogwood twigs supported deer and other wildlife. Before the Smokies became a national park, Cherokees used the roots to make a red dye, and mountain folk made weaving shuttles from the hard wood.[20]

Dogwood anthracnose first appeared in New York City in 1978 and reached the Cohutta Wilderness Area in northern Georgia by 1987. In the early 1990s, a plant pathologist at Virginia Polytechnic Institute and State University told a *Washington Post* reporter he feared the disease could "annihilate the species." Large tan and purple spots and holes appeared on the leaves before they wilted, and tiny cankers developed on the twigs. As the twigs died, the trees sprouted heavily off the trunk, in a process called epicormic branching. Dogwoods clustered in moist shady valleys, like the humid Smokies river valleys, died in a few years. Whereas dogwoods grown in sunny suburban yards can be protected by mulching, pruning, spraying fungicides, and improving air circulation, the dogwoods in the forest remained vulnerable.[21]

No one who visited the Smokies in April before 1998 can forget the soft clouds of white, which outlined the hillsides before the leafy canopy appeared. Because the four white dogwood leaf bracts grow in the shape of a cross (the flower forms a yellow center) and open at Easter time, local people said the tree commemorated the Christian story. North Carolina named the tree its state flower. In a touching article written for *Bioscience*, ecologist and hospital chaplain Phyllis Windle told of the grief she felt for the loss of this beautiful forest understory. Although scientists often claim detachment and objectivity toward their subjects, Windle declared a passion, an "ability and willingness to admire and care about other species," among her colleagues:

When I sit beside a hospital bed as a chaplain, I expect people to cry about the unwelcome changes they are experiencing. I expect and accept patients' feelings that are dark and intense—rage at life's unfairness and guilt for doing too little. . . . Honest conversations that come quite naturally at a bedside are far more difficult at a lab bench or conference table. Thus, it is harder for me to speak freely about my grief for dogwoods with ecological colleagues than with fellow chaplains."[22]

In the Smokies, one survey showed that dogwood death from the Asian fungus increased 21 percent between 1988 and 1992. Dogwoods along watersheds and northerly slopes surely looked wilted and dying. A hazard rating published by the Smokies resource-management team concluded in 1993 that "the future of flowering dogwood in the park is serious."[23] By 1997, half the monitored dogwoods were dead, although those in sunny locations survived the disease better than anyone expected. Like the trees well cared for by urban gardeners, they stood some chance of resisting the disease.

In 1993 two forest technicians, Ed Yost and Andy Finton, discovered another exotic pest in the forest. The smooth-bark beech bore edible beechnuts, consumed in large quantities by squirrels, raccoons, chipmunks, and bears, as well as by grouse and other birds. Often growing in pure stands, the beech favored moist rich soils in the gaps. Yost and Finton were hiking up Fork Ridge on their day off, when they noticed ugly-looking scales on the trees. Yost, who worked on an old-growth survey in the park, and Finton, who monitored rare plants, suspected that they saw more than a single infestation. They called USFS entomologist Steve Oak, who recognized another exotic, the beech bark scale insect from Europe. The insect, whose taxonomic name is *Cryptococcus fagisuga*, wounded the tree's inner bark, creating large cankers that provided a kind of "habitat" for the fungus *Nectria*, which infects the tree, effectively girdling it in one to four years. The disease first appeared in Nova Scotia in the 1890s, then by the 1930s spread to Maine and New Hampshire. To monitor the disease, park resource specialist Kristine Johnson established nine beech tree plots in 1994 and alerted University of Tennessee researchers, who began studying the scale. Each year that Yost and Finton returned to the plots, the disease had advanced.[24]

At the same time, Dutch elm disease attacked the American, slippery, and winged elms in the park. Widely planted as a shade tree in the United States, the American elm became one of the nation's most popular shade trees, because landscape architects in the Frederick Law Olmsted tradition planted the spreading tree in city parks and developments. In the forest, elms grow more distant from one another, which isolated them from the Dutch elm disease at first. First noticed in 1921 in the Netherlands (hence the name), the disease traveled to the Ohio River in 1932, on logs intended for veneers.[25] During the 1950s and 1960s, Dutch elm disease killed more than 90 percent of the 77 million elms in cities. Rangers noticed the disease in the park during these earlier decades, but not until the 1980s did the fungus attack slippery elm and winged elm. Slippery elm, which grows in a range and environment similar to that of American elm, has a mucilaginous inner bark that mountain people used for cough medicine and poultices. All three species, which grew widely along the Little River, yellowed and died during the 1990s.

Also in the 1990s, Johnson and Langdon discovered another European import, the mountain ash sawfly, in the park. A small tree with a spreading crown, the mountain ash sprouts showy white flowers in the early spring; the bright red clusters of tiny red "apples" against yellow leaves lend drama to bright blue October skies. The mountain ash sawfly defoliated these trees at high elevations, depleting their reserves. On still another hike, Johnson and Langdon noticed that the American holly suffered from several diseases, and started a monitoring program on the evergreen, much favored by songbirds.

At the end of the 1990s, Smokies resource managers also turned their attention to the great eastern hemlocks. The park contained an estimated 4,000 acres of old-growth hemlock, including a 169-foot hemlock near Ramsey Cascades, the largest of its kind in the world. Will Blozan, a forest ecologist who worked with Ed Yost and Kathie Johnson on an old-growth survey, found this champion during his research. After roaming the woods regularly for years, he developed a knack for finding champion trees; he claimed a special fondness for the hemlocks. Because of the balsam woolly adelgid and the chestnut blight, the hemlock forest remains "the closest we have to what was here 400 to 500 years ago," he said. "Every other ecosystem has something missing." Wildlife value the hemlock as protective cover; deer browse on its needles. Even brook trout prefer the shadowy border provided by hemlocks over streams, and many wildflowers, such as mayflower, blue cohosh, and wood sorrel, associate with the acidic soils under the tree.

The insect that threatens eastern hemlock, hemlock woolly adelgid, arrived in the United States as early as 1924 on Japanese hemlocks. Several eastern states reported outbreaks during the 1950s, when it began traveling south down the hemlocks on the Blue Ridge Parkway. Like the balsam woolly adelgid, the hemlock-specific insect spread rapidly and caused death quickly. In 1997 Johnson flew to China with a group of researchers to study predators of the adelgid, which is native to Asia, and researchers at the University of Tennessee and the North Carolina State University Department of Entomology began studying the insect as well. Dr. Dan Pittillo, a biologist at Western Carolina University, along with graduate students Aaron Cooper and Larissa Knebel started research plots on early park forester Frank Miller's 1934–35 sites in Cataloochee Valley to monitor the hemlocks. Meanwhile, in eleven states the adelgid sunk its daggerlike mouthparts into the bases of hemlock needles, draining them of vital fluids before they fell to the ground.[26]

Although Johnson and the other plant specialists in the park did *not* discover gypsy moths in the Smokies by the end of the twentieth century, they carefully monitored oak trees for this nettlesome exotic. Introduced by a French scientist living in Massachusetts in 1869 who wanted to promote the silk industry, the gypsy moth first infested the United States in 1889. The distinctive brownish gray larvae have tufts of hair on each segment and a double pair of blue and red spots. Young larvae eat holes in the oak tree; older larvae feed on leaf edges, eventually defoliating the entire tree. Because oaks leaf out all at once in the spring and do not grow leaves again until the following spring, a typical oak cannot survive many years of defoliation. Although they prefer oak, gypsy moths will also consume apple, alder, basswood, birch, poplar, sweet gum, willow, and hawthorn trees; in fact, they have been recorded on some 300 species.[27]

As early as 1913, *Southern Lumberman* warned about the gypsy moth's "devastating course" and urged northeastern states to make a "thorough investigation."[28] Easily transported by swinging from strands of silk in the wind, the larvae can attach themselves to cars or motor homes and travel great distances. By the end of the century, the gypsy moth was introduced as far west as California and as far south as Rabun County, Georgia. In

1981 the moths defoliated a record 12.9 million acres, an area larger than Rhode Island, Massachusetts, and Connecticut combined.[29] In the last two decades of the twentieth century, NPS technicians have set out pheromone traps in campgrounds, happily with few results. The Tennessee Division of Forestry treated outbreaks in Tennessee during the late 1990s with a naturally occurring bacterium and a virus specific to the gypsy moth.[30] Because the moths arrived so long ago, scientists in the southern mountains have had almost a century to work on the problem. Given the tremendous commercial value of oaks, entomologists found the funding to do the research.

Other Alien Invasions

All of these pests and diseases that threaten the native trees of the southern mountains shared something in common: they entered the country because of unrestricted world trade. Although the chestnut blight story proved that long-term biological consequences followed the expansion of world trade, legislators slowly took action. Regulations existed, but the Plant Quarantine Act of 1912, the Federal Plant Pest Act of 1957, and the Noxious Weed Act of 1974 did not receive much enforcement until the 1990s. The Animal and Plant Health Inspection Service (APHIS) supposedly took care of enforcement by inspecting imports, excluding contaminated products, detecting infestations, and eradicating the latter before they caused a problem. With a tiny budget, however, APHIS enforcement amounted to inspecting a few high-risk shipments for insects, plants, and animals.

When biological effects kept multiplying and government officials tallied the cost, Congress finally took action. One study estimated that exotic weeds alone cost the U.S. economy $13 billion per year in herbicides spent by farmers, golf courses, and industrial sites.[31] With a heightened awareness of the price tag, Congress boosted APHIS in 1992 to 1,929 employees. The agency spent $105 million on agricultural quarantines and increased inspections by 2,000 percent over 1984. The new inspectors found 1.3 million baggage violations and assessed $723,345 in penalties against passengers trying to smuggle in plant material. In one year they confiscated 1.6 million "unauthorized" plants. While the figures sound impressive, the APHIS staff still appeared small when confronted with the overwhelming growth of world trade. During the 1990s, for example, the United States greatly expanded trade with China. Items sent to the United States from China delivered more than trade goods, however: a wood-boring insect, the Asian long-horn beetle, infested solid wood packing material such as crates. In the hold of a typical oceangoing vessel, wood containers might be stacked ten high; when the importer arrived at a port, containers would be placed on semitrailers and driven all over the United States. Although an APHIS inspector might have seen this ship, it would have been physically impossible to inspect everything aboard. The discarded containers, crates, and pallets released the beetles, which began attacking maples, sycamore, horse chestnut, yellow poplar, and other species. "It's a big political issue," explained Steve Oak, an entomologist with the USFS. "We want the Chinese to fumigate or kiln-dry their packing material to eliminate exotic pests, but that adds cost and they don't want to do that." Free-trade advocates ask: Do we hamstring billions of dollars of trade because of the potential risk of the Asian long-horn beetle?[32]

And Congress expanded APHIS too late to control balsam woolly adelgid or butternut canker; at best, the agency improved control of new "noxious weeds."[33] When an exotic disease proved costly to the timber industry, money appeared for research; likewise, when a weed added costs to agriculture, it became "noxious" and a topic of much research. Just as exotic diseases moved from nurseries to natural areas such as national parks, exotics often planted as ornamentals spread across the lower elevations of the Smokies. As with diseases, no predators checked their growth. They changed surface temperature, the rate of erosion, and how nitrogen cycles in the ecosystem; in short, they threatened entire ecosystems and as a result, biodiversity.

Like pathogens invading the body through a wound, invasive exotic plants entered the park through almost any disturbance: horse manure following trail riders, seeds carried in the toe of a hiking boot, roadway plantings, and forbs in a field bordering the park. The more previous disturbance in the forest, the greater the chance invasives could gain a foothold. Since many exotics, including privet, honeysuckle, and lespedeza, possessed shade-tolerant qualities, they spread into even healthy old-growth forest ecosystems. Others, such as kudzu, mimosa, and multiflora rose, typically arrived along highways or riparian zones. All of these exotics, however, limited native plants by crowding out competitors and changing forest habitat.[34]

Johnson pointed out that most invasive plants arrived, ironically, because "somebody a long time ago thought they were a good idea." Some weeds, such as garlic mustard and purple loosestrife, came with European settlers who appreciated their medicinal properties. During the eighteenth and nineteenth centuries, gentlemen farmers and arboretum owners imported unusual plants to round out collections of flowering species from around the world. Botanist André Michaux, for example, first brought mimosa trees from the Far East in 1785 for his South Carolina garden, from which it escaped into the woodlands. Likewise, William Hamilton planted the first tree of heaven, another Asian exotic, on his Philadelphia estate in 1784. A favorite in eastern cities, tree of heaven probably came south with tourists and second-home owners, who wanted it in their yards, from which it entered the woodlands.[35]

When commercial nurseries proliferated in the nineteenth and twentieth centuries, they too lured customers with exotic plants with which to decorate their gardens. Nurserymen first imported multiflora rose from Japan and Korea in the 1860s. A large shrub that bears clusters of white flowers, multiflora rose seemed like an attractive ornamental, but soon it formed dense, impenetrable thickets that invaded old fields and choked wetlands on public lands. More recently, gardeners from New England to Georgia purchased Japanese spiraea from mail-order catalogs and local nurseries. A 3- to 6-foot shrub with bright pink, flat-topped flowers, spiraea infested streambanks and spread quickly into disturbed areas. Although planting multiflora rose and Japanese spiraea seemed like an effective way to create a quick-growing border, these exotics became a nightmare for rare plants and wildflowers. Both reproduce through vigorous, spreading roots as well as seeds; the more one cuts out the root, the more disturbance created for the plants to spread.[36]

In addition to arriving as nursery stock, invasive plants found their way to the Smokies through the U.S.D.A. Soil Conservation Service (SCS). Between 1935 and 1942, the SCS unleashed 85 million kudzu seedlings in the United States in an effort to control erosion along newly constructed roadways. SCS also used Japanese honeysuckle, multiflora rose, and buckthorn for roadside plantings. Dismissing the notion that the plants themselves might become pests, SCS officials proclaimed the wonders of the miracle vine kudzu that grew 12 inches a day with root systems that plunged 12 feet into the ground. The wonder plant returned nitrogen to the soil. As anyone who has traveled through the South since the 1950s knows, though, kudzu made a virtual topiary out of trees, hedges, walls, fences—even telephone poles. Unfortunately, the SCS even selected kudzu plants with "extra vigor." Kudzu first hit the Smokies in the 1950s, and by the end of the decade the park sent crews to Noland Creek and Fontana Lake to furiously remove kudzu from 46 acres.[37]

Because of congressional pressure to do something about harmful nonindigenous species, federal grants became available to public land managers. Between 1994 and 1997, Great Smoky Mountains National Park launched a massive control project against invasive exotic plants with an $800,000 grant from the Natural Resource Preservation and Protection program. "We want to preserve the diversity of the original plants native to the area," explained Johnson, who supervised the project. Because the Smokies contained more than 381 non-native plants, the park's Integrated Pest Management Plan could not realistically remove them all. And not all non-native plants become harmful. Jonquils, for example, which were planted by former park residents, do not rapidly multiply and colonize neighboring species. The Integrated Pest Management Plan targeted the thirty-five exotic weeds that demonstrated adverse impacts on native vegetation and could be controlled with reasonable success. Student Conservation Association (SCA) and seasonal technicians worked three summers to control the exotics on 600 sites—encompassing an area of about 1.5 million square meters. On Noland Creek, for example, they found kudzu roots thicker than their legs. One of the workers suggested creating a "champion" display, so the vegetative management office at Twin Creeks exhibited wisteria and oriental bittersweet roots 4 inches in diameter and privet and English ivy roots 8 inches in diameter. When funding ceased in 1996 the "veg crew" devoted most of its time to monitoring and maintenance.[38]

For three years technicians hacked, dug, ripped, and pulled the exotic pest plants. Musk thistle, garlic mustard, barberry, and Japanese grass can all be curtailed with mechanical methods. Because of the prolific nature of some exotics, such as kudzu, they also sprayed systemic herbicides on the plants. NPS policy permitted the use of pesticides for exotic control, though it stated that "chemical treatments should always be accompanied by non-chemical treatments."[39] Some environmental groups have been reluctant to get involved in exotic control because of the herbicides; and Johnson reported that a few of her SCA workers wouldn't touch the stuff. Those who watched exotics swallow up native species grew impatient with the environmentalists. "What the hell do they want?" asked Don Smitz, a Florida biologist who worked on exotic biocontrol. "Do they want a short-term environmental insult or a long-term ecological catastrophe?"[40]

In addition to control, the park worked to educate the public about preserving native species. As president of the Tennessee Exotic Pest Plant Council (TNEPPC), Johnson encouraged people to plant native species in their gardens and, if they planted exotics, to avoid species such as princess tree, purple loosestrife, and Japanese barberry, which easily become pests. "Everyone who plants should be aware of the invasive potential of some species," warned Johnson, who grew up in eastern Tennessee and plants a large vegetable garden herself. "Educated consumers will create a demand for native plant materials to use in responsible landscape design as well as revegetation and restoration projects."[41] In addition to publishing an exotics manual, TNEPPC has worked with North Carolina to help establish an exotic pest plant council in that state.

What is the cumulative effect of so many invasive plants and exotic diseases on the forests of the Smokies? No one knows, of course, but throughout the Southern Appalachians scientists acknowledged a major shift occurring in the ecology of the forest. West Virginia researcher Linda Butler studied oaks before the gypsy moth arrived in her state. Well known for her thorough taxonomic work, she expressed the feelings of many who do a lot of field identification research: "It seems like we're always moving ahead of some impending disaster," she remarked to fellow researchers at a conference. "Everywhere in the forest I see impacts of insects, tree diseases, pesticides, pollution, timber harvest, fire, development, roads, and recreation areas."[42] For hundreds of years human beings have used—adversely affected—the forest. Yet the sheer number of exotic plant diseases, all of them devastating, make everyone wonder about the long-term health of the forest. And that's even before considering air pollution.

Scenery without a View

As motorists in search of scenery made their daily pilgrimages to Clingmans Dome in the 1990s, increasingly they did not find what they came to see: a view. During the second half of the twentieth century, the average visibility in the Smokies decreased 80 percent in the summertime and 40 percent in the wintertime, according to regional airport records. Small particles of air pollution over the park lowered visibility to an annual average of just 25 miles. Even without monitoring equipment, an observant person noticed washed-out colors and fuzzy landscape features. Under the Organic Act of 1916, national parks have a mandate to maintain resources "unimpaired for future generations," but the dramatic increase in air pollution in the final decades of the twentieth century made that increasingly difficult to do. In a place tourists traveled hundreds and even thousands of miles to recreate, it became increasingly unhealthy to breathe.

Like the exotic pests and diseases, the air pollution problem resulted from circumstances largely outside the control of the park. Although the United States called itself an urban nation in 1920 (the first year in which more people lived in cities than in rural areas), the South did not become an urban region until 1960. During the Great Depression, New Deal projects, including TVA, pushed people off farms; during World War II army bases and defense manufacturers pulled them toward the city. The South's population grew 20 percent, about twice the national rate, during the "rush to the Sunbelt" between 1970 and 1980. With people came cars and an increased demand for electricity, which resulted in millions of tons of air pollutants emitted into the air.

The two chemical compounds most often indicted in air pollution are nitrogen oxides and sulfur dioxide (often referred to by their chemical symbols, NO_x and SO_2). Eighty percent of the sulfur dioxide comes from coal-burning power plants, and nitrogen oxides emitted from power plants, factories, and motor vehicles. Once into the air, both gaseous substances convert to tiny particles—nitrates and sulfates—that comprise that annoying haze, reducing visibility. When precipitation occurs, these particles reach the ground as acid rain or acid snow. Because this acidity can build up in the ecosystem over a long period of time, the more acid rain, the more threatened soils and plants. By the end of the 1990s, acid rain, acid clouds, and acid deposition dumped approximately 100 pounds of sulfate per acre annually at high elevations. The average annual acidity of rainfall in the park (measured on the pH scale, where 7 is neutral and everything below that acidic) is 4.5; individual clouds with acidities as low as 2.0 bathe the high-elevation forests of the Smokies in the summertime. Regularly during the 1990s, the Smokies received the highest sulfur and nitrogen deposits of any monitored location in North America.

Ozone, the third pollution problem, forms when nitrogen oxides react with hydrocarbons in the presence of sunlight. Most hydrocarbons are natural, as is of course sunshine in the South, so the best way to prevent ozone is to reduce nitrogen oxide levels. On ridgetops of the largest range of undeveloped mountains in the Southeast, ozone levels typically run two times higher than in nearby Knoxville or Nashville. That's because every day cities such as Knoxville and Nashville generate pollution, which at night rises into the atmosphere, where it joins with the polluted air transported from as far away as the Ohio River Valley. In the 1990s this residual layer kept moving at night, and because weather usually travels west to east in the region, ozone typically blanketed the ridgetops of the Smokies. For example, ozone concentrations at the Cove Mountain monitoring site, at 4,150 feet, averaged 60 parts per billion (ppb) all day long. Nearby Knoxville's concentrations were half that level.

In 1997 the Environmental Protection Agency (EPA) passed a new ozone standard to protect public health, defining an unhealthy day as one that reaches 85 ppb or greater over an eight-hour period.[43] In 1998, forty-four days were rated as unsafe for children, the elderly, people with asthma, or those engaged in vigorous outdoor activity. "And of course that's one of the reasons people come here: to hike, and bike, and backpack. [On unsafe days] those types of activities can cause coughing, wheezing, scratchy eyes, nose, and throats, that bad feeling that comes from ozone pollution," said Jim Renfro, air resource specialist for Great Smoky Mountains National Park. "If you can't meet public health standards, it's definitely going to bring a lot of attention to the park."[44]

Renfro first became involved with the park in 1984, when he served as a volunteer on the Appalachian Trail while completing his master's degree. A native of Illinois and a graduate of Southern Illinois University at Carbondale, Renfro joined John Peine's Uplands crew to do trail research, but he increasingly became involved in air quality research and monitoring. Now in charge of one of the oldest and most comprehensive air quality monitoring programs of any national park in the East, Renfro increasingly sees his work as educating the public about the scope of the problem. "This is a regional problem," he said. "Literally the eastern two-thirds of the United States affects the air quality here at the park." Coal-fired power plants as far away as Cleveland, Ohio, and Birmingham, Alabama, adversely affect the environment of the Great Smokies. Many of the coal-burning power plants in the Southeast are dinosaurs in terms of antipollution equipment and account for 37 percent of all the nitrogen oxides emitted. Motor vehicles produce an additional one-third.[45]

The nature of the problem pushed Renfro into the political arena. "It's important to understand this issue is an 'upstream-to-downstream' problem. If you want to fix the problem, you have to go to the sources. There's not much that can be done in terms of the Band-Aid effect. We can't put a bubble over the park. It's going to take policy changes to affect the source of the problem." Under the Clean Air Act of 1977, all national parks with more than 6,000 acres received a Class 1 rating, which means these areas should be the cleanest places in the country with the greatest air quality protection. Legislators ordered land managers, including the superintendent of the park, to take an "aggressive role" in protecting "air-quality related values," which specifically included visibility, plants, wildlife, water, and historic resources. Amendments to the Clean Air Act in 1990 called for a 40 percent reduction of SO_2 by the year 2010. "This will help, it's moving in the right direction," said Renfro. "But we've got a long way to go. For NO_x, there's still no cap. Even though cars are cleaner today, there's a lot more of them and people drive more miles. So emissions continue to go up." In the fall of 1998, the EPA called for a 30 percent reduction in NO_x in twenty-two eastern states by the year 2003. "That should help to lower ozone over the park," said Renfro. "But it won't completely protect sensitive plants."

The official NPS position on air quality supports the "strictest possible state regulations on autos and other emissions which contribute to the problem." Representing the Smokies, Renfro comments regularly on permit applications for new pollution sources; NPS policy requires that new permits be granted only when the new power plant or factory plans the "best available control technology" or reduces emissions elsewhere. Between 1980 and 1991, the NPS sent comments warning about the adverse effects of air pollution to the Tennessee Air Pollution Control Board on twenty-three permit applications covering projects near the park. "For a long time, we didn't get anywhere with our comments," said Renfro. In some cases, the NPS recommended specific control technology, but in all cases the states granted the permits. In 1991, for example, the U.S. Department of Interior objected to Tennessee Eastman's plans to build a $100 million coal-fired power plant in Kingsport. "Any increase in ozone levels would exacerbate the existing situation," said the regional director of the park service, "and would be unacceptable." Despite the strong stance taken by the park service, company spokesmen worried about the "future growth and preservation of the production we already have." And so in the old jobs-versus-the-environment struggle, Tennessee officials in charge of the permits countered that the park could always limit the traffic in the park, and, besides, how could they prove that ozone caused any damage? "I do know that heat and insects can cause damage, too," said the state director of the air pollution program.[46]

But the proof that ozone damages plants and affects human beings is already conclusive. In some locations, almost 100 percent of the black cherry trees and tall milkweed plants in the Great Smoky Mountains showed signs of ozone damage in the 1990s: yellowed flecking; and dark red, purple, or brown stippling on leaves. Tulip trees, sassafras, high-elevation blackberry (*Rubus canadensis*), cutleaf coneflower, and winged sumac all exhibited ozone damage. To understand potential effects on other plants, the park fumigated 46 species with ozone in a small greenhouse-like study site. Eleven of the species, including red maple and table mountain pine, were extremely sensitive to ozone.[47] Research showed that excessive ozone causes coughing, sinus inflammation, chest pains, asthma, reduced immune system function, and even permanent damage to lung tissue in human beings. "This is one of the most polluted national parks in the country," said Renfro. "It has the highest monitored deposition of nitrogen and sulfur pollution, which acidifies high elevation streams and forests and reduces visibility. It has the highest cumulative ozone pollution exposures in the East. But the good news is: we can do something about it."

Researchers did calculate and model the potential effects of car traffic in the park. Even the emissions from 1 million cars traveling across U.S. Highway 441, according to Renfro, release only 66 tons per year of No_x, a fraction of the over 4 million tons emitted in the Southeast. "It is cheaper to control stationary sources, such as power plants, than it is to control mobile sources (cars and trucks)," said Renfro. Park literature does, however, urge visitors to "use energy-efficient automobiles" and to "keep motor vehicles in good operating condition," but it stops short of recommending that people drive less or give up their cars. "I think it's appropriate for the park to do demonstration projects, such as shuttles to popular locations," said Renfro. "We're concerned with our sources, even the little ones, and we need to do all we can to reduce them. Most of our pollution, though, is transported from the rest of the region." But America's love affair with the automobile—the South's loyalty to big and multiple cars—played an integral role in the creation and continued success of the park, too.

Acid Rain Controversies

Whereas ozone damage can be easily verified, acid rain turned into a highly politicized issue during the last decades of the twentieth century. At a Forest Health Conference in Chattanooga (one of three such meetings in 1995), USFS officials talked about all the individual diseases, pests, and air pollution confronting the Southern Appalachians. A final speaker, however, presented a "comforting" talk about the natural ecological ebb and flow of forest ecosystems. To avoid doom and gloom prophesies, he discussed the severe disturbances in the early part of the century, including chestnut blight, abusive logging, and agriculture, as well as fire suppression by public agencies. This dynamic has led to an increase in fire sensitive species and a decrease in fire tolerant species, such as oak and hickory. One slide he showed during his presentation listed "winners" in the ecological flow, including scrubby second-growth species such as hackberry, serviceberry, red maple, black gum, sourwood, and poplar. The next slide listed the "losers" as the major components of an old-growth eastern forest: fir, oak, chestnut, hickory, hemlock, beech, dogwood, mountain ash, and elm. While the USFS appeared a little upbeat at what look like unprecedented changes, this summary accurately conveys the results of thirty years of research on forest dynamics. Forest health researchers don't see "forest decline," only fewer numbers of some species. The USFS joined thirteen state and federal organizations in an effort to monitor forest health in the southern mountains. Through the auspices of the Southern Appalachian Man and the Biosphere program (SAMAB), the agencies cooperated to begin answering questions such as the impact on soils, sustainability of native plants and animals, protection of water, and assessment of migrating species. "Although spot declines have been observed, there is no indication of widespread forest decline in the region," read the first official SAMAB literature on the program. Like the slides of "winners" and "losers," the glossy brochure seemed designed to reassure the public and to counter the worst-case scenerios projected by individual scientists and environmentalists.[48]

Because of Uplands Field Research Laboratory, the Smokies got an early boost in research on the effects of acid deposition. By 1982 two Uplands researchers, David Silsbee and Gary Larson, tried to collect "baseline information on natural water in the park." A lot of factors influenced water quality in the park, including airborne pollutants, the management of historical areas such as Cades Cove, construction, exotic animals, and visitor use. About 8 percent of the park, most of it in high elevations, is underlain by Anakeesta, a slate, phyllite, and schist formation that produces a significantly lower pH in the soil and water than occurs in other areas. Areas that were heavily logged in the past have an overall higher nitrate concentration than old-growth areas. In general, pH is lower in high elevations because they receive more rainfall and lower temperatures.[49] About this time, Gary Larson, Ray Matthews, and Silsbee also began monitoring acid precipitation in the Smokies. Although they had little to compare it with, in 1978 they recorded baseline data showing a pH of 3.2 for rain at the Twin Creeks location. (Distilled water has a pH of 5.6.) Summarizing the research on the effects of acid rain in other places, they wrote: "One could obviously conclude that the potential for acid precipitation to affect adversely the resources of the park is enormous."[50]

Their work encouraged Peter White to organize more comprehensive research on air quality by documenting pollutant loading on plants, identifying sensitive species, analyzing effects on larger ecosystems, and quantifying the loss in visibility. In 1982, White organized a symposium on the spruce-fir forest, which became a standard reference on the ecosystem; he also helped write major grants from the EPA and the USFS. Chris Eagar, who studied the balsam woolly adelgid for both his master's thesis and dissertation, began looking at the overall health of the spruce-fir forest.[51] The death of the Fraser fir, of course, affected its companion species, the red spruce. At first, undefended red spruce suffered blow-downs, then the red spruce abruptly produced less wood, measured in annual radial increments; the needles showed an odd flecking.[52] Because of national publicity about acid rain in Germany and the northeastern United States, funds became available from the USFS and EPA to survey and monitor the spruce-fir forest in the Smokies for acid deposition. Between 1985 and 1989, Eagar's research became part of the Spruce-Fir Cooperative, which coordinated findings with another station in the Blue Ridge, monitored by Virginia Tech. "We don't have strong documentation of decline in red spruce in the Southern Appalachians the way we do in the Northeast," said Eagar, who today works for the USFS in New Hampshire. In the Northeast, highly acidic cloud water envelops the high-elevation forests much of the time. "The clouds, in fact, are considerably more polluted than the rain," Eagar explained. This exposure leaches nutrients out of the foliage and affects the uptake of calcium by the cells; this in turn, makes the trees very susceptible to winter damage and other stresses. "In the Smokies, we just haven't seen that yet," said Eagar. "We think we documented thinning of the crowns, but nothing that could be called catastrophic." However, acid clouds have made the high-elevation soils more acidic, which releases aluminum from the soil minerals; aluminum, in turn, damages the roots of spruce, and, when it gets into the streams, becomes toxic to brook trout. Aluminum also inhibits the spruce's ability to take up calcium, which may explain the stunted growth. "This reduced calcium availability, caused by acidification of the soil, is stressing red spruce in some conditions," said Eagar. "But it probably won't kill it. We see a reduction in growth and a reduction in photosynthesis."[53]

While Eagar's careful description of the process reflected his years of research, he did not make pronouncements or grab headlines with such explanations. During the same period that Eagar worked to understand the spruce-fir forest, North Carolina State University ecologist Robert Bruck testified before Congress thirteen times about the increased stress on the forests of the southern mountains. In a dramatic slide presentation, he described scenes of forest death from eastern Europe, where few environmental controls exist, as a kind of warning and predictor of what could happen in the southeastern United States. He detailed the terrible acid rain in eastern Europe, then showed photos of his research site on Mount Mitchell, where he measured "cloud events" in 1988 at 3.54 on the acidity scale, or as he described them, "the acidity of Coke." He then showed photographs of the dead Fraser fir on Mount Mitchell, implying that the trees died from acid rain.

The scientific community distanced itself from Bruck's dramatic statements. "We know the balsam woolly adelgid is the sole reason for the extensive mortality of the Fraser fir [that Bruck shows in his pictures]," said Eagar. Because the balsam woolly adelgid attacked trees in unpolluted areas and gained a foothold before air pollution became a major problem, Eagar did not believe that acid rain was involved.[54] "Sure, there's no proof," Bruck countered, "How long do you want to wait for proof before we do something about it?" To a popular audience, Bruck claimed that the "holy tabernacle of science" acts as if its methods and research were a "holy grail." The "holy tabernacle," in fact, only asked to see his data.

Another voluntary partnership, the Southern Appalachian Mountains Initiative (SAMI), looked more specifically at air pollution. Coordinating state and federal agencies, industry, environmental groups, and academic scientists, SAMI was organized to help managers mitigate and prevent adverse air quality impacts to natural areas. In the Smokies, SAMI researchers have studied sulfate and nitrate deposition in the Noland Creek watershed since the mid-1980s and the impact on stream acidification and the neutralizing capacity of streams.[55]

Understanding the effects of acid rain in the Southern Appalachians, let alone the massive changes in the forest, is still years in the future. "Forest health is a hard thing to get at," remarked Dan Pittillo, biology professor at Western Carolina University. Plant species develop over such a long period of time; in most cases they coevolve with diseases, so that individual plants that do not have resistance will die. "Of course, we may be influencing their ability to develop resistance by introducing them to a situation with which they have no previous interaction—such as air pollution," explained Pittillo. "Now, you can't say that air pollution is killing the trees this year, because there's no hard data to back it. But the fact of the matter is, there are a lot of things happening in the forest that I don't think in my lifetime I've ever seen until now."

Because it is difficult to isolate a single cause, no one wants to assign blame to acid rain. Scientists generally get uncomfortable with apocalyptic forecasters; many distrust journalists and environmentalists who generalize from their research. Environmentalists, however, responded to Robert Bruck's call for action and demanded more attention from legislators. The Wilderness Society called Great Smoky Mountains National Park one of the ten "most endangered" parks in the United States. Wilderness Society President George Frampton Jr. recommended that $100 million of the $800 million park service budget be transferred to research on air pollution, acid rain, and forest fragmentation.[56] A group of environmentalists in western North Carolina grew impatient with USFS research, and in 1997 conducted a survey of their own in Virginia, eastern Tennessee, and southwest into the Great Smoky Mountains. With funding from the Z. Smith Reynolds Foundation and the Sierra Club, the survey began with aerial mapping of the areas, later ground-truthed by hiking teams. Wade Davidson, a University of Kentucky graduate student who led the teams, said the survey indicated that all northern hardwoods—yellow birch, sugar maple, beech, yellow buckeye, and other species—showed signs of decline, not just the spruce-fir forest. "This tells us that no longer can we explain the decline and death in terms of a bug here and a disease here," said Davidson. Harvard Ayers, an Appalachian State University sociologist who directed the study, echoed Davidson's remarks: "There's no doubt in my mind that air pollution is the dominant factor for killing these trees. The areas and elevations where these trees are dying are bombarded with air pollutants year-round."[57]

The tone of Ayers and Bruck, matched by the USFS, resulted in a perception among some environmentalists that government agencies have conspired to cover up the acid rain/air pollution issue. Although NPS and USFS entomologists and plant pathologists agreed that tree death is alarming, they still felt obligated to understand what combination of stresses, including drought, forest insects, diseases, and air quality, is harmful to the forest. Research scientists shy away from the bold statements made by Ayers and Bruck, but they express concern about the number of changes happening all at once. Whereas scientists may disagree about the role of air quality in specific tree deaths, by the end of the century they agreed that air pollution was beginning to transform the soils in the upper-elevation Smokies. Many named air pollution as the most important environmental issue facing the park. Murray Evans, a retired botanist who worked thirty-four years for the University of Tennessee, called atmospheric pollution the "number one environmental problem" facing the park. "Ozone, nitrogen oxides, and sulfur dioxide are clearly wreaking havoc at the higher elevations," he said.[58] "You can pick on the sweep of exotic plants and animals as having big near-term and long-term consequences," said Ed Clebsch, another retired biologist. "But I think deteriorating air quality standards are likely to have the biggest influence over the longest time. Because that's something you can't turn around. There are more automobiles burning more fossil fuels on the road every year, and I think we have very little understanding of what those products do biologically and ecologically." And air quality in general, Renfro argues, is related to the economic health of the region. On a simple level, if streams fail to support brook trout, no one will come to fish. From another perspective, if it's unsafe to hike in the park, who will come to visit? And what good is scenery without a view?

International Biosphere Conspiracies

While they share a common concern for air pollution, nature lovers, hikers, resource managers, and scientists generally roll their eyes when asked about the development in the gateway areas. Most people with a greater environmental sensitivity avoid the Sevierville-Gatlinburg artery and know the back roads to visit their favorite trails or watersheds. Those who deeply love the park, who experience its wintery seasons, its fragrant downpours, and its misty mornings, don't spend a lot of time in Gatlinburg. Those who care about the salamanders, mosses, old-growth forests, black bears, and Neotropical songbirds are not likely customers of the Dolly Parton Museum or Harrah's casino. And they avoid contact with the teeming crowds, which increasingly seem to be unconcerned with the wild place above them. The growing distance between those who appreciate the complex biology of the Smokies and the ordinary tourist/shopper portends an ominous disconnection, as a bizarre story from the end of the century forebodes.

During Evison's last months in the office, he accepted a certificate recognizing Great Smoky Mountains National Park as an International Biosphere Reserve. Developed in the 1970s, the Man and the Biosphere program was mostly a public relations program under the auspices of the United Nations Educational, Scientific, and Cultural Organization (UNESCO). Ecology and the environment became the key buzzwords in those days, and the UN didn't want to be left out of it. Spokespersons for Man and the Biosphere, mainly in honorary positions, talked to the media about the "vital importance between man and his environment" and the importance of monitoring natural ecosystems for change. When the park sponsored scientific conferences on aquatic problems, native black bears, the European wild boar, the park's grassy balds, and other subjects of interest to geologists, ecologists, botanists, and zoologists, Susan Bratton, director of Uplands Field Research Laboratory at the time, enthusiastically told the press that the park might become a "test area for the International Biosphere Reserve program." The principal result seemed to be the Man and the Biosphere logo, which began to appear on park publications. About a month earlier, Evison was one of a twelve-member U.S. team that traveled to the former Soviet Union for fourteen days to talk about the UNESCO program. The general purpose of the visit to then-communist Russia, Evison told a reporter, was to establish understanding between the two countries "so we can pool our knowledge of reserves of both countries," he said. "I think we made some real progress in that direction." No one gave it much thought after this publicity.[59]

During the 1980s, SAMAB organized scientific conferences and local education projects. Because so much research related to the Southern Appalachians takes place in far-flung locations and manifests through different state and federal agencies, park service leaders saw SAMAB as a possible umbrella that could facilitate discussion and exchange. As a coordinator, SAMAB could "take a leadership role in developing the scientific basis for solving interrelated ecological, social and economic problems by using ecosystem principles for the practical benefit of people."[60] SAMAB scientific conferences focused on specific problems, such as exotic pests or air quality, and the two-person SAMAB office solicited ideas for future meetings from major scientists.[61] Because the park's interpretive and education program declined markedly over the same period, Superintendent Dave Beal saw SAMAB as a possible way to pay for community outreach. Through SAMAB, the park funded ecological lesson plans for elementary school children and bibliographies for the interpretive staff.[62]

Despite these innocuous missions, SAMAB became the focus of a conspiracy theory in 1997. Individuals living in the region surrounding the park latched onto the theory, promulgated on the Internet, which accused SAMAB and the Man and the Biosphere program in general of being a socialist land-grab scheme. The accusations outrageously linked the cooperative research organization with an international scheme to take over all public lands. "This is just the first step in allowing the United Nations to control America's natural treasures in the name of protecting the world's environment," wrote Cliff Kincaid, director of the Citizens United Foundation in Fairfax, Virginia, in a letter printed off his web site, which was widely circulated that summer in Sevier County. "The bottom line is this: Bill Clinton and his Clintonistas are working night and day to hand over more and more of our nation's sovereignty and freedom to the socialist UN." The letter included a "citizens' order" for residents to sign that ordered congressmen to "reverse your shameful giveaway of American sovereignty and assets to the United Nations." The aim of this socialist land-grab deal, disguised, in the minds of the conspiracy theorists, as "a biosphere preserve," was to create a habitat where "most human activity is banned." In this nightmare of "One World Government," they believed, "people are the enemy."[63]

Since Great Smoky Mountains National Park received recognition as a Biosphere Reserve in 1976, visitation has grown steadily to a record 10 million, so it's difficult to see how the park has made people the "enemy."[64] Keith Dunnaway, a project manager at TVA in Chattanooga, still maintained that the park was headed for this apocalyptic vision in an editorial published in the *Chattanooga News-Free Press:*

> Imagine the United States carved up into wilderness reserves, with human beings herded into crowded metropolis areas known as human settlements. Imagine over half of the nation's land given over completely to wildlife, with human trespass on the land forbidden. Imagine all of the roads that once traversed that land ripped up to prevent human travel through the reserves.

Dunnaway accused the United Nations of coordinating a "Wildlands Project" that threatens individual property ownership. Evidence of this, he said, was the Foothills Land Conservancy, a Knoxville consortium buying up land around Great Smoky Mountains National Park.[65] Jack

Wadham, a Waynesville, North Carolina, businessman representing still another group, called Save Our Sovereignty, gave a presentation for the Macon County Republican Men's Club. Wadham claimed that the United Nations planned to evacuate Macon County as part of the biosphere program. "One million people in the area would lose their property," he told a local newspaper, if UN plans continued.[66]

Like all conspiracy theorists, the "Biosphere Reserve Takeover" alarmists take a few unrelated facts, then hold them under a magnifying glass of innuendo. The Foothills Land Conservancy was one of hundreds of such independent groups concerned with encroaching development. The Conservancy purchased land from voluntary sellers, however, as it has no powers of condemnation. Far from rejecting economic development, the Conservancy actually promoted it in an "environmentally sensitive manner." If, for example, a 100-acre farm could not be protected, the Conservancy tried to buy it, protect 75 acres, and sell 25 for development, explained member Rick Everett. In addition, the group supported conservation easements, voluntary legal documents in which landowners keep their land but agree not to develop it, preserving more green space and wildlife habitat in the buffer zone around the park. But the Foothills Land Conservancy forged no connections with SAMAB, let alone the United Nations or "One World Government."

Because so many environmental problems, such as air pollution, cross the boundaries of states, nations, and government agencies, the SAMAB program encouraged cooperation across these boundaries. "Various government agencies, operating only under their already existing authorities, agree to work together to coordinate their efforts, avoid costly duplication, and focus on the principal overriding problems," explained Don Barger, southeastern regional director of the National Parks and Conservation Association. "It's amazing how far a total lie can go if it's repeated enough times." The Man and the Biosphere program does encourage international cooperation, but it has no impact on national jurisdiction. In the 1990s, SAMAB worked on the Southern Appalachian Assessment, an inventory of resources in the region; environmental education programs for schools, resource-management workshops; forest health monitoring; support for protection of endangered species; and model community planning to make tourism development compatible with environmental protection. Understaffed and funded through a non-profit foundation, SAMAB can be accused of, if anything, being ineffectual or largely symbolic.[67]

Still, the conspiracy theory reminded us of the danger of an uninformed public, unaware of and uninterested in the natural world and historical moment in which it lives. Consuming a bland and sanitized version of their past in a Dollywood theme park, accepting a safe television version of nature, and reeling from bungee jumping to outlet mall shopping, people easily ignore threats of air pollution and exotic pests and diseases. As media critic Neil Postman put it, "we are amusing ourselves to death." If the mountains finally disappear from view, will anyone at Dollywood notice? Scientists and other scholars, increasingly isolated from the public, write for their colleagues and the advancement of their own careers and fail to play a role in public information or policy. At the beginning of a new millennium, the problems facing the Smokies *are* global ones, but they have nothing to do with bureaucrats and politicians at the United Nations. What makes a conspiracy theory emotionally satisfying is that it assigns blame; conveniently and not coincidentally, it takes attention away from us, our automobiles, and our power plants.

10.1. An exotic fungus, butternut canker, has infected nearly every butternut tree in the Southern Appalachians. Photo by author.

10.2. Gatlinburg before neon, circa 1911. Courtesy of Great Smoky Mountains National Park.

10.3. Gatlinburg post-neon, 1999. Photo by author.

10.4. View from Clingmans Dome, 1962. Courtesy of Great Smoky Mountains National Park.

10.5. View from Clingmans Dome, 1999, showing the effects of air pollution and the disease brought by the exotic balsam wooly adelgid. Photo by author.

10.6. U.S. 441 entrance to the Smokies through Pigeon Forge before Dollywood, 1952. Courtesy of Tennessee State Archives, Nashville, Tennessee, 1952.

10.7. Entrance to the Smokies through Pigeon Forge, 1999. Photo by author.

o.8. Rock wall along the Twin Creeks Road reminds visitors of the rich history contained within his biological treasure, Great Smoky Mountains National Park. Photo by author.

Epilogue to the 2024 Edition

Through interpretation, understanding; through understanding, appreciation; through appreciation, protection.

FREEMAN TILDEN, *Interpreting Our Heritage*

ON A MUGGY SUMMER DAY I traveled through Cades Cove, the most famous valley in the Great Smoky Mountains, to see how contemporary land managers have reimagined the "Drive-in Wilderness" of the 1950s.[1] The cattle that used to munch grass for tourists' photographs are gone. When the final agricultural lease expired in 2000, a team of rangers designed a plan to keep the open view of towering mountains that visitors love so much while supporting native species and honoring the mountain residents who once lived there. My guide for this day, Kris Johnson, who worked as supervisory forester before her retirement, stopped near a stand of Joe Pye weed, a giant pink flower buzzing with bees and other pollinators.

"We retained the historic look of a patchwork of small farms by conducting prescribed burns along the old fence lines," she said. "Early mountain residents farmed small lots of corn and wheat, not large herds of cattle. A combination of prescribed burns and bush-hogging keeps the view clear." Johnson's crews also created three large wetland restorations and regeneration of streambanks with willow, alders, and river cane, which helped mitigate damage to Abrams Creek from the agricultural lease era.[2]

We stopped to look for monarch butterflies. Johnson explained that to return pasture to meadows and wetlands, she used seeds hand-collected over 20 years to retain local genotypes, including a beautiful tall grass with red edging called big blue stem. Invited by this new habitat, short-eared owls, a threatened species in the Southeast, returned to Cades Cove. Named for short tufts of feathers that appear like ears on the top of their heads, these owls prefer open land and migrate from the tundra of Canada to the Smokies each year. "That was one of my happiest achievements," said Johnson, as the elusive monarch fluttered across the road behind her.[3]

In addition to the re-creation of Cades Cove, Johnson's team worked for three decades to control exotic and invasive plants in the national park. Seasonal crews ranged from 10 to 15 workers, supplemented with forestry technicians and volunteers. "We value and are mandated to protect native plant communities," explained Johnson. "These are essential for the wildlife that evolved with and are adapted to them." Thanks to federal grants that Johnson wrote over the past three decades, her crews of seasonal workers and volunteers spent 2,695 hours eliminating mimosa, privet, multiflora rose, Japanese honeysuckle, and garlic mustard from 110,000 square meters of the park.[4]

We also stopped to see a river-cane patch. Once the cattle and agricultural leases ended, the native plant expanded naturally. River cane provides important wildlife habitat and stabilizes streambanks against erosion. Park staff also worked with the Eastern Band to develop techniques for transplanting river cane from North Carolina Department of Transportation rights-of-way to the Oconaluftee River.[5] Ancient Cherokees depended upon the prolific plant for basketry, homebuilding, mats for wall coverings, and arrow shafts. River cane was devastated by development and grazing, and its restoration has strong historical meaning for the Cherokees.

It turns out that bears also like the new shoots of river cane, which are apparently good to eat.

At the John Oliver homesite, about a dozen tourists gathered around the front porch, where a ranger shared details about farm life. After listening, we circled to a path behind the house and found a quiet place to eat lunch. While we talked, we heard a snap and saw a rustle in the shrubs below us. Expecting to see a deer, we stood and craned our necks. To our surprise, a large black bear lumbered across the trail about 50 feet below, cutting us off from the Oliver site and an exit.

The size and power of a wild bear took my breath away. Her powerful paws and muscular shoulders steered her great weight across the path in a short moment of grace. Two cubs, roughhousing and tumbling, soon followed her through the ferns and sycamore shoots. Realizing that we were now isolated by a mother bear with cubs, we shoved cheese sticks and granola bars into our packs and hurried down the trail. We passed the spot she crossed, watching the movements in the nearby woods.

A family of four park visitors started coming up the path toward us from the Oliver house. They wore brand-new sunhats on the shady path, which made them look like tourists, but the parents in a charming way urged their children to notice all the green around them. I looked at Johnson. "Should we warn them off?" Neither of us wanted to scare the happy group.

"You have happened along at a lucky moment," Johnson told the family. "If you remain quietly here for a moment, you may get to see a mother bear and two cubs cross the trail above us." I could not tell if they were afraid as Johnson gave them tips for viewing bears in the wild. They stood very still.

Since the 1960s, when the National Park Service first adopted policies to better protect wild bears, the work also has involved retraining people. Do not feed bears; avoid getting too close; make yourself appear large and back away, facing them. The Great Smoky Mountains National Park today is surrounded by development. Rangers have to manage not only bears within the park but also educate the conglomeration of tourists, second-home owners, hunters, environmentalists, animal lovers, and rural residents in the surrounding area, all of whom have differing views about bears as neighbors. Nature cannot remain separate from the built world, as anyone who has seen a birdfeeder slashed to pieces knows all too well.

After what seemed like a long time, the mother bear ambled across the path again, now above us, followed by her two cubs. She did not acknowledge us, but of course she knew we were there. I thought to myself, *This is how it should be.* It is her home, her habitat, and we are doing our best to be polite guests. The family of tourists relaxed after their close encounters of the wild kind and asked questions about bears. This is what a national park experience is all about, learning about nature, encountering the deep beauty of wildness, and understanding why respect matters. The young family certainly went home to spread this story.

A Regional Nature Center

Because of its location near major urban areas, the Smokies hold the record as the most visited national park in the United States, with now more than 14 million visits in a single year, which is more than Yellowstone, Yosemite, and the Grand Canyon combined. U.S. Highway 441 from Cherokee to Gatlinburg and State Highway 73 both cut through park lands, and this is one reason for the high numbers. Significantly, creative thinkers within the park and nonprofits known as Park Partners have reimagined visitors' relationship to national parks. The Smokies have become a regional nature center for the Southeast, a place for researchers, schoolchildren, community scientists, and adult learners to reinforce their connection to the outdoors and their understanding of wild nature. In Haywood County, North Carolina, the park opened the Appalachian Highlands Science Learning Center, also known as "The Purchase." The picturesque site encompasses 535 acres at a misty 4,920-foot elevation where a house with a large porch has become a classroom, lab space, offices, and housing for visiting scientists.

The idea for this transformation was initiated in 1991 by landowner Kathryn McNeil, who approached the NPS about preserving a place she loved adjacent to the Smokies. McNeil and her husband had purchased a farm near the park in the 1960s and spent many happy seasons there with family.[6] On his first visit, Keith Langdon, the park's inventory and monitoring coordinator, noticed two things: the deeply rutted road that would challenge access but also a larkspur unusual on park land. On another visit he spotted a rare migrant, the vesper sparrow. "This is our chance," Langdon recalled thinking. "We have got to get this. We can create a center for both education and research in the park."[7] The old garage could become a lab; the master bedroom, a meeting room; the guest bedrooms, a dormitory. Langdon, along with park Superintendent Karen Wade, worked out an agreement to accept the donation in sections, then wrote NPS grants to accomplish a renovation in 2005.

Paul Super, the first head of research for the new center, came to the Smokies from Acadia National Park. In the beginning, Super noted, Wade wanted to facilitate better understanding of higher elevations, and The Purchase became one of the first such research and learning centers in the nation, with 17 by 2015. Super began to oversee research permits, identify research needs, recruit researchers, and find funding for them while building connections. "A lot of research was already being done in the park," he noted, "but we needed to improve connections between those who were doing it. We also needed to build a big picture for our own management out of all the individual studies being done by university scientists."[8]

The high-elevation location made this an excellent place to study ozone damage to plants such as the cutleaf coneflower (*Rudbeckia lacinata*), called sochan in Cherokee. Research by Appalachian State University, Auburn University, Oak Ridge National Laboratory, and the Environmental Protection Agency evolved into long-term monitoring. The staff then integrated monitoring into the local seventh-grade curriculum, so hundreds of middle-schoolers visit and do meaningful work for the scientists. Rangers help students learn to ask scientific questions: Does ozone impact seed production? How does drought impact ozone susceptibility? Sochan, popular in Cherokee cuisine, can be gathered in the park (with a permit) by tribal members. Learning this, the students also asked, "How does ozone impact the plant's vitamin C content?"[9]

"This park has been a leader in education and science," Super said. "There are things we can do, but we can't do it all ourselves, which is why we have encouraged citizen science. We start with students, then we get adult volunteers to finish collecting data on sochan. The Smokies have led the way in this area." He pointed out that he gets inquiries from many parks in the United States and around the world about to how to create community science.[10]

Susan Sachs, education branch coordinator for the Smokies, was hired to reach out to schools, create curriculum, sponsor teacher trainings, produce podcasts and webpages, and host schoolchildren to participate in the community science projects. "We have served 5,600 schoolchildren at this location in one year," Sachs said, most of them in May, September, and October. "We also have internships for high school students. Teachers know the program."[11]

The Purchase dovetails with Parks as Classrooms, which began in the early 1990s with a single school, Pi Beta Phi Elementary about a mile from the park border; by 2023 the program had extended to eighty schools spanning eighteen school districts in Tennessee and North Carolina. Parks as Classrooms celebrates the Smokies as both a historical setting and an ecological treasure, with lesson plans on Cherokee river cane, Civil War sentinels, and more; in a stream ecology lesson, students monitor soil moisture and temperature for a salamander species.[12]

"A very exciting thing we do here is to serve as intermediaries between scientists and students," Sachs said. She described a scientist studying flatworms. He was eagerly "adopted" by an advanced-placement biology class whose students ate meals with him and bombarded him with questions. "With every group we see this. They feed off each other's enthusiasm," she said.[13]

Sachs's and Super's enthusiasm is also contagious. Super said the results have been gratifying: "Interactions between students and graduate students, between students and researchers—this is what we hoped would happen, and it's happening."[14] Sachs likewise commented on the mutual learning. "There's so much we still don't know," she said. "We still have questions and our students and scholars help us ask better ones."[15]

On the Tennessee side of the park, the nonprofit Great Smoky Mountains Institute at Tremont has operated since 1969 as a residential environmental learning center for ages 4 through 93 as well as offering community outreach programs. "We practice regenerative education," said John DiDiego, who was education director at Yosemite Institute before taking on this role at Tremont. "Rather than talk *at* students, we want to know what they are curious about, what do they want to know? When we are successful, students have more questions and we have more energy than when we began. We model excitement for learning about nature."[16]

Tremont attracts as many as 5,000 children per year, ranging from fifth grade to high school and representing 13 states. The institute serves 1,000 adults in multiday programs in which they can work toward Appalachian Naturalist certification. Although the majority of adults come from Tennessee, 39 states are represented in their rosters. "You don't have to go on a safari to a foreign country," DiDiego emphasized. "The world is exciting right in front of you." One important learning experience many of Tremont's camps offer is silent solo hiking. Walkers start at staggered times on a trail so they can experience solitude safely and not have the anxiety some might feel with true isolation. "It's actually valuable to your brain to have this kind of connection to nature," DiDiego said. "Notice. Wonder. Put away your phone. Slow down the schedule, open yourself to being human."[17]

This wooded valley along the Middle Prong of the Little River once was home to Walker Valley Settlement School, part of a movement designed to bring literacy to remote areas of the United States. Mabel Ijams, the daughter of lumberman W. B. Townsend, operated the site until 1959 as a summer camp for girls through the Knoxville Girl Scout Council. For a short time during Lyndon Johnson's War on Poverty it became a Job Corps site, then Tremont Environmental Education Center. Ken Voorhis, director for 29 years, transformed Tremont into a center devoted to cooperative learning for adults and children using citizen science programs and establishing partnerships with local colleges and universities.[18]

To expand its reach into the community, in 2019 and 2020 the Great Smoky Mountains Institute at Tremont purchased two tracts of land outside the national park that comprise 196 acres. Staff met with architects to create designs that meet the standards of the Living Building Challenge, an international certification that pays close attention to the site and aims to meet the highest standards in sustainability. Jeremy Lloyd, manager of field and college programs, has been on the team working with architects to develop a place that goes beyond having the "appearance of being green" to actually giving back to the environment and the community. "Tremont's expansion campus will not only have a positive footprint," Lloyd said, "but will provide leadership for sustainability throughout the region in the development of best construction practices."[19]

Tremont now exists inside the park and closer to Knoxville, Tennessee. "We are proudest of our focus on people belonging in nature, helping them learn new things about themselves and the planet," said Catey McClary, Tremont president and CEO. "With the addition of our second campus, we will have the opportunity to engage in larger systems thinking, how we are all connected and how we can all connect to benefit our local communities and the environment."[20]

Tremont and Purchase Knob help educators and children connect as they continue to build bridges between local communities and the Smokies. During the park's 75th anniversary celebration, Superintendent Dale Ditmanson formally acknowledged the painful history of removing mountain people by honoring families of those removed. Cherokee elders, park families, longtime park employees, and park lovers gathered at Newfound Gap to rejoice in the tremendous biodiversity but remember the sacrifices that made the day possible. In 2010 Swain County officials, Congressman Heath Schuler, and the National Park Service finally settled the North Shore Road issue (described in chapter 5) by agreeing to compensate the county with $52 million for the broken promise of North Shore access. And park history has been remembered differently since the first edition of *The Wild East* was published, through the Parks as Classrooms program and the Oconaluftee Visitor Center and administrative building, opened in 2011, that maintains oral histories of mountain people about life before the park. Through all these measures, the park has gained stronger relations with local communities since the first edition of *The Wild East*.

Science in Service to Us

On a blue-sky autumn day I joined a group of park enthusiasts for a "bioblitz," an event led by Discover Life in America (DLIA) in which participants try to help scientists by identifying as many species as possible in a couple of hours. We listened to instructions at the Cosby Creek campground shelter, and our leader, Will Kuhn, helped people download iNaturalist on their phones. Kuhn is the organization's director of science and research and has a PhD in evolutionary biology from Rutgers, but he is patient and kind with amateurs who get excited about wooly caterpillars and worried about copperheads. He refers to himself modestly as a "budding naturalist."[21]

While others in the group conferred about tree species or insects captured by Kuhn, I found myself looking for mushrooms. According to iNaturalist, I recorded a frilly fungus called *Stereum*, a glob of orange that might be *higher Basidiomycetes*, and a fat mushroom with yellow gills that would look good made in ceramics but hails from the Boletaceae family. More than this, I felt the joy of being in the woods with quiet companions who noticed everything and shared my fascination with a fungus (*Artomyces pyxidatus*) that looked like a land-loving white sea anemone.

The next day on a hike without my fellow bioblitz colleagues, I could tell that I had changed. My eyes fell on mushrooms everywhere, a virtual paradise of mushrooms. I also discovered small creatures that appeared to thrive on fungal environments. A striped beetle from the Megalodacne family. Red toads. Black toads. Brown toads. Porters Creek trail is beautiful but also home for amazing creatures like the white-lip globe snail.

DLIA originated in 1997 when Keith Langdon and Becky Nichols with the park's resource management division, along with U.S. Geological Survey scientist Chuck Parker and UNC professor Peter White, began discussing the loss of habitat outside the park due to development, ozone levels, and acid deposition. White and Langdon wrote that they were "increasingly being forced to make many resource-impacting decisions without an adequate basis to judge the impacts on native species."[22] Inspired by a similar project in Costa Rica, more than 120 interested scientists met in December 1997 to help launch the All Taxa Biodiversity Initiative, and in a 1998 Earth Day ceremony, the NPS deputy director sanctioned the effort. Langdon and others at that first meeting realized that staffing, publicizing, and funding the initiative would be beyond the resources of the NPS. For the ambitious project to prosper, they needed a nonprofit to accomplish these tasks, and thus Discover Life in America came into being.[23]

Kuhn, our guide on the bioblitz, said he first learned about DLIA when he was in graduate school. "Anyone could see that it was a cool project," he said, "so while I earned a postdoc at the University of Tennessee, I started volunteering." When DLIA grew to the size of needing staff positions, Kuhn joined the effort. With a background in entomology, he is singlehandedly responsible for finding more than 50 records of new species in the park. "During Covid, I went through collections made on iNaturalist in the location of the 2016 fire," he said, referring to the Chimney Tops wildfires that raged through part of the park and nearby Gatlinburg. "I found a bee not previously found in the park, and the person who first identified that species contacted me. Because fire had devastated that area, [the discovery] received a lot of media attention."[24]

At the turn of the twenty-first century, the national park with the greatest biodiversity in the United States could claim an impressive 9,696 species. The scientists present at Langdon's original meeting thought that as many as 10,000 more might be found, but they emphasized the need to understand also where in the Smokies to find them and how they interacted with each other and habitats. By 2023 the DLIA website boasted 21,669 species in the park; 10,894 were newly found in the park although present in other places, and 1,079 were newly identified and named species. These species include a lot of microbes and insects but also 64 lichens, 43 spiders, and 3 new species of salamanders. Equally important are the 74 mammals, 233 birds, and 71 fish species that existed in other places but are now known to live in the Smokies, too.

Any visitor can use the iNaturalist application on their phone to locate known species and help identify newly found species.[25] Any visitor may find one of the species on the "Smokies Most Wanted List" and add to the scientific record from their hiking trail or campsite. DLIA also leads bioblitz events like the one I attended and sponsors an outreach program where middle-schoolers bioblitz their school grounds. "We not only want people to become aware of biodiversity in the park; we want them to see the biodiversity everywhere," said Kuhn. "We are training future observers, enthusiasts, and advocates for nature."[26]

Discovery builds relations with science, but science in the Great Smoky Mountains National Park has improved all of our lives in the Southeast through air-quality monitoring. When I first met Jim Renfro and interviewed him for

The Wild East, he was a new air-quality specialist collecting air-quality data for the National Park Service and summarizing weather conditions. "We were not then meeting public health standards for ozone and particulate matter," he recalled.[27] In a 2002 report, Appalachian Voices, National Parks Conservation Association, and Our Children's Earth Foundation named the Smokies the most polluted national park in the country. In his steadfast way, however, Renfro kept collecting and summarizing what became one of the most detailed and comprehensive collections of data on air quality in the National Park Service.[28] Armed with "accurate, timely, and precise" data, Renfro created PowerPoint presentations about the data and took them on the road. He put 30 years of data about air quality in front of lawmakers, citizens groups, park staff, scientists, the media, and students. Renfro is careful to credit the data, not himself, as persuasive in documenting a decline in air quality; the numbers he gave EPA and state air programs motivated some of the region's largest power producers, including TVA, to redesign smokestacks. Charts and graphs pushed neighboring states to adopt plans for improving air quality.

"We've got bluer skies and greener mountains, and what a huge difference this makes in everything from real estate values to our basic health," Renfro said. Visibility on the haziest days has improved from 9 miles to 48 miles, and ground-level ozone has declined by 27 percent. Annual sulfur dioxide (SO_2) emissions from regional power plants declined 75 percent from 1990 to 2014. "Every state has a draft plan of reasonable, affordable measures for reducing SO_2 and NO_2 [nitrogen dioxide]. The goal is restoring even the 'most impaired days' to natural conditions."[29]

Any visitor can check the air quality at one of the webcams on the Great Smoky Mountains National Park website: Look Rock, Newfound Gap, Clingmans Dome, Twin Creeks, Leconte Creek, and Purchase Knob. (The sunset image on the cover of this edition was taken by one of these webcams.) The site provides hourly photographs and readings for ozone, particulate matter, wind, precipitation, temperature, and humidity. The archived data from these sites determine whether the Smokies meet public health and environmental standards; the data establish baseline conditions to identify areas of concerns; detect long-term trends; help target new research, understanding, and models; and provide the foundation for rule-making. "We've made incredible progress in a short time," Renfro said, "but we need to maintain our momentum and ask 'What else can we do?' Mercury is still an issue, for example. Acid deposition in streams is still a problem." A 2006 University of Tennessee study analyzing stream water showed that all 12 major streams were still pH-impaired. And returning clear views of the landscapes to natural conditions is still needed.[30]

What can we do? Renfro sees positive change happening with the growth of new technology, both for power sources and cars as well as a new parking permit system, but the unending growth and sprawl in the region continue to impact the air. He sees hope in all the education and outreach being done, including very active Park Partners and cooperating and philanthropic associations such as Smokies Life and Friends of the Smokies.[31]

Toward More Secure Financial Footing

The oldest Park Partner central to the success of the Smokies is Smokies Life (formerly the Great Smoky Mountains Association), created by Congress in 1953 to provide programs and services such as the ubiquitous *Smokies Guide* and to enhance visitors' experiences and share the proceeds from these activities with the park. Smokies Life raised $3 million for the construction of the new Oconaluftee Visitor Center. By 2023 aid from Smokies Life topped $1.75 million annually. The organization also helps the park by paying the salaries of staff working at all four visitor centers. "The big western parks not only have entrance fees, but they make up a large part of their budget through payments by food service, gift-shop sales, and hotel concessions," explained Smokies Life CEO Laurel Rematore, who came to the Smokies after working at Mesa Verde and Yosemite. "The Smokies has almost three times as many visitors as the Grand Canyon but does not have the same concession income."[32]

Lack of income other than federal funding has plagued the Smokies in part because of a Tennessee requirement that required Highway 441 between Gatlinburg and Cherokee to remain open at all times with no tolls. After researching the legality of a parking fee, in 2022 Superintendent Cassius Cash took the bold step of requiring a parking pass for any vehicle that stops more than 15 minutes. The first African American superintendent and one of the longest-staying leaders, he built respect by meeting with and listening to local leaders. He then selected Smokies Life to design the tags and help sell them in the visitor centers. "It was at first controversial," remarked Rematore. "In its first year [2023], Park It Forward is already generating more funding than park managers projected and is being used to rebuild critically needed park staffing levels that have eroded over many years."[33]

The other growing Park Partner is Friends of the Smokies, which began in 1993. Superintendent Randy Pope had been watching the success of the Yosemite Fund for many years when he had a phone call from two prominent Tennesseans, Tommy Trotter and Gary Wade.[34] Wade, a Sevierville native and retired justice of the Tennessee Supreme Court, first became interested in helping the Smokies when Trotter, a childhood friend, challenged him to hike all the trails on the Tennessee side of the park. At the top of Mount Cammerer they explored the historic fire tower, a stone structure with a remarkable view, but grew alarmed at its condition, with graffiti, a leaky roof, and a damaged floor. Trotter said they should go see the superintendent about this.[35]

In Superintendent Pope's office, Wade learned that the National Park Service had a mandate to preserve historic structures but often struggled to fund regular maintenance. Trotter offered to do the architectural drawings, and Wade raised $35,000 for repairs. On September 3, 1993, Superintendent Pope called together Gary Wade and nine others from North Carolina and Tennessee to create Friends of the Smokies. The 156 charter members donated $1,000 each to create the organization, then followed up with a campaign to refurbish Tremont. In 1995 the state of Tennessee, followed by North Carolina, allowed Friends of the Smokies to raise money through a specialty license plate, and the revenue from the plates ensured that the organization could have a staff.[36] "We still have a couple of core principles," said Wade, who has spent more than 30 years on the Friends of the Smokies board. "We never take a position on park issues, and we let the park superintendents take the lead, explaining their priorities."[37]

By 2020 Friends of the Smokies had raised $70 million in support of the Great Smoky Mountains National Park. The organization also started the Parks Forever endowment to raise money for the maintenance of historic buildings. Then Friends of the Smokies started the Trails Forever endowment for trail maintenance. "Fulfilling these needs is a great honor," said Dana Soehn, Friends of the Smokies president and CEO. "No matter what happens, we will be able to preserve park buildings. No matter what happens, 850 miles of trails will be maintained."[38] After the 2016 fire, Friends of the Smokies raised money to get a new radio communication system that can interface with police, fire, and emergency personnel in neighboring jurisdictions.

More park partnerships have sprung up because of very specific needs. The increase in traffic along major corridors like Interstate I-40, for instance, has led to an increase in accidents involving black bears, elk, deer, bobcats, and other species. More than 28,500 cars travel down the 28 miles of the Pigeon River Gorge on the east side of the park every day, and this endangers animals that need to cross the road to find food, shelter, and mates. Besides killing 162 large mammals between 2018 and 2022, crashes put human life at risk and devastate the vehicles involved. Six organizations—the Conservation Fund, Defenders of Wildlife, National Parks and Conservation Association, North Carolina Wildlife Federation, Wilderness Society, and Wildlands Network—have worked with Smokies Life to create Safe Passage. The groups have coordinated with more than two dozen state and federal agencies to establish corridors for wildlife and to prevent traffic fatalities. When the North Carolina Department of Transportation replaced the bridge at Harmon Den on I-40 near the state line in 2022, it included a wildlife underpass to help prevent these crashes.[39]

Park Partnerships can sometimes bridge conflicts more easily than an agency of the federal government. Rematore serves on a committee called Bear Wise with local businesspeople to help solve the ongoing difficulties that development has caused for black bears. Research over the past three decades shows that black bears can become habituated to raiding trash cans. They can't be trained to not raid the cans, and if bears are relocated, they will travel hundreds of miles to return to the Smokies, potentially being hurt or killed on the journey. "The best approach is to educate humans," said Rematore. "We are working with the City of Gatlinburg to expand availability of bear-resistant dumpsters by providing them for rent. Gatlinburg can set an example for Sevier County and East Tennessee businesses and residents. Rather than being dictated to change by the National Park Service, we can help residents come up with solutions."[40]

Necessary Symbiosis All across Nature

The Great Smoky Mountains National Park faced an even greater challenge in 2016 from an abrupt change in the weather. In June of that year University of Tennessee Professor Karen Hughes noticed that the trails in the Smokies seemed dry, "very dry" for a normally wet month. An evolutionary biologist, Hughes studies fungi; in fact, at that time she already had helped locate 3,500 species in the Smokies for DLIA. Mushrooms do not thrive in dry weather. By August, she recalled, the situation was dire. "We were in a terrible drought," she said. Mycologists, she explained, are naturally attuned to the weather, and she felt downright anxious about the dry condition of the trees.[41]

Small fires started in many places in October and November, during what Steve Norman, an ecologist with the US Forest Service, called a "hot drought," as average temperatures were two degrees warmer than the norm. During this unusual situation—unusual for the southern rainforest—the wet leaves, fallen limbs, and rotted logs that are an ordinary part of the Smokies became dry enough to become fuel for a fire. The air in Asheville, Knoxville, and beyond grew hazy and filled with soot.[42]

What would become the notorious Chimney Tops 2 fire seemed at first like just another fire in a terrible year. Named for a craggy rock formation at the top of the mountain that looks something like the ruins of an enormous chimney, Chimney Tops has a popular if strenuous trail from one of the busiest picnic areas in the park. The narrow ridge below the famous peak filled with smoke on the evening of the day before Thanksgiving 2016, but officials who hiked to the base of the fire realized that a fire line would be impossible due to the rocky terrain. By Saturday the weather forecast called for strong winds but also rain, which might help put the fire out. On Monday, November 28, a cold front from the south hit the Blue Ridge, then rose toward the stable air in the upper atmosphere, dropping down again over the mountains with greater turbulence. "The arms of Leconte [a nearby mountain] acted like fire arms, exaggerating the wind wave by wave," Norman said. Over the course of the day the wind speed kept rising, and the fire spread faster than anyone predicted.[43]

"We rarely have crown fires here," explained Jennifer Franklin, a University of Tennessee professor and a specialist in forest restoration. "Fire typically creeps along the ground." The exceptionally dry season combined with the dry leaves in the crowns of the trees plus the high winds caused whole treetops to burst into flames. When the treetops hit powerlines, the fire expanded and hopscotched down the mountains toward Gatlinburg.[44]

Carey Woods, principal of Pi Beta Phi Elementary School in Gatlinburg, remembered that before the Thanksgiving break, the air quality—hazy with a strong smoky smell—put the school into Code Orange, which meant students stayed inside for recess. She described the school as having a very diverse student population from pre-K to eighth grade "with great community support, a loving place to work, and a dedicated staff." By the time they graduate, children from Pi Beta Phi spend 40 hours in the Great Smoky Mountains through the Parks as Classroom program.[45]

Monday, November 28, when Woods stood at the door greeting students coming off the buses, the air was filled with thick smoke and illuminated by a strange amber light. Later, she said, "we would become a vortex of wind and smoke and debris." By 9 a.m. some parents returned to pick up their children, and Woods began to confer with the superintendent of schools on how the remaining students could be evacuated.[46]

Just after noon, buses arrived and began transporting more than 500 students to Rocky Top Sports World, which agreed to receive the students until parents picked them up. The reality of what was happening in Gatlinburg did not hit Woods until the next day because she was so busy organizing the students' safe pick-up. By that time, Rocky Top Sports World had become a refugee center. Nearly one fourth of those associated with the school, 98 families and seven staff members, lost their homes and all of their belongings in the terrible fire. When a police escort took the principal into town to see the school, the building had been well watered by the fire department and was smoky but intact. Once the policeman started driving back through the town to check addresses, however, "it looked like a bomb had gone off behind the school." The trip through the rubble of homes and now destroyed landmarks made her sick to her stomach.[47]

By the end of the week, Woods learned that two students and their mother perished in the wildfire. Fourteen people total lost their lives in the tragic Chimney Tops 2 wildfire. About 11,410 acres burned inside the park, and in Gatlinburg 2,000 homes were destroyed. "It seemed like layer upon layer of tragedy," Woods recalled.[48]

The rest of the week Woods spent helping those in the refugee center and restoring classes in three locations. Her staff needed counseling and supplies, and her students needed counseling and supplies, and with the help of the community and donations from around the United States, by Thursday she was able to provide all of them with not only the routine of school but services and supplies. Dolly Parton established the My People Fund, which would eventually give more than $8 million to those who lost their homes in the fire.[49]

Friday night at the end of an extraordinary week, the principal stood in the borrowed school's gymnasium, where 98 piles of clothing, household items, and other supplies awaited her students' families. At 10 p.m., it was finally silent, and Woods said she felt overcome by the outpouring of generosity. "For one second [in this country] it did not matter what race you were, what religion, or what political beliefs you have. These human beings needed you and you were there. Kindness was there."[50]

As soon as the fire hit Gatlinburg, the media broadcast terrifying images and voices from the red inferno. Mary Ann Hitt, national director of campaigns for the Sierra Club, frantically tried to locate her parents, who lived in nearby Pittman Center. Her father was formerly a director of the Uplands Research Lab, now the Twin Creeks Science Center, in the Smokies. Both were elderly and did not move quickly. On Facebook, Hitt watched as flames flew out of the Park Vista Hotel. In the morning, she discovered that her parents were okay, but old friends had lost their entire home not far from the hotel.[51]

Although Hitt has worked on climate change issues for ten years, the extreme weather events associated with a warmer climate had always seemed far away—fires in California, floods on a little-known island far away. The record-breaking drought and sudden high winds that caused the Chimney Tops fire, she realized, was exactly the kind of extreme weather events that scientists have been predicting will increase in the coming decade. "It was a life-changing experience for me because I realized that there's no place that is going to be safe from climate change, and we're not safe now. It's not just a problem for our grandchildren, it's a problem for us today, and it's a problem for my children today."[52]

Karen Hughes, the University of Tennessee biologist who studies fungi, recalled how scientists felt when news about the massive impact on the park and Gatlinburg filled the media. "I was really sad," she said. "All those people and animals! I was devastated. I couldn't think about research."[53]

The following year, though, in 2017, Hughes wrote a grant to study what happened to fungi in the Great Smoky Mountains National Park. At first all she witnessed was devastation. A fire-adaptive species, Table Mountain pine, has cones that open in the heat, so she kept looking for it. Some individual trees that survived the fire indeed had open pine cones, which meant they would reseed. But Table Mountain pine is in a symbiotic relationship with a fungus in the soil; neither can live without each other, and the organic layer in many places she studied was nothing but pits of hard mud. "For a long time, I didn't think anything would be left in the soil," Hughes said. "Fire specialists talk about the soil being sterilized eight inches down."[54]

Hughes and teams of volunteers kept returning every couple of weeks to three of the most severely burned sites in the park. Finally, in March 2017 they started to see fungi, mushrooms that looked like little cups. These species were completely new to the park. Had they always existed in the soil, waiting for a fire? Or did they travel there when conditions were right? Through genetic research the teams found that many fire-responsive fungi were endophytes, which lie inside the leaves and stems. It's as if they hide out in plants and come out when they are most needed![55]

In what seemed like a miraculous turn of events, in June 2017, Hughes's team found Table Mountain pine sprouting on the most devastated sites, and they tested and discovered the necessary fungus around its roots. Fungi, clearly, will be an important part of the recovery of the soil and forest of the Smokies. Mushrooms, those often disregarded plants on a trail, are, in Hughes words, "beautiful and edible and medicinal, yet so little is known about them." They may end up being incredibly important as we prepare for a future of extreme weather. Hughes marvels at what she calls a "necessary symbiosis all across nature."[56]

When I wrote *The Wild East*, I described the contemporary 540,000 acres of the Great Smoky Mountains as an "island wilderness." In 2001 I saw the misty ridges of the Smokies surrounded by a sea of second homes, condominiums, and commercial development. Reflecting upon the Chimney Tops 2 fire, however, as well as a massive downpour in Greenbriar Valley in July 2022 (8.72 inches in a matter of hours), I believe that "island" is the wrong metaphor.

Through the growth of scientific research and education, we are more aware than at any time in human history of the extraordinary wealth of biodiversity that exists in the Great Smoky Mountains. Through the sacrifices of many and the diligence of others for more than a hundred years, Americans have managed to create an extraordinary treasure of beauty and wildness in the southeastern United States near the major urban areas of Knoxville and Asheville. Clearly, the words "preserved" and "preservation" fail to cover the complex story of restoration and recovery in this magnificent place and mistakenly put it under glass—or on an island—in our minds. Thinking this way may fool us into believing our work is done.

Although we humans are capable of terrible destruction, such as the lumbermen who cleared the hillsides during the early twentieth century, we're also capable of protecting that land and the refuge it gives bear, elk, river otters, and salamanders as well as rare and unknown mushrooms. In the past two decades, we have learned that this protection has also improved our lives; the air we breathe is clearer and cleaner because of the Great Smoky Mountains. In an era when authors warn of the "last child to play outside," the park has become a regional nature center, both literally and virtually. And when extreme weather events struck, human beings proved themselves heroic and generous and adaptive. After the Chimney Tops 2 fire there were arrests and lawsuits, but the surrounding communities also have improved everything from fire and rescue protocols to radio equipment and communication with the park.

The biography of the Great Smoky Mountains reveals that for better or worse the future of this treasure is in our hands. There are hundreds of small actions that everyone can take from walking a wooded trail with a child to installing solar panels on a home to shifting a lawn to native plants. In 2022 Lavita Hill and Mary Crow, two members of the Eastern Band of Cherokee, took a small action to move mountains. They decided to support the idea of restoring the name "Kuwohi" to the highest peak in the Great Smoky Mountains, which was known as Clingmans Dome. White mountain people called the peak "Smoky Dome" or "Old Smoky," but it was renamed in 1859 for Thomas Lanier Clingman, a Confederate general who promoted the peak as the tallest in the southern mountains. "Kuwohi" translates as "mulberry place," and it figures prominently as a setting in the Cherokee myth "The Origin of Disease and Medicine." In July 2022 the tribal council passed legislation in support of the name change. In August, the Buncombe County Board of Commissioners voted to support the name change. In 2023 the application was submitted to the US Board on Geographic Names. For years to come, I hope to celebrate this place where the bears meet. What we do matters to a cutleaf coneflower at 5,000 feet in the Great Smoky Mountains but also to the future of our great green planet.

Notes to the Epilogue

1. Freeman Tilden, *Interpreting Our Heritage* (Chapel Hill: UNC Press, 1957). Many thanks to Laurel Rematore for pointing out this quote.

2. Kris Johnson, interview with the author, Cades Cove, July 14, 2022.

3. Johnson, interview.

4. Martha Hunter, "Preserving the Landscape through Invasive Species Management," *Smokies Life* 16 (Spring 2022): 34–36.

5. Johnson, interview.

6. Kathryn McNeil to Keith Langdon, October 21, 1991, II.A.1.H Lands, The Purchase Historical Reference Material 1966–2005, box 5, folder 115, Great Smoky Mountains National Park (GSMNP).

7. Keith Langdon, interview with the author, Gatlinburg, TN, July 15, 2022. Memo to files by chief, Resource Management and Science Division, The Purchase vertical file, GSMNP.

8. Paul Super, interview with the author, Appalachian Highlands Science Learning Center, August 1, 2022. The universities with the most research permits in the Smokies have been the University of Tennessee, Western Carolina University, the University of North Carolina at Chapel Hill, Clemson University, North Carolina State University, Duke University, Appalachian State University, Virginia Tech University, the University of Georgia, and Tennessee Tech University.

9. Super, interview.

10. Super, interview.

11. Susan Sachs, interview with the author, Appalachian Highlands Science Learning Center, August 1, 2022.

12. Sachs, interview.

13. Sachs, interview.

14. Super, interview.

15. Sachs, interview.

16. John DiDiego, interview with the author, Great Smoky Mountains Institute at Tremont, August 1, 2022.

17. DiDiego, interview.

18. Jeremy Lloyd, *Great Smoky Mountains Institute at Tremont: Connecting People with Nature.* (Townsend, TN: Great Smoky Mountains Institute at Tremont, 2019), 22, 28.

19. Jeremy Lloyd, interview with the author, Maryville, TN, August 2, 2022.

20. Catey McClarey, Zoom interview with the author, August 18, 2022.

21. Will Kuhn, phone interview with the author, August 9, 2023.

22. Peter White and Keith Langdon, "The ATBI in the Smokies: An Overview," *George White Forum* 23 (2006): 18–19.

23. Langdon, interview.

24. Kuhn, interview. The DLIA website https://dlia.org/ provides everything from free topographic maps and a digitized catalog of the GSMNP herbarium to the NPS DataStore, with 430 scientific articles and papers about ATBI.

25. For protection, iNaturalist automatically obscures the specific locations of sensitive species in the park.

26. Kuhn, interview.

27. Jim Renfro, phone interview with the author, September 23, 2022.

28. David Brill, "Breathing in the Smokies: a Remarkable Success Story," *Smokies Life* 7 (Fall 2013): 34.

29. Renfro, interview. Renfro also shared one of his PowerPoint presentations, "The Role of Long-term Monitoring for Program and Policy Evaluation at the Great Smoky Mountains National Park."

30. Renfro, interview.

31. Renfro, interview. The US Congress is the original source of Park Partners, as legislation allowed for philanthropic partnership agreements in the Department of the Interior.

32. Laurel Rematore, phone interview with the author, August 30, 2023.

33. Rematore, interview. About one third of the parking passes are sold by Smokies Life in the visitor centers. The rest are sold through Recreation.gov and ticket dispensers in the lots.

34. Randall R. Pope, "Friends of the Smokies," signed notes in the possession of Friends of the Smokies. The Yosemite Fund merged with the Yosemite Association in 2010 to form the Yosemite Conservancy, which is currently Yosemite National Park's philanthropic and cooperating association.

35. Gary Wade, phone interview with the author, October 11, 2023.

36. Wade, interview.

37. Wade, interview.

38. Dana Soehn, phone interview with the author, October 16, 2023.

39. Frances Figart, "Reconnecting a Living Landscape," *Smokies Life* 16 (Fall 2022): 13–15.

40. Rematore, interview.

41. Karen Hughes, interview by Casey Kaufman, November 7, 2019, Rising from the Ashes: The Chimney Tops 2 Wildfires Oral History Project, University of Tennessee Special Collections, https://rfta.lib.utk.edu.

42. Steve Norman, interview by Ken Wise, June 6, 2020, Rising from the Ashes: The Chimney Tops 2 Wildfires Oral History Project, University of Tennessee Special Collections, https://rfta.lib.utk.edu.

43. Norman, interview.

44. Jennifer Franklin, interview by Ken Wise, November 7, 2019, Rising from the Ashes: The Chimney Tops 2 Wildfires Oral History Project, University of Tennessee Special Collections, https://rfta.lib.utk.edu.

45. Carey Woods, interview by Ken Wise, January 11, 2020, Rising from the Ashes: The Chimney Tops 2 Wildfires Oral History Project, University of Tennessee Special Collections, https://rfta.lib.utk.edu.

46. Woods, interview.

47. Woods, interview.

48. Woods, interview.

49. Woods, interview.

50. Woods, interview.

51. Mary Ann Hitt, interview by Casey Kaufman, September 24, 2020, Rising from the Ashes: The Chimney Tops 2 Wildfires Oral History Project, University of Tennessee Special Collections, https://rfta.lib.utk.edu.

52. Hitt, interview.

53. Hughes, interview.

54. Hughes, interview.

55. Hughes, interview.

56. Hughes, interview.

Introduction

1. Paris Lambdin, "Biodiversity in Selected Ecosystems and the Importance of Systematics." Paper presented at Forty-second Southern Forest Insect Work Conference, 4 August 1998.

2. R. H. Whittaker, "Vegetation of the Great Smoky Mountains," *Ecological Monographs* 26 (January 1956): 45–56.

3. As this work goes to press, forthcoming books by Dan Pierce and Stephen Taylor will help remedy the lack of serious scholarship about the Smokies. In 1987, however, there was not much besides Frome and Campbell.

4. For Spanish contact see Charles Hudson, *The Juan Pardo Expeditions: Explorations of the Carolinas and Tennessee, 1566–1568* (Washington, D.C.: Smithsonian Institution Press, 1990) and Hudson et al., "The Tristan de Luna Expedition, 1599–1561," *Southeastern Archaeology* 8 (1989): 31–45; also Marvin Smith, *Archaeology of Aboriginal Culture Change in the Interior Southeast* (Gainesville: University of Florida Press, 1989). On cattle-raising, see Brad Alan Bays, "The Historical Geography of Cattle Herding, 1761–1861" (master's thesis, University of Tennessee, 1991).

5. For Cherokee involvement in the fur trade, see David Corkran, *Cherokee Frontier: Conflict and Survival, 1740–1762* (Norman: University of Oklahoma Press, 1962); Mary W. Rothrock, "Cherokee Traders among the Overhill Cherokee," *East Tennessee Historical Society's Publications* 4 (1929): 3–18; and Neil W. Franklin, "Virginia and the Cherokee Indian Trade, 1673–1752," *East Tennessee Historical Society's Publications* 7 (January 1932): 3–21.

6. Lieutenant Francis Marion, "Sowing Tears of Hate," *Journal of Cherokee Studies* 2 (Summer 1977): 333.

7. For a detailed discussion see Ronald N. Satz, *American Indian Policy in the Jacksonian Era* (Lincoln: University of Nebraska Press, 1975); Joel Martin, *Sacred Revolt* (Boston: Beacon Press, 1991); and William Gerald McLoughlin, *Cherokee Renascence in the New Republic* (Princeton: Princeton University Press, 1984).

8. John R. Finger, *The Eastern Band of Cherokees, 1819–1900* (Knoxville: University of Tennessee Press, 1984), 20–59.

9. John R. Finger, *Cherokee Americans* (Lincoln: University of Nebraska Press, 1991), 16; George H. Smathers, *The History of Land Titles in Western North Carolina* (Asheville, N.C.: Miller Publishing, 1938), 91.

10. Robert S. Lambert, "The Pioneer History of the Great Smoky Mountains National Park" (unpublished manuscript, GSMNP, n.d.), 24–25.

11. *Code of Tennessee* (1858), 353–54; *Code of Tennessee* (1884), 384; *Code of Tennessee* (1917), 1124.

12. Lewis Laska, "The Law of Squirrels, Robins, Snakes, Cats, Raccoons and Elephants," *Tennessee Bar Journal* 35 (1990): 14.

13. Jonathan Woody, interview by Sam Easterby, 1973, Oral History Collection, GSMNP.

14. Durwood Dunn, *Cades Cove: The Life and Death of a Southern Appalachian Community, 1818–1937* (Knoxville: University of Tennessee Press, 1988), 1–21; Steven G. Platt and Christopher G. Brantley, "Canebrakes: An Ecological and Historical Perspective," *Castanea* 62 (March 1997): 8–21. For nineteenth-century attitudes toward the wilderness, see Roderick Nash, *Wilderness and the American Mind* (New Haven: Yale University Press, 1967), 67–83.

1. Forest Economics

1. Lands Transferred to the Federal Government, GSMNP; Lucinda Oakley Ogle, interview by Paul Sagan, 1990, Oral History Collection, GSMNP.

2. William L. Hall, "New National Forests in the Southern Appalachians," *Southern Lumberman* 69 (21 December 1912): 104.

3. Henry Graves, *Forest Conditions in Western North Carolina*, North Carolina Economic Survey, Bulletin 23 (Raleigh, N.C.: Edwards, Broughton and Company, 1911).

4. Winfred Cagle, interview by William Weaver, 1973, Oral History Collection, GSMNP; Elizabeth Engelman Black, "A Study of the Diffusion of Culture in a Relatively Isolated Mountain Community" (Ph.D. diss., University of Chicago, 1928).

5. Neely, 27; Finger, *Cherokee Americans*, 1–16; U. S. Federal Population Census, 1900; John Gulick, "The Acculturation of Cherokee Community Organization," *Social Forces*, 246–50.

6. Cherokee Census Books, Record Group 75, Series 16, Box 1; Dewitt Harris to Cherokee Indian Agency, 6 August 1906, Record Group 75, CIA, Box 5, FRCEP.

7. Robert Etheridge, "Tobacco among the Cherokees," *Journal of Cherokee Studies* (Spring 1978): 76–77; Douglas A. Rossman, *Where the Legends Live* (Cherokee, N.C.: Cherokee Publications, 1988), 21, 27; Census Books, Record Group 75, Series 16, Box 1, FRCEP.

8. Joseph S. Hall, *Smoky Mountain Folks and Their Lore* (Asheville, N.C.: Cataloochee Press and Great Smoky Mountains Natural History Association, 1960), 10,

57–59, 62–63, 65. See also Dunn, 143–78, and Michael Ann Williams, *Great Smoky Mountains Folklife* (Jackson: University Press of Mississippi, 1995).

9. Catherine Albanese, *American Religious Experience and Religions* (Belmont, Calif.: Wadsworth, 1992), 332; see also James L. Peacock and Ruel W. Tyson Jr., *Pilgrims of Paradox: Calvinism and Experience among the Primitive Baptists of the Blue Ridge* (Washington, D.C.: Smithsonian Institution Press, 1989), 7.

10. Nora De Armond, *So High the Sun* (Clarksville, Tenn.: Jostens Publications, 1982), 31.

11. S. B. Buckley, "Mountains of North Carolina and Tennessee," *American Journal of Science and Arts* 27 (May 1959): 286–94. Buckley recorded trappers with otter, mink, black fox, red fox, raccoon, and muskrat in 1858.

12. Clon Ownby, interview by Bill Landry, 1989, Landry Collection, GSMNP; Lona Parton Tyson, *Reflections of the Pinnacle: The Story of Parton Roots* (Gatlinburg, Tenn.: Tyson, 1982), 18; J. Roy Whaley and Sam Whaley, interview by V. R. Bender and R. Madden, 1969, Oral History Collection, GSMNP.

13. P. Audley Whaley, interview by William Alston, 1975; Robert Woody, interview by Sam Easterby, 1973; Alie Newman Maples, interview by Jane Whitney, 1973, Oral History Collection, GSMNP; Raymond Caldwell, interview by Bill Landry, 1989; Henry Posey, interview by Bill Landry, 1989; Gudger Palmer, interview by Bill Landry, 1988, Landry Collection, GSMNP.

14. *1896 Code of Tennessee*, 669; *1905 Code of Tennessee*, 738, 1009–10; Seymour D. Thompson, *A Compilation of the Statute Laws of Tennessee* (St. Louis: Gilbert, 1873), 809–10; Mooney, 307, 375; Elizabeth Powers and Mark Hannah, *Cataloochee: Lost Settlement of the Smokies* (Charleston, N.C.: Powers-Hannah, 1982), 344–45; Thomas B. Womack, *Revisal of 1905 Code of North Carolina* (Raleigh, N.C.: E. M. Uzzell, 1905), 344–45.

15. John Preston Arthur, *Western North Carolina: A History, 1730–1930* (Raleigh, N.C.: Edwards, Broughton and Company, 1914), 520.

16. *Public Statutes of North Carolina* (Raleigh, N.C.: State Printer, 1872), 474; Womack, 571–73; similar laws included Swain County after 1909; see *North Carolina Code of 1927* (Raleigh, N.C.: State Printer, 1927), 741.

17. Robert S. Woody, interview by Sam Easterby, 1973; Newton Ownby, interview by Joseph Hall, 1939; Eunice Smelcer, interview by Joseph Hall, 1939; Herman Matthews, interview by Glenn Cardwell, 1979; Eugene Lowe, interview by Bill Landry, 1989, Oral History Collection, GSMNP; Raymond Fogelson, "The Conjuror in Eastern Cherokee Society," *Journal of Cherokee Studies* (Fall 1980): 73; Mooney, 370–71; Elsie Martin in *The Cherokee Perspective*, ed. Laurence French and Jim Hornbuckle (Boone, Tenn.: Appalachian Consortium Press, 1981), 202.

18. Hattie Caldwell Davis, *Cataloochee Valley: Vanished Settlement of the Great Smoky Mountains* (Alexandria, Va.: Worldcom, 1997), 31, 121. Hiding meat for a future meal is actually typical bear behavior.

19. Frank M. Thompson, *Code of Tennessee* (Louisville: Baldwin Law Book Company, 1917); Hall, 21; S. J. Hunnicutt, *Twenty Years of Hunting and Fishing in the Great*

Smoky Mountains (Knoxville: S. B. Newman, 1926); Wiley Oakley, *Roamin' and Restin'* (Gatlinburg, Tenn.: Oakley Enterprises, 1940); Fonz Cable, interview by Joseph Hall, 1939; Charley Myers, interview by Jane Whitney, 1973; Seymour Calhoun, interview by William Alston, 1975; Fred Newman, interview by Jane Whitney, 1973; P. Audley Whaley, interview by William F. Alston, 1975, Oral History Collection, GSMNP; Maynard Ledbetter, interview by Bill Landry, 1989, Landry Collection, GSMNP.

20. Mooney, 260. For an excellent study of bald history, see Phil Gersmehl, "A Geographic Approach to a Vegetative Problem: The Case of the Southern Appalachian Grassy Balds" (Ph.D. diss., University of Georgia, 1970).

21. Mary Lindsay and Susan Power Bratton, "The Vegetation of Grassy Balds and Other High Elevation Disturbed Areas in the Great Smoky Mountains National Park," *Bulletin of the Torrey Botanical Club* 196 (October–December 1979): 269; Mary Lindsay, "History of the Grassy Balds in the Great Smoky Mountains National Park," Management Report No. 4 (April 1976): 8–9; Maynard Ledbetter, interview by Bill Landry, 1989; Paul Woody, interview by Kathleen Manscill, 1984; Herb Clabo, interview by Jane Whitney, 1973; Jim Shelton, interview by Mary Lindsay, 75, Oral History Collection, GSMNP; superintendent to Miss Estelle Reed, 29 July 1902, Record Group 75, Series 6, Box 4, FRCEP.

22. W. S. Campbell to H. L. Moody, 23 July 1904; H. W. Spray to commissioner, Bureau of Indian Affairs, 24 September 1902; H. W. Spray to A. E. Holton, 24 September 1902; H. W. Spray to B. P. Howell, 13 April 1903; W. S. Campbell to H. L. Moody, 23 July 1904, Record Group 75, CA, Series 6, Box 4, FRCEP. See also Dunn, 33–34.

23. H. W. Spray to commissioner, Bureau of Indian Affairs, 4 April 1901, Record Group 75, CA, Series 6, Box 4, FRCEP; Bessie Jumper, interview by Lois Calone-huskie, in *Journal of Cherokee Studies* 14 (1989): 24–35; Lindsay, "History of the Grassy Balds," 12–13; Paul Woody, interview by Kathleen Manscill, 1984; Raymond J. Caldwell, interview by Bill Landry, 1989; Henry Posey, interview by Bill Landry, 1989, Oral History Collection, GSMNP.

24. Horace Kephart, *Our Southern Highlanders* (New York: McMillan, 1921), 53–54; Mark MacKenzie, "Location of Areas within the Great Smoky Mountains National Park with a High Dominance of Chestnut during the 1930s and therefore a High Probability of Present Day Chestnut Regeneration," technical report, National Park Service, 1987, 8; Gifford Pinchot and W. W. Ashe, *Timber Trees and Forests of North Carolina* (Winston, N.C.: M. I. and J. C. Stewart, 1897), 224.

25. Notebook, Charles Grossman Papers; Paul Woody, interview by Kathleen Manscill, 1984; Alie Newman Maples, interview by Jane Whitney, 1973; Johnny Manning, interview by Glenn Cardwell, 1980, Oral History Collection, GSMNP; Delce Mae Carver Bryant, interview by Bill Landry, 1989, Landry Collection; GSMNP; Vic Weals, "Gourmet Hogs Fattened on Mountain Chestnuts," *Knoxville Journal* (8 October 1981): A3.

26. Walter Cole, interview by Charles Grossman, 1965, Oral History Collection, GSMNP; Maynard Ledbetter, interview by Bill Landry, 1989, Landry Collection,

GSMNP; Wildlife Resources Commission, Tennessee, "A Strategic Plan for Wildlife Resource Management" (Washington, D.C.: U.S. Department of Interior, 1990), 7.

27. Seymour Calhoun, interview by William F. Alston, 1973, Oral History Collection, GSMNP; Martha Wachacha, interview by Lois Calonehuskie, in *Journal of Cherokee Studies* 14 (1989): 51–57.

28. Herb Clabo, interview by Jane Whitney, 1973, Oral History Collection, GSMNP; Lands Transferred to the Federal Government, GSMNP; Maggie Wachacha, interview by Lois Calonehuskie, Earl Davis, and Tom Hill, in *Journal of Cherokee Studies* (1989): 50; Powers, 289.

29. North Carolina's fence law started in 1777, *Revisal of Public Statutes of North Carolina* (Raleigh, N.C.: Edwards, Broughton and Company, 1873). Tennessee adopted a similar law in 1873, *West's Tennessee Digest* (St. Paul: West Law Book Company, 1987). For the stock laws, see *North Carolina Code of 1927* (1928), 681, and *Acts of Tennessee* (1903), 315. See also Forest McDonald and Grady McWhiney, "The Antebellum Southern Herdsman: A Reinterpretation," *Journal of Southern History* 41 (May 1975): 147–66; John E. Roland, interview by Robert Madden, 1969; Henry Davis, interview by Robert Madden, 1969, Oral History Collection, GSMNP; Henry Posey, interview by author, 1990, tape recording in author's possession.

30. Herbert L. Stoddard, "The Use of Controlled Fire in Southeastern Game Management" (Thomasville, Ga.: Cooperative Quail Study Association, 1939), 21; Ayres and Ashe, 176–77; Charlotte Pyle, "Predictions of Forest Type and Productivity Index on Disturbed Sites in the Great Smoky Mountains National Park" (master's thesis, University of Tennessee, 1988), 35; Sarah H. Hill, *Weaving New Worlds: Southeastern Cherokee Women and Their Basketry* (Chapel Hill: University of North Carolina Press, 1997), 118; Seymour Calhoun, interview by William F. Alston, 1975, Oral History Collection, GSMNP.

31. H. W. Spray to commissioner, Bureau of Indian Affairs, Record Group 75, Series 6, Box 3, FRCEP.

32. Dunn, 226; Jarvis Connor, interview by Rosemary Nichols, 1974, Oral History Collection, GSMNP; H. W. Spray to commissioner, Bureau of Indian Affairs, 17 August 1900, Record Group 75, Series 6, Box 3, FRCEP.

33. *Directory & Shipping Guide, Lumber Mills and Lumber Dealers* (Chicago: Rand McNally, 1884), 327–33, 338–42, 429–30, 438–49; Robert S. Lambert, "Logging in the Great Smokies, 1880–1930," *Tennessee Historical Quarterly* (December 1961): 351–52; Abstracts of Titles, North Carolina, vol. 2, GSMNP.

34. Lambert, 34; Weaver H. McCracken III, "Comparison of Forest Cover prior to and following Disturbance in Two Areas of the Great Smoky Mountains National Park" (master's thesis, University of Tennessee, 1978), 9–10; *Asheville Citizen-Times*, 18 March 1991.

35. Inez Burns, *History of Blount County, Tennessee, 1795–1955* (Nashville: Tennessee Historical Commission, 1957), 244. See also Clon Ownby, interview by Bill Landry, 1989, Landry Collection, GSMNP; Winfred Cagle, interview by William Weaver, 1973, Oral History Collection, GSMNP.

36. Dewitt Harris to commissioner, Bureau of Indian Affairs, 25 January 1905, Bureau of Indian Affairs, Cherokee Indian Agency, Box 5; superintendent to Cover & Sons, 28 May 1902, Superintendent's Letterbooks, Bureau of Indian Affairs, Cherokee Indian Agency, Box 4, FRCEP. Some home tanning of hides did occur in 1900 as well, though most people bought their shoes at the store. Dewitt Harris to commissioner, 12 February 1907, Box 5, FRCEP.

37. H. W. Spray to Cherokee Indian Agency, 15 January 1900; H. W. Spray to Cherokee Indian Agency, 10 January 1903; W. S. Campbell to A. E. Holten, 7 June 1904, Record Group 75, Series 6, Box 4, FRCEP. See also Smathers, 8; Dewitt Harris to W. A. Jones, 21 September 1904; Dewitt Harris to Cherokee Indian Agency, 19 April 1905, Record Group 75, Series 6, Box 5, FRCEP; testimony of John Thomas Walker, 1 May 1939; copy in Land Acquisition Files, 3, GSMNP.

38. Cope, 64; Lucy Black Ownby, interview by Bill Landry, 1989, Landry Collection, GSMNP; John Witthoft, "Cherokee Indian Use of Potherbs," *Journal of Cherokee Studies* 2 (Spring 1977): 251–52; Williams, 97.

39. Juanita Ownby, interview by Glenn Cardwell, 1974, Oral History Collection, GSMNP; Laura C. Martin, *Wildflower Folklore* (Charlotte, N.C.: East Woods Press, 1984), 69, 113. Little brown jug is also called heart leaf or wild ginger. See also notebook, Charles Grossman Papers, GSMNP.

40. Hall, 46; Cope, 15.

41. Mooney, 425; Turkey George Palmer, interview by Joseph Hall, 1938, Oral History Collection, GSMNP; Powers, 292–93.

42. Lucinda Oakley Ogle, "I Wanted to Go to School Forever," *Appalachian Journal* 14 (1987): 240–41; Delce Mae Carver Bryant, interview by Bill Landry, 1989, Landry Collection, GSMNP.

43. Charles P. Nicholson, *Atlas of the Breeding Birds of Tennessee* (Knoxville: University of Tennessee Press, 1997), 246–47, 264, 279–87, 322.

44. Kathleen E. Franzreb and Ricky A. Phillips, *Neotropical Migratory Birds of the Southern Appalachians*, Southern Research Station General Technical Report SE-96 (USDA, 1996), 16; Christopher J. Haney, "Spatial Incidence of Barred Owl Reproduction in Old-Growth Forests of the Appalachian Plateau," *Journal of Raptor Research* 31 (1997): 10; Powers, 347–49; Mooney, 281, 284.

45. Census Records, Record Group 75, CA, Series 16, Box 1, FRCEP; Census of Agriculture, North Carolina and Tennessee, 1925.

46. William H. Banks Jr., *Ethnobotany of the Cherokee Indians* (master's thesis, University of Tennessee, 1953), 11.

47. Charles Grossman Maps, GSMNP. These 1927 U.S. Geological Survey quadrangles show the presence of homes by creeks and springs; Gladys Trentham Russell, *Call Me Hillbilly* (Alcoa, Tenn.: Russell Printing Company, 1974), 17. Russell remembers sixteen outbuildings on her farm in 1921 in the Sugarlands. Ed Trout, "Rock and Timber" (unpublished manuscript, GSMNP, 1992), 56–57; Marian Moffett, *East Tennessee Cantilever Barns* (Knoxville: University of Tennessee Press, 1993), 27, 47–48.

48. Delce Dyer, "The Farmstead Yards at Cades Cove: Restoration and Manage-

ment Alternatives for the Domestic Landscape of the Southern Appalachian Mountaineer" (master's thesis, University of Georgia, 1988), 30–33; Mooney, 286.

49. John Solomon Otto, "The Decline of Forest Farming in Southern Appalachia," *Journal of Forest History* 27 (1983): 22–23; Charlotte Pyle, "Prediction of Forest Type and Productivity Index on Disturbed Sites in the Great Smoky Mountains National Park" (master's thesis, University of Tennessee, 1988), 36.

50. Emmaline Diver in *The Cherokee Perspective*, 195; *Waynesville Mountaineer* 10 April 1987. See also Evolena Ownby, "Evolena Remembers Big Greenbrier and Other Communities of Living" (unpublished manuscript, Vertical Files, GSMNP, 1979), 6; Tyson, 27.

51. Comments of foresters and agricultural experts can be analyzed in USDA soil surveys as well as in the Biltmore Collection, FHS; H. W. Spray to commissioner, Bureau of Indian Affairs, 19 February 1903, Record Group 75, CA, Series 6, Box 4, FRCEP. Eugene Lowe, interview by Bill Landry, 1989, Landry Collection, GSMNP; Charles L. Doughty, "Report of Work of the County Agent," Sevier County, 1916, Agricultural Records, GSMNP.

52. "Report of Work of the County Agent," Sevier County, 1916, Agricultural Records, GSMNP; Joseph Hart to commissioner, Bureau of Indian Affairs, 12 July 1897, Record Group 75, CA, Series 6, Box 3, FRCEP; Wesley Reagen, interview by Robert Madden and Glenn Cardwell, 1969; Lem Ownby, interview by Orlie Trentham, 1972; Paul Woody, interview by Kathleen Manscill, 1984; Herb Clabo, interview by Jane Whitney, 1973; Oral History Collection, GSMNP; Evolena Ownby, 25, and Lona Parton Tyson, 19.

53. Joseph Hart to W. N. Hailmann, 25 January 1898, Record Group 75, CA, Series 6, Box 2, FRCEP; Van Noppen, 270; Ed Trout, "Milling in the Smokies" (unpublished manuscript, GSMNP, 1978), 28. Trout states that a "groundhog thresher," which required eight horses to pull, was used in Cades Cove in 1900, but most smaller farms continued to use hand methods.

54. Herb Clabo, interview by Jane Whitney, 1973; Jim Shelton, interview by Robert Madden, 1968, Oral History Collection, GSMNP; Girard, B1; Bessie Jumper, interview by Lois Calonehuskie, *Journal of Cherokee Studies* 14 (1989): 24–35.

55. Dora Proffit Williams and Velma Ownby Lamons in Jerry Wear, ed., *Lost Communities of Sevier County: Greenbrier* (Sevierville, Tenn.: Sevierville Heritage Committeee, 1985), 12, 41; Lucy Black Ownby, interview by Bill Landry, 1989; Jonathon Woody, interview by Sam Easterby, 1973, Oral History Collection, GSMNP; Neely, 35–36; Frank Kyleska to commissioner, Bureau of Indian Affairs, 6 December 1910, Record Group 75, CA, Series 6, Box 7, FRCEP.

56. Charles Grossman to M. Robert Ripley, 3 November 1936; Charles Grossman Papers, GSMNP; Trout, "Milling in the Smokies," 33–35; Andy Cline, interview by Robert Madden, 1969; Herb Clabo and "Preacher" Moore, interviews by Jane Whitney, 1973, Oral History Collection, GSMNP.

57. Seymour Calhoun, interview by William F. Alston, 1975; J. Roy Whaley and Sam Whaley, interview by Robert Madden, 1969; Jim Shelton, interview by Robert

Madden, 1968, Oral History Collection, GSMNP; Dora Proffit Williams, 13; Tyson, 22.

58. Laura Dulcie Abbott McCauley, interview by Mary Robinson, 1981; Winfred Cagle, interview by William Weaver, 1973; Herman Matthews, interview by Glenn Cardwell, 1979; Fred Newman, interview by Jane Whitney, 1973; Bert Crisp, interview by Robert Madden, 1968, Oral History Collection, GSMNP; see also Lela King Gobble in *Lost Communities of Sevier County: Greenbrier*, ed. Jerry Wear, 35; Callie Wachacha, interview by Lois Calonehuskie, Earl Davis, Marty Catolster, and Susan Crowe, 1986; Ella Jackson, interview by Lois Calonehuskie and Bill Jackson, 1987; *Journal of Cherokee Studies* 14 (1989): 17–23, 58–62.

59. Birgie Manning, interview by Mary Ruth Chiles, 1981; Paul Woody, interview by Kathleen Manscill, 1984; Winfred Cagle, interview by William Weaver, 1973, Oral History Collection, GSMNP; Dora Proffit Williams, 31–32; *Asheville Citizen-Times*, 24 July 1981, and *Asheville Citizen-Times*, 30 March 1980.

60. Lucy Black Ownby, interview by Bill Landry, 1989; Paul Woody, interview by Kathleen Manscill, 1984; Wesley Reagen, interview by Robert Madden and Glenn Cardwell, 1969; Walter Cole, interview by Charles Grossman, 1965; Oral History Collection, GSMNP; Dewitt Harris to William Taylor, 27 October 1904, and Dewitt Harris to Professor Herbert Webber, 4 February 1907, Record Group 75, CA, Series 6, Box 5, FRCEP; *Sevier County Times*, 26 February 1976; Wilma Dykeman and Jim Stokely, *Highland Homeland: The People of the Great Smokies* (Washington, D.C.: National Park Service, 1978), 49.

61. Seymour Calhoun, interview by William Alston, 1975; Robert Woody, interview by Sam Easterby, 1973; Clon Ownby, interview by Glenn Cardwell, 1974; J. Roy Whaley and Sam Whaley, interview by V. R. Bender and R. Madden, 1969, Oral History Collection, GSMNP. See also W. W. Ashe, *The Possibilities of a Maple Sugar Industry in Western North Carolina* (Winston, N.C.: M. I. and J. C. Stewart, 1897), 1.

62. Alie Newman Maples, interview by Jane Whitney, 1973; Jim Shelton, interview by Mary Lindsay, 1975; Winfred Cagle, interview by William Weaver, 1973; Oral History Collection, GSMNP; Alice Moore Posey, interview by author, 1990, tape recording in author's possession; Margaret Lynn Brown and Donald Edward Davis, "Great Smoky Mountains Trail History" (unpublished manuscript, GSMNP, 1992), 103. H. W. Spray to commissioner, Bureau of Indian Affairs, 24 October 1902; Dewitt Harris to Cherokee Indian Agency, 30 June 1906, Record Group 75, Series 6, Boxes 4 and 5, FRCEP.

63. Unfortunately, such records were not kept again until the 1920s; Tyson, 5; Lucinda Oakley Ogle, "I Wanted to Go to School Forever," *Appalachian Journal* 14 (1987): 240–41; Russell, 55.

64. Henry Posey, interview by author, 1990; Winfred Cagle, interview by William Weaver, 1973; Paul Woody, interview by Kathleen Manscill, 1984, Oral History Collection; Henry Posey, interview by Bill Landry, 1989, Landry Collection, GSMNP; Catherine Albanese, *American Religious Experience and Religions* (Belmont, Calif.: Wadsworth, 1992), 332; Paul Salstrom, "Appalachia's Informal Economy and the Transition to Capitalism," *Journal of Appalachian Studies* 4 (Fall 1996): 227.

65. Robert Woody, "Cataloochee Homecoming," *South Atlantic Quarterly* 49 (January 1950): 16.

66. Harold Brookfield and Christine Padoch, "Appreciating Agrodiversity," *Environment* 36 (June 1995): 8–13.

67. Author acknowledges Carolyn Merchant, *Ecological Revolutions: Nature, Gender, and Science in New England* (Chapel Hill: University of North Carolina Press, 1989), 153–97; Timothy Silver, "In Search of Iron Eyes: A Historian Reflects on the Cherokees as Environmentalists," *Appalachian Voice* (Winter 1996): 3; and Ronald D Eller, e-mail message, 22 June 1998, printout in author's possession, in developing this conclusion.

2. A Lumberman's Dream

1. William L. Hall, "To Remake the Appalachians," *World's Work* 28 (July 1914): 335; John and Ina Woetemeyer Van Noppen, "The Genesis of Forestry in the Southern Appalachians: A Brief History," *Appalachian Journal* 1 (Autumn 1972): 67n.

2. Roy Carroll and Raymond H. Pulley, *Historic Structures Report: Little Cataloochee, North Carolina* (Gatlinburg, Tenn.: Great Smoky Mountains Natural History Association, 1976), 10, 12; H. B. Ayres and W. W. Ashe, 155–56. For typical yields, see Michael Williams, *Americans and Their Forests: A Historical Geography* (New York: Cambridge University Press, 1989), 239–41; W. R. Mattoon, "William Willard Ashe," *Journal of Forestry* (May 1932): 652–53.

3. William L. Hall, "New National Forests in the Southern Appalachians," *Southern Lumberman* 69 (21 December 1912): 107.

4. *Asheville Citizen-Times*, 31 August 1980; "In North Carolina," *Southern Lumberman*, 7 January 1911, 13; Ronald G. Schmidt and William S. Hooks, *Whistle over the Mountain: Timber, Track, and Trails in the Tennessee Smokies* (Yellow Springs, Ohio: Graphicom Press, 1994), 56.

5. Herbert Knox Smith, "Report of the Commissioner of Corporations on the Lumber Industry," February 13, 1911. Reprint (Washington, D.C.: U.S. Government Printing Office, 1931).

6. Abstracts of Title, North Carolina, GSMNP; Robert S. Lambert, "Logging the Great Smokies, 1880–1930," *Tennessee Historical Quarterly* (December 1961): 354; Dewitt Harris to Cherokee Indian Agency, 22 December 1906, 28 December 1908, Record Group 75, Series 6, Box 5, FRCEP; Minutes Book, Parsons Pulp & Paper Company, Whitmer-Parsons Pulp and Lumber Company, Box 3, Logging Records, GSMNP; *Directory of American Sawmills and Planing Mills* (Nashville: Southern Lumberman, 1928), 721.

7. Dennis E. Reedy, *W. M. Ritter Lumber Company Family History Book* (self-published, n.d.), 10, FHS; Abstracts of Title, North Carolina, GSMNP.

8. Prescott, 31–33. Though some companies used band saws as early as 1880, not until patents were issued in the 1890s did the band saw become accurate enough to produce quantities of straight boards for large-scale operations. See also Frothingham, 8–10.

9. Vic Weals, *The Last Train to Elkmont* (Knoxville: Olden Press, 1991), 17. Weals

substantiated the story by the deed on file at the Blount County Court House; Dollie Lee Burchfield Nelson to W. E. Mize, 9 December 1938, Land Acquisition Files, GSMNP.

10. Ray Garrett, "In Less Than a Life Span," *American Forests* 58 (October 1952): 23; Dewitt Harris to commissioner, Bureau of Indian Affairs, 28 December 1908, 19 September 1908, Record Group 75, Series 6, Boxes 5 and 8, FRCEP.

11. W. J. Damtoft, interview by Elwood R. Maunder, 1959, FHS. Damtoft was hired by the National Forest Service to clear up titles on Little River Lumber Company lands for possible purchase. *North Carolina vs. Suncrest*, Box 4, Logging Records, GSMNP.

12. Reuben Robertson, interview by Jerry Maunder, 1959, FHS. See also Richard Bartlett's *Troubled Waters: Champion International and the Pigeon River Controversy* (Knoxville: University of Tennessee Press, 1995).

13. U.S. Department of Labor, *U.S. Wages and Hours of Labor in the Lumber, Millwork, and Furniture Industries* (Washington, D.C.: U.S. Government Printing Office, 1913); Daniel A. Cornfield, *Workers and Dissent in the Redwood Empire* (Philadelphia: Temple University Press, 1987), 5–6, 172–75; *Southern Lumberman*, 25 April 1908, 26; 21 March 1908, 22; 9 September 1911, 32. Started in 1881 by Dan Baird, *Southern Lumberman* was the oldest lumber trade paper in the United States. In 1915, circulation was between 5,000 and 6,000, according to the publication.

14. Eller, 93–112; Frome, 168; Lambert, "Logging the Great Smokies," 355; Rogers, 73–78.

15. T. G. Murdock, memorandum to Dr. Willis King, 25 February 1942; Willa Mae Hall Trull, "Adams v. Westfelt" (unpublished manuscript, Mining File, GSMNP, n.d.). See also Oliver, 51–52.

16. W. J. Damtoft, interview by Elwood R. Maunder, 1959, FHS; *Southern Lumberman*, 23 December 1911, 83–84.

17. Eller, 94–111; Ayres and Ashe, *Southern Appalachian Forests*, 170, 216–18, 172; Inman F. Eldredge, interview by Elwood Maunder, 1959, in *Voices From the South: Recollections of Four Foresters* (Santa Cruz, Calif.: Forest History Society, 1977), 54–55. Eldredge was educated in the Biltmore School.

18. "Timber Supply of the United States," *Southern Lumberman*, 31 July 1909, 30–31.

19. *Southern Lumberman*, 25 May 1907, 33.

20. *Mountain Press*, 8 March 1999.

21. Schmidt and Hooks, 107–9; *Asheville Citizen-Times*, 20 March 1922, 15A.

22. Weals, 79–80; photo collection, FHS; Joe Barnes, interview by Weaver McCracken, 1974, transcript in Weaver McCracken Collection, GSMNP.

23. Jennie Bradshaw Abbott, interview by C. Bren Martin, Little River Railroad and Lumber Museum, Townsend, Tenn.; McCracken, 49–52, 65–73; Pyle and Schafale, "Land Use History of Three Spruce-Fir Forest Sites in Southern Appalachia," 16; Bret Wallach, "The Slighted Mountains of Upper East Tennessee," *Journal of the Association of American Geographers* 71 (September 1981): 363–64, 3n; Laurence C. Walker, *The Southern Forest* (Austin: University of Texas Press, 1991),

102; Curt McCarter and Louis McCarter, interview by Weaver McCracken, 1974, McCracken Collection, GSMNP.

24. Paul M. Fink, *Backpacking Was the Only Way,* 65.

25. John Parton, interview by Robert Lambert, 1958; Seymour Calhoun, interview by W. F. Alston, 1975; Oral History Collection, GSMNP.

26. Albert Siler, interview by Weaver McCracken, 1974, transcript in Weaver McCracken Collection; Louis McCarter, interview by Robert Lambert, 1958, Oral History Collection (Shea Brothers contracted with Little River Lumber Company); Horace Trentham, interview by Weaver McCracken, 1974, transcript in Weaver McCracken Collection; Lucy Black Ownby, interview by Bill Landry, 1989, Landry Collection; William T. Rolen, interview by Weaver McCracken, 1974, transcript in Weaver McCracken Collection, GSMNP.

27. Lambert, 34; J. S. Holmes, state forester, "Forest Fires in North Carolina during 1918, 1919, and 1920," Economic Paper No. 51 (Raleigh, N.C.: Mitchell Printing Company, 1921), 25, 32–36; *Code of Tennessee* 1134 (1917); "Forest Fire Problems in Southern States," *Southern Lumberman,* 13 April 1912, 32–33.

28. J. Keith Esser, photo album, 1912, Biltmore Collection, FHS; Cope, 134–35.

29. Pyle and Schafale, "Land Use History of Three Spruce-Fir Forest Sites in Southern Appalachia," 20.

30. Womack, 1027; Frank M. Thompson, *Code of Tennessee* (Louisville: Baldwin Law Book Company, 1917), 1132; *North Carolina Code* (1927), 726, 729–43; *Code of Tennessee* (1917), 1129–33; *Code of Tennessee* (1931), 1156.

31. D. S. Wilgrove, "Nest Predation in Forest Tracts and the Decline of Migratory Songbirds," *Ecology* 66: 1211–14.

32. James W. Petranka, "Recovery of Salamanders after Clearcutting in the Southern Appalachians," *Conservation Biology* 13 (February 1999): 203–5.

33. James W. Petranka, Matthew Eldridge, and Catherine Haley, "Effects of Timber Harvesting on Southern Appalachian Salamanders," *Conservation Biology* 7 (June 1993): 363–79. Petranka et al. were criticized by Andrew N. Ash and Richard Bruce in "Impacts of Timber Harvesting on Salamanders," *Conservation Biology* 8 (March 1994): 300–301 for their methodology and their failure to consider that salamanders could relocate to nearby areas. In the Smokies, at least, there would have been few unaffected areas nearby.

34. "Lumbermen and the Appalachian Reserve," *Southern Lumberman,* 18 June 1908, 21. The newspaper's estimate was conservative compared with that of foresters, such as R. S. Kellogg, with the USFS, who estimated sixteen years for hardwoods in 1907. See "Future of the Appalachian Forests," *Southern Lumberman,* 21 December 1907, 54, and "Why Some Birds and Animals Become Extinct," *Southern Lumberman,* 16 May 1908.

35. *Baldwin's Cumulative Code Supplement* (1920), 334; *Code of Tennessee* (1917), 1125–30; Walter Cole, interview by Charles Grossman, 1965, Oral History Collection, GSMNP.

36. *Asheville Citizen-Times,* 10 April 1977.

37. Seymour Calhoun, interview by W. F. Alston, 1975, Oral History Collection;

Raymer Brackin, interview by Weaver McCracken, 1974, transcript in Weaver McCracken Collection, vol. 15; D. R. Beeson Papers, AAETSU.

38. McCracken, 59.

39. David Cameron Duffy and Albert J. Meier, "Do Appalachian Herbaceous Understories Ever Recover from Clearcutting?" *Conservation Biology* 6 (June 1992): 196–201. Duffy and Meier have drawn considerable criticism for their conclusions (A. Sydney Johnson, William M. Ford, and Philip E. Hale, "The Effects of Clearcutting on Herbaceous Understories Are Still Not Fully Known," *Conservation Biology* 7 [June 1993]: 433–35). More recent defenders, however, argue that their results are consistent with other studies and "the existence of such effects should be beyond debate" (Glenn Matlack, "Plant Demography, Land-Use History, and the Commercial Use of Forests," *Conservation Biology* 8 [March 1994]: 298–99). See also Susan P. Bratton, "Logging and Fragmentation of Broadleaved Deciduous Forests," *Conservation Biology* 8 (March 1994): 295–97.

40. Charlotte Pyle, "Vegetation Disturbance History of Great Smoky Mountains National Park: An Analysis of Archival Maps and Records" (Gatlinburg, Tenn.: Uplands Field Research Laboratory, 1985), 13–19. Estimate is from Lambert, "Logging in the Great Smoky Mountains National Park," 13. I consider Lambert's estimate "conservative," because by his own admission he did not include timber shipped in the log, timber cut for tanbark, timber destroyed by machinery and fire, and timber used in construction or for fuel. See also E. H. Frothingham, "Timber Growing and Logging Practices in the Southern Appalachian Region," U.S. Technical Bulletin 250 (Washington, D.C.: U.S. Department of Agriculture, 1931), 17.

41. "W. M. Ritter Honored by Friends and Associates in Fiftieth Anniversary Dinner," *Southern Lumberman*, 1 March 1940; John Parris, "Reuben Robertson Was Industrial Giant," *Asheville Citizen-Times*, 27 December 1972, 13.

42. W. M. Ritter, "An Address before the Chamber of Commerce of Bluefield, West Virginia," December 3, 1943, Vertical Files, AAETSU; W. M. Ritter, "Big Columbus Lumberman Honored," *Southern Lumberman*, 20 June 1917, 25, Charles C. Tiller Collection, AAETSU. The company later invested in coal and produced 5 million tons a year during the 1950s. Ritter was taken over by Georgia-Pacific in 1960.

43. *American Lumberman*, 8 June 1901, 1.

44. Robert Woody, interview by Sam Easterby, 1973, Oral History Collection, GSMNP. *Summaries, Census of Agriculture* (Washington, D.C.: U.S. Department of Commerce, 1925), 447–95, 604–11; U.S. Department of Commerce, Bureau of the Census, Twelfth Census of the U.S., 1900, and Thirteenth Census of the U.S., 1910, Population Schedules, Haywood County, N.C.

45. Carroll and Pulley, 26; Delce Mae Carver Bryant, interview by Bill Landry, 1989, Landry Collection, GSMNP; Walter O Sharp, "Report of the County Agent, Sevier County, 1917," Agricultural Records, GSMNP.

46. Jesse F. House to commissioner, Bureau of Indian Affairs, 14 December 1903, Record Group 75, Series 6, Box 4, FRCEP; Black, 25–27.

47. Lindsay, "History of the Grassy Balds," 12–13.

48. Black, 91; *North Carolina vs. Suncrest Lumber Operations*, Logging Records, GSMNP.

49. *Southern Lumberman*, 19 June 1915, 1050. P. Audley Whaley, interview by Weaver McCracken, 1974; Horace Trentham, interview by Weaver McCracken, 1974, McCracken Collection, GSMNP.

50. Fink, *Backpacking Was the Only Way* (Johnson City, Tenn.: Research Advisory Council, 1975), 115.

51. Sam Whaley, interview by Glen Cardwell, 1973, Oral History Collection; Johnny Manning, interview by Glen Cardwell, 1981, Oral History Collection, GSMNP.

52. Dewitt Harris to Gifford Pinchot, 2 January 1907; Frank Kyselka to commissioner, Bureau of Indian Affairs, 23 June 1909, Record Group 75, Series 6, Boxes 5 and 6, FRCEP; Maggie Wachacha, interview by Lois Calonehuskie, Earl Davis, and Tom Hill, 1987, in *Journal of Cherokee Studies* 14 (1989): 46–47; Neely, 27; Dewitt Harris to Cherokee Indian Agency, 19 April 1905, Box 5; Frank Kyselka to Cherokee Indian Agency, 22 July 1909, Record Group 75, Series 6, Box 6, FRCEP.

53. Paul Woody, interview by Kathleen Manscill, 1984, Oral History Collection, GSMNP.

54. Mark Hannah, interview by Bill Landry, 1989, Landry Collection, GSMNP.

55. Henry Canby, "Top of Ol' Smoky," *Harper's* (March 1916): 574–83, NC Collection, UNC Chapel Hill.

56. Arnold Thompson, interview by Weaver McCracken, 1974, Weaver McCracken Collection, GSMNP; McCracken, 40.

57. Robert E. Dils, "Influence of Forest Cutting and Mountain Farming on Some Vegetation, Surface Soil, and Surface Runoff Characteristics," Southeastern Forest Experiment Station, Paper No. 24 (Washington, D.C.: U.S. Forest Service, 1953).

58. Ronald L. Lewis, "Railroads, Deforestation and the Transformation of Agriculture in the West Virginia Back Counties, 1880–1920," in *Appalachia in the Making: The Mountain South in the Nineteenth Century* (Chapel Hill: University of North Carolina Press, 1995), 316; see also Ron Lewis, *Transforming the Appalachian Countryside: Railroads, Deforestation, and Social Change in West Virginia, 1880–1920* (Chapel Hill: University of North Carolina Press, 1998), 263–92.

59. Holmes, 67, 79–81, 90.

60. J. S. Holmes, "Forest Conditions in Western North Carolina," North Carolina Geological and Economic Survey, Bulletin 23 (Raleigh, N.C.: Edwards, Broughton and Company, 1911), 9–14, 38.

3. Scenery in the Eminent Domain

1. Harvey Broome, *Out under the Sky of the Great Smokies: A Personal Journey* (Knoxville: Greenbrier Press, 1975), 5, 17; Broome, "Origins of the Wilderness Society," *The Living Wilderness* 31 (Winter 1967): 10–11; Raymond S. Spears, *Camping, Woodcraft and Wildcraft* (Girard, Kans.: Haldeman-Julius, 1924), 29.

2. Horace Kephart, "The Need for a National Park in the Smokies," *Knoxville News-Sentinel*, 2 August 1925, 4.

3. C. H. Longwell, quoted in *The Great Smoky Mountains National Park in Tennessee and North Carolina* (Knoxville: Greenbrier Press, 1975), 5, 17; Kephart, *Our Southern Highlanders*, 50; John Willy, "Ten Days in the Proposed Great Smoky Mountains National Park," *Hotel Monthly* (1926): 44–58.

4. Kenneth Thompson, "Wilderness and Health in the Nineteenth Century," *Journal of Historical Geography* 2 (1976): 145–161; Robin Dial, "Montvale is Experience for Campers," *Knoxville News-Sentinel*, 29 June 1975, 1B; *Maryville-Alcoa Times*, 18 July 1968, 1B; Charles V. Patton, "Scene of Popular Summer Resort Lures Former Guests," *Knoxville Journal*, 3 July 1949, 1B.

5. "Star Points to . . . Seaton Springs," *The Star*, 6 April 1981, 8B; Pat Lamon, "The Original Charm of Seaton Springs," *Sevier County News-Record*, 1 June 1978, 1B.

6. For an excellent discussion of local-color writers and their encounters with Cades Cove folk culture, see Dunn, 156–63; Charles Egbert Craddock, *The Prophet of the Great Smokies* (Boston and New York: Houghton Mifflin, 1885 [1913]), 30, 185; and *In the Tennessee Mountains* (Boston: Houghton Mifflin, 1885), 1, 18, 81, 117, 322.

7. Joan and Wright Langley, *Yesterday's Asheville* (Miami: E. A. Seeman Publishing, 1975), 57.

8. Jesse R. Lankford, "The Campaign for a National Park in Western North Carolina" (master's thesis, Western Carolina University, 1978), 2, 8, 13, 37.

9. Charles Dennis Smith, "The Appalachian National Park Movement, 1885–1901," *North Carolina Historical Review* 37 (January 1960): 41–42, 44, 46, 50, 62–63. Smathers later moved to Swain County. He regularly helped land speculators and lumber companies untangle title problems and eventually became a lawyer for Champion; "Memorial of the Appalachian National Park Association," *Senate Journal*, Fifty-sixth Congress, First Session, 4 January 1900.

10. George Ellison, introduction to *Our Southern Highlanders*. Reprint (New York: MacMillan, 1976), ix–xxxiii.

11. Kephart, *Our Southern Highlanders*, 50–74; 321–22, 450.

12. Paul M. Fink, "Early Explorers in the Great Smokies," *East Tennessee Historical Society's Publications* 51 (1979): 40–53; James Harlean, "The Great Smokies, Site of a Proposed National Park," *Review of Reviews* (October 1928): 373; Broome, 8.

13. Michael McDonald and Bruce Wheeler, *Knoxville: Continuity and Change in an Appalachian City* (Knoxville: University of Tennessee Press, 1988), xx; "Historic Inns and Hotels of the Smokies" (unpublished manuscript, Mary Ruth Chiles Collection, GSMNP).

14. Elizabeth Timmons, "Stories About Walland Shared," *Maryville-Alcoa Times*, 3 October 1979, 1B; Burns, 94; George Preston, interview by Bill Landry, 1989, Landry Collection, GSMNP; Christopher Branden Martin, "Selling the Southern Highlands: Tourism and Community Development in the Mountain South" (Ph.D. diss., University of Tennessee, 1997), 123.

15. Elizabeth Skaggs Bowman, *Land of High Horizons* (Kingsport, Tenn.: Southern Publishers, 1938), 67–69; Mary Ruth Chiles Collection, GSMNP.

16. Rellie Dodgen, interview by Bill Landry, 1990, Oral History Collection,

GSMNP; "Andy Huff Keeps with the Times," *Knoxville News-Sentinel,* 18 May 1930, A6.

17. Robert Lindsay Mason, *The Lure of the Great Smokies* (New York: Houghton Mifflin, 1927), 301–2; Harvey Broome, *Some Miscellaneous Writings* (Knoxville: Greenbrier Press, 1970), 12–13; Glenn Shultz, quoted in Chiles, 28; Edward Hunt, "Indian Gap Hotel: A Luxury Hotel in the Middle of the Smokies" (unpublished manuscript, Mary Ruth Chiles Collection, n.d., GSMNP).

18. John Gulick, "The Acculturation of Eastern Cherokee Community Organization," *Social Forces* (1935): 249. See also Finger, *Cherokee Americans,* 32.

19. Thomas J. Blumer, "Rebecca Youngbird: An Independent Cherokee Potter," *Journal of Cherokee Studies* 5 (Spring 1980): 43; Sarah Hitch Hill, "Cherokee Patterns: Interweaving Women and Baskets in History" (Ph.D. diss., Emory University, 1991), 380.

20. Alie Newman Maples, interview by Jane Whitney, 1973, Oral History Collection, GSMNP; D. R. Beeson Diary, 28 August 1914, AAETSU.

21. Paul J. Adams to Carson Brewer, 16 March 1965, Paul J. Adams Papers, Box 5, TSTATE.

22. Uplands Field Research Laboratory, "European Wild Hogs in the Great Smoky Mountains National Park" (Gatlinburg, Tenn.: Uplands Field Research Laboratory, 1985). Mountain men who once hunted feral hogs slowly adapted to this more elusive prey.

23. Office of Technology Assessment, *Harmful Non-Indigenous Species in the United States* (Washington, D.C.: U.S. Government Printing Office, 1993), 75; Hill, 319, 322, 332, 380.

24. Betsy Beeler Creekmore, *Knoxville* (Knoxville: University of Tennessee Press, 1958), 214; Morrell, 3.

25. Alfred Runte, *National Parks: The American Experience* (Lincoln: University of Nebraska Press, 1987), 83, 97–102.

26. Carlos Campbell, "Willis P. Davis and Anne May Davis," Davis Collection, GSMNP. Davis made his fortune in iron and steel; Mrs. Davis went on to serve in the Tennessee House of Representatives. For an excellent discussion of the Knoxville park promoters and how they fit into national conservation movements, see Daniel S. Pierce, "The Park Panacea: The Movement for a National Park in the Great Smoky Mountains of East Tennessee, 1923–1928" (unpublished paper, Knoxville, 1994), 9–20.

27. John Thomas Whaley, "A Timely Idea at an Ideal Time: Knoxville's Role in Establishing the Great Smoky Mountains National Park" (master's thesis, University of Tennessee, 1984), 38; Carlos C. Campbell, "Biography of Colonel David C. Chapman" (unpublished manuscript, n.d.), Chapman Collection, GSMNP.

28. Campbell, 22–30; U.S. Department of Interior, *Final Report of the Southern Appalachian National Park Commission to the Secretary of the Interior* (Washington, D.C.: U.S. Government Printing Office, 1931).

29. *Knoxville Journal,* 15 December 1924 and 17 August 1925.

30. "Report on Subscriptions, North Carolina and Tennessee," 13 February

1926, Great Smoky Mountains Conservation Association Collection, GSMNP; letters to the editor, *Montgomery's Vindicator*, 5 February 1930; "Why Mr. Gaskell is Fighting the Park Commission," 13 March 1931, scrapbook, George Masa Collection, Hunter Library, Western Carolina University, Cullowhee, N.C.

31. Campbell, 31; Joe Barnes, interview by Weaver McCracken, 1974, Oral History Collection, GSMNP; W. B. Townsend to Austin Peay, September 1924, Austin Peay Papers, Box 84, Folder 1; brochure, "A State Park Every 100 Miles," Austin Peay Papers, Container 99, Folder 2, TSTATE.

32. *Knoxville News-Sentinel* and *Knoxville Journal*, 7 December 1925; Reuben Robertson, interview by Jerry Maunder, 1959, Forest History Society, Durham, N.C.; "Report of Committee Appointed by the Western Carolina Lumber and Timber Association," 25 July 1925, Vertical Files, GSMNP; Verne Rhoades, *North Carolina Geological and Economic Survey, Federal Forest Purchases and Forest Recreation* (Chapel Hill: North Carolina State Government, 1924), 7.

33. James B. Wright, "Great Smoky Mountains National Park," statement elicited by the Park Investigating Committee of the Sixty-sixth General Assembly, 1929, North Carolina Collection, University of North Carolina, Chapel Hill, 14.

34. *Knoxville News-Sentinel*, 1 November 1925; *Great Smoky Mountains* (Knoxville: Great Smoky Mountains Conservation Association, 1928), 6, 10; *Knoxville News-Sentinel*, 1 April 1929; *Knoxville News-Sentinel*, 17 May 1924; "Great Smoky Mountains National Park Would Be an Asset to the State," *UNC Newsletter* 12 (17 March 1926): 1.

35. Jesse M. Shaver, "Flowers of the Great Smoky Mountains," *Journal of the Tennessee Academy of Science* 1 (April 1926): 17; G. R. Mayfield, "Magni Fumosi, Conservandi Sunt," *Journal of the Tennessee Academy of Science* 1 (April 1926): 27; *Great Smoky Mountains*, 6, 11; *Knoxville News-Sentinel*, 13 December 1925; *Asheville Citizen-Times*, 24 August 1930.

36. *Knoxville Journal*, 29 November 1925. For full development of the stereotyping issue, see Margaret Lynn Brown, "Captains of Tourism: Selling a National Park in the Great Smoky Mountains," *Journal of the Appalachian Studies Association* 4 (1992): 42–49; *New York Times*, 25 January 1926; Harlean, 373; *Knoxville News-Sentinel*, 3 March 1926, 4; "Tentative Area for National Park in Smoky Mountains," *Kuhlman's Pepper Box* (November 1925): 8. The precedent was established almost simultaneously at Shenandoah National Park in Virginia; see Charles L. Perdue Jr. and Nancy J. Martin-Perdue, "Appalachian Fables and Facts: A Case Study of the Shenandoah National Park Removals," *Appalachian Journal* (Autumn–Winter 1979–1980): 84–104. One previous national park in the East, Lafayette (later renamed Acadia), was for the most part a donation of land from John D. Rockefeller.

37. *Southern Lumberman*, 25 April 1908, 657; William E. Shands and Robert G. Healy, *The Lands Nobody Wanted: A Conservation Foundation Report* (Washington, D.C.: The Conservation Foundation, 1977), 15; Opal Snyder, "History of the Great Smoky Mountains National Park" (master's thesis, George Peabody College for Teachers), 11–13.

38. *Knoxville News-Sentinel*, 13 April 1927; Campbell, 36. For details on the "Cammerer Line," see map, Paul Adams Papers, TSTATE.

39. *Great Smoky Mountains*, back page; *Knoxville Free Press*, 20 April 1927; *New York Times*, 25 January 1926; *Great Smoky Mountains*, 12.

40. *Progressive Labor*, 20 April 1927; *Knoxville News-Sentinel*, 19 April 1927; Carlos Campbell, correspondence to J. Ross Eakin, 3 March 1932, Land Acquisition Files, Box XV-2, GSMNP.

41. *An Act to Provide for the Acquisition of Parks and Recreational Facilities in the Great Smoky Mountains of North Carolina*, 25 February 1927 (Asheville, N.C.: Jarrett's Press, 1927), 10; *Knoxville Journal*, 21 April 1927; *Knoxville News-Sentinel*, 22 April 1927; *Knoxville News-Sentinel*, 6 April 1928.

42. Newhall, Nancy, *A Contribution to the Heritage of Every American: The Conservation Activities of John D. Rockefeller, Jr.* (New York: Alfred A. Knopf, 1957), ix; Joseph W. Ernest, ed., *Worthwhile Places: Correspondence of John D. Rockefeller, Jr. and Horace M. Albright* (New York: Fordham University Press, 1991), 5–6.

43. Darwin Lambert, *The Undying Past of Shenandoah National Park* (Boulder, Colo.: Roberts, Rinehart, 1989), 239–41.

44. Cammerer to Mark Squires, 21 April 1928; Jorn R. Aust to Beardsley Ruml, 15 November 1928; memorandum from Cammerer, 11 February 1929; Laura Spelman Rockefeller Memorial, Record Group III, Subseries 4, Box 13, Folders 144 and 145, Rockefeller Archives, New York.

45. James B. Wright, "Testimony of James B. Wright" (manuscript, North Carolina Collection, Wilson Library, University of North Carolina, Chapel Hill, n.d.).

46. *Knoxville News-Sentinel*, 9 March 1931, 2 April 1929, and 9 April 1929. The actual number of attendees at this "mass meeting" was not given. See also Cammerer to Kenneth Chorley, Laura Spelman Rockefeller Memorial, Record Group III, Subseries 4, Box 13, Folder 145, Rockefeller Archives, New York; Campbell, 77–78. Horace Albright, director of the National Park Service 1929–1933, held slightly more paternal attitudes toward the mountain people, but he did not oppose condemnation. See Horace Albright, interview by Michael Frome, 1964, Oral History Collection, GSMNP.

47. W. J. Damtoft, interview by Elwood R. Maunder, 1959, Forest History Society, Durham, N.C.; Robertson, interview by Elwood P. Maunder, 1959, Forest History Society, Durham, N.C.; Smathers, X; Campbell, 83.

48. John Oliver, letter to John Jones, 17 July 1928, Land Acquisition Files, Individual Tracts, Box III-30, GSMNP; *Knoxville Journal*, 29 July 1929.

49. W. H. Woodbury to Zebulon Weaver, 26 March 1932, Zebulon Weaver Papers, Hunter Library, Western Carolina University, Cullowhee, N.C.; Dunn, 249–51; "Data for Mr. Rhoades Report," North Carolina National Park Commission Records, North Carolina State Archives, Raleigh; Zenith Whaley, interview by author, 1989, tape recording in author's possession.

50. Winfred Cagle, interview by William Weaver, 1973; Alie Newman Maples, interview by Jane Whitney, 1973, Oral History Collection, GSMNP. See also J. R.

Eakin to David C. Chapman, 15 December 1933, Land Acquisition Files, GSMNP, for additional examples of life savings lost in bank failures.

51. This estimate was compiled from Lands Transferred to the Federal Government and Land Acquisition Files, GSMNP; North Carolina Park Commission Records, North Carolina State Archives, Raleigh.

52. Appraisals of Interior Holdings, Land Acquisition Files, GSMNP; North Carolina Park Commission Records, North Carolina State Archives, Raleigh.

53. A. C. Shaw, "Synopsis of Land Status," 25 October 1926, Land Acquisition Files; D. C. Chapman to E. D. Demaray, 27 July 1934, Chapman Collection, GSMNP.

54. J. Ross Eakin to Arno Cammerer, 19 September 1931; Arno Cammerer to J. Ross Eakin, 20 May 1932, Land Acquisition Files, GSMNP.

55. Minutes of meeting of the North Carolina Park Commission, 14 December 1929, North Carolina Park Commission Records, North Carolina State Archives, Raleigh; J. R. Eakin to director, National Park Service, 8 October 1932; Eakin to director, 21 January 1935; memorandum, Hillory Tolson, acting director, National Park Service, 16 August 1943, Land Acquisition Files, Box XIV, Folders 3, 7, and 10, GSMNP.

56. This estimate was compiled from Lands Transferred to the Federal Government and Land Acquisition Files, GSMNP; North Carolina Park Commission Records, North Carolina State Archives, Raleigh. Population was figured by using the average farm population statistics from the U.S. Department of Commerce and multiplying by the number of farms. Tenancy was figured by multiplying the average tenancy rate in each county by the number of farms in that county.

57. Ray Lyman Wilbur, letter to Verne Rhoades, 16 May 1929, North Carolina Park Commission Records, North Carolina State Archives, Raleigh; *U.S. Code*, 16, 403E; Cammerer to Chapman, 28 May 1928; Land Acquisition Files, Individual Tracts, Box III, Folder 43; Cammerer to Chapman, 24 May 1933, Great Smoky Mountains Conservation Association, Box XI, Folder 15, GSMNP; Clifford Elmore Oakley, interview by Bill Landry, 19 May 1990, Landry Collection, GSMNP.

58. Testimony of Colonel Chapman, September 1939, Box I–29, Great Smoky Mountains Conservation Association Collection, GSMNP. Those disgruntled over his control of construction efforts called him the "Czar of Elkmont." See also Morrell, 7–8.

59. O. C. Goodwin, "A History of Forestry in North Carolina," in North Carolina Forest History Series, Keith A. Argow, ed., vol. 1, no. 3 (North Carolina State University, Raleigh, January 1969), 12; G. F. Gravatt, "Chestnut Blight," U.S. Department of Agriculture, Farmers' Bulletin No. 1641 (Washington, D.C.: U.S. Government Printing Office, 1930), 3.

60. G. G. Copp, "A Disease Which Threatens the American Chestnut Tree," *Scientific American* 95 (15 December 1906): 451; George H. Hepting, "Death of the American Chestnut," *Journal of Forest History* (July 1974): 62, 65; *Southern Lumberman*, 6 August 1910, 38C; 20 August 1910, 27; Haven Metcalf, "The Chestnut

Tree Blight: An Incurable Disease That Has Destroyed Dollars Worth of Trees," *Scientific American* 106 (16 March 1912): 241–42; "Fighting the Chestnut Bark Disease," *Scientific American* 108 (5 April 1913): 314; *Southern Lumberman*, 1 February 1913, 21.

61. Steve Oak, interview by author, March 1999, tape recording in author's possession.

62. "Report of Committee Appointed by Western Carolina Lumber and Timber Association," 25 July 1925, 4; Ellen Mason Exum, "Tree in a Coma," *American Forests* (November–December 1992): 20; D. V. Baxter, "Deterioration of Chestnut in the Southern Appalachians," Technical Bulletin No. 257 (Washington, D.C.: U.S. Department of Agriculture, 1931), 19; Reuben Robertson, interview by Jerry Mander, 1959, FHS.

63. Frank W. Woods and Royal E. Shanks, "Natural Replacement of Chestnut by Other Species in the Great Smoky Mountains National Park," *Ecology* 40 (July 1969): 350.

64. Walter Cole, interview by Charles Grossman, 1965, Oral History Collection, GSMNP; James M. Hill, "Wildlife Value of *Castanea dentata* and the Historical Decline of the Chestnut and its Future Use in Restoration of Natural Areas" (unpublished manuscript, Randolph-Macon College, 1993); Stephen Nash, "The Blighted Chestnut," *National Parks* (July–August 1988): 16.

65. Gudger Palmer, interview by Bill Landry, 1988, Landry Collection; Paul Woody, interview by Kathleen Manscill, 1984, and J. Roy Whaley, interview by V. R. Bender and Robert Madden, 1973, Oral History Collection, GSMNP.

66. See W. O. Whittle, "Movement of Population from the Smoky Mountains Area" (Knoxville: University of Tennessee, 1934). Whittle attempted to establish the success of mountaineers by surveying only those mountain people who stayed in the area. Typical newspaper coverage can be seen in the *Knoxville News-Sentinel*, 27 September 1931.

67. Eakin to Frank Bond, chairman, U.S. Geographic Board, 25 October 1932, "Suggested Changes of Local Names in the Great Smoky Mountains National Park," Vertical Files, and Mary Ruth Chiles, "Geographic Place Names in the Great Smoky Mountains National Park," GSMNP; *Greensboro News*, 22 July 1930. Kephart also was on the North Carolina committee until his death in an automobile accident.

68. Chapman to Horace Kephart, 20 February 1930, Great Smoky Mountains Conservation Association Collection, GSMNP.

4. Landscaping a Park out of the Wilderness

1. *Superintendent's Report*, March 1933, GSMNP.

2. *Superintendent's Report*, February 1931, December 1931. For a description of Eakin, see Horace Albright, interview by Michael Frome, 1964, and George Preston, interview by Bill Landry, 1989, Landry Collection, GSMNP.

3. Laura Thornborough, "Smoky Mountain Park," *Washington Star* (1 April

1929): 5; Guy Bell, "Two Mountain Flower Festivals Set for June in the Great Smokies," *Southeastern Flower Grower* (April 1933): 9, 13, Vertical Files, GSMNP; *Superintendent's Report*, November 1936, GSMNP.

4. Joe Frank Manley, interview by Bill Landry, 1988, Landry Collection, GSMNP [Manley's emphasis].

5. Horace Albright, "Research in the National Parks," *Scientific Monthly* 36 (June 1933): 483–501.

6. *Superintendent's Report*, November 1931, December 1931, February 1932, July 1932, October 1932, and January 1936, GSMNP. E. V. Romarok's remarks do not take into account that the New England cottontail (*Sylvilagus transitionalis*), also found in the Smokies, lives in more wooded areas.

7. *Superintendent's Report*, May and June 1932, May and June 1935, August and November 1936, June and July 1937, GSMNP; Lucy Black Ownby, Delce Mae Carver Bryant, interviews by Bill Landry, 1989, Landry Collection, GSMNP; Fred Chappell, "The Storyteller," in *I Am One of You Forever* (Baton Rouge: Louisiana State University Press, 1985), 99–100. Of course, in Chappell's book this is a fictional incident and therefore may not relate to this actual fence at all, but it seems an accurate depiction of the attitudes of mountain people and bears.

8. Lucy Ownby, interview by Bill Landry, 1989, Landry Collection, GSMNP; P. Audley Whaley, interview by William Alston, 1975, Oral History Collection, GSMNP; *Superintendent's Report*, January 1937 and October 1938; December 1939; January, February, November, and December 1940, GSMNP.

9. National Park Service, *Manual of the Branch of Forestry* (Washington, D.C.: Government Printing Office, 19 July 1935); Printed Materials Collection, FDRL.

10. *Superintendent's Report*, March 1931, April 1931, May 1931, November 1931, August 1932, November 1932, March 1933, June 1934, and August 1934; John Ise, *Our National Park Policy: A Critical History* (Baltimore: Johns Hopkins Press, 1961), 594.

11. *Superintendent's Report*, April 1935 and May 1936; Laura Thornborough, *Great Smoky Mountains* (New York: Crowell Publishing, 1942), 34. See also Campbell, "The Great Smoky Mountains National Park," 23.

12. Press release, 20 February 1939, in *Superintendent's Report*, February 1939, GSMNP; Thornborough, 34.

13. Press release, 23 February 1933, in *Superintendent's Report*, February 1933, GSMNP. A year later the limit fell to a maximum of ten trout, 10 inches minimum, with only artificial bait. See also *Superintendent's Report*, February and November 1934, GSMNP.

14. Raymond J. Caldwell, interview by Bill Landry, 1989, Landry Collection, GSMNP.

15. *Superintendent's Report*, April, September, and November 1931; January 1932; and August 1933, GSMNP.

16. *Superintendent's Report*, October 1932.

17. *Superintendent's Report*, January and February 1934.

18. H. C. Wilburn to John T. Needham, 20 May 1931, North Carolina Park Commission Collection; *Superintendent's Report*, March 1931; July and September 1932, GSMNP.

19. *Superintendent's Report*, August 1931, January 1932, and August 1936, GSMNP.

20. Chapman to J. R. Eakin, 26 July 1933, Chapman Collection, GSMNP.

21. Eakin to Chapman, 15 December 1933, Land Acquisition Files, GSMNP.

22. Charles L. Perdue Jr. and Nancy Martin-Perdue, "Appalachian Facts and Fables: A Case Study of the Shenandoah National Park Removals," *Appalachian Journal* 7 (Autumn–Winter 1979–1980): 90.

23. *Tulsa World*, 31 July 1930; *National Geographic News Bulletin*, 7 December 1936, 1–2; *Winston-Salem Sentinel*, 27 April 1930; *State Magazine* (19 September 1936): 3; *Asheville Citizen-Times*, 6 December 1936.

24. *Knoxville News-Sentinel*, 25 August 1929, 25 May 1930; Ise, 620–21. The National Park Service in those early years thought it could be self-supporting. Once roads and administration facilities were established, auto permits, concessions, receipts from public utilities, and the sale of timber or mineral rights would bring in enough appropriations to cover operation costs.

25. *Superintendent's Report*, May 1931, GSMNP.

26. *Superintendent's Report*, July 1931, January and February 1932, GSMNP; Donald C. Swain, *Wilderness Defender* (Chicago: University of Chicago Press, 1970), 210; summary of communication to Thomas H. McDonald, 15 July 1935, Official Files, U.S. Department of Interior, FDRL; Arno B. Cammerer to Charles Webb, 12 October 1937, Laura Spelman Rockefeller Memorial, Series III, Subseries 4, Box 13, Folder 149, Rockefeller Archives.

27. FDR to Frederic Delano, 22 January 1936, President's Personal File, Box 430; FDR to Joseph Black, 21 September 1937, President's Personal File, Box 349, FDRL.

28. *Superintendent's Report*, 1932, GSMNP.

29. *Knoxville Journal*, 30 October 1932; Earl Huskey and Bob Brown, interview by Bill Landry, 1990, Landry Collection, GSMNP.

30. Franklin D. Roosevelt, "The President's Greeting," *The Civilian Conservation Corps, "Builder of Men"* (Washington, D.C.: Happy Days Publishing Company, 1934), 32. FDR to Robert Fechner, 5 April 1938, President's Personal File, Box 349, FDRL.

31. Walter W. Miller, "The Civilian Conservation Corps in East Tennessee and the Great Smoky Mountains National Park, 1933–1942" (unpublished research paper, GSMNP, 1974), 2–8; *Superintendent's Report*, July 1934.

32. *Superintendent's Report*, August 1933; "Narrative Report on Emergency Conservation Work, January 1934," CCC Records, GSMNP; Charles J. Weeks, "The Eastern Cherokee and the New Deal," *North Carolina Historical Review* 53 (July 1976): 310.

33. Charlotte Pyle, "CCC Camps in the Great Smoky Mountains National Park"

(unpublished manuscript, GSMNP, 1979). *Superintendent's Report*, May 1933 and January 1934.

34. *Superintendent's Report*, June 1933, December 1934, July 1935, January 1936, July 1937, May 1938, and May 1939.

35. Arthur Stupka, interview by Bill Landry, Landry Collection, GSMNP.

36. Robert W. Blythe, "Draft, Historic Resource Study: Great Smoky Mountains National Park" (unpublished manuscript, Southeast Support Office, National Park Service, 13 April 1998), 85–89.

37. *Superintendent's Report*, April 1934, May and June 1935, March and October 1937.

38. *Superintendent's Report*, January 1932, February 1933, and April 1935; Frank Jackson, interview by Glenn Cardwell and Kathleen Manscill, 1981, Oral History Collection, GSMNP.

39. *Superintendent's Report*, May 1932, May 1933, March 1934, and April 1936, GSMNP. Although other historians have noted that sometimes foresters mistook traditional burning practices—to keep down snakes, bugs, and ticks—for arson, there was no evidence of this in the early management records. It is certainly possible, however, that controlled burning "got out of hand" and the rangers recorded it as intentional or malicious. See John Shea, "Our Pappies Burned the Woods," *American Forests* 46 (April 1940): 159–62.

40. *Superintendent's Report*, March 1931, January 1932, February 1932, March 1932, September 1932, November 1932, December 1932, January 1934, March 1935, April 1936, December 1936, March 1937, April 1937, November 1937, February 1938, April 1938, October 1938, and April 1939. With the strong relationship between mountain men and their dogs, the park practice of dispatching dogs "running loose" may have been another cause, according to Jim Shelton, interviewed by Mary Lindsay, 1985, Oral History Collection, GSMNP.

41. *Superintendent's Report*, October and November 1936, November 1938, GSMNP.

42. *Superintendent's Report*, January 1937 and November 1940; P. Audley Whaley, interview by William Alston, 1975, Oral History Collection, GSMNP; Paul J. Adams, *Mount LeConte* (Knoxville: Holston Printing, 1966), 48.

43. *Superintendent's Report*, June 1932, November 1933, February 1935, June 1936, October 1936, February 1937, July 1934, October 1934, November 1934, March 1934, October 1934, June 1939, and April 1940, GSMNP.

44. *Superintendent's Report*, February 1934 and September 1935; Blythe, 101–2.

45. See Phoebe Cutler, *The Public Landscape of the New Deal* (New Haven: Yale University Press, 1985), 57, 64; Blythe, 90–94; Frank A. Waugh, *Landscape Conservation* (Washington, D.C.: U.S. Department of Interior, 1935), 3.

46. *Superintendent's Report*, March 1935, GSMNP.

47. *Superintendent's Report*, September 1936, GSMNP.

48. The park received a PWA allotment of $28,250; *Superintendent's Report*, November 1933 and September 1935, GSMNP.

49. *Superintendent's Report*, September 1934; Amos Reagen, interview by Joseph Hall, 1939, Oral History Collection, GSMNP.

50. H. M. Jennison, Brushy Trail and Hughes Ridge, 1935, photo collection, GSMNP.

51. *Superintendent's Report*, July 1933, December 1934, and August 1937, GSMNP.

52. *Report, Emergency Conservation Work, April 1, 1934 to June 30, 1934*, CCC Records; *Superintendent's Report*, June 1937, August and September 1938, and January 1939, GSMNP.

53. *Superintendent's Report*, September 1933; January, June, and November 1934; June 1937, GSMNP.

54. William C. Tweed and Laura E. Soulliere, *National Park Rustic Architecture, 1916–1942* (National Park Service, Western Regional Office, 1977), 35.

55. Blythe, 110, 124, 126.

56. See Williams, 130–32; *Asheville Citizen-Times*, 24 December 1936; and *Superintendent's Report*, January 1937, GSMNP; Hall, 6.

57. *Superintendent's Report*, May 1936, November 1937, and January 1939, GSMNP; Paul Adams to A. F. Ganier, 20 November 1934, Paul J. Adams Papers, Box 5, TSTATE.

58. Alden B. Stevens, "A Preliminary Report on a General Museum Development Plan for the Great Smoky Mountains National Park," 31 July 1935; H. C. Wilburn to J. Ross Eakin, 22 March 1939, 29 March 1939, 6 June 1939, and 11 June 1940, H. C. Wilburn Papers, GSMNP.

59. H. C. Wilburn to J. Ross Eakin, 24 March 1939; Wilburn to Eakin, 24 March 1939, H. C. Wilburn Papers, Hunter Library, Western Carolina University, Cullowhee, N.C.

60. Robert Sterling Yard to Mr. MacRaye, 1 November 1934; Harvey Broome to Gordon L. Browning, 31 May 1937, Harvey Broome Papers, GSMNP; Robert Sterling Yard, "Will the States Control the Great Smokies?" *National Park Bulletin* (June 1937): 15, Vertical Files, GSMNP. Yard, director of the new National Parks and Conservation Association, was a close friend of Cammerer.

61. Campbell, 117–21; Ickes to FDR, 28 July 1933, Cammerer to Governor Browning, 26 July 1937, Official Files, U.S. Department of Interior, Boxes 14 and 15, FDRL; Federal Writers' Project, *North Carolina: A Guide to the Old North State* (Chapel Hill: University of North Carolina Press, 1939), 559–61; Isabelle F. Story, *Our National Parks* (U.S. Government Printing Office, 1936), 86–88.

62. Frome, 217–21; Campbell, 121–25; Ise, 255, 260–61.

63. *Superintendent's Report*, April 1940, GSMNP.

64. Frank W. Woods, "Natural Replacement of Chestnut in the Great Smoky Mountains Following the Chestnut Blight." Paper presented at the Annual Meeting of the Tennessee Academy of Science (28 November 1952), 2–3; Paul J. Adams, "Birds of LeConte" (unpublished manuscript, Paul J. Adams Papers, Box 6, TSTATE).

65. Paul J. Adams, "Birds of LeConte" (unpublished manuscript, Paul J. Adams Papers, Box 6, TSTATE).

66. *Superintendent's Report*, April 1940, GSMNP.

67. *Superintendent's Report*, April, May, June, October, and November 1939; February, April, and September 1940, GSMNP.

68. *Superintendent's Report*, December 1937, GSMNP.

69. P. Audley Whaley, interview by William Alston, 1975, Oral History Collection, GSMNP.

70. *Superintendent's Report*, September 1934; Carlos Campbell, "The Great Smoky Mountains National Park: The Rooftop of Eastern America," *Tennessee Wildlife* 3 (December 1939): 23G; Alan Kelly, J. S. Griffith, and Ronald D. Jones, "Changes in Distribution of Trout in Great Smoky Mountains National Park, 1900–1977," Technical Papers of the U.S. Fish and Wildlife Service, No. 102 (Washington, D.C.: U.S. Fish and Wildlife Service, 1980).

71. *Superintendent's Report*, July 1935; D. J. Kucken, J. S. Davis, J. W. Petranka, and C. K. Smith, "Anakeesta Stream Acidification and Metal Contamination: Effects on a Salamander Community," *Journal of Environmental Quality* 23 (November–December 1994): 1311–77.

72. *Superintendent's Report*, March and April 1934, February 1936, and July 1939, GSMNP.

73. Harold Ickes to FDR, 3 April 1944, Official Files, U.S. Department of Interior, Box 16, FDRL.

74. *New York Herald Tribune*, 1 September 1940.

75. *New York Times*, 5 August 1998.

76. *Superintendent's Report*, June 1934, June and December 1940.

77. Press release, 20 February 1939, in *Superintendent's Report*, February 1939; *Superintendent's Report*, July 1936, June 1935, May and July 1937, GSMNP.

78. *Superintendent's Report*, October 1939 and October 1940, GSMNP.

79. *Smoky Mountains Hiking Club Handbook* (Knoxville: Smoky Mountains Hiking Club, 1942), 56. Stephen George Myers, *The Smokies Guide* (Asheville, N.C.: Stephens Press, 1941); Roderick Peattie, *The Great Smokies and the Blue Ridge: The Story of the Southern Appalachians* (New York: Vanguard Press, 1943).

80. Lucinda Oakley Ogle, interview by Paul Sagan, 1990, Oral History Collection; *Superintendent's Report*, November 1938, GSMNP; *Knoxville Journal*, 21 September 1939.

81. Arno Cammerer, "Excerpts from Speeches, Letters and Press Releases Concerning the Great Smoky Mountains National Park Which May be Used in Fashioning a Dedication Address," President's Personal File, Box 2265, FDRL.

82. Thornborough, 9; Campbell, 129–30.

83. *Asheville Citizen-Times*, 3 September 1940; Franklin Delano Roosevelt, "Address of the President," President's Personal File, Box 2260, FDRL; see also FDR to Director McEntee, 28 March 1942, President's Personal File, Box 2265, FDRL.

5. A Lake in the National Defense

1. C. M. Terry, "Recent Developments in Water Recreation," Division of Reservoir Properties, general correspondence, Box 38, TVA Records, FRCEP; National Park Service, "A Study of the Park and Recreation Problems of the United States" (Washington, D.C.: U.S. Government Printing Office, 1941), 22, 39.

2. Fred J. Cohn, "Big Majority of County's People on Relief," *Asheville Citizen-Times* (19 February 1939): 1A.

3. C. T. Barker, "Navigation Benefits from Fontana Reservoir, March 20, 1936," records of the TVA, U.S. Department of Commerce, Box 107, FRCEP; Wilmon Henry Droze, *High Dams and Slack Waters: TVA Rebuilds a River* (Baton Rouge: Louisiana State University Press, 1965), 19–41, 53–54.

4. To understand early-twentieth-century attitudes toward flooding, see George Fillmore Swain, *Conservation of Water by Storage* (New Haven: Yale University Press, 1914), 242–84; Roy Talbert Jr., *FDR's Utopian: Arthur Morgan of the TVA* (Jackson: University of Mississippi Press, 1987), 108–27. For Morgan's opinion of the Army Corps of Engineers, see Arthur Morgan, *Dams and Other Disasters: A Century of the Army Corps of Engineers in Civil Works* (Boston: Porter Sargent, 1971); Michael J. McDonald and John Muldowny, *TVA and the Dispossessed: The Resettlement of Population in the Norris Dam Area* (Knoxville: University of Tennessee Press, 1982), 4, 217.

5. Chapman to Eakin, 12 July 1934; W. R. Mize to Chapman, 2 October 1934; Subject File, Box I–16, Chapman Collection, GSMNP.

6. Arthur E. Morgan, *The Making of TVA* (Buffalo: Prometheus Books, 1974), 106, 108, 113; Walter L. Creese, *TVA's Public Planning: The Vision, the Reality* (Knoxville: University of Tennessee Press, 1990), 192–93. For a detailed look at the issues between Lilienthal and Morgan, see the President's Secretary Files, Box 166, FDRL.

7. Lilienthal, *The Journals of David Lilienthal* (New York: Harper & Row, 1964), 115. See also *TVA: Democracy on the March* (New York: Harper and Row, 1944); Morgan, *The Making of TVA*, 178.

8. David Lilienthal, "The Restoration of Economic Equality among the Regions of the U.S." Address before the Thirty-eighth Annual Meeting of Newspaper Publishers, 21 May 1940; J. L. Harris Papers, Special Collections, Robert W. Woodruff Library, Emory University, Atlanta; *Jackson County Journal*, 11 June 1942.

9. *Bryson City Times*, 17 October 1940, 22 May 1941, 29 May 1941, and 10 July 1941; *Jackson County Journal*, 13 March 1941, 29 May 1941. For pronunciation, Alberta and Carson Brewer, *Valley So Wild: A Folk History* (Knoxville: East Tennessee Historical Society, 1975), 258. In the nineteenth century, people called the community Welch after a prominent family, but after Whiting Lumber Company arrived, an unknown employee named the post office Japan, presumably because it was so far from everything else, and the name stuck. After Pearl Harbor, a patriotic war committee from New York state tried to get the residents to change the name Japan on their post office. Residents supported patriotic efforts and appreciated the concern, but they were happy with the name as it was.

10. Creese, 191–93; Morgan, *The Making of TVA*, 174; Lilienthal, *Journals*, 350. See also Russell D. Parker, "Alcoa, Tennessee: The Early Years, 1919–1939," *East Tennessee Historical Society's Publications* 48 (1976): 84–103; TVA, *The Fontana Project*, 301, 478. The estimated cost (Lilienthal's) was $28 million, but the final project cost was just short of $70 million. TVA, *Annual Report for 1945* (Washington, D.C.: U.S. Government Printing Office, 1945), appendix.

11. David Lilienthal, "Politics and the Management of the Public's Business." Address before Knoxville Kiwanis Club, 9 July 1942; J. L. Harris Papers, Box 22, Special Collections, Robert Woodruff Library, Emory University, Atlanta. In recent years, several writers have reported the Fontana was needed for Oak Ridge, the Tennessee site of the Manhattan Project. However, the author searched the National Archives, Top Secret Correspondence of Manhattan District Engineers, 1942–1946, Reel 5, Files 11–19, and no reference to Fontana could be found among the TVA reports.

12. *Bryson City Times*, 20 November 1941, 27 November 1941, 2 October 1941, 15 January 1942, 22 January 1942, 5 February 1942, 17 June 1943, 22 July 1943, and 29 July 1943.

13. *Bryson City Times*, 9 October 1941; Schlemmer quote reprinted in *North Shore Historical Association* (Spring 1994): 4; memorandum, Maurice Heale to H. L. Fruend, 13 February 1941, TVA Record Group 142: 138, FRCEP.

14. TVA, *The Fontana Project*, 346, 351. Mary Jane Loue, *Voices in the Valley: Remembering World War II, Excerpts from TVA Oral History Interviews* (Knoxville: TVA, 1993), 5; TVA, *Annual Report for 1942* (Washington, D.C.: U.S. Government Printing Office, 1943), 22. For an excellent account of Fontana, see Stephen Wallace Taylor, "Building the Back of Beyond: Government Authority, Community Life, and Economic Development in the Upper Little Tennessee Valley, 1880–1992" (Ph.D. diss., University of Tennessee, 1996); Taylor does a fine job on the trials of black workers, 112–17; "slacking off" quote, 135.

15. Lucile Kirby Royden, *The Village of Five Lives: Fontana of the Great Smoky Mountains* (Fontana Dam: Government Services, Inc., 1964), 18–21. Fontana was named for an Italian naturalist, Felice Fontana, who visited the Smokies during the nineteenth century, according to the *Bryson City Times*, 28 January 1943; TVA, *The Fontana Project*, 193–236.

16. John K. Baily, "Shack Development Control, Fontana Area," TVA-Reservoir Property Management Division (1 May 1944), TVA Record Group 142: 6, FRCEP; Arnold Monteith, interview by Bill Landry, 1989, Landry Collection, GSMNP.

17. James B. Light, memorandum to superintendent, 8 January 1942; J. R. Eakin, memorandum to director, 13 January 1942; J. R. Eakin to L. F. Simons, TVA, 30 January 1942, Management Files, Box VIII, GSMNP. This was neither the first nor the last concession made by the park to national defense during World War II. One company of army officers and men occupied the park for a year, and a group of conscientious objectors was stationed in an old CCC camp. The National Park Service also offered to permit the development of any mineral deposits found in the national park needed "during the period of emergency," but none apparently were

taken. *Superintendent's Report*, January 1942; H. C. Amick to Arthur Stupka, 13 January 1942, and E. M. Lisle to national park superintendents, 22 May 1941, Mining, Vertical Files, GSMNP.

18. The dam, located in Nevada and Arizona, is today called Hoover Dam. Started under the administration of an unpopular president, Hoover Dam did not receive the name of its founder until 1947. U.S. Department of Interior, *The Construction of Hoover Dam* (Las Vegas: KC Publications, 1976 [28th edition]), 2, 13, 18.

19. R. A. Wilhelm, memorandum to superintendent, 31 December 1941, Management Files, Box VIII, GSMNP; TVA, *The Fontana Project*, 261; TVA, *Annual Report for 1943* (Washington, D.C.: U.S. Government Printing Office, 1943), 22; *Sylva Herald and Ruralite*, 12 July 1944.

20. TVA, *The Fontana Project*, 357–88, 494, 466; Arnold Monteith, interview by Bill Landry, 1989, Landry Collection, GSMNP; W. M. Broadfoot and H. L Williston, "Flooding Effects on Southern Forests," *Journal of Forestry* (September 1973): 584–88.

21. James B. Light, memorandum to superintendent, 16 February 1942, Management Files, Box VIII; J. T. Needham, memorandum to superintendent, 12 December 1942; J. R. Eakin to H. V. Gass, 4 January 1943; Howard Ellis Davis to J. R. Eakin, 15 January 1943, Management Files, Box VIII; J. J. Goulden, memorandum, 19 January 1943, Management Files, Box VIII, GSMNP.

22. *Superintendent's Report*, 16 July 1943.

23. Conrad Wirth, memorandum to director, 15 September 1942, Management Files, Box VIII, GSMNP.

24. Walter H. Sheffield, memorandum to regional chief of planning, 12 July 1943, Management Files, Box VIII; D. E. Lee, memorandum to director, 3 October 1941, Management Files, Box VIII, GSMNP. For more on overpurchase policy, see McDonald and Muldowny, 127–36.

25. Agreement reprinted in *Transportation Concepts* (Washington, D.C.: U.S. Department of Interior, 1971), 47–49.

26. *Jackson County Journal*, 33 April 1943; J. R. Eakin to regional director, National Park Service, 27 July 1942; J. R. Eakin to regional director, 3 August 1942; memorandum for the files, Ben H. Thompson, 10 September 1942, Management Files, Box VIII, GSMNP. Retirement of "marginal lands" was also part of TVA's stated management goals. *Bryson City Times*, 3 December 1942, 24 December 1942; *Sylva Herald*, 4 August 1943; resume of status, H. J. Spelman, division engineer, 11 June 1946, Management Files, Box VII, GSMNP; Taylor, 156.

27. T. J. Woofter Jr., "Preliminary Work Memorandum: Submarginal Counties of the Southeast" and "Statistical Summary of Agriculture" (25 October 1938), TVA Record Group 142: 18, FRCEP; TVA, "Tentative Outline of Material to Be Presented before Special Committee Investigating the Interstate Migration of Destitute Citizens" (25 October 1940), TVA Record Group 142: 38, FRCEP. For more about mountaineer stereotyping under Lilienthal, see David Whisnant, *Modernizing the Mountaineer* (Boone, N.C.: Appalachian Consortium Press, 1980), 43–69.

28. Arnold J. Hyde, "Almond-Judson Community, Fontana Area" (TVA: 1 June

1944, Reservoir Property Management Department, Population Readjustment Division), 2, 12, TVA Record Group 142, FRCEP; see also Arnold Monteith, interview by Bill Landry, 1989, Landry Collection, GSMNP; TVA, *The Fontana Project*, 486.

29. Hyde, "Almond-Judson," 4–5; Arnold Monteith, interview by Bill Landry, 1989, Landry Collection, GSMNP.

30. Hyde, "Stecoah Community-Fontana Area" (TVA, Reservoir Property Management Department, 1 October 1944), 3–5, TVA Record Group 142, FRCEP.

31. Alice Moore Posey, interview by author, 1990, tape recording in author's possession.

32. Hyde, "Almond-Judson," 1–2; hearings, Subcommittee of the Committee on Agriculture and Forestry, 16–19 March 1942 (Washington, D.C.: U.S. Government Printing Office, 1942), 211.

33. Wayne Moore, "TVA and Farm Communities of the Lower Tennessee Valley" (Ph.D. diss., University of Rochester, 1990); Charles J. McCarthy, "Land Acquisition Policies and Proceedings in TVA: A Study of the Role of Land Acquisition in a Regional Agency," *Ohio State Law Journal* 10 (Winter 1949): 46–63; Eugene Lowe, interview by Bill Landry, 1989, Landry Collection, GSMNP. At Fontana, 8.2 percent of the landowners were forced to leave through a declaration of taking. This represents a relatively high figure for TVA dams. TVA, *The Fontana Project*, 478.

34. Oliver, 92.

35. Minutes of staff meeting, Population Readjustment Division personnel, 20 March 1941; TVA, "Property Taxes, Improvement Taxes, Property Sold to the State for Delinquent Taxes," TVA Record Group 142; minutes of staff meeting, Population Readjustment Division personnel, 20 March 1941, TVA Record Group 142: 138, FRCEP.

36. Hyde, "Almond-Judson," 6–7, 12; case files, TVA Regional Property Management Division, TVA Record Group 142, FRCEP.

37. Minutes of staff meeting, Population Readjustment Division personnel, 13 May 1941, TVA Record Group 142: 138, FRCEP.

38. Case files, TVA Regional Property Management Division, TVA Record Group 142, FRCEP.

39. J. R. Eakin to E. W. Cowling Jr., 25 August 1943; Philip G. Rust to J. R. Eakin, 11 September 1943; J. R. Eakin to Philip G. Rust, 16 September 1943, Management Files, Box VIII, GSMNP; *Superintendent's Report*, November and December 1944; Louise Oliver, interview by Bill Landry, 1989, Landry Collection, GSMNP.

40. *Sylva Herald and Ruralite*, 25 October 1944.

41. Rome C. Sharp, "TVA Readjustment: Proctor Community, Fontana Area" (TVA, 1 May 1944), 1–3, TVA Record Group 142, FRCEP; Henry Posey, interview by author and Michael Kline, 1990, tape recording in author's possession.

42. Case files, TVA Regional Property Management Division; Sharp, "TVA Population Readjustment: Proctor Community," TVA Record Group 142: 5, FRCEP.

43. Hillory A. Tolson to Howard K. Menhinick, 5 April 1944, Management Files, Box VIII, GSMNP. Memorandum, park ranger Morrell to superintendent, 17 January 1950, Management Files, Box VIII, GSMNP.

44. Oliver, 92–93.

45. *Asheville Citizen-Times*, 17 March 1945; *Knoxville Journal*, 22 July 1945; *Knoxville News-Sentinel*, 22 July 1945.

46. File notes, A. H. Zimmerman, 29 September 1944; Gordon R. Clapp to J. Ross Eakin, 16 October 1944, Division of Reservoir Properties, general correspondence, TVA Record Group 142: 30, FRCEP; Herbert Hudson to J. Ed Campbell, 21 March 1945 and 28 July 1945; E. B. Whitaker to Herbert Hudson, 27 August 1945; HEB to JJG, 5 June 1945; Felix A. Grisette to Allard J. Gray, 28 May 1946, Division of Reservoir Properties, general correspondence, TVA Record Group 142: 30, FRCEP.

47. *TVA vs. Welch*, 25 March 1946, No. 528. Interestingly, most of the legal precedents used to support TVA's case involved railroad rights-of-way. It is important to note that by 1946 five of the justices, including Black, were Roosevelt appointees. See also William E. Leuchtenburg, *Franklin D. Roosevelt and the New Deal* (New York: Harper & Row, 1963), 238.

48. Case files, TVA Regional Property Management Division, TVA Record Group 142, FRCEP; TVA, *The Fontana Project*, 486; Alice Moore Posey, interview by author and Michael Kline, 1990, tape recording in author's possession; Henry Posey, interview by author and Michael Kline, 1991, tape recording in author's possession.

49. Division of Reservoir Properties, "Family Removal and Relocation," general correspondence, 1940–1965, TVA Record Group 142: 52; "Annual Report, Reservoir Property Management Department," TVA Record Group 142: 8, FRCEP.

50. TVA, *Annual Report for 1945* (Washington, D.C.: U.S. Government Printing Office, 1945), 1; *Superintendent's Report*, January 1945; Indian mounds, photos by H. C. Wilburn, GSMNP; Daniel J. Lenihan, ed., *The Final Report of the National Reservoir Inundation Study* 1 (Santa Fe: U.S. Department of Interior, 1989), 4–5.

51. International Council of Scientific Unions, Scientific Committee on Problems of the Environment, *Man-Made Lakes as Modified Ecosystems* (Paris: International Council of Scientific Unions, 1972), 50–52; Jim Gasque, *Hunting and Fishing in the Great Smokies* (New York: Alfred A. Knopf, 1948), 78.

52. William Stolzenburg, "The Mussels' Message," *The Nature Conservancy Magazine* (November–December 1992): 18–19.

53. Document, "Identification of Specimens Collected by Carl L. Hubbs Family and Assistants, June 1940," Fishery Studies, Vertical Files, GSMNP; Robert A. Kuehne and Roger W. Barbour, *American Darters* (Lexington: University of Kentucky Press, 1983), 53, 83, 100. David Etnier, interview with author, 8 April 1999, tape recording in author's possession.

54. Etnier and Starnes, *The Fishes of Tennessee* (Knoxville: University of Tennessee Press, 1994), 153–54, 311–12; Mark Alston et al., "Historical Overview of Fisheries Studies and Sport Fisheries Monitoring," Resources Management Report (Gatlinburg, Tenn.: Uplands Field Research Laboratory, 1984), 11.

55. Etnier and Starnes, *The Fishes of Tennessee*, 12, 99, 104–5. See also Etnier and Starnes, "An Analysis of Tennessee's Jeopardized Fish Taxonomy," *Journal of Tennessee Academy of Science* 66 (1991): 129–33. Until the 1960s, official fishery studies of

Great Smoky Mountains National Park did not include Hazel Creek and the other tributaries of Fontana Dam. Until the 1970s, scientists themselves took little notice of reservoir ecology at all, so it is difficult to reconstruct scientifically what happened when the Little Tennessee River became the Fontana Reservoir. Reeve M. Bailey to Arthur Stupka, 3 April 1952, Freshwater Fisheries, Vertical Files, GSMNP; Samuel Eddy, *The Freshwater Fishes* (Dubuque, Iowa: William C. Brown Company, 1974), 42–43; "Fish of Tennessee," *Tennessee Wildlife* 1 (August 1937): 14.

56. Arthur Stupka, *The Birds of the Great Smoky Mountains National Park* (Knoxville: University of Tennessee Press, 1963), 5; Francis H. Kortright, *Ducks, Geese, and Swans of North America* (Harrisburg: Stackpole Company, 1967), 47–49.

57. David Etnier, interview by author, 8 April 1999.

58. Conrad L. Wirth to R. Bruce Etheridge, 25 September 1944; Howard K. Menhinick to Blair Ross, 25 September 1945, Management Files, Box VIII, GSMNP; Howard K. Menhinick, "Tennessee Valley Forecast: Fishery and Wildlife Resources" (TVA: Regional Studies Department, 1943), C-3 and C-4, TVA Record Group 142: 138, FRCEP; Darrell E. Louder and W. Donald Baker, "Some Limnological Aspects of Fontana Reservoir." Paper presented at the Annual Meeting of the Southern Division of the American Fisheries Society, 24, 25, and 26 October 1966, 9.

59. Mallory G. Martin, North Carolina Wildlife Resource Commission, correspondence with author, 11 April 1995. Mallory also included the commission's stocking records for Fontana Lake.

60. TVA, *The First Fifty Years: Changed Land, Changed Lives* (Chattanooga: TVA, 1983), 70, 77; Louder and Baker, 9; A. R. Abernathy, G. L. Larson, and R. C. Matthews Jr., "Heavy Metals in the Surficial Sediments of Fontana Lake, North Carolina," *Water Resources* 18 (1984): 351–54; Todd Buchta, "Vintage Lakes Face Murky Future," *Knoxville News-Sentinel*, 6 August 1984; S. O. Ryding and W. Rast, *The Control of Eutrophication of Lakes and Reservoirs* (Paris: Parthenon, 1989), 37, 42, 179–80.

6. Drive-in Wilderness

1. Harvey Broome, "Mountain Notebook . . . 1950," *The Living Wilderness* 29 (Autumn 1965): 3–13.

2. Elizabeth Skaggs Bowman, *Land of High Horizons* (Kingsport, Tenn.: Southern Publishers, 1938), 78; Blackwell Robinson, ed., *North Carolina Guide* (Chapel Hill: University of North Carolina Press, 1955), 607.

3. State Advertising Division, *North Carolina: Variety Vacationland* (Raleigh, N.C.: Department of Conservation and Development, 1946), 3; Edward Meeman, "Conservation Wins—Great Smokies More Beautiful Than Ever," *Memphis Press-Scimitar*, Rockefeller Family Archives, Records Group 2: 93: 852; *Orlando Sentinel*, 6 June 1954; *Christian Science Monitor*, 15 March 1955; Gordon Young, "Great Smoky Mountains National Park," *National Geographic* (October 1968): 522–49.

4. Larry Dilsaver, *America's National Park System: The Critical Documents* (Lanham, Md.: Rowman & Littlefield), 63.

5. William C. Everhardt, *The National Park Service* (Boulder, Colo.: Westview Press, 1983), 24–25; Dilsaver, 194.

6. Press Releases and Clippings File, 1–2, GSMNP.

7. North Carolina State Highway and Public Works Commission, Tennessee State Department of Highways and Public Works, and U.S. Bureau of Public Roads, *Great Smoky Mountains National Park Travel Study* (Washington, D.C.: U.S. Government Printing Office, 1956), 5, 23, 26; Laura Thornborough, *Great Smoky Mountains* (New York: Crowell, 1942), 170.

8. Broome, 13.

9. Campbell, 25–30; John O. Morrell, *The Mirth of a National Park* (self-published, 1981), 4–5. According to retired veteran ranger Morrell, Campbell wrongly places the blame for this incident on Paul Adams, who would have known the difference between Grassy Gap and Grassy Patch, the meeting place. He and the author agree that Chapman was the more likely cause of this faux pas.

10. Tom Alexander, *Mountain Fever* (Asheville, N.C.: Bright Books, 1995), 1, 73, 77, 87.

11. Jeanette S. Greve, *The Story of Gatlinburg* (Strasburg, Va.: Shenandoah Publishing House, 1941), 134; memorandum, superintendent to regional director, 9 January 1953; Management Files, Box XIV–6, GSMNP; Hattie Caldwell Davis, *Cataloochee Valley* (Alexandria, Va.: Worldcom, 1997), 184.

12. Alexander, 88.

13. Memorandum, superintendent to regional director, 9 January 1953; Management Files, Box XIV–6, GSMNP.

14. Summary of Survey on Stock-Killing Bears, Management Files, Box XIV–6, GSMNP; memorandum to superintendent from assistant chief ranger, 1 September 1941, Black Bear Management Plans, Vertical Files, GSMNP.

15. Assistant chief ranger to superintendent, 2 June 1952; statement by Tom Alexander, 2 June 1952; Management Files, Box XIV–6, GSMNP.

16. *Knoxville News-Sentinel,* Press Releases and Clippings File, 1951, GSMNP.

17. Fred M. Packard to Ben Hibbs, 16 October 1952; John Preston to Mrs. J. W. McGovern, 20 October 1952; John Preston to regional director, 8 August 1952; Management Files, Box XIV–6, GSMNP; *Mountain Press,* 13 November 1952.

18. Memorandum, chief ranger to acting superintendent, 14 November 1952; memorandum, Edward Hummel to regional director, 15 December 1952, Management Files, Box XIV–6, GSMNP; *Asheville Citizen-Times,* 13 November 1952.

19. Regional director to director, National Park Service, 20 November 1952; Thomas A. Alexander to Hon. Willis Smith, 26 February 1953; Willis Smith to Conrad Wirth, 3 March 1953; acting director to Hon. Willis Smith, 11 March 1953, Management Files, Box XIV–6, GSMNP.

20. *Superintendent's Report,* May 1954 and October 1961, GSMNP.

21. Dilsaver, 87–88.

22. E. V. Komarek to J. R. Eakin, 12 October 1934; Eakin to director, 15 October 1934; Thomas to Eakin, 19 December 1934; K. E. Steinmetz to Eakin, 31 December 1934; Demaray to Eakin, 10 May 1935, Watersnakes, Vertical Files, GSMNP.

23. Bernard S. Martof, William M. Palmer, Joseph R. Bailey, and Julian R.

Harrison II, *Amphibians and Reptiles of the Carolinas and Virginia* (Chapel Hill: University of North Carolina Press, 1980), 221–22.

24. Robert Burrows Jr. "Biological Survey of Streams in the Great Smoky Mountains National Park" (unpublished manuscript, Vertical Files, GSMNP, April 1935), 12; *Superintendent's Report*, September 1936; "Brook Trout Restoration, 1979," Brook Trout, Vertical Files, GSMNP.

25. Willis King, "A Program for the Management of Fish Resources in the Great Smoky Mountains National Park," *Transactions of the American Fisheries Society* 68 (1938): 88–95.

26. Mark Alston et al., "Historical Overview of Fisheries Studies and Sports Fisheries Monitoring" (Resources Management Report, Series-78, Uplands Field Research Laboratory, 1984), 5; *Knoxville Journal*, 17 May 1953.

27. Daniel Reinhold and Othello Wallis, "Development and Success of Catch and Release Angling Programs," 1961, memorandum, superintendent to Region One director, Fishing, Recreational, Vertical Files, GSMNP.

28. *Superintendent's Report*, July 1957, GSMNP.

29. Robert E. Lennon and Phillip S. Parker, "The Reclamation of Indian and Abrams Creek," Scientific Fisheries Report No. 306 (Washington, D.C.: 1959); Robert E. Lennon, "An Annual Report of Progress" (Leestown, W.Va.: U.S. Fish and Wildlife Service, 1959); *Superintendent's Report*, June 1958, GSMNP.

30. *Superintendent's Report*, November 1956, GSMNP.

31. Frank Richardson to Philip Douglas, 2 February 1966, Fisheries, Vertical Files, GSMNP.

32. Office Order No. 323, Fish Policy, 13 April 1936, reprinted in Dilsaver, 149.

33. Robert Lennon, "Brook Trout of the Great Smoky Mountains National Park," Technical Papers of the Bureau of Sports Fisheries and Wildlife, U.S. Department of Interior, 1967; Annual Summary of Fish Planting for 1971, U.S. Department of Interior, National Park Service, Resource Management Files, Box II–20; Annual Summary of Fish Planting for 1975, Vertical Files, Stocking, GSMNP.

34. *Knoxville Journal*, 11 June 1953; Ed Trout, *Gatlinburg: Cinderella City* (Pigeon Forge, Tenn.: Griffen Graphics, 1985).

35. *Christian Science Monitor*, 1955, in Press Releases and Clippings File, GSMNP; William H. Gilbert, "The Cherokees of North Carolina: Living Memorials to the Past," *Smithsonian Report for 1956* (Washington, D.C.: Smithsonian Institution Press, 1957), 529–55; *Cherokee Community Development Content, Cherokee Indian Reservation, 1953*, Joe Jennings Collection, AAETSU.

36. For a valuable critique of the work done by Appalachian settlement schools such as the Pi Phi School, see David Whisnant, *All That is Native and Fine: The Politics of Culture in an American Region* (Chapel Hill: University of North Carolina Press, 1983).

37. The irony of these goals can be understood with the addition of the words by the county agent, who noted that the majority of residents managed to live on a small

spot of land cultivating corn, beans, and potatoes. "They seem to be able to live on less than any people it has been my privilege to observe," he wrote. *Annual Report, Sevier County*, 1930, Record Group 75: 6: 24, FRCEP; Narrative Summary of Annual Report Home Demonstration Work, Sevier County, 1935, Agricultural Records, GSMNP; *Asheville Citizen-Times*, 18 January 1937.

38. Greve, 136; "Children of Tourism," *Now and Then*, 34; Oakley, 6–8.

39. Russell Shaw, *The Gatlinburg Story* (Gatlinburg, Tenn.: self-published, 1960), 12, 27, 28.

40. Jerome Dobson, "The Changing Control of Economic Activity in the Gatlinburg, Tennessee, Area, 1930–1973" (Ph.D. diss., University of Tennessee, 1975); H. B. Teeter, "Gatlinburg Eyes the Future," *Nashville Tennessean Magazine*, 28 June 1953, 2; George Fry's autobiography, *George Fry: The Legend* documents how much time superintendents spent socializing with local businessmen. The *Knoxville News-Sentinel* article (in Individuals, John C. Preston, GSMNP, n.d.) revealed that the paper worried that Preston might come "under obligations that could become embarrassing to him and damaging to the park."

41. *Orlando Sentinel*, 6 June 1954; Trout, 116–17.

42. Phyllis Gordon, "The Lure of the Great Smokies," *Healthways* (June 1954): 46–48, Vertical Files, GSMNP; *Philadelphia Inquirer*, 28 January 1952.

43. *Knoxville News-Sentinel*, 22 November 1940; *Knoxville Journal*, 28 November 1940.

44. Neil Maher, "Hold Up That Road: Let Uncle Sam Build It, Auto Tourism, Wilderness, and the Evolution of the Great Smoky Mountains National Park's Motor Road System" (unpublished manuscript, GSMNP, 1996), 78–80.

45. Jerome E. Dobson, "The Changing Control of Economic Activity in the Gatlinburg, Tennessee, Area, 1930–1973" (Ph.D. diss., University of Tennessee, 1975), 18, 21, 79–81; Trout, *Cinderella City*, 121; *Chicago Tribune*, 11 June 1967.

46. Robinson, 578.

47. Finger, *Cherokee Americans*, 87–90.

48. Hill, 290–302; *Asheville Citizen-Times*, 14 August 1938; *Superintendent's Report*, September 1932, GSMNP.

49. *Asheville Citizen-Times*, 17 June 1939; Superintendent Fought to editor, *Asheville Citizen-Times*, 11 June 1937, Joe Jennings Collection, AAETSU; Frances M. Young, "Annual Indian Festival," WPA Records, Box 13, 87-A., North Carolina State Archives, Raleigh.

50. Hill, 254–57, 303, 313.

51. Jennings to William Zimmerman, Bureau of Indian Affairs, 10 July 1947, Jennings Collection, AAETSU.

52. Hill, 304; correspondence, Joe Jennings, "Public Relations—Cherokee Indian Reservation"; Business Enterprise Statistics, Aubrey Jennings, "Eastern Cherokee Indians Recent Progress, 1954," Jennings Collection, AAETSU; *Nashville Tennesseean*, 3 August 1952.

53. *The Cherokee Indians of the Qualla Reservation: How They Live Today* (Knoxville: J. L. Caton, 1937), 4; Laura Thornborogh, *The Great Smoky Mountains*, 72–73.

54. Press release by John Parris, 9 November 1951, WNCAC, Joe Jennings Collection, AAETSU.

55. Finger, *Cherokee Americans*, 114–15.

56. *Asheville Citizen-Times*, 29 February 1948.

57. Memorandum, Joe Jennings to Harry E. Buchanan, n.d., Joe Jennings Collection, AAETSU; Jennings, 8–9; William A. McCall, *Cherokees and Pioneers* (Asheville, N.C.: Stephens Press, 1952), 84; Duane H. King, "History of the Museum of the Cherokee Indian," *Journal of Cherokee Studies* 1 (Summer 1976): 60–64.

58. Dykeman and Stokely, 159; Jennings, 10; Finger, *Cherokee Americans*, 102–3; Big Cove, 69.

59. *The Guide Book to Cherokee: 1000 Facts and Answers to Questions about the Cherokee* (Cherokee, N.C.: Official Publications, 1953), 9.

60. Oscar Chapman from John Collier, 9 February 1950; Alfred Mynders to Jennings, October 1954; Jennings to Mynders, 21 October 1954; Joe Jennings Collection, AAETSU.

61. E. M. Lisle, acting director to director, 10 October 1940, Vertical Files, Cades Cove, GSMNP.

62. Memorandum to regional director from O. B. Taylor, 29 July 1946, Resource Management Files, Box III–1, GSMNP.

63. Memorandum to regional director from O. B. Taylor, 29 July 1946; memorandum for the files, 8 May 1946, Resource Management Files, Box III–1, GSMNP; Susan Power Bratton, Raymond C. Matthews Jr., and Peter S. White, "Agricultural Area Impacts within a Natural Area: Cades Cove, A Case History," *Environmental Management* 4 (1980): 433–48.

64. Memorandum to regional director, 22 November 1946, Resource Management Files, Box III–1, GSMNP.

65. *Daily (Maryville) Times*, 1 May 1953.

66. "The Cades Cove Story," *Ranger Manual*, chapter 2, part 4: 1, Vertical Files, Cades Cove, GSMNP.

67. "The Cades Cove Story," *Ranger Manual*, chapter 2, part 4: 2, Vertical Files, Cades Cove, GSMNP.

68. Quoted in full, *Daily (Maryville) Times*, 1 May 1953.

69. *Knoxville Journal*, 19 October 1941.

70. "My Great-Great-Grandfather," *Friends* (October 1962): 14–15, Vertical Files, GSMNP; Bart Leiper, "Time Stands Still in Cades Cove," *Tennessee Conservationist* (December 1957): 8–9, Vertical Files, GSMNP; Warner Ogden, *Cades Cove: A Drive-in Look at Mountain Pioneers* (April 1961): 44–47.

71. Andrew Sparks, "Cades Cove . . . A Pioneer Paradise," *Atlanta Journal and Constitution*, 23 April 1961; William O. Douglas, "The People of Cades Cove," *National Geographic Magazine* (July 1962): 60–88.

72. Report, "Channel Conditions and Recommended Improvement Abrams Creek," 1964, Vertical Files, Cades Cove, GSMNP; Bratton et al., 445.

73. "Proposed Management Plan for Former Hay Lease Area in Cades Cove," 1997, Cades Cove, Vertical Files, GSMNP; John Bull and John Farrand Jr., *Audubon*

Society Field Guide to North American Birds (New York: Alfred A. Knopf, 1977), 392, 492–93.

74. Memorandum to superintendent from chief ranger, 8 February 1954, Ranger Activities, Box II–1, GSMNP; *Superintendent's Report*, March 1960, GSMNP; Thomas L. Burst and Michael R. Pelton, "Some Population Parameters of the Cades Cove Deer Herd, Great Smoky Mountains National Park," *Proceedings, Annual Conference South Eastern Association Fish & Wildlife Agencies* 32 (1980): 339–44; Susan P. Bratton, "Impacts of White-tailed Deer on the Vegetation of Cades Cove, Great Smoky Mountains National Park," *Proceedings, Annual Conference South Eastern Association Fish & Wildlife Agencies* 33 (1981): 305–12; Houk, 176.

75. Frome, 331; *Smoky Mountains Hiking Club Guide*, 1956, 6–13.

76. *Superintendent's Report*, August 1955, November 1955 to November 1966; see especially May 1965, GSMNP.

77. Broome, 13.

78. State Advertising Division, *State Advertising Bulletin* (Raleigh, N.C., 10 November 1951): 1.

7. Bearly Managing Tourons

1. Michael Ann Williams, *Great Smoky Mountains Folklife*, 133–35.

2. Morrell, 34.

3. Newton B. Drury to Howard K. Menhinick, 12 September 1944, Management Files, Box VIII–6, GSMNP.

4. National Park Service, *A Study of the Park and Recreation Problems of the U.S.* (Washington, D.C.: U.S. Government Printing Office, 1941), 22.

5. Alston Chase, *Playing God in Yellowstone* (New York: Harcourt Brace Jovanovich, 1987), 202.

6. Richard Sellars, *Preserving Nature in the National Parks* (New Haven: Yale University Press, 1998), 206, 208–9; Chase, 202.

7. George Fry, *George Fry: The Legend* (self-published, 1994), 221, 229, 238, 250–51. The book is based on a diary Fry kept from high school through his retirement from the National Park Service; Morrell, 20–21.

8. Taylor, 175–76; Bob Matthews, "Tourist Activity Expansion Need Is Stressed by WNCAC Leaders," *Asheville Citizen-Times*, 13 October 1953; *Superintendent's Report*, September 1947.

9. *Superintendent's Report*, August 1963, August 1965, GSMNP; Michael Frome, *Battle for the Wilderness* (Salt Lake City: University of Utah Press, 1997), 19–20.

10. Fry, 233.

11. Shireen Parsons, "Wilderness Warrior," *Appalachian Voice* (Summer 1998): 8, 14.

12. Ernest Dickerman to Harvey and Anne Broome, 18 July 1957; Judson C. Dickerman to Anne Broome, 19 July 1956; Ernest M. Dickerman folder, Harvey Broome Collection, McClung Collection, Knoxville; Ernie Dickerman, 1911–1998, A Memorial, Leroy Fox Collection, unprocessed records, Great Smoky Mountains Collection, Hodges Library, University of Tennessee, Knoxville.

13. Dickerman to Hummel, 7 May 1957, Ernest M. Dickerman folder, Harvey Broome Collection, McClung Collection, Knoxville.

14. *New York Times*, 5 August 1998.

15. John Opie, *Nature's Nation: An Environmental History of the United States* (New York: Harcourt Brace Jovanovich, 1997), 391–92, 405–6, 417–22; Frome, 24, 26.

16. Leroy Fox, interview by author, 27 February 1998, tape recording in author's possession.

17. Leroy Fox, interview by author, 27 February 1998, tape recording in author's possession; Ray Payne, interview by author, August 1998, tape recording in author's possession.

18. Fry, 209.

19. *Superintendent's Report*, May 1964 and September 1964, GSMNP.

20. Wilderness Society, "Wilderness for the Smokies," and Smoky Mountains Hiking Club, "A Wilderness Plan for the Smokies," in *The Living Wilderness* 29 (Summer 1965): 2, 32–36.

21. *Knoxville News-Sentinel*, 24 October 1965.

22. Paul Adams to George Fry, 17 August 1964, Box 5, Paul Adams Papers, TSTATE.

23. *Knoxville News-Sentinel*, 21 November 1965.

24. *Knoxville News-Sentinel*, 12 June 1966; Fry 237.

25. Robert Cahn, "Will Success Spoil the National Parks?" *Christian Science Monitor* 1968, 18. Visitor Use, Vertical Files, GSMNP.

26. *Knoxville News-Sentinel*, 11 April 1966, 17 April 1966.

27. *Chicago Tribune*, editorial reprinted in the *Knoxville Journal*, 7 March 1966; *Knoxville News-Sentinel*, 5 June 1966.

28. *Knoxville News-Sentinel*, 24 January 1966.

29. *Knoxville News-Sentinel*, 27 March 1966; *Knoxville Journal*, 25 May 1966; *Knoxville News Sentinel*, 25 May 1966.

30. *Knoxville News-Sentinel*, 13 June 1966, 14 June 1966; "Wilderness Areas in the Great Smokies," *Appalachian Trailway News* (September 1966): 41–44; Fry, 238.

31. *Superintendent's Report*, July 1966, GSMNP; proceedings, wilderness hearing on Great Smoky Mountains National Park, Bryson City, N.C., 15 June 1966, Vertical Files, Wilderness, GSMNP.

32. *Asheville Citizen-Times*, 24 June 1966.

33. *Superintendent's Report*, November 1966, GSMNP; Fry, 250; Leroy Fox, interview by author, 17 February 1999, tape recording in author's possession. Fox still has the counter he used, stopped at 234.

34. Ted Snyder, interview by author, 12 August 1998, tape recording in author's possession.

35. "Roster of Great Smoky Mountains Delegation Meeting with Secretary of the Interior Walter Hickel," Leroy Fox Collection, unprocessed records, Great Smoky Mountains Collection, Hodges Library, University of Tennessee, Knoxville.

36. Leroy G. Fox, "Memorandum"; Edward C. Clebsch, "Remarks Prepared for Presentation to Secretary of the Interior Walter J. Hickel"; Frank Bell, "Statement

for Secretary Hickel Conference," 23 June 1969; Leroy Fox Collection, unprocessed records, Great Smoky Mountains Collection, Hodges Library, University of Tennessee, Knoxville.

37. Leroy Fox, interview by author, tape recording in author's possession; Fox, "A Brief Statement on the Great Smoky Mountains Wilderness and Roads Controversy," Leroy Fox Collection, unprocessed records, Great Smoky Mountains Collection, Hodges Library, University of Tennessee, Knoxville.

38. TVA, "Lease of Fontana Village, Contract No. TV–92173," TVA, Division of Reservoir Properties, general correspondence, 1940–1965, TVA Record Group 142: 29, FRCEP; State Advertising Bulletin (Raleigh, N.C.: State Administration Division, Department of Conservation and Development, 19 June 1950); Great Smoky Mountains National Park, *Transportation Concepts*, 2, 24. George Ellison, "Road to Nowhere Offers Interesting Holiday Outing," *Asheville Citizen-Times*, 29 December 1993.

39. Fry, 239.

40. Jane Tate Eagar and Michael R. Pelton, "Pandhandler Black Bears in the Great Smoky Mountains National Park," report to National Park Service, Southeast Region, 1979, Vertical Files, Black Bears, GSMNP.

41. *Superintendent's Report*, June and August 1938, GSMNP.

42. *Superintendent's Report*, May, June, and August 1940, GSMNP.

43. *Superintendent's Report*, June 1941, GSMNP.

44. Chief ranger to superintendent, 11 July 1963, Ranger Activities, Box II–10, GSMNP; Bill Sharpe, "Visitors to Smoky Mountains Park Are Warned Not to Feed Bears," *The New Cherokee Phoenix* (21 August 1951): 4; Nelson Beecher Keyes, *America's National Parks* (Garden City, N.Y.: Doubleday, 1957), 15–19.

45. *Superintendent's Report*, June 1942, GSMNP.

46. *Superintendent's Report*, August, September, October, and November 1941, GSMNP; *Bryson City Times*, 9 April 1942; *Jackson County Journal*, 14 August 1941; Morrell, 36.

47. *Superintendent's Report*, July 1949, July 1950, August 1950, August 1951, August 1954, July 1955, and September 1957, GSMNP; Bill Sharpe, "Visitors to Smoky Mountains Park Are Warned Not to Feed Bears, *The New Cherokee Phoenix* 1 (1951): 4.

48. Dilsaver, 222, 242.

49. Summary of Bear Incidents, 1960–1969, Great Smoky Mountains National Park, memorandum, Radio Room to Mr. Fry, 17 May 1968, Management Files, Box XV–20, GSMNP.

50. Stephen Herrero, *Bear Attacks: Their Causes and Avoidance* (New York: Lyons and Burford), 226–27.

51. *Knoxville News-Sentinel*, 11 July 1965, GSMNP.

52. Emmett Watson, "Menace in Our Northern Parks," *Sports Illustrated* 27 (30 October 1967): 62–74.

53. "Night of Terror," *Time* 90 (25 August 1967): 19; "Oh My God, I'm Dead!" *Newsweek* (28 August 1967): 26.

54. Chase, 142–53.

55. *Knoxville News-Sentinel*, 21 April 1968; 1968 Bear Management Program, Management Files, Box XV–20, GSMNP.

56. Mrs. Robert Wagoner to George Fry, 26 April 1968; June Simpson to Mr. Udall, 15 May 1968; Frances Watkins to superintendent, 2 May 1968; Miss Susan Chadwell to chief park ranger, 25 April 1968; Parks Department from Paul Coleman, 8 May 1968; Mrs. Earl McDuffie to Fry, 25 June 1968; Ruth B. Owens to George Fry, 3 May 1968; J. N. Blake to Fry, 8 July 1968; Sevier Countians to Fry, n.d., Management Files, Box XV–20, GSMNP.

57. George Fry to Mrs. Robert Wagner, Management Files, Box XV–20, GSMNP; *Knoxville Journal*, 11 June 1968.

58. Gordon Burghardt et al. to George Fry, n.d.; Fry to Gordon Burghardt, 1 May 1968, Management Files, Box XV–20, GSMNP.

59. Gairdner B. Moment to Karl T. Gilbert, 25 January 1969, Management Files, Box XV–20, GSMNP; Gairdner B. Moment, "Bears: The Need for a New Sanity in Wildlife Conservation," *Bioscence* 12 (December 1968): 1105–08.

60. Mrs. N. H. Bunting to park naturalist, 30 June 1969; postcard to Superintendent Fry from Sam Lessie, 12 July 1968; George Fry to Wesley L. Kinser, 28 August 1968, Management Files, Box XV–20, GSMNP.

61. *Waynesville Mountaineer*, 26 February 1969.

62. Bill Hensley, director of travel and promotion, to George Fry, 24 May 1968.

63. *Knoxville Journal*, 14 June 1968.

64. Fry, 262.

65. Roland H. Wauer, "The Greening of Natural Resource Management," *Trends* 19 (1982): 2–6.

66. Chief ranger to superintendent, 11 July 1963, Ranger Activities, Box II–10; Tom Ringenberg to superintendent, 2 April 1968; Richard Safran to supervisor, 30 September 1968; Lisa Lofland to superintendent, 13 June 1968; Emily H. Earley to George Fry, 31 July 1968; Management Files, Box XV–20, GSMNP.

67. Dwight McCarter, *Lost: A Ranger's Diary of Search and Rescue* (Yellow Springs, Ohio: Graphicom Press, 1998), 22–43; Fry, 262.

8. Still Not a Wilderness

1. Arthur Stupka, interview by Bill Landry, 1989, Landry Collection, GSMNP; Susan Bratton, interview by author, 9 December 1998, e-mail printout in author's possession; Don Defoe, interview by author, tape recording in author's possession.

2. Sellars, 214–15.

3. Sellars, 215–16; Dilsaver, 249; Chase, 33–34.

4. Susan Bratton, interview by author, 8 November 1998, e-mail printout in author's possession.

5. Susan Bratton, interview by author, 9 December 1998, e-mail printout in author's possession; *Maryville-Alcoa Times*, 24 February 1978.

6. Susan Bratton, interview by author, 5 February 1999, e-mail printout in author's possession; *Knoxville News-Sentinel*, 14 September 1976.

7. Susan Bratton, interview by author, 9 December 1998, e-mail printout in author's possession.

8. Susan Power Bratton, Matthew Hickler, and James Graves, "Trail and Campsite Erosion Survey for the Great Smoky Mountains National Park," 1 (Gatlinburg, Tenn.: Uplands Field Research Laboratory, 1978), 1.

9. Susan Power Bratton, Matthew Hickler, and James H. Graves, "Trail and Campsite Erosion Survey for the Great Smoky Mountains National Park," 3 (Gatlinburg, Tenn.: Uplands Field Research Laboratory, 1978), 24.

10. Susan Power Bratton, Matthew G. Hickler, James H. Graves, "Trail and Campsite Erosion Survey for the Great Smoky Mountains National Park," 2 (Gatlinburg, Tenn.: Uplands Field Research Laboratory, 1978), 37.

11. *New Orleans States-Item*, 12 November 1976; *Wall Street Journal*, 15 September 1976; "Fact Sheet Implementation of a Campground Reservation System," 1 July 1974, Visitor Use, Vertical Files, GSMNP.

12. Russ Olson, *Administrative History: Organizational Structures of the National Park Service, 1917 to 1985* (Washington, D.C.: U.S. Government Printing Office, 1985), 96–99.

13. Sellars, 347n.

14. John Rogers to G. E. Mernin, 22 September 1967, Resource Management Files, Box III–10, GSMNP.

15. Smoky Mountains Hiking Club, quote in Houk, 106.

16. *Superintendent's Report*, March 1960, October 1960, March 1962, September 1962; James R. Fox and Michael R. Pelton, "An Evaluation of Control Techniques for the European Wild Hog in the Great Smoky Mountains National Park," Draft, 1978, European Wild Hog, Vertical Files, GSMNP.

17. *Superintendent's Report*, March 1964, GSMNP.

18. Resource Study Proposal, European Wild Hog, Collection Permits, Boxes II–2 and II–7, GSMNP.

19. George Matschke and John P. Hardister, "Movements of Transplanted European Wild Boar in North Carolina and Tennessee," 1965, European Wild Boar, Vertical Files, GSMNP.

20. Fox and Pelton, 30–31.

21. Aaron J. Sharp, "European Wild Boar Management, Great Smoky Mountains National Park," January 1978, European Wild Boar, Vertical Files, GSMNP.

22. Susan Power Bratton, "An Integrated Ecological Approach to the Management of the European Wild Boar in the Great Smoky Mountains National Park," 1974, European Wild Boar, Vertical Files, GSMNP.

23. Sellars, 237–38; *Charlotte Observer*, 19 September 1976.

24. *Gatlinburg Press*, 25 May 1967; Robert Cahn, "Will Success Spoil the National Parks?" A series of sixteen articles in the *Christian Science Monitor*, reprint, 1968, Press Releases and Clippings File, GSMNP; *U.S. News and World Reports* (13 June 1977): 36.

25. Boyd Evison, interview by author, 20 August 1998, e-mail printout in author's possession.

26. *Akron Beacon-Journal,* 30 May 1976; personal data sheet, Boyd Evison, GRSM 39354, GSMNP; *Gatlinburg Press,* 24 June 1975; *Knoxville Journal,* 11 June 1975.

27. *Charlotte Observer,* 19 September 1976; *Raleigh News and Observer,* 14 August 1977.

28. *Gatlinburg Press,* 19 August 1975.

29. Boyd Evison, interview by author, 20 August 1998, e-mail printout in author's possession; Susan Bratton, interview by author, 8 February 1999, e-mail printout in author's possession; Uplands Field Research Laboratory, pamphlet, Uplands Field Research Laboratory scrapbook, GSMNP.

30. *Smoky Mountain Times,* 1 April 1976; *Knoxville News-Sentinel,* 19 February 1976; press release, 16 January 1976 and 16 August 1977, Press Releases and Clippings File, 1970s, GSMNP; Leroy Fox, interview by author, 27 February 1999, tape recording in author's possession.

31. *Maryville-Alcoa Daily Times,* 6 February 1978; *Gatlinburg Press,* 10 February 1976; *Knoxville Journal,* 18 February 1976; *Gatlinburg Press,* 15 April 1976.

32. Boyd Evison, interview by author, 21 August 1998, e-mail printout in author's possession.

33. *Sevier County Times,* 26 February 1976; *Asheville Times,* 3 March 1976.

34. Boyd Evison, interview by author, 21 August 1998, e-mail printout in author's possession.

35. Press release, 16 August 1977, Press Releases and Clippings File, GSMNP; Boyd Evison, interview by author, 21 August 1998, e-mail printout in author's possession. The practice of mowing trails was resumed some time during the 1980s.

36. Susan P. Bratton, Linda L. Stromberg, and Mark E. Harmon, "Firewood-Gathering Impacts in Backcountry Campsites in the Great Smoky Mountains National Park," *Environmental Management* 6 (1982): 62–71; Susan P. Bratton, Matthew G. Hickler, and James H. Graves, "Visitor Impacts on Backcountry Campsites in the Great Smoky Mountains," *Environmental Management* (1978): 431–42; press releases, 16 March 1978, 22 May 1978, and 16 May 1978, Press Releases and Clippings File, Box II–21, GSMNP.

37. *Knoxville News-Sentinel,* 25 January 1976; *Knoxville Journal,* 31 August 1976.

38. *Asheville Citizen-Times,* 11 January 1976.

39. Susan Bratton, "The Decline of the Smokies Trout," *Tennessee Conservationist* 43 (July–August 1977): 2–3; *Gatlinburg Press,* 13 January 1976; long distance phone call record, 4 March 1976; correspondence, Ben Dalton to Whom It May Concern, 4 February 1976, Resource Management Files, Box II–20, GSMNP; *Citizen Tribune,* 9 June 1989.

40. Interim Brook Management Plan, Great Smoky Mountains National Park, June 1978, Vertical Files, Brook Trout, GSMNP.

41. Memorandum, Boyd Evison to regional director, 16 March 1978; Interim Brook Management Plan, Great Smoky Mountains National Park, June 1978, Vertical Files, Brook Trout, GSMNP.

42. *Knoxville News-Sentinel,* 26 July 1978; Sharon Simpson to Boyd Evison, 27 July 1978, correspondence, 1970s, Resource Management Files, GSMNP.

43. Alan Kelly, Gary Larson, Mike Myers, environmental assessment, "Proposed Recovery Plan of Brook Trout, 1978," 3 March 1978, Vertical Files, Brook Trout, GSMNP.

44. Boyd Evison to regional director, National Park Service, 5 July 1978, Vertical Files, Brook Trout, GSMNP.

45. Long Range Wildlife and Habitat Management Plan, 1967–1971, Management Files, Box XV–20, GSMNP.

46. Sharp, 5.

47. *Asheville Citizen-Times*, 6 March 1977.

48. Boyd Evison to Carlos Campbell, 24 March 1978; Tanner, Box I–5, GSMNP.

49. *Knoxville News-Sentinel*, 13 January 1978, 29 March 1978, 22 June 1978, and 18 June 1978; *Knoxville Journal*, 30 March 1978.

50. Sheila D. Minim, "The European Wild Boar Issue in the Great Smoky Mountains National Park," February 1978, European Wild Boar, Vertical Files, GSMNP.

51. Boyd Evison to Lamar Gudger, 6 September 1977; James Bainbridge to John Duncan, 25 November 1977; Tanner, Box I–V, GSMNP.

52. Vince Ellis, "Wilderness Recommendation," Management Files, Box XVII–2; "Wilderness Issues," Management Files, Box V–16, GSMNP.

53. Frank Bell, "Statement for Secretary Hickel Conference Regarding Great Smoky Mountains National Park Wilderness Designation under the Wilderness Act," 23 June 1969, Leroy Fox Collection, unprocessed records, Great Smoky Mountains Collection, Hodges Library, University of Tennessee, Knoxville.

54. *Knoxville News-Sentinel*, 20, 21, 23 February 1975.

55. "Action Alert," insert in *Tenne-sierran* 5 (February 1975).

56. *Asheville Citizen-Times*, 4 July 1975; Ted Snyder, interview by author, 12 August 1998, tape recording in author's possession.

57. *Asheville Citizen-Times*, 21 November 1976.

58. *Knoxville News-Sentinel*, 8 February 1977.

59. Paul Adams to Boyd Evison, 11 April 1977, Paul Adams Papers, Box 5, TSTATE.

60. *Knoxville News-Sentinel*, 11 February 1977.

61. *Knoxville News-Sentinel*, 10 February 1977.

62. *Mountaineer*, 8 June 1977.

63. *Kingston Free-Press*, 31 July 1977.

64. *Nashville Tennesseean*, 24 January 1978; *Waynesville Mountaineer*, 20 February 1978.

65. *Smoky Mountain Times*, 3 August 1978.

66. *Knoxville News-Sentinel*, 9 August 1978; *Asheville Citizen-Times*, 11 August 1978.

67. *Smoky Mountain Times*, 10 August 1978.

68. *Knoxville Journal*, 25 October 1978; *Asheville Citizen-Times*, 25 October 1978.

69. Boyd Evison, interview by author, 4 September 1998, e-mail printout in author's possession.

70. *Knoxville Journal*, 25 October 1978.

71. *Knoxville News-Sentinel*, 27 November 1978; *Maryville-Alcoa Times*, 7 November 1978.

72. *Smoky Mountain Times*, 14 September 1978.

73. Leroy Fox to Bill Rolen, 27 June 1979, Leroy Fox Collection, unprocessed records, Great Smoky Mountains Collection, Hodges Library, University of Tennessee, Knoxville.

74. Leroy Fox, "Draft Plan of Alternatives Available to Swain County to Resolve the 1943 Agreement," Leroy Fox Collection, unprocessed records, Great Smoky Mountains Collection, Hodges Library, University of Tennessee, Knoxville; Leroy Fox, interview by author, tape recording in author's possession.

75. *General Management Plan, Great Smoky Mountains National Park* (Washington, D.C.: U.S. Government Printing Office, 1982).

76. Susan Bratton, interview by author, 15 February 1999, e-mail printout in author's possession.

77. *Knoxville News-Sentinel*, 17 November 1985; *U.S. Supreme Court Reports* 84 L Ed 2d.

9. *In Search of the Wild East*

1. Law Enforcement Case Incident Report 599.744, Eastern Mountain Lion, Vertical Files, GSMNP.

2. Susan Bratton, "Is the Panther Making a Comeback?" *National Parks & Conservation Magazine* (July 1978): 13.

3. Susan Bratton, interview by author, 8 April 1999, e-mail printout in author's possession.

4. George Fry to Jack Horan, 6 February 1967, Eastern Mountain Lion, Vertical Files, GSMNP.

5. Nicole Culbertson, "Status and History of the Mountain Lion in the Great Smoky Mountains National Park," Management Report No. 15 (Gatlinburg, Tenn.: Uplands Field Research Laboratory, 1977), 51–56.

6. Sellers, 232–33.

7. Peter S. White and Susan P. Bratton, "After Preservation: Philosophical and Practical Problems of Change," *Biological Conservation* 18 (1980): 241–55.

8. *Gatlinburg Press*, 5 July 1978; Robert L. Downing to cooperator, 18 December 1978, Vertical Files, Panther, GSMNP; *Knoxville Journal*, 28 July 1987; Mike Pelton, interview by author, 8 April 1999, tape recording in author's possession.

9. W. H. Camp, "The Grass Balds of the Great Smoky Mountains of Tennessee and North Carolina," *Ohio Journal Science* 31 (1931): 157–64; R. H. Whittaker, "Vegetation of the Great Smoky Mountains," *Ecological Monographs* 26 (1956): 1–80; D. M. Brown, "Vegetation on Roan Mountain: A Psytosociological and Successional Study," *Ecological Monographs* 11 (1941): 61–97; B. W. Wells, "Origin of the Southern Appalachian Grass Balds," *Science* 83 (1936): 283; Philip Gersmehl, "A Geographic Approach to a Vegetation Problem: The Case of the Southern Appalachian Grassy Balds" (Ph.D. diss., University of Georgia, 1970).

10. *Knoxville News-Sentinel*, 17 March 1963; *Maryville Alcoa Daily Times*, 6 March 1963.

11. *Knoxville News-Sentinel*, 23 May 1976.

12. Mary Lindsay, "History of the Grassy Balds in Great Smoky Mountains National Park," Management Report No. 4 (U.S. Department of Interior, National Park Service, Southeast Region, Uplands Field Research Laboratory, 1976); Susan Bratton, "The Management of Historic Ecosystems and Landscapes in National Parks," *Proceedings of the Conference on Science in the National Parks* 4 (1986), 3–43.

13. *Knoxville News-Sentinel*, 16 July 1976.

14. Mary M. Lindsay and Susan Power Bratton, "Grassy Balds of the Great Smoky Mountains: Their History and Flora in Relation to Potential Management," *Environmental Management* 3 (1979): 427–28.

15. Susan P. Bratton and Peter S. White, "Grassy Balds Management and Nature Preserves: Issues and Problems" (Gatlinburg, Tenn.: Uplands Field Research Laboratory, n.d.), 103; Peter White to Superintendent Beal, 9 December 1982; summary, "Grassy Balds of the Great Smoky Mountains National Park," 1 May 1983; memorandum, park ranger to Vegetation Management crew, 13 June 1986, Balds, Vertical Files, GSMNP; Rudy Abramson, "Nature's Bald Spots," *Audubon* (March–April 1995): 38–39.

16. Larry Richardson, "Salute to a Pioneer: Paul J. Adams," *The Tennessee Conservationist* 34 (February 1973): 2–3.

17. *Knoxville Journal*, 21 February 1975.

18. Donald J. Bogucki, "Debris Slides in the Mt. Le Conte Area, Great Smoky Mountains National Park, U.S.A.," *Geografiska Annaler* 3 (1976): 179–91.

19. Paul L. Whittaker, "Comparison of Surface Damage by Horses and Hikers," Investigator's Annual Report; "Work Plan for Comparison of Damage by Horses and Hikers," 10 November 1977; and "Comparison of Surface Impact by Hiking and Horseback Riding in the Great Smoky Mountains National Park," Management Report No. 24, Uplands Field Research Laboratory, Box I–5, GSMNP.

20. Leroy Fox, interview by author, 27 February 1999, tape recording in author's possession.

21. *Knoxville News-Sentinel*, 76 or 77, Brewer column; *Gatlinburg Extra*, 18 September 1976.

22. *Knoxville News-Sentinel*, 28 April 1978; Leroy Fox, interview by author, 27 February 1999, tape recording in author's possession.

23. Dave Beal, "Abstract of Remarks by Dave Beal, Wilderness Management Symposium, 14 November 1980," Management Files, Box XVII–2, GSMNP.

24. *Knoxville News-Sentinel*, 8 February 1984.

25. Chris Eagar, interview by author, 16 April 1999, tape recording in author's possession.

26. Susan Bratton, interview by author, 28 February 1999, e-mail printout in author's possession.

27. Peter S. White, interview by author, 2 April 1999, tape recording in author's possession.

28. Chris Eagar, interview by author, 16 April 1999, tape recording in author's possession.

29. James A. Allen and Virginia Burkett, "The National Biological Service: Emphasis on Partnership," *Journal of Forestry* (March 1995): 15–17.

30. Steve Moore, interview by author, August 1998, tape recording in author's possession.

31. Stephen Moore and Bromfield Ridley, "Standing Crops of Brook Trout Concurrent with Removal of Rainbow Trout from Selected Streams in the Great Smoky Mountains National Park," *North American Journal of Fisheries Management* 3 (1983): 72–80; Jerry West, Stephen Moore, and M. Randall Turner, "Evaluation of Electrofishing as a Management Technique in Restoring Brook Trout in the Great Smoky Mountains," National Park Service Research/Resources Management Report, 1990.

32. Gary Larson, Stephen Moore, and Danny Lee, "Angling and Electrofishing for Removing Non-Native Rainbow Trout from a Stream in a National Park," *North American Journal of Fisheries Management* 6 (Fall 1986): 580–85.

33. John P. Hayes, Stanley Guffey, Frank Kriegler, Gary McCracken, and Charles Parker, "Genetic Diversity of Native, Stocked, and Hybrid Populations of Brook Trout in the Southern Appalachians," *Conservation Biology* 10 (October 1996): 1403–12.

34. *Chattanooga Free-Press*, 9 February 1992; *Knoxville News-Sentinel*, 26 July 1998.

35. *Cherokee One Feather*, 4 May 1988; press release, "Herbst to Keynote Brook Trout Celebration," 6 May 1988, Vertical Files, GSMNP; Steve Moore, interview by author, August 1998, tape recording in author's possession.

36. David Etnier, interview by author, 8 April 1999, tape recording in author's possession; Damien J. Simbeck, "Distribution of the Fishes of the Great Smoky Mountains National Park" (master's thesis, University of Tennessee, 1990).

37. Gerald R. Dinkins, "Aspects of the Life History of the Smoky Madtom, *Noturus baileyi* Taylor, in Citico Creek" (master's thesis, University of Tennessee, 1984).

38. Peggy W. Shute, "Ecology of the Rare Yellowfin Madtom, *Nocturus flavipinnis* Taylor, in Citico Creek" (master's thesis, University of Tennessee, 1984).

39. *Mountain Press*, 27 September 1988; David Etnier, interview by author, 8 April 1999, tape recording in author's possession.

40. *Knoxville News-Sentinel*, 22 September 1988; *Knoxville News-Sentinel*, 4 October 1989.

41. Carroll Schell, interview by author, 17 March 1999, tape recording in author's possession.

42. *Knoxville News-Sentinel*, 15 May 1980; handwritten notes, River Otter, Vertical Files, GSMNP.

43. *Mountain Press*, 28 February 1986; Jane Griess, "Progress Report: River Otter Project, October 1986," River Otter, Vertical Files, GSMNP.

44. Jane M. Griess, "River Otter Reintroduction in the Great Smoky Mountains National Park" (master's thesis, University of Tennessee, 1987).

45. *Knoxville News-Sentinel*, 9 July 1992.

46. *Asheville Citizen-Times*, 26 January 1994, and *Knoxville News-Sentinel*, 15 January 1994; *Citizen Tribune*, 9 July 1989; Carroll Schell, interview by author, March 17 1999, tape recording in author's possession.

47. Warren T. Parker, "A Historic Perspective of *Canis rufus* and Its Recovery Potential," Red Wolf Management Series, Technical Report No. 3, May 1988, Red Wolf, Vertical Files, GSMNP.

48. Gary Henry, interview by author, 7 April 1999, tape recording in author's possession.

49. Gary Henry, interview by author, 7 April 1999, tape recording in author's possession; *Metro Pulse* (Knoxville), April 1999, 8–15.

50. Arthur Stupka, interview by Bill Landry, 1989, Landry Collection; Arthur Stupka to Joseph Hickey, 11 August 1939, Peregrine Falcons, Vertical Files, GSMNP.

51. "Reintroduction of Peregrines, Great Smoky Mountains National Park," 1984; memorandum, field supervisor, U.S. Fish and Wildlife Service, to superintendent, 20 July 1984; Rick Knight and Robert Shumate, "Greenbrier Pinnacle," 14 September 1984, Peregrines, Vertical Files, GSMNP.

52. *Mountain Press*, 2 July 1990, 11 May 1997; Dick Dickinson, "Peregrine Falcon Growth and Behavior from Nesting to Dispersal States at a Smoky Mountain Eyrie," August 1997, Peregrine Falcon, Vertical Files, GSMNP.

53. *Gatlinburg Press*, 1 May 1975, 19 August 1975.

54. *Waynesville Mountaineer*, 29 July 1977; *Miami News*, 26 September 1978; press release, 19 August 1977; "Bear Management Plan," June 1977, Vertical Files, Bears, GSMNP.

55. Kim Delozier, interview by author, August 1998; "Bare Facts," *Resource Management Newsletter*, 27 April 1981, Bears, Vertical Files, GSMNP.

56. *The Tennessean*, 10 October 1989; Case Incident Record 894155; Bear Incidents, Great Smoky Mountains National Park, Bears, Vertical Files, GSMNP.

57. Kim Delozier, interview by author, August 1998; Mike Pelton, interview by author, 8 April 1999, tape recordings in author's possession.

58. *Knoxville News-Sentinel*, 16 April 1991.

59. *Mountain Press*, 17 February 1998; Trout, 133.

60. John C. Peine and James R. Renfro, "Visitor Use Patterns in the Great Smoky Mountains National Park," Resource Management Report SER-90 (Gatlinburg, Tenn.: Uplands Field Research Laboratory, 1988).

61. Dobson, 123, 127, 128; *Knoxville News-Sentinel*, 20 July 1995.

62. *Mountain Press*, 17 February 1998; Pat Arnow, "Dollywood: The Changing Profile of Pigeon Forge," *Now and Then* 8 (Spring 1991): 8–10.

63. Dolly Parton, *My Life and Other Unfinished Business* (New York: HarperCollins, 1994), 313.

64. Michael Smith, *Behind the Glitter: The Impact of Tourism on Rural Women in the Southeast* (Lexington, Ky.: Southeast Women's Employment Coalition, 1989), 47, 48–49, 51.

65. Smith, 60–61.

66. *Asheville Citizen-Times,* 31 January 1988.

67. *Knoxville News-Sentinel,* 31 January 1988.

68. *Knoxville Journal,* 19 May 1983.

69. *Asheville Citizen-Times,* 18 October 1998.

70. Southeast Women's Employment Coalition, *Women of the Rural South* (Lexington, Ky.: Southeast Women's Employment Coalition, 1986); *Performance Audit: Department of Tourist Development* (Nashville: Division of State Audit, 1989).

71. *Mountain Press,* 23 November 1993.

72. *Mountain Press,* 1 July 1998.

73. *Mountain Press,* 30 January 1999.

74. Lucinda Oakley Ogle, interview by Paul Sagan, 1990, Oral History Collection, GSMNP.

75. *Knoxville News-Sentinel,* 11 September 1994.

76. Leroy Fox, interview by author, 27 February 1999, tape recording in author's possession.

77. Superintendent to regional director, 18 November 1983, Leroy Fox Collection, unprocessed records, Great Smoky Mountains Collection, Hodges Library, University of Tennessee, Knoxville.

78. *Smoky Mountain Times,* 27 March 1984.

79. *Smoky Mountain Times,* 15 March 1984; Leroy Fox, interview by author, March 1999.

80. "Briefing Statement, Director's Visit," 29 April 1987, Management Files, Box XVIII–7, GSMNP.

81. "Wilderness Proposal '87," 8 April 1987, Wilderness, Vertical Files, GSMNP.

82. *Cherokee One Feather,* 29 June 1988.

83. *Senate Subcommittee Hearings,* 23 June 1987.

10. Global Threats, Local Conspiracy Theories

1. *Superintendent's Report,* September 1963; memorandum, chief ranger to superintendent, 9 September 1963 and 6 November 1963, Ranger Activities, Box II–10, GSMNP.

2. *Superintendent's Report,* December 1963, June 1964 and 1965, GSMNP.

3. Peter S. White, "Biodiversity and the Exotic Species Threat," *Exotic Pests of Eastern Forests: Conference Proceedings,* ed. Kerry O. Britton (Nashville: USDA Forest Service and Tennessee Exotic Pest Plant Council, 8–10 April 1997), 1.

4. Stagner Report, reprinted in Dilsaver, 217.

5. Sellers, 262–64; National Resource Council, *Science and the National Parks* (Washington, D.C.: National Academy Press, 1992), 41–57.

6. Kristine Johnson, interview by author, 27 January 1999, e-mail printout in author's possession.

7. H. L. Lambert and W. M. Ciesla, "Status of the Balsam Woolly Aphid in the Southern Appalachians—1996," Report No. 6-7-3, USDA Forest Service, Southeastern Area, BWA, Vertical Files, GSMNP.

8. U.S. Forest Service Research Note SE-32, "Release of Predators of the Balsam Woolly Aphid in North Carolina," October 1963, Vertical Files, BWA, GSMNP.

9. Lambert and Ciesla, 6–10.

10. Ann Sutton and Myron Sutton, *Eastern Forests* (New York: Alfred A. Knopf, 1993), 363.

11. C. H. Claridge, state forester, to R. K. Smith et al., 26 November 1963; James P. Wiggins, "Cost of Controlling the Balsam Woolly Aphid on Road Mountain," n.d., BWA, Vertical Files, GSMNP; George S. Puritch, "The Toxic Effects of Fatty Acids and Their Salts on the Balsam Woolly Aphid," *Canadian Journal of Forest Resources* 5 (1975): 515–22.

12. Mrs. Cornelia D. Hollister to person working on saving Fraser fir trees, 25 August 1983, BWA, Vertical Files, GSMNP.

13. *Charlotte Observer*, 20 September 1982.

14. *Waynesville Mountaineer*, 9 September 1987.

15. *Waynesville Mountaineer*, 27 July 1984; Kristine Johnson to Garrett Smathers, 25 November 1997; Peter White to Chris Eagar, 20 October 1985, BWA, Vertical Files, GSMNP; Kristine Johnson, interview by author, 29 January 1999, e-mail printout in author's possession.

16. N. S. Nicholas and P. S. White, "The Effect of Balsam Woolly Aphid Infestation on Fuel Levels in Spruce-Fir Forests of the Great Smoky Mountains National Park," Research/Resource Management Report SER-74, January 1985, Uplands Field Research Laboratory, National Park Service, BWA, Vertical Files, GSMNP.

17. Dr. Fred J. Alsop III, and Thomas F. Laughlin, "Censuses of a Breeding Bird Population in a Virgin Spruce-Fir Forest on Mt. Guyot, Great Smoky Mountains National Park before and after Balsam Wooly Aphid Infestation," April 1986, BWA, Vertical Files, GSMNP.

18. Paris Lambdin, "Biodiversity in Selected Ecosystems and the Importance of Systematics." Paper presented at Forty-second Southern Forest Insect Work Conference, 4 August 1998.

19. Scott E. Schlarbaum, Frederick Hebard, Pauline Spaine, and Joseph Kamalay, "Three American Tragedies: Chestnut Blight, Butternut Canker, and Dutch Elm Disease," in *Exotic Pests of Eastern Forests: Conference Proceedings*, ed. Kerry O. Britton (Nashville: USDA Forest Service and Tennessee Exotic Pest Plant Council, 8–10 April 1997): 48–50; Southern Appalachian Assessment: Terrestrial Technical Report, July 1996, Southern Appalachian Man and the Biosphere Cooperative, 112; Sutton, 431; Johnson, 2; Kristine Johnson, interview by author, 1 February 1998, e-mail printout in author's possession.

20. Raleigh *News and Observer*, 26 February 1997; Johnson, "Summary of Forest Insect and Disease Impacts," 1; Sutton, 375.

21. Johnson, 1–2; "How to Identify and Control Dogwood Anthracnose," brochure, USDA Forest Service (Washington, D.C.: U.S. Government Printing Office, 1990).

22. Phyllis Windle, "The Ecology of Grief," *Bioscience* 42 (May 1992): 363–67; *Washington Post*, 8 April 1990.

23. K. Langdon, Charles Parker, Mark Windham, Sue Powell, and Kristine Johnson, "A Preliminary Hard Rating for Dogwood Anthracnose in the Southern Appalachians," and M. Windham, M. Montgomery-Dee, and K. Langdon, "Increased Dogwood Anthracnose in Great Smoky Mountains National Park from 1988–1992" and "Factors Affecting Dogwood Anthracnose Severity in Great Smoky Mountains National Park," both in *Results of the 1992 Dogwood Anthracnose Impact Assessment and Pilot Test in the Southeastern United States*, John L. Knighten and Robert L. Anderson, eds. (Asheville, N.C.: USDA Forest Service, Southern Region, 1993), 35–52.

24. David Houston, "Beech Bark Disease," *Exotic Pests of Eastern Forests: Conference Proceedings*, ed. Kerry O. Britton (Nashville: USDA Forest Service and Tennessee Exotic Pest Plant Council, 8–10 April 1997): 29–41; *Southern Appalachian Assessment: Terrestrial Technical Report*, July 1996, Southern Appalachian Man and the Biosphere Cooperative, 111; Sutton, 399; Johnson, 3; Kristine Johnson, interview by author, 1 February 1999, e-mail printout in author's possession.

25. *Popular Science* 243 (July 1993): 72.

26. Mark McClure, "Hemlock Woolly Adelgid," USDA Forest Service Pest Alert, Northeastern Area (Durham, N.H.: USDA Forest Service 1991); *Transylvania Times*, 28 January 1999; "Giant Hemlocks Face Predator," *National Parks* 73 (January–February 1999): 16–19.

27. USDA Forest Service, Southern Region, *Insects and Diseases of Trees in the South*, Protection Report R8-PR 16 (June 1989): 12.

28. *Southern Lumberman* 68 (15 March 1913): 912.

29. University of Tennessee *Daily Beacon*, 28 September 1992; *Asheville Citizen-Times*, 21 December 1998.

30. Kristine Johnson, "Summary of Forest Insect and Disease Impacts, Great Smoky Mountains National Park," October 1997.

31. Randy G. Westbrooks, Lee Otteni, and Robert E. Eplee, "New Strategies for Weed Prevention," in *Exotic Pests of Eastern Forests: Conference Proceedings*, ed. Kerry O. Britton (Nashville: USDA Forest Service and Tennessee Exotic Pest Plant Council, 8–10 April 1997), 13–21.

32. Steve Oak, interview by author, 23 February 1999, tape recording in author's possession.

33. U.S. Congress, Office of Technology Assessment, *Harmful Non-Indigenous Species in the United States* (Washington, D.C.: U.S. Government Printing Office, 1993), 170–75.

34. Kristine Johnson, "Exotic Plant Management in the Great Smoky Mountains National Park," handout, Exotic Species, Vertical Files, GSMNP, 2–4; *Johnson City Press*, 28 May 1997; James H. Miller, "Exotic Invasive Plants in Southeastern Forests," in *Exotic Pests of Eastern Forests: Conference Proceedings*, ed. Kerry O. Britton (Nashville: USDA Forest Service and Tennessee Exotic Pest Plant Council, 8–10 April 1997), 97–105.

35. Stephen Spongberg, *A Reunion of Trees* (Cambridge: Harvard University Press, 1990), 90, 225–26; R. C. Anderson and S. S. Dhilion, "Acclimatization of Garlic Mustard," *American Journal of Botany* 78 (1991): 129–30.

36. John M. Randall and Janet Marinelli, eds., *Invasive Plants: Weeds of the Global Garden* (Brooklyn: Brooklyn Botanic Garden Publications, 1996), 66, 69; D. T. Patterson, "The History and Distribution of Five Exotic Weeds in North Carolina," *Castenea* 41 (1976): 177–80.

37. Ted Williams, "Invasion of the Aliens," *Audubon* (September–October 1994): 24–32; *Superintendent's Report*, March, June, and July 1958; July and September 1962; J. H. Miller and E. Boyd, "Kudzu: Where Did It Come From and How Can We Stop It?" *Southern Journal of Applied Forestry* 7 (1983): 165–69.

38. Kristine Johnson, "Exotic Plant Management in the Great Smoky Mountains National Park," handout, Exotic Species, Vertical Files, GSMNP, 2–4; *Johnson City Press*, 28 May 1997.

39. Michael A. Ruggiero, "The Rational Use of Pesticides in Park and Recreation Areas," *Trends* 23 (1986): 10–14.

40. Robert Devine, "Botanical Barbarians," *Sierra* (January–February 1994): 50–71.

41. "Exotic Pest Plants and Their Effects on Natural Areas," Western North Carolina Tomorrow, pamphlet, Exotic Pests, Vertical Files, GSMNP; Kris Johnson to author, 6 April 1999, e-mail printout in author's possession.

42. Linda Butler, "Biodiversity Studies in West Virginia: Problems and Challenges." Paper presented at Forty-second Annual Forest Insect Work Conference, 4 August 1998.

43. Joe Bowman, "Mountain Air Not Safe to Breathe," *Tennessee Star-Journal*, 25–31 July 1997, A1.

44. Jim Renfro, interview by author, 19 August 1998, tape recording in author's possession.

45. Great Smoky Mountains Natural History Association and National Park Service, "Great Smoky Mountains National Park Management, Folio No. 2," n.d., Air Quality, Vertical Files, GSMNP.

46. Richard Powelson, "Planned Boiler Steams Up Federal Agency," *Knoxville News-Sentinel*, 14 November 1991; Randall R. Pope, "Briefing Statement," 15 November 1991, Air Quality, Vertical Files, GSMNP.

47. James R. Renfro, "Ozone and Visibility Monitoring and Research at Great Smoky Mountains National Park" (Gatlinburg, Tenn.: Twin Creeks Natural Resource Center, 12 August 1994), 12.

48. TVA, "Forest Health Monitoring in Southern Appalachia," brochure, SAMAB, n.d.

49. D. G. Silsbee and G. L. Larson, "Water Quality of Streams in the Great Smoky Mountains National Park," *Hydrobiologia* 89 (1982): 97–115.

50. Gary Larson, David Silsbee, and Raymond C. Matthews Jr., "A Brief Review of Causes and Consequences of Acid Participation in Relation to Potential Effects on

the Resources of the Great Smoky Mountains National Park" (Gatlinburg, Tenn.: Uplands Field Research Laboratory, n.d.), 9, 19.

51. Peter White, "An Outline of Air Quality Related Research in GRSM," May 1985, Uplands Field Research Laboratory, Box I–13, GSMNP.

52. Christopher Eagar, "Forest Damage on Clingman's Dome, Great Smoky Mountains National Park," BWA, Vertical Files, GSMNP.

53. Chris Eagar, interview by author, 16 April 1999, tape recording in author's possession.

54. *Waynesville Mountaineer,* 9 September 1987.

55. Stephen C. Nodvin and Niki S. Nicholas, "Watershed, Forest Health, and Air Quality Research in the Great Smoky Mountains." Paper presented at Forty-fifth AIBS Annual Meeting, 12 August 1994, Knoxville; Patricia F. Brewer, Kathy Tonnessen, Jack Cosby, Ron Munson, and Tim Sullivan, "Watershed Responses to Changes in Deposition of Sulfur, Nitrogen, and Base Cations: A Modeling Exercise by SAMI." Paper presented at Ninth Annual SAMAB Conference, Gatlinburg, Tenn., 4–6 November 1998.

56. *Knoxville News-Sentinel,* 25 May 1988.

57. *Appalachian Voice* (Early Winter 1997): 11.

58. Murray Evans, phone interview by author, 7 July 1998.

59. *Knoxville News-Sentinel,* 23 May 1976; *Gatlinburg Press,* 24 June 1976; *Maryville-Alcoa Daily Times,* 18 November 1976; *Knoxville News-Sentinel,* 24 October 1978.

60. William P. Gregg to Frank B. Golley, 31 January 1983, Uplands Field Research Laboratory, Box II–6, GSMNP.

61. Peter White to Bill Greg, 29 December 1987, Uplands Field Research Laboratory, Box II–6, GSMNP.

62. Memorandum, Beal to regional director, 16 July 1985, Uplands Field Research Laboratory, Box II–6, GSMNP.

63. *Mountain Press,* 30 June 1997.

64. *Maryville-Alcoa Daily Times,* 18 November 1976.

65. *Chattanooga Free Press,* 21 June 1998.

66. *Mountain Press,* 1 July 1997.

67. *Mountain Press,* 30 June 1997; *Foothills News: Newsletter of the Foothills Land Conservancy* 1 (1992): 4–5; brochure, SAMAB, "Finding Solutions That Enhance Economic and Environmental Health," n.d.

Epilogue

1. Sevierville *Mountain Press,* 23 July 1997; *Knoxville News-Sentinel,* 2 October 1997.

2. Sevierville *Mountain Press,* 15 November 1997.

3. Sevierville *Mountain Press,* 25 September 1997.

4. Sevierville *Mountain Press,* 22 November 1997.

5. *Nashville Banner,* 24 November 1997.

6. Sevierville *Mountain Press*, 27 September 1997.

7. Alfred Runte, *National Parks: The American Experience*. 3d ed. (Lincoln and London: University of Nebraska Press, 1997).

8. Mark David Spence, "Crown of the Continent, Backbone of the World," *Environmental History* 1 (July 1996): 29–49, 33–34.

9. William Cronon, "The Trouble with Wilderness; or, Getting Back to the Wrong Nature," in *UnCommon Ground: Rethinking the Human Place in Nature* (New York: W. W. Norton, 1996), 69–90. For more on Native American issues, see Robert H. Keller and Michael F. Turek, *American Indians and National Parks* (Tucson: University of Arizona Press, 1998).

10. Excerpts from the Final Environmental Impact Statement, General Management Plan for Great Smoky Mountains National Park, January 1982, Vertical Files, Elkmont, GSMNP.

11. *Chattanooga Times*, 29 November 1991; *National Parks* (March–April 1992): 19.

12. *Mountain Press*, 26 May 1992.

13. *Mountain Press*, 26 May 1992 and 30 June 1992; Mrs. Burl Watson to Congressman Jimmy Quillen, 26 December 1991; Mrs. Mrytle Fox and Miss Zelma Ownby to Hon. James Quillen, 13 February 1992, Vertical Files, Elkmont, GSMNP.

14. Dilsaver, 46.

15. John Nolt, Athena Bradley, Mike Knapp, Donald E. Lampard, and Jonathon Scherch, *What Have We Done?* (Washborn, Tenn.: Foundation for Global Sustainability, 1998), 248.

16. John Nolt et al., 183.

17. Stephen C. Trombulak, "The Restoration of Old Growth: Why and How," in *Eastern Old-Growth Forests: Prospects for Rediscovery and Recovery*, ed. Mary Byrd Davis (Washington, D.C: Island Press, 1996), 305–18.

18. Keith Langdon, "The ATVI," public talk at Transylvania County Sierra Club meeting, 15 April 1999.

19. *Asheville Citizen-Times*, vol. 129, no. 168, 1998.

20. Richard M. Stapleton, "A Call to Action," *National Parks* (March–April 1994): 39.

Abbreviations

AAETSU	Archives of Appalachia, East Tennessee State University, Johnson City, Tennessee
FHS	Forest History Society, Durham, North Carolina
FRCEP	Federal Record Center, East Point, Atlanta, Georgia
GSMNP	Great Smoky Mountains National Park Archives, Gatlinburg, Tennessee
NCSTATE	North Carolina State Archives, Raleigh, North Carolina
TSTATE	Tennessee State Archives, Nashville, Tennessee
UTK	Hodges Library, University of Tennessee, Knoxville, Tennessee

I. Primary Sources

A. MANUSCRIPTS

Atlanta, Georgia. East Point Record Center for the National Archives.
   Cherokee Indian Agency Collection.
   Tennessee Valley Authority Records.
Atlanta, Georgia. Emory University. Robert W. Woodruff Library.
   J. L. Harris Papers.
Berkeley, California. Bancroft Library. Sierra Club Collection.
   Theodore Snyder Jr. Papers.
Chapel Hill, North Carolina. University of North Carolina.
   North Carolina Collection.
Cullowhee, North Carolina. Western Carolina University.
   George Masa Collection.

Horace Kephart Collection.

Zebulon Weaver Collection.

Durham, North Carolina. Forest History Society.

Biltmore Collection.

Photo Collection.

Gatlinburg, Tennessee. Great Smoky Mountains National Park Archives.

Abstracts of Title, North Carolina.

Agricultural Records.

Charles S. Grossman Papers.

Civilian Conservation Corps Records.

David C. Chapman Collection.

Davis Collection.

Harvey Broome Papers.

H. C. Wilburn Papers.

Hook Photography Collection.

Great Smoky Mountains Conservation Association Papers.

Land Acquisition Files.

Lands Transferred to the Federal Government, Files.

Logging Records.

Management Files.

Mary Ruth Chiles Collection.

Photo Collection.

Smoky Mountains Hiking Guide Collection.

Uplands Field Research Laboratory Files. Vertical Files.

Hyde Park, New York. Franklin and Eleanor Roosevelt Library.

President's Personal Files.

Johnson City, Tennessee. East Tennessee State University.

Archives of Appalachia.

Charles C. Tiller Collection.

D. R. Beeson Papers.

Joe Jennings Papers.

Knoxville, Tennessee. University of Tennessee Archives, Hodges Library.

Great Smoky Mountains National Park Collection.

Knoxville, Tennessee. McClung Collection.

Broome Papers.

Thompson Photograph Collection.

Nashville, Tennessee. Tennessee State Archives.

Austin Peay Papers.

Paul J. Adams Papers.

New York, New York. Rockefeller Archive Center.

Laura Spellman Rockefeller Memorial Collection.

Rockefeller Family Collection.

Raleigh, North Carolina. North Carolina State Archives.

North Carolina Park Commission Collection.

Cherokee, North Carolina. Living Voices Project.

Jackson, Ella. Interview by Lois Calonehuskie and Bill Jackson, 1987.

    Jumper, Bessie. Interview by Lois Calonehuskie, 1987.

Wachacha, Maggie. Interview by Lois Calonehuskie, Earl Davis, and Tom Hill, 1987.

Dilsaver, Larry M. *America's National Park System: The Critical Documents.* Lanham, Md.: Rowman & Littlefield, 1994.

Ernest, Joseph W., ed. *Worthwhile Places: Correspondence of John D. Rockefeller, Jr. and Horace M. Albright.* New York: Fordham University Press, 1991.

Fry, George. *George Fry: The Legend.* Self-published, 1994.

Lilienthal, David. *The Journals of David Lilienthal.* New York: Harper & Row, 1964.

Marion, Lieutenant Francis. "Sowing Tears of Hate." *Journal of Cherokee Studies* 2 (Summer 1977): 333–34.

Loue, Mary Jane. *Voices in the Valley: Remembering World War II, Excerpts from TVA Oral History Interviews.* Knoxville, Tenn.: TVA, 1993.

Durham, North Carolina. Forest History Society. Tape recordings.

    Damtoft, W. J. Interview by Elwood R. Maunder, 1959.

    Robertson, Reuben. Interview by Jerry Maunder, 1959.

Gatlinburg, Tennessee. Great Smoky Mountains National Park Library. Tape recordings.

    Albright, Horace. Interview by Michael Frome, 1964.

    Burchfield, John. Interview by Joseph Hall, 1939.

    Cable, Fonz. Interview by Joseph Hall, 1939.

    Calhoun, Granville. Interview by William F. Alston, 1975.

    Calhoun, Seymour. Interview by William F. Alston, 1975.

    Carver, Jarvis. Interview by Rosemary Nichols, 1974.

    Clabo, Herbert. Interview by Jane Whitney, 1973.

    Cline, Andy. Interview by Robert Madden, 1969.

    Cole, Nancy. Interview by Charles S. Grossman, 1965.

    Cole, Walter. Interview by Charles S. Grossman, 1965.

    Conner, Jarvis. Interview by Rosemary Nichols, 1974.

    Crisp, Bert. Interview by Robert Madden, 1968.

    Crisp, Zeb. Interview by Joseph Hall, 1938.

    Davis, Henry and John. Interview by Robert Madden, 1969.

    Husky, Ethel. Interview by Glenn Cardwell, 1974.

    Jackson, Frank. Interview by Glenn Cardwell and Kathleen Manscill, 1981.

    McCarter, Louis. Interview by Robert S. Lambert, 1958.

    McCauley, Laura Dulcie Abbott. Interview by Mary Robinson, 1981.

    Manning, Birgie. Interview by Mary Ruth Chiles, 1981.

    Manning, Johnny. Interview by Mary Ruth Chiles, 1981.

Maples, Alie Newman. Interview by Jane Whitney, 1973.
Matthews, Herman. Interview by Glenn Cardwell, 1979.
Moore, "Preacher." Interview by Jane Whitney, 1973.
Myers, Charley. Interview by Jane Whitney, 1973.
Newman, Fred. Interview by Jane Whitney, 1973.
Ogle, Lucinda Oakley. Interview by Jane Whitney, 1973.
Ogle, Lucinda Oakley. Interview by Paul Sagan, 1990.
Ownby, Clon. Interview by Glenn Cardwell, 1974.
Ownby, Enslie. Interview by Glenn Cardwell, 1974.
Ownby, Juanita. Interview by Glenn Cardwell, 1974.
Ownby, Lem. Interview by Orlie Trentham, 1972.
Ownby, Newton. Interview by Joseph Hall, 1939.
Palmer, Mrs. George. Interview by Joseph Hall, 1938.
Palmer, "Turkey" George. Interview by Joseph Hall, 1938.
Palmer, Will. Interview by Joseph Hall, 1939.
Parton, John. Interview by Robert Lambert, 1958.
Reagan, Amos. Interview by Joseph Hall, 1938.
Reagan, Wesley. Interview by Robert Madden and Glenn Cardwell, 1969.
Roland, John. Interview by Robert Madden, 1969.
Shelton, Jim. Interview by Robert Madden, 1968.
Shelton, Jim. Interview by Jane Whitney, 1972.
Shelton, Jim. Interview by Mary Lindsay, 1975.
Smelcer, Eunice. Interview by Joseph Hall, 1939.
Stinnett, Leola. Interview by Joseph Hall, 1938.
Woody, Paul. Interview by Kathleen Manscill, 1984.
Woody, Robert. Interview by Sam Easterby, 1973.

Transcripts in the Weaver McCracken Collection.

Barnes, Joe. Interview by Weaver McCracken, 1974.
Brackin, Raymer. Interview by Weaver McCracken, 1974.
Cagle, Winfred. Interview by William Weaver, 1973.
McCarter, Curt. Interview by Weaver McCracken, 1974.
Rolen, William T. Interview by Weaver McCracken, 1978.
Siler, Albert. Interview by Weaver McCracken, 1974.
Sutton, Pink. Interview by Weaver McCracken, 1974.
Thompson, Arnold. Interview by Weaver McCracken, 1974.
Trentham, Horace. Interview by Weaver McCracken, 1974.
Whaley, P. Audley. Interview by Weaver McCracken, 1974.
Wiggins, Dave. Interview by Weaver McCracken, 1974.

Video Recordings in the Landry Collection.

Brown, Bob. Interview by Bill Landry, 1990.
Bryant, Delce Mae Carver. Interview by Bill Landry, 1989.

Caldwell, Raymond J. Interview by Bill Landry, 1989.

Dodgen, Rellie. Interview by Bill Landry, 1990.

Dorsey, "Pot." Interview by Bill Landry, 1989.

Hannah, Mark. Interview by Bill Landry, 1989.

Honeycutt, Dan L. Interview by Bill Landry, 1989.

Hunt, Edward. Interview by Bill Landry, 1989.

Huskey, Earl. Interview by Bill Landry, 1989.

Ledbetter, Maynard. Interview by Bill Landry, 1989.

Lowe, Eugene. Interview by Bill Landry, 1989.

Manley, Joe Frank. Interview by Bill Landry, 1988.

Monteith, Arnold. Interview by Bill Landry, 1988

Oakley, Clifford Elmore. Interview by Bill Landry, 1990.

Oliver, Louise. Interview by Bill Landry, 1989.

Ownby, Lucy Black. Interview by Bill Landry, 1989.

Palmer, Gudger. Interview by Bill Landry, 1988.

Palmer, Riley. Interview by Bill Landry, 1988.

Posey, Henry. Interview by Bill Landry, 1989.

Preston, George. Interview by Bill Landry, 1989.

Reagan, Ode. Interview by Bill Landry, 1989.

Stupka, Arthur. Interview by Bill Landry, 1989.

Vance, Clarence. Interview by Bill Landry, 1989.

Webb, Dewey. Interview by Bill Landry, 1989.

TAPE RECORDINGS AND E-MAIL TRANSCRIPTS
IN THE AUTHOR'S POSSESSION.

Bratton, Susan. Interviews by author, 1998, 1999.

Cardwell, Glenn. Interview by author, 1988.

Clebsch, Ed. Interview by author, 1999.

Defoe, Don. Interview by author, 1998.

Delozier, Kim. Interview by author, 1998.

Eagar, Chris. Interview by author, 1999.

Etnier, David. Interview by author, 1999.

Evans, Murray. Interview by author, 1998.

Evison, Boyd. Interview by author, 1998.

Fox, Leroy. Interview by author, 1999.

Henry, Gary. Interview by author, 1999.

Johnson, Kristine. Interview by author, 1999.

Langdon, Keith, Interview by author, 1999.

Moore, Stephen. Interview by author, 1998.

Oak, Steve. Interview by author, 1999.

Payne, Ray. Interview by author, 1998.

Pelton, Mike. Interview by author, 1999.

Pittillo, Dan. Interview by author, 1998.

Posey, Alice Moore. Interview by author and Michael Kline, 1990.
Posey, Henry. Interview by author and Michael Kline, 1990.
Renfro, James R. Interview by author, 1998.
Schell, Carroll. Interview by author, 1999.
Snyder, Ted. Interview by author, 1998.
Whaley, Zenith. Interview by author, 1989.
White, Peter S. Interview by author, 1999.

D. GOVERNMENT DOCUMENTS

Alston, Mark, et al. *Historical Overview of Fisheries Studies and Sport Fisheries Monitoring*. Gatlinburg, Tenn.: Uplands Field Research Laboratory, 1984.
Ashe, W. W. "Chestnut in Tennessee." *Bulletin 10, Forest Studies in Tennessee.* Nashville, Tenn.: Baird-Ward Printing Company, 1912.
———. *Forest Fires: Their Destructive Work, Causes and Prevention.* Raleigh, N.C.: State Printer, 1895.
———. *The Possibilities of a Maple Sugar Industry in Western North Carolina.* Winston-Salem, N.C.: M. I. and J. C. Stewart, 1897.
Ayres, H. B., and W. W. Ashe. *The Southern Appalachian Forests: Professional Paper No. 37.* Washington, D.C.: GPO, 1905.
Battle, William Horn. *Battle's Revisal of Public Statutes of North Carolina.* Raleigh, N.C.: Edwards, Broughton and Company, 1873.
Baxter, D. V. "Deterioration of Chestnut in the Southern Appalachians." *Technical Bulletin No. 257.* Washington, D.C.: U.S. Department of Agriculture, 1931.
Bratton, Susan Power, Matthew G. Hickler, and James H. Graves. *Trail and Campsite Erosion Survey for the Great Smoky Mountains National Park.* 3 vols. Gatlinburg, Tenn.: Uplands Field Research Laboratory, 1978.
Bratton, Susan Power, and Peter S. White. *Grassy Balds Management and Nature Preserves: Issues and Problems.* Gatlinburg, Tenn.: Uplands Field Research Laboratory, n.d.
Code Commission. *The Code of Tennessee.* Kingsport, Tenn.: Southern Publishers, 1931.
Culbertson, Nicole. "Status and History of the Mountain Lion in the Great Smoky Mountains National Park." *Management Report No. 15.* Gatlinburg, Tenn.: Uplands Field Research Laboratory, 1977.
Dils, Robert E. "Influence of Forest Cutting and Mountain Farming on Some Vegetation, Surface Soil, and Surface Runoff Characteristics." *Southeast Forest Experiment Station Paper No. 24.* Washington, D.C.: USDA Forest Service, 1953.
Dykeman, Wilma, and Jim Stokely. *Highland Homeland: The People of the Great Smokies.* Washington, D.C.: National Park Service, 1978.
Fanzreb, Kathleen E., and Ricky A. Phillips. "Neotropical Migratory Birds of the Southern Appalachians." *Southern Research Station General Technical Report SE-96.* Washington, D.C.: U.S. Department of Agriculture, 1996.

Federal Writer's Project. North Carolina: *The WPA Guide to the Old North State.* Chapel Hill: University of North Carolina, 1939.

Frothingham, E. H. "Timber Growing and Logging Practices in the Southern Appalachian Region." *Technical Bulletin No. 250.* Washington, D.C.: U.S. Department of Agriculture, 1931.

Gilbert, William H. "The Cherokees of North Carolina: Living Memorials to the Past." *Smithsonian Report for 1956.* Washington, D.C.: Smithsonian Institution Press, 1957, 529–55.

Gravatt, G. F. "Chestnut Blight." *Farmer's Bulletin No. 1641.* Washington, D.C.: GPO, 1930.

Graves, Henry. Forest Conditions in Western North Carolina. *North Carolina Economic Survey, Bulletin No. 23.* Raleigh, N.C.: Edwards, Broughton and Company, 1911.

Great Smoky Mountains National Park. *Transportation Concepts.* Washington, D.C.: U.S. Department of Interior, 1971.

Harber, V. L., Bernard Frank, and W. E. McQuilkin. "Forest Practices and Productivity." *Yearbook of Agriculture, 1957.* Washington, D.C.: GPO, 1957.

Holmes, J. S. "Forest Conditions in Western North Carolina." *North Carolina Geological and Economic Survey, Bulletin No. 23.* Raleigh, N.C.: Edwards, Broughton and Company, 1911.

———. "Forest Fires in North Carolina during 1918, 1919, and 1920." *Economic Paper No. 51.* Raleigh, N.C.: Mitchell Printing Co., 1921.

Kelly, G. Alan, G. S. Griffith, and Ronald D. Jones. "Changes in Distribution of Trout in the Great Smoky Mountains National Park, 1900–1977." *Technical Paper of the U.S. Fish and Wildlife Service No. 102.* Washington, D.C.: U.S. Fish and Wildlife Service, 1980.

Knighten, John L., and Robert L. Anderson, eds. *Results of the 1992 Dogwood Anthracnose Impact Assessment and Pilot Test in the Southeastern United States.* Asheville, N.C.: USDA Forest Service, Southern Region, 1993.

Lambert, H. L., and W. M. Ciesla. "Status of the Balsam Woolly Aphid in the Southern Appalachians—1966." *Report No. 6–7–3.* USDA Forest Service, Southeastern Area, 1966.

Lambert, Robert S. "Logging in the Great Smoky Mountains National Park, a Report to the Superintendent." Manuscripts in Great Smoky Mountains National Park Archives, 1958.

———. "The Pioneer History of the Great Smoky Mountains National Park." Manuscripts in Great Smoky Mountains National Park Archives, n.d.

Lenihan, Daniel J., ed. *Final Report of the National Reservoir Inundation Study, I.* Santa Fe, N.M.: U.S. Department of Interior, 1989.

Lennon, Robert E. *An Annual Report of Progress.* Leestown, W. Va.: U.S. Fish and Wildlife Service, 1959.

———. "Brook Trout of the Great Smoky Mountains National Park." *Technical Papers of the Bureau of Sports Fisheries and Wildlife.* Washington, D.C.: U.S. Department of Interior, 1967.

Lennon, Robert E., and Philip S. Parker. "The Reclamation of Indian and Abrams Creek." *Scientific Fisheries Report No. 306*. Washington, D.C.: U.S. Department of Interior, 1959.

Lindsay, Mary M. "History of the Grassy Balds in Great Smoky Mountains National Park." *Management Report No. 4*. U.S. Department of Interior, National Park Service, Southeast Region. Gatlinburg, Tenn.: Uplands Field Research Laboratory, 1976.

McClure, Mark. "Hemlock Woolly Adelgid." *USDA Forest Service Pest Alert, Northeastern Area*. Durham, N.H.: USDA Forest Service, 1991.

Madden, Robert R. *Mountain Home: The Walker Family Farmstead*. Washington, D.C.: GPO, 1977.

Meigs, Return J., and William F. Cooper. *Code of Tennessee*. Nashville, Tenn.: E. G. Eastman and Company, 1858.

Michie, A. Hewson. *The North Carolina Code of 1927*. Charlottesville, Va.: Michie Company, 1928.

Milliken, W. A. *Code of Tennessee*. Nashville, Tenn.: Marshall & Bruce, 1884.

National Park Service. *Manual of the Branch of Forestry*. Washington, D.C.: GPO, 1935.

———. *A Study of the Park and Recreation Problems of the U.S.* Washington, D.C.: GPO, 1941.

North Carolina State Advertising Division. *North Carolina: Variety Vacationland*. Raleigh, N.C.: Department of Conservation and Development, 1946.

North Carolina State Highways and Public Works Commission, Tennessee State Department of Highways and Public Works, and U.S. Bureau of Public Roads. *Great Smoky Mountains National Park Travel Study*. Washington, D.C.: GPO, 1956.

Olson, Russ. *Administrative History: Organizational Structures of the National Park Service, 1917 to 1985*. Washington, D.C.: GPO, September 1985.

Peine, John C., and James R. Renfro. "Visitor Use Patterns in the Great Smoky Mountains National Park." *Resource Management Report SER-90*. Gatlinburg, Tenn.: Uplands Field Research Laboratory, 1988.

Pinchot, Gifford, and W. W. Ashe. *Timber Trees and Forests of North Carolina*. Winston, N.C.: M. I. and J. C. Stewart, 1897.

Pyle, Charlotte. *Vegetation Disturbance History of the Great Smoky Mountains National Park: An Analysis of Archival Maps and Records*. Gatlinburg, Tenn.: Uplands Field Research Laboratory, 1985.

Renfro, James R. "Ozone and Visibility Monitoring and Research at Great Smoky Mountains National Park." Gatlinburg, Tenn.: Twin Creeks Natural Resource Center, 12 August 1994.

Rhoades, Verne. *North Carolina Geological and Economic Survey, Federal Forest Purchases and Forest Recreation*. Chapel Hill, N.C.: North Carolina State Government, 1924.

Roosevelt, Franklin D. "The President's Greeting." *The Civilian Conservation Corps, Builder of Men*. Washington, D.C.: Happy Days Publishing Company, 1933.

Shannon, R. T. *Annotated Code of Tennessee*. Nashville, Tenn.: Marshall and Bruce, 1896.

Smith, Herbert Knox. *Report of the Commissioner of Corporations on the Lumber Industry, February 13, 1911*. Washington, D.C.: GPO, 1931.

Spahr, Neal B., and Charles Seymour. *Baldwin's Cumulative Supplement*. Cleveland, Ohio: Baldwin Law Book Company, 1920.

Story, Isabel F. *Our National Parks*. Washington, D.C.: GPO, 1936.

Superintendent's Monthly Reports, 1931–1945. Contained in Great Smoky Mountains National Park Archives.

Tennessee Acts. Nashville, Tenn.: Albert B. Tavel, 1891.

Tennessee Valley Authority. *Annual Report for 1938*. Washington, D.C.: GPO, 1938.

———. *Annual Report for 1939*. Washington, D.C.: GPO, 1939.

———. *Annual Report for 1940*. Washington, D.C.: GPO, 1940.

———. *Annual Report for 1941*. Washington, D.C.: GPO, 1941.

———. *Annual Report for 1942*. Washington, D.C.: GPO, 1942.

———. *Annual Report for 1943*. Washington, D.C.: GPO, 1943.

———. *Annual Report for 1944*. Washington, D.C.: GPO, 1944.

———. *Annual Report for 1945*. Washington, D.C.: GPO, 1945.

———. *The First Fifty Years: Changed Lands, Changed Lives*. Chattanooga, Tenn.: TVA, 1983.

———. *The Fontana Project*. Technical Report No. 12. Washington, D.C.: GPO, 1950.

Thompson, Frank M. *Thompson's Shannon's Code of Tennessee*. Louisville, Ky.: Baldwin Law Book Company, 1917.

Thompson, Seymour D. *A Compilation of the State Laws of Tennessee*. St. Louis, Mo.: Gilbert Publishing, 1873.

U.S. Census. *Twelfth Census of the United States, 1900*. Population Schedules. Haywood County, North Carolina.

———. *Thirteenth Census of the United States, 1910*. Population Schedules. Haywood County, North Carolina.

U.S. Congress, Office of Technology Assessment. *Harmful Non- Indigenous Species in the United States*. Washington, D.C.: GPO, 1993.

U.S. Department of Agriculture, Forest Service, Southern Region. *Insects and Diseases of Trees in the South*. Protection Report R8-PR16. Asheville, N.C.: USDA Forest Service, Southern Region, 1989.

U.S. Department of Commerce. *Directory of American Sawmills*. Washington, D.C.: GPO, 1915.

U.S. Department of Interior. *The Construction of Hoover Dam*. Las Vegas, Nev.: KC Publications, 1976 (28th edition).

———. *Final Report of the Southern Appalachian National Park Commission to the Secretary of the Interior*. Washington, D.C.: GPO, 1931.

U.S. Department of Labor. *Wages and Hours of Labor in the Lumber, Millwork, and Furniture Industries, 1890–1912*. Washington, D.C.: GPO, 1913.

U.S. Forest Service. *The South's Fourth Forest: Alternatives for the Future*. Washington, D.C.: U.S. Forest Service, 1988.

Waugh, Frank A. *Landscape Conservation*. Washington, D.C.: U.S. Department of Interior, 1935.

Wests Tennessee Digest. St. Paul, Minn.: West Law Book Company, 1987.

Wildlife Resources Commission, Tennessee. *A Strategic Plan for Wildlife Resource Management*. Washington, D.C.: U.S. Department of Interior, 1990.

Womack, Thomas B. *Revisal of 1905 Code of North Carolina*. Raleigh, N.C.: E.M. Uzzell, 1905.

II. Secondary Works

A. BOOKS

Adams, Paul J. *Mount LeConte*. Knoxville, Tenn.: Holston Printing, 1966.

Albanese, Catherine. *American Religious Experience and Religions*. Belmont, Calif.: Wadsworth, 1992.

Alexander, Tom. *Mountain Fever*. Asheville, N.C.: Bright Books, 1995.

Allen, Barbara, and Thomas Schlereeth, eds. *Sense of Place: American Regional Cultures*. Lexington: University of Kentucky Press, 1990.

Anderson, William L., ed. *Cherokee Removal, Before and After*. Athens: University of Georgia Press, 1984.

Arthur, John Preston. *Western North Carolina: A History, 1730–1930*. Spartanburg, N.C.: John Preston Arthur, 1914.

Barclay, R. E. *Ducktown Back in Raht's Time*. Chapel Hill: University of North Carolina Press, 1946.

Bartlett, Richard. *Troubled Waters: Champion International and the Pigeon River Controversy*. Knoxville: University of Tennessee Press, 1995.

Bookchin, Murray. *The Ecology of Freedom*. Palo Alto, Calif.: Cheshire Books, 1982.

———. *Remaking Society: Pathways to a Green Future*. Boston: South End Press, c. 1990.

———. *Toward an Ecological Society*. Montreal: Black Rose Books, 1980.

Bowman, Elizabeth Skaggs. *Land of High Horizons*. Kingsport, Tenn.: Southern Publishers, 1938.

Brewer, Alberta, and Carson Brewer. *Valley So Wild: A Folk History*. Knoxville: East Tennessee Historical Society, 1975.

Broome, Harvey. *Out Under the Sky of the Great Smokies: A Personal Journey*. Knoxville, Tenn.: Greenbrier Press, 1975.

———. *Some Miscellaneous Writings*. Knoxville, Tenn.: Greenbrier Press, 1970.

Bull, John, and John Farrand Jr. *Audubon Society Field Guide to North American Birds*. New York: Alfred A. Knopf, 1977.

Burns, Inez. *History of Blount County, Tennessee, 1795–1955*. Nashville: Tennessee Historical Commission, 1957.

Buxton, Barry M., ed. *The Great Forest: An Appalachian Story*. Boone, N.C.: Appalachian Consortium Press, 1985.

Campbell, Carlos. *Birth of a National Park in the Great Smoky Mountains*. Knoxville: University of Tennessee Press, 1960.

Campbell, John C. *The Southern Highlander and His Homeland*. Lexington: University of Kentucky Press, 1969.

Cantu, Rita. *Great Smoky Mountains: The Story Behind the Scenery*. Las Vegas, Nev.: KC Publications, 1979.

Carroll, Roy, and Raymond H. Pulley. *Historic Structures Report: Little Cataloochee, North Carolina*. Gatlinburg, Tenn.: Great Smoky Mountains Natural History Association, 1976.

Chappell, Fred. *I Am One of You Forever*. Baton Rouge: Louisiana State University Press, 1985.

Chase, Alston. *Playing God in Yellowstone: The Destruction of America's First National Park*. New York: Atlantic Monthly Press, 1986.

Conkin, Paul, and Erwin Hargrove, eds. *TVA: Fifty Years of Grass-Roots Bureaucracy*. Urbana: University of Illinois Press, 1983.

Cope, Florence Bush. *Dorie: Woman of the Mountains*. Knoxville: University of Tennessee Press, 1992.

Corkran, David H. *Cherokee Frontier: Conflict and Survival, 1740–1762*. Norman: University of Oklahoma Press, 1962.

Cornfield, Daniel A. *Workers and Dissent in the Redwood Empire*. Philadelphia: Temple University Press, 1987.

Craddock, Charles Egbert (Mary Noilles Murphree). *In the Tennessee Mountains*. Boston: Houghton Mifflin, 1885.

———. *The Prophet of the Great Smokies*. Boston and New York: Houghton Mifflin, 1885.

Creekmore, Betsey Beeler. *Knoxville*. Knoxville: University of Tennessee Press, 1958.

Creese, Walter L. *TVA's Public Planning: The Vision, the Reality*. Knoxville: University of Tennessee Press, 1990.

Cronon, William. *Changes in the Land: Indians, Colonists, and the Ecology of New England*. New York: Hill & Wang, 1983.

Crosby, Alfred. *The Columbian Exchange: Biological and Cultural Consequences of 1492*. Westport, Conn.: Greenwood Publishing, 1972.

Cunningham, Rodger. *Apples on the Flood*. Knoxville: University of Tennessee Press, 1987.

Cutler, Phoebe. *The Public Landscape of the New Deal*. New Haven: Yale University Press, 1985.

Davidson, Donald. *The Tennessee*. Vol. 2, *The New River: The Civil War to TVA*. New York: Rinehart, 1948.

Davis, Hattie Caldwell. *Cataloochee Valley*. Alexander, N.C.: World Comm, 1997.

Davis, Mary Byrd, ed. *Eastern Old Growth Forests: Prospects for Rediscovery and Recovery*. Washington, D.C.: Island Press, 1996.

DeArmond, Nora. *So High the Sun*. Clarksville, Tenn.: Jostens Publications, 1982.

Droze, Wilmon Henry. *High Dams and Slack Waters: TVA Rebuilds a River*. Baton Rouge: Louisiana State University Press, 1965.

Dunn, Durwood. *Cades Cove: The Life and Death of a Southern Appalachian Community, 1818–1937*. Knoxville: University of Tennessee Press, 1988.

Eaton, Allen. *Handicrafts of the Southern Highlands*. New York: Dover Publications, 1973.

Eddy, Samuel. *The Freshwater Fishes*. Dubuque, Iowa: William C. Brown Co., 1974.

Eller, Ronald D. *Miners, Millhands, and Mountaineers: Industrialization of the Appalachian South, 1880–1930*. Knoxville: University of Tennessee Press, 1982.

Etnier, David, and Wayne Starnes. *The Fishes of Tennessee*. Knoxville: University of Tennessee Press, 1994.

Everhardt, William C. *The National Park Service*. Boulder, Colo.: Westview Press, 1983.

Finger, John. *Cherokee Americans: The Eastern Band of Cherokees in the Twentieth Century*. Lincoln: University of Nebraska Press, 1991.

———. *The Eastern Band of Cherokees, 1819–1900*. Knoxville: University of Tennessee Press, 1984.

Fink, Paul M. *Backpacking Was the Only Way*. Johnson City, Tenn.: Research Advisory Council, East Tennessee State University, 1975.

French, Laurence, and Jim Hornbuckle, eds. *The Cherokee Perspective*. Boone, N.C.: Appalachian Consortium Press, 1981.

Frome, Michael. *Battle for the Wilderness*. Salt Lake City: University of Utah Press, 1997.

———. *Strangers in High Places: The Story of the Great Smoky Mountains*. Garden City, N.Y.: Doubleday, 1966.

Gasque, Jim. *Hunting and Fishing in the Great Smokies*. New York: Alfred A. Knopf, 1948.

Gates, William H. *Observations on the Possible Origins of the Balds of the Southern Appalachians*. Baton Rouge: Louisiana State University Press, 1941.

Great Smoky Mountains Conservation Association. *The Great Smoky Mountains in North Carolina and Tennessee*. Knoxville: Great Smoky Mountains Publishing Company, 1928.

Great Smoky Mountains Natural History Association. *Hiking Trails of the Smokies*. Gatlinburg, Tenn.: Great Smoky Mountains Natural History Association, 1994.

Greve, Jeanette S. *The Story of Gatlinburg*. Strasburg, Va.: Shenandoah Publishing House, 1941.

Hall, Joseph S. *Smoky Mountain Folks and Their Lore*. Asheville, N.C.: Great Smoky Mountains Natural History Association, 1960.

Hays, Samuel P. *Beauty, Health, and Permanence: Environmental Politics in the U.S., 1955–1985*. New York: Cambridge University Press, 1987.

———. *Conservation and the Gospel of Efficiency: The Progressive Movement, 1890–1920*. Cambridge: Harvard University Press, 1959.

Herrero, Stephen. *Bear Attacks: Their Causes and Avoidance.* New York: Lyons and Burford, 1985.

Hill, Sarah H. *Weaving New Worlds: Southeastern Cherokee Women and their Basketry.* Chapel Hill: University of North Carolina Press, 1997.

Houk, Rose. *Great Smoky Mountains National Park.* New York: Houghton Mifflin, 1994.

Hudson, Charles. *The Juan Pardo Expeditions: Explorations of the Carolinas and Tennessee, 1566–1568.* Washington, D.C.: Smithsonian Institution Press, 1990.

Hunnicutt, S. J. *Twenty Years of Hunting and Fishing in the Great Smoky Mountains.* Knoxville, Tenn.: S. B. Newman, 1926.

International Council of Scientific Unions, Scientific Committee on Problems of the Environment. *Man-Made Lakes as Modified Ecosystems.* Paris: International Council of Scientific Unions, 1972.

Ise, John. *Our National Park Policy: A Critical History.* Baltimore: Johns Hopkins Press, 1961.

Keller, Robert H., and Michael F. Turek. *American Indians and National Parks.* Tucson: University of Arizona Press, 1998.

Kephart, Horace. *Our Southern Highlanders.* New York: MacMillan, 1921. Reprint. Knoxville: University of Tennessee Press, 1976.

Keyes, Nelson Beecher. *America's National Parks.* Garden City, N.Y.: Doubleday, 1957.

Kortright, Francis H. *Ducks, Geese, and Swans of North America.* Harrisburg, Pa.: Stackpole Co., 1967.

Kuehne, Robert A., and Roger W. Barbour. *American Darters.* Lexington: University of Kentucky Press, 1983.

Lambert, Darwin. *The Undying Past of Shenandoah National Park.* Boulder, Colo.: Roberts, Rinehart, Inc., 1989.

Langley, Joan, and Wright Langley. *Yesterday's Asheville.* Miami: E. A. Seeman Publishing, 1975.

Leopold, Aldo. *A Sand County Almanac* (reprint of 1949 edition). London: Oxford University Press, 1966.

Leuchtenburg, William E. *Franklin D. Roosevelt and the New Deal.* New York: Harper and Row, 1963.

Lilienthal, David. *TVA: Democracy on the March.* New York: Harper and Row, 1944.

McCall, William A. *Cherokees and Pioneers.* Asheville, N.C.: Stephens Press, 1952.

McCarter, Dwight. *Lost: A Ranger's Diary of Search and Rescue.* Yellow Springs, Ohio: Graphicom Press, 1998.

McDonald, Michael J., and John Muldowny. *TVA and the Dispossessed: The Resettlement of Population in the Norris Dam Area.* Knoxville: University of Tennessee Press, 1982.

McDonald, Michael J., and William Bruce Wheeler. *Knoxville: Continuity and Change in an Appalachian City.* Knoxville: University of Tennessee Press, 1988.

McEvoy, Arthur. *Fisherman's Problem: Ecology and Law in the California Fisheries.* New York: Cambridge University Press, 1986.

McLoughlin, William Gerald. *Cherokee Renascence in the New Republic*. Princeton: Princeton University Press, 1984.

Martin, A. C., H. S. Zim, and A. L. Nelson. *American Wildlife and Plants: A Guide to Wildlife Food Habits*. New York: Dover Publications, 1951.

Martin, Joel. *Sacred Revolt*. Boston: Beacon, 1991.

Martin, Laura. *Wildflower Folklore*. Charlotte, N.C.: East Woods Press, 1984.

Martof, Bernard S., William M. Palmer, Joseph R. Bailey, and Julian R Harrison II. *Amphibians and Reptiles of the Carolinas and Virginia*. Chapel Hill: University of North Carolina Press, 1980.

Mason, Robert Lindsay. *The Lure of the Great Smokies*. New York: Houghton-Mifflin, 1927.

Mayer, John J., and I. Lehr Brisbin. *Wild Pigs of the United States: Their History, Comparative Morphology, and Current Status*. Athens: University of Georgia Press, 1991.

Medford, W. Clark. *The Early History of Haywood County*. Waynesville, N.C.: W. Clark Medford, 1961.

Merchant, Carolyn. *Ecological Revolutions: Nature, Gender, and Science in New England*. Chapel Hill: University of North Carolina Press, 1989.

Mitchell, Robert. *Appalachian Frontiers*. Lexington: University of Kentucky Press, 1991.

Moffett, Marian. *East Tennessee Cantilever Barns*. Knoxville: University of Tennessee Press, 1993.

Mooney, James. *Myths of the Cherokee and Sacred Formula of the Cherokee*. Nashville, Tenn.: Charles and Randy Elder, 1982.

Morgan, Arthur E. *Dams and Other Disasters: A Century of the Army Corps of Engineers in Civil Works*. Boston: Porter Sargent, 1971.

———. *The Making of TVA*. Buffalo, N.Y.: Prometheus Books, 1974.

Morgan, John. *The Log House of East Tennessee*. Knoxville: University of Tennessee Press, 1990.

Morrell, John O. *The Mirth of a National Park*. John O. Morrell, 1981.

Myers, Stephen George. *The Smokies Guide*. Asheville, N.C.: Stephens Press, 1941.

Nash, Roderick. *Wilderness and the American Mind*. New Haven: Yale University Press, 1967.

National Resource Council. *Science and the National Parks*. Washington, D.C.: National Academy Press, 1992.

Neely, Sharlotte. *Snowbird Cherokee*. Athens: University of Georgia Press, 1991.

Newhall, Nancy. *A Contribution to the Heritage of Every American: The Conservation Activities of John D. Rockefeller, Jr*. New York: Alfred A. Knopf, 1957.

Nicholson, Charles P. *Knoxville: Atlas of the Breeding Birds of Tennessee*. Knoxville: University of Tennessee Press, 1997.

Nolt, John, Athena Bradley, Mike Knapp, Donald E. Lampard, and Jonathan Scherch. *What Have We Done?* Washburn, Tenn.: Earth Knows, 1997.

Oakley, Wiley. *Roamin' and Restin'*. Gatlinburg, Tenn.: Oakley Enterprises, 1940.

Oliver, Duane. *Hazel Creek from Then til Now*. Hazelwood, N.C.: Duane Oliver, 1989.

Opie, John. *Nature's Nation: An Environmental History of the United States*. New York: Harcourt Brace, 1997.

Parton, Dolly. *My Life and Other Unfinished Business*. New York: Harper-Collins, 1994.

Peacock, James L., and Ruel W. Tyson Jr. *Pilgrims of Paradox: Calvinism and Experience among the Primitive Baptists of the Blue Ridge*. Washington, D.C.: Smithsonian Institution Press, 1989.

Peattie, Roderick. *The Great Smokies and the Blue Ridge: The Story of the Southern Appalachians*. New York: Vanguard Press, 1943.

Perdue, Theda. *Slavery and the Evolution of Cherokee Society, 1540–1866*. Knoxville: University of Tennessee Press, 1979.

Pinchot, Gifford, and W. W. Ashe. *Timber Trees and Forests of North Carolina*. Winston, N.C.: M. I. and J. C. Steward, 1897.

Powers, Elizabeth, and Mark Hannah. *Cataloochee: Lost Settlement of the Smokies*. Charleston, N.C.: Powers-Hannah, 1982.

Prescott, De Witt. *The Evolution of Modern Band Saw Mills*. Menominee, Mich.: Prescott, 1910.

Pyne, Stephen. *Fire in America*. Princeton: Princeton University Press, 1988.

Raitz, Karl B., and Richard Ulack. *Appalachia: A Regional Geography*. Boulder, Colo.: Westview Press, 1984.

Rand McNally. *Directory & Shipping Guide, Lumber Mills and Lumber Dealers*. Chicago: Rand McNally, 1884.

Randall, John M., and Janet Marinelli, eds. *Invasive Plants: Weeds of the Global Garden*. Brooklyn, N.Y.: Brooklyn Botanic Garden Publications, 1996.

Robinson, Blackwell, ed. *North Carolina Guide*. Chapel Hill: University of North Carolina Press, 1955.

Rossman, Douglas A. *Where the Legends Live*. Cherokee, N.C.: Cherokee Publications, 1988.

Royden, Lucile Kirby. *The Village of Five Lives: Fontana of the Great Smoky Mountains*. Fontana, N.C.: Government Services, Inc., 1964.

Runte, Alfred. *National Parks: The American Experience*. 3d ed. Lincoln: University of Nebraska Press, 1997.

Russell, Gladys Trentham. *Call Me Hillbilly*. Alcoa, Tenn.: Russell Printing Company, 1974.

Ryding, S. O., and W. Rast. *The Control of Eutrophication of Lakes and Reservoirs*. Paris: Parthenon, 1989.

Salstrom, Paul. *Appalachia's Path to Dependency*. Lexington: University of Kentucky Press, 1994.

Satz, Ronald N. *American Indian Policy in the Jacksonian Era*. Lincoln: University of Nebraska Press, 1975.

Schmidt, Ronald G., and William S. Hooks. *Whistle over the Mountain: Timber, Track, and Trails in the Tennessee Smokies*. Yellow Springs, Ohio: Graphicom Press, 1994.

Sevier County Heritage Committee. *Sevier County, Tennessee, and Its Heritage*. Waynesville, N.C.: Walsworth, 1994.

Shands, William E., and Robert G. Healy. *The Lands Nobody Wanted: A Conservation Foundation Report*. Washington, D.C.: The Conservation Foundation, 1977.

Shaw, Russell. *The Gatlinburg Story*. Gatlinburg, Tenn.: Russell Shaw, 1960.

Silver, Timothy. *A New Face on the Countryside: Indians, Colonists, and Slaves in South Atlantic Forests, 1500–1800*. New York: Cambridge University Press, 1990.

Smathers, George H. *The History of Land Titles in Western North Carolina*. Asheville, N.C.: Miller Publishing, 1938.

Smith, Marvin. *Archaeology of Aboriginal Culture Change in the Interior Southeast*. Gainesville: University of Florida Press, 1989.

Smith, Michael. *Behind the Glitter: The Impact of Tourism on Rural Women in the Southeast*. Lexington, Ky.: Southeast Women's Employment Coalition, 1989.

Southeast Women's Employment Coalition. *Women of the Rural South*. Lexington, Ky.: Southeast Women's Employment Coalition, 1986.

Southern Lumberman. *Southern Lumberman's Directory of American Sawmills and Planing Mills*. Nashville, Tenn.: Southern Lumberman, 1928.

Spears, Raymond S. *Camping, Woodcraft, and Wild Craft*. Girard, Kans.: Haldeman-Julius, 1924.

Spongberg, Stephen. *A Reunion of Trees*. Cambridge: Harvard University Press, 1990.

Stoddard, Herbert L. *The Use of Controlled Fire in Southeastern Game Management*. Thomasville, Ga.: Cooperative Quail Study Association, 1939.

Stupka, Arthur. *Notes on the Birds of the Great Smoky Mountains National Park*. Knoxville: University of Tennessee Press, 1963.

Sutton, Ann, and Myron Sutton. *Eastern Forests*. New York: Alfred A. Knopf, 1993.

Swain, Donald C. *Wilderness Defender*. Chicago: University of Chicago Press, 1970.

Swain, George Fillmore. *Conservation of Water by Storage*. New Haven: Yale University Press, 1914.

Swanson, Robert E. *A Field Guide to the Trees and Shrubs of the Southern Appalachians*. Baltimore: Johns Hopkins University Press, 1994.

Talbert, Roy, Jr. *FDR's Utopian: Arthur Morgan of the TVA*. Jackson: University of Mississippi Press, 1987.

Thomasson, Lillian. *Swain County: Early History and Development*. Bryson City, N.C.: Miller Publishing, 1965.

Thornborough, Laura. *Great Smoky Mountains*. New York: Crowell Publishing, 1942.

Thornton, W. W. *The Law of Railroad Fences and Private Crossings*. Indianapolis: Bowen-Merrill Company, 1892.

Trout, Ed. *Gatlinburg: Cinderella City*. Pigeon Forge, Tenn.: Griffen Graphics, 1985.

Tweed, William C., and Laura E. Soulliere. *National Park Rustic Architecture, 1916–1942*. Denver: National Park Service, Western Regional Office, 1977.

Tyson, Lona Parton. *Reflections from the Pinnacle: The Story of Parton Roots*. Gatlinburg, Tenn.: Tyson, 1982.

Von Noppen, Ina W., and John J. Von Noppen. *Western North Carolina Since the Civil War*. Boone, N.C.: Appalachian Consortium Press, 1973.

Walker, Laurence. *The Southern Forest: A Chronicle.* Austin: University of Texas Press, 1991.

Waller, Altina. *Feud: Hatfields, McCoys, and Social Change in Appalachia, 1860–1900.* Chapel Hill: University of North Carolina Press, 1988.

Walton, George E. *Mineral Springs of the U.S. and Canada.* New York: D. Appleton and Company, 1874.

Weals, Vic. *The Last Train to Elkmont.* Knoxville, Tenn.: Olden Press, 1991.

Wear, Jerry, ed. *Lost Communities of Sevier County: Greenbrier.* Sevierville, Tenn.: Sevierville Heritage Committee, 1985.

Weller, Jack. *Yesterday's People.* Lexington: University of Kentucky Press, 1965.

Whisnant, David. *All That is Native and Fine: The Politics of Culture in an American Region.* Chapel Hill: University of North Carolina Press, 1983.

———. *Modernizing the Mountaineer: People, Power, and Planning in Appalachia.* Boone, N.C.: Appalachian Consortium Press, 1980.

White, Richard. *The Middle Ground.* New York: Cambridge University Press, 1991.

Williams, Michael Ann. *Americans and Their Forests: A Historical Geography.* New York: Cambridge University Press, 1989.

———. *Great Smoky Mountains Folklife.* Jackson: University of Mississippi Press, 1995.

———. *Homeplace: The Social Use and Meaning of the Folk Dwelling in Southwestern North Carolina.* Athens: University of Georgia Press, 1991.

Worster, Donald. *Dust Bowl: The Southern Plains in the 1930s.* New York: Oxford University Press, 1979.

———. *Nature's Economy: The Roots of Ecology.* San Francisco: Sierra Club Books, 1977.

B. ARTICLES

Abernathy, A. R., G. L. Larson, and R. C. Matthews Jr. "Heavy Metals in the Surficial Sediments of Fontana Lake, North Carolina." *Water Resources* 18 (1984): 351–54.

Abramson, Rudy. "Nature's Bald Spots." *Audubon* 97 (March–April 1995): 38–39.

Albright, Horace. "Research in the National Park." *Scientific Monthly* 36 (June 1933): 483–501.

Allen, James A., and Virginia Burkett. "The National Biological Service: Emphasis on Partnership." *Journal of Forestry* 93 (March 1995): 15–17.

Anderson, R. C., and S. S. Dhilion. "Acclimatization of Garlic Mustard." *American Journal of Botany* 78 (1991): 129–30.

Armstrong, Anne Wetzell. "The Southern Mountaineers." *Yale Review* 24 (October 1935): 539–540.

Arnow, Pat. "Dollywood: The Changing Profile of Pigeon Forge." *Now and Then* 8 (Spring 1991): 8–10.

Ash, Andrew N., and Richard Bruce. "Impacts of Timber Harvesting on Salamanders." *Conservation Biology* 8 (March 1994): 300–301.

Berry, Wendell. "Decolonizing Rural America." *Audubon* 95 (March/April 1993): 100–105.

Blumer, Thomas J. "Rebecca Youngbird: An Independent Cherokee Potter." *Journal of Cherokee Studies* 5 (Spring 1980): 41–47.

Bogucki, Donald J. "Debris Slides in the Mt. Le Conte Area, Great Smoky Mountains National Park, U.S.A." *Geografiska Annaler* 3 (1976): 179–91.

Bowman, Joe. "Mountain Air Not Safe to Breathe." *Tennessee Star-Journal* (25–31 July 1997): A1.

Bratton, Susan P. "The Decline of the Smokies Trout." *Tennessee Conservationist* 43 (July–August 1977): 2–4.

———. "Impacts of White-Tailed Deer on the Vegetation of Cades Cove, Great Smoky Mountains National Park." In *Proceedings of the Annual Conference of the South Eastern Association of Fish & Wildlife Agencies* 33 (1981): 305–12.

———. "Is the Panther Making a Comeback?" *National Parks & Conservation Magazine* (July 1978): 13.

———. "Logging and Fragmentation of Broadleaved Deciduous Forests." *Conservation Biology* 8 (March 1994): 295–97.

———. "The Management of Historic Ecosystems and Landscapes in National Parks." In *Proceedings of the Conference on Science in the National Parks* 4 (1986): 3–43.

Bratton, Susan P., Raymond C. Matthews Jr., and Peter S. White. "Agricultural Area Impacts within a Natural Area: Cades Cove, a Case History." *Environmental Management* 4 (1980): 433–48.

Bratton, Susan P., Linda L. Stromberg, and Mark E. Harmon. "Firewood-Gathering Impacts in Backcountry Campsites in the Great Smoky Mountains National Park." *Environmental Management* 6 (1982): 62–71.

Britton, Kerry O., ed. *Exotic Pests of Eastern Forests: Conference Proceedings.* Nashville: Tennessee Exotic Pest Plant Council and USDA Forest Service, 8–10 April, 1997.

Broadfoot, W. M., and H. L. Williston. "Flooding Effects on Southern Forests." *Journal of Forestry* 71 (September 1973): 584–88.

Brookfield, Harold, and Christine Padoch. "Appreciating Agrodiversity." *Environment* 36 (June 1993): 8–13.

Broome, Harvey. "Mountain Notebook . . . 1950." *The Living Wilderness* 29 (Autumn 1965): 3–13.

———. "Origins of the Wilderness Society." *The Living Wilderness* 31 (Winter 1967): 10–11.

Brown, D. M. "Vegetation on Roan Mountain: A Psychosociological and Successional Study." *Ecological Monographs* 11 (1941): 61–97.

Brown, Margaret Lynn. "Captains of Tourism: Selling a National Park in the Great Smoky Mountains." *Journal of the Appalachian Studies Association* 4 (1992): 42–49.

Burst, Thomas L., and Michael R. Pelton. "Some Population Parameters of the Cades Cove Deer Herd, Great Smoky Mountains National Park." In *Proceedings* of the *Annual Conference of the South Eastern Association of Fish & Wildlife Agencies* 32 (1980): 339–44.

Cain, Stanley. "Ecological Studies of the Vegetation of the Great Smoky Mountains of North Carolina and Tennessee." *Botanical Gazette* 91 (1931): 13.

Camp, W. H. "The Grassy Balds of the Great Smoky Mountains of Tennessee and North Carolina." *Ohio Journal of Science* 31 (1931): 157–64.

Campbell, Carlos. "The Great Smoky Mountains National Park: The Rooftop of Eastern America." *Tennessee Wildlife* 3 (December 1939): 1–10.

"Chestnut Tree Blight, The." *Scientific American* 106 (1912): 241–42.

Clebsch, Edward E. C., and R. T. Busing. "Secondary Succession, Gap Dynamics, and Community Structure in a Southern Appalachian Cove Forest." *Ecology* 70 (1989): 728–35.

Cole, William E. "Urban Development in the Tennessee Valley." *Social Forces* 26 (October 1947): 67–75.

Copp, A. "A Disease Which Threatens the American Chestnut Tree." *Scientific American* 95 (15 December 1906): 451.

Cronon, William. "Mode of Prophecy and Production: Placing Nature in History." *Journal of American History* 76 (March 1990): 1122–31.

———. "A Place for Stories: Nature, History, and Narrative." *Journal of American History* 78 (March 1992): 1347–76.

———. "The Trouble With Wilderness, or, Getting Back to the Wrong Nature." In *Uncommon Ground: Rethinking the Human Place in Nature,* 69–90. New York: W. W. Norton, 1996.

———. "The Uses of Environmental History." *Environmental History Review* 17 (Fall 1993): 1–22.

Cummings, Joe. "Community and the Nature of Change: Sevier County, Tennessee, in the 1890s." *East Tennessee Historical Society's Publications* 59 (1985–1986): 63–88.

Day, Gordon. "The Indian as an Ecological Factor in the Northeastern Forest." *Ecology* 34 (1953): 329–46.

Devine, Robert. "Botanical Barbarians." *Sierra* 79 (January–February 1994): 50–71.

Douglas, William O. "The People of Cades Cove." *National Geographic Magazine* 122 (July 1962): 60–95.

Duffy, David Cameron, and Albert J. Meier. "Do Appalachian Herbaceous Understories Ever Recover from Clearcutting?" *Conservation Biology* 6 (1992): 196–201.

Etheridge, Robert. "Tobacco among the Cherokees." *Journal of Cherokee Studies* 3 (Spring 1978): 76–84.

Etnier, David, and Wayne Starnes. "An Analysis of Tennessee's Jeopardized Fish Taxonomy." *Journal of the Tennessee Academy of Science* 66 (1991): 129–33.

Exum, Ellen Mason. "Tree in a Coma." *American Forests* 98 (November–December 1992): 20–26.

Fink, Paul M. "Early Explorers of the Great Smokies." *East Tennessee Historical Society's Publications* 51 (1979): 40–53.

————. "A Forest Enigma." *American Forests* 37 (1931): 538.

Flores, Dan. "Place: An Argument for Bioregional History." *Environmental History Review* 18 (Winter 1994): 3–11.

Fogelson, Raymond. "The Conjuror in Eastern Cherokee Society." *Journal of Cherokee Studies* 5 (Fall 1980): 60–87.

Foreman, Dave. "Around the Campfire." *Wild Earth* (Winter 1996–1997): 3–4.

Franklin, Neil W. "Virginia and the Cherokee Indian Trade, 1673–1752." *East Tennessee Historical Society's Publications* 7 (1932): 3–21.

Frost, William. "Our Contemporary Ancestors." *Atlantic Monthly* 83 (March 1899): 311–19.

Garrett, Ray. "In Less Than a Life Span." *American Forests* 58 (October 1952): 23.

Gove, William. "Sidewinders in the Great Smokies." *Northern Logger and Timber Processor* 19 (February 1971): 15–16.

Green, Joan, and H. F. Robinson. "Maize Was Our Life: A History of Cherokee Corn." *Journal of Cherokee Studies* 11 (Spring 1986): 40–52.

Gulick, John. "The Acculturation of Cherokee Community Organization." *Social Forces* (1930): 246–50.

Hall, William L. "New National Forests in the Southern Appalachians." *Southern Lumberman* 69 (21 December 1912): 104–7.

————. "To Remake the Appalachians." *World's Work* 28 (July 1914): 335.

Haney, Christopher J. "Spatial Incidence of Barred Owl Reproduction in Old-Growth Forests of the Appalachian Plateau." *Journal of Raptor Research* 31 (1997): 10–15.

Harlean, James. "The Great Smokies, Site of a Proposed National Park." *Review of Reviews* (October 1928): 373–77.

Hart, John Fraser. "Land Rotation in Appalachia." *The Geographical Review* 67 (April 1977): 151–60.

Hayes, John P., Stanley Guffey, Frank Kriegler, Gary McCracken, and Charles Parker. "Genetic Diversity of Native, Stocked, and Hybrid Populations of Brook Trout in the Southern Appalachians." *Conservation Biology* 10 (October 1996): 1403–12.

Hepting, George H. "Death of the American Chestnut." *Journal of Forest History* (July 1974): 61–67.

Hudson, Charles, et al. "The Tristan de Luna Expedition, 1561–1599." *Southeastern Archaeology* 8 (1989): 31–45.

Jacobs, Jane. "Why TVA Failed." *New York Review of Books* 31 (May 1984): 41–47.

Johnson, A. Sydney, William M. Ford, and Philip E. Hale. "The Effects of Clearcutting on Herbaceous Understories Are Still Not Fully Known." *Conservation Biology* 7 (June 1993): 433–35.

Journal of Cherokee Studies 14 (1989). The entire volume is devoted to the Fading Voices Project.

King, Duane H. "History of the Museum of the Cherokee Indian." *Journal of Cherokee Studies* 1 (Summer 1976): 60–64.

King, Willis. "A Program for the Management of Fish Resources in the Great Smoky Mountains National Park." *Transactions of the American Fisheries Society* 68 (1938): 88–95.

Kucken, D. J., J. S. Davis, J. W. Petranka, and C. K. Smith. "Anakeesta Stream Acidification and Metal Contamination: Effects on a Salamander Community." *Journal of Environmental Quality* 23 (November–December 1994): 1311–77.

Lambert, Robert S. "Logging the Great Smokies, 1880–1930." *Tennessee Historical Quarterly* (December 1961): 351–52.

———. "Logging on the Little River, 1890–1940." *East Tennessee Historical Society's Publications* 31 (1961): 32–42.

Larson, Gary, Stephen Moore, and Danny Lee. "Angling and Electrofishing for Removing Non-Native Rainbow Trout from a Stream in a National Park." *North American Journal of Fisheries Management* 6 (Fall 1986): 580–85.

Laska, Lewis. "The Law of Squirrels, Robins, Snakes, Cats, Raccoons and Elephants." *Tennessee Bar Journal* 35 (1990): 14–36.

Lindsay, Mary M., and Susan Power Bratton. "The Grassy Balds of the Great Smoky Mountains: Their History and Flora in Relation to Potential Management." *Environmental Management* 3 (1979): 417–30.

———. "The Vegetation of Grassy Balds and Other High Elevation Disturbed Areas in the Great Smoky Mountains National Park." *Bulletin of the Torrey Botanical Club* 196 (October–December 1979): 264–74.

McCarthy, Charles J. "Land Acquisition Policies and Proceedings in TVA: A Study of the Role of Land Acquisition in a Regional Agency." *Ohio State Law Journal* 10 (Winter 1949): 46–63.

McDonald, Forrest, and Grady McWhiney. "The Antebellum Southern Herdsman: A Reinterpretation." *Journal of Southern History* 41 (May 1975): 146–66.

Matlack, Glenn. "Plant Demography, Land-Use History, and the Commercial Use of Forests." *Conservation Biology* 8 (March 1994): 298–99.

Mattoon, W. R. "William Willard Ashe." *Journal of Forestry* (May 1932): 652–53.

Mayfield, G. R. "Magni Fumosi, Conservandi Sunt." *Journal of Tennessee Academy of Science* 1 (April 1926): 27–35.

Metcalf, Haven. "The Chestnut Tree Blight: An Incurable Disease That Has Destroyed Dollars Worth of Trees." *Scientific American* 106 (16 March 1912): 241–42.

Miller, James H. "Exotic Invasive Plants in Southeastern Forests." In *Proceedings of the Conference on Exotic Pests of Eastern Forests*, 97–105. Nashville: Tennessee Exotic Pest Plant Council, USDA Forest Service, 1997.

Miller, James H., and E. Boyd. "Kudzu: Where Did It Come From, and How Can We Stop It?" *Southern Journal of Applied Forestry* 7 (1983): 165–69.

Moment, Gairdner B. "Bears: The Need for a New Sanity in Wildlife Conservation." *Bioscience* 12 (December 1968): 1105–8.

Moore, Stephen, and Bromfield Ridley. "Standing Crops of Brook Trout Concurrent with Removal of Rainbow Trout from Selected Streams in the Great Smoky

Mountains National Park." *North American Journal of Fisheries Management* 3 (1983): 72–80.

Nash, Stephen. "The Blighted Chestnut." *National Parks* 62 (July–August 1988): 14–19.

Ogle, Lucinda Oakley. "I Wanted to Go to School Forever." *Appalachian Journal* 14 (1987): 240–41.

Otto, John Solomon. "The Decline of Forest Farming in Southern Appalachia." *Journal of Forest History* 27 (1983): 18–27.

Parker, Russell D. "Alcoa, Tennessee: The Early Years, 1919–1939." *East Tennessee Historical Society's Publications* 48 (1976): 84–103.

Parsons, Shireen. "Wilderness Warrior." *Appalachian Voice* (Summer 1998): 8, 14.

Patterson, D. T. "The History and Distribution of Five Exotic Weeds in North Carolina." *Castanea* 41 (1976): 177–80.

Perdue, Charles L., and Nancy J. Martin-Perdue. "Appalachian Fables and Facts: A Case Study of the Shenandoah National Park Removals." *Appalachian Journal* 7 (Autumn–Winter 1979–1980): 84–104.

Peterson, Ron. "Two Early Boundary Lines with the Cherokee Nation." *Journal of Cherokee Studies* 6 (1981): 14–29.

Petranka, James W., Matthew Eldridge, and Catherine Haley. "Effects of Timber Harvesting on Southern Appalachian Salamanders." *Conservation Biology* 7 (1993): 363–79.

Platt, Stephen G., and Christopher G. Brantley. "Canebrakes: An Ecological and Historical Perspective." *Castanea* 62 (March 1997): 8–21.

Puritch, George S. "The Toxic Effects of Fatty Acids and Their Salts on the Balsam Woolly Aphid." *Canadian Journal of Forest Resources* 5 (1975): 515–22.

Pyle, Charlotte, and Michael Schafale. "Land Use History of Three Spruce-Fir Forest Sites in Southern Appalachia." *Journal of Forest History* 32 (January 1988): 4–21.

Richardson, Larry. "Salute to a Pioneer: Paul J. Adams." *The Tennessee Conservationist* 34 (February 1973): 2–3.

Rothrock, Mary W. "Cherokee Traders among the Overhill Cherokee." *East Tennessee Historical Society's Publications* 4 (1929): 3–18.

Ruggiero, Michael A. "The Rational Use of Pesticides in Park and Recreation Areas." *Trends* 23 (1986): 10–14.

Shaver, Jesse M. "Flowers of the Great Smoky Mountains." *Journal of the Tennessee Academy of Science* 1 (April 1926): 17–20.

Shea, John. "Our Pappies Burned the Woods." *American Forests* 46 (April 1940): 159–62.

Silsbee, D. G., and G. L. Larson. "Water Quality of Streams in the Great Smoky Mountains National Park." *Hydrobiologia* 89 (1982): 97–115.

Silver, Timothy. "In Search of Iron Eyes: A Historian Reflects on the Cherokees as Environmentalists." *Appalachian Voice* (Winter 1996): 3, 18.

Smith, Charles Dennis. "The Appalachian National Park Movement, 1885–1901." *North Carolina Historical Review* 37 (January 1960): 41–63.

Spence, Mark David. "Crown of the Continent, Backbone of the World." *Environmental History* 1 (July 1996): 29–49.

Stapleton, Richard M. "A Call to Action." *National Parks* (March/April 1994): 39.

Stolzenburg, William. "The Mussels' Message." *The Nature Conservancy Magazine* (November/December 1992): 18–19.

Thompson, Kenneth. "Wilderness and Health in the Nineteenth Century." *Journal of Historical Geography* 2 (1976): 145–61.

Van Noppen, John, and Ina Woetemeyer Van Noppen. "The Genesis of Forestry in the Southern Appalachians: A Brief History." *Appalachian Journal* 1 (Autumn 1972): 63–71.

Wallach, Bret. "The Slighted Mountains of Upper East Tennessee." *Journal of the Association of American Geographers* 71 (September 1981): 363–65.

Watson, Emmett. "Menace in Our Northern Parks." *Sports Illustrated* 27 (30 October 1967): 62–74.

Wauer, Roland H. "The Greening of Natural Resource Management." *Trends* 19 (1982): 2–6.

Weeks, Charles J. "The Eastern Cherokee and the New Deal." *North Carolina Historical Review* 53 (July 1976): 303–19.

Wells, B. W. "Origin of the Southern Appalachian Grass Balds." *Science* 83 (1936): 283.

———. "Southern Appalachian Grass Balds." *Journal of the Elisha Mitchell Scientific Study* 53 (1937): 24–25.

White, Peter S., and Susan P. Bratton. "After Preservation: Philosophical and Practical Problems of Change." *Biological Conservation* 18 (1980): 241–55.

Whittaker, R. H. "Vegetation of the Great Smoky Mountains." *Ecological Monographs* 26 (1956): 1–80.

Wilcrove, D. S. "Nest Predation in Forest Tracts and the Decline of Migratory Songbirds." *Ecology* 66 (1985): 1211–14.

Wilderness Society. "Wilderness for the Smokies." *The Living Wilderness* 29 (Summer 1965): 2, 32–36.

Williams, Michael Ann. "Pride and Prejudice: The Appalachian Boxed House in Southwestern North Carolina." *Winterthur Portfolio* 25 (Winter 1990): 217–30.

Williams, Ted. "Invasion of the Aliens." *Audubon* (September–October 1994): 24–32.

Willy, John. "Ten Days in the Proposed Great Smoky Mountains National Park." *Hotel Monthly* (1926): 44–58.

Windle, Phyllis. "The Ecology of Grief." *Bioscience* 42 (May 1992): 363–67.

Witthoft, John. "Cherokee Indian Use of Potherbs." *Journal of Cherokee Studies* 2 (Spring 1977): 251–52.

Woods, Frank W., and Royal E. Shanks. "Natural Replacement of Chestnut by Other Species in the Great Smoky Mountains National Park." *Ecology* 40 (July 1969): 349–61.

Woody, Robert. "Cataloochee Homecoming." *South Atlantic Quarterly* 49 (January 1950): 16.

Worster, Donald. "Toward an Agroecological Perspective in History." *Journal of American History* 76 (May 1990): 1087–1106.

Young, Gordon. "Great Smoky Mountains National Park." *National Geographic* 134 (October 1968): 522–49.

C. UNPUBLISHED WORKS

Arends, Ernesto. "Vegetation Patterns a Half Century Following the Chestnut Blight in the Great Smoky Mountains National Park." Master's thesis, University of Tennessee, 1981.

Bays, Brad Alan. "The Historical Geography of Cattle Herding, 1761–1861." Master's thesis, University of Tennessee, 1991.

Black, Ellen Engelman. "A Study of the Diffusion of Culture in a Relatively Isolated Mountain Community." Ph.D. diss., University of Chicago, 1928.

Blythe, Robert W. "Draft, Historic Resource Study: Great Smoky Mountains National Park." Unpublished manuscript, Southeast Support Office, National Park Service, 13 April 1998.

Brewer, Patricia F., Kathy Tonnessen, Jack Cosby, Ron Munson, and Tim Sullivan. "Watershed Responses to Changes in Deposition of Sulfur, Nitrogen, and Base Cations: A Modeling Exercise by SAMI," 4–6. Paper presented at Ninth Annual SAMAB Conference, Gatlinburg, Tenn., November 1998.

Brown, Margaret Lynn, and Donald Edward Davis. "Great Smoky Mountains Trail History." Unpublished manuscript, GSMNP Archives, 1992.

Bruhn, Mary Ellen. "Vegetational Succession on the Grassy Balds of the Great Smoky Mountains." Master's thesis, University of Tennessee, 1964.

Burrows, Robert Jr. "Biological Survey of Streams in the Great Smoky Mountains National Park." Unpublished manuscript, vertical file, GSMNP Archives, April 1935.

Butler, Linda. "Biodiversity Studies in West Virginia: Problems and Challenges." Paper presented at Forty-second Southern Forest Insect Work Conference, 4 August 1998.

Davis, Donald Edward. "Where There Be Mountains: Environmental and Cultural Change in the Appalachian South, 1500–1800." Ph.D. diss., University of Tennessee, 1993.

Dinkins, Gerald R. "Aspects of the Life History of the Smoky Madtom, *Noturus baileyi* Taylor, in Citico Creek." Master's thesis, University of Tennessee, 1984.

Dobson, Jerome. "The Changing Control of Economic Activity in the Gatlinburg, Tennessee, Area, 1930–1973." Ph.D. diss., University of Tennessee, 1975.

Dyer, Delce. "The Farmstead Yards at Cades Cove: Restoration and Management Alternatives for the Domestic Landscape of the Southern Appalachian Mountaineer." Master's thesis, University of Georgia, 1988.

Fink, Paul. "Trips Manuscript: To the Great Smokies Area." Typed manuscript, vertical files, GSMNP, n.d.

Gersmehl, Philip. "A Geographic Approach to a Vegetation Problem: The Case of the Southern Appalachian Grassy Balds." Ph.D. diss., University of Georgia, 1970.

Gilbert, V. C. "Vegetation of the Grassy Balds of the Great Smoky Mountains National Park." Master's thesis, University of Tennessee, 1954.

Griess, Jane M. "River Otter Reintroduction in the Great Smoky Mountains National Park." Master's thesis, University of Tennessee, 1987.

Hill, James M. "Wildlife Value of *Castanea dentata* and the Historical Decline of the Chestnut and Its Future Use in Restoration of Natural Areas." Unpublished manuscript, Randolph-Macon College, 1993.

Hill, Sarah Hitch. "Cherokee Patterns: Interweaving Women and Baskets in History." Ph.D. diss., Emory University, 1991.

Hunt, Edward. "Indian Gap Hotel: A Luxury Hotel in the Middle of the Smokies." Unpublished manuscript, Mary Ruth Chiles Collection, GSMNP, n.d.

Lambdin, Paris. "Biodiversity in Selected Ecosystems and the Importance of Systematics." Paper presented at Forty-second Southern Forest Insect Work Conference, 4 August 1998.

Lankford, Jesse R. "The Campaign for a National Park in Western North Carolina." Master's thesis, Western Carolina University, 1978.

Lennon, Robert. "Fishes of the Great Smoky Mountains National Park." Unpublished manuscript, GSMNP, 1960.

Louder, Darrell E., and W. Donald Baker. "Some Limnological Aspects of Fontana Reservoir." Paper presented at Annual Meeting of the Southern Division of the American Fisheries Society, 24–26 October 1966.

McCracken, Weaver H. III. "Comparison of Forest Cover Prior to and following Disturbance in Two Areas of the Great Smoky Mountains National Park." Master's thesis, University of Tennessee, 1978.

Martin, Christopher Branden. "Selling the Southern Highlands: Tourism and Community Development in the Mountain South." Ph.D. diss., University of Tennessee, 1997.

Miller, Walter M. "The Civilian Conservation Corps in East Tennessee and the Great Smoky Mountains National Park, 1933–1942." Unpublished manuscript, GSMNP, 1974.

Moore, Wayne. "TVA and Farm Communities of the Lower Tennessee Valley." Ph.D. diss, University of Rochester, 1990.

Nodvin, Stephen C., and Niki S. Nicholas. "Watershed, Forest Health, and Air Quality Research in the Great Smoky Mountains." Paper presented at Forty-fifth AIBS Annual Meeting, Knoxville, Tenn., 12 August 1994.

Norburn, Mary Elizabeth. "The Influence of the Physiographic Features of Western North Carolina on the Settlement and Development of the Region." Master's thesis, University of North Carolina, 1932.

Ownby, Evolena. "Evolena Remembers Big Greenbrier and Other Communities of Living." Unpublished manuscript, vertical file, GSMNP, 1979.

Pierce, Daniel S. "The Park Panacea: The Movement for a National Park in the

Great Smoky Mountains of East Tennessee, 1923–1928." Unpublished paper, Knoxville, Tenn., 1994.

Pyle, Charlotte. "CCC Camps in the Great Smoky Mountains National Park." Unpublished manuscript, GSMNP, 1979.

———. "Predictions of Forest Type and Productivity: Index on Disturbed Sites in the Great Smoky Mountains National Park." Master's thesis, University of Tennessee, 1988.

Reeves, W. Thomas. "A History of Haywood County." Master's thesis, Duke University, 1937.

Shute, Peggy W. "Ecology of the Rare Yellowfin Madtom, *Nocturus flavipinnis* Taylor, in Citico Creek." Master's thesis, University of Tennessee, 1984.

Simbeck, Damien J. "Distribution of the Fishes of the Great Smoky Mountains National Park." Master's thesis, University of Tennessee, 1990.

Snyder, Opal. "History of the Great Smoky Mountains National Park." Master's thesis, George Peabody College for Teachers, 1935.

Taylor, Stephen Wallace. "Building the Back of Beyond: Government Authority, Community Life, and Economic Development in the Upper Little Tennessee Valley, 1880–1992." Ph.D. diss., University of Tennessee, 1996.

Trout, Ed. "Milling in the Smokies." Unpublished manuscript, GSMNP, 1978.

———. "Rock and Timber: The Historic Structures of the Great Smoky Mountains National Park." Unpublished manuscript, GSMNP, 1991.

Trull, Willa Mae Hall. "Adams v. Westfelt." Unpublished manuscript, Mining File, GSMNP, n.d.

Whaley, John Thomas. "A Timely Idea at an Ideal Time: Knoxville's Role in Establishing the Great Smoky Mountains National Park." Master's thesis, University of Tennessee, 1984.

Whittle, W. O. "Movement of Population from the Smoky Mountains Area." Unpublished manuscript, University of Tennessee, 1934.

Woods, Frank. "Natural Replacement of Chestnut in the Great Smoky Mountains following the Chestnut Blight." Paper presented at Annual Meeting of the Tennessee Academy of Science, 28 November 1952.

Bradley Fork, 187
Bradshaw, Arnold, 162, 163, 164
Bratton, Susan Power, 248–52, 254–57, 273, 270, 287, 339, 355
Brevard, N.C., 25, 441
Brewer, Carson, 221, 271, 285
Brock, Bill, 258
Brock, N.C., 149, 157
Broome, Anne, 219–20
Broome, Harvey, 6, 78–79, 83, 85, 90, 109, 133, 174, 178, 208–9, 219–21, 225–26, 245, 355
Brotherhood of Timber Workers, 57
Brown, Charles M., 189
Bruck, Robert, 335–36
Brushy Mountain Trail, 130
Bryant, Delce Mae Carver, 22, 29, 37, 68, 115
Bryant, Harold, 185
Bryson City, N.C., 23, 69, 89, 157, 161, 164, 218, 227, 230, 247, 260, 269, 309–11
Bryson City Times, 149–50
Buckeye, 16, 53–54, 129, 337
Buckeye Gap, 225
Buckthorn, 326
Buncombe County, 7, 81
Bureau of Indian Affairs, 26, 85, 138, 196
Bureau of Public Roads, 120, 128
Burke County, N.C., 8
Burningbush, 208
Burns, Gamey, 154
Burns, John, 163
Burrows, Robert, 185
Bushnell, N.C., 93, 152, 154–58, 160
Butler, Linda, 328
Butler, Marion, 81
Butterflies, 3
Butternut trees, 37, 54; canker, 319–20, 343

Cabin Flats, 180
Cable, Fonz, 114
Cable, Samuel, 7
Cable Cove, 156
Cable Mill, 132
Cades Cove, Tenn.: farming community in, 7, 9, 13, 19, 20, 22, 24, 30, 32, 35, 40, 50–51, 69, 80, 84; flooding for lake, 120, 133, 147; NPS management of, 125, 139, 144,

202–9, 178, 186, 187–88, 212, 215, 222, 231, 254, 293–94, 297, 300; why in national park, 93–99, 109
Cagle, Winfred, 25, 28, 40, 97
Cain, Stanley, 247
Caldwell, Pearl, 29
Caldwell, Raymond, 20, 117
Caldwell Fork, 182
California medfly, 317
Calhoun, Granville, 25, 82, 105
Calhoun, Seymour, 18, 22, 24, 60, 61, 65
Cammerer, Arno, 92–93, 95, 116–17, 120, 133, 140, 379n.46, 385n.60
Cammerer line, 93
Campbell, Carlos, 5, 193, 224, 265, 283
Campbell, Tom, 139
Campgrounds, 127–28, 133, 139, 208, 222, 229, 234, 251, 258, 261–62
Camping, 16, 85, 106, 117, 176–77, 229–31, 251, 283, 311
Candler, N.C., 261
Cane, 9
Cantilever barns, 31
Canton, N.C., 51, 73
Carolina Mountain Club, 225, 226, 267
Carolina silverbell, 4
Carson, Rachel, 218
Carter, Jimmy, 272
Carver, Blake, 191
Cash, W. J., xiii
Cathey, Charley, 153
Catons Grove, Tenn., 13
Cataloochee Creek, 295
Cataloochee Divide, 222
Cataloochee Ranch, 179–84, 210
Cataloochee Valley, N.C.: farming community, 9, 13, 17, 18, 19, 23, 30, 40, 46; logging and, 50, 51, 56, 68, 69, 71, 101, 117; NPS management, 136, 222, 300, 317–18. *See also* Cataloochee Ranch
Catfish, 167, 184, 293, 295
Cathcart, William, 7
Cats, 35–36, 114
Cattle, 6, 9, 18, 19–21, 68, 114, 181, 182–84, 204, 206–7, 212, 231, 354
Caughron, Kermit, 204, 206
Cedar, 31

—descriptions of: by Ayres and Ashe, 50–51; in 1900, 7, 11; in 1933, 113; in 1950, 174

Great Smoky Mountains Conservation Association (GSMCA), 79, 88–93, 189

Great Smoky Mountains Natural History Association (GSMNHA), 247, 281, 292, 295

Great Smoky Mountains Wilderness Advocates, 267, 268, 284

Greenbrier, Tenn.: farming community, 13, 16, 22, 27, 51, 84, 97, 120, 126; NPS management, 219, 222, 258

Greenbrier Pinnacle, 126, 219, 298

Greens, 26–27

Gregory Bald, 14, 109, 115, 178, 253, 282–83

Gregory, Russell, 282

Griess, Jane, 295

Gristmills, 30, 35, 132

Grossman, Charles, 132

Groundhogs, 33, 66, 118, 174

Grouse, 86

Gudger, Lamar, 268, 270

Guides, 80, 191

Guineas, 31

Gunnar, George, 157

Gunnar Branch, 157

Hackberry, 333

Hacking, 298–99

Hall, William, 50

Hamilton, William, 326

Hannah, Mack, 97

Hannah, Mark, 23, 71, 181

Hardwood Manufacturers' Association, 58

Harmon, Mark, 187

Harrington, Joel E., 268

Harris, William O., 278

Harshbarger, Tom, 261

Hartzog, George, Jr., 216–18, 220, 222, 239, 226–27, 248, 251, 309, 358

Hatcheries. See Trout

Haw Gap, 252

Hawkins, George, 307

Hawks, 36, 101

Haywood County, N.C., 7, 13, 17, 20, 69, 182

Hazel Creek, N.C.: farming community in, 7, 13, 25, 39, 105, 157, 158, 161, 295; and Fontana removal, 149, 154, 161–66, 188; in logging era, 51–52, 58, 59, 65, 75, 82; NPS management of, 220

Headquarters. See Sugarlands Headquarters

Hearts-a-bustin', 191

Heintooga, 225, 251

Helgeson, Julie, 233

Helms, Jesse, 309–11, 356

Hemlock, eastern, 2, 4, 12, 26, 51, 53–54, 129, 134, 321–22, 333; woolly adelgid, 322

Henderson Springs, 84, 86

Henry, Gary, 296–297

Herders, 20

Hermann, Ray, 249, 250

Hickel, Walter, 226–27

Hickory, 12, 38, 53–54, 333, 349

Higdon, Stephen, 352

Hikers, hiking, 61, 70, 78, 84, 109, 126, 132, 138, 189, 225–26, 233–34, 238–40, 250, 255, 270, 281–83, 298, 321

Hill, Sarah, 197

History: Cherokees and, 199–201; and environmentalists, 283–86; NPS vision of, xvi, 131–33, 138, 202–9; nostalgia and, 5, 78–79; and scientists, 279–80, 281–83, 351. See also Frontier; Museums; North Shore Road

Hoey, Clyde, 140

Hogs, 9, 22–23, 33, 38, 40, 68, 114, 231

Holhouser, James, 268

Holly, 29, 322

Holmes, J. S., 73–74, 82

Honeybees, 38, 117

Honeysuckle, Japanese, 87, 325

Hooper Bald, 86, 252

Hoover, Herbert, 67, 122

Hoover Dam, 152–53, 389n.18

Horace M. Albright Training Center, 234, 255, 259

Horn, Stanley, 49, 59

Hornbeam, American, 129

Horses, horseback riding, 24, 33, 60, 122, 176, 179, 184, 210, 229, 250, 284, 286, 311, 354

Hotel LeConte, 84, 85

Whaley, J. Roy, 16, 101
Whaley, J. W., 85
Whaley, P. Audley, 18, 27, 70, 115–16, 126, 136
Whaley, Sam, 70
Whaley, Stephen, 192
Whaley, Zenith, 97
Wharton, C. H., 225
Wheatley, Marie, 305
Whelan, William, 264, 266
Whip-poor-will, 30
Whiskey. *See* Moonshine
White, Peter S. 280, 287–88, 334–35
White Oak Flats, 190
White pine blister rust, 135
Whiting Lumber Company, 50, 159, 387n.9
Whitmer, William, 52, 67
Whitmer-Parsons Pulp and Lumber Company, 54
Whittaker, Paul, 284–85
Whittaker, Robert, 248, 281
Whittle, W. O., 68
Wilburn, H. C., 132–33, 203, 354
Wild cat. *See* Mountain lion
Wilderness: automobiles and, 202, 221–27; Boyd Evison perspective of, 255–56; in Cades Cove, 202–9; "de facto" wilderness management, 273; early perceptions of, 8, 42, 247, 364n.14; early positive associations with, 81–83, 179; and grassy balds, 281–83; lake, 169; NPS view of, 140, 285–86, 308; reclaiming the term, 361; and re-creating the pre-Columbian scene, 279–83; views of 1950s tourists, 174–78, 209
—campaign to gain designation as: 1966, 6, 219–27, 245; 1975–78, 267–74; 1984, 309–11
Wilderness Act (1964), 219, 220
Wilderness Society, 79, 174, 218, 223–24, 226, 309, 337, 353
Wildflowers, 214, 246, 252, 323. *See also* individual names
Wildlife. *See* individual species
Wildlife Federation, 224
Wildlife management, 113–14. *See also* individual species

Wilkes County, N.C., 8
Williams, Dora Proffit, 27–28
Williamson, Wayne, 263–64
Wilson, John, 224
Windle, Phyllis, 320
Wine, 29
Wirth, Conrad, 176, 216–17, 248
Wisteria, 327
Witch hazel, 129
Wolves, red, 6, 8–9, 18, 114, 296–98, 313
Women: Cherokee, 27, 35–37, 70–71; mountain white, 26–28, 34, 36–37, 70–71; in the NPS, 249; and tourism, 190, 194, 304–5
Wonderland Club, 87, 93, 107; lease arrangement, 98–99, 352–53
Wood, Dillard, 60
Woodland grazing, 22–23
Woodland pasture. *See* Woodland grazing
Woods, Leeunah Vance, 311
Woody, Carl, 71
Woody, Paul, 19, 20, 21, 34, 37, 40–41, 101
Woody, Robert, 17, 40, 67
Woody, Jonathan, 9
Work, Hubert, 88
Works Progress Administration (WPA), 121, 124, 128, 134
World systems. *See* Global economy
World trade. *See* Global economy
World War I, 57, 71
World War II, 123, 141, 148, 150, 165, 176, 197, 388n.17
Worster, Donald, 348, 356, 358
Wright, James B., 87–88, 93, 95–96
Wrens, 319
Writers, local color, 80–83
Yard, Robert Sterling, 385n.60
Yards, 31
Yellow Creek, 61
Yellowstone National Park, 88, 94, 175, 179, 209, 234, 247
Yost, Ed, 321, 322
Youngbird, Rebecca, 85

Zodiac, 37
Z. Smith Reynolds Foundation, 337

Margaret Lynn Brown is professor emeritus of history at Brevard College in North Carolina. She is also an essayist and reviewer.

NEW PERSPECTIVES ON THE HISTORY OF THE SOUTH
Edited by John David Smith

New Perspectives on the History of the South
Edited by John David Smith

"In the Country of the Enemy": The Civil War Reports of a Massachusetts Corporal, edited by
    William C. Harris (1999)
The Wild East: A Biography of the Great Smoky Mountains, by Margaret Lynn Brown (2000; first
    paperback edition, 2001; revised edition, 2024)
*Crime, Sexual Violence, and Clemency: Florida's Pardon Board and Penal System in the Progressive
    Era*, by Vivien M. L. Miller (2000)
*The New South's New Frontier: A Social History of Economic Development in Southwestern North
    Carolina*, by Stephen Wallace Taylor (2001)
Redefining the Color Line: Black Activism in Little Rock, Arkansas, 1940–1970, by John A. Kirk
    (2002)
The Southern Dream of a Caribbean Empire, 1854–1861, by Robert E. May (2002)
Forging a Common Bond: Labor and Environmental Activism during the BASF Lockout, by
    Timothy J. Minchin (2003)
*Dixie's Daughters: The United Daughters of the Confederacy and the Preservation of Confederate
    Culture*, by Karen L. Cox (2003; first paperback edition, 2006; second paperback edition,
    2018)
The Other War of 1812: The Patriot War and the American Invasion of Spanish East Florida, by
    James G. Cusick (2003)
"Lives Full of Struggle and Triumph": Southern Women, Their Institutions, and Their Communities,
    edited by Bruce L. Clayton and John A. Salmond (2003)
German-Speaking Officers in the U.S. Colored Troops, 1863–1867, by Martin W. Öfele (2004)
Southern Struggles: The Southern Labor Movement and the Civil Rights Struggle, by John A.
    Salmond (2004)
Radio and the Struggle for Civil Rights in the South, by Brian Ward (2004; first paperback edition,
    2006)
Luther P. Jackson and a Life for Civil Rights, by Michael Dennis (2004)
Southern Ladies, New Women: Race, Region, and Clubwomen in South Carolina, 1890–1930, by
    Joan Marie Johnson (2004)
Fighting Against the Odds: A History of Southern Labor since World War II, by Timothy J. Minchin
    (2005; first paperback edition, 2006)
*"Don't Sleep with Stevens!": The J. P. Stevens Campaign and the Struggle to Organize the South,
    1963–80*, by Timothy J. Minchin (2005)
"The Ticket to Freedom": The NAACP and the Struggle for Black Political Integration, by Manfred
    Berg (2005; first paperback edition, 2007)
"War Governor of the South": North Carolina's Zeb Vance in the Confederacy, by Joe A. Mobley
    (2005)
Planters' Progress: Modernizing Confederate Georgia, by Chad Morgan (2005)
The Officers of the CSS Shenandoah, by Angus Curry (2006)
The Rosenwald Schools of the American South, by Mary S. Hoffschwelle (2006; first paperback
    edition, 2014)
*Honor in Command: Lt. Freeman S. Bowley's Civil War Service in the 30th United States Colored
    Infantry*, edited by Keith Wilson (2006)
A Black Congressman in the Age of Jim Crow: South Carolina's George Washington Murray, by John
    F. Marszalek (2006)
The Spirit and the Shotgun: Armed Resistance and the Struggle for Civil Rights, by Simon Wendt
    (2007; first paperback edition, 2010)
Making a New South: Race, Leadership, and Community after the Civil War, edited by Paul A.
    Cimbala and Barton C. Shaw (2007)

From Rights to Economics: The Ongoing Struggle for Black Equality in the U.S. South, by Timothy J. Minchin (2007)

Slavery on Trial: Race, Class, and Criminal Justice in Antebellum Richmond, Virginia, by James M. Campbell (2007; first paperback edition, 2010)

Welfare and Charity in the Antebellum South, by Timothy James Lockley (2007; first paperback edition, 2009)

T. Thomas Fortune, the Afro-American Agitator: A Collection of Writings, 1880–1928, edited by Shawn Leigh Alexander (2008; first paperback edition, 2010)

Francis Butler Simkins: A Life, by James S. Humphreys (2008)

Black Manhood and Community Building in North Carolina, 1900–1930, by Angela Hornsby-Gutting (2009; first paperback edition, 2010)

Counterfeit Gentlemen: Manhood and Humor in the Old South, by John Mayfield (2009; first paperback edition, 2010)

The Southern Mind Under Union Rule: The Diary of James Rumley, Beaufort, North Carolina, 1862–1865, edited by Judkin Browning (2009; first paperback edition, 2011)

The Quarters and the Fields: Slave Families in the Non-Cotton South, by Damian Alan Pargas (2010; first paperback edition, 2011)

The Door of Hope: Republican Presidents and the First Southern Strategy, 1877–1933, by Edward O. Frantz (2011; first paperback edition, 2012)

Painting Dixie Red: When, Where, Why, and How the South Became Republican, edited by Glenn Feldman (2011; first paperback edition, 2014)

After Freedom Summer: How Race Realigned Mississippi Politics, 1965–1986, by Chris Danielson (2011; first paperback edition, 2013)

Dreams and Nightmares: Martin Luther King Jr., Malcolm X, and the Struggle for Black Equality in America, by Britta Waldschmidt-Nelson (2012)

Hard Labor and Hard Time: Florida's "Sunshine Prison" and Chain Gangs, by Vivien M. L. Miller (2012)

Ain't Scared of Your Jail: Arrest, Imprisonment, and the Civil Rights Movement, by Zoe A. Colley (2013; first paperback edition, 2014)

After Slavery: Race, Labor, and Citizenship in the Reconstruction South, edited by Bruce E. Baker and Brian Kelly (2013; first paperback edition, 2014)

Stinking Stones and Rocks of Gold: Phosphate, Fertilizer, and Industrialization in Postbellum South Carolina, by Shepherd W. McKinley (2014; first paperback edition, 2017)

The Path to the Greater, Freer, Truer World: Southern Civil Rights and Anticolonialism, 1937–1955, by Lindsey R. Swindall (2014; first paperback edition, 2019)

Printed in the USA
CPSIA information can be obtained
at www.ICGtesting.com
CBHW020521200824
13324CB00005B/14

9 780813 080864